D0070310

The
WILKINSON
& BOA
BIBLE HANDBOOK

The WILKINSON & BOA

BIBLE HANDBOOK

*The Ultimate Guide to Help You
Get More Out of the Bible*

BRUCE WILKINSON
and
KENNETH BOA

THOMAS NELSON PUBLISHERS
Nashville, Tennessee

Copyright © 1983, 2002 by Thomas Nelson Publishers
All rights reserved. Written permission must be secured from the publisher to use or
reproduce any part of this book, except for brief quotations in critical reviews or
articles.

This book is a compilation of material from the following:

Talk Thru the Old Testament
Copyright © 1980 by Walk Thru the Bible Ministries, Inc.

Talk Thru the New Testament
Copyright © 1981 by Walk Thru the Bible Ministries, Inc.

Charts are from the *Walk Thru the Old Testament* and *Walk Thru the New Testament*
seminar notebooks, copyrighted by Walk Thru the Bible Ministries, © 1974, 1976,
1979. These charts may not be reproduced without written permission.

Unless otherwise indicated, all Scripture quotations are from The Holy Bible, New
King James Version, copyright © 1979, 1980, 1982 by Thomas Nelson, Inc., Publishers.

Published in Nashville, Tennessee, by Thomas Nelson, Inc.

Printed in the United States of America

To our wives

Darlene and Karen

*"An excellent wife is the
crown of her husband." (Prov. 12:49)*

Contents

New Testament

Preface

The Beauty of the Bible

The Bible is unique in its production, preservation, proclamations, and product. In its production, it is a harmonious and unified message of redemption that has emerged out of diversity of authors, circumstances, and literary forms. In its preservation, it has miraculously withstood the ravages of time, persecution, and criticism, and continues to be the best selling book in the world. In its proclamations, it stands alone in its revelation of God's plan from eternity to eternity and in its life-giving message. In its product, it has changed the course of history, reached more people, and transformed more lives than any other book.

The Doorway to a New Domain

Scripture tells us that there are really two realms: that which is seen and that which is unseen. The first is the realm of apparent reality, the world we know through our minds and our five senses. If it were not for divine revelation, we would be locked into this level without any way of breaking through to the second realm, the world of ultimate reality. Bound to the level of the finite, the relative, and the temporal, we would be unable to find the meaning and purpose we long for that can only come from the level of the infinite, the absolute, and the eternal. There would be no hope of finding answers to the basic questions of life: Who am I? Where did I come from? Why am I here? Where am I going?

God gave us His Word to deliver us from the power of darkness and to translate us to the domain of light, "the kingdom of the Son of His love" (Col. 1:13). The Bible reveals the full scope of the Lord's creative and redemptive plan for His people. Only in its pages can we gain a perspective on our corporate past, present, and future and realize the overwhelming significance of our new identity as the recipients of "every spiritual blessing in the heavenly places in Christ" (Eph. 1:3).

By drinking deeply and regularly from the well of God's Word, our entire value system will be gradually transformed from the temporal to the eternal. The study of Scripture sets our minds on the things above (Col. 3:2), the source of all biological and spiritual life. It enables us to look not "at the things which are seen, but at the things which are not seen. For the things which are seen are temporary, but the things which are not seen are eternal" (2 Cor. 4:18).

This is the heart of wisdom—plugging into the realm of ultimate reality and walking in the light, life, and love of the Lord. By pursuing the precepts and principles of the Bible, we gain the most important skill of all: the ability to live each area of life under the dominion of the King. The Bible does not tell us to live and learn; it exhorts us to learn and live.

The Pathway to a Better Life

There are several reasons for getting into the Word and letting the Word get into us. Here are six:

1. Nourishment and Growth

The Bible was not merely written for our information, but for our transformation. "All Scripture is given by inspiration of God, and profitable for doctrine, for reproof, for correction, for instruction in righteousness, that the man of God may be complete, thoroughly equipped for every good work" (2 Tim. 3:16–17). While the Bible is an inspired revelation from the living God, it requires our response before it can have an impact upon our lives. Scripture is indeed "profitable for doctrine," but its profit does not stop on the level of doctrine; it must move from the head to the heart to accomplish the purpose for which it was given.

God loves us and desires nothing less than our highest good: conformity to the character of His Son. A dynamic relationship with the truth of His Word provides us with the spiritual nourishment we will need to grow into the maturity of Christlikeness.

EXERCISE: Study 2 Peter 1:2–8 to trace the progressive effect that the knowledge of God and His promises has upon the life of a believer.

2. New Priorities and Values

The study of Scripture can deliver us from the bondage of a temporal perspective and provide us with an eternal value system. By frequently renewing our minds with the Word (Rom. 12:2), our thinking and behavior come more into conformity with God's view of significance, purpose, identity, and success. The pursuit of God's value system leads to fulfillment and joy in contrast to the frustration and unhappiness that result from the pursuit of the world's value system. See Psalm 5:11; 16:5–8; 105:3–4; Jeremiah 9:23–24; Matthew 6:33; 2 Corinthians 4:16–18; Philippians 1:21; Colossians 1:10–12.

3. Overcoming Temptation

The study of Scripture provides us with both corrective and preventive medicine. It warns us in advance of the kinds of temptations we can expect (e.g., Prov. 4:10–27; 5:1–23; 1 John 2:15–16), tells us about the process of temptation (see Jas. 1:12–17), and shows us how to deal with temptation (1 Cor. 10:13; Eph. 6:10–18).

4. Guidance for Decision Making

The Scriptures reveal God's moral will for practically every area of life. A working knowledge of the commands, prohibitions, and principles of the Bible will give us wisdom and guidance in the decisions that shape the course of our earthly existence (Ps. 119:105; Prov. 1:2–5), and a divine perspective that will enable us to respond in the right way to our circumstances and rise above them (Jas. 1:5).

5. *Knowledge of God*

The Bible is a progressive revelation of the person, plan, character, mind, love, and will of our Creator. We cannot hope to know Him and His ways apart from time spent in His revealed Word.

EXERCISE: All but three verses in Psalm 119 contain a reference to the Word of God (variously referred to as God's laws, decrees, precepts, promises, testimonies, statutes, judgments, ordinances, commands, and words). Read this psalm and record your observations of the beneficial effects of the Scriptures in cultivating a relationship with God.

6. *Knowledge of Ourselves*

"For the word of God is living and powerful, and sharper than any two-edged sword, piercing even to the division of soul and spirit, and of joints and marrow, and is a discerner of the thoughts and intents of the heart" (Heb. 4:12). The Bible cuts below the façade of appearances and lays bare our secret motivations and plans (cf. 1 Sam. 16:7). As we read it, the Word becomes a mirror that exhibits our true character, exposes areas of self-delusion, and exhorts us to change (see Jas. 1:21–25).

Kenneth Boa and Bruce Wilkinson

The Scarlet Thread of Redemption

W. A. Criswell

THE BIBLE IS A BOOK OF REDEMPTION. It is that or nothing at all. It is not a book of history, science, anthropology, or cosmogony. It is a book of salvation and deliverance for lost mankind.

The idea in the word "redemption" is twofold: it refers to a deliverance; and it refers to the price paid for that deliverance, a ransom. We are redeemed from the penalty of sin and from the power of Satan and evil by the price Jesus paid on the Cross for us; and we are redeemed to a new freedom from sin, to a new relationship to God, and to a new life of love by the appropriation of that atonement for our sins.

The whole of the Bible, whether the Old Testament or the New Testament, looks to the mighty redemptive atonement of Christ. His blood sacrifice is the ransom paid for our deliverance. He took our sinful nature upon Himself in order that He might satisfy the demands of the Law. His sacrifice is accepted as the payment for the debt the sinner man owes to God, and His death is accepted as the full payment for man's deliverance.

Our Lord's redemptive work for us is threefold: (1) It is closely associated with forgiveness, since we receive forgiveness through the redemptive price of Christ's death. (2) It involves justification, since the deliverance establishes us in a restored position of favor before God. (3) It promises final deliverance from the power of sin at the coming of the Lord. The story of this redemption is "The Scarlet Thread of Redemption."

I. The Creation and the Fall

When God made the heavens and the earth, they must have been beautiful, perfect, and pure, as only God could create them. But sin entered through the pride of Satan, and the beautiful creation was destroyed. Sin always destroys. It did so again after the perfect re-creation described in the first chapter of Genesis. In the Garden of Eden, through a denial of the Word of God and through Satan's deception of the woman, our first parents fell. When Eve was deceived, Adam chose to die by the side of the woman whom God had created and placed in his arms. As the Lord came to visit the man and his wife in the cool of the day, he could not find them. They were afraid and hid themselves from the Lord because they were naked and ashamed. To hide their guilt, they made for themselves aprons of fig leaves, but when God looked upon the covering, He said, "This will not do." Covering for sin (atonement for sin) cannot be woven by human hands. Therefore, somewhere in the Garden of Eden, the Lord took an innocent animal; and before the eyes of Eve and Adam, God killed that innocent animal as the ground drank up its blood. This is the beginning of "The Scarlet Thread of Redemption." Through the slaughter of an innocent victim, God took coats of skin and covered over the shame and the nakedness of the man and his wife. This is the first sacrifice, and it was offered by the hand of almighty God. I have often thought that when Adam saw the gasping, spent life of that innocent creature, and when he saw the crimson stain which soiled the ground, it was his first experience of what it meant to die because of sin. Thus, the story of atonement and sacrifice begins and unfolds throughout the Word of God, until finally in glory we shall see great throngs of the saints who have washed their robes and made them white in the Blood of the Lamb. This is "The Scarlet Thread of Redemption."

II. From the Seventh Day in Eden to the Call of Abraham

In the Garden of Eden, as the Lord covered the nakedness of the man and the woman, He turned to Satan and said, "The seed of this woman, whom you have deceived and through whom you have destroyed the human race, will crush your head." For centuries the old rabbis pored over the word of Yahweh God to Satan: "The seed of the woman." Seed is masculine; seed belongs to the man. A woman does not have seed. The old rabbis, not understanding, looked in amazement at that word and the promise of God that the seed of the woman would crush Satan's head. We now know that the promise relates to the virgin birth and to the long conflict and struggle between the hatred of Lucifer and the love of God in Christ Jesus. It speaks of Jesus at Calvary. Jesus suffered. His heel was bruised. But in that bruising, He defeated once and for all the power of that old serpent, the devil, whose head He crushed.

As the man Adam and his wife Eve made their first home in an earth cursed for their sakes, in the passing of time there were born to them two sons. One was named Cain and the other Abel. In jealousy and insane fury, the older brother killed the younger brother. But the seed of God must be preserved. The Lord, therefore, gave to Eve another son, named Seth. Seth was a man of faith as Cain was a man of the world. When the children of Seth, the godly remnant, intermarried with the children of Cain, the seed of the world, the result was a fallen progeny that filled the earth with violence. Finally, God said, "It is enough. One hundred twenty years from now, I am going to destroy this world by a flood." But a member of the line of Seth found grace in the sight of the Lord. His name was Noah. To preserve the righteous seed, God told Noah to build an ark; and into that ark of safety, salvation, and hope, Noah brought his family. After the passing of the awesome judgment of the flood, the earth once again began its story of redemption through the lives of this one man and his three sons.

It was not long, however, before the ravages of sin began to waste the select family of God. Instead of carrying out the great commission of the Lord for mankind to inhabit the whole earth, the people drew together into one plain and announced their purpose to build a tower around which they were to center their civilization and their collective, communal unity. When God looked down and saw the pride of men in their hearts, He confused their speech and caused them to "babble." From this "Tower of Babel," therefore, the different component parts of the human race, being unable to understand each other, scattered in different directions and so fathered the nations of the earth that grew up from those three great family lines of Noah.

III. From the Call of Abraham Through the Times of the Judges

We begin the story of Abraham in a dark, dark day. The whole world had been plunged into abysmal idolatry, but God called out this man to leave his home, his place, his country, and his family to go into another country, which he should afterward receive for an inheritance. In obedience, Abraham left the Mesopotamian Valley and came as a pilgrim, a stranger, and a sojourner into the promised land of Canaan. There he dwelt and there God gave him two sons. But the Lord God said to Abraham that Ishmael, the child of the flesh and the son of a slave woman, would not be the promised seed. When Abraham was one hundred years old and when Sarah was ninety years old, God miraculously placed into the arms of the parents the child and seed of promise whom they named Isaac. Isaac was the father of two sons, Esau and Jacob. The Lord, refusing Esau, chose Jacob, whom He renamed, after Jacob's deep conversion experience, "The Prince of God," even "Israel."

Because of a severe famine in Canaan and because of the presence of Joseph, the son of Israel, in Egypt, the entire household of Jacob went down to live in the land of the Nile. In the passing of the years, there arose a pharaoh who did not know Joseph. The chosen family became slaves to this new ruler of Egypt, and their heavy groaning ascended to the ears of the Lord God in heaven. The Lord, therefore, raised up a mighty prophet by the name of Moses to deliver his people from the bondage and slavery of the Egyptians. God wrought this deliverance by a marvelous miracle called the Passover. For the Lord had said, "When I see the blood, I will pass over you and will spare you and your home." This way of salvation through the blood is once again "The Scarlet Thread of Redemption."

After the Lord God delivered the chosen family out of Egypt, He brought them by the hand of Moses through the parting of the Red Sea into the Sinai Peninsula, to the base of Mount Horeb. There for forty days and forty nights Moses was with God, and there the Lord gave to Moses the Ten Commandments, the pattern of the tabernacle, the ritual instructions of holy worship, and all of the other marvelous things in the Book of Leviticus that portray and prophesy the sacrifice of the Son of God.

After the death of Moses, Joshua crossed over the Jordan and completed the wars of conquest. In the first confrontation at Jericho an incident occurred which gave rise to the title of this summary. The scouts sent by Joshua to spy out Jericho were saved by the faith and the kindness of Rahab. The men of Israel promised life and safety, both for her and her father's house, if she would bind a scarlet cord in her window. This she faithfully did, and, when Jericho was delivered into the hands of Joshua by the mighty intervention of God, Rahab and her family were spared because of that scarlet cord, "The Scarlet Thread of Redemption."

After the conquest of Canaan through the military prowess and genius of Joshua, we have the story of the judges. The difference between a judge and a king is this: a king gives his throne to his son, but a judge is raised up in a time of crisis and endowed with special gifts from God for that one period of time. The days of the judges end with the birth of Samuel.

IV. From the First of the Prophets to the Founding of the Kingdom

During the time of Samuel, the people began to cry for a king. It was the purpose of God in the beginning for the children of Israel to have a king (Deut. 17:1–20), but it hurt the heart of the Lord that the request should come in so vain and rebellious a way as they presented it to Samuel. But according to the Word and instruction of God, Samuel anointed Saul to be king over Israel. In his early ministry, Saul was a mighty man and carried out the mandates of heaven, but he soon fell away from the instruction of Samuel and fell into gross disobedience to the will of God. The Word of the Lord, therefore, came to Samuel that he anoint a man after God's own heart. That anointing came upon a lad from the shepherd field, a son of Jesse by the name of David.

V. David and the Kingdoms of Israel and Judah

The first part of David's life as king of Israel was magnificent. Then, in the very prime of his life, at the very height of his glory, he turned aside from the will of God and became soft and indulgent and lustful like other Oriental kings. This brought to David an infinite tragedy, one by which the name of God was blasphemed and has been injured ever since. Nevertheless, God forgave the sin of David and chose him to be the father of that marvelous Son who would sit upon His throne as King forever. A type of that glorious son of David, called Jesus the Christ, was the immediate son of David, called Solomon. Solomon also began his reign gloriously and triumphantly, but like his father, Solomon fell into tragic decline. Upon his death, the kingdom was torn in two.

Thereafter, the people of God were divided into two kingdoms, that of the North called the kingdom of Israel, and that of the South called the kingdom of Judah. The northern kingdom of Israel was taken away into captivity by the cruel and ruthless Assyrians in 722 B.C. The southern kingdom was carried away into captivity in 586 B.C. by the Babylonians. In the days of the Babylonian captivity, Jeremiah prophesied in Jerusalem, while Daniel, the prophet-statesman, and Ezekiel, the holy seer, comforted and strengthened the people of God in Mesopotamia.

Out of the Bablyonian captivity came three great establishments by which God has blessed our world. First, the Jews were never idolatrous again. Second, the synagogue was born, and from the synagogue came the church. The services of the synagogue are the same type of services we have today. Third, out of the captivity came the canon of the Old Testament. Out of tears and suffering come our greatest blessings, "The Scarlet Thread of Redemption."

VI. From the Prophets to the Christ to the Preaching of Paul

Out of the agonies of the days of the kingdoms of Israel and Judah came the depiction by the prophets of a more glorious Savior and King whom God would send to His people. When we read a passage like Psalm 22 or Isaiah 53, we seem to be standing by the cross of the Son of God. More and more as the days went by, the great spiritual leaders of Israel and Judah began to outline and to depict the coming of a Redeemer who would save the people from their sins and bring to them the everlasting hope and righteousness of God in a promised messiah. This messianic hope became stronger and more gloriously received as the centuries passed.

From the Babylonian captivity in 539 B.C., Cyrus the Persian gave the people the right to return to their homeland in Judah and to build their holy temple in Jerusalem. Thus the remnant of the captivity returned under Zerubbabel, the political leader, and Joshua, the high priest. This holy remnant, seeking to restore the worship of the true God in Jerusalem and to recreate the political life of Judah, was encouraged by God's messengers Haggai, Zechariah, and Malachi.

Of the three great restoration prophets, Zechariah is far and away the greatest. Zechariah spoke much about Israel, about the end time, and about the conversion of the people of the Lord. The last prophet, of course, is Malachi. He delivered his message of hope and messianic promise from c. 433–430 B.C.

The four-hundred-year period between the Old Testament and the New Testament marks the rise of the Hellenistic Empire. God used Alexander the Great to spread abroad throughout the civilized world one culture and one language, which made possible the preaching of Christ to all men everywhere.

In that interbiblical period also arose the might of the Roman Empire. When Augustus Caesar was the Roman emperor and when Rome had the entire world in her hand, the great prophecy of Isaiah and the great prophecy of Micah and the great prophecy of Nathan to David and the great prophecy of Jacob to his son Judah and the great promise of God Almighty to Eve in the Garden of Eden came to pass. In the Seed of the woman and through the seed of Abraham all the families of the earth are to be blessed-and our Savior is thus born into the world. "The Scarlet Thread of Redemption" has led us to the birth of Him who has come to redeem the human race from its fallen estate.

In His ministry, Jesus began early to teach His disciples that He should suffer and die. When He was transfigured, there appeared Moses and Elijah, talking with Him about His death, which He should accomplish in Jerusalem. When He was anointed by Mary of Bethany, He said it was for His burial. When the Greeks came to see Him from afar, He said, "And I, if I am lifted up from the earth, will draw all peoples to Myself" (John 12:32). At the Last Supper He said, "This is My body; eat in remembrance of Me." And again He said, "This is My blood; drink in remembrance of Me." Before He went to the Cross, He gave Himself in Gethsemane in labor of soul for our redemption (Is. 53:11). And when He bowed His head and died He said, "It is finished" (John 19:30). When we proclaim the Cross, when we preach the blood, and when we announce the sacrificial death of Christ, we are preaching the meaning of His Coming into the world. The sacrifice of Christ consummated the great redemptive plan and purpose of God in the earth. This is "The Scarlet Thread of Redemption."

After the Resurrection of our Lord, after the giving of the Great Commission to the apostles, and after the Ascension of our Savior into heaven, the Lord poured out the Holy Spirit upon His church in Jerusalem on the day of Pentecost. Thereafter the disciples of Jesus and the preachers of the redemptive message of Christ began to make known throughout the earth the Good News of our hope and salvation.

The epistles of Paul are chided into four distinct groups. The first group he wrote from Athens and Corinth, during his second missionary journey. They are 1 and 2 Thessalonians. The second group of letters were born during his third missionary journey. While he was in Ephesus, he wrote 1 Corinthians. Somewhere in Macedonia between Ephesus and Corinth, he wrote 2 Corinthians. Then, either in Antioch or on his way to Antioch, he wrote Galatians and Romans. First and Second Corinthians, Galatians, and Romans, therefore, center around the city of Ephesus. The third group of epistles Paul wrote during his first Roman imprisonment. They are Philippians, Philemon, Colossians, and Ephesians. The fourth and last group of his epistles, which were written after his first Roman imprisonment, were 1 Timothy, Titus, and 2 Timothy, called the "Pastoral Epistles." In all Paul's letters there is the constant theme of redemptive love. It is a part of "The Scarlet Thread of Redemption."

VII. The Apocalypse and the Consummation of the Age

We come now to the conclusion of the Bible.

On the Isle of Patmos, a rocky little point in the sea several miles southwest of Ephesus, John was exiled to die of exposure and starvation. But even there the Lord appeared to John in an incomparable and glorious vision. The vision is called the Revelation, that is, "the unveiling." The Apocalypse, the uncovering of Jesus Christ in His glory, in His majesty, and in His kingdom, is the reward that God gave to Jesus for saving us, Adam's fallen children, from our sins.

After the vision of the exalted and glorified Christ in chapter 1 and after the prophetic words concerning the church age in chapters 2 and 3, we have the rapture of John through an open door into heaven. While John, the translated saint, is with the Savior in heaven, there are poured out upon the earth the judgments of Almighty God called the "Great Tribulation." They are depicted in the opening of the seven seals, the seven trumpets, and the seven bowls. In those dark days John sees a vision in Revelation, chapter 7, concerning the blood-washed, blood-bought redeemed of the Lord in glory. Announcement is made to him through one of the elders that these are they who have come out of the Great Tribulation and have washed their robes and made them white in the blood of the Lamb. This is "The Scarlet Thread of Redemption" that began with the blood of covering in the Garden of Eden and finds its ultimate and final consummation in the blood-washed throng before the throne of God in glory.

After the seven seals and the judgments thereof, the seven trumpets and the judgments thereof, the seven bowls and the judgments thereof, and the seven angels and the judgments thereof, we come to the final great Judgment Day of Almighty God. The Antichrist, who professes to be the leader of the nations of the world, is gathering the armies of the entire earth together. They are converging from the north in Russia, from the east in China, from the south in Africa, and from the west in Europe and the islands of the sea. They are converging for that great day of the Lord. That is the Battle of Armageddon, the last great war the world is going to fight. At Megiddo, the armies of the earth by the millions and the millions will converge to face that rendezvous with God. In the midst of this unimaginable holocaust, Christ intervenes in human history. He comes with His saints. He delivers His people, who have been shut up in the holy city, and takes Satan and binds him for a thousand years in the bottomless pit.

After the binding of Satan for a thousand years, which is called the "glorious Millennium," Satan is released and thereafter goes forth once again to lead men in rebellion against God. This is the final conflict, which ends forever men's refusal to accept the will of God for their lives. At the end time in the final resurrection of the wicked dead and the Great White Throne Judgment, the books are opened, and those whose names are not found written in the Lamb's Book of Life are cast out and rewarded according to their deeds. Into the abyss of hell are flung Satan and his angels along with those who choose Satan and his way of life, plus death and the grave—all are hurled into the fiery flames where the beast and the false prophet already will have been for a thousand years.

After the earth is purged of Satan and his minions, after the judgment upon those who reject Christ and His grace, and after the earth is cleansed of the heartache and tears of sickness, sin, death, and the grave, there will come the renovation of this earth and this heaven. It is a new creation with a new heaven and a new earth, remade according to the fullness of the glory and wonder of God. In it is the new and holy city, the heavenly Jerusalem, and in it is the dwelling place of God Himself. Tears, death, sorrow, pain, crying are all passed away. There are no graves on the hillsides of glory and no funeral wreaths on the doors of those mansions in the sky.

The book closes with the incomparable message of the hope and salvation we have in the personal coming and presence of the Lord Christ Himself. This is "The Scarlet Thread of Redemption" that leads to glory.[1]

---

[1]W.A. Criswell, *Believer's Study Bible [computer file]*, electronic ed., *Logos Library System*, (Nashville: Thomas Nelson) 1997, c1991 by the Criswell Center for Biblical Studies.

Introduction to the Bible

ON AN EARTHBOUND LEVEL, there are two fundamental sources of human knowledge: reason and experience. Both are essential to our understanding of the world about us, but they are limited. They leave unanswered the most crucial questions that can be raised—Who am I? Where did I come from? Where am I going? Is there any purpose to human existence? Where is history going? Unless there is a third source of knowledge, a source that carries us beyond the limits of reason and experience, there is no hope of finding answers to these basic issues of meaning and significance.

The Bible claims to provide this third source of knowledge. It is *revelation,* and the belief that God has revealed Himself and His ways to man in Holy Scripture is the underlying axiom of the Christian world view. In it we have direct access to a revelation from a personal Being Who created all things and Who is not subject to our limitations as fragile, finite creatures.

The Bible describes two forms of revelation; these are usually called general and special revelation. According to Psalm 19:1–6 and Romans 1:20, God has revealed truths about "His invisible attributes . . . His eternal power and Godhead" to us through His creation, and this *general* revelation is available to all. In addition to the external revelation of nature, He has also implanted the knowledge of His existence in every human heart, although many have chosen to suppress this truth in (Rom. 1:18). God's *special* revelation involves His more direct means of communicating to some people in a variety of ways, including dreams, visions, and angels, but most clearly in the Person of Christ (Heb. 1:1–2) and in the pages of Scripture.

The sovereign Lord of history is intimately involved in the affairs of mankind, and the Scriptures record the panoramic story of His plan to bring redemption to the earth and ultimately to make all things new in Christ. The God of the Bible is both the Creator and the Redeemer, and the Cross is portrayed as the central event of history. The Old Testament anticipates the work of Messiah in many ways, and the New Testament points back to Jesus as the Author and Perfector of faith (Heb. 12:2). He is the Alpha and the Omega, the First and the Last, the Beginning and the End (Rev. 22:13). Indeed, Christ claimed to be the Key to the Scriptures, the One of Whom the entire Old Testament spoke (Luke 24:44–46).

God chose to reveal Himself in a progressive way, and His written Word gradually unfolded more and more truth about His Person and work. It has been said that the New is in the Old concealed, and the Old is in the New revealed. The thirty-nine books of the Old Testament provide the foundation upon which the superstructure of the twenty-seven books of the New Testament is built.

Mysteriously, the Scriptures claim to be completely divine and completely human. There is a parallel here to the God-man, Jesus Christ, who is fully God and fully man. God joined with sinful humanity to produce the sinless living Word, and in a similar sense joined with sinful humanity to produce the inspired written Word.

This process of inspiration was best described by Peter when he wrote that "men of God spoke as they were moved by the Holy Spirit" (2 Pet. 1:21). The styles, personalities, and vocabularies of the different biblical writers are quite distinct, but their work is nevertheless the Word of God. Paul added that all Scripture is God-breathed, that is, inspired by God (2 Tim. 3:16).

One of the evidences of the divine origin of the Bible is its uniqueness. First, it is unique in its *production*. It is one book ("the Bible" simply means "the Book"; it is derived from the Greek word *biblos* which means "book, scroll") and yet many books. It is not merely a collection of historical narratives, letters, stories, and poetry. It is a perfect unity that is composed of many diverse elements. The Bible is a progressive revelation which harmoniously traces redemption from Genesis to Revelation. It is a unified and self-consistent portrait that centers on the Person and work of Jesus Christ as its primary theme.

Yet the Bible was produced over a time span of about one thousand five hundred years. Century after century men added to this book, unaware for the most part of one another's writings and sometimes in the dark as to the meaning of some of their own words (1 Pet. 1:10–12). In addition, the backgrounds of its more than forty authors could hardly have been more diverse. They include Samuel the judge, Amos the sheep breeder, Ezra the priest, Nehemiah the statesman, and a host of other scribes, kings, prophets, poets, musicians, philosophers, farmers, and teachers. The New Testament writers include a tax collector, a physician, a tentmaker, two fishermen, and two carpenters. Some, like Moses, Isaiah, and Paul, were highly educated, while others were unschooled. The Bible contains the work of freeman and slave, landholder and yeoman, prosperous and poor. Its chapters were written in palaces and in prisons, in cities and in wildernesses, in times of war and peace, and in every other circumstance. It was written in three languages (Hebrew, Aramaic, and Greek) and on three continents. The Bible is a divine library which contains prophecy, history, law, poetry, hymns, wisdom literature, stories, biography, letters, oratory, parables, philosophy, drama, exposition, and sermons. Its literary styles and themes are diverse, but it is all interwoven into a composite and unified whole.

Second, the Bible is unique in its *preservation*. In spite of persecution, perversion, criticism, abuse, and time, the Bible has survived virtually intact. It is an anvil that has worn out many hammers. There is no ancient document which has manuscript support that even approximates that of the New Testament. The Scriptures are unique in the quantity, quality, and antiquity of their manuscripts. Many have sought to ban and destroy the Bible, but their efforts have been futile. The Bible is by far the most popular book in the world. Portions have been translated in over one thousand seven hundred languages, and it has been copied and circulated more extensively than any other literature. Recent archaeological, historical, and linguistic evidences have refuted destructive critical theories in favor of the trustworthiness of Scripture.

Third, the Bible's *proclamations* are unique. Over a quarter of the Bible was prophetic at the time it was written, and these prophecies stand alone in their graphic detail, accuracy, and scope. The subject matter of the Bible covers the whole range from heaven to hell, from the divine to the demonic, and from eternity past to eternity future. Its portrait of God as the infinite-personal triune Creator is unique. So also is its description of man in his originally perfect state, as well as his fall and sinfulness. Its message of salvation by faith and not by works, and the whole concept of the sacrifice of the God-man on our behalf, is without parallel. The Bible is also unique in its historical emphasis. Other religious books and mythical accounts are written in the format of the "long ago and far away." Thus, they are completely unverifiable; there is no way to examine them or support them with historical evidence. But the Bible is locked into space and time in such a way that we can know, with impressive accuracy, where and when its events took place (e.g., Jer. 1:1–3; Ezek. 1:1–3; Luke 3:1–2).

Fourth, the Bible is unique in its *product*. No other book has so profoundly influenced the culture, thought, and history of the world. It has molded and dominated the art, music, morality, oratory, law, politics, philosophy, and literature of Western civilization. It has not only changed history, but it has also changed millions of lives. Its witness to redemption in Christ has provided hope, joy, and purpose for all who have appropriated it.

As a revelation of God's love, the Bible requires a response. We must not only respond intellectually to its message, but also volitionally and morally. The Bible was divinely designed to change lives in a radical way, and it is perpetually relevant to all times and cultures. Far from being provincial or culturally bound, "the Word of our God stands forever" (Is. 40:8). "For the Word of God is living and powerful, and sharper than any two-edged sword, and piercing even to the division of soul and spirit, and of joints and marrow, and is a discerner of the thoughts and intents of the heart" (Heb. 4:12).

Nevertheless, many people have difficulty in putting the pieces of the Bible together. It is easy to get lost in the legal codes of Leviticus and Deuteronomy and in the oracles of the Old Testament prophets. Without broad overview, we will miss the harmony, grandeur, and significance of the Bible. If we limit ourselves to a snippet here and there, instead of pursuing a systematic plan to read the Bible through on a regular basis, we will be unable to appreciate the riches of this divine revelation. *Talk Thru the Bible* was developed to help the reader gain a synthetic perspective on the message of the Bible by providing an introduction, overview, and outline of each book.

The dove Noah released from the ark soared across the wide seas that engulfed the world, found no roost, and sought again the refuge of the great vessel. So man has departed from the truths of the Bible, using wings of independence to seek distant horizons. But like the weary dove, through the years many have returned to the changeless certainty of God's Word following years of aimless flight. As one generation begins to drift from the gospel, the following generation finds its worth anew, clinging tenaciously to its teachings as though they were the first to discover them.

As the vivid rainbow hearkens every eye to an upward glance, so the Bible draws men irresistibly to its message. The rainbow does not distinguish between the eye of a poor man and the eye of a king. Its attraction and promise are the same for all who behold, if only they have the eyes to see. Men and women of all times and lands and stations in life have sought the pages of this Book for comfort, wisdom, and challenge. Pioneers on horseback, truck drivers in their semis, and astronauts circling the moon have pondered its truths. Gang leaders in Harlem and headhunters in the Amazon have been transformed by its message. Though its colors are many and its spectrum is wide, it is, nonetheless one graceful arch of hope over a storm-darkened planet, varied in its appeal—singular in its beauty.

Introduction to the
Old Testament

THE BIBLE IS THE GREATEST WORK of literature, history, and theology ever written. In its production, preservation, proclamation, and product (changed history, changed lives), it stands as the most unique book in existence. It is a unity out of a diversity of authors, time span, and literary forms. The Old and New Testaments smoothly blend to create a bold sweep from eternity past to eternity future, from the heights of heaven to the depths of hell. In these sixty-six books we discover our past, understand our present, and attain hope for our future.

The Old Testament is a redemptive history that lays the foundation upon which the New Testament is built. There is a progressive revelation in the Scriptures, and what is anticipated in the Old Testament is unfolded in the New. The Old points ahead and the New points back to the central event in all history—the substitutionary death of the Messiah.

The Old Testament was originally divided into two sections: the Law and the Prophets (see Matt. 7:12; Luke 16:16,29,31). This was later expanded into a threefold division of the Law, the Prophets, and the Writings (Luke 24:44). All thirty-nine books in our Old Testament are contained in the twenty-four books of the Hebrew Bible.

The Greek translation of the Old Testament arranged the books in the four divisions that we use today: Law (5); History (12); Poetry (5); and Prophecy (17). The five Books of the Law can be combined with the twelve historical books to get the structure on the following page.

The seventeen historical books trace the entire history of Israel from its inception to the time of the prophet Malachi. In the Pentateuch Israel was chosen, redeemed, disciplined, and instructed. The remaining twelve historical books record the conquest of the land, the period of the judges, the formation of a united kingdom, and the division of that kingdom into the North (Israel) and the South (Judah). Each kingdom was taken into captivity but many of the people eventually returned.

The five poetical books focus on a right relationship with God as the basis for a life of meaning, skill, and beauty.

The seventeen prophetical books have a two-pronged message of condemnation (because of Israel's iniquity and idolatry) and consolation (future hope in spite of present judgment). Often at great personal cost, these men refused to dilute God's strong words.

	HISTORICAL (17)	POETICAL (5)	PROPHETICAL (17)	
PENTATEUCH (5)	Genesis	Job	Isaiah	**MAJOR (5)**
	Exodus	Psalms	Jeremiah	
	Leviticus	Proverbs	Lamentations	
	Numbers	Ecclesiastes	Ezekiel	
	Deuteronomy	Song of Solomon	Daniel	
HISTORICAL (12)	Joshua		Hosea	**MINOR (12)**
	Judges		Joel	
	Ruth		Amos	
	First Samuel		Obadiah	
	Second Samuel		Jonah	
	First Kings		Micah	
	Second Kings		Nahum	
	First Chronicles		Habakkuk	
	Second Chronicles		Zephaniah	
	Ezra		Haggai	
	Nehemiah		Zechariah	
	Esther		Malachi	

Events	Experience	Expectation
Past	Present	Future
God's Work	God's Ways	God's Will
Narrative	Poetry	Prophecy
Covenant People	Covenant Practice	

Introduction to the
Pentateuch

THE FIVE BOOKS OF MOSES are variously known as the Law, the Torah (Hebrew for Law), the Law of Moses, the "five-fifths of the Law," and the Pentateuch. The word "Pentateuch" is derived from the Greek words *penta* (five) and *teuchos* (scroll or book).

Although there is much external and internal evidence that supports the Mosaic authorship of these five books, many critics in the last two centuries have challenged this. The usual scenario is that Israel's religion evolved through several stages and various literary strands appeared along the way. These were edited during the divided kingdom and after the Babylonian exile. These theories, however, are built upon assumptions that have since been proven false or remain unproven.

Is the Pentateuch Mosaic or is it a mosaic? These books show a clear continuity of content, theme, purpose, and style that point to a single author. They make up a unity, not a late and unreliable patchwork. Each book smoothly picks up where the previous book left off. There is a completeness about the Pentateuch not only in its consecutive history but also in its progressive spiritual development:

BOOK	KEY IDEA	THE NATION	THE PEOPLE	GOD'S CHARACTER	GOD'S ROLE	GOD'S COMMAND
Genesis	Beginnings	Chosen	Prepared	Powerful Sovereign	Creator	"Let there be!"
Exodus	Redemption	Delivered	Redeemed	Merciful	Deliverer	"Let My people go!"
Leviticus	Worship	Set Apart	Taught	Holy	Sanctifier	"Be holy!"
Numbers	Wandering	Directed	Tested	Just	Sustainer	"Go in!"
Deuteronomy	Renewed	Made Ready	Retaught	Loving Lord	Rewarder	"Obey!"

Genesis

This book provides the foundation for the entire Bible in its history and theology. Its first eleven chapters give a sweeping survey of primeval events: God's work of creation, the fall of man, the judgment of the Flood, and the spread of the nations. There is a sudden shift in chapter 12 as God singles out one man through whom He would bring salvation and bless all nations. The remainder of Genesis traces the story of Abraham and his descendants Isaac, Jacob, and Joseph.

Exodus

Jacob's descendants have moved from Canaan to Egypt and are suffering under the bondage of a new pharaoh. After a period of four hundred years they cry to God for deliverance. God responds by empowering Moses to stand before Pharaoh and create the ten devastating plagues. After their redemption in the Passover, the Israelites leave Egypt, cross the sea, and journey to Mount Sinai. There God reveals His covenant law and gives them the pattern for the building of the tabernacle.

Leviticus

Now that the people have been redeemed and delivered, they must be set apart to God to live holy lives. God gives them instructions for the sacrificial system and the priesthood. The remainder of Leviticus teaches the people how to become ceremonially and morally pure. The emphasis is on sanctification, service, and obedience.

Numbers

Still at Mount Sinai, the people receive additional directions before proceeding to the promised land of Canaan. When they are on the verge of entering the land, their faith crumbles and God disciplines them by making them wander in the wilderness until the disbelieving generation dies out. The new generation then reaches Moab, the doorway to the land of Canaan. It is here that God begins to instruct the people who are about to inherit the land.

Deuteronomy

Moses is at the end of his life and Joshua has been appointed as his successor. In his farewell messages to the generation that grew up in the wilderness, Moses reminds them of God's dealings in the past, reviews the need for righteousness and integrity in the present, and reveals what will happen in the near and distant future. Moses then blesses the people and views the Promised Land from Mount Nebo before his death.

Genesis

GENESIS IS THE BOOK of beginnings. Its fifty chapters sketch human history from creation to Babel (chs. 1—11) and from Abraham to Joseph (chs. 12—50). The first eleven chapters introduce the Creator God and the beginnings of life, sin, judgment, family, worship, and salvation. The remainder of the book focuses on the lives of four patriarchs of the faith: Abraham, Isaac, Jacob, and Joseph, from whom will come the nation of Israel and ultimately the Savior, Jesus Christ.

Focus	Four Events				Four People			
	1:1 ———————————— 11:9				11:10 ———————————————— 50:26			
Divisions	Creation	Fall	Flood	Nations	Abraham	Isaac	Jacob	Joseph
	1:1 — 2:25	3:1 — 5:32	6:1 — 9:29	10:1 — 11:9	11:10 — 25:8	25:19 — 26:35	27:1 — 36:43	37:1 — 50:26
Topics	Beginning of the Human Race				Beginning of the Hebrew Race			
	Historical				Biographical			
Place	Fertile Crescent (Eden-Haran)				Canaan (Haran–Canaan)			Egypt (Canaan–Egypt)
Time	c. 2000+ Years (c. 4004–2090 B.C.)				193 Years (2090–1897 B.C.)			93 Years (1897–1804 B.C.)

GENESIS

—5—

Introduction and Title

The first part of Genesis focuses on the beginning and spread of sin in the world and culminates in the devastating Flood in the days of Noah. The second part of the book focuses on God's dealings with one man, Abraham, through whom God promises to bring salvation and blessing to the world. Abraham and his descendants learn firsthand that it is always safe to trust the Lord in times of famine and feasting, blessing and bondage. From Abraham . . . to Isaac . . . to Jacob . . . to Joseph . . . God's promises begin to come to fruition in a great nation possessing a great land.

Genesis is a Greek word meaning "origin, source, generation, or beginning." The original Hebrew title *Bereshith* means "In the Beginning."

The literary structure of Genesis is clear and is built around eleven separate units, each headed with the word *generations* in the phrase "These are the generations" or "The book of the generations": (1) Introduction to the Generations (1:1—2:3); (2) Heaven and Earth (2:4—4:26); (3) Adam (5:1—6:8); (4) Noah (6:9—9:29); (5) Sons of Noah (10:1—11:9); (6) Shem (11:10–26); (7) Terah (11:27—25:11); (8) Ishmael (25:12–18); (9) Isaac (25:19—35:29); (10) Esau (36:1—37:1); (11) Jacob (37:2—50:26).

Author

Although Genesis does not directly name its author, and although Genesis ends some three centuries before Moses was born, the whole of Scripture and church history are unified in their adherence to the Mosaic authorship of Genesis.

The Old Testament is replete with both direct and indirect testimonies to the Mosaic authorship of the entire Pentateuch (see Ex. 17:14; Lev. 1:1–2; Num. 33:2; Deut. 1:1; Josh. 1:7; 1 Kin. 2:3; 2 Kin. 14:6; Ezra 6:18; Neh. 13:1; Dan. 9:11–13; Mal 4:4). The New Testament also contains numerous testimonies (see Matt. 8:4; Mark 12:26; Luke 16:29; John 7:19; Acts 26:22; Rom. 10:19; 1 Cor. 9:9; 2 Cor. 3:15).

The early church openly held to the Mosaic authorship, as does the first-century Jewish historian Josephus. As would be expected the Jerusalem Talmud supports Moses as author.

It would be difficult to find a man in all the range of Israel's life who was better prepared or qualified to write this history. Trained in the "wisdom of the Egyptians" (Acts 7:22), Moses had been providentially prepared to understand and integrate, under the inspiration of God, all the available records, manuscripts, and oral narratives.

Date and Setting

Genesis divides neatly into three geographical settings: (1) the Fertile Crescent (1—11); (2) Israel (12—36); (3) Egypt (37—50).

The setting of the first eleven chapters changes rapidly as it spans more than two thousand years and fifteen hundred miles, and paints the majestic acts of the Creation, the Garden of Eden, the Noahic Flood, and the towering citadel of Babel.

The middle section of Genesis rapidly funnels down from the broad brim of the two millenia spent in the Fertile Crescent to less than two hundred years in the little country of Canaan. Surrounded by the rampant immorality and idolatry of the Canaanites, the godliness of Abraham rapidly degenerates into gross immorality in some of his descendants.

In the last fourteen chapters, God dramatically saves the small Israelite nation from extinction by transferring the "seventy souls" to Egypt so that they may grow and multiply. Egypt is an unexpected womb for the growth of God's chosen nation Israel, to be sure, but one in which they are isolated from the maiming influence of Canaan.

Genesis spans more time than any other book in the Bible; in fact, it covers more than all sixty-five other books of the Bible put together.

Utilizing the same threefold division noted above, the following dates can be assigned:

A. 2000 or more years, 4000–2090 B.C. (1—11)
  1. Creation, 4000 B.C. or earlier (1:1)
  2. Death of Terah, 2090 B.C. (11:32)
B. 193 years, 2090–1897 B.C. (12—36)
  1. Death of Terah, 2090 B.C. (11:32)
  2. Joseph to Egypt, c. 1897 B.C. (37:2)
C. 93 years, 1897–1804 B.C. (37—50)
  1. Joseph to Egypt, c. 1897 B.C. (37:2)
  2. Death of Joseph, 1804 B.C. (50:26)

Theme and Purpose

The theme of Genesis is God's choice of a nation through whom He would bless all nations.

Over two thousand years are covered in Genesis 1—11, but this represents only one-fifth of the book. By contrast, four-fifths of Genesis (12—50) covers less than three hundred years. It is clear that Genesis is highly thematic, concentrating on the course of God's redemptive work. Genesis is not a complete or universal history.

Genesis was written to present the beginning of everything except God: the universe (1:1); man (1:27); the Sabbath (2:2–3); marriage (2:22–24); sin (3:1–7); sacrifice and salvation (3:15,21); the family (4:1–15); civilization (4:16–21); government (9:1–6); nations (11); Israel (12:1–3). It was also written to record God's choice of Israel and His covenant plan for the nation, so that the Israelites would have a spiritual perspective. Genesis shows how the sin of man is met by the intervention and redemption of God.

Keys to Genesis

Key Word: Beginnings

Key Verses (3:15; 12:3)—"And I will put enmity between you and the woman, and between your seed and her Seed; He shall bruise your head, and you shall, bruise His heel" (3:15).

"I will bless those who bless you, and I will curse him who curses you; and; in you all the families of the earth shall be blessed" (12:3).

Key Chapter (15)—Central to all of Scripture is the Abrahamic covenant, which is given in 12:1–3 and ratified in 15:1–21. Israel receives three specific promises: (1) the promise of a great land—"from the river of Egypt to the great river, the River Euphrates" (15:18); (2) the promise of a great nation—"and I will make your descendants as the dust of the earth" (13:16); and (3) the promise of a great blessing— "I will bless you and make your name great; and you shall be a blessing" (12:2).

Christ in Genesis

Genesis moves from the general to the specific in its messianic predictions: Christ is the Seed of the woman (3:15), from the line of Seth (4:25), the son of Shem (9:27), the descendant of Abraham (12:3), of Isaac (21:12), of Jacob (25:23), and of the tribe of Judah (49:10).

Christ is also seen in people and events that serve as types. (A "type" is a historical fact that illustrates a spiritual truth.) Adam is "a type of Him who was to come" (Rom. 5:14). Both entered the world through a special act of God as sinless men. Adam is the head of the old creation; Christ is the Head of the new creation. Abel's acceptable offering of a blood sacrifice points to Christ, and there is a parallel in his murder by Cain. Melchizedek ("righteous king") is. "made like the Son of God" (Heb. 7:3). He is the king of Salem ("peace") who brings forth bread and wine and is the priest of the Most High God. Joseph is also a type of Christ. Joseph and Christ are both objects of special love by their fathers, both are hated by their brethren, both are rejected as rulers over their brethren, both are conspired against and sold for silver, both are condemned though innocent, and both are raised from humiliation to glory by the power of God.

Contribution to the Bible

Genesis provides a historical perspective for the rest of the Bible by covering more time than all the other biblical books combined. Its sweeping scope from Eden to Ur to Haran to Canaan to Egypt makes it the introduction not only to the Pentateuch but to the Scriptures as a whole. Genesis gives the foundation for all the great doctrines of the Bible. It shows how God overcomes man's failure under different conditions. Genesis is especially crucial to an understanding of Revelation, because the first and last three chapters of the Bible are so intimately related.

Survey of Genesis

Genesis is not so much a history of man as it is the first chapter in the history of the *redemption* of man. As such, Genesis is a highly selective spiritual interpretation of history. Genesis is divided into four great events (1—11) and four great people (12—50).

The Four Great Events: Chapters 1—11 lay the foundation upon which the whole Bible is built and center on four key events. (1) *Creation:* God is the sovereign Creator of matter, energy, space, and time. Man is the pinnacle of the Creation. (2)

Fall: Creation is followed by corruption. In the first sin man is separated from God (Adam from God), and in the second sin, man is separated from man (Cain from Abel). In spite of the devastating curse of the Fall, God promises hope of redemption through the seed of the woman (3:15). (3) *Flood:* As man multiplies, sin also multiplies until God is compelled to destroy humanity with the exception of Noah and his family. (4) *Nations:* Genesis teaches the unity of the human race: we are all children of Adam through Noah, but because of rebellion at the Tower of Babel, God fragments the single culture and language of the post-Flood world and scatters people over the face of the earth.

The Four Great People: Once the nations are scattered, God focuses on one man and his descendants through whom He will bless all nations (12—50). (1) *Abraham:* The calling of Abraham (12) is the pivotal point of the book. The three covenant promises God makes to Abraham (land, descendants, and blessing) are foundational to His program of bringing salvation upon the earth. (2) *Isaac:* God establishes His covenant with Isaac as the spiritual link with Abraham. (3) *Jacob:* God transforms this man from selfishness to servanthood and changes his name to Israel, the father of the twelve tribes. (4) *Joseph:* Jacob's favorite son suffers at the hands of his brothers and becomes a slave in Egypt. After his dramatic rise to the rulership of Egypt, Joseph delivers his family from famine and brings them out of Canaan to Goshen.

Genesis ends on a note of impending bondage with the death of Joseph. There is great need for the redemption that is to follow in the Book of Exodus.

Outline of Genesis

Part One: Primeval History (1:1—11:9)

I. The Creation, 1:1—2:25
    A. Creation of the World, 1:1—2:3
    B. Creation of Man, 2:4–25

II. The Fall, 3:1—5:32
    A. The Fall of Man, 3:1–24
        1. Temptation of Man, 3:1–5
        2. Fall of Man, 3:6–7
        3. Judgment on Man, 3:8–24
    B. After the Fall: Conflicting Family Lines, 4:1—5:32
        1. The Initial Conflict, 4:1–15
        2. The Ungodly Line of Cain, 4:16–24
        3. The Godly Line of Seth, 4:25—5:32

III. The Judgment of the Flood, 6:1—9:29
    A. Causes of the Flood, 6:1–5
        1. The Ungodly Multiply, 6:1–4
        2. The Ungodly Sin Continually, 6:5

    B. Judgment of the Flood, 6:6–22
        1. Ungodly to Be Destroyed, 6:6–7
        2. Godly to Be Saved, 6:8–22
    C. The Flood, 7:1—8:19
        1. The Ark Is Entered, 7:1–10
        2. The Earth Is Flooded, 7:11–24
        3. The Flood Recedes, 8:1–19
    D. Results of the Flood, 8:20—9:17
        1. Noah Worships God, 8:20–22
        2. God's Covenant to Noah, 9:1–17
    E. After the Flood: The Sin of the Godly Line, 9:18–29
        1. The Sons of Noah, 9:18–19
        2. Ham's Sin, 9:20–24
        3. The Curse on Canaan, 9:25–27
        4. Noah's Death, 9:28–29

IV. The Judgment on the Tower of Babel, 10:1—11:9
    A. Family Lines after the Flood, 10:1–32
        1. The Family of Japheth, 10:1–5
        2. The Family of Ham, 10:6–14
        3. The Family of Canaan, 10:15–20
        4. The Family of Shem, 10:21–32
    B. Judgment on all the Family Lines, 11:1–9
        1. Construction of the Tower, 11:1–3
        2. Rebellion at the Tower, 11:4
        3. Judgment on all the Family Lines, 11:5–9

Part Two: Patriarchal History (11:10—50:26)

I. The Life of Abraham, 11:10—25:18
    A. Introduction of Abram, 11:10–32
        1. Abram's Family Line, 11:10–26
        2. Abram's Past, 11:27–32
    B. The Covenant of God with Abram, 12:1—25:18
        1. Initiation of the Covenant, 12:1–20
        2. Separation to the Covenant, 13:1—14:24
            a. Abram's Separation from Lot, 13:1–13
            b. God's Promise to Abram, 13:14–18
            c. Abram Rescues Lot, 14:1–16
            d. Abram Refuses Reward, 14:17–24
        3. Ratification of the Covenant, 15:1—16:16
            a. God's Promise of Children, 15:1–21
            b. A Carnal Plan for Children, 16:1–16
        4. Institution of the Covenant: Circumcision, 17:1–27
        5. Testing of the Covenant, 18:1—20:18
            a. Sarah's Faith Is Tested, 18:1–15
            b. Abraham's Faith Is Tested, 18:16–33

c. Destruction of Sodom and Gomorrah, 19:1–29
d. The Sin of Lot, 19:30–38
e. The Test of Abimelech, 20:1–18
6. Consummation of the Covenant, 21:1—25:18
  a. Birth of Isaac, 21:1–34
  b. Offering of Isaac, 22:1–24
  c. Death of Sarah, 23:1–20
  d. Isaac's Marriage, 24:1–67
  e. Abraham Dies, 25:1–18

II. The Life of Isaac, 25:19—26:35
A. The Family of Isaac, 25:19–34
B. The Failure of Isaac, 26:1–33
C. The Failure of Esau, 26:34–35

III. The Life of Jacob, 27:1—36:43
A. Jacob Gains Esau's Blessing, 27:1—28:9
B. Jacob's Life at Haran, 28:10—31:55
  1. Jacob's Dream, 28:10–22
  2. Jacob's Labors, 29:1—30:43
  3. Jacob's Flight, 31:1–55
C. Jacob's Return, 32:1—33:20
  1. Jacob Fights with the Angel, 32:1–32
  2. Jacob Makes Peace with Esau, 33:1–20
D. Jacob's Residence in Canaan, 34:1—35:29
  1. The Defilement of Dinah, 34:1–31
  2. The Devotion at Bethel, 35:1–15
  3. The Deaths of Rachel and Isaac, 35:16–29
E. The History of Esau, 36:1–43

IV. The Life of Joseph, 37:1—50:26
A. The Corruption of Joseph's Family, 37:1—38:30
  1. Joseph's Family Sins against Him, 37:1–36
  2. Joseph's Family Sins with the Canaanites, 38:1–30
B. The Exaltation of Joseph, 39:1—41:57
  1. Joseph's Test with the Egyptian Woman, 39:1–23
  2. Joseph's Test with the Egyptian Society, 40:1–23
  3. Joseph's Test with Pharaoh's Dreams, 41:1–36
  4. Joseph's Exaltation over Egypt, 41:37–57
C. The Salvation of Jacob's Family, 42:1—50:26
  1. Joseph's Brothers Visit Egypt, 42:1–38
  2. Joseph's Brothers' Second Journey to Egypt, 43:1—45:28
  3. Jacob's Family Safe in Egypt, 46:1—47:26
  4. Jacob Blesses the Family in Egypt, 47:27—49:32
  5. Jacob Dies in Egypt, 49:33—50:14
  6. Joseph Dies in Egypt, 50:15–26

Exodus

AFTER NEARLY FOUR HUNDRED YEARS of growth in Egypt, the infant nation Israel is now ready to leave behind the chains of slavery and seek a new homeland. Exodus narrates the liberation of Israel from Egyptian captivity and the migration of God's new nation to the wilderness of Sinai. Moses, the great deliverer, announces ten devastating plagues of judgment upon Egypt, then leads the Israelites on the first leg of their journey to the Promised Land.

Chapters 1—18 relate Israel's exodus from bondage in Egypt, while chapters 19—40 record the instructions given by God on Mount Sinai to direct the life and worship of the nation.

EXODUS

Focus	Redemption from Egypt				Revelation from God	
	1:1 — 18:27				19:1 — 40:38	
Divisions	Need for Redemption	Preparation for Redemption	Redemption of Israel	Preservation of Israel	Revelation of the Covenant	Response of Israel to the Covenant
	1:1 — 1:22	2:1 — 4:31	5:1 — 15:21	15:22 — 18:27	19:1 — 31:18	32:1 — 40:38
Topics	Narration				Legislation	
	Subjection		Redemption		Instruction	
Place	Egypt		Wilderness		Mount Sinai	
	1:1 — 13:16		13:17 — 18:27		19:1 — 40:38	
Time	430 Years		2 Months		10 Months	

Introduction and Title

Exodus is the record of Israel's birth as a nation. Within the protective "womb" of Egypt, the Jewish family of seventy rapidly multiplies. At the right time, accompanied by severe "birth pains," an infant nation, numbering between two and three million people, is brought into the world where it is divinely protected, fed, and nurtured.

The Hebrew title, *We'elleh Shemoth,* "And These Are the Names," comes from the first phrase in 1:1. Exodus begins in the Hebrew with "And" to show it as a continuation of Genesis. The Greek title is *Exodus,* a word meaning "exit, departure, or going out." The Septuagint uses this word to describe the book by its key event (see 19:1, "gone out"). In Luke 9:31 and in Second Peter 1:15, the word *exodus* speaks of physical death (Jesus and Peter). This embodies Exodus' theme of redemption, because redemption is accomplished only through death. The Latin title is *Liber Exodus,* "Book of Departure," taken from the Greek title.

Author

Critics have challenged the Mosaic authorship of Exodus in favor of a series of oral and written documents that were woven together by editors late in Israel's history. Their arguments are generally weak and far from conclusive, especially in view of the strong external and internal evidence that points to Moses as the author.

External Evidence: Exodus has been attributed to Moses since the time of Joshua (see 20:25; Josh. 8:30–32). Other biblical writers attribute Exodus to Moses: Malachi (Mal. 4:4), the disciples (John 1:45), and Paul (Rom. 10:5). This is also the testimony of Jesus (see Mark 7:10; 12:26; Luke 20:37; John 5:46–47; 7:19, 22–23). Jewish and Samaritan traditions consistently hold to the Mosaic authorship of Exodus.

Internal Evidence: Portions of Exodus are directly attributed to Moses (see 15; 17:8–14; 20:1–17; 24:4, 7, 12; 31:18; 34:1–27). Moses' usual procedure was to record events soon after they occurred in the form of historical annals. It is clear from Exodus that the author must have been an eyewitness of the Exodus and an educated man. He was acquainted with details about the customs and climate of Egypt and the plants, animals, and terrain of the wilderness. A consistency of style and development also points to a single author. Its antiquity is supported by the frequent use of ancient literary constructions, words, and expressions.

Date and Setting

If the early date for the Exodus (c. 1445 B.C.) is assumed, this book was composed during the forty-year wilderness journey, between 1445 B.C. and 1405 B.C. Moses probably kept an account of God's work, which he then edited in the plains of Moab shortly before his death. Exodus covers the period from the arrival of Jacob in Egypt (c. 1875 B.C.) to the erection of the tabernacle 431 years later in the wilderness (c. 1445 B.C.).

Theme and Purpose

There are two basic themes in Exodus, and both tie in together. The first theme is redemption, portrayed in the Passover, and the second theme is deliverance, portrayed in the Exodus from Egypt (see 6:6; 15:13,16; Deut. 7:8). This redemption and deliverance was accomplished through the shedding of blood and by the power of God.

Exodus was written to portray the birth of Israel as the nation that would bring God's rule on earth. It records the story of Israel's redemption under the leadership of Moses. It also serves as an exposé of the falsehood of idolatry. Yahweh is revealed as infinitely superior to any so-called "gods." Exodus also teaches that obedience to God is necessary for a redeemed and set apart people.

Keys to Exodus

Key Word: Redemption
Key Verses (6:6; 19:5–6)—"Therefore say to the children of Israel: 'I *am* the LORD; I will bring you out from under the burdens of the Egyptians, I will rescue you from their bondage, and I will redeem you with an outstretched arm and with great judgments'" (6:6).

"'Now therefore, if you will indeed obey My voice and keep My covenant, then you shall be a special treasure to Me above all people; for all the earth *is* Mine. And you shall be to Me a kingdom of priests and a holy nation'" (19:5–6).

Key Chapters (12—14)—The climax of the entire Old Testament is recorded in chapters 12—14: the salvation of Israel through blood (the Passover) and through power (the Red Sea). The Exodus is the central event of the Old Testament as the Cross is of the New Testament.

Christ in Exodus

Exodus contains no direct messianic prophecies, but it is full of types and portraits of Christ. Here are seven: (1) *Moses:* In dozens of ways Moses is a type of Christ (Deut. 18:15). Both Moses and Christ are prophets, priests, and kings (although Moses was never made king, he functioned as the ruler of Israel); both are kinsman-redeemers; both are endangered in infancy; both voluntarily renounce power and wealth; both are deliverers, lawgivers, and mediators. (2) *The Passover:* John 1:29, 36 and First Corinthians 5:7 make it clear that Christ is our slain God and the Passover Lamb. (3) *The seven feasts:* Each of these feasts portrays some aspect of the ministry of Christ. (4) *The Exodus:* Paul relates baptism to the Exodus event because baptism symbolizes death to the old and identification with the new (see Rom. 6:2–3; 1 Cor. 10:1–2). (5) *The manna and water:* The New Testament applies both to Christ (see John 6:31–35, 48–63; 1 Cor. 10:3–4). (6) *The tabernacle:* In its materials, colors, furniture, and arrangement, the tabernacle clearly speaks of the person of Christ and the way of redemption. The development is progressive from suffering, blood, and death, to beauty, holiness, and the glory of God. The tabernacle is theology in a physical form. (7) *The high priest:* In several ways the high priest foreshadows the ministry of Christ, our Great High Priest (see Heb. 4:14–16; 9:11–12, 24–28).

Contribution to the Bible

Exodus accounts for many of the religious ceremonies and customs of Israel, the creation of the tabernacle, the formation of the priesthood, the Mosaic Law, and the sacrificial system. As such, Exodus is foundational for the following history of Israel. It describes how the Israelites escaped from Egypt, became the covenant people of God, and came to know His presence and His ways. Exodus stands at the heart of the Old Testament as the greatest example of the saving acts of God before Christ. It provides the framework for the rest of the Old Testament message. The Passover, the Exodus, Moses, the Law, and the tabernacle dominated the thought of Israel for centuries to come.

Survey of Exodus

Exodus abounds with God's powerful redemptive acts on behalf of His oppressed people. It begins in pain and ends in liberation; it moves from the groaning of the people to the glory of God. It is the continuation of the story that begins in Genesis with the seventy descendants of Jacob who move from Canaan to Egypt. They have multiplied under adverse conditions to a multitude of over two million people. When the Israelites finally turn to God for deliverance from their bondage, God quickly responds by redeeming them "with an outstretched arm and with great judgments" (6:6). God faithfully fulfills His promise made to Abraham centuries before (Gen. 15:13–14).

The book falls into two parts: (1) redemption from Egypt (1—8); and (2) revelation from God (19—40).

Redemption from Egypt (1—18): After four centuries of slavery, the people of Israel cry to the God of Abraham, Isaac, and Jacob for deliverance. God has already prepared Moses for this purpose, and has commissioned him at the burning bush to stand before Pharaoh as the advocate for Israel. However, Pharaoh hardens his heart: "Who is the LORD, that I should obey His voice to let Israel go?" (5:2).

God soon reveals Himself to Pharaoh through a series of object lessons, the ten plagues. These plagues grow in severity until the tenth brings death to the firstborn of every household of Egypt. Israel is redeemed through this plague by means of the Passover lamb. The Israelites' faith in God at this point becomes the basis for their national redemption. As they leave Egypt, God guides them by a pillar of fire and smoke, and saves them from Egypt's pursuing army through the miraculous crossing of the sea. In the wilderness He protects and sustains them throughout their journeys.

Revelation from God (19—40): Now that the people have experienced God's deliverance, guidance, and protection, they are ready to be taught what God expects of them. The redeemed people must now be set apart to walk with God. This is why the emphasis moves from narration in chapters 1—18 to legislation in chapters 19—

40. On Mount Sinai, Moses receives God's moral, civil, and ceremonial laws, as well as the pattern for the tabernacle to be built in the wilderness. After God judges the people for their worship of the golden calf, the tabernacle is constructed and consecrated. It is a building of beauty in a barren land and reveals much about the person of God and the way of redemption.

Outline of Exodus

Part One: Redemption from Egypt (1:1—18:27)

I. The Need for Redemption from Egypt, 1:1–22
   A. Israel's Rapid Multiplication, 1:1–7
   B. Israel's Severe Affliction, 1:8–14
   C. Israel's Planned Extinction, 1:15–22

II. The Preparation of the Leaders of the Redemption, 2:1—4:31
   A. Moses Is Redeemed from Murder, 2:1–10
   B. Moses Tries to Redeem by Murder, 2:11–22
   C. Israel Calls upon God, 2:23–25
   D. God Calls upon Moses, 3:1—4:17
      1. God Miraculously Appears, 3:1–6
      2. God Calls Moses to Leadership, 3:7–10
      3. God Answers Moses' Objections, 3:11—4:17
         a. "Who Am I?", 3:11–12
         b. "What Is His Name?", 3:13–22
         c. "They Will Not Believe Me," 4:1–9
         d. "I Am Slow of Speech," 4:10–17
   E. Moses Accepts the Call, 4:18–26
      1. Moses Returns to Egypt, 4:18–23
      2. Moses Reinstitutes Circumcision, 4:24–26
   F. Israel Accepts the Call of Moses as Deliverer, 4:27–31

III. The Redemption of Israel from Egypt by God, 5:1—15:21
   A. Moses Confronts Pharaoh by Word, 5:1—6:9
      1. Pharaoh Rejects Moses, 5:1–14
      2. Israel Rejects Moses, 5:15–21
      3. Moses Questions God's Plan, 5:22–23
      4. God Reassures Moses, 6:1–8
      5. Moses Reassures Israel, 6:9
   B. Moses Confronts Pharaoh with Miracles, 6:10—7:13
      1. God Recommissions Moses, 6:10–27
      2. Moses Objects, 6:28–30
      3. God Reassures Moses, 7:1–7
      4. Aaron's Rod Swallows Pharaoh's Rods, 7:8–13

C. Moses Confronts Pharaoh Through Plagues, 7:14—11:10
   1. First Plague: Blood, 7:14–25
   2. Second Plague: Frogs, 8:1–15
   3. Third Plague: Lice, 8:16–19
   4. Fourth Plague: Flies, 8:20–32
   5. Fifth Plague: Disease on Beasts, 9:1–7
   6. Sixth Plague: Boils on Man and Beast, 9:8–12
   7. Seventh Plague: Hail, 9:13–35
   8. Eighth Plague: Locusts, 10:1–20
   9. Ninth Plague: Darkness, 10:21–29
   10. Tenth Plague: Death Announced, 11:1–10
D. Israel Redeemed by Blood through the Passover, 12:1—13:16
   1. Instructions for the Passover, 12:1–20
   2. Participation in the Passover, 12:21–28
   3. Redemption through the Passover, 12:29–36
   4. Freedom because of the Passover, 12:37–51
   5. Sanctification as a Result of the Passover, 13:1–16
E. Israel Redeemed by Power from Egypt, 13:17—15:21
   1. God Leads Israel, 13:17—14:2
   2. Pharaoh Follows Israel, 14:3–9
   3. Israel Rebels against God, 14:10–12
   4. God Opens the Red Sea, 14:13–31
   5. Israel Praises God, 15:1–21

IV. The Preservation of Israel in the Wilderness, 15:22—18:27
A. Preserved from Thirst, 15:22–27
B. Preserved from Hunger, 16:1–36
C. Preserved from Thirst Again, 17:1–7
D. Preserved from Defeat, 17:8–16
E. Preserved from Chaos, 18:1–27

Part Two: Revelation from God (19:1—40:38)

I. The Revelation of the Old Covenant, 19:1—31:18
A. The Preparation of the People, 19:1–25
   1. Location of the Giving of the Covenant, 19:1–2
   2. Purpose of the Covenant, 19:3–6
   3. Israel Accepts the Covenant, 19:7–8
   4. Israelites Sanctify Themselves, 19:9–25
B. The Revelation of the Covenant, 20:1–26
   1. The Ten Commandments, 20:1–17
      a. Commandments Relating to God, 20:1–11
      b. Commandments Relating to Man, 20:12–17
   2. The Response of Israel, 20:18–21
   3. Provision for Approaching God, 20:22–26

C. The Judgments, 21:1—23:33
   1. Social Regulations, 21:1—22:15
      a. Rights of Persons, 21:1–32
      b. Rights of Property, 21:33—22:15
   2. Moral Regulations, 22:16—23:9
      a. Proper Conduct, 22:16–31
      b. Proper Justice, 23:1–9
   3. Religious Regulations, 23:10–19
      a. Sabbatical Year, 23:10–13
      b. Three National Feasts, 23:14–19
   4. Conquest Regulations, 23:20–33
D. The Formal Ratification of the Covenant, 24:1–11
   1. The Covenant Is Ratified through Blood, 24:1–8
   2. The God of the Covenant Is Revealed, 24:9–11
E. The Tabernacle, 24:12—27:21
   1. The Revelation Is Given on Mount Sinai, 24:12–18
   2. The Offering for the Tabernacle, 25:1–7
   3. The Revelation of the Tabernacle, 25:8—27:21
      a. The Purpose of the Tabernacle, 25:8–9
      b. The Ark of the Covenant, 25:10–22
      c. The Table of Showbread, 25:23–30
      d. The Golden Lampstand, 25:31–40
      e. The Curtains of Linen, 26:1–14
      f. The Boards and Sockets, 26:15–30
      g. The Inner Veil, 26:31–35
      h. The Outer Veil, 26:36–37
      i. The Bronze Altar, 27:1–8
      j. The Court of the Tabernacle, 27:9–19
      k. The Oil for the Lamp, 27:20–21
F. The Priests, 28:1—29:46
   1. The Clothing of the Priests, 28:1–43
      a. The Command to Make the Priests' Clothes, 28:1–5
      b. The Ephod, 28:6–14
      c. The Breastplate, 28:15–29
      d. The Urim and Thummim, 28:30
      e. The Robe of the Ephod, 28:31–35
      f. The Holy Crown, 28:36–38
      g. The Priest's Coat, 28:39–43
   2. The Consecration of the Priests, 29:1–37
   3. The Continual Offerings of the Priests, 29:38–46
G. Institution of the Covenant, 30:1—31:18
   1. Instructions for Using the Tabernacle, 30:1–38
      a. The Altar of Incense, 30:1–10
      b. The Ransom Money, 30:11–16
      c. The Laver of Bronze, 30:17–21

Leviticus

LEVITICUS FOCUSES ON THE WORSHIP and walk of the nation of God. In Exodus, Israel was redeemed and established as a kingdom of priests and a holy nation. Leviticus shows how God's people are to fulfill their priestly calling. They have been led out of bondage (Exodus), and into the sanctuary of God (Leviticus); now they must move on from redemption to service, from deliverance to dedication.

Leviticus is God's guidebook for His newly redeemed people, showing them how to worship, serve, and obey a holy God. Both access to God (through the sacrifices) and fellowship with God (through obedience) show the awesome holiness of the God of Israel. Indeed "you shall be holy; for I [the Lord] am holy" (11:44).

Focus	Sacrifice				Sanctification				
	1:1 .... 17:16				18:1 .... 27:34				
Divisions	Laws of Acceptable Approach to God	Laws of the Priests	Laws of Israel Regarding Purity	Laws of National Atonement	Laws of Sanctification for the People	Laws of Sanctification for the Priesthood	Laws of Sanctification in Worship	Laws of Sanctification in the Land of Canaan	Laws of Sanctification through Vows
	1:1 — 7:38	8:1 — 10:20	11:1 — 15:33	16:1 — 17:16	18:1 — 20:27	21:1 — 22:33	23:1 — 24:23	25:1 — 26:46	27:1 — 27:34
Topics	Way to God				Walk with God				
	Laws of Acceptable Approach to God				Laws of Continued Fellowship with God				
Place	Mount Sinai								
Time	c. 1 Month								

LEVITICUS

Introduction and Title

Leviticus is God's guidebook for His newly redeemed people, showing them how to worship, serve, and obey a holy God. Fellowship with God through sacrifice and obedience show the awesome holiness of the God of Israel. Indeed, " 'You shall be holy, for I the LORD your God *am* holy' " (19:2).

Leviticus focuses on the worship and walk of the nation of God. In Exodus, Israel was redeemed and established as a kingdom of priests and a holy nation. Leviticus shows how God's people are to fulfill their priestly calling.

The Hebrew title is *Wayyiqra,* "And He Called." The Talmud refers to Leviticus as the "Law of the Priests," and the "Law of the Offerings." The Greek title appearing in the Septuagint is *Leuitikon,* "that which pertains to the Levites." From this word, the Latin Vulgate derived its name *Leviticus* which was adopted as the English title. This title is slightly misleading because the book does not deal with the Levites as a whole but more with the priests, a segment of the Levites.

Author

The kind of arguments used to confirm the Mosaic authorship of Genesis and Exodus also apply to Leviticus because the Pentateuch is a literary unit. In addition to these arguments, others include the following:

External Evidence: (1) A uniform ancient testimony supports the Mosaic authorship of Leviticus. (2) Ancient parallels to the Levitical system of trespass offerings have been found in the Ras Shamra Tablets dating from about 1400 B.C. and discovered on the coast of northern Syria. (3) Christ ascribes the Pentateuch (which includes Leviticus) to Moses (cf. Matt. 8:2–4 and Lev. 14:1–4; Matt. 12:4 and Lev. 24:9; see also Luke 2:22).

Internal Evidence: (1) Fifty-six times in the twenty-seven chapters of Leviticus it is stated that God imparted these laws to Moses (see 1:1; 4:1; 6:1, 24; 8:1). (2) The Levitical code fits the time of Moses. Economic, civil, moral, and religious considerations show it to be ancient. Many of the laws are also related to a migratory life-style.

Date and Setting

No geographical movement takes place in Leviticus: the children of Israel remain camped at the foot of Mount Sinai (see 25:1–2; 26:46; 27:34). The new calendar of Israel begins with the first Passover (Ex. 12:2); and, according to Exodus 40:17, the tabernacle is completed exactly one year later.

Leviticus picks up the story at this point and takes place in the first month of the second year. Numbers 1:1 opens at the beginning of the second month. Moses probably wrote much of Leviticus during that first month and may have put it in its final form shortly before his death in Moab, about 1405 B.C.

Theme and Purpose

The clear theme of Leviticus is holiness (11:45; 19:2). It teaches that one must approach a holy God on the basis of sacrifice and priestly mediation, and that one can only walk with a holy God on the basis of sanctification and obedience. God's chosen people must approach Him in a holy manner.

Leviticus was written to show Israel how to live as a priestly kingdom and a holy nation in fellowship with God. It provides a guide for worship, a law code, and a handbook on holiness for the priests. In Genesis man was ruined and Israel was born; in Exodus people were redeemed and Israel delivered; in Leviticus people were cleansed and Israel consecrated to the service of God.

Keys to Leviticus

Key Word: Holiness

Key Verses (17:11; 20:7–8)—" 'For the life of the flesh *is* in the blood, and I have given it to you upon the altar to make atonement for your souls; for it *is* the blood *that* makes atonement for the soul' " (17:11).

"Sanctify yourselves therefore, and be holy, for I *am* the LORD your God. And you shall keep My statutes, and perform them: I *am* the LORD who sanctifies you" (20:7–8).

Key Chapter (16)—The Day of Atonement (*"Yom Kippur"*) was the most important single day in the Hebrew calendar as it was the only day the high priest entered into the Holy of Holies to "make atonement for you, to cleanse you, *that* you may be clean from all your sins before the LORD" (16:30).

Christ in Leviticus

The Book of Leviticus is replete with types and allusions to the person and work of Jesus Christ. Some of the more important include: (1) *The five offerings:* The burnt offering typifies Christ's total offering in submission to His Father's will. The meal offering typifies Christ's sinless service. The peace offering is a type of the fellowship believers have with God through the work of the Cross. The sin offering typifies Christ as our guilt-bearer. The trespass offering typifies Christ's payment for the damage of sin. (2) *The high priest:* There are several comparisons and contrasts between Aaron, the first high priest, and Christ, our eternal High Priest. (3) *The seven feasts:* Passover speaks of the substitutionary death of the Lamb of God. Christ died on the day of Passover. Unleavened Bread speaks of the holy walk of the believer (1 Cor. 5:6–8). Firstfruits speaks of Christ's resurrection as the firstfruit of the resurrection of all believers (1 Cor. 15:20–23). Christ rose on the day of the Firstfruits. Pentecost speaks of the descent of the Holy Spirit after Christ's ascension. Trumpets, the Day of Atonement, and Tabernacles speak of events associated with the second advent of Christ. This may be why these three are separated by a long gap from the first four in Israel's annual cycle.

Contribution to the Bible

For some readers Leviticus appears dull. It has no action or plot except for the death of Nadab and Abihu in chapter 10. It is heavy with rules, regulations and repetition. Its content seems outmoded and difficult to apply. But in reality Leviticus is rich in spiritual truth. It develops a number of doctrinal and practical themes centering on the questions of pardon for guilt and fellowship with God. It reveals how God in His grace accepts the death of a substitute as payment for the penalty of sin. And it has a number of types and portraits of the coming Messiah.

Leviticus is to Exodus what the Epistles are to the Gospels:

Exodus	Leviticus
Pardon	Purity
God's approach to man	Man's approach to God
Man's guilt	Man's defilement
Salvation	Sanctification
A great act	A long process

The predictive types and symbols in this book are fulfilled in the New Testament, particularly in Hebrews.

Survey of Leviticus

It has been said that it took God only one night to get Israel out of Egypt, but it took forty years to get Egypt out of Israel. In Exodus, Israel is redeemed and established as a kingdom of priests and a holy nation; and in Leviticus, Israel is taught how to fulfill their priestly call. They have been led out from the land of bondage in Exodus and into the sanctuary of God in Leviticus. They move from redemption to service, from deliverance to dedication. This book serves as a handbook for the Levitical priesthood, giving instructions and regulations for worship. Used to guide a newly redeemed people into worship, service, and obedience to God, Leviticus falls into two major sections: (1) sacrifice (1—17), and (2) sanctification (18—27).

Sacrifice (1—17): This section teaches that God must be approached by the sacrificial offerings (1—7), by the mediation of the priesthood (8—10), by the purification of the nation from uncleanness (11—15), and by the provision for national cleansing and fellowship (16—17). The blood sacrifices remind the worshipers that because of sin the holy God requires the costly gift of life (17:11). The blood of the innocent sacrificial animal becomes the substitute for the life of the guilty offerer: "without shedding of blood there is no remission" (Heb. 9:22).

Sanctification (18—27): The Israelites serve a holy God who requires them to be holy as well. To be holy means to be "set apart" or "separated." They are to be separated *from* other nations *unto* God. In Leviticus the idea of holiness appears eighty-seven times, sometimes indicating ceremonial holiness (ritual requirements), and at other times moral holiness (purity of life). This sanctification extends to the people of Israel (18—20), the priesthood (21—22), their worship (23—24), their life in Canaan (25—26), and their special vows (27). It is necessary to remove the defilement that separates the people from God so that they can have a walk of fellowship with their Redeemer.

Outline of Leviticus

Part One: The Laws of Acceptable Approach to God: Sacrifice (1:1—7:16)

I. The Laws of Acceptable Approach to God, 1:1—7:38
 A. Laws of Approach to God When in Fellowship, 1:1—3:17
  1. The Burnt Offering, 1:1–17
  2. The Meal Offering, 2:1–16
  3. The Peace Offering, 3:1–17
 B. Laws of Approach to God When out of Fellowship, 4:1—6:7
  1. The Sin Offering, 4:1—5:13
  2. The Trespass Offering, 5:14—6:7
 C. Laws for Administering Offering, 6:8—7:38
  1. The Burnt Offering, 6:8–13
  2. The Meal Offering, 6:14–23
  3. The Sin Offering, 6:24–30
  4. The Trespass Offering, 7:1–10
  5. The Peace Offering, 7:11–36
  6. The Summary of the Offerings, 7:37–38

II. The Laws of the Priests, 8:1—10:20
 A. The Consecration of the Priesthood, 8:1–36
  1. Consecration Commanded by God, 8:1–5
  2. Cleansing the Priests with Water, 8:6
  3. Special Garments, 8:7–9
  4. Anointing with Oil, 8:10–13
  5. Consecrating with Blood, 8:14–30
  6. The Priests Are to Remain in the Tabernacle, 8:31–36
 B. The Ministry of the Priesthood, 9:1–24
  1. Offerings for the Priest, 9:1–14
  2. Offerings for the People, 9:15–21
  3. The Lord Accepts the Offerings, 9:22–24
 C. Failure of the Priesthood, 10:1–20
  1. The Sin of Nadab and Abihu, 10:1–11
  2. The Sin of Eleazar and Ithamar, 10:12–20

III. The Laws of Israel Regarding Purity, 11:1—15:33
 A. Laws Concerning Clean and Unclean Food, 11:1–47
  1. Animals of the Earth, 11:1–8
  2. Living Things in the Waters, 11:9–12
  3. Birds of the Air, 11:13–19

4. Winged Insects, 11:20–23
5. The Carcasses of the Unclean Animals, 11:24–28
6. Creeping Things, 11:29–38
7. The Carcasses of the Clean Animals, 11:39–40
8. The Purpose of Dietary Laws, 11:41–47
B. Laws Concerning Childbirth, 12:1–8
C. Laws Concerning Leprosy, 13:1—14:57
    1. Laws Concerning the Examination of Leprosy, 13:1–59
       a. Examination of People, 13:1–46
       b. Examination of Garments, 13:47–59
    2. Laws Concerning the Cleansing of Leprosy, 14:1–57
       a. Cleansing of People, 14:1–32
       b. Cleansing of Houses, 14:33–53
       c. The Purpose of the Laws of Leprosy, 14:54–57
D. Laws Concerning Discharge, 15:1–33
    1. Discharge of the Man, 15:1–18
    2. Discharge of the Woman, 15:19–30
    3. The Purpose of the Laws of Discharge, 15:31–33

IV. The Laws of National Atonement, 16:1—17:16
A. Laws Concerning National Cleansing through the Day of Atonement, 16:1–34
    1. Preparation of the High Priest, 16:1–5
    2. Identification of the Sacrifices, 16:1–5
    3. Atonement for the Priest, 16:11–14
    4. Atonement for the Tabernacle, 16:15–19
    5. Atonement for the People, 16:20–28
    6. Purpose of the Day of Atonement, 16:29–34
B. Laws Concerning the Location of Sacrifices, 17:1–9
C. Laws Concerning the Use of Blood, 17:10–16

Part Two: The Laws of Acceptable Walk with God: Sanctification (18:1—27:34)

I. The Laws of Sanctification for the People, 18:1—20:27
A. Laws of Sexual Sin, 18:1–30
B. Laws of Social Order, 19:1–37
C. Laws of Penalties, 20:1–27
    1. The Penalty for Worshiping Molech, 20:1–5
    2. The Penalty for Consulting Spirits, 20:6–8
    3. The Penalty for Cursing Patents, 20:9
    4. The Penalty for Committing Sexual Sins, 20:10–21
    5. The Purpose of the Laws of Sanctification of the People, 20:22–27

II. The Laws of Sanctification for the Priesthood, 21:1—22:33
A. Prohibited Practices of the Priests, 21:1–15
    1. Laws Concerning Priests, 21:1–9
    2. Laws Concerning the High Priest, 21:10–15
B. People Prohibited from the Priesthood, 21:16–24

    C. Things Prohibited of the Priesthood, 22:1–16
    D. Sacrifices Prohibited of the Priesthood, 22:17–30
    E. The Purpose of the Laws of the Priesthood, 22:31–33

III. The Laws of Sanctification in Worship, 23:1—24:23
    A. Laws of the Sanctified Feasts of Worship, 23:1–44
        1. The Weekly Sabbath, 23:1–3
        2. Yearly Feasts, 23:4–44
            a. Passover, 23:4–5
            b. Unleavened Bread, 23:6–8
            c. Firstfruits, 23:9–14
            d. Pentecost, 23:15–22
            e. Trumpets, 23:23–25
            f. Day of Atonement, 23:26–32
            g. Tabernacles, 23:33–44
    B. Laws of the Sanctified Elements of Worship, 24:1–9
        1. Oil for the Lamps, 24:1–4
        2. The Showbread, 24:5–9
    C. Law of the Sanctified Name of God, 24:10–23

IV. The Laws of Sanctification in the Land of Canaan, 25:1—26:46
    A. Laws of the Sanctification of the Land of Canaan, 25:1–55
        1. Law of the Sabbath Year, 25:1–7
        2. Law of the Year of Jubilee, 25:8–55
    B. Results of Obedience and Disobedience in the Land of Canaan, 26:1–46
        1. Basic Requirements of Obedience, 26:1–2
        2. Conditions and Results of Obedience, 26:3–13
        3. Conditions and Results of Disobedience, 26:14–39
        4. The Promise of Restoration, 26:40–46

V. The Laws of Sanctification through Vows, 27:1–34
    A. The Special Consecrating of Acceptable Things, 27:1–25
        1. Consecration of Persons, 27:1–8
        2. Consecration of Animals, 27:9–13
        3. Consecration of Houses, 27:14–15
        4. Consecration of Fields, 27:16–25
    B. Things Excluded from Consecration, 27:26–34
        1. Firstborn Clean Animals, 27:26–27
        2. Devoted Things, 27:28–29
        3. Tithes, 27:30–33
    C. The Conclusion of Leviticus, 27:34

Numbers

ONLY A YEAR HAS PASSED since the exodus from Egypt when the Book of Numbers opens. Numbers, the book of divine discipline, shows the painful consequences of unbelief and irresponsible decisions on the part of God's chosen people. Numbers begins with the old generation (chs. 1—12), moves through a tragic transition period (chs. 13—20), and ends with the new generation (chs. 21—36) poised at the doorstep to the land of Canaan. The book contains the records of two generations, two censuses, and two sets of instructions for enjoying the land of promise. God's love is kind, but it can also be severe. His people must learn they can move forward only as they trust and depend on Him.

Focus	Old Generation		Tragic Transition				New Generation		
	1:1 — 10:10		10:11 — 25:18				26:1 — 36:13		
Divisions	Organization of Israel	Sanctification of Israel	To Kadesh-barnea	At Kadesh-barnea	In Wilderness	To Moab	Reorganization of Israel	Regulations of Offerings and Vows	Conquest and Division of Israel
	1:1 — 4:49	5:1 — 10:10	10:11 — 12:16	13:1 — 14:45	15:1 — 19:22	20:1 — 25:18	26:1 — 27:23	28:1 — 30:16	31:1 — 36:13
Topics	Order		Disorder				Reorder		
	Preparation		Postponement				Preparation		
Place	Mount Sinai		Wilderness				Plains of Moab		
Time	20 Days		38 Years, 3 Months, 10 Days				c. 5 Months		

NUMBERS

Introduction and Title

Numbers is the book of wanderings. It takes its name from the two numberings of the Israelites—the first at Mount Sinai and the second on the plains of Moab. Most of the book, however, describes Israel's experiences as they wander in the wilderness. The lesson of Numbers is clear. While it may be necessary to pass through wilderness experiences, one does not have to live there. For Israel, an eleven-day journey became a forty-year agony.

The title of Numbers comes from the first word in the Hebrew text, *Wayyedabber,* "And He Said." Jewish writings, however, usually refer to it by the fifth Hebrew word in 1:1, *Bemidbar,* "In the Wilderness," which more nearly indicates the content of the book. The Greek title in the Septuagint is *Arithmoi,* "Numbers." The Latin Vulgate followed this title and translated it *Liber Numeri,* "Book of Numbers." These titles are based on the two numberings: the generation of Exodus (1) and the generation that grew up in the wilderness and conquered Canaan (26). Numbers has also been called the "Book of the Journeyings," the "Book of the Murmurings," and the "Fourth Book of Moses."

Author

The evidence that points to Moses as the author of Numbers is similar to that for the previous books of the Pentateuch. These five books form such a literary unit that they rise or fall together on the matter of authorship.

External Evidence: The Jews, the Samaritans, and the early church give testimony to the Mosaic authorship of Numbers. Also a number of New Testament passages cite events from Numbers and associate them with Moses. These include John 3:14; Acts 7; 13; First Corinthians 10:1–1; Hebrews 3–4 and Jude 11.

Internal Evidence: There are more than eighty claims that "the LORD spoke to Moses" (the first is 1:1). In addition, Numbers 33:2 makes this clear statement: "Now Moses wrote down the starting points of their journeys at the command of the LORD." Moses kept detailed records as an eyewitness of the events in this book. As the central character in Exodus through Deuteronomy, he was better qualified than any other man to write these books.

Some scholars have claimed that the third person references to Moses point to a different author. However, use of the third person was a common practice in the ancient world. Caesar, for example, did the same in his writings.

Date and Setting

Leviticus covers only one month, but Numbers stretches over almost thirty-nine years (c. 1444–405 B.C.). It records Israel's movement from the last twenty days at Mount Sinai (1:1; 10:11), the wandering around Kadesh-barnea, and finally the arrival in the plains of Moab in the fortieth year (see 22:1; 26:3; 33:50; Deut. 1:3). Their tents occupy several square miles whenever they camp since there are probably over two-and-a-half million people (based on the census figures in chapters 1 and 26).

God miraculously feeds and sustains them in the desert—He preserves their clothing and gives them manna, meat, water, leaders, and a promise (14:34).

Theme and Purpose

The theme of Numbers is the consequence of disbelief and disobedience to the holy God. The Lord disciplined His people but remained faithful to His covenant promises in spite of their fickleness. Numbers displays the patience, holiness, justice, mercy, and sovereignty of God toward His people. It teaches that there are no shortcuts to His blessings—He uses trials and tests for specific purposes.

Numbers was written to trace the history of Israel's wanderings from Sinai to Moab. But the fact that there is almost no record of the thirty-eight years of wandering shows that Numbers is a very thematic history. It selects those events that are important to the development of God's redemptive program. The sins of the first generation were written as a reminder and a warning to the second generation. They must implicitly trust God before they can possess the Land of Blessing.

Keys to Numbers

Key Word: Wanderings

Key Verses (14:22–23; 20:12)—"Because all these men who have seen My glory and the signs which I did in Egypt and in the wilderness, and have put Me to the test now these ten times, and have not heeded My voice, they certainly shall not see the land of which I swore to their fathers, nor shall any of those who rejected Me see it" (14:22–23).

"Then the LORD spoke to Moses and Aaron, 'Because you did not believe Me, to hallow Me in the eyes of the children of Israel, therefore you shall not bring this congregation into the land which I have given them'" (20:12).

Key Chapter (14)—The critical turning point of Numbers may be seen in chapter 14 when Israel rejects God by refusing to go up and conquer the Promised Land. God judges Israel "according to the number of the days in which you spied out the land, forty days, for each day you shall bear your guilt one year, *namely* forty years, and you shall know My rejection" (14:34).

Christ in Numbers

Perhaps the clearest portrait of Christ in Numbers is the bronze serpent on the stake, a picture of the Crucifixion (21:4–9): "And as Moses lifted up the serpent in the wilderness, even so must the Son of Man be lifted up" (John 3:14). The rock that quenches the thirst of the multitudes is also a type of Christ: "they drank of that spiritual Rock that followed them, and that Rock was Christ" (1 Cor. 10:4). The daily manna pictures the Bread of Life who later comes down from heaven (John 6:31–3).

Balaam foresees the rulership of Christ: "I see Him, but not now; I behold Him, but not near; a Star shall come out of Jacob; a Scepter shall rise out of Israel" (24:17). The guidance and presence of Christ is seen in the pillar of cloud and fire, and the sinner's refuge in Christ may be seen in the six cities of refuge. The red heifer sacrifice (19) is also considered a type of Christ.

Contribution to the Bible

In Genesis God elected a people, in Exodus He redeemed them, in Leviticus He sanctified them, and in Numbers He directed them. Numbers takes up the story where Leviticus left off, on Mount Sinai. Leviticus describes the believers' worship, Numbers their walk:

Leviticus	Numbers
Sanctuary	Wilderness
Purity	Pilgrimage
Fellowship	Faithlessness
Legislative	Narrative
Ceremonial	Historical

Numbers teaches the important lesson that biblical faith often requires trusting God against appearances (in this case, the prospect of annihilation by superior enemy forces). Two extensive New Testament passages turn to this wilderness experience for illustrations of spiritual truth. In First Corinthians 10:1-2 it illustrates the danger of self-indulgence and immorality, and in Hebrews 3:7—4:6 it illustrates the theme of entering God's rest through belief. "Now all these things happened to them as examples, and they were written for our admonition, on whom the ends of the ages have come" (1 Cor. 10:11).

Survey of Numbers

Israel as a nation is in its infancy at the outset of this book, only thirteen months after the Exodus from Egypt. In Numbers, the book of divine discipline, it becomes necessary for the nation to go through the painful process of testing and maturation. God must teach His people the consequences of irresponsible decisions. The forty years of wilderness experience transforms them from a rabble of ex-slaves into a nation ready to take the Promised Land. Numbers begins with the old generation (1:1—10:10), moves through a tragic transitional period (10:11—25:18), and ends with the new generation (26—36) at the doorway to the land of Canaan.

The Old Generation (1:1—10:10): The generation that witnessed God's miraculous acts of deliverance and preservation receives further direction from God while they are still at the foot of Mount Sinai (1:1—10:10). God's instructions are very explicit, reaching every aspect of their lives. He is the Author of order, not confusion; and this is seen in the way He organizes the people around the tabernacle. Turning from the outward conditions of the camp (1—4) to the inward conditions (5—10), Numbers describes the spiritual preparation of the people.

The Tragic Transition (10:11—25:18): Israel follows God step by step until Canaan is in sight. Then in the crucial moment at Kadesh they draw back in unbelief. Their murmurings had already become incessant, "Now *when* the people complained, it displeased the LORD; for the LORD heard *it*" (11:1). But their unbelief after sending out the twelve spies at Kadesh-barnea is something God will not tolerate. Their rebellion at Kadesh marks the pivotal point of the book. The generation of the Exodus will not be the generation of the conquest.

Unbelief brings discipline and hinders God's blessing. The old generation is doomed to literally kill time for forty years of wilderness wanderings—one year for every day spent by the twelve spies in inspecting the land. They are judged by disinheritance and death as their journey changes from one of anticipation to one of aimlessness. Only Joshua and Caleb, the two spies who believed God, enter Canaan. Almost nothing is recorded about these transitional years.

The New Generation (21—36): When the transition to the new generation is complete, the people move to the plains of Moab, directly east of the Promised Land (22:1). Before they can enter the land they must wait until all is ready. Here they receive new instructions, a new census is taken, Joshua is appointed as Moses' successor, and some of the people settle in the Transjordan.

Numbers records two generations (1—14; 21—36), two numberings (1; 26), two journeyings (10—14; 21—27), and two sets of instructions (5—9; 28—36). It illustrates both the kindness and severity of God (Rom. 11:22) and teaches that God's people can move forward only as they trust and depend on Him.

Outline of Numbers

Part One: The Preparation of the Old Generation to Inherit the Promised Land (1:1—10:10)

I. The Organization of Israel, 1:1–49
    A. Organization of the People, 1:1—2:34
        1. The First Census of Israel, 1:1–54
        2. Arrangement of the Camp, 2:1–34
          a. On the East, 2·1–9
          b. On the South, 2:10–16
          c. On the Middle, 2:17
          d. On the West, 2:18–24
          e. On the North, 2:25–31
          f. The Camp Is Arranged, 2:32–34
    B. Organization of the Priests, 3:1—4:49
        1. The Census of the Levites, 3:1–39
          a. The Family of Aaron, 3:1–5
          b. The Ministry of the Levites, 3:6–13
          c. The Census Is Commanded, 3:14–20
          d. The Census of Gershon, 3:21–6

      e. The Census of Kohath, 3:27–32
      f. The Census of Merari, 3:33–37
      g. The Summary of the Census, 3:38–39
    2. The Substitution of the Levites for the Firstborn, 3:40–51
    3. The Ministry of the Levites, 4:1–49
      a. The Ministry of Kohath, 4:1–20
      b. The Ministry of Gershon, 4:21–28
      c. The Ministry of Merari, 4:29–33
      d. The Census of the Working Levites, 4:34–49

II. Sanctification of Israel, 5:1—10:10
  A. Sanctification through Separation, 5:1–31
    1. Separation of Unclean Persons, 5:1–4
    2. Separation in Restitution for Sin, 5:5–10
    3. Separation from Suspected Infidelity, 5:11–31
  B. Sanctification through the Nazirite Vow, 6:1–27
  C. Sanctification through Worship, 7:1—9:14
    1. Israel Gives Donations, 7:1–89
    2. The Levites Are Consecrated, 8:1–26
    3. The Passover Is Celebrated, 9:1–14
  D. Sanctification through Divine Guidance, 9:15—10:10
    1. Guidance of the Cloud, 9:15–23
    2. Guidance of the Silver Trumpets, 10:1–10

Part Two: The Failure of the Old Generation to Inherit the Promised Land (10:11—25:18)

I. The Failure of Israel En Route to Kadesh, 10:11—12:16
  A. Israel Departs Mount Sinai, 10:11–36
  B. Failure of the People, 11:1–9
    1. Israel Complains about Circumstances, 11:1–3
    2. Israel Complains about Food, 11:4–9
  C. Failure of Moses, 11:10–15
    1. Moses Complains about the People, 11:10–13
    2. Moses Complains about His Own Life, 11:14–15
  D. God Provides for Moses, 11:16–30
  E. God Provides for the People, 11:31–35
    1. God Provides Quail 11:31–32
    2. God Sends Plagues, 11:33–35
  F. Failure of Miriam and Aaron, 12:1–16
    1. Miriam and Aaron Rebel, 12:1–3
    2. Miriam Is Punished, 12:4–10
    3. Moses Intercedes, 12:11–13
    4. Miriam Is Restored, 12:14–16

II. The Climactic Failure of Israel at Kadesh, 13:1—14:45
  A. Investigation of the Promised Land, 13:1–33
  B. Israel Rebels against God, 14:1–10

    C. Moses Intercedes, 4:11–19

    D. God Judges Israel, 14:20–38

        1. Israel to Wander and Die, 14:20–35

        2. Spies Die Immediately, 14:36–38

    E. Israel Rebels against the Judgment of God, 14:39–45

        1. Moses Warns Israel, 14:39–44

        2. Amalekites Defeat Israel 14:45

III. The Failure of Israel in the Wilderness, 15:1—19:22

    A. Review of the Offerings, 15:1–41

        1. Offerings to Thank the Lord, 15:1–21

        2. Offerings for Unintentional Sins, 15:22–29

        3. No Offering for Intentional Sins, 15:30–36

        4. The Tassel on the Garment, 15:37–41

    B. Rebellion of Korah 16:1–40

        1. Korah Rebels against Moses and Aaron, 16:1–4

        2. God Judges Korah, 16:15–40

    C. Rebellion of Israel against Moses and Aaron, 16:41–50

        1. Israel Rebels against Moses and Aaron, 16:41

        2. God Judges Israel, 16:42–50

    D. Role of the Priesthood, 17:1—19:22

        1. Confirmation of the Divine Call, 17:1–13

        2. Remuneration of the Priesthood, 18:1–32

        3. Purification of the Red Heifer, 19:1–22

IV. The Failure of Israel En Route to Moab, 20:1—25:18

    A. Miriam Dies, 20:1

    B. Moses and Aaron Fail, 20:2–13

        1. The Sin of Israel, 20:2–6

        2. The Command of God, 20:7–8

        3. The Sin of Moses, 20:9–13

    C. Edom Refuses Passage, 20:14–21

    D. Aaron Dies20:22–29

    E. Israel's Victory over the Canaanites, 21:1–3

    F. The Failure of Israel, 21:4–9

        1. Israel Complains 21:4–5

        2. God Judges with Serpents, 21:6

        3. The Bronze Serpent, 21:7–9

    G. Journey to Moab, 21:10–20

    H. Israel's Victory over Ammon, 21:21–32

    I. Israel's Victory over Bashan, 21:33–35

    J. Failure with the Moabites, 22:1—25:18

        1. Balaam Is Sought by Balak, 22:1–40

        2. Balaam Blesses Israel, 22:41—24:25

            a. The First Oracle of Balaam, 22:41–23:12

            b. The Second Oracle of Balaam, 3:13–26

  c. The Third Oracle of Balaam, 23:27—24:13

  d. The Fourth Oracle of Balaam, 24:14–25

 3. The Sin of Israel with the Moabites, 25:1–18

  a. Israel Commits Harlotry, 25:1–2

  b. Phinehas Stays the Plague, 25:3–15

  c. Israel to Destroy Moab, 25:16–18

Part Three: The Preparation of the New Generation to Inherit the Promised Land (26:1—36:13)

I. The Reorganization of Israel, 26:1—27:23

 A. The Second Census, 26:1–51

 B. Method for Dividing the Land, 26:52–56

 C. Exceptions for Dividing the Land, 26:57—27:11

  1. The Levites Have No Inheritance, 26:57–62

  2. The Old Generation Has No Inheritance, 26:63–65

  3. The Special Laws of Inheritance, 27:1–11

 D. Appointment of Israel's New Leader, 27:12–23

  1. Moses Is Set Aside, 27:12–14

  2. Joshua Is Appointed, 27:15–23

II. The Regulations of Offerings and Vows, 28:1—30:16

 A. The Regulations of Sacrifices, 28:1—29:40

  1. Daily Offering, 28:1–8

  2. Weekly Offering, 28:9–10

  3. Monthly Offering, 28:11–15

  4. Yearly Offering, 28:16—29:40

   a. Passover, 28:16

   b. Unleavened Bread, 28:17–25

   c. Firstfruits, 28:26–31

   d. Trumpets, 29:1–6

   e. Atonement, 29:7–11

   f. Tabernacle, 29:12–40

 B. The Regulations of Vows, 30:1–16

III. The Conquest and Division of Israel, 31:1—36:13

 A. Victory over Midian, 31:1–54

  1. Destruction of the Midianites, 31:1–18

  2. Purification of Israel, 31:19–24

  3. Distribution of the Spoils, 31:25–54

 B. Division of the Land East of Jordan, 32:1–42

 C. The Summary of Israel's Journeys, 33:1–49

  1. From Egypt to Sinai, 33:1–15

  2. From Sinai to Kadesh, 33:16–17

  3. The Wilderness Wanderings, 33:18–36

  4. From Kadesh to Moab, 33:37–49

Deuteronomy

DEUTERONOMY, MOSES' "UPPER DESERT DISCOURSE," consists of a series of farewell messages by Israel's 120-year-old leader. It is addressed to the new generation destined to possess the Land of Promise—those who survived the forty years of wilderness wandering. Deuteronomy, like Leviticus, contains a vast amount of legal detail, but its emphasis is on the laymen rather than the priests and sacrifices. Moses reminds the new generation of the importance of obedience if they are to learn from the sad example of their predecessors. Moving from the past (Israel's history) to the present (Israel's holiness and homeland) to the future (Israel's new leader), Moses stresses the faithfulness of Israel's God, who "brought us out . . . to give us the land" (6:23).

Focus	**First Sermon**	**Second Sermon**				**Third Sermon**			
	1:1　　4:43	4:44　　　　　　　　　　26:19				27:1　　　　　　　　　34:12			
Divisions	Review of God's Acts for Israel	The Exposition of the Decalogue	Ceremonial Laws	Civil Laws	Social Laws	Ratification of Covenant	Palestinian Covenant	Transition of Covenant Mediator	
	1:1　　4:43	4:44　　11:32	12:1　16:17	16:18　20:20	21:1　26:19	27:1　28:68	29:1　30:20	31:1　34:12	
Topics	What God Has Done	What God Expected of Israel				What God Will Do			
	Historical	Legal				Prophetical			
Place	Plains of Moab								
Time	c. 1 Month								

DEUTERONOMY

Introduction and Title

Deuteronomy, Moses' "Upper Desert Discourse," consists of a series of farewell messages by Israel's 120-year-old leader. It is addressed to the new generation destined to possess the Land of Promise—those who survived the forty years of wilderness wandering.

Like Leviticus, Deuteronomy contains a vast amount of legal detail, but its emphasis is on the laymen rather than the priests. Moses reminds the new generation of the importance of obedience if they are to learn from the sad example of their parents.

The Hebrew title of Deuteronomy is *Haddebharim,* "The Words," taken from the opening phrase in 1:1, "These *are* the words." The parting words of Moses to the new generation are given in oral and written form so that they will endure to all generations. Deuteronomy has been called "five-fifths of the Law" since it completes the five books of Moses. The Jewish people have also called it *Mishneh Hattorah,* "repetition of the Law," which is translated in the Septuagint as *To Deuteronomion Touto,* "This Second Law." Deuteronomy, however, is not a second law but an adaptation and expansion of much of the original law given on Mount Sinai. The English title comes from the Greek title *Deuteronomion,* "Second Law." Deuteronomy has also been appropriately called the "Book of Remembrance."

Author

The Mosaic authorship of Deuteronomy has been vigorously attacked by critics who claim that Moses is only the originator of the tradition on which these laws are based. Some critics grant that part of Deuteronomy may have come from Mosaic times through oral tradition. The usual argument is that it was anonymously written not long before 621 B.C. and used by King Josiah to bring about his reform in that year (2 Kin. 22—23). There are several reasons why these arguments are not valid.

External Evidence: (1) The Old Testament attributes Deuteronomy and the rest of the Pentateuch to Moses (see Josh. 1:7; Judg. 3:4; 1 Kin. 2:3; 2 Kin. 14:6; Ezra 3:2; Neh. 1:7; Ps. 103:7; Dan. 9:11; Mal. 4:4). (2) Evidence from Joshua and First Samuel indicates that these laws existed in the form of codified written statutes and exerted an influence on the Israelites in Canaan. (3) Christ quotes it as God's Word in turning back Satan's three temptations (see Matt. 4:4, 7, 10) and attributes it directly to Moses (see Matt. 19:7–9; Mark 7:10; Luke 20:28; John 5:45–47). (4) Deuteronomy is cited more than eighty times in seventeen of the twenty-seven New Testament books. These citations support the Mosaic authorship (see Acts 3:22; Rom. 10:19). (5) Jewish and Samaritan traditions point to Moses.

Internal Evidence: (1) Deuteronomy includes about forty claims that Moses wrote it (see 31:24–26; cf. 1:1–5; 4:44–46; 29:1; 31:9). (2) Deuteronomy fits the time of Moses, not Josiah: Canaan is viewed from the outside; the Canaanite religion is seen as a future menace; it assumes the hearers remember Egypt and the wilderness; Israel is described as living in tents; and there is no evidence of a divided kingdom. (3) A serious problem of misrepresentation and literary forgery would arise if this book were written in the seventh century B.C. (4) Geographical and historical details indicate a firsthand knowledge. (5) Deuteronomy follows the treaty form used in the fifteenth and fourteenth centuries B.C. (6) Moses' obituary in Chapter 34 was probably written by Joshua.

Date and Setting

Like Leviticus, Deuteronomy does not progress historically. It takes place entirely on the plains of Moab due east of Jericho and the Jordan River (see 1:1; 29:1; Josh. 1:2). It covers about one month: combine Deuteronomy 1:3 and 34:8 with Joshua 5:6–12. The book was written at the end of the forty-year period in the wilderness (c. 1405 B.C.) when the new generation was on the verge of entering Canaan. Moses wrote it to encourage the people to believe and obey God in order to receive God's blessings.

Theme and Purpose

"Beware lest you forget" is a key theme in Deuteronomy. Moses emphasizes the danger of forgetfulness because it leads to arrogance and disobedience. They must remember two things: (1) when they prosper, it is God who has caused it, and (2) when they disobey God, He will discipline them as He did when the previous generation failed to believe Him at Kadesh-barnea. Deuteronomy is a call to obedience as a condition to blessing. God has always been faithful to His covenant and He now extends it to the new generation. Deuteronomy is a covenant renewal document that uses the same format as Near Eastern treaties in the time of Moses. These treaties had the following elements: (1) a preamble (a list of the parties making the treaty; 1:1–5), (2) a historical prologue (the benevolent dealings of the king in the past; 1:6—4:43), (3) stipulations (conditions of the covenant; 4:44—26:19), (4) ratification (blessings and cursings; 27–30), and (5) continuity (provisions for maintaining the covenant; 31—34). There is an emphasis on choice, and the people are urged to choose life rather than death (30:19–20). They are told to "hear" (50 times) and "do," "keep," "observe" (177 times) God's commands out of a heart of "love" (21 times).

Keys to Deuteronomy

Key Word: Covenant

Key Verses (10:12–13; 30:19–20)—"And now, Israel, what does the LORD your God require of you, but to fear the LORD your God, to walk in all His ways and to love Him, to serve the LORD your God with all your heart and with all your soul *and* to keep the commandments of the LORD and His statutes which I command you today for your good?" (10:12–13).

"I call heaven and earth as witnesses today against you, *that* I have set before you life and death, blessing and cursing; therefore choose life, that both you and your descendants may live; that you may love the LORD your God, that you may obey His voice, and that you may cling to Him: for He *is* your life and the length of your days; and that you may dwell in the land which the LORD swore to your fathers, to Abraham, Isaac, and Jacob, to give them" (30:19–20).

Key Chapter (27)—The formal ratification of the covenant occurs in chapter 27 as Moses, the priests, the Levites, and all of Israel "Take heed and listen, O Israel: This day you have become the people of the LORD your God" (27:9).

Christ in Deuteronomy

The most obvious portrait of Christ is found in chapter 18, verse 15: "The LORD your God will raise up for you a Prophet like me from your midst, from your brethren. Him you shall hear" (see also 18:16–19; Acts 7:37). Moses is a type of Christ in many ways as he is the only biblical figure other than Christ to fill the three offices of prophet (34:10–12), priest (Ex. 32:31–35), and king (although Moses was not king, he functioned as ruler of Israel; 33:4–5). Both are in danger of death during childhood; both are saviors, intercessors, and believers; and both are rejected by their brethren. Moses is one of the greatest men who ever lived, combining not just one or two memorable virtues but many.

Contribution to the Bible

Deuteronomy is a supplementary book to the rest of the Pentateuch and fills a role similar to that of the Gospel of John compared to the synoptic Gospels. It fills in missing elements and gives the spiritual significance of the history found in the other books of Moses. Genesis to Numbers portray God's ways, Deuteronomy reveals God's love:

Genesis to Numbers	Deuteronomy
Development of Israel's History	Philosophy of Israel's history
Divine performances	Divine principles
God speaks to Moses	Moses speaks to the people

The emphasis on God's love in this book (4:37; 7:7–8; 10:15; 23:5) was a crucial step for Israel's understanding.

Deuteronomy was perhaps Christ's favorite book. He quoted from it often (see Matt. 4:4,7,10; 22:37–38; Mark 7:10; 10:19, 29—30).

Survey of Deuteronomy

Deuteronomy, in its broadest outline, is the record of the renewal of the old covenant given at Mount Sinai. This covenant is reviewed, expanded, enlarged, and finally ratified in the plains of Moab. Moses accomplishes this primarily through three sermons that move from a retrospective, to an introspective, and finally to a prospective look at God's dealings with Israel.

Moses' First Sermon (1:1—4:43): Moses reaches into the past to remind the people of two undeniable facts in their history: (1) the moral judgment of God upon Israel's unbelief, and (2) the deliverance and provision of God during times of obedience. The simple lesson is that obedience brings blessing, and disobedience brings punishment.

Moses' Second Sermon (4:44—26:19): This moral and legal section is the longest in the book because Israel's future as a nation in Canaan will depend upon a right relationship with God. These chapters review the three categories of the Law: (1) *The testimonies (5—11).* These are the moral duties—a restatement and expansion of the Ten Commandments plus an exhortation not to forget God's gracious deliverance. (2) *The statutes (12:1—16:17).* These are the ceremonial duties—sacrifices, tithes, and feasts. (3) *The ordinances (16:18—26:19).* These are the civil (16:18—20:20) and social (21—26) duties—the system of justice, criminal laws, laws of warfare, rules of property, personal and family morality, and social justice.

Moses' Third Sermon (27—34): In these chapters Moses writes history in advance. He predicts what will befall Israel in the near future (blessings and cursings) and in the distant future (dispersion among the nations and eventual return). Moses lists the terms of the covenant soon to be ratified by the people. Because Moses will not be allowed to enter the land, he appoints Joshua as his successor and delivers a farewell address to the multitude. God Himself buries Moses in an unknown place, perhaps to prevent idolatry. Moses finally enters the Promised Land when he appears with Christ on the Mount of Transfiguration (Matt. 17:3). The last three verses of the Pentateuch (34:10–12) are an appropriate epitaph for this great man.

Outline of Deuteronomy

Part One: Moses' First Sermon:
"What God Has Done for Israel" (1:1–43)

I. The Preamble of the Covenant, 1:1–5

II. The Review of God's Acts for Israel, 1:6—4:43
   A. From Mount Sinai to Kadesh, 1:6–18
   B. At Kadesh, 1:19–46
   C. From Kadesh to Moab, 2:1–23
      1. "Do Not Meddle with Edom," 2:1–8
      2. "Do Not Harass Moab," 2:9–15
      3. "Do Not Harass Ammon," 2:16–23
   D. Conquest of East Jordan, 2:24—3:20
      1. The Conquest of Sihon, 2:24–37
      2. The Conquest of Og, 3:1–11
      3. Land Is Granted to Two-and-a-Half Tribes, 3:12–20
   E. Transition of Leadership, 3:21–29
   F. Summary of the Covenant, 4:1–43

Part Two: Moses' Second Sermon:
"What God Expects of Israel" (4:44—26:19)

I. The Introduction to the Law of God, 4:44–49

II. The Exposition of the Decalogue, 5:1—11:32
    A. The Covenant of the Great King, 5:1–33
        1. Setting of the Covenant, 5:1–5
        2. Commandments of the Covenant, 5:6–21
        3. Response of Israel, 5:22–27
        4. Response of God, 5:28–33
    B. The Command to Teach the Law, 6:1–25
    C. The Command to Conquer Canaan, 7:1–26
    D. The Command to Remember the Lord, 8:1–20
    E. The Commands about Self-Righteousness, 9:1—10:11
        1. Moses Rehearses Israel's Rebellion, 9:1–29
        2. Moses Rehearses God's Mercy, 10:1–11
    F. The Commands Regarding Blessings and Cursings, 10:12—11:32
        1. Love God, 10:12–22
        2. Study and Obey the Commands, 11:1–21
        3. Victory Depends upon Obedience, 11:22–32

III. The Exposition of the Additional Laws, 12:1—26:19
    A. The Exposition of the Ceremonial Laws, 12:1—16:17
        1. Law of the Central Sanctuary, 12:1–28
        2. Law of Idolatry, 12:29—13:18
        3. Law of Food, 14:1–21
        4. Law of the Tithes, 14:22–29
        5. Law of the Debts, 15:1–11
        6. Law of the Slaves, 15:12–18
        7. Law of Firstborn, 15:19–23
        8. Law of the Feasts, 16:1–17
    B. The Exposition of the Civil Laws, 16:18—20:20
        1. Law of the Administration of the Judges, 16:18—17:13
        2. Law of the Administration of the King, 17:17–20
        3. Law of the Administration of the Priest and Prophet, 18:1–22
        4. Cities of Refuge, 19:1–14
        5. Law of Witnesses, 19:15–21
        6. Law of Warfare, 20:1–20
    C. The Exposition of the Social Laws, 21:1—26:19
        1. Law of Unknown Murder, 21:1–9
        2. Law of the Family, 21:10—22:30
            a. Law of Marriage, 21:10–17
            b. Law of the Rebellious Son, 21:18–23
            c. Law of the Brother's Property, 22:1–4
            d. Law of Separation, 22:5–12
            e. Law of Marriage, 22:13–30

3. Law of Acceptance into the Congregation, 23:1–23
4. Laws for Harmony in the Nation, 23:24—25:19
5. Law of the Tithe, 26:1–15
6. Vow of Israel and of God, 26:16–19

Part Three: Moses' Third Sermon: "What God Will Do for Israel" (27:1—34:12)

I. The Ratification of the Covenant in Canaan, 27:1—28:68
  A. Erection of the Altar, 27:1–8
  B. Admonition to Obey the Law, 27:9–10
  C. Proclamation of the Curses, 27:11–26
  D. Warnings of the Covenant, 28:1–68
    1. Promised Blessings for Obedience, 28:1–14
    2. Promised Curses for Disobedience, 28:15–68

II. The Institution of the Palestinian Covenant, 29:1—30:20
  A. The Covenant Is Based on the Power of God, 29:1–9
  B. Parties of the Covenant, 29:10–15
  C. Warnings of the Covenant, 29:16—30:10
    1. Scattering of Israel, 29:16–29
    2. Restoration of Israel, 30:1–10
  D. Ratification of the Palestinian Covenant, 30:11–20

III. The Transition of the Covenant Mediator, 31:1—34:12
  A. Moses Charges Joshua and Israel, 31:1–13
  B. God Charges Israel, 31:14–21
  C. The Book of the Law Is Deposited, 31:22–30
  D. The Song of Moses, 32:1–47
  E. The Death of Moses, 32:48—34:12
    1. Moses Is Ordered to Mount Nebo, 32:48–52
    2. Moses Blesses the Tribes, 33:1–29
    3. Moses Views the Promised Land, 34:1–4
    4. Moses Dies and Is Mourned, 34:5–8
    5. Moses Is Replaced by Joshua, 34:9
    6. Moses Is Extolled in Israel, 34:10–12

The Feasts of Israel

THE FIRST COMING OF CHRIST

Month	Day(s)	Feast	Looks Back On . . .	Looks Ahead To . . .	Scripture
1st	14	Passover	Redemption of Firstborn	Christ's Redeeming Death	1 Corinthians 5:7 1 Peter 1:18–19
1st	15–21	Un-leavened Bread	Separation from Other Nations	Holy Walk of Believers	1 Corinthians 5:7–8 Galatians 5:9,16–17
1st	16	Firstfruits	Harvest in the Land	Resurection of Christ	1 Corinthians 15:20–23 Revelation 1:5
3rd	6	Pentecost	Completion of Harvest	Sending of the Holy spirit	Acts 2:1–47 1 Corinthians 12:13

The Summer Gap (John 4:35)

THE SECOND COMING OF CHRIST

Month	Day(s)	Feast	Looks Back On . . .	Looks Ahead To . . .	Scripture
7th	1	Trumpets	Israel's New Year	Israel's Regathering	Isaiah 27:12–13 Matthew 24:21–31
7th	10	Day of Atonement	Israel's National Sin	Israel's National Conversion	Zechariah 12:10 Romans 11:26–27
7th	15–22	Tabernacles	Israel in the Wilderness	Israel in the Kingdom	Zechariah 14:14–16 Revelation 7:9–19

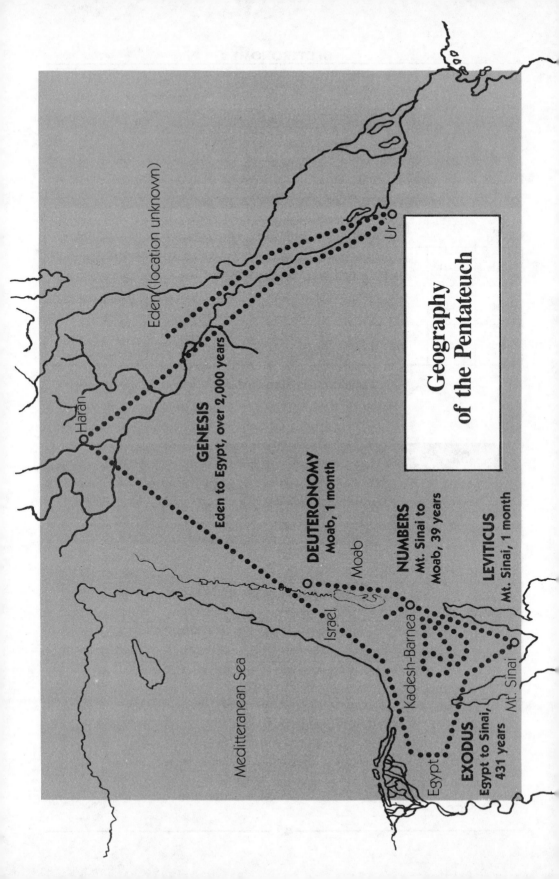

**Geography
of the Pentateuch**

Eden (location unknown)

Ur

Haran

GENESIS
Eden to Egypt, over 2,000 years

DEUTERONOMY
Moab, 1 month

Moab

NUMBERS
Mt. Sinai to
Moab, 39 years

LEVITICUS
Mt. Sinai, 1 month

Israel

Kadesh-Barnea

Mt. Sinai

Mediterranean Sea

Egypt

EXODUS
Egypt to Sinai,
431 years

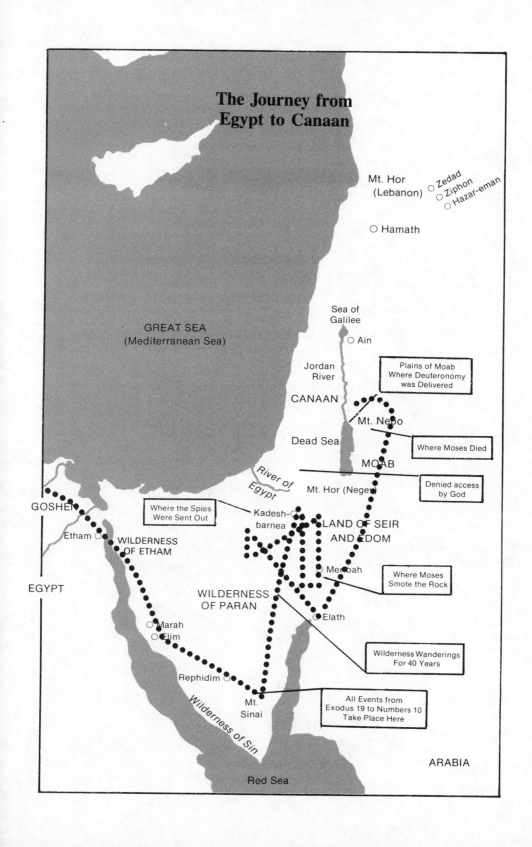

The Journey from Egypt to Canaan

Mt. Hor
(Lebanon)   ○ Zedad
             ○ Ziphon
              ○ Hazar-eman

○ Hamath

GREAT SEA
(Mediterranean Sea)

Sea of
Galilee
   ○ Ain

Jordan
River

CANAAN

Plains of Moab
Where Deuteronomy
was Delivered

Mt. Nebo

Where Moses Died

Dead Sea

MOAB

River of Egypt

Mt. Hor (Negev)

Denied access
by God

GOSHEN

Etham ○

WILDERNESS
OF ETHAM

Where the Spies
Were Sent Out

Kadesh-
barnea

LAND OF SEIR
AND EDOM

EGYPT

Meribah

Where Moses
Smote the Rock

WILDERNESS
OF PARAN

○ Marah
○ Elim

Rephidim ○

Mt.
Sinai

Wilderness of Sin

○ Elath

Wilderness Wanderings
For 40 Years

All Events from
Exodus 19 to Numbers 10
Take Place Here

ARABIA

Red Sea

Introduction to the
Historical Books

THE TWELVE HISTORICAL BOOKS pick up the story of Israel where it left off at the end of Deuteronomy. These books describe the occupation and settlement of Israel in the Promised Land, the transition from judges to the monarchy, the division and decline of the kingdom, the captivities of the northern and southern kingdom, and the return of the remnant.

The historical books break into three divisions: (1) the theocratic books (Joshua, Judges, Ruth), (2) the monarchical books (Samuel, Kings, Chronicles), and (3) the restoration books (Ezra, Nehemiah, Esther).

THE THEOCRATIC BOOKS

These books cover the conquest and settlement of Canaan and life during the time of the judges. During these years (1405–1043 B.C.), Israel was a nation ruled by God (a theocracy).

Joshua

The first half of Joshua describes the seven-year conquest of the Land of Promise through faith and obedience on the past of Joshua and the people. After their spiritual and physical preparation, the Israelites took the land in three campaigns: central, southern, and northern. The last half of the book details the partitioning of the land among the twelve tribes and closes with Joshua's challenge to the people.

Judges

The disobedience in Judges stands in contrast to the faithful obedience found in Joshua. The Israelites did not drive out all the Canaanites and began to take part in their idolatry. Judges records seven cycles of foreign oppression, repentance, and deliverance. The people failed to learn from these cycles, and the book ends with two illustrations of idolatry and immorality.

Ruth

This little book sheds a ray of light in an otherwise dark period. The story of Ruth occurred in the days of the judges, but it is a powerful illustration of righteousness, love, and faithfulness to the Lord.

THE MONARCHICAL BOOKS

These six books trace the history of Israel's monarchy from its inception in 1043 B.C. to its destruction in 586 B.C.

First Samuel

The prophet Samuel carried Israel across the transition from the judges to the monarchy. The people clamored for a king and God told Samuel to anoint Saul. Saul began well but soon degenerated into an ungodly tyrant. David became God's king-elect but he was pursued by the jealous Saul whose murderous intentions were checked only by death.

Second Samuel

Upon the demise of Saul, David reigned for seven years over Judah and another thirty-three years over the twelve reunited tribes. His reign was characterized by great blessing until he committed adultery and murder. From that point until his death he was plagued by personal, family, and national struggles.

First Kings

Solomon brought the kingdom to its political and economic zenith, but this wisest of men played the fool in his multiple marriages with foreign women. After his death in 931 B.C., the kingdom was tragically divided when the ten northern tribes of Israel set up their own king. Only the southern kingdom of Judah (two tribes) remained subject to the Davidic dynasty.

Second Kings

The story of the divided kingdom continues in Second Kings as it carries Israel and Judah to their bitter ends. None of the nineteen kings of Israel did what was right in the sight of God, and their corruption led to captivity at the hands of the Assyrians in 722 B.C. Judah lasted longer because eight of its twenty rulers followed the Lord. But Judah also fell in judgment and was carried away by the Babylonians between 605 B.C. and 586 B.C.

First Chronicles

The Books of Chronicles give a divine perspective on the history of Israel from the time of David to the two captivities. The first book begins with a nine-chapter genealogy from Adam to the family of Saul, followed by a spiritually oriented account of the life of David.

Second Chronicles

This book continues the narrative with the life of Solomon, and focuses on the construction and dedication of the temple. It then traces the history of the kings of Judah only, giving the spiritual and moral reasons for its ultimate downfall.

THE RESTORATION BOOKS

The last three historical books describe the return of a remnant of the Jews to their homeland after seventy years (605–536 B.C.) of captivity. They were led in the period from 536–420 B.C. by Zerubbabel, Ezra, and Nehemiah.

Ezra

Babylon was conquered by Persia in 539 B.C. and Cyrus issued a decree in 536 B.C. that allowed the Jews to return to Palestine. Zerubbabel led about fifty thousand to Jerusalem to rebuild the temple, and years later (458 B.C.), Ezra the priest returned with almost two thousand Jews.

Nehemiah

The temple was built, but the wall of Jerusalem still lay in ruins. Nehemiah obtained permission, supplies, and money from the king of Persia to rebuild the walls (444 B.C.). After the walls were built, Ezra and Nehemiah led the people in revival and reforms.

Esther

The story of Esther took place between chapters 6 and 7 of Ezra. Most of the Jews chose to remain in Persia, but their lives were in danger because of a plot to exterminate them. God sovereignly intervened and used Esther and Mordecai to deliver the people.

Joshua

JOSHUA, THE FIRST OF THE TWELVE historical books (Joshua—Esther), forges a link between the Pentateuch and the remainder of Israel's history. Through three military campaigns involving more than thirty enemy armies, the people of Israel learn a crucial lesson under Joshua's capable leadership: victory comes through faith in God and obedience to His Word, rather than military might or numerical superiority.

The first half of Joshua (chs. 1—12) describes the seven-year conquest of the land; the second half (chs. 13—24) relates the partitioning and settlement of the land among the twelve tribes.

Focus	Conquest of Canaan		Settlement in Canaan				
	1:1 13:37		13:8 24:33				
Divisions	Preparation of Israel for Conquest	Conquest of Canaan by Israel	Settlement East of the Jordan	Settlement West of the Jordan	Settlement of Religious Community	Conditions for Continued Settlement	
	1:1 5:15	6:1 13:7	13:8 13:33	14:1 19:51	20:1 21:45	22:1 24:33	
Topics	Entering Canaan	Conquering Canaan	Dividing Canaan				
	Preparation	Subjection	Possession				
Place	Jordan River	Canaan	2½ Tribes—East Jordan 9½ Tribes—West Jordan				
Time	c. 1 Month	c. 7 Years	c. 18 Years				

51

Introduction and Title

Joshua, the first of the twelve historical books (Joshua-Esther), forges a link between the Pentateuch and the remainder of Israel's history. Through three major military campaigns involving more than thirty enemy armies, the people of Israel learn a crucial lesson under Joshua's capable leadership: victory comes through faith in God and obedience to His word, rather than through military might or numerical superiority.

The title of this book is appropriately named after its central figure, Joshua. His original name is *Hoshea*, "salvation" (Num. 13:8); but Moses evidently changes it to *Yehoshua* (Num. 13:16), "Yahweh Is Salvation." He is also called *Yeshua*, a shortened form of *Yehoshua*. This is the Hebrew equivalent of the Greek name *Iesous* (Jesus). Thus, the Greek title given to the book in the Septuagint is *Iesous Naus*, "Joshua the Son of Nun." The Latin title is *Liber Josue*, the "Book of Joshua."

His name is symbolic of the fact that although he is the leader of the Israelite nation during the conquest, the Lord is the Conqueror.

Author

Although it cannot be proven, Jewish tradition seems correct in assigning the authorship of this book to Joshua himself. Chapter 24, verse 26 makes this clear statement: "Then Joshua wrote these words in the Book of the Law of God." This refers at least to Joshua's farewell charge, if not to the book as a whole (see also 18:9). Joshua, as Israel's leader and an eyewitness of most of the events, was the person best qualified to write the book. He even uses the first person in one place ("us," 5:6). "We" appears in some manuscripts of chapter 5, verse 1. The book was written soon after the events occurred: Rahab was still alive (6:25). Other evidences for early authorship are the detailed information about Israel's campaigns and use of the ancient names of Canaanite cities.

The unity of style and organization suggest a single authorship for the majority of the book. Three small portions, however, must have been added after Joshua's death. These are: (1) Othniel's capture of Kirjath Sepher (15:13–19; cf. Judg. 1:9–15), (2) Dan's migration to the north (19:47; cf. Judg. 18:27–29), and (3) Joshua's death and burial (24:29–33). These may have been inserted early in the time of the judges by Eleazer the priest and his son Phinehas (24:33).

Joshua, born a slave in Egypt, becomes a conqueror in Canaan. He serves as personal attendant to Moses, as one of the twelve spies (of whom only he and Caleb believed God), and as Moses' successor. His outstanding qualities are obedient faith, courage, and dedication to God and His Word.

Date and Setting

Joshua divides neatly into three geographical settings: (1) the Jordan River (1—5); (2) Canaan (6—13:7); and (3) the twelve tribes situated on both sides of the Jordan (13:8—24:33).

The setting of the first five chapters begins east of the Jordan as Joshua replaces Moses, crosses the Jordan on dry land, and finally prepares for war west of the Jordan.

Like a wise general, Joshua utilizes the divide-and-conquer strategy; and his campaign leads him to central Canaan (6—8), southern Canaan (9—10), and finally to northern Canaan (11—12).

After listing those areas yet to be conquered (13:1–7), Joshua undertakes the long task of dividing the Promised Land to all the tribes. First, he settles those two-and-a-half tribes east of the Jordan (13:8–33) and then the nine-and-a-half tribes west of the Jordan (14:1—19:51). Completing this, he is free to assign the six Cities of Refuge and the forty-eight Cities of Levites, which are scattered among all the tribes.

The Book of Joshua cannot be dated precisely, but utilizing the same threefold division noted above, the following dates can be assigned:

A. One month, March-April, 1405 B.C. (1—5)
   1. Death of Moses, March, 1405 B.C. (Deut. 34:5–9)
   2. Crossing the Jordan, April 10, 1405 B.C. (4:19)
B. Seven years, April 1405–1398 B.C. (6:1—13:7)
   1. Caleb forty years old at Kadesh (14:7)
   2. Caleb eighty-five years old at that time (14:10)
    Note: Forty-five years less thirty-eight years of wandering leaves seven years.
C. Eight years, 1398/7–1390 B.C. (13:8–23)
   1. Division begun, 1398/7 B.C. (14:7–10)
   2. Joshua dies at 110, c. 1390 B.C. (24:29)

Theme and Purpose

The theme of Joshua is Israel's possession of the Promised Land and enjoyment of God's blessings through obedient faith.

Joshua's historical purpose is to document the conquest of Canaan by the Israelites under Joshua's leadership. As such, Joshua joins the eleven out of seventeen historical books that carry on the geographical and chronological story of Israel from the time of Abraham to Malachi. The other ten are: Genesis, Exodus, Numbers, Judges, First and Second Samuel, First and Second Kings, Ezra, and Nehemiah. The remaining six—Leviticus, Deuteronomy, Ruth, First and Second Chronicles, and Esther—are supplementary in nature. Out of the list of eleven, only Joshua does *not* record a massive failure by Israel or its leadership (the sin in chapter 7 was quickly remedied).

Theologically, Joshua teaches that victory and blessing come through obedience and trust in God. Active faith leads to obedience which in turn brings blessing. God required the people to attempt the impossible in submission to His directions before He made it possible for them to succeed. The book emphasizes God's covenant faithfulness to His promises regarding a land for Israel, and God's holiness in bringing judgment upon the immoral Canaanites.

Keys to Joshua

Key Word: Conquest

Key Verses (1:8; 11:23)—"This Book of the Law shall not depart from your mouth, but you shall meditate in it day and night, that you may observe to do according to all that is written in it. For then you will make your way prosperous, and then you will have good success" (1:8).

"So Joshua took the whole land, according to all that the LORD had said to Moses; and Joshua gave it as an inheritance to Israel according to their divisions by their tribes. Then the land rested from war" (11:23).

Key Chapter (24)—Some of the most critical periods in Israel's history are the transitions of leadership: Moses to Joshua; Joshua to the judges; the judges to the kings, and so on. Before his death and in preparation for a major transition of leadership by one man (Joshua) to many (the judges), Joshua reviews for the people God's fulfillment of His promises and then challenges them to review their commitment to the covenant (24:24–25), which is the foundation for all successful national life.

Christ in Joshua

Although there are no direct messianic prophecies in the book, Joshua is clearly a type of Christ. His name *Yeshua* ("Yahweh Is Salvation") is the Hebrew equivalent of the name *Jesus*. In his role of triumphantly leading his people into their possessions, he foreshadows the One who will bring "many sons to glory" (Heb. 2:10). "Now thanks *be* to God who always leads us in triumph in Christ" (2 Cor. 2:14; see Rom. 8:37). Joshua succeeds Moses and wins the victory unreached by Moses. Christ will succeed the Mosaic Law and win the victory unreachable by the Law (see John 1:17; Rom. 8:2–4; Gal. 3:23–25; Heb. 7:18–19).

The "Commander of the army of the LORD" (5:13–15) met by Joshua is evidently a preincarnate appearance of Christ (cf. 5:15 with Ex. 3:5).

Rahab's scarlet cord (2:21) portrays safety through the blood (Heb. 9:19–22); and amazingly, this gentile woman is found in Christ's genealogy (Matt. 1:5).

Contribution to the Bible

Joshua acts as a historical link that continues the story left off in the Pentateuch. It is a theological history that teaches moral and spiritual lessons as it brings Israel from the wilderness up to the time of the judges. In Genesis God's people were prepared, in Exodus they were redeemed, in Leviticus they were taught, and in Numbers they failed God's test at Kadesh-barnea. The new generation was taught in Deuteronomy and tested in Joshua (Jericho). This time they passed the test of belief and received God's blessings. Israel moved from prospect to possession, from vision to venture. One of the key concepts in Joshua is the importance of the *written Word* of God (see 1:8; 8:32–35; 23:6–16; 24:26–27).

Survey of Joshua

Joshua resumes the narrative where Deuteronomy left off, and takes Israel from the wilderness to the Promised Land. Israel has now reached its climactic point of fulfilling the centuries-old promise in Genesis of a homeland. The first half of Joshua (1:1—13:7) describes the seven-year conquest of the land, and the second half (13:8—24:33) gives the details of the division and settlement of the land.

Conquest (1:1—13:7): The first five chapters record the spiritual, moral, physical, and military preparation of Joshua and the people for the impending conquest of Canaan. Joshua is given a charge by God to complete the task begun by Moses (1:2). After being encouraged by God, Joshua sends out two spies who come back with a favorable report (in contrast to the spies of the previous generation). Obedience and faith are united in the miraculous crossing of the Jordan River (3:1—4:24).

Joshua's campaign in central Canaan (6:1—8:35) places a strategic wedge between the northern and southern cities preventing a massive Canaanite alliance against Israel. This divide-and-conquer strategy proves effective, but God's directions for taking the first city (Jericho) sound like foolishness from a military point of view. The Lord uses this to test the people and to teach them that Israel's success in battle will always be by His power and not their own might or cleverness. Sin must be dealt with at once because it brings severe consequences and defeat at Ai (7:1–26).

The southern and northern campaigns (9:1—13:7) are also successful, but an unwise oath made to the deceptive Gibeonites forces Israel to protect them and to disobey God's command to eliminate the Canaanites.

Settlement (13:8—24:33): Joshua is growing old, and God tells him to divide the land among the twelve tribes. Much remains to be won, and the tribes are to continue the conquest by faith after Joshua's death. The allocation of the land to the various tribes is described (13:8—21:45) as well as the inheritances of Caleb (14—15) and the Levites (21).

The last chapters (22:1—24:33) record the conditions for continued successful settlement in Canaan. Access to God, as well as His forgiveness, come only through the divinely established sacrificial system; and civil war almost breaks out when the eastern tribes build an altar that is misinterpreted by the western tribes.

Realizing that blessing comes from God only as Israel obeys His covenant, Joshua preaches a moving sermon, climaxed by Israel's renewal of her allegiance to the covenant.

Outline of Joshua

Part One: The Conquest of Canaan (1:1—13:7)

I. Israel Is Prepared for the Conquest, 1:1—5:15
  A. Joshua Replaces Moses, 1:1–18
    1. Joshua Is Commissioned by God, 1:1–9
    2. Joshua Commands Israel, 1:10–15
       a. Joshua Commands the Tribes West of the Jordan, 1:10–11
       b. Joshua Commands the Tribes East of the Jordan, 1:12–15
    3. Joshua Is Accepted by Israel, 1:16–18

   B. Joshua Prepares Israel Militarily, 2:1—5:1
      1. Joshua Spies Canaan, 2:1–24
        a. The Faith of Rahab, 2:1–21
        b. The Faith of the Spies, 2:22–24
      2. Joshua Leads Israel into Canaan, 3:1—5:1
        a. The Miraculous Crossing of the Jordan, 3:1–17
        b. The Memorial of the Crossing, 4:1–24
        c. The Canaanites Fear Israel, 5:1
   C. Joshua Prepares Israel Spiritually, 5:2–12
      1. Circumcision Is Practiced, 5:2–9
      2. Passover Is Celebrated, 5:10–11
      3. From Manna to Corn, 5:12
   D. The Commander of the Lord Appears, 5:13–15

II. The Conquest of Canaan by Israel, 6:1—13:7
   A. Conquest of Central Canaan, 6:1—8:35
      1. Victory at Jericho, 6:1–27
      2. Defeat at Ai, 7:1–26
      3. Victory at Ai, 8:1–29
      4. Result of the Victories, 8:30–35
        a. Israel Worships the Lord, 8:30–31
        b. Israel Renews the Covenant, 8:32–35
   B. Conquest of Southern Canaan, 9:1—10:43
      1. Failure with the Gibeonites, 9:1–27
      2. Victory over the Amorites, 10:1–43
   C. Conquest of Northern Canaan, 11:1–15
   D. Conquest of Canaan Is Summarized, 11:16—12:24
      1. The Summary of Conquered Territory, 11:16–23
      2. The Summary of Conquered Kings, 12:1–24
        a. Kings Are Conquered by Moses, 12:1–6
        b. Kings Are Conquered by Joshua, 12:7–24
   E. Unconquered Parts of Canaan, 13:1–7

Part Two: The Settlement in Canaan (13:8—24:33)

I. The Settlement East of the Jordan, 13:8–33
   A. Geographical Boundaries, 13:8–13
   B. Tribal Boundaries, 13:14–33
      1. Boundaries of Levi, 13:14
      2. Boundaries of Reuben, 13:15–23
      3. Boundaries of Gad, 13:24–28
      4. Boundaries of the Half-Tribe of Manasseh, 13:29–33

II. The Settlement West of the Jordan, 14:1—19:51
   A. The First Settlement Done at Gilgal, 14:1—17:18
      1. Method of Setting Tribal Boundaries, 14:1–5
      2. Boundaries of Judah, 14:6—15:63

      a. Boundaries of Caleb, 14:6–15

      b. Boundaries of the Remainder of Judah, 15:1–63

    3. Boundaries of the Tribes of Joseph, 16:1—17:18

      a. Boundaries of Joseph, 16:1–4

      b. Boundaries of Ephraim, 16:5–10

      c. Boundaries of the Half-Tribe of Manasseh, 17:1–18

  B. The Second Settlement Done at Shiloh, 18:1—19:51

    1. The Remaining Tribes Move to Shiloh, 18:1

    2. New Method of Setting Tribal Boundaries, 18:2–10

    3. Boundaries of Benjamin, 18:11–28

    4. Boundaries of Simeon, 19:1–9

    5. Boundaries of Zebulun, 19:10–16

    6. Boundaries of Issachar, 19:17–23

    7. Boundaries of Asher, 19:24–31

    8. Boundaries of Naphtali, 19:32–39

    9. Boundaries of Dan, 19:40–48

   10. Boundaries of Joshua, 19:49–51

III. The Settlement of the Religious Community, 20:1—21:45

  A. Six Cities of Refuge, 20:1–9

  B. Selection of the Levitical Cities, 21:1–42

    1. The Families To Be Assigned Cities, 21:1–7

    2. Cities for the Kohathites, 21:8–26

    3. Cities for the Gershonites, 21:27–33

    4. Cities for the Merarites, 21:34–42

  C. The Settlement of Israel Is Completed, 21:43–45

IV. The Conditions for Continued Settlement, 2:1—24:33

  A. The Altar of Witness, 22:1–34

    1. Joshua Challenges the Eastern Tribes, 22:1–9

    2. Construction of the Altar, 22:10

    3. Misunderstanding of the Altar, 22:11–20

    4. Explanation of the Altar, 22:21–29

    5. Celebration by the Western Tribes, 22:30–34

  B. Blessings of God Come only through Obedience, 23:1—24:28

    1. A Reminder from History, 23:1–16

    2. Renewal of the Covenant, 24:1–28

  C. Joshua and Eleazar Die, 24:29–33

Judges

THE BOOK OF JUDGES STANDS in stark contrast to Joshua. There, an obedient people conquered the land through trust in the power of God. But in Judges, a disobedient and idolatrous people are frequently defeated because of their rebellion against God. In seven distinct cycles of sin, Judges shows how the nation has set aside God's law and in its place "everyone did what was right in his own eyes" (21:25). Result: corruption from within and oppression from without. From time to time God raises up military champions to throw off the yoke of bondage and restore the nation to pure worship. But all too soon the "sin cycle" begins again as the nation's spiritual temperature grows steadily colder.

JUDGES

Focus	Deterioration		Deliverance						Depravity		
	1:1 3:4		3:5 16:31						17:1 21:25		
Divisions	Failure of Israel to Complete the Conquest	Judgment of God for the Failure	Southern Campaign	Northern Campaign I	Central Campaign	Eastern Campaign	Northern Campaign II	Western Campaign	Sin of Idolatry	Sin of Immorality	Sin of Civil War
	1:1 1:36	2:1 3:4	3:5 3:31	4:1 5:31	6:1 10:5	10:6 12:7	12:8 12:15	13:1 16:31	17:1 18:31	19:1 19:30	20:1 21:25
Topics	Causes of the Cycles		Curse of the Cycles						Conditions in the Cycles		
	Living with the Canaanites		War with the Canaanites						Living Like the Canaanites		
Place	Canaan										
Time	c. 350 Years										

Introduction and Title

The Book of Judges stands in stark contrast to Joshua. In Joshua an obedient people conquered the land through trust in the power of God. In Judges, however, a disobedient and idolatrous people are defeated time and time again because of their rebellion against God.

In seven distinct cycles of sin to salvation, Judges shows how Israel had set aside God's law and in its place substituted *"what was* right in his own eyes" (21:25). The recurring result of abandonment from God's law is corruption from within and oppression from without. During the nearly four centuries spanned by this book, God raises up military champions to throw off the yoke of bondage and to restore the nation to pure worship. But all too soon the "sin cycle" begins again as the nation's spiritual temperature grows steadily colder.

The Hebrew title is *Shophetim,* meaning "judges, rulers, deliverers, or saviors." *Shophet* not only carries the idea of maintaining justice and settling disputes, but it is also used to mean "liberating and delivering." First the judges deliver the people; then they rule and administer justice. The Septuagint used the Greek equivalent of this word, *Kritai* ("Judges"). The Latin Vulgate called it *Liber Judicum,* the "Book of Judges." This book could also appropriately be titled "The Book of Failure."

Author

The author of Judges is anonymous, but Samuel or one of his prophetic students may have written it. Jewish tradition contained in the Talmud attributes Judges to Samuel, and certainly he was the crucial link between the period of the judges and the period of the kings.

It is clear from two verses (18:31; 20:27) that the book was written after the ark was removed from Shiloh (1 Sam. 4:3–11). The repeated phrase "In those days *there was* no king in Israel" (17:6; 18:1; 21:25; cf. 19:1) shows that Judges was also written after the commencement of Saul's reign but before the divided kingdom. The fact that the Jebusites were dwelling in Jerusalem "to this day" (1:21) means that it was written before 1004 B.C. when David dispossessed the Jebusites (2 Sam. 5:5–9). Thus, the book was written during the time of Samuel; and it is likely that Samuel compiled this book from oral and written source material. His prophetic ministry clearly fits the moral commentary of Judges, and the consistent style and orderly scheme of Judges point to a single compiler.

Chapter 18, verse 30 contains a phrase that poses a problem to this early date of composition: "until the day of the captivity of the land." If this refers to the 722 B.C. Assyrian captivity of Israel it could have been inserted by a later editor. It is more likely a reference to the Philistine captivity of the land during the time of the judges. This event is described as "captivity" in Psalm 78:61.

Date and Setting

If Judges was not written by Samuel it was at least written by one of his contemporaries between 1043 B.C. (the beginning of Saul's reign) and 1004 B.C. (David's capture of Jerusalem).

Joshua's seven-year conquest is general in nature; much of the land remains to be possessed (Josh. 13:1). There are still important Canaanite strongholds to be taken by the individual tribes. Some of the nations have been left to "test Israel" (3:1, 4). During this time, the Egyptians maintain strong control along the coastal routes, but they are not interested in the hill country where Israel is primarily established.

The events covered in Judges range from about 1380 B.C.–1045 B.C. (c. 335 years), but the period of the judges extends another thirty years since it includes the life of Samuel (1 Sam. 1:1—5:1). Evidently, the rulerships of some of the judges overlap because not all of them ruled over the entire land. Judges describes the cycles of apostasy, oppression, and deliverance in the southern region (3:7–31), the northern region (4:1—5:31), the central region (6:1—10:5), the eastern region (10:6—12:15), and the western region (13:1—16:31). The spread of apostasy covers the whole land.

Theme and Purpose

The historical purpose of Judges is to carry the story of Israel from the death of Joshua to the time of Samuel and the beginning of the united kingdom. It was written during the reign of Saul (1043–1011 B.C.) or during the first seven years of David's reign (1011–1004 B.C.), and it gives an explanation and defense of Israel's monarchy (see 17:6; 18:1; 19:1; 21:25). The nation needed to be unified under a righteous king.

Like the other historical books of the Bible, Judges presents the historical facts in a very selective and thematic way. For example, chapters 17–21 actually preceded most of chapters 3–16, but these chapters appear at the end of the book to illustrate the moral conditions that were prevailing during the period. Judges gives a geographical survey of apostasy to illustrate its spread and a chronological survey to illustrate its growing intensity. The book reaches a climax in chapters 17–21 with the last verse as a fitting summary.

Theologically, Judges makes a clear contrast between the idolatry, immorality, and violence of Israel and Yahweh's covenant faithfulness and gracious deliverance of the people. In His patient love, God forgave the people every single time they repented. Israel often acted in foolishness, ingratitude, stubbornness, and rebellion, and this led to defeat. Sin always leads to suffering, and repentance always leads to deliverance.

Keys to Judges

Key Word: Cycles
Key Verses (2:20–21; 21:25)—"Then the anger of the Lord was hot against Israel; and He said, 'Because this nation has transgressed My covenant which I commanded their fathers, and has not heeded My voice, I also will no longer drive out before them any of the nations which Joshua left when he died'" (2:20–21).

"In those days *there was* no king in Israel; everyone did *what was* right in his own eyes" (21:25).

Key Chapter (2)—The second chapter of Judges is a miniature of the whole book as it records the transition of the godly to the ungodly generation, the format of the cycles, and the purpose of God in not destroying the Canaanites.

Christ in Judges

Each judge is a savior and a ruler, a spiritual and political deliverer. Thus, the judges portray the role of Christ as the Savior-King of His people. The Book of Judges also illustrates the need for a righteous king.

Including First Samuel, seventeen judges are mentioned altogether. Some are warrior-rulers (e.g., Othniel and Gideon), one is a priest (Eli), and one is a prophet (Samuel). This gives a cumulative picture of the three offices of Christ, who excelled all his predecessors in that He was the ultimate Prophet, Priest, and King.

Contribution to the Bible

Judges records the failure of the theocracy due to lack of faith and obedience. They were disloyal to their divine King and would later find it easier to follow an earthly king. Judges stands in bold contrast to Joshua:

Joshua	Judges
Freedom	Bondage
Progress	Decline
Conquest through belief	Defeat through disbelief
"Far be it from us that we should forsake the LORD to serve other gods" (24:16)	"So the children of Israel did evil in the sight of the LORD. They forgot the LORD their God, and served the Baals and Asherahs" (3:7).
Israel served God (24:31)	Israel served self (21:25)
Israel knew the person of God and the power of God (24:16–18, 31)	Israel knew neither the person of God nor the power of God (2:10)
Objective morality	Subjective morality
Israel pressing onward	Israel spiralling downward
Sin judged	Sin tolerated
Faith and obedience	Lack of both

Survey of Judges

Following the death of Joshua, Israel plunges into a 350-year Dark Age. After Joshua and the generation of the conquest pass on, "another generation arose after them who did not know the LORD nor the work which He had done for Israel" (2:10; see also 2:7–10; Josh. 24:31). Judges opens with a description of Israel's deterioration, continues with seven cycles of oppression and deliverance, and concludes with two illustrations of Israel's depravity.

Deterioration (1:1—3:4): Judges begins with short-lived military successes after Joshua's death, but quickly turns to the repeated failure of all the tribes to drive out their enemies. The people feel the lack of a unified central leader, but the primary reasons for their failure are a lack of faith in God and a lack of obedience to Him (2:1–3). Compromise leads to conflict and chaos. Israel does not drive out the inhabitants (1:21, 27, 29–30); instead of removing the moral cancer spread by the inhabitants of Canaan, they contract the disease. The Canaanite gods literally become a snare to them (2:3). Chapter 2, verses 11–23 are a microcosm of the pattern found in chapters 3–16 of Judges.

Deliverances (3:5—16:31): This section describes seven apostasies (fallings away from God), seven servitudes, and seven deliverances. Each of the seven cycles has five steps: sin, servitude, supplication, salvation, and silence. These also can be described by the words rebellion, retribution, repentance, restoration, and rest. The seven cycles connect together as a descending spiral of sin (2:19). Israel vacillates between obedience and apostasy as the people continually fail to learn from their mistakes. Apostasy grows, but the rebellion is not continual. The times of rest and peace are longer than the times of bondage. The monotony of Israel's sins can be contrasted with the creativity of God's methods of deliverance.

The judges are military and civil leaders during this period of loose confederacy. Thirteen are mentioned in this book, and four more are found in First Samuel (Eli, Samuel, Joel, and Abijah).

Cycle	Oppressor	Years of Oppression	Deliverer	Years of Peace
1 (3:7–11)	Mesopotamians	8	Othniel	40
2 (3:12–30)	Moabites	18	Ehud	80
Parenthesis (3:31)	Philistines	—	Shagmar	—
3 (4:1—5:31)	Canaanites	20	Deborah/Barak	40
4 (6:1—8:32)	Midianites	7	Gideon	40
5 (8:33—10:5)	Abimelech	3	Tola/Jair	45
6 (10:6—12:15)	Ammonites	18	Jepthah/Ibzan/Elon/Abdon	6,7,10,8
7 (13:1—16:31)	Philistines	40	Samson	20

Depravity (17:1—21:25): These chapters illustrate (1) religious apostasy (17-18) and (2) social and moral depravity (19-21) during the period of the judges. Chapters 19–21 contain one of the worst tales of degradation in the Bible. Judges closes with a key to understanding the period: "every man did *what was* right in his own eyes" (21:25). The people are not doing what is wrong in their own eyes, but what is "evil in the sight of the LORD."

Outline of Judges

Part One: The Deterioration of Israel and Failure to Complete the Conquest of Canaan (1:1—3:4)

I. The Failure of Israel to Complete the Conquest, 1:1–36
  A. Failure of Judah, 1:1–20
  B. Failure of Benjamin, 1:21
  C. Failure of Tribes of Joseph, 1:22–29
  D. Failure of Zebulum, 1:30
  E. Failure of Asher, 1:31–32
  F. Failure of Naphtali, 1:33
  G. Failure of Dan, 1:34–36

II. The Judgment of God for Not Completing the Conquest, 2:1—3:4
  A. Angel Announces Judgment, 2:1–5
  B. Godly Generation Dies, 2:6–10
  C. Judgment of God Is Described, 2:11–19
  D. Enemy Is Left as a Test, 2:20—3:4

Part Two: The Deliverance of Israel During the Seven Cycles (3:5—16:31)

I. The Southern Campaign, 3:5–31
  A. The Judge Othniel, 3:5–11
  B. The Judge Ehud, 3:12–30
  C. The Judge Shamgar, 3:31

II. The Northern Campaign: The Judges Deborah and Barak, 4:1—5:31
  A. Deborah and Barak Are Called, 4:1–11
  B. Canaanites Are Defeated, 4:12–24
  C. Song of Deborah and Barak, 5:1–31

III. The Central Campaign, 6:1—10:5
  A. The Judge Gideon, 6:1—8:32
    1. Israel Sins, 6:1–10
    2. Gideon Called, 6:11–40
    3. Midianites Defeated, 7:1—8:21
    4. Gideon Judges, 8:22–32
  B. The Judge Abimelech, 8:33—9:57
    1. Confusion after Gideon Dies, 8:33–35
    2. Deception of Abimelech, 9:1–6
    3. Revelation of Jotham, 9:7–21

    4. Destruction of Shechem, 9:22–49
    5. Death of Abimelech, 9:50–57
  C. The Judge Tola, 10:1–2
  D. The Judge Jair, 10:3–5

IV. The Eastern Campaign: The Judge Jephthah, 10:6—12:7
  A. Israel Sins, 10:6–18
  B. Salvation: Jephthah, 11:1—12:6
    1. Jephthah Is Called, 11:1–11
    2. Jephthah Judges, 11:12–28
    3. Jephthah Vows, 11:29–40
    4. Ephraim Is Conquered, 12:1–7

V. The Second Northern Campaign, 12:8–15
  A. The Judge Ibzan, 12:8–10
  B. The Judge Elon, 12:11–12
  C. The Judge Abdon, 12:13–15

VI. The Western Campaign: The Judge Samson, 13:1—16:31
  A. Miraculous Birth of Samson, 13:1–25
  B. Sinful Marriage of Samson, 14:1–20
  C. Judgeship of Samson, 15:1–20
  D. Failure of Samson, 16:1–31

Part Three: The Depravity of Israel in Sinning Like the Canaanites (17:1—21:25)

I. The Failure of Israel through Idolatry, 17:1—18:31
  A. Example of Personal Idolatry, 17:1–13
  B. Example of Tribal Idolatry, 18:1–31

II. The Failure of Israel through Immorality, 19:1–30
  A. Example of Personal Immorality, 19:1–10
  B. Example of Tribal Immorality, 19:11–30

III. The Failure of Israel through the War between the Tribes, 20:1—21:25
  A. War between Israel and Dan, 20:1–48
  B. Failure of Israel after the War, 21:1–25
    1. Israel's Foolish Vow, 21:1–7
    2. Men at Jabesh Gilead Murdered, 21:8–15
    3. Women of Shiloh Kidnapped, 21:16–25

Ruth

RUTH IS A BEAUTIFUL "interlude of love" set in the period of the judges in Israel—an era marked by immorality, idolatry, and war. This heartwarming story of devotion and faithfulness records the life of Ruth, a Moabite widow who leaves her homeland to live with her widowed Jewish mother-in-law in Bethlehem. God honors her commitment by guiding her to the field of Boaz (a near kinsman) where she gathers grain and eventually finds a husband! The book closes with a brief genealogy in which Boaz's name is prominent as the great-grandfather of King David, through whom would come the Christ.

RUTH

Focus	Ruth's Love Demonstrated		Ruth's Love Rewarded	
	1:1 2:23		3:1 4:22	
Divisions	Ruth's Decision to Remain with Naomi	Ruth's Devotion to Care for Naomi	Ruth's Request for Redemption by Boaz	Ruth's Reward of Redemption by Boaz
	1:1 1:18	1:19 2:23	3:1 3:18	4:1 4:22
Topics	Ruth and Naomi		Ruth and Boaz	
	Death of Family	Ruth Cares for Naomi	Boaz Cares for Ruth	Birth of Family
Place	Moab	Fields in Bethlehem	Threshing Floor in Bethlehem	Bethlehem
Time	c. 30 Years			

Introduction and Title

Ruth is a cameo story of love, devotion, and redemption set in the black context of the days of the judges. It is the story of a Moabite woman who forsakes her pagan heritage in order to cling to the people of Israel and to the God of Israel. Because of her *faithfulness* in a time of national *faithlessness,* God rewards her by giving her a new husband (Boaz), a son (Obed), and a privileged position in the lineage of David and Christ (she is the great-grandmother of David).

Ruth is the Hebrew title of this book. This name may be a Moabite modification of the Hebrew word *reuit,* meaning "friendship or association." The Septuagint entitles the book *Routh,* the Greek equivalent of the Hebrew name. The Latin title is *Ruth,* a transliteration of *Routh.*

Author

The author of Ruth is not given anywhere in the book, nor is he known from any other biblical passage. Talmudic tradition attributes it to Samuel but this is unlikely since David appears in Ruth (4:17, 22), and Samuel died before David's coronation (1 Sam. 25:1). Ruth was probably written during David's reign since Solomon's name is not included in the genealogy. The anonymity of the book, however, should not detract from its spiritual value or literary beauty.

Date and Setting

Ruth divides neatly into four distinct settings: (1) the country of Moab (1:1–18); (2) a field in Bethlehem (1:19—2:23); (3) a threshing floor in Bethlehem (3:1–18); and (4) the city of Bethlehem (4:1–22).

The setting of the first eighteen verses is Moab, a region northeast of the Dead Sea. The Moabites, descendants of Lot, worship Chemosh and other pagan gods. Scripture records two times when they fight against Israel (see Judg. 3:12–30; 1 Sam. 14:47). Ruth takes place about two centuries after the first war and approximately eighty years before the record.

Ruth 1:1 gives the setting of the remainder of the book: "Now it came to pass, in the days when the judges ruled." This is a time of apostasy, warfare, decline, violence, moral decay, and anarchy. Ruth provides a cameo of the other side of the story—the godly remnant who remain true to the laws of God.

Because Ruth is written more to tell a beautiful story than to give all the historical facts of that period, the assignment of time is somewhat difficult. Utilizing the same fourfold division noted above, the following can be assigned:

A. Ruth 1:1–18 (note 1:4): The country of Moab (c. ten years)
B. Ruth 1:19—2:23 (note 1:22; 2:23): A field in Bethlehem (months)
C. Ruth 3:1–18 (note 3:2, 8, 14, 18): A threshing floor in Bethlehem (one day)
D. Ruth 4:1–22 (note 4:13–16): The city of Bethlehem (c. one year)

Theme and Purpose

Chapters 17—21 form an appendix to the Book of Judges, offering two illustrations of unrighteousness during the time of the judges. Ruth serves as a third illustration of life during this time, but it is an illustration of godliness. It is a positive picture of real faith and obedience (1:16–17; 3:10) that leads to blessing (4:13, 17). Ruth also teaches that Gentiles could believe in the true God (three out of the four women mentioned in Christ's genealogy in Matthew 1 were Gentiles—Tamar, Rahab, and Ruth). Ruth explains how a gentile woman could become a member of the royal lineage of David and shows the divine origin of the Davidic dynasty (4:18–22).

The theme of Ruth is redemption, especially as it relates to the Kinsman-Redeemer. It reveals Yahweh's gracious character and sovereign care for His people (2:12). It stresses God's providential rewards for faithfulness. Not all was lost during this chaotic period—there was always a faithful remnant of those who did what was right in the sight of the Lord.

Keys to Ruth

Key Word: Kinsman-Redeemer

Key Verses (1:16; 3:11)—"But Ruth said: 'Entreat me not to leave you, *or to* turn back from following after you; for wherever you go, I will go; and wherever you lodge, I will lodge; your people *shall be* my people, and your God, my God" (1:16).

"And now, my daughter, do not fear. I will do for you all that you request, for all the people of my town know that you *are* a virtuous woman" (3:11).

Key Chapter (4)—In twenty-two short verses, Ruth moves from widowhood and poverty to marriage and wealth (2:1). In exercising the law regulating the redemption of property (Lev. 25:25–34) and the law concerning a brother's duty to raise up seed (children) in the name of the deceased (Deut. 25:5–10), Boaz brings a Moabite woman into the family line of David and eventually of Jesus Christ.

Christ in Ruth

The concept of the Kinsman-Redeemer or *goel* (3:9, "close relative") is an important portrayal of the work of Christ. The *goel* must: (1) be related by blood to those he redeems (see Deut. 25:5, 7–10; John 1:14; Rom. 1:3; Phil. 2:5–8; Heb. 2:14–15); (2) be able to pay the price of redemption (see 2:1; 1 Pet. 1:18–19); (3) be willing to redeem (see 3:11; Matt. 20:28; John 10:15, 18; Heb. 10:7); and (4) be free himself (Christ was free from the curse of sin). The word *goel,* used thirteen times in this short book, presents a clear picture of the mediating work of Christ.

Contribution to the Bible

(1) Literary—Ruth is a book of simplicity but profundity. It is one of literature's best examples of filial love and piety. (2) Historical—Ruth provides a bridge between the judges and the monarchy (its last word is "David"). It illustrates faithfulness amid infidelity. (3) Doctrinal—Ruth teaches that the Gentiles are not outside the scope of redemption. (4) Moral—Ruth communicates high ideals of integrity in relationships and marriage.

Ruth is one of the two biblical books named after a woman:

Ruth	Esther
A gentile woman	A Jewish woman
Lived among the Jews	Lived among the Gentiles
Married a Jewish man in the royal line of David	Married a gentile man who ruled an empire
A story of faith and blessing	A story of faith and blessing

The book of Ruth contrasts with Judges in several ways:

Ruth	Judges
Fidelity, righteousness, purity	Immorality
Following the true God	Idolatry
Devotion	Decline, debasement, disloyalty
Love	Lust
Peace	War
Kindness	Cruelty
Obedient faith leads to blessing	Disobedience leads to sorrow
Spiritual light	Spiritual darkness

Survey of Ruth

Ruth is the story of a virtuous woman who lives above the norm of her day. Although it was probably written during the time of David, the events take place during the time of the judges. This period in Israel's history was generally a desert of rebellion and immorality, but the story of Ruth stands in contrast as an oasis of integrity and righteousness.

Ruth is "a virtuous woman" (3:11) who shows loyal love to her mother-in-law Naomi and her near-kinsman Boaz. In both relationships, goodness and love are clearly manifested. Her love is demonstrated in chapters 1—2 and rewarded in chapters 3—4.

Ruth's Love Is Demonstrated (1—2): The story begins with a famine in Israel, a sign of disobedience and apostasy (Deut. 28—30). An Israelite named Elimelech ("My God Is King") in a desperate act moves from Bethlehem ("House of Bread"—note the irony) to Moab. Although he seeks life in that land, he and his two sons Mahlon ("Sick") and Chilion ("Pining") find only death. The deceased sons leave two Moabite widows, Orpah ("Stubbornness") and Ruth ("Friendship"). Elimelech's widow, Naomi, hears that the famine in Israel is over and decides to return, no longer as Naomi ("Pleasant") but as Mara ("Bitter"). She tells her daughters-in-law to remain in Moab and remarry since there was no security for an unmarried woman in those days. Orpah chooses to leave Naomi and is never mentioned again. Ruth, on the other hand, resolves to cling to Naomi and follow Yahweh, the God of Israel. She therefore gives up her culture, people, and language because of her love.

Naomi's misfortune leads her to think that God is her enemy, but He has plans she does not yet realize. In her plight, she must let Ruth glean at the edge of a field. This is a humiliating and dangerous task because of the character of many of the reapers. However, God's providential care brings her to the field of Boaz, Naomi's kinsman. Boaz ("In Him Is Strength") begins to love, protect, and provide for her.

Ruth's Love Is Rewarded (3—4): Boaz takes no further steps toward marriage, so Naomi follows the accepted customs of the day and requests that Boaz exercise his right as Kinsman-Redeemer. In chapter 3, verses 10–13, Boaz reveals why he has taken no action: he is older than Ruth (perhaps twenty years her senior), and he is not the nearest kinsman. Nevertheless, God rewards Ruth's devotion by giving her Boaz as a husband and by providing her with a son, Obed, the grandfather of David.

Outline of Ruth

Part One: Ruth's Love Is Demonstrated (1:1—2:23)

I. **Ruth's Decision to Remain with Naomi,** 1:1–18
   A. Ruth's Need to Remain with Naomi, 1:1–5
   B. Ruth's Opportunity to Leave Naomi, 1:6–15
   C. Ruth's Choice to Remain with Naomi, 1:16–18

II. **Ruth's Devotion to Care for Naomi,** 1:19—2:23
   A. Ruth and Naomi Return to Bethlehem, 1:19–22
   B. Ruth Gleans for Food, 2:1–23
      1. Boaz Meets Ruth, 2:1–7
      2. Boaz Protects Ruth, 2:8–16
      3. Boaz Provides for Ruth, 2:17–23

Part Two: Ruth's Love Is Rewarded (3:1—4:22)

I. **Ruth's Request for Redemption by Boaz,** 3:1–18
   A. Naomi Seeks Redemption for Ruth, 3:1–5
   B. Ruth Obeys Naomi, 3:6–9
   C. Boaz Desires to Redeem Ruth, 3:10–18

II. **Ruth's Reward of Redemption by Boaz,** 4:1–22
   A. Boaz Marries Ruth, 4:1–12
   B. Ruth Bears a Son, Obed, 4:13–15
   C. Naomi Receives a New Family, 4:16
   D. Ruth Is the Great-grandmother of David, 4:17–22

First Samuel

SAMUEL, THE LAST JUDGE and first great prophet in Israel, anoints the first king. Though Saul's physical credentials are impressive, his indifferent heart attitude toward God results in the kingdom being taken away from his family. In his place Samuel anoints young David as the king-elect. David becomes a growing threat to the insanely jealous Saul, eventually fleeing to the wilderness for his very life. But God's hand of protection is clearly upon David, even as God's hand of judgment is being felt by Saul and his family. Foolishly consulting a medium at En Dor, Saul hears his own doom pronounced. True to the prophet's word, Saul and his sons are killed the next day in combat.

FIRST SAMUEL

Focus	Samuel			Saul		
	1:1 — 7:17			8:1 — 31:13		
Divisions	Transition of Leadership #1 Eli—Samuel	Judgeship of Samuel	Transition of Leadership #2 Samuel—Saul	Reign of Saul	Transition of Leadership #3 Saul—David	
	1:1 — 3:21	4:1 — 7:17	8:1 — 12:25	13:1 — 15:9	15:10 — 31:13	
Topics	Decline of Judges		Rise of Kings			
	Eli	Samuel	Saul		David	
	1:1 — 3:21	4:1 — 7:17	8:1 — 15:9		15:10 — 31:13	
Place	Canaan					
Time	c. 94 Years					

Introduction and Title

The First Book of Samuel describes the transition of leadership in Israel from judges to kings. Three characters are prominent in the book: Samuel, the last judge and first prophet; Saul, the first king of Israel; and David, the king-elect, anointed but not yet recognized as Saul's successor.

The books of First and Second Samuel were originally one book in the Hebrew Bible, known as the "Book of Samuel" or simply "Samuel." This name has been variously translated "The Name of God," "His Name Is God," "Heard of God," and "Asked of God." The Septuagint divides Samuel into two books even though it is one continuous account. This division artificially breaks up the history of David. The Greek (Septuagint) title is *Bibloi Basileion,* "Books of Kingdoms," referring to the later kingdoms of Israel and Judah. First Samuel is called *Basileion Alpha,* "First Kingdoms." Second Samuel and First and Second Kings are called "Second, Third, and Fourth Kingdoms." The Latin Vulgate originally called the books of Samuel and Kings *Libri Regum,* "Books of the Kings." Later the Latin Bible combined the Hebrew and Greek titles for the first of these books, calling it *Liber I Samuelis,* the "First Book of Samuel," or simply "First Samuel."

Author

The author of First and Second Samuel is anonymous, but Jewish talmudic tradition says that it was written by Samuel. Samuel may have written the first portion of the book, but his death recorded in First Samuel 25:1 makes it clear that he did not write all of First and Second Samuel. Samuel did write a book (10:25), and written records were available. As the head of a company of prophets (see 10:5; 19:20), Samuel would be a logical candidate for biblical authorship.

First Chronicles 29:29 refers to "the Book of Samuel the Seer," "the Book of Nathan the Prophet," and "the Book of Gad the Seer." All three men evidently contributed to these two books; and it is very possible that a single compiler, perhaps a member of the prophetic school, used these chronicles to put together the Book of Samuel. This is also suggested by the unity of plan and purpose and by the smooth transitions between sections.

Date and Setting

If Samuel wrote the material in the first twenty-four chapters, he did so soon before his death (c. 1015 B.C.). He was born around 1105 B.C., and ministered as a judge and prophet in Israel between about 1067 and 1015 B.C. The books of Samuel end in the last days of David; so they must have been compiled after 971 B.C. The reference in First Samuel 27:6 to the divided monarchy in which Judah is separate from Israel indicates a compilation date after Solomon's death in 931 B.C. However, the silence regarding the Assyrian captivity of Israel in 722 B.C. probably means that First Samuel was written before this key event.

First Samuel covers the ninety-four-year period from the birth of Samuel to the death of Saul (c. 1105–1101 B.C.). The Philistines strongly oppress Israel from 1087

B.C. until the battle of Ebenezer in 1047 B.C. (7:10–14). However, even after this time the Philistines exercise military and economic control. They live in the coastal plains; and the hill country in which the Israelites dwell protects them from total conquest by the Philistines.

Theme and Purpose

The books of Samuel give a prophetically oriented history of Israel's early monarchy. The First of these books picks up the story of Israel left off in Judges 16:31. Samuel followed Samson, and he too had to deal with the Philistines since Samson did not accomplish a permanent victory. First Samuel traces the transition of leadership in Israel from judges to kings, from a theocracy to a monarchy. The monarchy brought greater stability because the people found it easier to follow an earthly king. Samuel was the kingmaker who anointed the first two rulers of the united kingdom. Saul quickly disobeyed God and became a tyrant. David became the first real theocratic king—he allowed God to rule through him.

In their actions during the period of the judges, the people rejected Yahweh as their King. The clamor for an earthly king in First Samuel was the natural outcome of this practical rejection (8:7). God had intended to give Israel a king (see Gen. 49:10; Deut. 17:14–20), but the people insisted on the king of their choice instead of waiting for God's king. Nevertheless, this book teaches the sovereign control of Yahweh who establishes and removes kings. Saul was rejected by the Lord because he failed to learn the truth that "to obey is better than sacrifice" (15:22). He became characterized by mental imbalance, raging jealousy, foolishness, and immorality. David illustrated the principle that "the LORD does not see as man sees" (16:7). The Lord established the Davidic dynasty because of David's obedience, wisdom, and dependence on God.

Samuel also reveals the critical role of the prophets in their divinely commissioned exhortations to the kings and the people of Israel.

Keys to First Samuel

Key Word: Transition
Key Verses (13:14; 15:22)—"But now your kingdom shall not continue. The LORD has sought for Himself a man after His own heart, and the LORD has commanded him *to be* commander over His people, because you have not kept what the LORD commanded you" (13:14).

"Then Samuel said: 'Has the LORD *as great* delight in burnt offerings and sacrifices, as in obeying the voice of the LORD? Behold, to obey is better than sacrifice, and to heed than the fat of rams.'" (15:22).

Key Chapter (15)—First Samuel 15 records the tragic transition of kingship from Saul to David. As in all three changes recorded in First Samuel, God removes His blessing from one and gives it to another because of sin. "Because you have rejected the word of the LORD, He also has rejected you from *being* king" (15:23).

Christ in First Samuel

Samuel is a type of Christ in that he is a prophet, priest, and judge. Highly revered by the people, he brings in a new age.

David is one of the primary Old Testament portrayals of the person of Christ. He is born in Bethlehem, works as a shepherd, and rules as king of Israel. He is the anointed king who becomes the forerunner of the messianic King. His typical messianic psalms are born of his years of rejection and danger (Ps. 22). God enables David, a man "after His own heart" (13:14), to become Israel's greatest king. The New Testament specifically calls Christ the "seed of David according to the flesh" (Rom. 1:3) and "the Root and the Offspring of David" (Rev. 22:16).

Contribution to the Bible

Historically, First Samuel provides the crucial link from the judges to the monarchy. It is a fast-moving narrative that gives a spiritual perspective on three very different personalities whose lives were interwoven: Samuel, Saul, and David.

This is the first book to use the word *Messiah* ("anointed," 2:10). It is also the first to call God the "LORD of hosts" (e.g., 1:3). The well-known words *Ichabod* ("no glory," 4:21) and *Ebenezer* ("stone of help," 7:12) come from this book. Our Lord alluded to First Samuel on at least two occasions (viz., 21:6 in Matt. 12:3–4 and 16:7 in Luke 16:15).

Survey of First Samuel

First Samuel records the crucial transition from the theocracy under the judges to the monarchy under the kings. The book is built around three key men: Samuel (1—7), Saul (8—31), and David (16—31).

Samuel (1—7): Samuel's story begins late in the turbulent time of the judges when Eli is the judge-priest of Israel. The birth of Samuel and his early call by Yahweh are found in chapters 1–3. Because of his responsiveness to God (3:19), he is confirmed as a prophet (3:20–21) at a time when the "word of the LORD was rare in those days; *there was* no widespread revelation" (3:1).

Corruption at Shiloh by Eli's notoriously wicked sons leads to Israel's defeat in the crucial battle with the Philistines (4:1–11). The ark of the covenant, God's "throne" among the people, is lost to the Philistines; the priesthood is disrupted by the deaths of Eli and his sons; and the glory of God departs from the tabernacle (Ichabod, "glory has departed," 4:21). Samuel begins to function as the last of the judges and the first in the order of the prophets (Acts 3:24). His prophetic ministry (7:3–17) leads to a revival in Israel, the return of the ark, and the defeat of the Philistines. When Samuel is old and his sons prove to be unjust judges, the people wrongly cry out for a king. They want a visible military and judicial ruler so they can be "like all the nations" (8:5–20).

Saul (8—15): In their impatient demand for a king, Israel chooses less than God's best. Their motive (8:5) and criteria (9:2) are wrong. Saul begins well (9—11), but his good characteristics soon degenerate. In spite of Samuel's solemn prophetic warning (12), Saul and the people begin to act wickedly. Saul presumptuously assumes the role of a priest (2 Chr. 26:18) and offers up sacrifices (13). He makes a foolish vow (14) and disobeys God's command to destroy the Amalekites (15). Samuel's powerful words (15:22–23) evoke a pathetic response (15:24–31).

Saul and David (16—31): When God rejects Saul, He commissions Samuel to anoint David as Israel's next king. God's king-elect serves in Saul's court (16:14—23:29) and defeats the Philistine Goliath (17). Jonathan's devotion to David leads him to sacrifice the throne (20:30–31) in acknowledgment of David's divine right to it (18). David becomes a growing threat to the insanely jealous Saul; but he is protected from Saul's wrath by Jonathan, Michal, and Samuel (19).

Saul's open rebellion against God is manifested in his refusal to give up what God has said cannot be his. David is protected again by Jonathan from Saul's murderous intent (20), but Saul becomes more active in his pursuit of David. The future king flees to a Philistine city where he feigns insanity (21), and flees again to Adullam where a band of men forms around him (22).

David continues to escape from the hand of Saul, and on two occasions spares Saul's life when he has the opportunity to take it (24—26). David again seeks refuge among the Philistines, but is not allowed to fight on their side against Israel. Saul, afraid of impending battle against the Philistines, foolishly consults a medium at Endor to hear the deceased Samuel's advice (28). The Lord rebukes Saul and pronounces his doom; he and his sons are killed by the Philistines on Mount Gilboa (31).

Outline of First Samuel

Part One: Samuel, the Last Judge (1:1—7:17)

I. The First Transition of National Leadership: Eli-Samuel, 1:1—3:21
   A. The Birth of the New Leader, 1:1—2:11
      1. Hannah's Barrenness, 1:1–18
      2. Samuel's Birth, 1:19–28
      3. Hannah's Prophetic Prayer, 2:1–11
   B. The Need of the New Leader, 2:12–36
      1. Sinfulness of Eli's Son, 2:12–21
      2. Compromise of Eli as Father, 2:22–36
   C. The Transition from Eli to Samuel, 3:1–18
      1. The Word of the Lord Does Not Come to Eli, 3:1
      2. The Word of the Lord Comes to Samuel, 3:2–18
   D. Samuel Is Recognized as the New Leader of Israel, 3:19–21

II. The Judgeship of Samuel, 4:1—7:17
   A. The Need for Samuel's Leadership, 4:1—6:21
      1. Conquest of Israel by Philistia, 4:1–10
      2. Eli and His Sons Die, 4:11–22

3. The Sin with the Ark, 5:1—7:2
   a. The Philistines' Sin with the Ark, 5:1—6:9
   b. The Israelites' Sin with the Ark, 6:10–21
B. The Victories under Samuel's Leadership, 7:1–17
   1. The Acceptable Return of the Ark, 7:1–2
   2. Israel Returns to the Lord, 7:3–6
   3. Israel's Victory over Philistia, 7:7–17

Part Two: Saul, the First King (8:1—31:13)

I. The Second Transition of National Leadership: Samuel-Saul, 8:1—12:25
A. The Causes of the Transition, 8:1–9
   1. Israel Rejects Samuel's Sons as Leaders, 8:1–5
   2. Israel Rejects God as King, 8:6–9
B. The Transition from Samuel to Saul, 8:10—12:25
   1. Samuel Warns Israel, 8:10–22
   2. God Chooses Saul, 9:1—10:16
   3. Samuel Anoints Saul, 10:17–27
   4. Israel Makes Saul King, 11:1–15
   5. Samuel Confirms Saul, 12:1–25

II. The Reign of King Saul, 13:1—15:9
A. The Early Success of King Saul, 13:1–4
B. The Failures of King Saul, 13:5—15:9
   1. Saul's Sinful Sacrifices, 13:5–23
   2. Saul's Selfish Curse, 14:1–52
   3. Saul's Incomplete Obedience, 15:1–9

III. The Third Transition of National Leadership: Saul-David, 15:10—31:13
A. The Transition of Kingship from Saul to David, 15:10—18:9
   1. God Rejects Saul as King, 15:10–35
   2. God Anoints David as King, 16:1–13
   3. God Takes His Spirit from Saul, 16:14–23
   4. God Confirms David over Saul, 17:1—18:9
      a. David Defeats Goliath, 17:1–58
      b. Jonathan Loves David, 18:1–4
      c. Israel Elevates David over Saul, 18:5–9
B. The Attempts of Saul to Slay David, 18:10—20:42
   1. By Throwing a Spear at David, 18:10–16
   2. By Tricking David to Fight the Philistines, 18:17–30
   3. By Commanding His Servants to Kill David, 19:1–7
   4. By Throwing a Spear at David Again, 19:8–10
   5. By Sending His Messengers to Kill David, 19:11–17
   6. By Coming to Kill David at Samuel's House, 19:18–24
   7. By Commanding Jonathan to Bring David to Be Killed, 20:1–42
C. The Rise of David in Exile, 21:1—28:2
   1. David Is Protected by the Priest, 21:1–9
   2. David Pretends to Be Mad, 21:10–15

3. David Builds an Army in the Wilderness, 22:1—26:25
    a. David Flees to Adullam, 22:1–5
    b. Saul Slays the Priests of God, 22:6–23
    c. David Smites the Philistines, 23:1–12
    d. Saul Chases David, 23:13–29
    e. David Saves Saul's Life, 24:1–22
    f. Samuel the Judge Dies, 25:1
    g. David Marries Abigail, 25:2–44
    h. David Saves Saul's Life Again, 26:1–20
    i. Saul Admits His Guilt, 26:21–25
4. David Joins with the Philistines, 27:1—28:2
D. The Final Decline of Saul, 28:3—31:13
    1. God Does Not Answer Saul, 28:3–6
    2. Saul Visits the Medium, 28:7–25
    3. David Is Spared from Fighting Saul, 29:1–11
    4. God Answers David, 30:1–8
    5. David Kills the Enemy, 30:9–31
    6. The Enemy Kills Saul, 31:1–13

Second Samuel

SOON AFTER THE DEATH of Saul, David the king-elect becomes monarch first over Judah (where he reigns with Hebron as his capital for seven and one-half years) and finally over all Israel (where he makes Jerusalem his capital and reigns for thirty-three years). Thus, Second Samuel chronicles the forty-year reign of the man who lived at the halfway point between Abraham and Christ—about 1000 B.C. David's triumphs bring the nation to the very zenith of its power. But his dual sins of adultery and murder bring personal and national chastening from the Lord. Throughout his life, David seeks God zealously and confesses his sins promptly—actions befitting the one called by God "a man after My own heart" (Acts 13:22).

Focus	David's Triumphs			David's Transgressions	Troubles	
	1:1 10:19			11:1 11:27	12:1 24:25	
Divisions	Political Triumphs	Spiritual Triumphs	Military Triumphs	Sins of Adultery and Murder	Troubles in David's House	Troubles in David's Kingdom
	1:1 5:25	6:1 7:29	8:1 10:19	11:1 11:27	12:1 13:36	13:37 24:25
Topics	Success			Sin	Failure	
	Obedience			Disobedience	Judgment	
Place	David in Hebron	David in Jerusalem				
Time	7½ Years	33 Years				

SECOND SAMUEL

Introduction and Title

The Second Book of Samuel records the highlights of David's reign, first over the territory of Judah, and finally over the entire nation of Israel. It traces the ascension of David to the throne, his climactic sins of adultery and murder, and the shattering consequences of those sins upon his family and the nation.

See First Samuel for details on the titles of the books of Samuel. The Hebrew title for both books (originally one) is *Samuel*. The Greek title for Second Samuel is *Basileion Beta*, "Second Kingdoms." The Latin title is *Liber II Samuelis*, the "Second Book of Samuel," or simply "Second Samuel."

Author

Second Samuel was probably compiled by one man who combined the written chronicles of Nathan the prophet and Gad the seer (1 Chr. 29:29). In addition to these written sources, the compiler evidently used another source called "the Book of Jasher" (1:18). (See comments under First Samuel.)

Date and Setting

The date of the composition for First and Second Samuel was sometime after the death of Solomon (931 B.C.) but before the Assyrian captivity of the northern kingdom (722 B.C.). It is likely that Samuel was composed early in the divided kingdom, perhaps around 900 B.C.

The story of David begins in First Samuel 16 and ends in First Kings 2. Second Samuel records the major events of David's forty-year rule. His reign in Hebron begins in 1011 B.C. and ends in 1004 B.C. (5:5). His thirty-three year reign over the united Judah and Israel lasts from 1004 B.C. to 971 B.C.

Theme and Purpose

There is no real break in the narrative between First Samuel 31:13 and Second Samuel 1:1. The two books of Samuel were originally one book written to provide a divine perspective on the establishment of the united kingdom under Saul and its expansion under David. These books repeatedly illustrate the hostility between the ten northern and two southern tribes and the difficulty of keeping them united. The final split between Israel and Judah that occurred after the death of Solomon in 931 B.C. comes as no surprise in light of First and Second Samuel.

The Book of Second Samuel offers a very candid portrait of the strengths and weaknesses of David's forty-year reign. God is no respecter of persons, and the heroes of the Bible like David are not glorified to the neglect of their sin. This balanced presentation of the life of Israel's greatest king reveals the origin of a perpetual dynasty (7:16).

Several spiritual truths are reinforced and illustrated in the life of David. The most obvious of these is the cause and effect principle stressed in every book since Genesis: obedience (1—7) brings God's blessings (8—10), and disobedience (11) leads to God's judgment (12—24). The consequences of sin cannot be avoided; "sin, when it is full-grown, brings forth death" (James 1:15), in this case, many.

Keys to Second Samuel

Key Word: David

Key Verses (7:12–13; 22:21)—"When your days are fulfilled and you rest with your fathers, I will set up your seed after you, who will come from your body, and I will establish his kingdom. He shall build a house for My name, and I will establish the throne of his kingdom forever" (7:12–13).

"The LORD rewarded me according to my righteousness; according to the cleanness of my hands He has recompensed me" (22:21).

Key Chapter (11)—The eleventh chapter of Second Samuel is pivotal for the entire book. This chapter records the tragic sins of David regarding Bathsheba and her husband Uriah. All of the widespread blessings on David's family and his kingdom are quickly removed as God chastises His anointed one.

Christ in Second Samuel

As seen in the introduction to First Samuel, David is one of the most important types of Christ in the Old Testament. In spite of his sins, he remains a man after God's own heart because of his responsive and faithful attitude toward God. He sometimes fails in his personal life, but he never flags in his relationship to the Lord. Unlike most of the kings who succeed him, he never allows idolatry to become a problem during his reign. He is a true servant of Yahweh, obedient to His Law, and an ideal king. His rule is usually characterized by justice, wisdom, integrity, courage, and compassion. Having conquered Jerusalem, he sits upon the throne of Melchizedek, the "righteous king" (cf. Gen. 14:18). David is the standard by which all subsequent kings are measured.

Of course, David's life as recorded in chapters 1—10 is a far better portrayal of the future Messiah than is his life as it is seen in chapters 11—24. Sin mars potential. The closest way in which he foreshadows the coming King can be seen in the important covenant God makes with him (7:4–17). David wants to build a house for God; but instead, God makes a house for David. The same three promises of an eternal kingdom, throne, and seed are later given to Christ (Luke 1:32–33). There are nine different dynasties in the northern kingdom of Israel, but there is only one dynasty in Judah. The promise of a permanent dynasty is fulfilled in Christ, the "son of David" (Matt. 21:9; 22:45), who will sit upon the throne of David (see Is. 9:7; Luke 1:32).

Contribution to the Bible

First Samuel reveals how the kingdom was established and Second Samuel shows how it was consolidated. This book tells us how the nation was unified, how it obtained Jerusalem as its royal capital, how it subdued its enemies and extended its boundaries, and how it achieved economic prosperity. It records the beginning of an endless dynasty and the life of a man about whom more is known than any other individual in the Old Testament.

Survey of Second Samuel

Second Samuel continues the account of the life of David at the point where First Samuel concludes. Soon after the death of Saul, the king-elect becomes the king enthroned, first over Judah when he reigns in Hebron for seven-and-a-half years and finally over all Israel when he reigns in Jerusalem for thirty-three years. This book reviews the key events in the forty-year reign of the man who is the halfway point between Abraham and Christ. It can be surveyed in the three divisions: the triumphs of David (1—10), the transgressions of David (11), and the troubles of David (12—24).

The Triumphs of David (1—10): Chapters 1—4 record the seven-year reign of David over the territory of Judah. Even though Saul is David's murderous pursuer, David does not rejoice in his death because he recognizes that Saul has been divinely anointed as king. Saul's son Ishbosheth is installed by Abner as a puppet king over the northern tribes of Israel. David's allies led by Joab defeat Abner and Israel (see 2:17; 3:1). Abner defects and arranges to unite Israel and Judah under David, but Joab kills Abner in revenge. The powerless Ishbosheth is murdered by his own men, and David is made king of Israel (5:3). David soon captures and fortifies Jerusalem and makes it the civil and religious center of the now united kingdom. Under David's rule the nation prospers politically, spiritually, and militarily. David brings the ark to Jerusalem and seeks to build a house for God (7). His obedience in placing the Lord at the center of his rule leads to great national blessing (8—10). "And the LORD preserved David wherever he went" (8:14).

The Transgressions of David (11): David's crimes of adultery and murder mark the pivotal point of the book. Because of these transgressions, David's victories and successes are changed to the personal, family, and national troubles which are recorded throughout the rest of Second Samuel.

The Troubles of David (12—24): The disobedience of the king produces chastisement and confusion at every level. David's glory and fame fade, never to be the same again. Nevertheless, David confesses his guilt when confronted by Nathan the prophet and is restored by God. A sword remains in David's house as a consequence of the sin: the baby born to David and Bathsheba dies, his son Amnon commits incest, and his son Absalom murders Amnon.

The consequences continue with Absalom's rebellion against his father. He shrewdly "stole the hearts of the men of Israel" (15:6). David is forced to flee from Jerusalem, and Absalom sets himself up as king. David would have been ruined, but God keeps Absalom from pursuing him until David has time to regroup his forces. Absalom's army is defeated by David's, and Joab kills Absalom in disobedience of David's orders to have him spared.

David seeks to amalgamate the kingdom, but conflict breaks out between the ten northern tribes of Israel and the two southern tribes of Judah and Benjamin. Israel decides to follow a man named Sheba in a revolt against David, but Judah remains faithful to him. This leads to war, and Joab defeats the rebels.

The closing chapters are actually an appendix to the book because they summarize David's words and deeds. They show how intimately the affairs of the people as a whole are tied to the spiritual and moral condition of the king. The nation enjoys God's blessing when David is obedient to the Lord, and suffers hardship when David disobeys God.

Outline of Second Samuel

Part One: The Triumphs of David (1:1—10:19)

I. **The Political Triumphs of David,** 1:1—5:25
  A. The Reign of David in Hebron over Judah, 1:1—4:12
    1. King Saul Dies, 1:1–27
    2. David Is Anointed as King over Judah, 2:1–7
    3. Ishbosheth Is Made King over Israel, 2:8–11
    4. David and Ishbosheth Fight, 2:12—4:12
      a. David's Victory over Ishbosheth, 2:12–32
      b. David's Growth over Ishbosheth, 3:1–5
      c. Abner's Murder, 3:6–39
      d. Ishbosheth's Murder, 4:1–8
      e. Judgment on the Murder of Ishbosheth, 4:9–12
  B. The Reign of David in Jerusalem, 5:1–25
    1. David Is Anointed to Reign over Israel, 5:1–5
    2. Conquest of Jerusalem, 5:6–10
    3. Alliance with Tyre, 5:11–12
    4. David's Family, 5:13–16
    5. Conquest of Philistia, 5:17–25

II. **The Spiritual Triumphs of David,** 6:1—7:29
  A. The Transportation of the Ark, 6:1–23
    1. Incorrect Transportation of the Ark, 6:1–11
    2. Correct Transportation of the Ark, 6:12
    3. David Rejoices over the Ark, 6:13–15
    4. Michal Despises David, 6:16–23
  B. The Institution of the Davidic Covenant, 7:1–29
    1. David Is Forbidden to Build God a House, 7:1–3
    2. God Promises David an Eternal House, 7:4–17
    3. David Praises God, 7:18–29

III. **The Military Triumphs of David,** 8:1—10:19
  A. The Triumphs of David over His Enemies, 8:1–12
    1. David Defeats Philistia, 8:1
    2. David Defeats Moab, 8:2
    3. David Defeats Zobah and Syria, 8:3–8
    4. David Receives Spoil from His Enemies, 8:9–12
  B. The Righteous Rule of David, 8:13—9:13
    1. David's Righteous Rule over Israel, 8:13–18
    2. David's Righteous Rule over Mephibosheth, 9:1–13

    C. The Triumphs of David over Ammon and Syria, 10:1–19
        1. Insult of Ammon, 10:1–5
        2. Ammon Is Defeated, 10:6–14
        3. Syria Is Defeated, 10:15–19

Part Two: The Transgressions of David (11:1–27)

I. The Sin of Adultery, 11:1–5

II. The Sin of Murder, 11:6–27
    A. Uriah Does Not Sleep with Bathsheba, 11:6–13
    B. David Commands Uriah's Murder, 11:14–25
    C. David and Bathsheba Marry, 11:26–27

Part Three: The Troubles of David (12:1—24:25)

I. The Troubles in David's House, 12:1—13:36
    A. Prophecy by Nathan, 12:1–14
        1. Prophecy of the Sword, 12:1–12
        2. David Repents for His Sin, 12:13–14
    B. David's Son Dies, 12:15–25
        1. God Takes away the Son of Adultery, 12:15–23
        2. God Gives Another Son, 12:24–25
    C. Joab's Loyalty to David, 12:26–31
    D. Incest in David's House, 13:1–20
    E. Amnon Is Murdered, 13:21–36

II. The Troubles in David's Kingdom, 13:37—24:25
    A. Rebellion of Absalom, 13:37—17:29
        1. Flight of Absalom, 13:37–39
        2. Return of Absalom, 14:1–24
        3. Deceit of Absalom, 14:25—15:6
        4. Rebellion of Absalom, 15:7–12
        5. Flight of David, 15:13—16:14
        6. Reign of Absalom, 16:15—17:29
    B. Absalom's Murder, 18:1–33
    C. David Is Restored as King, 19:1—20:26
        1. Reproof of Joab, 19:1–7
        2. Restoration of David, 19:8—20:26
    D. The Commentary on the Reign of David, 21:1—24:25
        1. Famine, 21:1–14
        2. War with Philistia, 21:15–22
        3. Psalms of Thanksgiving, 22:1—23:7
        4. Deeds of David's Mighty Men, 23:8–39
        5. The Census and the Plague, 24:1–25

First Kings

THE FIRST HALF OF First Kings traces the life of Solomon. Under his leadership, Israel rises to the peak of her size and glory. Solomon's great accomplishments, including the unsurpassed splendor of the temple which he constructs in Jerusalem, bring him worldwide fame and respect. But Solomon's zeal for God diminishes in his later years, as pagan wives turn his heart away from the worship of God in the temple of God. Result: the king with the divided heart lives behind a divided kingdom. For the next century, the Book of First Kings, traces the twin histories of two sets of kings and two nations, of disobedient people who are growing indifferent to God's prophets and precepts.

FIRST KINGS

Focus	United Kingdom			Divided Kingdom				
	1:1 · · · 11:43			12:1 · · · 22:53				
Divisions	Establishment of Solomon	Rise of Solomon	Decline of Solomon	Division of the Kingdom	Reigns of Various Kings	Reign of Ahab with Elijah	Reign of Jehoshaphat in Judah	Reign of Ahaziah in Israel
	1:1 — 2:46	3:1 — 8:66	9:1 — 11:43	12:1 — 14:31	15:1 — 16:28	16:29 — 22:40	22:41 — 22:50	22:51 — 22:53
Topics	Solomon			Many Kings				
	Kingdom in Tranquility			Kingdoms in Turmoil				
Place	Jerusalem: Capital of United Kingdom			Samaria: Capital of Israel / Jerusalem: Capital of Judah				
Time	40 Years			90 Years				

Introduction and Title

The first half of First Kings traces the life of Solomon. Under his leadership Israel rises to the peak of her size and glory. Solomon's great accomplishments, including the unsurpassed splendor of the temple which he constructs in Jerusalem, bring him worldwide fame and respect. However, Solomon's zeal for God diminishes in his later years, as pagan wives turn his heart away from worship in the temple of God. As a result, the king with the divided heart leaves behind a divided kingdom. For the next century, the Book of First Kings traces the twin histories of two sets of kings and two nations of disobedient people who are growing indifferent to God's prophets and precepts.

Like the two books of Samuel, the two books of Kings were originally one in the Hebrew Bible. The original title was *Melechim,* "Kings," taken from the first word in 1:1, *Vehamelech,* "Now King." The Septuagint artificially divided the Book of Kings in the middle of the story of Ahaziah into two books. It called the books of Samuel "First and Second Kingdoms" and the books of Kings "Third and Fourth Kingdoms." The Septuagint may have divided Samuel, Kings, and Chronicles into two books each because the Greek required a greater amount of scroll space than did the Hebrew. The Latin title for these books is *Liber Regum Tertius et Quartus,* "Third and Fourth Book of Kings."

Author

The author of First and Second Kings is unknown, but evidence supports the talmudic tradition that Kings was written by the prophet Jeremiah. The author was clearly a prophet/historian as seen in the prophetic expose of apostasy. Both First and Second Kings emphasize God's righteous judgment on idolatry and immorality. The style of these books is also similar to that found in Jeremiah. The phrase "to this day" in First Kings 8:8 and 12:19 indicates a time of authorship prior to the Babylonian captivity (586 B.C.). However, the last two chapters of Second Kings were written after the captivity, probably by a Jewish captive in Babylon.

Evidently, the majority of First and Second Kings was written before 586 B.C. by a compiler who had access to several historical documents. Some of these are mentioned: "the book of the acts of Solomon" (11:41) "the book of the chronicles of the kings of Israel" (14:19), and "the book of the chronicles of the kings of Judah" (14:29; 15:7). These books may have been a part of the official court records (2 Kin. 18:18). In addition, Isaiah 36—39 was probably used as a source (cf. 2 Kin. 18—20).

Date and Setting

The Book of Kings was written to the remaining kingdom of Judah before and after its Babylonian exile. The majority was compiled by a contemporary of Jeremiah, if not by Jeremiah himself (c. 646–570 B.C.). It is a record of disobedience, idolatry, and ungodliness which serves as an explanation for the Assyrian captivity of Israel (722 B.C.) and the Babylonian captivity of Judah (586 B.C.). First Kings covers the

120 years from the beginning of Solomon's reign in 971 B.C. through Ahaziah's reign ending in 851 B.C. The key date is 931 B.C., the year the kingdom was divided into the northern nation of Israel and the southern nation of Judah.

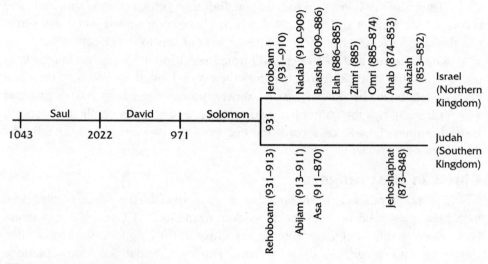

Theme and Purpose

The theme of First Kings is that the welfare of Israel and Judah depended upon the covenant faithfulness of the people and their king. Historically, it was written to give an account of the reigns of the kings from Solomon to Jehoshaphat (Judah) and Ahaziah (Israel). The two books of Kings as a whole trace the monarchy from the point of its greatest prosperity under Solomon to its demise and destruction in the Assyrian and Babylonian captivities.

Theologically, First Kings provides a prophetically-oriented evaluation of the spiritual and moral causes that led to political and economic effects in the two kingdoms. The material is too selective to be considered a biography of the kings. For example, Omri was one of Israel's most important rulers from a political point of view, but because of his moral corruption, his achievements are dismissed in eight verses. The lives of these kings are used to teach several basic principles: (1) Man cannot properly rule himself without conscious dependence on the help of God; (2) the kings had great responsibility as God's administrators, because the circumstances of the nation depended in large part upon their faithfulness to Yahweh; (3) the kings were illustrations of the people as a whole—just as they disregarded God's prophets, so did the people; and (4) observance of God's law produces blessing, but apostasy is rewarded by judgment.

Keys to First Kings

Key Word: Division of the Kingdom

Key Verses (9:4-4; 11:11)—"Now if you walk before Me as your father David walked, in integrity of heart and in uprightness, to do according to all that I have

---
85

commanded you, *and* if you keep My statutes and My judgments, then I will establish the throne of your kingdom over Israel forever, as I promised David your father, saying, 'You shall not fail to have a man on the throne of Israel.'" (9:4–5).

"Therefore the LORD said to Solomon, 'Because you have done this, and have not kept My covenant and My statutes, which I have commanded you, I will surely tear the kingdom away from you and give it to your servant'" (11:11).

Key Chapter (12)—The critical turning point in First Kings occurs in chapter 12 when the united kingdom becomes the divided kingdom. Solomon dies, and his son Rehoboam becomes king and unwisely leads the nation into a civil war which tragically rips the nation into two separate, and at times conflicting, nations. Instead of unity, First Kings records the history of the two kings, two capitals, and two religions.

Christ in First Kings

Solomon typifies Christ in a number of ways. His fabled wisdom points ahead to "Christ Jesus, who became for us wisdom from God" (1 Cor. 1:30). Solomon's fame, glory, wealth, and honor foreshadow Christ in His kingdom. Solomon's rulership brings knowledge, peace, and worship. However, despite Solomon's splendor, the Son of Man later says of His coming, "indeed a greater than Solomon is here" (Matt. 12:42).

The prophet Elijah is more typical of John the Baptist than of Christ, but his prophetic ministry and miraculous works illustrate aspects of the life of Christ.

Contribution to the Bible

In First Samuel the kingdom was established, and in Second Samuel it was consolidated. First Kings brings the kingdom from the height of its glory to a sudden abyss of division and decline. This book begins a set pattern in its portrayal of each king that is carried on in Second Kings. The account shifts between the kings of Israel and Judah in a way that synchronizes the two monarchies. The accession year of every king is dated in terms of its overlap with the ruler of the other kingdom. Introductory and concluding formulas are used, and a theological verdict on the reign of each king is passed. The life and reign of David is the standard by which the kings of Judah are judged.

First Kings also shows how the prophetic ministry came into its maturity at the end of the united kingdom and throughout the divided kingdom. This book describes the ministries of several of God's prophets.

Survey of First Kings

The first half of First Kings concerns the life of one of the most amazing men who ever lived. More than any man before or since, he knew how to amass and creatively use great wealth. With the sole exception of Jesus Christ, Solomon is the wisest man in human history. He brings Israel to the peak of its size and glory, and yet, the kingdom is disrupted soon after his death, torn in two by civil strife. This book divides clearly into two sections: the united kingdom (1—11) and the divided kingdom (12—22).

United Kingdom (1—11): These chapters give an account of Solomon's attainment of the throne, wisdom, architectural achievements, fame, wealth, and tragic unfaithfulness. In chapter 1 Solomon's half-brother Adonijah attempts to take the throne as David's death is nearing, but Nathan the prophet alerts David, who quickly directs the coronation of Solomon as coregent. Solomon still has to consolidate his power and deal with those who oppose his rule. Only when this is done is the kingdom "established in the hand of Solomon" (2:46). Solomon's ungodly marriages (cf. 3:1) eventually turn his heart from the Lord, but he begins well with a genuine love for Yahweh and a desire for wisdom. This wisdom leads to the expansion of Israel to the zenith of her power. Solomon's empire stretches from the border of Egypt to the border of Babylonia, and peace prevails.

From a theocratic perspective, Solomon's greatest achievement is the building of the temple. The ark is placed in this exquisite building, which is filled with the glory of God. Solomon offers a magnificent prayer of dedication and binds the people with an oath to remain faithful to Yahweh.

Because the Lord is with him Solomon continues to grow in fame, power, and wealth. However, his wealth later becomes a source of trouble when he begins to purchase forbidden items. He acquires many foreign wives who lead him into idolatry. It is an irony of history that this wisest of men acts as a fool in his old age. God pronounces judgment and foretells that Solomon's son will rule only a fraction of the kingdom (Judah).

Divided Kingdom (12—22): Upon Solomon's death, God's words come to pass. Solomon's son Rehoboam chooses the foolish course of promising more severe taxation. Jeroboam, an officer in Solomon's army, leads the ten northern tribes in revolt. They make him their king, leaving only Judah and Benjamin in the south under Rehoboam. This is the beginning of a chaotic period with two nations and two sets of kings. Continual enmity and strife exist between the northern and southern kingdoms. The north is plagued by apostasy (Jeroboam sets up a false system of worship) and the south by idolatry. Of all the northern and southern kings listed in this book, only Asa (15:9–24) and Jehoshaphat (22:41–50) do *"what was* right in the eyes of the Lord" (15:11; 22:43). All of the others are idolaters, usurpers, and murderers.

Ahab brings a measure of cooperation between the northern and southern kingdoms, but he reaches new depths of wickedness as a king. He is the man who introduces Jezebel's Baal worship to Israel. The prophet Elijah ministers during this low period in Israel's history, providing a ray of light and witness of the word and power of God. But Ahab's encounter with Elijah never brings him to turn from his false gods to God. Ahab's treachery in the matter of Naboth's vineyard causes a prophetic rebuke from Elijah (21). Ahab repents (21:27–29) but later dies in battle because of his refusal to heed the words of Micaiah, another prophet of God.

Outline of First Kings

Part One: The United Kingdom (1:1—11:43)

I. The Establishment of Solomon as King, 1:1—2:46
    A. Appointment of Solomon as King, 1:1–53
        1. Decline of David, 1:1–4
        2. Plot of Adonijah to Be King, 1:5–9
        3. Anointing of Solomon, 1:10–40
        4. Submission of Adonijah, 1:41–53
    B. Solidification of Solomon as King, 2:1–46
        1. David's Charge to Solomon, 2:1–9
        2. David Dies, 2:10–11
        3. Solomon Is Established as King, 2:12
        4. The Kingdom Is Purged, 2:13–46
            a. Adonijah Is Executed, 2:13–25
            b. Abiathar Is Removed, 2:26–27
            c. Joab Is Executed, 2:28–35
            d. Shimei Is Executed, 2:36–46

II. The Rise of Solomon as King, 8:66
    A. Solomon's Request for Wisdom, 3:1–28
        1. Unwise Marriage of Solomon, 3:1–2
        2. Request for Wisdom, 3:3–15
        3. Display of Solomon's Wisdom, 3:16–27
        4. National Recognition of Solomon's Wisdom, 3:28
    B. Solomon's Administration of Israel, 4:1–34
        1. Eleven Princes, 4:1–6
        2. Twelve Governors, 4:7–19
        3. Solomon Reigns in Wisdom, 4:20–34
    C. The Temple and Solomon's House Are Constructed, 5:1—8:66
        1. Construction of the Temple, 5:1—6:38
            a. Temple Materials, 5:1–12
            b. Temple Laborers, 5:13–18
            c. The Temple Is Completed, 6:1–38
        2. Construction of Solomon's House, 7:1–12
        3. Furnishings of the Temple, 7:13–51
        4. Dedication of the Temple, 8:1–66
            a. The Ark Returns, 8:1–9
            b. The Shekinah Returns, 10–11
            c. Solomon's Sermon, 8:12–21

    d. Solomon's Prayer, 8:22–61

    e. Israel Rejoices, 8:62–66

III. The Decline of Solomon as King, 9:1—11:43

  A. Reiteration of the Davidic Covenant, 9:1–9

  B. Disobedience of Solomon to the Covenant, 9:10—11:8

    1. Sale of Cities in Israel, 9:10–14

    2. Enslavement of the Canaanites, 9:15–28

    3. Multiplication of Wealth, 10:1–25

    4. Multiplication of Horses, 10:26–29

    5. Intermarriage with Foreign Women, 1:1–3

    6. Worship of Idols, 11:4–8

  C. Chastening of Solomon for Breaking the Covenant, 11:9–40

    1. The Rebuke of God, 11:9–13

    2. The Chastisement of God, 11:14–40

  D. Death of Solomon, 11:41–43

Part Two: The Divided Kingdom (12:1—22:53)

I. The Division of the Kingdom, 12:1—14:31

  A. Cause of the Division, 12:1–24

    1. Request of Israel to Rehoboam, 12:1–5

    2. Foolish Response of Rehoboam, 12:6–15

    3. Revolt of the Northern Tribes, 12:16–24

  B. Reign of Jeroboam in Israel, 12:25—14:20

    1. Sin of Jeroboam, 2:25–33

    2. Warning of the Prophet, 13:1–6

    3. Sin of the Prophet, 13:7–19

    4. Judgment on the Prophet, 13:20–32

    5. Continued Sin of Jeroboam, 13:33–34

    6. Judgment on Jeroboam, 14:1–20

  C. Reign of Rehoboam in Judah, 14:21–31

    1. Sin of Rehoboam, 14:21–24

    2. Judgment on Rehoboam, 14:25–31

II. The Reigns of Two Kings in Judah, 15:1–24

  A. Reign of Abijam in Judah, 15:1–8

  B. Reign of Asa in Judah, 15:9–24

    1. Obedience of Asa, 15:9–15

    2. Disobedience of Asa, 15:16–22

    3. Death of Asa, 15:23–24

III. The Reigns of Five Kings in Israel, 15:2—16:28

  A. Reign of Nadab in Israel, 15:25–31

  B. Reign of Baasha in Israel, 15:32—16:7

  C. Reign of Elah in Israel, 16:8–14

  D. Reign of Zimri in Israel, 16:15–20

  E. Reign of Omri in Israel, 16:21–28

IV. The Reign of Ahab in Israel, 16:29—22:40
    A. Sin of Ahab, 16:29–34
    B. The Ministry of Elijah, 17:1—19:21
        1. Miracle of the Drought, 17:1–16
            a. Prophecy of the Drought, 17:1
            b. Miracle of Food, 17:2–16
        2. Miracle of the Resurrection of the Gentile Son, 17:17–24
        3. Miracle of Fire on Mount Carmel, 18:1–40
            a. Challenge to Ahab, 18:1–19
            b. Victory on Mount Carmel, 18:20–40
        4. Miracle of the Rain, 18:41–46
        5. Failings of Elijah, 19:1–18
            a. Elijah Flees from Jezebel, 19:1–3
            b. Elijah Desires to Die, 19:4–8
            c. Elijah Has Self-pity, 19:9–18
        6. Call of Elisha, 19:19–21
    C. Wars with Syria, 20:1–43
        1. First Victory over Syria, 20:1–21
        2. Second Victory over Syria, 20:22–43
    D. Murder of Naboth, 21:1–16
    E. Death of Ahab, 21:17—22:40
        1. Prediction of Ahab's Death, 21:17–29
        2. Defeat by Syria, 22:1–36
            a. Promise of Victory by the False Prophets, 22:1–12
            b. Promise of Defeat by Micaiah, 22:13–28
            c. Defeat of Israel, 22:29–36
        3. Death of Ahab, 22:37–40

V. The Reign of Jehoshaphat in Judah, 22:41–50

VI. The Reign of Ahaziah in Israel, 22:51–53

Second Kings

SECOND KINGS, CONTINUES without interruption the "Tale of Two Kingdoms" begun in First Kings. The twin kingdoms and Judah pursue a collision course with captivity as the glory of the once United Kingdom becomes increasingly remote. Division leads to decline, and ultimately ends in double deportation. Israel is captured and dispersed by the Assyrians, while Judah is led off to exile in Babylonia. In spite of the best efforts of prophets like Elisha to shock the nations back to their religious senses, it is too late. The kingdom divided in First Kings becomes the kingdom dissolved in Second Kings. God's patience is long; God's pleading is persistent; but when ignored, God's love can also be severe.

SECOND KINGS								
Focus	**Divided Kingdom**				**Surviving Kingdom**			
	1:1			17:41	18:1			25:30
Divisions	Ministry of Elisha Under Ahaziah and Jehoram	Reign of Ten Kings of Israel and Eight Kings of Judah		Fall of Israel	Reign of Hezekiah and Two Evil Kings		Reign of Josiah and Four Evil Kings	Fall of Judah
	1:1	8:15	8:16 16:20	17:1 17:41	18:1 21:26		22:1 24:16	24:17 25:30
Topics	Israel and Judah				Judah			
	Ahaziah to Hoshea				Hezekiah to Zedekiah			
Place	Israel Deported to Assyria				Judah Deported to Babylonia			
Time	131 Years (853–722 B.C.)				155 Years (715–560 B.C.)			

Introduction and Title

The Book of Second Kings continues the drama begun in First Kings—the tragic history of two nations on a collision course with captivity. The author systematically traces the reigning monarchs of Israel and Judah, first by carrying one nation's history forward, then retracing the same period for the other nation.

Nineteen consecutive evil kings rule in Israel, leading to the captivity by Assyria. The picture is somewhat brighter in Judah, where godly kings occasionally emerge to reform the evils of their predecessors. In the end, however, sin outweighs righteousness and Judah is marched off to Babylonia. See "First Kings" for more detail concerning the title.

Author

See "Author" in First Kings for a discussion of authorship. If this now divided book was not written by Jeremiah, it probably was written by a prophetic contemporary of his. The majority of Second Kings was written before the Babylonian captivity (see "to this day," 17:34, 41).

The literary style of Second Kings is similar to that of the book of Jeremiah, and it has been observed that the omission of Jeremiah's ministry in the account of King Josiah and his successors may indicate that Jeremiah himself was the recorder of the events. However, the last two chapters were evidently added to the book after the Babylonian captivity and written by someone other than Jeremiah. The prophet Jeremiah was forced to flee to Egypt (Jer. 43:1–8), not to Babylonia. It is interesting that section 24:18—25:30 is almost the same as Jeremiah 52.

Date and Setting

The last recorded event in Second Kings is the release of Jehoiachin (25:27–30), which takes place in 560 B.C. Most of First and Second Kings probably was written just prior to 586 B.C., but chapters 24 and 25 were written after Jehoiachin's release, perhaps about 550 B.C.

Chapters 1—17 cover the 131 years from 853 B.C. (King Ahaziah of Israel) to 722 B.C. (the Assyrian captivity of Israel). Chapters 18—25 cover the 155 years from the beginning of Hezekiah's reign in 715 B.C. to the release of Jehoiachin in Babylonia in 560 B.C. The united kingdom lasts for 112 years (1043–931 B.C.), the northern kingdom of Israel exists for another 209 years (931–722 B.C.), and the southern kingdom of Judah continues for an additional 136 years (722–586 B.C.). During this 457-year kingdom period, there are great shifts of world power. Egyptian and Assyrian control over Palestine fluctuates; Assyria rises to preeminence, declines, and is finally conquered by Babylonia.

The books of Kings show that judgment comes to the kingdoms of Israel and Judah because of their idolatry, immorality, and disunity. Judah lasts 136 years longer than Israel because of the relative goodness of eight of its twenty kings. Israel never breaks away from Jeroboam's idolatrous calf worship, but Judah experiences some periods of revival in the worship of Yahweh. During these years, God sends many of His prophets. Elijah, Elisha, Amos, and Hosea are in the northern kingdom, while in the southern kingdom Obadiah, Joel, Isaiah, Micah, Nahum, Zephaniah, Jeremiah, and Habakkuk are prophesying.

Theme and Purpose

The two books of Kings were artificially divided in the middle of the reign of King Ahaziah of Israel. Because both books were originally one, they share the same theme and purpose (see "First Kings"). They record the pivotal events in the careers of the kings of Israel and Judah and show how disobedience and rebellion against God led to the failure and overthrow of the monarchy. Kings was written selectively, not exhaustively, from a prophetic viewpoint to teach that the decline and collapse of the two kingdoms occurred because of failure on the part of the rulers and people to heed the warnings of God's messengers. The spiritual climate of the nation determined its political and economic conditions.

The prophets of Yahweh play a prominent role in First and Second Kings as God uses them to remind the kings of their covenant responsibilities as His theocratic administrators. When the king kept the covenant, he and the nation would be richly blessed. But judgment consistently fell upon those who refused to obey God's law. God is seen in Kings as the controller of history who reveals His plan and purpose to His people. Tragically, the people were concerned more with their own plans, and their rejection of God's rule led to exile at the hands of the Assyrians and Babylonians.

Keys to Second Kings

Key Word: Captivities of the Kingdom

Key Verses (17:22–23; 23:27)—"For the children of Israel walked in all the sins of Jeroboam which he did; they did not depart from them, until the LORD removed Israel out of His sight, as He had said by all His servants the prophets. So Israel was carried away from their own land to Assyria, *as it is* to this day" (17:22–23).

"And the LORD said, 'I will also remove Judah from My sight, as I have removed Israel, and will cast off this city Jerusalem which I have chosen, and the house of which I said, "My name shall be there" ' " (23:27).

Key Chapter (25)—The last chapter of Second Kings records the utter destruction of the city of Jerusalem and its glorious temple. Only the poor of Israel are left, and even some of them flee for their lives to Egypt. Hope is still alive, however, with the remnant in the Babylonian captivity as Evil-Merodach frees Jehoiachin from prison and treats him kindly.

Christ in Second Kings

Unlike the nine different dynasties in the northern kingdom, the kings of Judah reign as one continuous dynasty. In spite of Queen Athaliah's attempt to destroy the house of David, God remains faithful to His covenant with David (2 Sam. 7) by preserving his lineage. Jesus the Messiah is his direct descendant.

While Elijah is a type of John the Baptist (see Matt. 11:14; 17:10–12; Luke 1:17),

Elisha reminds us of Christ. Elijah generally lives apart from the people and stresses law, judgment, and repentance. Elisha lives among the people and emphasizes grace, life, and hope.

Contribution to the Bible

Second Kings continues and completes the history of Israel and Judah as nations. The kingdom was established in First Samuel and consolidated in Second Samuel. First Kings records its division and decline, and Second Kings its deterioration and destruction.

First Kings	Second Kings
Opens with David, King of Israel	Closes with Nevuchadnezzar, King of Babylonia
Solomon's glory	Jehoiachin's shame
The temple built and consecrated	The temple violated and destroyed
Begins with blessings for obedience	Ends with judgment for disobedience
The growlth of apostasy	The consequences of apostasy
The united kingdom is divided	The two kingdoms are destroyed

Theologically, Kings stresses that God is the sovereign Lord over the history of Israel and the other nations. He predicts and controls history and uses various nations as His instruments of judgment for Israel's failure to keep the covenant. The king was to act as the servant of God by leading the nation into righteousness and fellowship with the Lord, but most of the kings perverted the purpose of their office because of their moral and spiritual rebellion.

Survey of Second Kings

Without interruption Second Kings continues the narrative of First Kings. The twin kingdoms of Israel and Judah pursue a collision course with captivity as the glory of the once united kingdom becomes increasingly diminished. Division has led to decline and now ends in double deportation with Israel captured by Assyria and Judah by Babylonia. This book traces the history of the divided kingdom in chapters 1—17 and the history of the surviving kingdom in chapters 18—25.

Divided Kingdom (1—17): These chapters record the story of Israel's corruption in a relentless succession of bad kings from Ahaziah to Hoshea. The situation in Judah during this time (Jehoram to Ahaz) is somewhat better, but far from ideal. This dark period in the northern kingdom of Israel is interrupted only by the ministries of such godly prophets as Elijah and Elisha. At the end of Elijah's miraculous ministry, Elisha is installed and authenticated as his successor. He is a force for righteousness in a nation that never served the true God or worshiped at the temple in Jerusalem. Elisha's ministry is characterized by miraculous provisions of sustenance and life.

Through him God demonstrates His gracious care for the nation and His concern for any person who desires to come to Him. However, like his forerunner Elijah, Elisha is basically rejected by Israel's leadership.

Elisha instructs one of his prophetic assistants to anoint Jehu king over Israel. Jehu fulfills the prophecies concerning Ahab's descendants by putting them to death. He kills Ahab's wife Jezebel, his sons, and also the priests of Baal. But he does not depart from the calf worship originally set up by Jeroboam. The loss of the house of Ahab means the alienation of Israel and Judah and the weakening of both. Israel's enemies begin to get the upper hand. Meanwhile, in Judah, Jezebel's daughter Athaliah kills all the descendants of David, except for Joash, and usurps the throne. However, Jehoiada the priest eventually removes her from the throne and places Joash in power. Joash restores the temple and serves God.

Syria gains virtual control over Israel, but there is no response to God's chastisement: the kings and people refuse to repent. Nevertheless, there is a period of restoration under Jeroboam II, but the continuing series of wicked kings in Israel leads to its overthrow by Assyria.

Surviving Kingdom (18—25): Of Israel's nineteen kings, not one is righteous in God's sight. All but one of its nine dynasties are created by murdering the previous king. In Judah, where there is only one dynasty, eight of its twenty rulers do what is right before God. Nevertheless, Judah's collapse finally comes, resulting in the Babylonian exile. Chapters 18—25 read more easily than chapters 1—17 because alternating the histories of the northern and southern kingdoms is no longer necessary. Only Judah remains.

Six years before the overthrow of Israel's capital of Samaria, Hezekiah becomes king of Judah. Because of his exemplary faith and reforms, God spares Jerusalem from Assyria and brings a measure of prosperity to Judah. However, Hezekiah's son Manasseh is so idolatrous that his long reign leads to the downfall of Judah. Even Josiah's later reforms cannot stem the tide of evil, and the four kings who succeed him are exceedingly wicked. Judgment comes with three deportations to Babylonia. The third occurs in 586 B.C. when Nebuchadnezzar destroys Jerusalem and the temple. Still, the book ends on a note of hope with God preserving a remnant for Himself.

Outline of Second Kings

Part One: The Divided Kingdom (1:1—17:41)

I. The Reign of Ahaziah in Israel, 1:1–18
    A. Political Situation under Ahaziah, 1:1
    B. Death of Ahaziah, 1:2–18

II. The Reign of Jehoram in Israel, 2:1—8:15
    A. Transition from Elijah to Elisha, 2:1–25
       1. Chariot of Fire Takes Elijah, 2:1–11
       2. Authority of Elijah Is Taken by Elisha, 2:12–25

    B. Spiritual Evaluation of Jehoram, 3:1–3

    C. Political Situation under Jehoram, 3:4–27

    D. Ministry of Elisha, 4:1—8:15

        1. Miracle of the Increase of the Widow's Oil, 4:1–7

        2. Miracle of the Shunammite's Son, 4:8–37

        3. Miracle of the Deadly Stew, 4:38–41

        4. Miracle of the Multiplication of the Loaves, 4:42–44

        5. Miracle of the Healing of Naaman, 5:1–27

        6. Miracle of the Floating Ax Head, 6:1–7

        7. Miracles during the First Syrian Attack, 6:8–23

           a. Syria's War Plan, 6:8–12

           b. God's Chariots and Horses, 6:13–17

           c. Syria's Army Is Blinded, 6:18–23

        8. Miracles of Elisha during the Second Syrian Attack, 6:24—7:20

           a. Siege of Samaria Causes Famine, 6:24–29

           b. Elisha's Prophecies, 6:30—7:20

        9. Elisha's Ministry with the Shunammite Woman, 8:1–6

      10. Elisha's Ministry with the King of Syria, 8:7–15

III. The Reign of Jehoram in Judah, 8:16–24

IV. The Reign of Ahaziah in Judah, 8:25–9:29

    A. Spiritual Evaluation of Ahaziah, 8:25–27

    B. Political Situation under Ahaziah, 8:28—9:26

        1. Battle against Syria, 8:28–29

        2. Anointing of Jehu King over Israel, 9:1–13

        3. Execution of Joram, 9:14–26

    C. Death of Ahaziah, 9:27–29

V. The Reign of Jehu in Israel, 9:30—10:36

    A. Fulfillment of Elisha's Prophecy, 9:30—10:28

    B. Spiritual Evaluation of Jehu, 10:29–31

    C. Political Situation under Jehu, 10:32–33

    D. Death of Jehu, 10:34–36

VI. The Reign of Queen Athaliah in Judah, 11:1–16

    A. Salvation of Joash, 11:1–3

    B. Overthrow of Athaliah by Jehoiada, 11:4–12

    C. Death of Athaliah, 11:13–16

VII. The Reign of Joash in Judah, 11:17—12:21

    A. Renewal of the Covenant, 11:17–21

    B. Spiritual Evaluation of Joash, 12:1–3

    C. Spiritual Situation under Joash, 12:4–16

    D. Political Situation under Joash, 12:17–18

    E. Death of Joash, 12:19–21

VIII. The Reign of Jehoahaz in Israel, 13:1–9

     5. Judah's Wealth Is Exposed to Babylon, 20:12–13
     6. Babylonian Exile Is Prophesied, 20:14–19
  C. Death of Hezekiah 20:20–21

II. The Reign of Manasseh in Judah, 21:1–18
  A. Spiritual Evaluation of Manasseh, 21:1–15
  B. Political Situation under Manasseh, 21:16
  C. Death of Manasseh, 21:17–18

III. The Reign of Amon in Judah, 21:19–26

IV. The Reign of Josiah in Judah, 22:1—23:30
  A. Spiritual Evaluation of Josiah, 22:1–2
  B. Renewal of the Covenant by Josiah, 22:3—23:27
     1. The Temple Is Repaired, 22:3–7
     2. The Book of the Law Is Discovered, 22:8–10
     3. Repentance of Josiah, 22:11–14
     4. Prophecy of Blessing, 22:15–20
     5. Institution of the Covenant, 23:1–3
     6. Reforms Because of the Covenant, 23:4–27
  C. Political Situation under Josiah, 23:28–29
  D. Death of Josiah, 23:30

V. The Reign of Jehoahaz in Judah, 23:31–34

VI. The Reign of Jehoiakim in Judah, 23:35—24:7

VII. The Reign of Jehoiachin in Judah, 24:8–16

VIII. The Reign of Zedekiah in Judah, 24:17—25:21
  A. Spiritual Evaluation of Zedekiah, 24:17–19
  B. Political Situation under Zedekiah, 24:20—25:21

IX. The Governorship of Gedaliah, 25:22–26

X. The Release of Jehoiachin in Babylon, 25:27–30

First Chronicles

THE BOOKS OF FIRST AND Second Chronicles cover the same period of Jewish history described in Second Samuel through Second Kings but the perspective of Chronicles is different. These books are no mere repetition of the same material, but rather are a divine editorial on the history of God's people. While Second Samuel and Kings give political history of Israel and Judah, Chronicles gives a religious history of the Davidic dynasty of Judah. The former were written from a prophetic and moral viewpoint, the latter from a priestly and spiritual perspective. The Book of First Chronicles begins with the royal line of David, then traces the spiritual significance of David's righteous reign.

FIRST CHRONICLES

Focus	Royal Line of David		Reign of David					
	1:1 — 9:44		10:1 — 29:30					
Divisions		The Genealogies of David & Israel	Accession of David as King	Acquisition of the Ark	Victories of David	Preparation for the Temple	Last Days of David	
	1:1	9:44	10:1 12:40	13:1 17:27	18:1 20:8	21:1 27:34	28:1 29:30	
Topics	Genealogy		History					
	Ancestry		Activity					
Place	Israel							
Time	Thousands of Years		c. 33 Years					

Introduction and Title

The books of First and Second Chronicles cover the same period of Jewish history described in Second Samuel through Second Kings, but the perspective is different. These books are no mere repetition of the same material, but rather form a divine editorial on the history of God's people. While Second Samuel and First and Second Kings give a political history of Israel and Judah, First and Second Chronicles present a religious history of the Davidic dynasty of Judah. The former are written from a prophetic and moral viewpoint, and the latter from a priestly and spiritual perspective. The Book of First Chronicles begins with the royal line of David and then traces the spiritual significance of David's righteous reign.

The books of First and Second Chronicles were originally one continuous work in the Hebrew. The title was *Dibere Hayyamim,* meaning "The Words (accounts, events) of the Days." The equivalent meaning today would be "The Events of the Times." Chronicles was divided into two parts in the third century B.C. Greek translation of the Hebrew Bible (the Septuagint). At that time it was given the name *Paraleipomenon,* "Of Things Omitted," referring to the things omitted from Samuel and Kings. Some copies add the phrase, *Basileon Iouda,* "Concerning the Kings of Judah." The First Book of Chronicles was called *Paraleipomenon Primus,* "The First Book of Things Omitted." The name "Chronicles" comes from Jerome in his Latin Vulgate Bible (A.D. 385–405): *Chronicorum Liber.* He meant his title in the sense of "The Chronicles of the Whole of Sacred History."

Author

Although the text does not identify the author, several facts seem to support the tradition in the Jewish Talmud that Ezra the priest was the author. The content points to a priestly authorship because of the emphasis on the temple, the priesthood, and the theocratic line of David in the southern kingdom of Judah. The narrative also indicates that Chronicles was at least written by a contemporary of Ezra. Chronicles is quite similar in style to the Book of Ezra, and both share a priestly perspective: genealogies, temple worship, ministry of the priesthood, and obedience to the law of God. In addition, the closing verses of Second Chronicles (36:22–23) are repeated with minor changes as the opening verses of Ezra (1:1–3). Thus, Chronicles and Ezra may have been one consecutive history as were Luke and Acts.

Ezra was an educated scribe (Ezra 7:6), and according to the apocryphal Book of Second Maccabees, chapter 2, verses 13–15, Nehemiah collected an extensive library which was available to Ezra for his use in compiling Chronicles. Many of these documents and sources are listed in the book (see "Author" in Second Chronicles). Scholars of Israel accumulated and compared historical material, and the author of Chronicles was actually a compiler who drew from many sources under the guidance and inspiration of the Holy Spirit.

Date and Setting

The genealogies in chapters 1—9 cover the time from Adam to David, and chapters 10—29 focus on the thirty-three years of David's rule over the united kingdoms of Israel and Judah (1004–971 B.C.). However, the genealogies extend to about 500 B.C., as seen in the mention of Zerubbabel, grandson of King Jeconiah, who leads the first return of the Jews from exile in 538 B.C., and also Zerubbabel's two grandsons Pelatiah and Jesaiah (3:21).

Ezra probably completed Chronicles between 450 and 430 B.C. and addressed it to the returned remnant. Ezra leads some of the exiles to Jerusalem in 457 B.C. and ministers to the people as their spiritual leader. During Ezra's time, Nehemiah is the political leader and Malachi is the moral leader. Chronicles spends a disproportionate time on the reigns of David and Solomon because they bring the nation to its pinnacle. The book is written to the people of Israel's "Second Commonwealth" to encourage them and to remind them that they must remain the covenant people of God. This would remind the Jews of their spiritual heritage and identity during the difficult times they were facing.

Theme and Purpose

Chronicles was written to provide a spiritual perspective on the historical events from the time of David to Cyrus' decree in 538 B.C. It traces Israel's lineage back to the dawn of the human race and forward to the end of the Babylonian captivity to reveal God's faithfulness and continuing purpose for His people. Because it was written to the returning remnant, Chronicles has a more positive thrust than Samuel or Kings. It does not deny failures but concentrates on the messianic line, the temple, and spiritual reforms. The readers needed encouragement in rebuilding their heritage. Chronicles teaches that Yahweh is still with them—He brought them back and enabled them to rebuild the temple. All is not lost; though the glory has departed and they are under the control of Gentile powers, God still has a future for them. The throne of David was gone but the line of David still stood.

Chronicles emphasizes the role of the Law, the priesthood, and the temple. Although Solomon's temple was gone, the second temple could be regarded as the remnant's link to the first. This book also taught that the past was pregnant with lessons for their present. Apostasy, idolatry, intermarriage with Gentiles, and lack of unity were the reasons for their recent ruin. It is significant that after the Exile, Israel never again worshiped foreign gods.

Keys to First Chronicles

Key Word: Davidic Covenant

Key Verses (17:11–14; 29:11)—"And it shall be, when your days are fulfilled, when you must go to *be* with your fathers, that I will set up your seed after you, who will be of your sons; and I will establish his kingdom. He shall build Me a house, and I will establish his throne forever. I will be his Father, and he shall be My son; and I will not take My mercy away from him, as I took *it* from *him* who was before you. And I will establish him in My house and in My kingdom forever; and his throne shall be established forever" (17:11–14).

"Yours, O LORD, *is* the greatness, the power and the glory, the victory and the majesty; For all *that is* in heaven and in earth *is Yours;* Yours *is* the kingdom, O LORD, and You are exalted as head over all" (29:11).

Key Chapter (17)—Pivotal for the book of First Chronicles as well as for the rest of the Scriptures is the Davidic covenant recorded in Second Samuel 7 and First Chronicles 17. God promises David that He will "establish him (David's ultimate offspring, Jesus Christ) in My house and in My kingdom forever; and his throne shall be established forever" (1 Chr. 17:14).

Christ in First Chronicles

See the introductions to First and Second Samuel for descriptions of David as a type of Christ. The Davidic covenant of Second Samuel 7 is found again in First Chronicles 7:11–14. Solomon fulfilled part, but the promise of the eternality of David's throne can only point to the coming of the Messiah.

The tribe of Judah is placed first in the national genealogy in First Chronicles because the monarchy, temple, and Messiah (Gen. 49:10) will come from this tribe. Since the books of Chronicles are the last books of the Hebrew Bible, the genealogies in chapters 1—9 are a preamble to the genealogy of Christ in the first book of the New Testament.

Contribution to the Bible

What Deuteronomy is to the rest of the Pentateuch and John is to the synoptic Gospels, Chronicles is to Israel's history in Samuel and Kings. Although there is overlap between Chronicles and the earlier kingdom books, the following table emphasizes some of the differences:

Samuel and Kings	Chronicles
The continuation of Israel's history from the united kingdom to the two captivities	Focuses on the southern kingdom and the Davidic line
Political history	Religious history
Prophetic authorship: emphasizes the prophetic ministry and moral concerns	Priestly authorship: emphasizes the priestly ministry and spiritual concerns
Written by authors soon after the events	Written by Ezra many years after the events
More negative—rebellion and tragedy	More postive—apostasy, but hope in spite of tragedy
Message of judgment	Message of hope
Man's failings	God's faithfulness
Emphasizes kings and prophets	Emphasizes the temple and the priests

The English Bible follows the arrangement of the Septuagint by placing Chronicles after Kings. But Chronicles appears at the end of the Hebrew Bible. Thus, "Abel to . . . Zechariah" (Matt. 23:35; Luke 11:51) is like saying "Genesis to Chronicles," the equivalent of our saying "Genesis to Malachi."

Survey of First Chronicles

Chronicles retraces the whole story of Israel's history up to the return from captivity in order to give the returned remnant a divine perspective on the developments of their past. The whole book of First Chronicles, like Second Samuel, is dedicated to the life of David. It begins with the royal line of David (1—9) before surveying key events of the reign of David (10—29).

Royal Line of David (1—9): These nine chapters are the most comprehensive genealogical tables in the Bible. They trace the family tree of David and Israel as a whole, but in a highly selective manner. The genealogies place a disproportionate emphasis on the tribes of Judah and Benjamin because Chronicles is not concerned with the northern kingdom but with the southern kingdom and the Davidic dynasty. They show God at work in selecting and preserving a people for Himself from the beginning of human history to the period after the Babylonian exile. The genealogies move from the patriarchal period (Adam to Jacob; 1:1—2:2) to the national period (Judah, Levi, and the other tribes of Israel; 2:3—9:44). They demonstrate God's keeping of His covenant promises in maintaining the Davidic line through the centuries. The priestly perspective of Chronicles is evident in the special attention given to the tribe of Levi.

Reign of David (10—29): Compared with Second Samuel, David's life in First Chronicles is seen in an entirely different light. This is clear from both the omissions and the additions. Chronicles completely omits David's struggles with Saul, his seven-year reign in Hebron, his various wives, and Absalom's rebellion. It also omits the event in Second Samuel that hurt the rest of his life—his sin with Bathsheba. Chronicles is written from a more positive perspective, emphasizing God's grace and forgiveness, in order to encourage the Jews who have just returned from captivity. Chronicles adds events not found in Second Samuel, such as David's preparations for the temple and its worship services.

Only one chapter is given to Saul's reign (10), because his heart was not right with God. David's story begins with his coronation over all Israel after he had already reigned for seven years as king over Judah. Chronicles stresses his deep spiritual commitment, courage, and integrity. It emphasizes his concern for the things of the Lord, including his return of the ark and his desire to build a temple for God. God establishes His crucial covenant with David (17), and the kingdom is strengthened and expanded under his reign (18—20). His sin in numbering the people is recorded to teach the consequences of disobeying God's law. Most of the rest of the book (22—29) is concerned with David's preparations for the building of the temple and the worship appreciated with it. The priestly perspective of Chronicles can be seen in the disproportionate space given to the temple and the priests. David is not allowed to build the temple (28:3), but he designs the plans, gathers the materials, prepares the site, and arranges for the Levites, priests, choirs, porters, soldiers, and stewards. The book closes with his beautiful public prayer of praise and the accession of Solomon.

Outline of First Chronicles

Part One: The Royal Line of David (1:1—9:44)

I. The Genealogy from Adam to Abraham, 1:1–27
    A. The Genealogy from Adam to Noah, 1:1–4
    B. The Genealogy from Noah to Abraham, 1:5–27
        1. Sons of Japheth, 1:5–7
        2. Sons of Ham, 1:8–16
        3. Sons of Shem, 1:17–27

II. The Genealogy from Abraham to Jacob, 1:28–54
    A. The Genealogy from Abraham to Isaac, 1:28–34
    B. The Genealogy from Isaac to Jacob, 1:35–54
        1. Sons of Esau, 1:35–42
        2. Kings of Edom, 1:43–50
        3. Chiefs of Edom, 1:51–54

III. The Genealogy from Jacob to David, 2:1–55
    A. The Genealogy of the Sons of Jacob, 2:1–2
    B. The Genealogy of the Sons of Judah, 2:3–55

IV. The Genealogy from David to the Captivity, 3:1–24
    A. The Genealogy of the Sons of David, 3:1–9
    B. The Genealogy of the Sons of Solomon, 3:10–24

V. The Genealogies of the Twelve Tribes, 4:1—8:40
    A. The Genealogy of Judah, 4:1–23
    B. The Genealogy of Simeon, 4:24–43
    C. The Genealogy of Reuben, 5:1–10
    D. The Genealogy of Gad, 5:11–22
    E. The Genealogy of Manasseh, 5:23–26
    F. The Genealogy of Levi, 6:1–81
        1. The High Priestly Line, 6:1–15
        2. The Levitical Line, 6:16–30
        3. The Musicians' Guild, 6:31–48
        4. The Generations of Aaron, 6:49–53
        5. Cities of the Priests and Levites, 6:54–81
    G. The Genealogy of Issachar, 7:1–5
    H. The Genealogy of Benjamin, 7:6–12
    I. The Genealogy of Naphtali, 7:13
    J. The Genealogy of Manasseh, 7:14–19

III. The Military Victories of King David, 18:1—20:8
  A. David's Early Victories Are Summarized, 18:1–17
    1. Victory over Philistia, 18:1
    2. Victory over Moab, 18:2
    3. Victory over Zobah, 18:3–4
    4. Victory over Syria, 18:5–11
    5. Victory over Edom, 18:12–17
  B. David's Latter Victories Are Summarized, 19:1—20:8
    1. Humiliation of David's Servants, 19:1–5
    2. Victory over the Ammonites, 19:6–15
    3. Victory over the Syrians, 19:16–19
    4. Victory over the Ammonites, 20:1–3
    5. Victory over the Philistine Giants, 20:4–8

IV. The Preparation and Organization of Israel for the Temple, 21:1—27:34
  A. Sinful Census of David, 21:1–30
    1. Temptation of David by Satan, 21:1–4
    2. Enumeration of Israel, 21:5–6
    3. Judgment of God, 21:7–17
      a. Prayer of David, 21:7–8
      b. Three Choices of David, 21:9–13
      c. Judgment of Pestilence, 21:14–17
    4. Withholding of Judgment by Sacrifices, 21:18–30
  B. Material Provisions for the Temple's Construction, 22:1–5
  C. Leaders Are Charged to Construct the Temple, 22:6–19
    1. David's Charge to Solomon, 22:6–16
    2. David's Charge to the Leaders, 22:17–19
  D. Organization of the Temple Leaders, 23:1—26:32
    1. Organizations of the Levitical Houses, 23:1–32
      a. Enumeration of the Levites, 23:1–6
      b. Organization of the Gershonites, 23:7–11
      c. Organization of the Kohathites, 23:12–20
      d. Organization of the Merarites, 23:21–23
      e. Duties of the Levites, 23:24–32
    2. Organization of the Courses of the Priests, 24:1–31
      a. Divisions of the Sons of Aaron, 24:1–19
      b. Organization of the Kohathites, 24:20–25
      c. Organization of the Merarites, 24:26–31
    3. Organization of the Orders of the Musicians, 25:1–31
    4. Organization of the Gatekeepers, 26:1–19
    5. Organization of the Treasuries of the Temple, 26:20–28
    6. Organization of the Officers outside the Temple, 26:29–32
  E. Organization of the Leaders of the Nation of Israel, 27:1–34
    1. The Twelve Captains of Israel, 27:1–15
    2. The Leaders of the Twelve Tribes, 27:16–24
    3. The Royal Officers of David, 27:25–31
    4. The Counselors of David, 27:32–34

V. The Last Days of David, 28:1—29:30
- A.   Final Exhortations of David, 28:1–10
  - 1.   Charge to Israel, 28:1–8
  - 2.   Charge to Solomon, 28:9–10
- B.   Final Provisions for the Temple, 28:11—29:9
  - 1.   Pattern for the Temple, 28:11–21
  - 2.   Provisions of David for the Temple, 29:1–5
  - 3.   Provisions of Israel for the Temple, 29:6–9
- C.   David's Final Prayer of Thanksgiving, 29:10–19
- D.   Coronation of Solomon, 29:20–25
- E.   Death of King David, 29:26–30

Second Chronicles

THE BOOK OF SECOND CHRONICLES parallels First and Second Kings but virtually ignores the northern kingdom of Israel because of its false worship and refusal to acknowledge the temple in Jerusalem. Chronicles focuses on those kings who pattern their life and reign after that of godly king David. It gives extended treatment to such zealous reformers as Asa, Jehoshaphat, Joash, Hezekiah, and Josiah. The temple and temple worship are central throughout the book, as befitting a nation whose worship of God is central to its very survival. The book begins with Solomon's glorious temple, and concludes with Cyrus' edict to rebuild the temple more than four hundred years later!

Focus	**Reign of Solomon**			**Reigns of the Kings of Judah**		
	1:1　　　　　　　　　9:31			10:1　　　　　　　　36:23		
Divisions	Inaguration of Solomon	Completion of the Temple	Glory of Solomon's Reign	Division of the Kingdom	Reforms under Asa, Jehoshaphat, Joash, Hezekiah and Josiah	Fall of Judah
	1:1　　1:17	2:1　　7:22	8:1　　9:31	10:1　　13:22	14:1　　35:27	36:1　　36:23
Topics	Temple Is Constructed			Temple Is Destroyed		
	Splendor			Disaster		
Place	Judah					
Time	c. 40 Years			c. 393 Years		

SECOND CHRONICLES

Introduction and Title

The Book of Second Chronicles parallels First and Second Kings but virtually ignores the northern kingdom of Israel because of its false worship and refusal to acknowledge the temple in Jerusalem. Chronicles focuses on those kings who pattern their lives and reigns after the life and reign of godly King David. It gives extended treatment to such zealous reformers as Asa, Jehoshaphat, Joash, Hezekiah, and Josiah.

The temple and temple worship, central throughout the book, befit a nation whose worship of God is central to its very survival. The book begins with Solomon's glorious temple and concludes with Cyrus's edict to rebuild the temple more than four hundred years later.

See "First Chronicles" for more detail on the title.

Author

For a discussion of the author of First and Second Chronicles, see "The Author of First Chronicles." The sources of First and Second Chronicles include official and prophetic records: (1) The Book of the Kings of Israel and Judah (or Judah and Israel) (see 1 Chr. 9:1; 2 Chr. 16:11; 20:34; 25:26; 27:7; 28:26; 32:32; 35:27; 36:8); (2) A Commentary on the Book of the Kings (2 Chr. 24:27); (3) Chronicles of Samuel the Seer (1 Chr. 29:29); (4) Chronicles of Nathan the Prophet (see 1 Chr. 29:29; 2 Chr. 9:29); (5) Chronicles of Gad the Seer (1 Chr. 29:29); (6) The Prophecy of Ahijah the Shilonite (2 Chr. 9:29); (7) The Visions of Iddo the Seer (see 2 Chr. 9:29; 12:15; 13:22); (8) Records of Shemaiah the Prophet (2 Chr. 12:15); (9) Records of Iddo the Prophet on Genealogies (2 Chr. 12:15); (10) Treatise of the Prophet Iddo (2 Chr. 13:22); (11) The Annals of Jehu the Son of Hanani (2 Chr. 20:34); (12) The Acts of Uzziah by Isaiah the Prophet (2 Chr. 26:22); (13) The Vision of Isaiah the Prophet (2 Chr. 32:32); (14) The Records of the Hozai (2 Chr. 33:19); (15) The Account of the Chronicles of King David (1 Chr. 27:24); and (16) The Writing of David and His Son Solomon (2 Chr. 35:4). In addition to these, the author-compiler had access to genealogical lists and documents, such as the message and letters of Sennacherib (2 Chr. 32:10–17).

Date and Setting

See "The Time of First Chronicles" for the back-ground of First and Second Chronicles. Chapters 1—9 cover the forty years from 971 B.C. to 931 B.C., and chapters 10—36 cover the 393 years from 931 B.C. to 538 B.C. Jeremiah's prediction of a seventy-year captivity in Babylonia (36:21; Jer. 29:10) is fulfilled in two ways: (1) A political captivity in which Jerusalem is overcome from 605 B.C. to 536 B.C.; and (2) a religious captivity involving the destruction of the temple in 586 B.C. and the completion of the new temple in 516 or 515 B.C.

Theme and Purpose

The Book of Second Chronicles provides a topical history of the end of the united kingdom (Solomon) and the kingdom of Judah. Chronicles is more than historical annals; it is a divine editorial on the spiritual characteristics of the Davidic dynasty. This is Why it focuses on the southern rather than the northern kingdom. Most of the kings failed to realize that apart from its true mission as a covenant nation called to bring others to Yahweh, Judah had no calling, no destiny, and no hope of becoming great on its own. Only what was done in accordance with God's will had any lasting value. Chronicles concentrates on the kings who were concerned with maintaining the proper service of God and the times of spiritual reform. But growing apostasy inevitably led to judgment.

The temple in Jerusalem is the unifying theme of First and Second Chronicles. Much of the material found in Second Samuel to Second Kings was omitted in Chronicles because it does not develop this theme. In First Chronicles 11—29, the central message is David's preparation for the construction and service of the temple. Most of Second Chronicles 1—9 is devoted to the building and consecration of the temple. Chapters 10—36 omit the kings of Israel in the north because they had no ties with the temple. Prominence is given to the reigns of Judah's temple restorers (Asa, Jehoshaphat, Joash, Hezekiah, and Josiah). The temple symbolically stood for God's presence among His people and their high calling. It was the spiritual link between their past and future. Thus, Ezra wrote this book to encourage the people to accept the new temple raised on the site of the old and to remind them of their true calling and God's faithfulness in spite of their low circumstances. The Davidic line, temple, and priesthood were still theirs.

Keys to Second Chronicles

Key Word: Priestly View of Judah

Key Verses (7:14; 16:9)—"If My people who are called by My name will humble themselves, and pray and seek My face, and turn from their wicked ways, then I will hear from heaven, and will forgive their sin and heal their land" (7:14).

"For the eyes of the LORD run to and fro throughout the whole earth, to show Himself strong on behalf of *those* whose heart *is* loyal to Him. In this you have done foolishly; therefore from now on you shall have wars" (16:9).

Key Chapter (34)—Second Chronicles records the reforms and revivals under such kings as Asa, Jehoshaphat, Joash, Hezekiah, and Josiah. Chapter 34 traces the dramatic revival that takes place under Josiah when the "Book of the Law" is found, read, and obeyed.

Christ in Second Chronicle

The throne of David has been destroyed, but the line of David remains. Murders, treachery, battles, and captivity all threaten the messianic line; but it remains clear and unbroken from Adam to Zerubbabel. The fulfillment in Christ can be seen in the genealogies of Matthew 1 and Luke 3.

The temple also prefigures Christ. Jesus says, "in this place there is *One* greater than the temple" (Matt. 12:6). He also likens His body to the temple: "Destroy this temple, and in three days I will raise it up" (John 2:19). In Revelation 21:22 He replaces the temple: "But I saw no temple in it, for the Lord God Almighty and the Lamb are its temple."

Contribution to the Bible

Chronicles begins with Adam and ends with the decree of Cyrus (538 B.C.). In this respect Chronicles touches upon more history than any other Old Testament book. It focuses on the period from David to the captivity of Judah and looks at the reigns of twenty-one kings and one queen. At the time it was written it taught lessons from the past, illustrated God's faithfulness in the present (the return from captivity and the new temple), and anticipated the fulfillment of God's promises in the future (the messianic line).

As a chronicle of the temple, the book surveys its conception (David), construction and consecration (Solomon), corruption and cleansing (the kings of Judah), and conflagration (Nebuchadnezzar).

Survey of Second Chronicles

Second Chronicles continues First Chronicles' spiritual commentary on Israel's kingdom period. It parallels First and Second Kings but virtually ignores the northern kingdom because of its false worship and refusal to acknowledge the temple in Jerusalem. Second Chronicles focuses on Judah's fortunes and, in particular, on those kings who do what is right in the sight of the Lord. It devotes considerable space to the spiritual reformations under Asa (14—15), Jehoshaphat (17—20), Joash (23:16—24:16), Hezekiah (29—32), and Josiah (34—35). This book repeatedly teaches that whenever God's people forsake Him, He withdraws His blessings, but trust in and obedience to the Lord bring victory. Since everything in Chronicles is related to the temple, it is not surprising that this concludes with Cyrus's edict to rebuild it. Solomon's glory is seen in chapters 1—9, and Judah's decline and deportation in chapters 10—36.

Solomon's Reign (1—9): The reign of Solomon brings in Israel's golden age of peace, prosperity, and temple worship. The kingdom is united and its boundaries extend to their greatest point. Solomon's wealth, wisdom, palace, and temple become legendary. His mighty spiritual, political, and architectural feats raise Israel to her zenith. However, it is in keeping with the purpose of Chronicles that six of these nine chapters concern the construction and dedication of the temple.

The Reign of Judah's Kings (10—36): Unfortunately, Israel's glory is short-lived. Soon after Solomon's death the nation is divided, and both kingdoms begin a downward spiral that can only be delayed by the religious reforms. The nation generally forsakes the temple and the worship of Yahweh, and is soon torn by warfare and unrest. The reformation efforts on the part of some of Judah's kings are valiant, but never last beyond one generation. Nevertheless, about 70 percent of chapters 10—36 deals with the eight good kings, leaving only 30 percent to cover the twelve evil rulers. Each king is seen with respect to his relationship to the temple as the center of worship and spiritual strength. When the king serves Yahweh, Judah is blessed with political and economic prosperity.

Here is a brief survey of Judah's twenty rulers: (1) *Rehoboam*—Although he is not righteous, he humbles himself before God and averts His wrath (12:12). (2) *Abijah*—He enjoys a short and evil reign, but he conquers Israel because "the children of Judah . . . relied on the LORD God" (13:18). (3) *Asa*—Although he destroys foreign altars and idols, conquers Ethiopia against great odds through his trust in God, and restores the altar of the Lord, yet he fails to trust God when threatened by Israel. (4) *Jehoshaphat*—He brings in a great revival; "his heart took delight in the ways of the LORD" (17:6). Jehoshaphat overthrows idols, teaches God's Word to the people, and trusts in God before battle. (5) *Jehoram*—A wicked king, he follows the ways of Ahab and marries his daughter. He leads Judah into idolatry and when he dies in pain, departs "to no one's sorrow" (21:20). (6—7) *Ahaziah* and *Athaliah*—Ahaziah is as wicked as his father, as is his mother Athaliah. Both are murdered. (8) *Joash*—Although he repairs the temple and restores the worship of God, when Jehoiada the priest dies, Joash allows the people to abandon the temple and return to idolatry. (9) *Amaziah*—Mixed in his relationship to God, he later forsakes the Lord for the gods of Edom. He is defeated by Israel and later murdered. (10) *Uzziah*—He begins well with the Lord and is blessed with military victories. However, when he becomes strong, he proudly and presumptuously plays the role of a priest by offering incense in the temple and therefore is struck with leprosy. (11) *Jotham*—Because he rebuilds the gate of the temple and reveres God, the Lord blesses him with prosperity and victory. (12) *Ahaz*—A wicked king and an idolator, he is oppressed by his enemies and forced to give tribute to the Assyrians from the temple treasures. (13) *Hezekiah*—He repairs and reopens the temple and puts away the altars and idols set up by his father Ahaz. Judah is spared destruction by Assyria because of his righteousness. His reforms are given only a few verses in Kings but three chapters in Chronicles. (14—15) *Manasseh* and *Amon*—Manasseh is Judah's most wicked king. He sets up idols and altars all over the land. However, he repents when he is carried away by Assyria. God brings him back to Judah and he makes a halfway reform, but it comes too late. Amon follows in his father's wickedness. Both kings are murdered. (16) *Josiah*—A leader in reforms and spiritual revival, he centers worship around the temple, finds the Law and obeys it, and reinstitutes the Passover. (17—19) *Jehoahaz, Jehoiakim, Jehoiachin*—Their relentless evil finally brings the downfall of Judah. The temple is ravaged in each of their reigns. (20) *Zedekiah*—Judah's last king is also wicked. Jerusalem and the temple are destroyed, and the Captivity begins. Second Chronicles nevertheless ends on a note of hope at the end of the Captivity, when Cyrus issues the decree for the restoration of Judah: "Who *is there* among you of all His people? May the LORD his God *be* with him, and let him go up!" (36:23).

Outline of Second Chronicles

Part One: The Reign of Solomon (1:1—9:31)

I. The Inauguration of Solomon as King, 1:1–17
  A. The Worship of Solomon, 1:1–6
  B. The Petition for Wisdom, 1:7–10
  C. The Provision of Wisdom, 1:11–12
  D. The Wealth of Solomon, 1:13–17

II. The Completion of the Temple, 2:1—7:22
  A. Preparation to Build the Temple, 2:1–18
    1. Selection of the Temple Builders, 2:1–2
    2. Selection of the Temple Materials, 2:3–18
  B. Construction of the Temple, 3:1—5:1
  C. Dedication of the Temple, 5:2—7:22
    1. The Installation of the Ark, 5:2–12
    2. The Glory of the Lord Fills the Temple, 5:13–14
    3. The Sermon of Solomon, 6:1–11
    4. The Prayer of Solomon, 6:12–42
    5. The Fire of the Lord Consumes the Sacrifices, 7:1–3
    6. The Nation Offers Sacrifices, 7:4–7
    7. The Nation Celebrates the Feasts of Tabernacles, 7:8–11
    8. The Lord Confirms the Covenant, 7:12–22

III. The Glory of the Reign of Solomon, 8:1—9:28
  A. Enlargement of Solomon's Territory, 8:1–6
  B. Subjugation of the Enemies of Solomon, 8:7–10
  C. Religious Practices of Solomon, 8:11–16
  D. Economic Operations of Solomon, 8:17–18
  E. The Queen of Sheba Visits, 9:1–12
  F. Solomon's Wealth, 9:13–28

IV. The Death of Solomon, 9:29–31

Part Two: The Reigns of the Kings of Judah (10:1—36:23)

I. The Reign of Rehoboam, 10:1—12:16
  A. Division of the Kingdom, 10:1–19
  B. Kingdom of Judah Is Strengthened, 11:1–23
  C. Kingdom of Judah Is Weakened, 12:1–12
  D. Death of Rehoboam, 12:13–16

II. The Reign of Abijah, 13:1–22
  A. War of Abijah and Jeroboam, 13:1–20
  B. Death of Abijah, 13:21–22

III. The Reign of Asa, 14:1—16:14
  A. Evaluation of Asa, 14:1–8
  B. Victory over the Ethiopians, 14:9–15
  C. Exhortation of Azariah, 15:1–7
  D. Reforms of Asa, 15:8–19
  E. Victory over the Syrians, 16:1–6
  F. Rebuke of Hanani, 16:7–10
  G. Death of Asa, 16:11–14

IV. The Reign of Jehoshaphat, 17:1—20:37
  A. Evaluation of Jehoshaphat, 7:1–6
  B. Instruction by the Priests and Levites, 17:7–9
  C. Expansion of the Kingdom, 17:10–19
  D. Alliance with Ahab, 18:1—19:4
  E. Organization of the Kingdom, 19:5–11
  F. Victory over Moab and Ammon, 20:1–30
  G. Summary of the Reign of Jehoshaphat, 20:31–34
  H. The Sin and Death of Jehoshaphat, 20:35–37

V. The Reign of Jehoram, 21:1–20
  A. Evaluation of Jehoram, 21:1–7
  B. Revolt by Edom and Libnah, 21:8–11
  C. Warning of Elijah, 21:12–15
  D. Invasion by Philistia and Arabia, 21:16–17
  E. Death of Jehoram, 21:18–20

VI. The Reign of Ahaziah, 22:1–9

VII. The Reign of Athaliah, 22:10—23:15

VIII. The Reign of Joash, 23:16—24:27
  A. Revival of Jehoiada, 23:16–21
  B. Evaluation of Joash, 24:1–3
  C. Repair of the Temple, 24:4–14
  D. Death of Jehoiada, 24:15–16
  E. Murder of Jehoiada's Son, 24:17–22
  F. Destruction of Judah by Syria, 24:23–24
  G. Death of Joash, 24:25–27

IX. The Reign of Amaziah, 25:1–28
  A. Evaluation of Amaziah, 25:1–4
  B. Victory over Edom, 25:5–13
  C. Idolatry of Amaziah, 25:14–16
  D. Defeat of Judah by Israel, 25:17–24
  E. Death of Amaziah, 25:25–28

X. The Reign of Uzziah, 26:1–23
  A. Evaluation of Uzziah, 26:1–5
  B. Victories of Uzziah, 26:6–15

Ezra

EZRA CONTINUES THE OLD TESTAMENT narrative of Second Chronicles by showing how God fulfilled His promise to return His people to the Land of Promise after seventy years of exile. Israel's "second exodus," this one from Babylonia, is less impressive than the Egyptian bondage because only a remnant choose to leave. Ezra relates the story of two returns from Babylonia, the first led by Zerubbabel to rebuild the temple (chs. 1—6), and the second under the leadership of Ezra to rebuild the spiritual condition of the people (chs. 7—10). Sandwiched between these two accounts is a gap of nearly six decades during which Esther lives and rules as queen in Persia.

EZRA					
Focus	**Restoration of the Temple**		**Reformation of the People**		
	1:1 6:22		7:1 10:44		
Divisions	First Return to Jerusalem	Construction of the Temple	Second Return to Jerusalem	Restoration of the People	
	1:1 2:70	3:1 6:22	7:1 8:36	9:1 10:44	
Topics	Zerubbabel		Ezra		
	First Return of 49,897		Second Return of 1,754		
Place	Persia to Jerusalem		Persia to Jerusalem		
Time	22 Years (538–516 B.C.)		1 Year (458–457 B.C.)		

Introduction and Title

Ezra continues the Old Testament narrative of Second Chronicles by showing how God fulfills His promise to return His people to the Land of Promise after seventy years of exile. Israel's "second exodus," this one from Babylonia, is less impressive than the return from Egypt because only a remnant chooses to leave Babylonia.

Ezra relates the story of two returns from Babylonia—the first led by Zerubbabel to rebuild the temple (1—6), and the second under the leadership of Ezra to rebuild the spiritual condition of the people (7—10). Sandwiched between these two accounts is a gap of nearly six decades, during which Esther lives and rules as queen in Persia.

Ezra is the Aramaic form of the Hebrew word *ezer,* "help," and perhaps means "Jehovah helps." Ezra and Nehemiah were originally bound together as one book because Chronicles, Ezra, and Nehemiah were viewed as one continuous history. The Septuagint, a Greek-language version of the Old Testament translated in the third century B.C. Calls Ezra-Nehemiah, *Esdras Deuteron,* "Second Esdras." First Esdras is the name of the apocryphal Book of Esdras. The Latin title is *Liber Primus Esdrae,* "First Book of Ezra." In the Latin Bible, Ezra is called First Ezra and Nehemiah is called Second Ezra.

Author

Although Ezra is not specifically mentioned as the author, he is certainly the best candidate. Jewish tradition (the Talmud) attributes the book to Ezra, and portions of the book (7:28—9:15) are written in the first person, from Ezra's point of view. The vividness of the details and descriptions favors an author who was an eyewitness of the later events of the book. As in Chronicles, there is a strong priestly emphasis, and Ezra was a direct priestly descendant of Aaron through Eleazar, Phinehas, and Zadok (7:1–5). He studied, practiced, and taught the law of the Lord as an educated scribe (7:1–12). Also according to Second Maccabees 2:13–15, he had access to the library of written documents gathered by Nehemiah. Ezra no doubt used this material in writing Ezra 1—6 as he did in writing Chronicles. Some think that Ezra composed Nehemiah as well by making use of Nehemiah's personal diary.

Ezra was a godly man marked by strong trust in the Lord, moral integrity, and grief over sin. He was a contemporary of Nehemiah (see Neh. 8:1–9; 12:36) who arrived in Jerusalem in 444 B.C. Tradition holds that Ezra was the founder of the Great Synagogue where the canon of Old Testament Scripture was settled. Another tradition says that he collected the biblical books into a unit and that he originated the synagogue form of worship.

Ezra wrote this book probably between 457 B.C. (the event of Ezra 7—10) and 444 B.C. (Nehemiah's arrival in Jerusalem). During the period covered by the Book of Ezra, Gautama Buddha (c. 560–480 B.C.) is in India, Confucius (551–479 B.C.) is in China, and Socrates (470–399 B.C.) is in Greece.

Date and Setting

The following table shows the chronological relationship of the books of Ezra, Nehemiah, and Esther:

538–515 B.C.	483–473 B.C.
Zerubbabel	Esther
Ezra 1—6	Book of Esther
First Return	—

457 B.C.	444–c. 425 B.C.
Ezra	Nehemiah
Ezra 7—10	Book of Nehemiah
Second Return	Third Return

These books fit against the background of these Persian kings:

Cyrus	(559–530 B.C.)
Cambyses	(530–522 B.C.)
Smerdis	(522 B.C.)
Darius I	(521–486 B.C.)
Ahasuerus	(486–464 B.C.)
Artaxerxes I	(464–423 B.C.)
Darius II	(423–404 B.C.)

Cyrus the Persian overthrows Babylonia in October, 539 B.C. and issues his decree allowing the Jews to return in 538 B.C. The temple is begun in 536 B.C. The Exile lasts only fifty years after 586 B.C., but the seventy-year figure for the Captivity is taken from a beginning date of 606 B.C. when the first deportation to Babylonia takes place. The rebuilding of the temple is discontinued in 534 B.C., resumed in 520 B.C., and completed in 515 B.C. It is begun under Cyrus and finished under Darius I. The two intervening kings, Cambyses and Smerdis, are not mentioned in any of these books. The prophets Haggai and Zechariah minister during Zerubbabel's time, about 520 B.C. and following years. Esther's story fits entirely in the reign of Xerxes, and Ezra ministers during the reign of Artaxerxes I, as does Nehemiah. There were three waves of deportation to Babylonia (606, 597, and 586 B.C.) and three returns from Babylonia: 538 B.C. (Zerubbabel), 457 B.C. (Ezra), and 444 B.C. (Nehemiah).

Theme and Purpose

The basic theme of Ezra is the spiritual, moral, and social restoration of the returned remnant in Jerusalem under the leadership of Zerubbabel and Ezra. Israel's worship was revitalized and its people were purified. God's faithfulness is seen in the way He sovereignly protected His people by a powerful empire while they were in captivity. They prospered in their exile and God raised up pagan kings who were sympathetic to their cause and encouraged them to rebuild their homeland. God also provided zealous and capable spiritual leaders who directed the return and the rebuilding. He kept the promise He made in Jeremiah 29:14: "'I will be found by you,' says the LORD, 'and I will bring you back from your captivity; I will gather you from all the nations and from all the places where I have driven you,' says the LORD, 'and I will bring you to the place from which I cause you to be carried away captive.'"

Keys to Ezra

Key Word: Temple

Key Verses (1:3; 7:10)—"Who *is there* among you of all His people? May his God be with him! Now let him go up to Jerusalem, which is in Judah, and build the house of the LORD God of Israel (He *is* God), which is in Jerusalem" (1:3).

"For Ezra had prepared his heart to seek the Law of the LORD, and to do *it*, and to teach statutes and ordinances in Israel" (7:10).

Key Chapter (6)—Ezra 6 records the completion and dedication of the temple which stimulates the obedience of the remnant to keep the Passover and separate themselves from the "filth of the nations of the land" (6:21).

Christ in Ezra

Ezra reveals God's continued fulfillment of His promise to keep David's descendants alive. Zerubbabel himself is part of the messianic line as the grandson of Jeconiah (Jehoiachin, I Chr. 3:17–19; see Matt. 1:12–13). There is a positive note of hope in Ezra and Nehemiah because the remnant has returned to the Land of Promise. In this land the messianic promises will be fulfilled, because they are connected with such places as Bethlehem, Jerusalem, and Zion. Christ will be born in Bethlehem (Mic. 5:2), not in Babylonia.

The Book of Ezra as a whole also typifies Christ's work of forgiveness and restoration.

Contribution to the Bible

Ezra fills in the history of the first two returns from the Babylonian captivity, and Nehemiah covers the third. This book forcefully emphasizes the power of the Word of God and the crucial need to obey it on every level of life (see 1:1; 3:2; 6:14,18; 7:6,10,14; 9:4; 10:3,5). Ezra follows Second Chronicles in the English Bible because it carries the story on from that point. But in the Hebrew Bible it appears with Nehemiah as one book just preceding Chronicles, the last book.

Survey of Ezra

Ezra continues the story exactly where Second Chronicles ends and shows how God's promise to bring His people back to their land is fulfilled (Jer. 29:10–14). God is with these people; and although their days of glory seem over, their spiritual heritage still remains and God's rich promises will be fulfilled. Ezra relates the story of the first two returns from Babylonia, the first led by Zerubbabel and the second led decades later by Ezra. Its two divisions are the restoration of the temple (1—6) and the reformation of the people (7—10), and they are separated by a fifty-eight year gap during which the story of Esther takes place.

The Restoration of the Temple (1—6): King Cyrus of Persia overthrows Babylonia in 539 B.C. and issues a decree in 538 B.C. that allows the exiled Jews to return to their homeland. Isaiah prophesied two centuries before that the temple would be rebuilt and actually named Cyrus as the one who would bring it about (Is. 44:28—45:4). Cyrus may have read and responded to this passage.

Out of a total Jewish population of perhaps two or three million, only 49,897 choose to take advantage of this offer. Only the most committed are willing to leave a life of relative comfort in Babylonia, endure a trek of nine hundred miles, and face further hardship by rebuilding a destroyed temple and city. Zerubbabel, a "prince" of Judah (a direct descendant of King David), leads the faithful remnant back to Jerusalem. Those who return are from the tribes of Judah, Benjamin, and Levi; but it is evident that representatives from the other ten tribes eventually return as well. The ten "lost tribes" are not entirely lost.

Zerubbabel's priorities are in the right place: he first restores the altar and the religious feasts before beginning work on the temple itself. The foundation of the temple is laid in 536 B.C., but opposition arises and the work ceases from 534 to 520 B.C. While Ezra 4:1–5, 24 concerns Zerub-babel, 4:6–23 concerns opposition to the building of the wall of Jerusalem some time between 464 and 444 B.C. These verses may have been placed here to illustrate the antagonism to the work of rebuilding. The prophets Haggai and Zechariah exhort the people to get back to building the temple (5:1–2), and the work begins again under Zerubbabel and Joshua the high priest. Tattenai, a Persian governor, protests to King Darius I about the temple build-ing and challenges their authority to continue. King Darius finds the decree of Cyrus and confirms it, even forcing Tattenai to provide whatever is needed to complete the work. It is finished in 515 B.C.

The Reformation of the People (7—10): A smaller return under Ezra takes place in 457 B.C., eighty-one years after the first return under Zerubbabel. Ezra the priest is given authority by King Artaxerxes I to bring people and contributions for the temple in Jerusalem. God protects this band of less than two thousand men and they safely reach Jerusalem with their valuable gifts from Persia. Many priests but few Levites return with Zerubbabel and Ezra (see 2:36–42; 8:15–19). God uses Ezra to rebuild the people spiritually and morally. When Ezra discovers that the people and the priests have intermarried with foreign women, he identifies with the sin of his people and offers a great intercessory prayer on their behalf. During the gap of fifty-eight years between Ezra 6 and 7, the people fall into a confused spiritual state and Ezra is alarmed. They quickly respond to Ezra's confession and weeping by making a covenant to put away their foreign wives and to live in accordance with God's law. This confession and response to the Word of God brings about a great revival and changes lives.

Outline of Ezra

Part One: The Restoration of the Temple of God (1:1—6:22)

I. The First Return to Jerusalem under Zerubbabel, 1:1—2:70
  A. Decree of Cyrus, 1:1–4
  B. Gifts from Israel and Cyrus, 1:5–11
  C. Census of the Returning People, 2:1–63
    1. The People of Known Descent, 2:1–58
      a. The Leaders, 2:1–2
      b. The People, 2:3–35
      c. The Priests, 2:36–39
      d. The Levites, 2:40–42
      e. The Servants, 2:43–58
    2. The People of Unknown Descent, 2:59–63
      a. The People, 2:59–60
      b. The Priests, 2:61–63
  D. The Return Completed, 2:64–70
    1. The People Who Returned, 2:64–67
    2. The Gifts the People Gave, 2:68–70

II. The Construction of the Temple, 3:1—6:22
  A. Construction of the Temple Foundation, 3:1–13
    1. Spiritual Preparation of the People, 3:1–6
    2. Completion of the Temple Foundation, 3:7–13
  B. Interruption of the Temple Construction, 4:1–24
    1. Present Opposition under Darius, 4:1–5
    2. Later Opposition under Ahasuerus, 4:6
    3. Later Opposition under Artaxerxes, 4:7–23
    4. Present Interruption of Construction under Darius, 4:24
  C. Completion of the Temple, 5:1—6:18
    1. Resumption of the Temple Construction, 5:1–2
    2. Opposition to the Construction, 5:3–17
      a. Opposition by Tattenai, 5:3–5
      b. The Letter to Darius, 5:6–17
    3. Confirmation of the Temple Construction, 6:1–12
    4. Completion of the Temple, 6:13–15
    5. Dedication of the Temple, 6:16–18
  D. Celebration of the Passover, 6:19–22

Part Two: The Reformation of the People of God (7:1—10:44)

I. The Second Return to Jerusalem under Ezra, 7:1—8:36

    A. The Decree of Artaxerxes, 7:1–28

        1. Ezra's Qualifications, 7:1–10

        2. Artaxerxes' Letter, 7:11–26

        3. Ezra's Response, 7:27–28

    B. Census of the Returning Israelites, 8:1–14

    C. Spiritual Preparation for the Return, 8:15–23

        1. Acquisition of Temple Leadership, 8:15–20

        2. Proclamation of a Fast, 8:21–23

    D. The Return Is Completed 8:24–36

II. The Restoration of the People, 9:1—10:44

    A. Israel Intermarries, 9:1–2

    B. Ezra Intercedes with God, 9:3–15

        1. Lamentation of Ezra, 9:3–4

        2. Confession of Ezra, 9:5–15

            a. God's Faithfulness, 9:5–9

            b. Israel's Unfaithfulness, 9:10–15

    C. Reformation of Israel, 10:1–44

        1. Israel Laments, 10:1–2

        2. The Covenant Is Instituted, 10:3–5

        3. Solution for Intermarriage, 10:6–44

            a. Separation Is Accepted, 10:6–17

            b. Separation of Priests, 10:18–22

            c. Separation of Levites, 10:23–24

            d. Separation of People, 10:25–44

Nehemiah

NEHEMIAH, CONTEMPORARY OF EZRA and cupbearer to the king in the Persian palace, leads the third and last return to Jerusalem after the Babylonian exile. His concern for the welfare of Jerusalem and its inhabitants prompts him to take bold action. Granted permission to return to his homeland, Nehemiah challenges his countrymen to arise and rebuild the shattered walls of Jerusalem. In spite of opposition from without and abuse from within, the task is completed in only fifty-two days—a feat which even the enemies of Israel must attribute to God's enabling. By contrast, the task of reviving and reforming the people of God within those rebuilt walls demands years of Nehemiah's godly life and leadership.

Focus	Reconstruction of the Wall		Restoration of the People	
	1:1 7:73		8:1 13:31	
Divisions	Preparation to Reconstruct the Wall	Reconstruction of the Wall	Renewal of the Covenant	Obedience to the Covenant
	1:1 2:30	3:1 7:73	8:1 10:39	11:1 13:31
Topics	Political		Spiritual	
	Construction		Instruction	
Place	Jerusalem			
Time	19 Years (444–425 B.C.)			

NEHEMIAH

Introduction and Title

Nehemiah, comtemporary of Ezra and cup-bearer to the king in the Persian palace, leads the third and last return to Jerusalem after the Babylonian exile. His concern for the welfare of Jerusalem and its inhabitants prompts him to take bold action. Granted permission to return to his homeland, Nehemiah challenges his countrymen to arise and rebuild the shattered wall of Jerusalem. In spite of opposition from without and abuse from within, the task is completed in only fifty-two days, a feat even the enemies of Israel must attribute to God's enabling. By contrast, the task of reviving and reforming the people of God within the rebuilt wall demands years of Nehemiah's godly life and leadership.

The Hebrew for Nehemiah is *Nehemyah,* "Comfort of Jehovah." The book is named after its chief character, whose name appears in the opening verse. The combined Book of Ezra-Nehemiah is given the Greek title *Esdras Deuteron,* "Second Esdras" (see "Ezra") in the Septuagint, a third-century B.C. Greek-language translation of the Hebrew Old Testament. The Latin title of Nehemiah is *Liber Secundus Esdrae,* "Second Book of Ezra" (Ezra was the first). At this point, it is considered a separate book from Ezra, and is later called *Liber Nehemiae,* "Book of Nehemiah."

Author

Clearly, much of this book came from Nehemiah's personal memoirs. The reporting is remarkably candid and vivid. Certainly some portions (1:1—7:5; 12:27–43; 13:4–31) are the "words of Nehemiah" (1:1). Some scholars think that Nehemiah composed those portions and compiled the rest. Others think that Ezra wrote two sections (7:6—12:26 and 12:44—13:3), and that he compiled the rest making use of Nehemiah's diary. A third view that neither wrote it seems least likely from the evidence. Nehemiah 7:5–73 is almost the same as Ezra 2:1–70, and both lists may have been taken from another record of the same period.

As cupbearer to Artaxerxes I, Nehemiah holds a position of great responsibility. His role of tasting the king's wine to prevent him from being poisoned places him in a position of trust and confidence as one of the king's advisers. As governor of Jerusalem from 444 to 432 B.C. (see 5:14; 8:9; 10:1; 13:6), Nehemiah demonstrates courage, compassion for the oppressed, integrity, godliness, and selflessness. He is willing to give up the luxury and ease of the palace to help his people. He is a dedicated layman who has the right priorities and is concerned for God's work, who is able to encourage and rebuke at the right times, who is strong in prayer, and who gives all glory and credit to God.

Date and Setting

See "Date and Setting" of Ezra, because both Ezra and Nehemiah share the same historical background. The Book of Nehemiah fits within the reign of Artaxerxes I of Persia (464–423 B.C.). Esther is Artaxerxes' stepmother, and it is possible that she is instrumental in Nehemiah's appointment as the king's cupbearer. Nehemiah leaves Persia in the twentieth year of Artaxerxes (2:1), returns to Persia in the thirty-second year of Artaxerxes (13:6), and leaves again for Jerusalem "after certain days" (13:6), perhaps about 425 B.C. This book could not have been completed until after his second visit to Jerusalem.

The historical reliability of this book is supported by the Elephantine papyri. These ancient documents mention Sanballat (2:19) and Jehohanan (6:18), and indicate that Bigvai replaces Nehemiah as governor of Judah by 410 B.C.

Malachi lives and ministers during Nehemiah's time, and a comparison of the books shows that many of the evils encountered by Nehemiah are specifically denounced by Malachi. The coldhearted indifference toward God described in both books remains a problem in Israel during the four hundred years before Christ, during which there is no revelation from God.

Theme and Purpose

While Ezra deals primarily with the religious restoration of Judah, Nehemiah is concerned with Judah's political and geographical restoration. The first seven chapters are devoted to the rebuilding of Jerusalem's walls because Jerusalem was the spiritual and political center of Judah. Without walls, Jerusalem could hardly be considered a city at all. As governor, Nehemiah also established firm civil authority. Ezra and Nehemiah worked together to build the people spiritually and morally so that the restoration would be complete. Thus, Nehemiah functions as the natural sequel to the Book of Ezra, and it is not surprising that the two books were regarded as a unit for centuries.

Nehemiah was also written to show the obvious hand of God in the establishment of His people in their homeland in the years after their exile. Under the leadership of Nehemiah, they accomplished in fifty-two days what had not been done in the ninety-four years since the first return under Zerubbabel. By obedient faith they were able to overcome what appeared to be insurmountable opposition.

Keys to Nehemiah

Key Word: Jerusalem Walls

Key Verses (6:15–16; 8:8)—"So the wall was finished on the twenty-fifth *day* of *the month* of Elul, in fifty-two days. And it happened, when all our enemies heard *of it,* and all the nations around us saw *these things,* that they were very disheartened in their own eyes; for they perceived that this work was done by our God" (6:15–16).

"So they read distinctly from the book, in the Law of God; and they gave the sense, and helped *them* to understand the reading" (8:8).

Key Chapter (9)—The key to the Old Testament is the covenant, which is its theme and unifying factor. Israel's history can be divided according to the nation's obedience or disobedience to God's conditional covenant: blessings from obedience and destruction from disobedience. Nehemiah records in chapter 9 that upon completion of the Jerusalem wall the nation reaffirmed its loyalty to the covenant.

Christ in Nehemiah

Like Ezra, Nehemiah portrays Christ in His ministry of restoration. Nehemiah illustrates Christ in that he gives up a high position in order to identify with the plight of his people; he comes with a specific mission and fulfills it; and his life is characterized by prayerful dependence upon God.

In this book, everything is restored except the king. The temple is rebuilt, Jerusalem is reconstructed, the covenant is renewed, and the people are reformed. The messianic line is intact, but the King is yet to come. The decree of Artaxerxes in his twentieth year (2:1) marks the beginning point of Daniel's prophecy of the Seventy Weeks (Dan. 9:25–27). "Know therefore and understand, *that* from the going forth of the command to restore and build Jerusalem until Messiah the Prince, *there shall be* seven weeks and sixty-two weeks; the street shall be built again, and the wall, even in troublesome times" (Dan. 9:25). The Messiah will come at the end of the sixty-nine weeks, and this is exactly fulfilled in A.D. 33 (see "Christ in Daniel").

Contribution to the Bible

Nehemiah fills in our understanding of a period that would otherwise be unclear. Along with Ezra it provides the background for the postexilic period and the three postexilic prophets (Haggai, Zechariah, and Malachi).

Ezra 1—6	Esther	Ezra 7—10		Nehemiah
Restoration under Zerubbabel		Reformation under Ezra		Reconstruction under Nehemiah
538–515	Fifty-eight Year Gap	457	Thirteen Year Gap	444–c. 425
Temple		People		Walls
Haggai, Zechariah		—		Malachi
First Return (about 50,000)		Second Return (about 2,000)		Third Return

The role of prayer in the life of Nehemiah is striking. It is instructive to study the series of problems, reactions, and prayers of Nehemiah presented in this book (see 1:5–11; 2:1–4, 19–20; 4:1–6, 7–10, 11–14; 6:9,14). Nehemiah demonstrated a balanced blend of dependence and discipline, prayer and planning. His prayers were generally short but fervent. Chapters 1—7 are filled with leadership principles, 8—10 with spiritual principles, and 11—13 with moral and social principles.

Survey of Nehemiah

Nehemiah is closely associated with the ministry of his contemporary, Ezra. Ezra is a priest who brings spiritual revival; Nehemiah is a governor who brings physical and political reconstruction and leads the people in moral reform. They combine to make an effective team in rebuilding the postexilic remnant. Malachi, the last Old Testament prophet, also ministers during this time to provide additional moral and spiritual direction. The Book of Nehemiah takes us to the end of the historical account in the Old Testament, about four hundred years before the birth of the promised Messiah. Its two divisions are: the reconstruction of the wall (1—7), and the restoration of the people (8—13).

The Reconstruction of the Wall (1—7): Nehemiah's great concern for his people and the welfare of Jerusalem leads him to take bold action. The walls of Jerusalem, destroyed by Nebuchadnezzar in 586 B.C., evidently have been almost rebuilt after 464 B.C. when Artaxerxes I took the throne of Persia (Ezra 3:6–23). When he hears that opposition led to their second destruction, Nehemiah prays on behalf of his people and then secures Artaxerxes' permission, provision, and protection for the massive project of rebuilding the walls.

The return under Nehemiah in 444 B.C. takes place thirteen years after the return led by Ezra, and ninety-four years after the return led by Zerubbabel. Nehemiah inspects the walls and challenges the people to "rise up and build" (2:18). Work begins immediately on the wall and its gates, with people building portions corresponding to where they are living.

However, opposition quickly arises, first in the form of mockery, then in the form of conspiracy when the work is progressing at an alarming rate. Nehemiah overcomes threats of force by setting half of the people on military watch and half on construction. While the external opposition continues to mount, internal opposition also surfaces. The wealthier Jews are abusing and oppressing the people, forcing them to mortgage their property and sell their children into slavery. Nehemiah again deals with the problem by the twin means of prayer and action. He also leads by example when he sacrifices his governor's salary. In spite of deceit, slander, and treachery, Nehemiah continues to trust in God and to press on with singleness of mind until the work is completed. The task is accomplished in an incredible fifty-two days, and even the enemies recognize that it can only have been accomplished with the help of God (6:16).

The Restoration of the People (8—13): The construction of the walls is followed by consecration and consolidation of the people. Ezra the priest is the leader of the spiritual revival (8—10), reminiscent of the reforms he led thirteen years earlier (Ezra 9—10). Ezra stands on a special wooden podium after the completion of the walls and gives the people a marathon reading of the Law, translating from the Hebrew into Aramaic so they can understand. They respond with weeping, confession, obedience, and rejoicing. The Levites and priests lead them in a great prayer that surveys God's past work of deliverance and loyalty on behalf of His people, and magnifies God's attributes of holiness, justice, mercy, and love. The covenant is then renewed with God as the people commit themselves to separate from the Gentiles in marriage and to obey God's commandments. Lots are drawn to determine who will remain in Jerusalem and who will return to the cities of their inheritance. One-tenth are required to stay in Jerusalem, and the rest of the land is resettled by the people and priests. The walls of Jerusalem are dedicated to the Lord in a joyful ceremony accompanied by instrumental and vocal music.

Unfortunately, Ezra's revival is short-lived; and Nehemiah, who returned to Persia in 432 B.C. (13:6), makes a second trip to Jerusalem about 425 B.C. to reform the people. He cleanses the temple, enforces the Sabbath, and requires the people to put away all foreign wives.

Outline of Nehemiah

Part One: The Reconstruction of the Wall (1:1—7:73)

I. The Preparation to Reconstruct the Wall, 1:1—2:20
    A. Discovery of the Broken Wall, 1:1–3
    B. Intercession of Nehemiah, 1:4—2:8
        1. Nehemiah Intercedes with God, 1:4–11
        2. Nehemiah Intercedes with Artaxerxes, 2:1–8
    C. Arrival of Nehemiah in Jerusalem, 2:9–11
    D. Preparation to Reconstruct the Wall, 2:12–20
        1. Nehemiah Inspects the Broken Walls, 2:12–16
        2. Nehemiah Exhorts the People, 2:17–18
        3. Nehemiah Answers the Enemies, 2:19–20

II. The Reconstruction of the Wall, 3:1—7:73
    A. Record of the Builders, 3:1–32
    B. Opposition to the Reconstruction, 4:1—6:14
        1. Opposition through Ridicule, 4:1–6
        2. Opposition through Threat of Attack, 4:7–9
        3. Opposition through Discouragement, 4:10–23
        4. Opposition through Extortion, 5:1–13
        5. Nehemiah's Unselfish Example, 5:14–19
        6. Opposition through Compromise, 6:1–4
        7. Opposition through Slander, 6:5–9
        8. Opposition through Treachery, 6:10–14
    C. Completion of the Reconstruction, 6:15–19
    D. Organization of Jerusalem, 7:1–4
    E. Registration of Jerusalem, 7:5–73
        1. The Plan, 7:5–6
        2. The Remnant of Known Descent, 7:7–60
            a. The Leaders, 7:7
            b. The Men of Israel, 7:8–38
            c. The Priests, 7:39–42
            d. The Levites, 7:43–45
            e. The Servants, 7:46–60
        3. The Remnant of Unknown Descent, 7:61–65
            a. The Men of Israel, 7:61–62
            b. The Priests, 7:63–65

4. The Total of the Remnant, 7:66–69
5. The Gifts of the Remnant for the Temple, 7:70–73

Part Two: The Restoration of the People, (8:1—13:31)

I. The Renewal of the Covenant, 8:1—10:39

   A. Interpretation of the Law, 8:1–18
      1. Reading of the Law, 8:1–8
      2. Response to the Reading, 8:9–18
         a. Israel Celebrates Her Understanding of the Law, 8:9–12
         b. Israel Obeys the Law, 8:13–18
   B. Reaffirmation of the Covenant, 9:1—10:39
      1. Spiritual Preparation of Israel, 9:1–3
      2. Reiteration of the Acts of Parties of the Covenant, 9:4–31
         a. The Great Deliverances of God, 9:4–15
         b. The Great Sins of Israel, 9:16–31
      3. Renewal of the Covenant, 9:32–38
      4. Ratifiers of the Covenant, 10:1–27
      5. Stipulations of the Covenant, 10:28–39

II. The Obedience to the Covenant, 11:1—13:31

   A. Resettlement of the People, 11:1–36
      1. Plan for the Resettlement, 11:1–2
      2. Resettlement within Jerusalem, 11:3–24
      3. Resettlement outside of Jerusalem, 11:25–36
   B. Register of the Priests and the Levites, 12:1–26
   C. Dedication of the Jerusalem Wall, 12:27–47
   D. Restoration of the People, 13:1–31
      1. Separation from the Heathen, 13:1–9
      2. Restoration of Levitical Support, 13:10–14
      3. Restoration of the Sabbath, 13:15–22
      4. Restoration from Mixed Marriages, 13:23–29
      5. Restoration in Summary, 13:30–31

Esther

THE STORY OF ESTHER'S LIFE fits between chapters 6 and 7 of Ezra, between the first return led by Zerubbabel and the second return led by Ezra. It provides the only biblical portrait of the vast majority of Jews who chose to remain in Persia rather than return to Palestine after the Exile. God's hand of providence and protection on behalf of His people is evident throughout the book, though His name does not appear once! Haman's plot which brings grave danger to the Jews (chs. 1—4) is countered by the courage of beautiful Esther and the counsel of her wise cousin Mordecai, resulting in a great deliverance (chs. 5—10). The Feast of Purim becomes an annual reminder of God's faithfulness on behalf of His people.

ESTHER

Focus	Threat to the Jews		Triumph of the Jews	
	1:1 — 4:17		5:1 — 10:3	
Divisions	Selection of Esther as Queen	Formulation of the Plot by Haman	Triumph of Mordecai over Haman	Triumph of Israel over Her Enemies
	1:1 — 2:20	2:21 — 4:17	5:1 — 8:3	8:4 — 10:3
Topics	Feasts of Ahasuerus		Feasts of Esther and Purim	
	Grave Danger		Great Deliverance	
Place	Persia			
Time	10 Years (483–473 B.C.)			

Introduction and Title

The story of Esther's life fits between chapters 6 and 7 of Ezra, between the first return led by Zerubbabel and the second return led by Ezra. It provides the only biblical portrait of the vast majority of Jews who choose to remain in Persia rather than return to Palestine after the Exile. God's hand of providence and protection on behalf of His people is evident throughout the book, though His name does not appear once. Haman's plot brings grave danger to the Jews and is countered by the courage of beautiful Esther and the counsel of her wise cousin Mordecai, resulting in a great deliverance. The Feast of Purim becomes an annual reminder of God's faithfulness on behalf of His people.

Esther's Hebrew name was *Hadassah,* "myrtle" (2:7), but her Persian name *Ester* was derived from the Persian word for "star" (*stara*). The Greek title for this book is *Esther,* and the Latin title is *Hester.*

Author

While the author's identity is not indicated in the text, the evident knowledge of Persian etiquette and customs, the palace in Susa, and details of the events in the reign of Ahasuerus indicate that the author lived in Persia during this period. The obvious Jewish nationalism and knowledge of Jewish customs further suggest that the author was Jewish. If this Persian Jew was not an eyewitness, he probably knew people who were. The book must have been written soon after the death of King Ahasuerus (464 B.C.), because chapter 10, verses 2–3 speak of his reign in the past tense. Some writers suggest that Mordecai himself wrote the book; this seems unlikely, for although Mordecai did keep records (9:20), the chapter 10 citation implies that his career was already over. Nevertheless, the author certainly made use of Mordecai's records and may have had access to the Book of the Chronicles of the Kings of Media and Persia (see 2:23; 10:2). Ezra and Nehemiah have also been suggested for authorship, but the vocabulary and style of Esther are dissimilar to that found in their books. It seems likely that a younger contemporary of Mordecai composed the book.

Date and Setting

Ahasuerus is the Hebrew name and Xerxes the Greek name of Khshayarsh, king of Persia in 486–464 B.C. According to chapter 1, verse 3, the feast of Xerxes took place in his third year, or 483 B.C. The historian Herodotus refers to this banquet as the occasion of Xerxes' planning for a military campaign against Greece. But in 479 B.C. he was defeated by the Greeks at Salamis, and Herodotus tells us that he sought consolation in his harem. This corresponds to the time when he held a "contest" and crowned Esther queen of Persia (2:16–17). Since the events of the rest of the book took place in 473 B.C. (3:7–12), the chronological span is ten years (483–473 B.C.). The probable time of authorship was between 464 B.C. (the end of Xerxes' reign; see 10:2–3) and about 435 B.C. The palace at Susa was destroyed by fire during that period, and such an event would probably have been mentioned. The historical and linguistic features of Esther do not support a date later than 400 B.C., as there is no trace of Greek influence.

Xerxes was a boisterous man of emotional extremes, whose actions were often strange and contradictory. This fact sheds light on his ability to sign a decree for the annihilation of the Jews, and two months later to sign a second decree allowing them to overthrow their enemies.

Esther was addressed to the many Jews who did not return to their homeland. Not all the godly people left—some did not return for legitimate reasons. Most were disobedient in staying in Persia. Nevertheless, God continued to care for His people in voluntary exile.

Keys to Esther

Key Word: Providence

Key Verses (4:14; 8:17)—"For if you remain completely silent at this time, relief and deliverance will arise for the Jews from another place, but you and your father's house will perish. Yet who knows whether you have come to the kingdom for *such* a time as this?" (4:14).

"And in every province and city, wherever the king's command and decree came, the Jews had joy and gladness, a feast and a holiday. Then many of the people of the land became Jews, because fear of the Jews fell upon them" (8:17).

Key Chapter (8)—According to the book of Esther, the salvation of the Jews is accomplished through the revised decree of King Ahasuerus, allowing the Jews to defend themselves against their enemies. Chapter 8 records this pivotal event with the accompanying result that "many of the people of the land became Jews."

Christ in Esther

Esther, like Christ, puts herself in the place of death for her people but receives the approval of the king. She also portrays Christ's work as Advocate on our behalf. This book reveals another satanic threat to destroy the Jewish people and thus, the messianic line. God continues to preserve His people in spite of opposition and danger, and nothing can prevent the coming of the Messiah.

Contribution to the Bible

Ezra deals primarily with the restoration of the Jewish people after the Exile, Nehemiah deals with their physical and spiritual reconstruction, and Esther deals with their preservation. Esther is more like a drama than any other portion of Scripture with its unexpected and ironic plot twists. Because of its unusual nature, Esther hopped from place to place in the canon of Scripture. The Septuagint even sandwiched it between two apocryphal books, the Wisdom of Sirach and Judith. It was found in the "Writings" section of the Hebrew Bible as one of the five rolls (*Megilloth*). The other four are Song of Solomon, Ruth, Lamentations, and Ecclesiastes. These books are read on Jewish holidays, and Esther is still read on the Feast of Purim.

There has been opposition to acceptance of Esther as divinely inspired, especially because no form of the name of God is used, and yet there are 187 references to the Persian king. Nor is there any mention of the Law, the offerings and sacrifices, prayer, or anything supernatural. Objections also appeared early in the Christian community because it is never quoted in the New Testament and because Esther gives the historical background for a nationalistic Jewish festival which has no connection with later Christian truth. It has also been challenged because of the blood-thirsty spirit of chapter 9. The Jews tried to overcome embarrassment by creating an apocryphal book called Additions to Esther which is full of references to God. Here are some reasons that combine to explain the omission of God: (1) The book was written in Persia and would be censored or profaned by substitution of a pagan god's name. (2) The general disobedience of the Jews in preferring the comfort of Persia to the hardships of rebuilding their homeland may be another factor. (3) The silence was intentional to illustrate the hidden but providential care of God in spite of outward appearances. This is a subtle form of revelation that shows the hand of God behind every event. (4) The name of Yahweh (YHWH) does appear in acrostic form four times in the Hebrew text (see 1:20; 5:4,13; 7:7). Incidentally, the word "Jews" appears forty-three times in the plural and eight times in the singular. It was derived from "Judah" because of the predominance of this tribe. The term was applied to all descendants of Jacob.

Survey of Esther

The clearly emerging message of Esther is that God uses ordinary men and women to overcome impossible circumstances to accomplish His gracious purposes. Chapters 1—4 describe the threat to the Jews, and chapters 5—10 describe the triumph of the Jews.

The Threat to the Jews (1—4): The story begins in Ahasuerus' winter palace at Susa. The king provides a lavish banquet and display of royal glory for the people of Susa, and proudly seeks to make Queen Vashti's beauty a part of the program. When she refuses to appear, the king is counseled to depose her and seek another queen, because it is feared that the other women will become insolent if Vashti goes unpunished. Esther later finds favor in the eyes of Ahasuerus and wins the royal "beauty pageant." At her uncle Mordecai's instruction, she does not reveal that she is Jewish. With her help, Mordecai is able to warn the king of an assassination plot, and his deed is recorded in the palace records. Meanwhile, Haman becomes captain of the princes, but Mordecai refuses to bow to him. When he learns that Mordecai is Jewish, Haman plots for a year to eliminate all Jews, as his rage and hatred grow. He casts lots (purim) daily during this period until he determines the best day to have them massacred. Through bribery and lies he convinces Ahasuerus to issue an edict that all Jews in the empire will be slain eleven months hence in a single day. Haman conceives his plot in envy and a vengeful spirit, and he executes it with malicious craft. The decree creates a state of confusion, and Mordecai asks Esther to appeal to the king to spare the Jews. At the peril of her life, Esther decides to see the king and reveal her nationality in a desperate attempt to dissuade Ahasuerus. Mordecai convinces her that she has been called to her high position for this purpose.

The Triumph of the Jews (5—10): After fasting, Esther appears before the king and wisely invites him to a banquet along with Haman. At the banquet she requests that they attend a second banquet, as she seeks the right moment to divulge her request. Haman is flattered but later enraged when he sees Mordecai. He takes his wife's suggestion to build a large gallows for Mordecai (he cannot wait the eleven months for Mordecai to be slain). That night Ahasuerus decides to treat his insomnia by reading the palace records. Reading about Mordecai's deed, he wants him to be honored. Haman, mistakenly thinking the king wants to honor him, tells the king how the honor should be bestowed, only to find out that the reward is for Mordecai. He is humbled and infuriated by being forced to honor the man he loathes. At Esther's second banquet Ahasuerus offers her as much as half of his kingdom for the third time. She then makes her plea for her people and accuses Haman of his treachery. The infuriated king has Haman hanged on the gallows that Haman intended for Mordecai. The gallows, seventy-five feet high, was designed to make Mordecai's downfall a city-wide spectacle, but it ironically provides Haman with unexpected public attention—posthumously.

Persian law sealed with the king's ring (3:12) cannot be revoked, but at Esther's request the king issues a new decree to all the provinces that the Jews may assemble and defend themselves on the day when they are attacked by their enemies. This decree changes the outcome intended by the first order and produces great joy. Mordecai is also elevated and set over the house of Haman. When the fateful day of the two decrees arrives, the Jews defeat their enemies in their cities throughout the Persian provinces, but do not take the plunder. The next day becomes a day of celebration and an annual Jewish holiday called the Feast of Purim. The word is derived from the Assyrian *puru,* meaning "lot," referring to the lots cast by Haman to determine the day decreed for the Jewish annihilation. The narrative closes with the advancement of Mordecai to a position second only to the king.

Outline of Esther

Part One: The Threat to the Jews (1:1—4:17)

I. The Selection of Esther as Queen, 1:1—2:20
    A. The Divorce of Vashti, 1:1–22
        1. The Feasts of Ahasuerus, 1:1–8
        2. Refusal of Queen Vashti, 1:9–12
        3. Removal of Vashti, 1:13–22
            a. Counsel to King Ahasuerus, 1:13–18
            b. Commandment of King Ahasuerus, 1:19–22

B. The Marriage to Esther, 2:1–20
   1. Decree to Search for Vashti's Replacement, 2:1–4
   2. Preparation of Esther, 2:5–14
   3. Selection of Queen Esther, 2:15–20

II. The Formulation of the Plot by Haman, 2:21—4:17
   A. Mordecai Reveals the Plot to Murder the King, 2:21–23
   B. Haman Plots to Murder the Jews, 3:1—4:17
      1. Haman Is Promoted, 3:1
      2. The Reason for Haman's Plot, 3:2–6
      3. Ahasuerus' Decree to Destroy the Jews, 3:7—4:17
         a. Presentation of the Plot, 3:7–9
         b. Publication of the Decree, 3:10–15
         c. Response of the Jews, 4:1–17
            (1) The Lamentation of the Jews, 4:1–3
            (2) The Plan of Mordecai, 4:4–14
            (3) The Promise of Queen Esther, 4:15–17

Part Two: The Triumph of the Jews, (5:1—10:3)

I. The Triumph of Mordecai over Haman, 5:1—8:3
   A. Setting for the Triumph, 5:1—6:3
      1. Esther's First Feast, 5:1–8
      2. Haman Plots to Kill Mordecai, 5:9–14
      3. King Ahasuerus' Plan to Honor Mordecai, 6:1–3
   B. Mordecai Is Honored, 6:4–14
      1. Haman's Plan to Honor Himself, 6:4–9
      2. Haman Is Forced to Honor Mordecai, 6:10–14
   C. Haman Dies on Gallows Prepared for Mordecai, 7:1–10
      1. Esther's Second Feast, 7:1–4
      2. Haman Is Indicted, 7:5–8
      3. Haman Is Hanged, 7:9–10
   D. Mordecai Is Given Haman's House, 8:1–3

II. The Triumph of Israel over Her Enemies, 8:4—10:3
   A. Preparation for the Victory of Israel, 8:4–17
      1. Esther's Petition to King Ahasuerus, 8:4–6
      2. King Ahasuerus' Counter-Decree, 8:7–14
      3. Many Gentiles Are Converted, 8:15–17
   B. Israel's Victory over Her Enemies, 9:1–16
      1. Victories on the First Day, 9:1–11
      2. Victories on the Second Day, 9:12–16
   C. Israel's Celebration, 9:17—10:3
      1. The Feast of Purim, 9:17–32
      2. The Fame of Mordecai, 10:1–3

Kings of Israel

Dynasty		Name (Character)	Length of Reign*	Relation to Predecessor	End of Reign	First & Second Kings	Second Chronicles
I	1	Jereboam I (Bad)	931/30–910/09 = 22		Stricken by God	1 Kin. 11:26—14:20	2 Chr. 9:29—13:22
	2	Nadab (Bad)	910/09–909/08 = 2	Son	Murdered by Baasha	1 Kin. 15:25–28	
II	3	Baasha (Bad)	909/08–886/85 = 24		Died	1 Kin. 15:27—16:7	2 Chr. 16:1–6
	4	Elah (Bad)	886/85–885/84 = 2	Son	Murdered by Zimri	1 Kin. 16:6–14	
III	5	Zimri (Bad)	885/84 = 7 days	Captian of Chariots	Suicide by fire	1 Kin. 16:9–20	
IV	6	Omri† (Bad)	855/84–874/73‡ = 12	Captain of Army	Died	1 Kin. 16:15–28	
	7	Ahab (Bad)	874/73–853 = 21	Son	Wounded in battle	1 Kin. 16:28—22:40	2 Chr. 18:1–34
	8	Ahaziah (Bad)	853–852 = 1	Son	Fell through lattice	1 Kin. 22:40 2 Kin. 1:18	2 Chr. 20:35–37
	9	Jehoram§ (Bad)	852–841 = 11	Brother	Murdered by Jehu	2 Kin. 3:1—9:25	2 Chr. 22:5–7
V	10	Jehu (Bad)	841–814/13 = 28		Died	2 Kin. 9:1—10:36	2 Chr. 22:7–12
	11	Jehoahaz (Bad)	814/13–796 = 16	Son	Died	2 Kin. 13:1–9	
	12	Jehoash‡ (Bad)	798–782/81 = 16	Son	Died	2 Kin. 13:10—14:16	2 Chr. 25:17–24
	13	Jeroboam II (Bad)	793/92–753‡ = 40	Son	Died	2 Kin. 14:23–29	
	14	Zechariah (Bad)	753–752 = 6 months	Son	Murdered by Shallum	2 Kin. 14:29—15:12	
VI	15	Shallum (Bad)	752 = 1 month		Murdered by Menaham	2 Kin. 15:10–15	
VII	16	Menahem (Bad)	752–742/41 = 10		Died	2 Kin. 15:14–22	
	17	Pekahiah (Bad)	742/41–740/39 = 2	Son	Murdered by Pekah	2 Kin. 15:22–26	
VIII	18	Pekah (Bad)	752–732/31‡ = 20	Captain of Army	Murdered by Hoshea	2 Kin. 15:27–31	2 Chr. 28:5–8
IX	19	Hoshea (Bad)	732/31–723/22 = 9		Deposed to Assyria	2 Kin. 15:30—17:6	

*According to Edwin R. Thiele. †Tibni coregency unsuccessful. ‡Overlapping/coregency. §Also Joram. ‡Also Joash.

Kings of Judah

Dynasty		Name (Character)	Length of Reign*	Relation to Predecessor	End of Reign	First & Second Kings	Second Chronicles
	1	Rehoboam (Bad)	931/30–913 = 17	Son	Died	1 Kin. 11:42—14:31	2 Chr. 9:31—12:16
	2	Abijam (Bad)	913–911/10 = 3	Son	Died	1 Kin. 14:34—15:8	2 Chr. 13:1–22
	3	Asa (Good)	911/10–870/69 = 41	Son	Died	1 Kin. 15:8–24	2 Chr. 14:1—16:14
	4	Jehoshaphat (Good)	873/72–848* = 25	Son	Died	1 Kin. 22:41–50	2 Chr. 17:1—20:37
	5	Jehoram (Bad)	853–841* = 8	Son	Stricken by God (Bowels)	2 Kin. 8:16–24	2 Chr. 21:1–20
	6	Ahaziah (Bad)	841 = 1	Son	Murdered by Jehu	2 Kin. 8:24—9:29	2 Chr. 22:1–9
	7	Athaliah (Bad)	841–835 = 6	Mother	Murdered by Army	2 Kin. 11:1–20	2 Chr. 22:1—23:21
	8	Joash (Good)	835–796 = 40	Grandson	Murdered by servants	2 Kin. 11:1—12:21	2 Chr. 22:10—24:27
	9	Amaziah (Good)	796–767 = 29	Son	Murdered by court members	2 Kin. 14:1–20	2 Chr. 25:1–28
	10	Azariah† (Good)	792/91–740/39* = 52	Son	Stricken by God (Leprosy)	2 Kin. 15:1–7	2 Chr. 26:1–23
	11	Jotham (Good)	750–732/31* = 18	Son	Died	2 Kin. 15:32–38	2 Chr. :27:1–9
	12	Ahaz (Bad)	735–716/15* = 19	Son	Died	2 Kin. 16:1–20	2 Chr. 28:1–27
	13	Hezekiah (Good)	716/15–687/86 = 29	Son	Died	2 Kin. 18:1—20:21	2 Chr. 29:1—32:33
	14	Manasseh (Bad)	697/96–643/42* = 55	Son	Died	2 Kin. 21:1–18	2 Chr. 33:1–20
	15	Amon (Bad)	643/42–641/40 = 2	Son	Murdered by servants	2 Kin. 21:19–26	2 Chr. 33:21–25
	16	Josiah (Good)	641/40–609 = 31	Son	Wounded in battle	2 Kin. 22:1—23:30	2 Chr. 34:1—35:27
	17	Johoahaz (Bad)	609 = 3 months	Son	Deposed to Egypt	2 Kin. 23:31–33	2 Chr. 36:1–4
	18	Jehoiakim (Bad)	609–596 = 11	Brother	Died in Babylonian Siege?	2 Kin. 23:34—24:5	2 Chr. 36:5–7
	19	Johoiachin (Bad)	598–597 = 3 months	Son	Deposed to Babylon	2 Kin. 24:6–16	2 Chr. 36:8–10
	20	Zedekiah (Bad)	597–586 = 11	Uncle	Deposed to Babylon	2 Kin. 24:17—25:30	2 Chr. 36:11–21

*According to Edwin R. Thiele. Some overlapping/coregencies. These are biblical numbers and do not always reflect coregencies. †Also Uzziah.

The Egyptian Empire

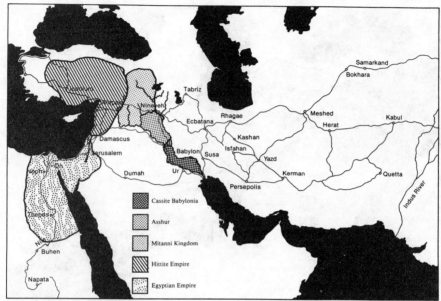

■	Cassite Babylonia
▨	Asshur
▨	Mitanni Kingdom
▨	Hittite Empire
▨	Egyptian Empire

© 1975. Bruce H. Wilkinson, Walk Thru the Bible Associates. Do not reproduce in any form.

The Assyrian Empire

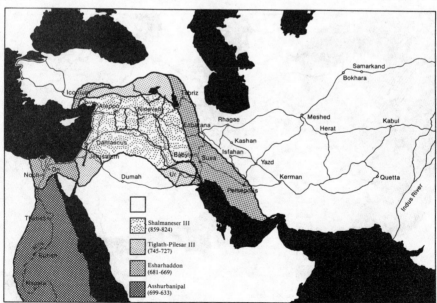

□	
▨	Shalmaneser III (859-824)
▨	Tiglath-Pilesar III (745-727)
▨	Esharhaddon (681-669)
■	Asshurbanipal (699-633)

© 1975. Bruce H. Wilkinson, Walk Thru the Bible Associates. Do not reproduce in any form.

The Babylonian Empire

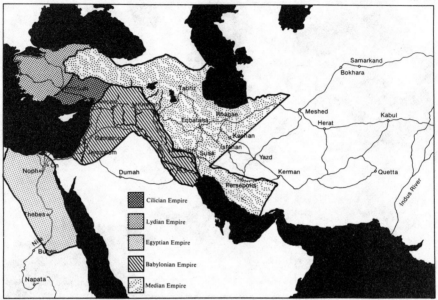

© 1975. Bruce H. Wilkinson, Walk Thru the Bible Associates. Do not reproduce in any form.

The Persian Empire

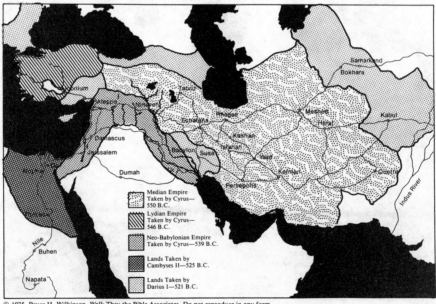

© 1975. Bruce H. Wilkinson, Walk Thru the Bible Associates. Do not reproduce in any form.

Introduction to the
Poetical Books

UNTIL RECENTLY, NOT MANY PEOPLE knew that fully one-third of the Hebrew Bible was written in poetry. This became more obvious when poetic sections were set off from prose sections in some English translations. In fact, there are only five Old Testament books that appear to have no poetry: Leviticus, Ruth, Ezra, Haggai, and Malachi. The five books now known as the poetical books serve as a hinge which links the past of the historical books to the future of the prophetical books. These books explore the experiential present and emphasize a lifestyle of godliness. Unlike the Pentateuch and twelve historical books, the poetical books do not advance the story of the nation Israel. Instead, they delve deeply into crucial questions about pain, God, wisdom, life, and love—all in the present tense.

Job

Job was a righteous man who was suddenly embroiled in an intense ordeal of every kind of suffering. He went through three cycles of debate with his friends who insisted that his misfortune must have been caused by sin. When God finally revealed Himself in His majesty and power to Job, it became obvious that the real issue was not Job's suffering but God's sovereignty. Job's questions were never answered but he willingly submitted to the wisdom and righteousness of God.

Psalms

The five books of psalms span the centuries from Moses to the postexilic period and cover the full range of human emotions and experiences. The wide variety of Psalms (lament, thanksgiving, praise, enthronement, pilgrimage, etc.) suited them for service as the temple hymnal for the people of Israel. The psalms were set to music and focused on worship.

Proverbs

The Book of Proverbs was designed to equip the reader in practical wisdom, discernment, discipline, and discretion. These maxims emphasize the development of skill in all the details of life so that beauty and righteousness will replace foolishness and evil as one walks in dependence upon God.

Ecclesiastes

The Preacher of Ecclesiastes applied his great mind and considerable resources to the quest for purpose and satisfaction in life under the sun. He found that wisdom, wealth, works, pleasure, and power all led to futility and striving after wind. The problem was compounded by the injustices and uncertainties of life and apparent absurdity of death. The only source of ultimate meaning and fulfillment is God Himself. One should therefore acknowledge his inability to understand all the ways of God, trust and obey Him, and enjoy His gifts.

Song of Solomon

This beautiful song portrays the intimate love relationship between Solomon and his Shulammite bride. It magnifies the virtues of physical and emotional love in marriage.

HEBREW POETRY

The five poetical books illustrate three kinds of poetry: (1) lyric poetry—originally accompanied by music on the lyre, this poetry often has strong emotional elements (most of Psalms); (2) didactic poetry—teaches principles about life by means of maxims (Proverbs, Ecclesiastes); and (3) dramatic poetry—dialogue in poetic form (Job, Song of Solomon).

Hebrew poetry is not based on assonance (rhyme) or meter. It has some rhythm which is produced by tonal stress, but this is not prominent. The real key to this kind of poetry is *parallelism,* which involves the "rhyming" of ideas through careful arrangement of parallel thoughts. At least six kinds of parallelism have been distinguished in Hebrew poetry: (1) *Synonymous parallelism.* Here the second line reinforces the thought of the first by using similar words and concepts (see Job 38:7; Ps. 3:1; 25:4; 49:1; Prov. 11:7,25; 12:28). (2) *Synthetic parallelism.* The second line adds to or completes the idea of the first line (see Ps. 1:1–2; 23:1,5; 95:3; Prov. 4:23). (3) *Antithetic parallelism.* The thought of the first line is contrasted in the second line (see Ps. 1:6; 18:27; Prov. 10:1; 14:34; 15:1). (4) *Emblematic parallelism.* The first line uses a figure of speech to illuminate the main point conveyed by the second line (see Ps. 42:1; Prov. 11:22; 25:25; 27:17). (5) *Climactic parallelism*. The second line repeats the first with the exception of the last term (see Ps. 29:1; Prov. 31:4). (6) *Formal parallelism*. The lines are joined solely by metric considerations (see Ps. 2:6). Parallelism is found not only in couplets (two lines), but also in triplets and quatrains (three and four lines), and sometimes in whole stanzas.

Hebrew poetry is also characterized by vivid figures of speech: (1) *Simile*. A comparison between two things that resemble one another in some way (see Ps. 1:3–4; 5:12; 17:8; 131:2). (2) *Metaphor*. A comparison in which one thing is declared to be another (see Ps. 23:1; 84:11; 91:4). (3) *Implication*. An implied comparison between two things in which the name of one thing is used in place of the other (see Ps. 22:16; Jer. 4:7). (4) *Hyperbole*. The use of exaggeration to emphasize a point (see Ps. 6:6; 78:27; 107:26). (5) *Rhetorical question*. The use of a question to confirm or deny a fact (see Ps. 35:10; 56:8; 94:6; 106:2). (6) *Metonymy*. One noun used in place of another because of some relationship between the two (see Ps. 5:9; 18:2; 57:9; 73:9). (7) *Anthropomorphism*. Assigning an appropriate part of the human body to God's Person to convey some truth about God (see Ps. 11:4; 18:15; 31:2; 32:8). (8) *Zoomorphism*. Assigning an appropriate part of an animal to God's Person to convey some truth about God (see Ps. 17:8; 36:7; 63:7; 91:4). (9) *Personification*. Assigning the characteristics of a human to lifeless objects (see Ps. 35:10; 77:16; 96:11; 104:19). (10) *Apostrophe*. Addressing lifeless objects (see Ps. 114:5). (11) *Synecdoche*. Representation of the whole by a part or a part by the whole (see Ps. 91:5). Visual imagery is clearly predominant in the poets.

Another technique in Hebrew poetry is the alphabetic acrostic— the first Hebrew letter in a line is the first letter of the alphabet, the second is the second letter of the alphabet, and so on. There are several variations on this technique (e.g., Ps. 119 and each chapter in Lamentations).

There are also three books of wisdom within the poets: Job, Proverbs, and Ecclesiastes. These books are denoted as such by the content, not the form. It is likely that there were schools of wisdom in Israel (see 1 Sam. 24:13; 1 Kin. 4:29–34). These wise men were practical observers of life who gave right answers in critical situations.

Job

THE BOOK OF JOB BEGINS in heaven with a conversation between God and Satan, then moves to earth for a detailed look at the life of an ancient patriarch named Job. Overnight, Job's blessings dissolve into heartaches as he suffers the loss of his health, wealth, family, and status. Left in turmoil over his sudden change of fortune, Job seeks an answer to the question, "Why?" Four human counselors are unable to provide the insight Job desperately needs. Finally it remains for Jehovah to teach Job some valuable lessons on the sovereignty of God and the need for complete trust in the Lord who is constantly at work behind the scenes.

Focus	Dilemma of Job	Debate of Job					Deliverance of Job
	1:1 2:13	3:1				37:24	38:1 42:17
Divisions	Controversy between God and Satan	First Cycle of Debate	Second Cycle of Debate	Third Cycle of Debate	Final Defense of Job	Solution of Elihu	Controversy of God and Job
	1:1 2:13	3:1 14:22	15:1 21:34	22:1 26:14	27:1 31:40	32:1 37:24	38:1 42:17
Topics	Conflict	Debate					Repentance
	Prose	Poetry					Prose
Place	Heaven and Earth	Land of Uz (North Arabia)					Heaven and Earth
Time	Patriarchal Period, c. 2000 B.C.						

Introduction and Title

Job is perhaps the earliest book of the Bible. Set in the period of the patriarchs (Abraham, Isaac, Jacob, and Joseph), it tells the story of a man who loses everything—his wealth, his family, his health—and wrestles with the question, Why?

The book begins with a heavenly debate between God and Satan, moves through three cycles of earthly debates between Job and his friends, and concludes with a dramatic "divine diagnosis" of Job's problem. In the end, Job acknowledges the sovereignty of God in his life and receives back more than he had before his trials.

Iyyōb is the Hebrew title for this book, and the name has two possible meanings. If derived from the Hebrew word for persecution, it means "persecuted one." It is more likely that it comes from the Arabic word meaning "to come back" or "repent." If so, it may be defined "repentant one." Both meanings apply to the book. The Greek title is *Iob,* and the Latin title is *Iob.*

Author

The author of Job is unknown, and there are no textual hints as to his identity. Commentators, however, have been generous with suggestions: Job, Elihu, Moses, Solomon, Isaiah, Hezekiah, Jeremiah, Baruch, and Ezra have all been nominated. The non-Hebraic cultural background of this book may point to gentile authorship. The rabbinic traditions are inconsistent, but one talmudic tradition suggests that Moses wrote the book. The land of Uz (1:1) is adjacent to Midian, where Moses lived for forty years, and it is conceivable that Moses obtained a record of the dialogue left by Job or Elihu.

Date and Setting

Chapter 4, verse 21 locates Uz in the area of Edom, southeast of the Dead Sea. This is also in the region of northern Arabia, and Job's friends come from nearby countries.

It is important to distinguish the date of the events in Job from the date of its writing. Accurate dating of the events is difficult because there are no references to contemporary historical occurrences. However, a number of facts indicate a patriarchal date for Job, perhaps between Genesis 11 and 12 or not long after the time of Abraham: (1) Job lived 140 years *after* the events in the book (42:16); his lifespan must have been close to 200 years. This fits the patriarchal period (Abraham lived 175 years, Gen. 25:7). (2) Job's wealth is measured in terms of livestock (1:3; 42:12) rather than gold and silver. (3) Like Abraham, Isaac, and Jacob, Job is the priest of his family and offers sacrifices. (4) There are no references to Israel, the Exodus, the Mosaic Law, or the tabernacle. (5) Fitting Abraham's time, the social unit in Job is the patriarchal family-clan. (6) The Chaldeans who murder Job's servants (1:17) are nomads and have not yet become city-dwellers. (7) Job uses the characteristic patriarchal name for God, *Shaddai* ("the Almighty"), thirty-one times. This early term is found only seventeen times in the rest of the Old Testament. The rare use of Yahweh "the LORD" also suggests a pre-Mosaic date. Ezekiel 14:14, 20 and James 5:11 show that Job was an historical person.

Several theories have been advanced for the date of writing: (1) It was written shortly after the events occurred, perhaps by Job or Elihu; (2) it was written by Moses in Midian (1485–1445 B.C.); (3) it was written in the time of Solomon (c. 950 B.C.—Job is similar to other Wisdom Literature of this time—compare the praises of wisdom in Job 28 and Proverbs 8. The problem here is the great time lag of about a thousand years.); or (4) it was written during or after the Babylonian captivity.

Theme and Purpose

The basic question of the book is, Why do the righteous suffer if God is loving and all-powerful? Suffering itself is not the central theme; rather, the focus is on what Job *learns* from his suffering—the sovereignty of God over all creation. The debate in chapters 3—37 regards whether God would allow this suffering to happen to a person who is innocent. The oversimplified solutions offered by Job's three friends are simply inadequate. Elihu's claim that God can use suffering to purify the righteous is closer to the mark. The conclusion at the whirlwind is that God is sovereign and worthy of worship in *whatever* He chooses to do. Job must learn to trust in the goodness and power of God in adversity by enlarging his concept of God. Even this "blameless" man (1:1) needs to repent when he becomes proud and self-righteous. He has to come to the end of his own resources, humble himself, and acknowledge the greatness and majesty of the Lord. Job teaches that God is Lord "of those in heaven, and of those on earth, and of those under the earth" (Phil. 2:10). He is omniscient, omnipotent, and good. As such, His ways are sometimes incomprehensible to men and women, but He can always be trusted. Without the divine perspective in chapters 1—2 and in 38—42, chapters 3—37 are a mystery. Job does not have access to chapters 1—2, but he is responsible to trust God when all appearances are contrary. Suffering is not always associated with sin; God often sovereignly uses it to test and teach.

Keys to Job

Key Word: Sovereignty

Key Verses (13:15; 37:23–24)—"Though He slay me, yet will I trust him. Even so, I will defend my own ways before Him" (13:15).

"*As for* the Almighty, we cannot find Him; *He is* excellent in power, *in* judgment and abundant justice; He does not oppress. Therefore men fear Him; He shows no partiality to any *who are* wise of heart" (37:23–24).

Key Chapter (42)—The last chapter of the book records the climax of the long and difficult struggle Job has with himself, his wife, his friends, and even his God. Upon Job's full recognition of the utter majesty and sovereignty of the Lord, he repents and no longer demands an answer as to the "why" of his plight.

Christ in Job

Job acknowledges a Redeemer (19:25–27) and cries out for a Mediator (9:33; 25:4; 33:23). The book raises problems and questions which are answered perfectly in Christ who identifies with our sufferings (Heb. 4:15). Christ is the believer's Life, Redeemer, Mediator, and Advocate.

Contribution to the Bible

Job is a book of dramatic poetry that is unsurpassed in beauty, depth, and intensity. It makes rich use of synonymous, antithetic, and synthetic parallelism. In its setting Job offers a glimpse of non-Hebrew culture in patriarchal times. Its universal flavor is appropriate to the universal theme it develops.

Job reveals five ways in which God uses hardships that are reflected in Deuteronomy 8: (1) To humble us (22:29; Deut. 8:2); (2) to test us (2:3; Deut. 8:2); (3) to rearrange our priorities (42:5–6; Deut. 8:3); (4) to discipline us (5:17; Deut. 8:5); and (5) to prepare us for future blessings (42:10; Deut. 8:7).

Chapters 38—42 give the most intensive survey of creation in the Bible. Among other things, Job teaches that the earth is suspended in empty space (26:7) and implies that the earth is a sphere (22:14).

Survey of Job

The Book of Job concerns the transforming crisis in the life of a great man who lived perhaps four thousand years ago. Job loses everything he has—wealth, family, and health—in a sudden series of catastrophes that force him to wrestle with the question, Why? The book begins with a heavenly debate between God and Satan, moves into an earthly debate between Job and his friends, and closes with a series of divine questions. Job's trust in God (1—2) changes to complaining and growing self-righteousness (3—31; cf. 32:1; 40:8), but his repentance (42:1–6) leads to his restoration (42:7–17). The trials bring about an important transformation. The man after the process is different from the man before the process. The Book of Job divides into three parts: (1) The dilemma of Job (1—2); (2) the debates of Job (3—37); and (3) the deliverance of Job (38—42).

The Dilemma of Job (1—2): Job is not a logical candidate for disaster (1:1, 8). His moral integrity and his selfless service to God heighten the dilemma. Behind the scene, Satan ("accuser") charges that no one loves God from pure motives, but only for material blessings (1:10). To refute Satan's accusations, God allows him to strike Job with two series of assaults. In his sorrow Job laments the day of his birth but does not deny God (1:21; 2:10).

The Debates of Job (3—37): Although Job's "comforters" reach wrong conclusions, they are his friends: of all who know Job, they are the only ones who come; they mourn with him in seven days of silent sympathy; and they confront Job without talking behind his back. However, after Job breaks the silence, a three-round debate follows in which his friends say Job must be suffering because of his sin. Job's responses to their simplistic assumptions make the debate cycles increase in emotional fervor. He first accuses his friends of judging him, and later appeals to the Lord as his judge and refuge.

The Three Cycles of Debate:

Bildad	Bildad	Bildad
Eliphaz Zophar	Eliphaz Zophar	Eliphaz (Zophar silent)
Job	Job	Job

Job's Response:

"You act as my judge"   "The Lord is my judge"   "The Lord is my refuge"

Job makes three basic complaints: (1) God does not hear me (13:3, 24; 19:7; 23:3–5; 30:20); (2) God is punishing me (6:4; 7:20; 9:17); and (3) God allows the wicked to prosper (21:7). His defenses are much longer than his friends' accusations; and in the process of defending his innocence, he becomes guilty of self-righteousness.

After Job's five-chapter closing monologue (27—31), Elihu freshens the air with a more perceptive and accurate view than those offered by Eliphaz, Bildad, or Zophar (32—37). He tells Job that he needs to humble himself before God and submit to God's process of purifying his life through trials.

	Eliphaz	Bildad	Zophar	Elihu
Characteristic:	Theologian	Historian, Legalist	Moralist, dogmatist	Young theologian, intellectual
Relies on:	Observation, Experience	Tradition	Assumption	Education
Personality:	Considerate	Argumentative	Rude, blunt	Perceptive, some conceit
Voice of:	Philosophy	History	Orthodoxy	Logic
Argument:	"*If* you sin, you suffer"	"You *must* be sinning"	"You *are* sinning"	"God purifies and teaches"
Advice to Job:	Only the wicked suffer	The wicked always suffer	The wicked are short-lived	Humble yourself and submit to God
Key Verse:	4:8; 5:17	8:8	20:5	37:23
Concept of God:	Righteous; punishes wicked, blesses good	Judge; immovable lawgiver	Unbending, merciless	Disciplinarian, teacher
Name:	"God is Gold" or "God Dispenses (Judgment)"	"Son of Contention"	"Rough" or "Chirper"	"He is My God"

The Deliverance of Job (38—42): After Elihu's preparatory discourse, God Himself ends the debate by speaking to Job from the whirlwind. In His first speech God reveals His power and wisdom as Creator and Preserver of the physical and animal world. Job responds by acknowledging his own ignorance and insignificance; he can offer no rebuttal (40:3–5). In His second speech God reveals His sovereign authority and challenges Job with two illustrations of His power to control the uncontrollable. This time Job responds by acknowledging his error with a repentant heart (42:1–6). If Job cannot understand God's ways in the realm of nature, how then can he understand God's ways in the spiritual realm? God makes no reference to Job's personal sufferings, and hardly touches on the real issue of the debate. However, Job catches a glimpse of the divine perspective; and when he acknowledges God's sovereignty over his life, his worldly goods are restored twofold. Job prays for his three friends who have cut him so deeply, but Elihu's speech is never rebuked. Thus, Satan's challenge becomes God's opportunity to build up Job's life. "Indeed we count them blessed who endured. You have heard of the perseverance of Job and seen the end *intended* by the Lord—that the Lord is very compassionate and merciful" (James 5:11; see also James 1:12).

Outline of Job

Part One: The Dilemma of Job (1:1—2:13)

I. The Circumstances of Job, 1:1–5

II. The First Assault of Satan, 1:6–22

III. The Second Assault of Satan, 2:1–10

IV. The Arrival of Job's Friends, 2:11–13

Part Two: The Debates of Job (3:1—37:24)

I. The First Cycle of Debate, 3:1—14:22
   A. Job's First Speech, 3:1–26
   B. Eliphaz's First Speech, 4:1—5:27
      1. Eliphaz Believes the Innocent Do Not Suffer, 4:1–21
      2. Eliphaz Calls Job Foolish, 5:1–7
      3. Eliphaz Encourages Job to Appeal to God, 5:8–16
      4. Eliphaz Encourages Job to Despise Not God's Discipline, 5:17–27
   C. Job's Reply to Eliphaz, 6:1—7:21
      1. Job's Deep Anguish, 6:1–13
      2. Job Seeks His Friends' Sympathy, 6:14–30
      3. Job Questions God's Continuing Trials, 7:1–21
   D. Bildad's First Speech, 8:1–22

E. Job's Response to Bildad, 9:1—10:22
   1. Job Argues His Case, 9:1–35
   2. Job Questions His Oppression, 10:1–22
F. Zophar's First Speech, 11:1–20
G. Job's Response to Zophar, 12:1—14:22
   1. Job Tells His Friends Only God Knows, 12:1–25
   2. Job Begs God to Speak to Him, 13:1–28
   3. Job Mourns That Man Has Only One Life, 14:1–22

II. The Second Cycle of Debate, 15:1—21:34
A. Eliphaz's Second Speech 15:1–35
   1. Job's Mouth Condemns Him, 15:1–13
   2. The Wicked Suffer, 15:14–35
B. Job's Response to Eliphaz, 16:1—17:16
   1. Job Calls His Friends Miserable Comforters, 16:1–5
   2. Job Laments His Situation, 16:6–14
   3. Job Defends His Innocence, 16:15–22
   4. God Makes Job a Byword, 17:1–16
C. Bildad's Second Speech, 18:1–21
D. Job's Response to Bildad, 19:1–29
E. Zophar's Second Speech, 20:1–29
F. Job's Response to Zophar, 21:1–34

III. The Third Cycle of Debate, 22:1—26:14
A. Eliphaz's Third Speech, 22:1–30
B. Job's Response to Eliphaz, 23:1—24:25
   1. Job Will Come Forth as Gold, 23:1–17
   2. God Seems Indifferent to the Wicked, 24:1–25
C. Bildad's Third Speech, 25:1–6
D. Job's Response to Bildad, 26:1–14

IV. The Final Defense of Job, 27:1—31:40
A. Job's First Monologue, 27:1—28:28
   1. Job Affirms His Righteousness, 27:1–23
   2. Job Observes That Man Cannot Discover Wisdom, 28:1–28
B. Job's Second Monologue, 29:1—31:40
   1. Job Remembers His Happy Past, 29:1–25
   2. Job Describes His Present Humiliation, 30:1–31
   3. Job Defends His Innocency, 31:1–34
      a. Innocent of Sensual Sins, 31:1–12
      b. Innocent of Abusing His Power, 31:13–23
      c. Innocent of Trusting in His Wealth, 31:24–28
      d. Innocent of Not Caring for His Enemies, 31:29–34
   4. Job Pleads to Meet God and Defend Himself, 31:35–40

V. The Solution of Elihu, 32:1—37:24
A. Elihu Intervenes in the Debate, 32:1–22
B. Elihu's First Rebuttal, 33:1–33

1. Elihu Challenges Job to Debate, 33:1–7
2. Elihu Quotes Job's Complaints, 33:8–11
3. Elihu Answers Job's Complaints, 33:12–33
C. Elihu's Second Rebuttal, 34:1–37
1. Elihu Challenges Job to Debate Again, 34:1–4
2. Elihu Quotes Job's Complaints, 34:5–9
3. Elihu Answers Job's Complaints, 34:10–37
D. Elihu's Third Rebuttal, 35:1–16
E. Elihu's Conclusion, 36:1—37:24
1. Elihu Believes That God Is Disciplining Job, 36:1–21
2. Elihu Reminds Job of the Greatness of God, 36:22—37:24

Part Three: The Deliverance of Job (38:1—42:17)

I. The First Controversy of God with Job, 38:1—40:5
A. God's First Challenge to Job, 38:1—40:2
1. God Questions Job from the Realm of Creation, 38:1–38
2. God Questions Job from the Realm of Animals, 38:39—39:30
3. God Demands an Answer to His Questions, 40:1–2
B. Job's First Answer to God, 40:3–5

II. The Second Controversy of God with Job, 40:6—42:6
A. God's Second Challenge to Job, 40:6—41:34
1. God Tells Job to Save Himself, 40:6–14
2. God Compares the Power of Job with That of the Behemoth, 40:15–24
3. God Compares the Power of Job with That of the Leviathan, 41:1–34
B. Job's Second Answer to God, 42:1–6
1. Job Confesses Lack of Understanding, 42:1–3
2. Job Repents of His Rebellion, 42:4–6

III. The Deliverance of Job and His Friends, 42:7–17

Psalms

THE BOOK OF PSALMS (from a Greek word meaning "a song sung to the accompaniment of a plucked instrument") was written and compiled over a period of perhaps a thousand years: from the time of Moses (Ps. 90) to the time of the return from exile (Ps. 126). The book was used as the temple hymnbook of the Kingdom Period, and stands as the longest, most oft-quoted, most diverse book of the Old Testament.

Book	Book 1 (1—41)	Book 2 (42—72)	Book 3 (73—89)	Book 4 (90—106)	Book 5 (107—150)
Chief Author	David	David/ Korah	Asaph	Anonymous	David/ Anonymous
Number of Psalms	41	31	17	17	44
Basic Content	Songs of Worship	Hymns of National Interest		Anthems of Praise	
Topical Likeness To Pentateuch	Genesis: Man and Creation	Exodus: Deliverance and Redemption	Leviticus: Worship and Sanctuary	Numbers: Wilderness and Wandering	Deuteronomy: Scripture and Praise
Closing Doxology	41:13	72:18–19	89:52	106:48	150:1–6
Possible Compiler	David	Hezekiah or Josiah		Ezra or Nehemiah	
Possible Dates of Compilation	c. 1020–970 B.C.	c. 970–610 B.C.		Until c. 430 B.C.	
Span of Authorship	About 1000 Years (c. 1410–430 B.C.)				

Introduction and Title

The Book of Psalms is the largest and perhaps most widely used book in the Bible. It explores the full range of human experience in a very personal and practical way. Its 150 "songs" run from the Creation through the patriarchal, theocratic, monarchical, exilic, and postexilic periods. The tremendous breadth of subject matter in the Psalms includes diverse topics, such as jubilation, war, peace, worship, judgment, messianic prophecy, praise, and lament. The Psalms were set to the accompaniment of stringed instruments and served as the temple hymnbook and devotional guide for the Jewish people.

The Book of Psalms was gradually collected and originally unnamed, perhaps due to the great variety of material. It came to be known as *Sepher Tehillim*—"Book of Praises"—because almost every psalm contains some note of praise to God. The Septuagint uses the Greek word *Psalmoi* as its title for this book, meaning poems sung to the accompaniment of musical instruments. It also calls it the *Psalterium* (a collection of songs), and this word is the basis for the term "Psalter." The Latin title is *Liber Psalmorum,* "Book of Psalms."

Author

Although critics have challenged the historical accuracy of the superscriptions regarding authorship, the evidence is strongly in their favor. Almost half (seventy-three) of the psalms are designated as Davidic: 3—9; 11—32; 34—41; 51—65; 68—70; 86; 101; 103; 108—110; 122; 124; 131; 133; and 138—145. David's wide experience as shepherd, musician, warrior, and king (1011–971 B.C.) is reflected in these psalms. The New Testament reveals that the anonymous psalms 2 and 95 were also written by this king whose name means "Beloved of Yahweh" (see Acts 4:25; Heb. 4:7). In addition to the seventy-five by David, twelve were by Asaph, "Collector," a priest who headed the service of music (see 50; 73—83; Ezra 2:41); ten were by the sons of Korah, "Bald," a guild of singers and composers (see 42; 44—49; 84—85; 87; Num. 26:9–11); two were by Solomon, "Peaceful," Israel's most powerful king (72; 127); one was by Moses, "Son of the Water," a prince, herdsman, and deliverer (90); one was by Heman, "Faithful," a wise man (see 88; 1 Kin. 4:31; 1 Chron. 15:19); and one was by Ethan, "Enduring," a wise man (see 89; 1 Kin. 4:31, 1 Chr. 15:19). The remaining fifty psalms are anonymous: 1; 2; 10; 33; 43; 66—67; 71; 91—100; 102; 104—107; 111—121; 123; 125—126; 128—130; 132; 134—137; and 146—150. Some of the anonymous psalms are traditionally attributed to Ezra.

Date and Setting

The Book of Psalms covers a wide time span from Moses (c. 1410 B.C.) to the postexilic community under Ezra and Nehemiah (c. 430 B.C.). Because of their broad chronological and thematic range, the psalms were written to different audiences under many conditions. They therefore reflect a multitude of moods and as such are relevant to every reader.

The five books were compiled over several centuries. As individual psalms were written, some were used in Israel's worship. A number of small collections were independently made, like the pilgrimage songs and groups of Davidic psalms (1—41, 51—70, 138—145). These smaller anthologies were gradually collected into the five books. The last stage was the uniting and editing of the five books themselves. David (1 Chr. 15:16) Hezekiah (2 Chr. 29:30; Prov. 25:1), and Ezra (Neh. 8) were involved in various stages of collecting the psalms. David was the originator of the temple liturgy of which his psalms were a part. The superscriptions of thirteen psalms specify key events in his life: First Samuel 19:11 (Ps. 59); 21:11 (Ps. 56); 21:13 (Ps. 34); 22:1 (Ps. 142); 22:9 (Ps. 52); 23:19 (Ps. 54); 24:3 (Ps. 57); Second Samuel 8:13 (Ps. 60); 12:13 (Ps. 51); 15:16 (Ps. 3); 15:23 (Ps. 63); 16:5 (Ps. 7); 22:2-51 (Ps. 18).

Here are four things to remember when interpreting the psalms: (1) When the superscription gives the historical event, the psalm should be interpreted in that light. When it is not given, there is little hope in reconstructing the historical occasion. Assuming occasions will probably hurt more than help the interpretive process. (2) Some of the psalms are associated with definite aspects of Israel's worship (e.g., 5:7; 66:13; 68:24–25), and this can help in understanding those psalms. (3) Many of the psalms use definite structure and motifs. (4) Many psalms anticipate Israel's Messiah and are fulfilled in Christ. However, care must be taken not to allegorize them and forget the grammatical-historical method of interpretation.

Theme and Purpose

There are several kinds of psalms, and they express different feelings and circumstances. But the common theme is worship—God is worthy of all praise because of who He is, what He has done, and what He will do. His goodness extends through all time and eternity. The psalms present a very personal response to the person and work of God as they reflect on His program for His people. There is a keen desire to see His program fulfilled and His name extolled. Many of the psalms survey the Word of God and the attributes of God, especially during difficult times. This kind of faith produces confidence in His power in spite of circumstances.

The psalms were used in the two temples and some were part of the liturgical service. They also served as an individual and communal devotional guide.

Keys to Psalms

Key Word: Worship
Key Verses (19:14; 145:21)—"Let the words of my mouth and the meditation of my heart be acceptable in Your sight, O LORD, my strength and my redeemer" (19:14):

"My mouth shall speak the praise of the LORD, and all flesh shall bless His holy name forever and ever" (145:21).

Key Chapter (100)—So many of the favorite chapters of the Bible are contained in the book of Psalms that it is difficult to select the key chapter among such psalms as Psalms 1; 22; 23; 24; 37; 72; 100; 101; 119; 121; and 150. The two central themes of worship and praise are beautifully wed in Psalm 100.

Christ in Psalms

Many of the psalms specifically anticipated the life and ministry of Jesus Christ, the One who came centuries later as Israel's promised Messiah ("anointed one"). The Psalms, like the four Gospels, give several perspectives on the person and work of Christ:

- *Jesus Christ, the King* (portrayed in Matthew)
    - 2: Christ rejected as King by the nations
    - 24: Christ is King of Glory
    - 18: Christ is Protector and Deliverer
    - 47: Christ rules in His kingdom
    - 20: Christ provides salvation
    - 110: Christ is King-Priest
    - 21: Christ is given glory by God
    - 132: Christ is enthroned
- *Jesus Christ, the Servant* (portrayed in Mark)
    - 17: Christ is Intercessor
    - 41: Christ is betrayed by a close friend
    - 22: Christ is the dying Savior
    - 69: Christ is hated without a cause
    - 23: Christ is Shepherd
    - 109: Christ loves those who reject Him
    - 40: Christ is obedient unto death
- *Jesus Christ, the Son of God* (portrayed in Luke)
    - 8: Christ is made a little lower than angels
    - 40: Christ's resurrection is realized
    - 16: Christ's resurrection is promised
- *Jesus Christ, the Son of God* (portrayed in John)
    - 19: Christ is Creator
    - 118: Christ is the Chief Cornerstone
    - 102: Christ is eternal

There are five different kinds of messianic psalms: (1) *Typical messianic.* The subject of the psalm is in some feature a type of Christ (34:20; 69:4,9). (2) *Typical prophetic.* The psalmist uses language to describe his present experience which points beyond his own life and becomes historically true only in Christ (22). (3) *Indirectly messianic.* At the time of composition the psalm referred to a king or the house of David in general, but awaits final fulfillment in Christ (2, 45, 72). (4) *Purely prophetic.* Refers solely to Christ without reference to any other son of David (110). (5) *Enthronement.* Anticipates the coming of Yahweh and the consummation of His kingdom—will be fulfilled in the person of Christ (96—99).

Here are some of the specific messianic prophecies in the Book of Psalms:

Psalm	Prophecy	Fulfillment
2:7	God will declare Him to be His Son	Matthew 3:17
8:6	All things will be put under His feet	Hebrews 2:8
16:10	He will be resurrected from the dead	Mark 16:6–7
22:1	God will forsake Him in His hour of need	Matthew 27:46
22:7–8	He will be scorned and mocked	Luke 23:35
22:16	His hands and feet will be pierced	John 20:25,27
22:18	Others will gamble for His clothes	Matthew 27:35–36
34:20	Not one of His bones will be broken	John 19:32–33,36
35:11	He will be accused by false witnesses	Mark 14:57
35:19	He will be hated without a cause	John 15:25
40:7–8	He will come to do God's will	Hebrews 10:7
41:9	He will be betrayed by a friend	Luke 22:47
45:6	His throne will be forever	Hebrews 1:8
68:18	He will ascend to God's right hand	Mark 16:19
69:9	Zeal for God's house will consume Him	John 2:17
69:21	He will be given vinegar and gall to drink	Matthew 27:34
109:4	He will pray for His enemies	Luke 23:34
109:8	His betrayer's office will be fulfilled by another	Acts 1:20
110:1	His enemies will be made subject to Him	Matthew 22:44
110:4	He will be a priest like Melchizedek	Hebrews 5:6
118:22	He will be the chief corrnerstone	Matthew 21:42
118:26	He will come in the name of the LORD	Matthew 21:9

Contribution to the Bible

The Book of Psalms is quoted more times in the New Testament than any other book. Our Lord frequently used the Psalms during the course of His earthly life (e.g., the Sermon on the Mount, teaching the multitudes, answering the Jewish leaders, cleansing the temple, during the Last Supper, and on the Cross). The singing of psalms was a regular part of worship in the early church (cf. 1 Cor. 14:26; Eph. 5:19; Col. 3:16).

In addition to the Book of Psalms, there are at least eleven other psalms in the Old Testament: (1) the song of the sea (Ex. 15:1–18); (2) the song of Moses (Deut. 32:1–43); (3) the song of Deborah (Judg. 5); (4) the song of Hannah (1 Sam. 2:1–10); (5) a psalm of David (2 Sam. 22:2–51; Ps. 18); (6) Job's lament psalms (Job 3, 7, 10); (7) a doxology in Isaiah (Is. 12:4–6); (8) the song of Hezekiah (Is. 38:9–20); (9) Jeremiah's lament psalms (Lam. 3:19–38; 5); (10) the prayer of Jonah (Jon. 2:1–9); and (11) the prayer of Habakkuk (Hab. 3:2–19).

Survey of Psalms

The Psalter is really five books in one, and each book ends with a doxology (see chart). The last psalm is the closing doxology for Book 5 and for the Psalter as a whole. After the Psalms were written, editorial superscriptions or instructions were added to 116 of them. These superscriptions are historically accurate and are even numbered as the first verses in the Hebrew text. They designate fifty-seven psalms as *mizmor,* "psalm"—a song accompanied by a stringed instrument. Another twenty-nine are called *shir,* "song" and thirteen are called *maskil,* "contemplative poem." Six are called *miktam,* perhaps meaning "epigram" or "inscription poem." Five are termed *tepillah,* "prayer" (Hab. 3), and only one is called *tehillah,* "praise" (145). In addition to these technical terms, the psalms can be classified according to certain themes: Creation psalms (8; 19), Exodus psalms (78), penitence psalms (6), pilgrimage psalms (120—134), and messianic psalms (see "Christ in Psalms"). There are even nine acrostic psalms in which the first verse or line begins with the first verse of the Hebrew alphabet, the next begins with the second, and so on (see 9; 10; 25; 34; 37; 111; 112; 119; 145).

First Chronicles 16:4 supports another approach to classification: "to invoke, to thank, and to praise the LORD, the God of Israel" (RSV). This leads to three basic types—lament, thanksgiving, and praise psalms. The following classification further divides the Psalms into ten types: (1) *Individual lament psalms:* Directly addressed to God, these psalms petition Him to rescue and defend an individual. They have these elements: (a) an introduction (usually a cry to God), (b) the lament, (c) a confession of trust in God, (d) the petition, (e) a declaration or vow of praise. Most psalms are of this type (e.g., 3—7; 12; 13; 22; 25—28; 35; 38—40; 42; 43; 51; 54—57; 59; 61; 63; 64; 69—71; 86; 88; 102; 109; 120; 130; 140—143). (2) *Communal lament psalms:* The only difference is that the nation rather than an individual makes the lament (e.g., 44; 60; 74; 79—80; 83; 85; 90; and 123). (3) *Individual thanksgiving psalms:* The psalmist publicly acknowledges God's activity on his behalf. These psalms thank God for something He has already done or express confidence in what He will yet do. They have these elements: (a) a proclamation to praise God; (b) a summary statement; (c) a report of deliverance; and (d) a renewed vow of praise (e.g., 18; 30; 32; 34; 40; 41; 66; 106; 116; and 138). (4) *Communal thanksgiving psalms:* In these psalms the acknowledgement is made by the nation rather than an individual (see 124; 129). (5) *General praise psalms:* These psalms revolve around the word "praise" and are more general than the thanksgiving psalms. The psalmist attempts to magnify the name of God and boast about His greatness (see 8; 19; 29; 103; 104; 139; 148; 150). The joyous exclamation "hallelujah" ("praise the LORD!") is found in several of these psalms. (6) *Descriptive praise psalms:* These psalms praise God for His attributes and acts (e.g., 33; 36; 105; 111; 113; 117; 135; 136; 146; 147). (7) *Enthronement psalms:* These psalms describe Yahweh's sovereign reign over all (see 47; 93; 96—99). Some anticipate the kingdom rule of Christ. (8) *Pilgrimage songs:* Also known as Songs of Zion, these psalms were sung by pilgrims traveling up to Jerusalem for the three annual religious feasts of Passover, Pentecost, and Tabernacles (see 43; 46; 48; 76; 84; 87; 120—134). (9) *Royal psalms:* The reigns of the earthly king and the heavenly King are portrayed in most of these psalms. (e.g.

2; 18; 20; 21; 45; 72; 89; 101; 110; 132; 144). (10) *Wisdom and didactic psalms:* The reader is exhorted and instructed in the way of righteousness (see 1; 37; 119).

There is a problem with the so-called imprecatory ("to call down a curse") psalms. These psalms invoke divine judgment on one's enemies (see 7; 35; 40; 55; 58; 59; 69; 79; 109; 137; 139; 144). Although some of them seem unreasonably harsh, a few things should be kept in mind: (1) They call for divine justice rather than human vengeance; (2) they ask for God to punish the wicked and thus vindicate His righteousness; (3) they condemn sin (in Hebrew thinking no sharp distinction exists between a sinner and his sin); and (4) even Jesus calls down a curse on several cities and tells His disciples to curse cities that do not receive the gospel (Matt. 10:14–15).

A number of special musical terms (some obscure) are used in the superscriptions of the psalms. "To the Chief Musician" appears in fifty-five psalms indicating that there is a collection of psalms used by the conductor of music in the temple, perhaps for special occasions. "Selah" is used seventy-one times in the Psalms and three times in Habakkuk 3. This word may mark a pause, a musical interlude, or a crescendo.

Outline of Psalms

Book One: Psalms 1—41

1. Two Ways of Life Contrasted
2. Coronation of the LORD's Anointed
3. Victory in the Face of Defeat
4. Evening Prayer for Deliverance
5. Morning Prayer for Guidance
6. Prayer for God's Mercy
7. Wickedness Justly Rewarded
8. God's Glory and Man's Dominion
9. Praise for Victory over Enemies
10. Petition for God's Judgment
11. God Tests the Sons of Men
12. The Pure Words of the LORD
13. The Prayer for God's Answer—Now
14. The Characteristics of the Godless
15. The Characteristics of the Godly
16. Eternal Life for One Who Trusts
17. "Hide Me Under the Shadow of Your Wings"
18. Thanksgiving for Deliverance by God
19. The Works and Word of God
20. Trust Not in Chariots and Horses but in God
21. Triumph of the King
22. Psalm of the Cross
23. Psalm of the Divine Shepherd

24. Psalm of the King of Glory
25. Acrostic Prayer for Instruction
26. "Examine Me, O LORD, and Prove Me"
27. Trust in the LORD and Be Not Afraid
28. Rejoice Because of Answered Prayer
29. The Powerful Voice of God
30. Praise for Dramatic Deliverance
31. "Be of Good Courage"
32. The Blessedness of Forgiveness
33. God Considers All Man's Works
34. Seek the LORD
35. Petition for God's Intervention
36. The Excellent Lovingkindness of God
37. "Rest in the LORD"
38. The Heavy Burden of Sin
39. Know the Measure of Man's Days
40. Delight to Do God's Will
41. The Blessedness of Helping the Poor

Book Two: Psalms 42—72

42. Seek After the LORD
43. "Hope in God"
44. Prayer for Deliverance by God
45. The Psalm of the Great King
46. "God Is Our Refuge and Strength"
47. The LORD Shall Subdue All Nations
48. The Praise of Mount Zion
49. Riches Cannot Redeem
50. The LORD Shall Judge All People
51. Confession and Forgiveness of Sin
52. The LORD Shall Judge the Deceitful
53. A Portrait of the Godless
54. The LORD Is Our Helper
55. "Cast Your Burden upon the LORD"
56. Fears in the Midst of Trials
57. Prayers in the Midst of Perils
58. Wicked Judges Will Be Judged
59. Petition for Deliverance from Violent Men
60. A Prayer for Deliverance of the Nation
61. A Prayer When Overwhelmed
62. Wait for God
63. Thirst for God
64. A Prayer for God's Protection
65. God's Provision through Nature
66. Remember What God Has Done

Book Three: Psalms 73—89

Book Four: Psalms 90—106

Book Five: Psalms 107—150

107. God Satisfies the Longing Soul
108. Awake Early and Praise the LORD
109. Song of the Slandered
110. The Coming of the Priest-King-Judge
111. Praise for God's Tender Care
112. The Blessings of Those Who Fear God
113. The Condescending Grace of God
114. In Praise for the Exodus
115. To God Alone Be the Glory
116. Love the LORD for What He Has Done
117. The Praise of All Peoples
118. Better to Trust God than Man
119. An Acrostic in Praise of the Scriptures
120. A Cry in Distress
121. God Is Our Keeper
122. "Pray for the Peace of Jerusalem"
123. Plea for the Mercy of God
124. God Is on Our Side
125. Trust in the LORD and Abide Forever
126. "Sow in Tears, Reap in Joy"
127. Children Are God's Heritage
128. Blessing on the House of the God-fearing
129. Plea of the Persecuted
130. "My Soul Waits for the LORD"
131. A Childlike Faith
132. Trust in the God of David
133. Beauty of the Unity of the Brethren
134. Praise the LORD in the Evening
135. God Has Done Great Things!
136. God's Mercy Endures Forever
137. Tears in Exile
138. God Answered My Prayer
139. "Search Me, O God"
140. Preserve Me from Violence
141. Set a Guard, O LORD, over My Mouth
142. "No One Cares for My Soul"
143. "Teach Me to Do Your Will"
144. "What Is Man?"
145. Testify to God's Great Acts
146. "Do Not Put Your Trust in Princes"
147. God Heals the Brokenhearted
148. All Creation Praises the LORD
149. "The LORD Takes Pleasure in His People"
150. "Praise the LORD"

Proverbs

PROVERBS IS PERHAPS the most practical book in the Old Testament because it teaches wisdom (lit., "skillful living") in the multiple aspects of everyday life. In short pithy statements, maxims, and stories, Solomon and other contributors set forth about nine hundred proverbs—inspired precepts dealing with wisdom and folly, pride and humility, justice and vengeance, laziness and work, poverty and wealth, friends and neighbors, love and lust, anger and strife, masters and servants, life and death. Reading a proverb takes only a few seconds; applying a proverb can take a lifetime!

PROVERBS

Focus	Purpose of Proverbs	Proverbs to Youth	Proverbs of Solomon	Proverbs of Solomon (Hezekiah)	Words of Agur	Words of Lemuel
	1:1 1:7	1:8 9:18	10:1 24:34	25:1 29:27	30:1 30:33	31:1 31:31
Divisions	Purpose and Theme	Father's Exhortations	First Collection of Solomon	Second Collection of Solomon	Numerical Proverbs	Wisdom for Leaders / Virtuous Wife
	1:1 1:7	1:8 9:18	10:1 24:34	25:1 29:27	30:1 30:33	31:1 31:9 / 31:10 31:31
Topics	Prologue	Principles of Wisdom			Epilogue	
	Commendation of Wisdom	Counsel of Wisdom			Comparisons of Wisdom	
Place	Judah					
Time	c. 950–700 B.C.					

161

Introduction and Title

The key word in Proverbs is *wisdom,* "the ability to live life skillfully." A godly life in an ungodly world, however, is no simple assignment. Proverbs provides God's detailed instructions for His people to deal successfully with the practical affairs of everyday life: how to relate to God, parents, children, neighbors, and government. Solomon, the principal author, uses a combination of poetry, parables, pithy questions, short stories, and wise maxims to give in strikingly memorable form the common sense and divine perspective necessary to handle life's issues.

Because Solomon, the pinnacle of Israel's wise men, was the principal contributor, the Hebrew title of this book is *Mishle Shelomoh,* "Proverbs of Solomon." (1:1). The Greek title is *Paroimiai Salomontos,* "Proverbs of Solomon." The Latin title *Liber Proverbiorum,* "Book of Proverbs," combines the words *pro* "for" and *verba* "words" to describe the way the proverbs concentrate many words into a few. The rabbinical writings called Proverbs *Sepher Hokhmah,* "Book of Wisdom."

Author

Solomon's name appears at the beginning of the three sections he authored: Chapter 1, verse 1 for chapters 1—9; chapter 10, verse 1 for chapters 10:1—22:16; and chapter 25, verse 1 for chapters 25—29. According to First Kings 4:32, he spoke 3,000 proverbs and 1,005 songs. Only about 800 of his 3,000 proverbs are included in the two Solomonic collections in this book. No man was better qualified than Solomon to be the principal contributor. He asked for wisdom (1 Kin. 3:5–9) and God granted it to him (1 Kin. 4:29–31) to such a degree that people from foreign lands came to hear him speak (1 Kin. 4:34; 10:1–13, 24). His breadth of knowledge, aptitude, skill, and perception were extraordinary. In every area Solomon brought prosperity and glory to Israel until his latter years (cf. 1 Kin. 11:4).

It is likely that Solomon collected and edited proverbs other than his own. According to Ecclesiastes 12:9, "he pondered and sought out *and* set in order many proverbs." The second collection of Solomonic proverbs in 25—29 was assembled by the scribes of King Hezekiah because of his interest in spiritually benefitting his subjects with the Word of God. The prophets Isaiah and Micah ministered during Hezekiah's time, and it has been suggested that they also might have been involved in this collection.

"The words of the wise" (22:17; cf. 24:23) are quite similar to those found in The Wisdom of Amenemope, a document of teachings on civil service by an Egyptian who probably lived between 1000 B.C. and 600 B.C. Wise men of this period went to hear one another, and it is probable that Amenemope borrowed certain aphorisms from Hebrew literature. If the *hakhamim* ("wise men") lived before Solomon's time, he may have been the collector and editor of his series of wise sayings.

There is no biblical information about Agur (30) or Lemuel (31). Agur teen Jakeh (30:1) is simply called an oracle, and Lemuel is called a king and an oracle (31:1). Both have been identified with Solomon, but there is no basis for this suggestion.

Date and Setting

Proverbs is a collection of topical maxims and is not a historical book. It is a product of the wisdom school in Israel. According to Jeremiah 18:18 and Ezekiel 7:26, three groups communicated to the people on behalf of God: the priests imparted the Law; the prophets communicated the divine word and visions; and the sages, or elders, gave counsel to the people. The sages provided the practical application of godly wisdom to specific problems and decisions. The "Preacher" of Ecclesiastes is a good example of the wisdom school (see Eccl. 1:1, 12; 7:27; 12:8–10). *Qoheleth,* or "Preacher," meant "one who addresses an assembly": he presided over a "school" of wise men and "taught the people knowledge" (Eccl. 12:9). "My son" in Proverbs and Ecclesiastes evidently refers to the pupil. This was parallel to Samuel's role of heading Israel's school of prophets.

Wisdom literature is also found in other countries of the ancient Near East. In Egypt, written examples can be found as early as 2700 B.C. Although the style was similar to Israel's Wisdom Literature, the proverbs and sayings of these countries differed from those of Israel in content because they lacked the character of the righteous standards of the Lord.

Solomon's proverbs were written by 931 B.C., and his proverbs in chapters 25—29 were collected by Hezekiah about 230 years later (Hezekiah reigned from 715 to 686 B.C.). Under Solomon Israel was at its spiritual, political, and economic summit. Solomon probably wrote his proverbs in his middle years, before his character began to decline into carnality, materialism, and idolatry.

Theme and Purpose

Proverbs is one of the few biblical books that clearly spells out its purpose. The purpose statement in chapter 1, verses 2—6 is twofold: (1) To impart moral discernment and discretion (1:2a,3–5); and (2) to develop mental clarity and perception (1:2b,6). The words "wisdom and instruction" (1:2a) complement each other because wisdom (*hokhmah*) means "skill," and instruction (*musar*) means "discipline." No skill is perfected without discipline, and when a person has skill he has freedom to create something beautiful. Proverbs deals with the most fundamental skill of all: practical righteousness before God in every area of life. This requires knowledge, experience, and a willingness to put God first (3:5–7). Chapters 1—9 are designed to create a felt need for wisdom and Proverbs as a whole is designed both to prevent and to remedy ungodly life-styles. The book served as a manual to impart the legacy of wisdom, prudence, understanding, discretion, knowledge, guidance, competence, correction, counsel, and truth from generation to generation.

The theme of Proverbs is: "The fear of the LORD is the beginning of knowledge" (1:7a). To fear God is to stand in awe of His righteousness, majesty, and power and to trust Him by humbly depending upon Him. There is a reciprocal relationship here, because "the fear of the LORD is the beginning [foundation] of wisdom" (9:10), but wisdom leads to the knowledge and fear of God (2:1–5).

Keys to Proverbs

Key Word: Wisdom

Key Verses (1:5–7; 3:5–6)—"A wise *man* will hear and increase learning, and a man of understanding will attain wise counsel, to understand a proverb and an enigma, the words of the wise and their riddles. The fear of the LORD is the beginning of knowledge, *but* fools despise wisdom and instruction" (1:5–7).

"Trust in the LORD with all your heart, and lean not on your own understanding; In all your ways acknowledge Him, and He shall direct your paths" (3:5–6).

Key Chapter (31)—The last chapter of Proverbs is unique in ancient literature, as it reveals a very high and noble view of women. The woman in these verses is: (1) A good woman (31:13, 15–16, 19, 25); (2) a good wife (31:11–12, 23–24); (3) a good mother (31:14–15, 18, 21, 27); and (4) a good neighbor (31:20–26). Her conduct, concern, speech, and life stand in sharp contrast to the woman pictured in chapter 7.

Christ in Proverbs

In chapter 8, wisdom is personified and seen in its perfection. It is divine (8:22–31), it is the source of biological and spiritual life (3:18; 8:35–36), it is righteous and moral (8:8–9), and it is available to all who will receive it (8:1–6, 32–35). This wisdom became incarnate in Christ "in whom are hidden all the treasures of wisdom and knowledge" (Col. 2:3). "But of Him you are in Christ Jesus, who became for us wisdom from God—and righteousness and sanctification and redemption" (1 Cor. 1:30; cf. 1 Cor. 1:22–24).

Contribution to the Bible

Proverbs along with Job and Ecclesiastes is the Wisdom Literature of the Old Testament. It is built upon the fear of Yahweh as the basis for practical holiness and skill in life. There is a universal and comprehensive tone in this book because it talks to everyone. The proverbs are generalized statements that are true to life even though individual cases may differ. Psalms emphasizes a walk before God and the devotional life, but Proverbs concentrates on a walk before men and the daily life. The proverbs are practical, moral, and concise—they should be read very slowly in small sections. Some are humorous as well (see 11:22; 19:24; 23:13,35; 24:33; 25:24; 26:13–16; 27:15–16; 30:15,21–23). There are at least fourteen New Testament quotations or allusions to the Proverbs.

James has a number of similarities to the Book of Proverbs. Compare Proverbs and James on the tongue: (a) Prov. 12:18–19 and James 1:26; (b) Prov. 15:1–2 and James 3:5; (c) Prov. 18:21; 21:6 and James 3:6; (d) Prov. 21:23 and James 1:19; 3:8; (e) Prov. 25:15 and James 3:3; and (f) Prov. 25:23 and James 4:1. The comparison of earthly and divine wisdom in James also resembles Proverbs. Man's wisdom in James 3:15–16 is: (1) earthly (Prov. 14:2); (2) natural (Prov. 7:18); (3) demonic (Prov. 27:20); (4) jealous (Prov. 6:34); (5) selfish (Prov. 28:25); (6) disorderly (Prov. 11:29); and (7) evil (Prov. 8:13). God's wisdom in James 3:17 is: (1) pure (Prov. 15:26); (2) peaceable (Prov. 3:1–2); (3) gentle (Prov. 11:2); (4) reasonable (Prov. 14:15); (5) full of mercy and good fruits (Prov. 11:17; 3:18), (6) unwavering (Prov. 21:6); and (7) without hypocrisy (Prov. 28:13).

Survey of Proverbs

Proverbs is the most intensely practical book in the Old Testament because it teaches skillful living in the multiple aspects of everyday life. Its specific precepts include instruction on wisdom and folly, the righteous and the wicked, the tongue, pride and humility, justice and vengeance, the family, laziness and work, poverty and wealth, friends and neighbors, love and lust, anger and strife, masters and servants, life and death. Proverbs touches upon every facet of human relationships, and its principles transcend the bounds of time and culture.

The Hebrew word for *proverb* (*mashal*) means "comparison, similar, parallel." A proverb uses a comparison or figure of speech to make a pithy and poignant observation. Proverbs have been defined as simple illustrations that expose fundamental realities about life. These maxims are not theoretical but practical; they are easily memorized, based on real-life experience, and designed for use in the mainstream of life. The proverbs are general statements and illustrations of timeless truth, which allow for, but do not condone, exceptions to the rule. The key word is *hokhmah,* "wisdom": it literally means "skill" (in living). Wisdom is more than shrewdness or intelligence. Instead, it relates to practical righteousness and moral acumen. The Book of Proverbs may be divided into six segments: (1) the purpose of Proverbs (1:1–7); (2) the proverbs to the youth (1:8—9:18); (3) the proverbs of Solomon (10:1—24:34); (4) the proverbs of Solomon copied by Hezekiah's men (25:1—29:27); (5) the words of Agur (30:1–33); and (6) the words of King Lemuel (31:1–31).

The Purpose of Proverbs (1:1–7): The brief prologue states the author, theme, and purpose of the book.

The Proverbs to the Youth (1:8—9:18): Following the introduction, there is a series of ten exhortations, each beginning with "My son" (1:8—9:18). These messages introduce the concept of wisdom in the format of a father's efforts to persuade his son to pursue the path of wisdom in order to achieve godly success in life. Wisdom rejects the invitation of crime and foolishness, rewards seekers of wisdom on every level, and wisdom's discipline provides freedom and safety (1—4). Wisdom protects one from illicit sensuality and its consequences, from foolish practices and laziness, and from adultery and the lure of the harlot (5—7). Wisdom is to be preferred to folly because of its divine origin and rich benefits (8—9). There are four kinds of fools, ranging from those who are naive and uncommitted to scoffers who arrogantly despise the way of God. The fool is not mentally deficient; he is self-sufficient, ordering his life as if there were no God.

The Proverbs of Solomon (10:1—24:34): There is a minimal amount of topical arrangement in these chapters. There are some thematic clusters (e.g., 26:1–12, 13–16, 20–22), but the usual units are one-verse maxims. It is helpful to assemble and organize these proverbs according to such specific themes as money and speech.

This Solomonic collection consists of 375 proverbs of Solomon. Chapters 10—15 contrast right and wrong in practice, and all but nineteen proverbs use antithetic parallelism, that is, parallels of paired opposite principles. Chapters 16:1—22:16 offer a series of self-evident moral truths and all but eighteen proverbs use synonymous parallelism, that is, parallels of paired identical or similar principles. The words of wise men (22:17—24:34) are given in two groups. The first group includes thirty distinct sayings (22:17—24:22), and six more are found in the second group (24:23–34).

The Proverbs of Solomon copied by Hezekiah's Men (25:1—29:27): This second Solomonic collection was copied and arranged by "the men of Hezekiah" (25:1). These proverbs in chapters 25—29 further develop the themes in the first Solomonic collection.

The Words of Agur (30:1–33): The last two chapters of Proverbs form an appendix of sayings by other otherwise unknown sages, Agur and Lemuel. Most of Agur's material is given in clusters of numerical proverbs.

The Words of King Lemuel (31:1–31): The last chapter includes an acrostic of twenty-two verses (the first letter of each verse consecutively follows the complete Hebrew alphabet) portraying a virtuous wife (31:10–31).

Outline of Proverbs

I. The Purpose of Proverbs, 1:1–7

II. Proverbs to the Youth, 1:8—9:18
    A. Obey Parents, 1:8–9
    B. Avoid Bad Company, 1:10–19
    C. Seek Wisdom, 1:20—2:22
    D. Benefits of Wisdom, 3:1–26
    E. Be Kind to Others, 3:27–35
    F. Father Says Get Wisdom, 4:1–13
    G. Avoid the Wicked, 4:14–22
    H. Keep Your Heart, 4:23–27
    I. Do Not Commit Adultery, 5:1–14
    J. Do Be Faithful to Your Spouse, 5:15–23
    K. Avoid Surety 6:1–5
    L. Do Not Be Lazy, 6:6–19
    M. Do Not Commit Adultery, 6:20—7:27
    N. Praise of Wisdom, 8:1—9:12
    O. Foolish Woman, 9:13–18

III. Proverbs of Solomon, 10:1—24:34
    A. Proverbs Contrasting the Godly and the Wicked, 10:1—15:33
    B. Proverbs Encouraging Godly Lives, 16:1—22:16
    C. Proverbs Concerning Various Situations, 22:17—24:34

Ecclesiastes

ECCLESIASTES IS A PROFOUND BOOK recording an intense search by the Preacher (traditionally understood to be Solomon) for meaning and satisfaction in life—in spite of the inequities, inconsistencies, and seeming absurdities of life on earth.

The key word in Ecclesiastes is vanity, the futile emptiness of trying to make sense out of life apart from God. Looked at "under the sun" (8:17), life's pursuits lead only to frustration. Power, prestige, pleasure—nothing can fill the God-shaped void in man's life—except God Himself. But seen from His perspective, life becomes meaningful and fulfilling. Skepticism and despair melt away when each day is viewed as a gift from God.

ECCLESIASTES	Focus	Thesis: "All Is Vanity"		Proof: "Life Is Vain"		Counsel: "Fear God"		
		1:1 — 1:11		1:12 — 6:12		7:1 — 12:14		
	Divisions	Introduction of Vanity	Illustration of Vanity	Proof from Scripture	Proof from Obsevations	Coping in a Wicked World	Counsel for Uncertainty	Conclusion: Fear & Obey God
		1:1 — 1:3	1:4 — 1:11	1:12 — 2:26	3:1 — 6:12	7:1 — 9:18	10:1 — 12:8	12:9 — 12:14
	Topics	Declaration of Vanity		Demonstration of Vanity		Deliverance from Vanity		
		Subject		Sermons		Summary		
	Place	Universe ("Under the Sun")						
	Time	c. 935 B.C.						

Introduction and Title

The key word in Ecclesiastes is *vanity,* the futile emptiness of trying to be happy apart from God. The Preacher (traditionally taken to be Solomon—1:1, 12—the wisest, richest, most influential king in Israel's history) looks at "life under the sun" and, from the human perspective, declares it all to be empty. Power, popularity, prestige, pleasure—nothing can fill the God-shaped void in man's life but God Himself! But once seen from God's perspective, life takes on meaning and purpose, causing Solomon to exclaim, "Eat . . . drink . . . rejoice . . . do good . . . live joyfully . . . fear God . . . keep His commandments!" Skepticism and despair melt away when life is viewed as a daily gift from God.

The Hebrew title *Qoheleth* is a rare term, found only in Ecclesiastes (see 1:1–2, 12; 7:27; 12:8–10). It comes from the word *qahal,* "to convoke an assembly, to assemble." Thus, it means "one who addresses an assembly, a preacher." The Septuagint used the Greek word *Ekklesiastes* as its title for this book. Derived from the word *ekklesia,* "assembly, congregation, church," it simply means "preacher." The Latin *Ecclesiastes* means "speaker before an assembly."

Author

There are powerful arguments that the author of Ecclesiastes was Solomon.

External Evidence: Jewish talmudic tradition attributes the book to Solomon but suggests that Hezekiah's scribes may have edited the text (see Prov. 25:1). Solomonic authorship of Ecclesiastes is the standard Christian position, although some scholars, along with the Talmud, believe the work was later edited during the time of Hezekiah or possibly Ezra.

Internal Evidence: The author calls himself "the son of David, king in Jerusalem" (1:1, 12). Solomon was the best qualified Davidic descendant for the quest in this book. He was the wisest man who ever taught in Jerusalem (see 1:16; 1 Kin. 4:29–30). The descriptions of Qoheleth's exploration of pleasure (2:1–3), impressive accomplishments (2:4–6), and unparalleled wealth (2:7–10) were fulfilled only by King Solomon. The proverbs in this book are similar to those in the Book of Proverbs (e.g., 7; 10). According to chapter 12, verse 9, Qoheleth collected and arranged many proverbs, perhaps referring to the two Solomonic collections in Proverbs. The unity of authorship of Ecclesiastes is supported by the seven references to Qoheleth.

Date and Setting

Some scholars argue that the literary forms in Ecclesiastes are postexilic; but they are, in fact, unique, and cannot be used in dating this book. The phrase "all who were before me in Jerusalem" (1:16) has been used to suggest a date after Solomon's time, but there were many kings and wise men in Jerusalem before the time of Solomon. However, Solomon was the only son of David who reigned over Israel from Jerusalem (1:12).

Ecclesiastes was probably written late in Solomon's life, about 935 B.C. If this is so, the great glory that Solomon ushered in early in his reign was already beginning to fade; and the disruption of Israel into two kingdoms would soon take place. Jewish tradition asserts that Solomon wrote Song of Solomon in his youthful years, Proverbs in his middle years, and Ecclesiastes in his last years. This book may be expressing his regret for his folly and wasted time due to carnality and idolatry (cf. 1 Kin. 11).

There are no references to historical events other than to personal aspects of Qoheleth's life. The location was Jerusalem (1:1, 12, 16), the seat of Israel's rule and authority.

Theme and Purpose

Eccclesiastes reports the results of a diligent quest for purpose, meaning, and satisfaction in human life. The Preacher poignantly sees the emptiness and futility of power, popularity, prestige, and pleasure apart from God. The word *vanity* appears thirty-seven times to express the many things that cannot be understood about life. All earthly goals and ambitions when pursued as ends in themselves lead to dissatisfaction and frustration. Life "under the sun" (used twenty-nine times) seems to be filled with inequities, uncertainties, changes in fortune, and violations of justice. But Ecclesiastes does not give an answer of atheism or skepticism; God is referred to throughout. In fact, it claims that the search for man's *summum bonum* must end in God. Satisfaction in life can only be found by looking beyond this world. Ecclesiastes gives an analysis of negative themes but it also develops the positive theme of overcoming the vanities of life by fearing a God who is good, just, and sovereign (12:13–14). Wisdom involves seeing life from a divine perspective and trusting God in the face of apparent futility and lack of purpose. Life is a daily gift from God and it should be enjoyed as much as possible (see 2:24–26; 3:12–13, 22; 5:18–20; 8:15; 9:7–10; 11:8–9). Our comprehension is indeed limited, but there are many things we *can* understand. Qoheleth recognized that God will ultimately judge all people. Therefore he exhorted: "fear God and keep His commandments" (12:13).

Keys to Ecclesiastes

Key Word: Vanity

Key Verses (2:24; 12:13–14)—"There is nothing better for a man *than* that he should eat and drink, and *that* his soul should enjoy good in his labor. This also, I saw, was from the hand of God" (2:24).

Let us hear the conclusion of the whole matter: "Fear God and keep His commandments, for this is the whole duty of man. For God will bring every work into judgment, including every secret thing, whether *it is* good or whether *it is* evil" (12:13–14).

Key Chapter (12)—At the end of the Book of Ecclesiastes, the Preacher looks at life through "binoculars." On the other hand, from the perspective of the natural man who only sees life "under the sun," the conclusion is, "all *is* vanity." Life's every activity, even though pleasant for the moment, becomes purposeless and futile when viewed as an end in itself.

The Preacher carefully documents the latter view with a long list of his own personal pursuits in life. No amount of activities or possessions has satisfied the craving of his heart. Every earthly prescription for happiness has left the same bitter aftertaste. Only when the Preacher views his life from God's perspective "above the sun" does it take on meaning as a precious gift "from the hand of God" (2:24).

Chapter 12 resolves the book's extensive inquiry into the meaning of life with the single conclusion, "Fear God and keep His commandments, for this is the whole duty of man" (12:13).

Christ in Ecclesiastes

Ecclesiastes convincingly portrays the emptiness and perplexity of life without a relationship with the Lord. Each person has eternity in his heart (3:11), and only Christ can provide ultimate satisfaction, joy, and wisdom. Man's highest good is found in the "one Shepherd" (12:11) who offers abundant life (see John 10:9–10).

Contribution to the Bible

Ecclesiastes is the most philosophical book in the Bible, and its perspective is that of human wisdom (1:13, 16–17) more than the divine "Thus says the LORD." Because of its point of view, the book contains several statements that contradict the general teaching of Scripture when used out of context (see 1:15; 2:24; 3:19–20; 7:16–17; 8:15; 9:2, 5; 10:19; 11:9). Thus, there was a running debate over officially recognizing it as part of the Old Testament canon until Jewish scholars finally settled it in the Council of Jamnia (c. A.D. 90). Different positions continue to be held concerning its inspiration. (1) Some believe it is uninspired because of its fatalism (3:15), pessimism (4:2), hedonism (2:24; 8:15), and materialism (3:19–21). It is a naturalistic work with some references to God. (2) Others believe the book is partly inspired as the best that the human mind can produce apart from God. The concluding exhortation to fear God (12:13–14) is the key to the book. (3) Ecclesiastes has difficult passages because of its vantage point, but it is inspired. For example, chapter 3, verses 19–20, say that the deaths of men and animals are alike; both go to the grave. But this does not teach that there is no afterlife. It is a true statement—humans and animals die, decompose, and disappear. The apparent problems caused by Ecclesiastes are overcome when the purpose of the author and the fact of progressive revelation are taken into account.

Ecclesiastes develops clear truths about God and man: God's existence (3:14; 5:2); God's sovereignty and power (6:2; 7:13; 9:1); God's justice (5:8; 8:12–13); man's sinfulness (7:20; 9:3); man's finiteness (8:8,17); man's duty (9:7–10; 12:13); man's immortality (3:11; 12:7); and divine punishment and rewards (2:26; 3:17; 8:12; 11:9; 12:14). The exclusive use of *Elohim* ("God," forty-one times) rather than *Yahweh* ("LORD") shows that the Creator/creature relationship rather than the Redeemer/redeemed relationship is being considered. Qoheleth's search shows that empiricism (1—2) and rationalism (3—12) are not enough without the third way of knowing—revelation.

This series of sermons by the Preacher illustrates that life under the sun is futile without a relationship with the One who made the sun.

Life Under the Sun	Life Under the *Son*
1:3 What advantage is work under the sun	He who has begun a good work in you will complete *it* until the day of Jesus Christ (Phil. 1:6)
1:9 Nothing new under the sun	Therefore, if anyone *is* in Christ, *he is* a creation . . . all things have become new (2 Cor. 5:17)
1:14 All deeds are vanity under the sun	Be steadfast, immovable . . . knowing that your labor is not in vain in the Lord (1 Cor. 15:58)
2:18 The fruit of labor is hated under the sun	Being fruitful in every good work and increasing in the knowledge of God (Col. 1:10)
6:12 Man is mortal under the sun	Whoever believes in Him should not perish but have everlasting life (John 3:16)
8:15 Pleasure is temporary under the sun	For it is God who works in you both to will and to do for *His* good pleasure (Phil. 2:13)
8:17 Man cannot discover God's work under the sun	Now I know in part, but then I shall know just as I also am known (1 Cor. 13:12)
9:3 All men die under the sun	God has given us eternal life, and this life is in His Son (1 John 5:11)
9:11 Strength and speed under the sun	God has chosen the weak things of the world to put to shame the things which are mighty (1 Cor. 1:27)
12:2 Life under the sun will cease	That you may know that you have eternal life (1 John 5:13)

Survey of Ecclesiastes

Ecclesiastes is a profound and problematic book. It is the record of an intense search for meaning and satisfaction in life on this earth, especially in view of all the iniquities and apparent absurdities that surround us. It takes the perspective of the greatest answers that wisdom under the sun can produce. If the Preacher is identified as Solomon, Ecclesiastes was written from a unique vantage point. Possessing the greatest mental, material, and political resources ever combined in one man, he was qualified beyond all others to write this book. Ecclesiastes is extremely difficult to synthesize, and several alternate approaches have been used. The one used here is:

the thesis that "all is vanity" (1:1–11), the proof that "all *is* vanity" (1:12—6:12), the counsel for living with vanity (7:1—12:14).

The Thesis that "All Is Vanity" (1:1–11): After a one-verse introduction, the Preacher states his theme: "Vanity of vanities, all *is* vanity" (1:2). Life under the sun appears to be futile and perplexing. Verses 3–11 illustrate this theme in the endless and apparently meaningless cycles found in nature and history.

The Proof that "All Is Vanity" (1:12—6:12): The Preacher describes his multiple quest for meaning and satisfaction as he explores his vast personal resources. He begins with wisdom (1:12–18) but finds that "he who increases knowledge increases sorrow." Due to his intense perception of reality he experiences just the reverse of "ignorance is bliss." The Preacher moves from wisdom to laughter, hedonism, and wine (2:1–3) and then turns to works, women, and wealth (2:4–11); but all lead to emptiness. He realizes that wisdom is far greater than foolishness, but both seem to lead to futility in view of the brevity of life and universality of death (2:12–17). He concludes by acknowledging that contentment and joy are found only in God.

At this point, Ecclesiastes turns from his situation in life to a philosophical quest; but the conclusion remains the same. The Preacher considers the unchanging order of events and the fixed laws of God. Time is short, and there is no eternity on earth (3:1–15). The futility of death seems to cancel the difference between righteousness and wickedness (3:16–22). Chapters 4—5 explore the futility in social relationships (oppression, rivalry, covetousness, power) and in religious relationships (formalism, empty prayer, vows). In addition, the world's offerings produce disappointment, not satisfaction. Ultimate meaning can be found only in God.

The Counsel for Living with Vanity (7:1—12:14): A series of lessons on practical wisdom (7:1—9:12) portrays levity and pleasure-seeking as superficial and foolish; it is better to have sober depth of thought. Wisdom and self-control provide perspective and strength in coping with life. One should enjoy prosperity, and consider in adversity that God made both. Avoid the twin extremes of self-righteousness and immorality. Sin invades all men, and wisdom is cut short by evil and death. The human mind cannot grasp ultimate meaning. Submission to authority helps one avoid unnecessary hardship, but real justice is often lacking on earth. The uncertainties of life and certainty of the grave show that God's purposes and ways often cannot be grasped. One should, therefore, magnify opportunities while they last, because fortune can change suddenly.

Wisdom, the most powerful human resource, is contrasted with the meaningless talk and effort of fools (9:13—11:6). In view of the unpredictability of circumstances, wisdom is the best course to follow in order to minimize grief and misfortune. Wisdom involves discipline and diligence. The Preacher offers exhortations on using life well (11:7—12:7). Youth is too brief and precious to be squandered in foolishness or evil. A person should live well in the fullness of each day before God and acknowledge Him early in life. This section closes with an exquisite allegory of old age (12:1–7).

The Preacher concludes that the "good life" is only attained by revering God. Those who fail to take God and His will seriously into account are doomed to lives of foolishness and futility. Life will not wait upon the solution of all its problems; nevertheless, real meaning can be found by looking not "under the sun" but beyond the sun to the "one Shepherd" (12:11).

Outline of Ecclesiastes

Part One: The Thesis that "All Is Vanity" (1:1–11)

I. Introduction of Vanity, 1:1–3

II. Illustrations of Vanity, 1:4–11

Part Two: The Proof that "All Is Vanity" (1:12—6:12)

I. Proof of "All Is Vanity" from Experience, 1:12—2:26
   A. Vanity of Striving after Wisdom, 1:12–18
   B. Vanity of Striving after Pleasure, 2:1–3
   C. Vanity of Great Accomplishments, 2:4–17
   D. Vanity of Hard Labor, 2:18–23
   E. Conclusion: Be Content, 2:24–26

II. Proof of "All Is Vanity" from Observation, 3:1—6:12
   A. Immutability of God's Program, 3:1–22
      1. God Predetermines the Events of Life, 3:1–9
      2. God Predetermines the Conditions of Life, 3:10–15
      3. God Judges All, 3:16–22
   B. Inequalities of Life, 4:1–16
      1. Evil Oppression, 4:1–3
      2. Folly of Hard Work, 4:4–12
      3. Transience of Popularity, 4:13–16
   C. Insufficiencies of Human Religion, 5:1–7
   D. Insufficiencies of Wealth, 5:8–20
      1. Wealth Does Not Satisfy, 5:8–12
      2. Wealth Brings Difficulties, 5:13–17
      3. Wealth Comes Ultimately from God, 5:18–20
   E. Inescapable Vanity of Life, 6:1–12
      1. No Satisfaction in Wealth, 6:1–2
      2. No Satisfaction in Children, 6:3–6
      3. No Satisfaction in Labor, 6:7–8
      4. No Satisfaction in the Future, 6:9–12

Part Three: The Counsel for Living with Vanity (7:1—12:14)

I. Coping in a Wicked World, 7:1—9:18
   A. Wisdom and Folly Contrasted, 7:1–14
   B. Wisdom of Moderation, 7:15–18

Song of Solomon

SONG OF SOLOMON IS A LOVE SONG written by Solomon (1:1) and abounding in metaphors and oriental imagery. Historically, it depicts the wooing and wedding of a shepherdess by King Solomon, and the joys and heartaches of wedded love.

Allegorically, it pictures Israel as God's espoused bride (see Hosea 2:19–20), and the church as the bride of Christ. As human life finds its highest fulfillment in the love of man and woman, so spiritual life finds its highest fulfillment in the love of God for His people and Christ for His church.

The book is arranged like scenes in a drama with three main speakers: the bride (Shulamite), the king (Solomon), and a chorus (daughters of Jerusalem).

SONG OF SOLOMON					
Focus	**Beginning of Love** 1:1 — 5:1		**Broadening of Love** 5:2 — 8:14		
Divisions	Falling in Love 1:1 — 3:5	United in Love 3:6 — 5:1	Struggling in Love 5:2 — 7:10	Growing in Love 7:11 — 8:14	
Topics	Courtship	Wedding	Problem	Progress	
	Fostering of Love	Fulfillment of Love	Frustration of Love	Faithfulness of Love	
Place	Israel				
Time	c. 1 Year				

Introduction and Title

The Song of Solomon is a love song written by Solomon and abounding in metaphors and oriental imagery. Historically, it depicts the wooing and wedding of a shepherdess by King Solomon, and the joys and heartaches of wedded love.

Allegorically, it pictures Israel as God's espoused bride (Hos. 2:19–20), and the church as the bride of Christ. As human life finds its highest fulfillment in the love of man and woman, so spiritual life finds its highest fulfillment in the love of God for His people and Christ for His Church.

The book is arranged like scenes in a drama with three main speakers: the bride (Shulamite), the king (Solomon), and a chorus (daughters of Jerusalem).

The Hebrew title *Shir Hashirim* comes from chapter 1, verse 1, "The song of songs." This is in the superlative and speaks of Solomon's most exquisite song. The Greek title *Asma Asmaton* and the Latin *Canticum Canticorum* also mean "Song of Songs" or "The Best Song." The name *Canticles* ("Songs") is derived from the Latin title. Because Solomon is mentioned in chapter 1, verse 1, the book is also known as the Song of Solomon.

Author

Solomonic authorship is rejected by critics who claim it is a later collection of songs. Many take chapter 1, verse 1, to mean "which is about or concerning Solomon." But the internal evidence of the book strongly favors the traditional position that Solomon is its author. Solomon is specifically mentioned seven times (1:1, 5; 3:7, 9, 11; 8:11–12), and he is identified as the groom. There is evidence of royal luxury and rich imported goods (e.g., 3:6–11). The king by this time also had sixty queens and eighty concubines (6:8). Solomon's harem at its fullest extent reached seven hundred queens and three hundred concubines (1 Kin. 11:3).

First Kings 4:32–33 says that Solomon composed 1,005 songs and had intimate knowledge of the plant and animal world. This greatest of his songs alludes to twenty-one species of plants and fifteen species of animals. It cites geographical locations in the north and in the south, indicating that they were still one kingdom. For example, chapter 6, verse 4, mentions both Tirzah and Jerusalem, the northern and southern capitals (after Solomon's time, Samaria became the northern capital). Because of the poetic imagery, the Song of Solomon uses forty-nine words that occur nowhere else in Scripture.

Date and Setting

This song was written primarily from the point of view of the Shulamite, but Solomon was its author, probably early in his reign, about 965 B.C. There is a problem regarding how a man with a harem of 140 women (6:8) could extol the love of the Shulamite as though she was his only bride. It may be that Solomon's relationship with the Shulamite was the only pure romance he ever experienced. The bulk of his marriages were political arrangements. It is significant that the Shulamite was a vineyard keeper of no great means. This book was also written before Solomon plunged into gross immorality and idolatry. "For it was so, when Solomon was old, that his wives turned his heart after other gods; and his heart was not loyal to the LORD his God" (1 Kin. 11:4).

The Shulamite addresses the king as "my beloved" and the king addresses his bride as "my love." The daughters of Jerusalem were probably attendants to the Shulamite. The term *Shulamite* appears only once (6:13), and it may be derived from the town of Shunem which was southwest of the Sea of Galilee in the tribal area of Issachar. The song refers to fifteen geographic locations from Lebanon in the north to Egypt in the south: Kedar (1:5); Egypt (1:9); En Gedi (1:14); Sharon (2:1); Jerusalem (2:7); Lebanon (3:9); Mount Gilead (4:1); Amana (4:8); Shenir (4:8); Hermon (4:8); Tirzah (6:4); Heshbon (7:4); Damascus (7:4); Mount Carmel (7:5); and Baal Hamon (8:11).

Theme and Purpose

The purpose of this book depends on the viewpoint taken as to its primary thrust. Is it fictional, allegorical, or historical? (1) *Fictional:* Some hold that this song is a fictional drama that portrays Solomon's courtship of and marriage to a poor but beautiful girl from the country. But the book gives every indication that the story really happened. (2) *Allegorical:* In this view, the primary purpose of the Song was to illustrate the truth of God's love for His people whether the events were fictional or not. Some commentators insist that the book is indeed historical but its primary purpose is typical, that is, to present Yahweh's love for His bride Israel and/or Christ's love for His Church. But this interpretation is subjective and lacking in evidence. There are other places in Scripture where the husband/wife relationship is used symbolically (cf. Ezek. 16; 23; Hos. 1—3), but these are always indicated as symbols. This may be an application of the book but it should not be the primary interpretation. (3) *Historical;* The Song of Songs is a poetic record of Solomon's actual romance with a Shulamite woman. The various scenes in the book exalt the joys of love in courtship and marriage and teach that physical beauty and sexuality in marriage should not be despised as base or unspiritual. It offers a proper perspective of human love and avoids the extremes of lust and asceticism. Only when sexuality was viewed in the wrong way as something akin to evil was an attempt made to allegorize the book. But this is part of God's creation with its related desires and pleasures, and it is reasonable that He would provide us with a guide to a pure sexual relationship between a husband and wife. In fact, the union of the two sexes was originally intended to illustrate the oneness of the Godhead (see Gen. 1:27; 2:24; 1 Cor. 6:16–20). Thus, the Song is a bold and positive endorsement by God of marital love in all its physical and emotional beauty. This interpretation does not mean that the book has no spiritual illustrations and applications. It certainly illustrates God's love for His covenant people Israel, and anticipates Christ's love for His bride, the church.

Keys to Song of Solomon

Key Word: Love

Key Verses (7:10; 8:7)—"I *am* my beloved's, and his desire *is* toward me" (7:10).

"Many waters cannot quench love, nor can the floods drown it. If a man would give for love all the wealth of his house, it would be utterly despised" (8:7).

Key Chapter—Since the whole book is a unity, there is no Key Chapter; rather, all eight beautifully depict the love of a married couple.

Christ in Song of Solomon

In the Old Testament, Israel is regarded as the bride of Yahweh (see Is. 54:5–6, Jer. 2:2; Ezek. 16:8–14; Hos. 2:16–20). In the New Testament, the church is seen as the bride of Christ (see 2 Cor. 11:2; Eph. 5:23–25; Rev. 19:7–9; 21:9). The Song of Solomon illustrates the former and anticipates the latter.

Contribution to the Bible

The Song is a unit rather than a collection of songs. It is a dramatic poem built on a dialogue between the same two characters (and an occasional chorus) throughout. There is a continuity of style, imagery, and expression in this unique biblical book. Solomon emphasized the intellect in Ecclesiastes, but the emotions clearly dominate his Song.

This book was one of the *antilegomena* ("spoken against")—its inclusion in the canon of Scripture was delayed because of questions over its religious value, its use of God's name only once (8:6), its unusual subject matter, and the lack of quotations of the Song in the rest of the Scripture. The Song has traditionally been read at the Feast of the Passover.

Survey of Song of Solomon

Solomon wrote 1,005 songs (1 Kin. 4:32), but this beautiful eulogy of love stood out among them as the "song of songs" (1:1). The great literary value of this song can be seen in its rich use of metaphor and oriental imagery as it extols the purity, beauty, and satisfaction of love. It is never crass, but often intimate, as it explores the dimensions of the relationship between two lovers: attraction, desire, companionship, pleasure, union, separation, faithfulness, and praise. Like Ecclesiastes, this little book is not easily outlined, and various schemes can be used. It abounds with sudden changes of speakers, and they are not identified. The beginning of love is seen first (1:1—5:1), and then broadening of love (5:2—8:14).

The Beginning of Love (1:1—5:1): King Solomon has a vineyard in the country of the Shulamite (6:13; 8:11). The Shulamite must work in the vineyard with her brothers (1:6; 8:11–12); and when Solomon visits the area, he wins her heart and eventually takes her to the palace in Jerusalem as his bride. She is tanned from hours of work outside in the vineyard, but she is "fairest among women" (1:8).

This song is arranged like scenes in a one-act drama with three main speakers—

the bride (the Shulamite), the king (Solomon), and a chorus (the daughters of Jerusalem). It is not always clear who is speaking, but this is a likely arrangement:

The bride: 1:2–4, 5–7, 12–14, 16–17; 2:1, 3–6, 8–17; 3:1–4; 4:16; 5:2–8, 10–16; 6:2–3, 11–12; 7:9–13; 8:1–3, 6–7, 10–12, 14.
The groom: 1:8–10, 15; 2:2, 7; 3:5; 4:1–15; 5:1; 6:4–10, 13; 7:1–9; 8:4–5, 13.
The chorus: 1:4, 11; 3:6–11; 5:9; 6:1, 13; 8:5, 8–9.

Chapters 1—3 give a series of recollections of the courtship: (1) The bride's longing for affection at the palace before the wedding (1:2–8); (2) expressions of mutual love in the banquet hall (1:9—2:7); (3) a springtime visit of the king to the bride's home in the country (2:8–17); (4) the Shulamite dream of separation from her beloved (3:1–5); and (5) the ornate wedding procession from the bride's home to Jerusalem (3:6–11).

Solomon praises his bride from head to foot with a superb chain of similes and metaphors (4:1—5:1). Her virginity is compared to "a garden enclosed" (4:12), and the garden is entered when the marriage is consummated (4:16—5:1). The union is commended, possibly by God, in 5:1.

The Broadening of Love (5:2—8:14): Some time after the wedding, the Shulamite has a troubled dream (5:2) in the palace while Solomon is away. In her dream Solomon comes to her door but she answers too late—he is gone. She panics and searches for him late at night in Jerusalem. Upon his return, Solomon assures her of his love and praises her beauty (6:4—7:10). The Shulamite begins to think of her country home and tries to persuade her beloved to return there with her (7:11—8:4). The journey takes place in 8:5–7 and their relationship continues to deepen. Their love will not be overthrown by jealousy or circumstances. At her homecoming (8:8–14) the Shulamite reflects on her brothers' care for her when she was young (8:8–9). She remains virtuous ("I *am* a wall," 8:10) and is now in a position to look out for her brothers' welfare (8:11–12). The song concludes with a dual invitation of lover and beloved (8:13–14).

Outline of Song of Solomon

I. The Beginning of Love, 1:1—5:1
  A. Falling in Love, 1:1—3:5
    1. Bride's Longing for Affection, 1:1–8
    2. Expressions of Mutual Love, 1:9—2:7
    3. Visit of the King to the Bride's Home, 2:8–17
    4. Bride's Dream of Separation, 3:1–5
  B. United in Love, 3:6—5:1
    1. Wedding Procession, 3:6–11
    2. Bride's Beauty Is Praised, 4:1–15
    3. The Marriage Is Consummated, 4:16—5:1

II. Broadening of Love, 5:2—8:14
- A. Struggling in Love, 5:2—7:10
  1. Bride's Second Dream of Separation, 5:2–7
  2. Bridegroom's Handsomeness Is Praised, 5:8—6:3
  3. Bride's Beauty Is Praised, 6:4—7:10
- B. Growing in Love, 7:11—8:14
  1. Bride's Desire to Visit Her Home, 7:11—8:4
  2. Journey and Homecoming, 8:5–14

The Feasts of Israel

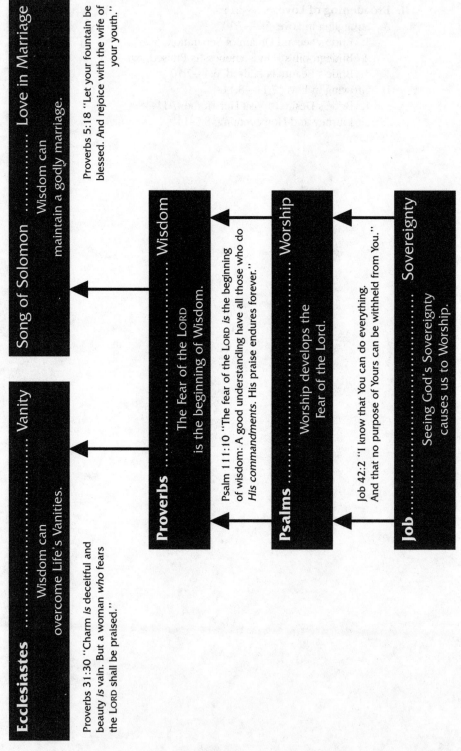

Ecclesiastes .... Vanity
Wisdom can overcome Life's Vanities.

Proverbs 31:30 "Charm *is* deceitful and beauty *is* vain. But a woman *who* fears the LORD shall be praised."

Song of Solomon .... Love in Marriage
Wisdom can maintain a godly marriage.

Proverbs 5:18 "Let your fountain be blessed. And rejoice with the wife of your youth."

Proverbs .... Wisdom
The Fear of the LORD is the beginning of Wisdom.

Psalm 111:10 "The fear of the LORD *is* the beginning of wisdom: A good understanding have all those who do *His commandments.* His praise endures forever."

Psalms .... Worship
Worship develops the Fear of the Lord.

Job 42:2 "I know that You can do everything. And that no purpose of Yours can be withheld from You."

Job .... Sovereignty
Seeing God's Sovereignty causes us to Worship.

Integration of the Old Testament

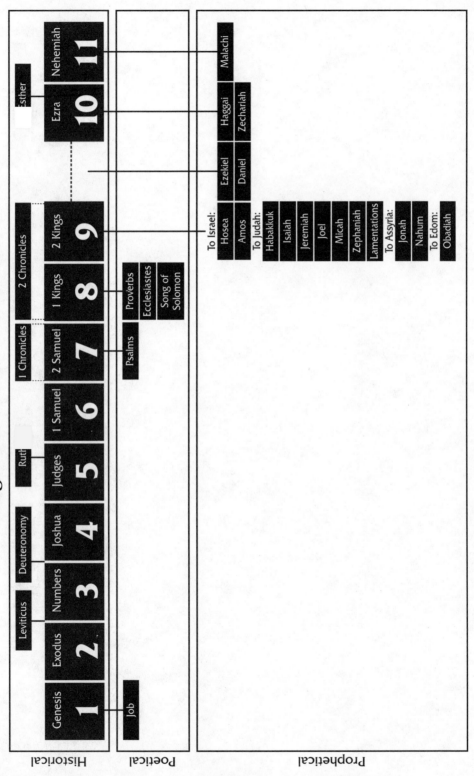

Historical

Genesis	Exodus	Leviticus	Numbers	Deuteronomy	Joshua	Judges	Ruth	1 Samuel	2 Samuel	1 Chronicles	1 Kings	2 Chronicles	2 Kings	Ezra	Esther	Nehemiah
1	**2**		**3**		**4**	**5**		**6**	**7**		**8**		**9**	**10**		**11**

Poetical

Job
Psalms
Proverbs
Ecclesiastes
Song of Solomon

Prophetical

To Israel:
Hosea
Amos

To Judah:
Habakkuk
Isaiah
Jeremiah
Joel
Micah
Zephaniah
Lamentations

To Assyria:
Jonah
Nahum

To Edom:
Obadiah

Ezekiel
Daniel

Haggai
Zechariah

Malachi

183

Introduction to the
Major Prophets

The Prophets as a Whole

THE SEVENTEEN PROPHETICAL BOOKS comprise about one-fourth of Scripture and are crucial from a theological and historical point of view. Yet their message and meaning evade more people than any other section of the Bible, principally because of neglect.

Designation

The second division of the Hebrew Bible was known as the Prophets and consisted of the Former Prophets and Latter Prophets. The Former Prophets were actually the historical books of Joshua, Judges, Samuel, and Kings. These books chronicled God's dealings with the theocratic nation from the time of Joshua to the Babylonian captivity. Thus, they furnish the background to the writing prophets. The Latter Prophets are Isaiah, Jeremiah, Ezekiel, and the twelve minor prophets. The term "latter" speaks more of their place in the canon than of chronology. These prophets left written records of their ministry, but the oral prophets (e.g., Nathan, Ahijah, Iddo, Jehu, Elijah, Elisha, Oded, Shemaiah, Azariah, Hanani, Jahaziel, and Huldah) left no records that survived. The writing prophets were later divided into the Major and Minor Prophets as we know them today. The Major Prophets were so designated because of their greater length (Lamentations excepted).

Characteristics

These men were called prophets, seers, watchmen, men of God, messengers, and servants of the Lord. The most frequently used title is *nabi,* "prophet" (over three hundred times), referring to one who has been called or appointed to proclaim the message of God Himself. The word *roeh,* "seer" speaks of one who perceives things that are not in the realm of natural sight or hearing. The English word "prophet" is derived from two Greek words that literally mean "speak for." This emphasizes the role of these people as divinely chosen spokesmen who received and related God's messages, whether in oral, visual, or written form. God communicated to them through a variety of means including dreams, visions, angels, nature, miracles, and an audible voice.

Samuel was, in a sense, the first of the real prophets (see Acts 3:24; 13:20; Heb. 11:32). He was the first to create a colony of prophets, and he presided over them at Ramah (1 Sam. 19:20). True prophets were divinely called and endowed with special abilities. Because of their moral and spiritual message which was grounded in the Law, their lives had to be consistent with their words. Deuteronomy 18:18–20 prescribed that a true prophet would speak in Yahweh's name and that his prophecies must be completely accurate.

Message

Although the prophets had a ministry of *foretelling* future events, their primary role was that of *forthtelling*. This demanded spiritual insight as well as foresight, because they proclaimed the consequences of specific attitudes and practices of their day. They dipped into the past for lessons and exhortations concerning the present. And they spoke of the need of present reforms to avert future judgment. The prophetic message had four major themes: (1) The prophets exposed the sinful practices of the people. It required considerable courage to tell the people what they needed to hear instead of succumbing to the temptation of telling them what they wanted to hear. God's messengers could not compromise their harsh treatment of sin as sin, knowing that the only hope for the people was a humble turning to the Lord and acknowledgment of their guilt. Like watchmen who alerted the people of coming danger, their messages were very practical. (2) The prophets called the people back to the moral, civil, and ceremonial law of God. They reminded the people about the character of God and urged them to trust Him with all their hearts. God has a rich purpose for them, but they must believe and obey Him. (3) They warned the people of coming judgment. God must condemn the nation if its princes, priests, and people continue to arrogantly reject God's moral and spiritual principles. They are responsible for their disobedience to their covenant commitment with God. Yahweh is the sovereign Lord of history, and the gentile nations will also be judged if they rebel against His dominion. (4) The prophets anticipated the coming Messiah. History is linear, not cyclical. It has a definite goal, and God will sovereignly move all things to a consummation in the messianic age. His name will be honored and His voice obeyed by all people of the earth. Biblical prophecy is unique because of its clarity and specific fulfillment. Over three hundred Old Testament prophecies were precisely fulfilled by Messiah in His first advent, and over four hundred more remain to be fulfilled when He comes again. "To Him all the prophets bear witness" (Acts 10:43).

In short, the prophetic message is twofold: condemnation because of the sin of man, but consolation because of the grace of God.

Interpretation

The prophets spoke in the context and background of their times, and it is important to understand their historical and cultural circumstances. They emphasized four chronological points—their own day, the Captivity and return, the first coming of Christ, and the messianic kingdom. The chronology was not as important in their minds as the events themselves, and they sometimes blurred the distinctions between these four periods. Some events were literally fulfilled, some were partially fulfilled, and some are yet unfulfilled. Their messages use symbols and figures of speech, but they point to real events.

There is a great diversity and individuality among the prophets ranging from the sophistication of Isaiah to the simplicity of Amos. Their personalities, backgrounds, interests, and writing styles vary widely, but they shared a common conviction, courage, and commitment. They wrote from the ninth to the fifth centuries B.C. and spanned God's program from their day to the new heaven and new earth. Of the seventeen prophetic books, twelve were preexilic, two were exilic, and three were postexilic.

THE MAJOR PROPHETS

Isaiah

This pinnacle of the prophets has a twofold message of condemnation (1—39) and consolation (40—66). Isaiah analyzes the sins of Judah and pronounces God's judgment on the nation. He broadens his scope to include judgment on the surrounding nations and moves to universal judgment followed by blessing. After a historical parenthesis concerning King Hezekiah, Isaiah consoles the people with a message of future salvation and restoration. Yahweh is the sovereign Savior who will rescue His people.

Jeremiah

Judah had reached the depths of moral and spiritual decay, and Jeremiah was called to the heartbreaking and unpopular ministry of declaring the certain judgment of God against the nation. Jeremiah faithfully ministered in spite of rejection and persecution, and the dreaded day finally came. Judah's defiance of God's holiness led to her downfall, but God graciously promised to establish a new covenant with His people.

Lamentations

This beautifully structured series of five lament poems is Judah's funeral for the fallen city of Jerusalem. After his forty years of warning, Jeremiah's awful words came true. His sorrow is obvious in his vivid descriptions of the defeat, destruction, and desolation of Jerusalem.

Ezekiel

The prophet Ezekiel ministered to the Jewish captives in Babylon before and after the fall of Jerusalem. Like Jeremiah, he had to convince the people that the city was doomed and that the Captivity would not be brief. Ezekiel also described the fate of Judah's foes and ended with a great apocalyptic vision of Judah's future.

Daniel

This crucial book abounds with detailed prophecies and visions of the future. It outlines God's sovereign plan for the gentile nations (2—7) and moves on to a portrait of Israel during the time of gentile domination (8—12). At a time when the Jews had little hope, Daniel provided encouragement by revealing God's power and plans for their future.

Isaiah

ISAIAH, THE "MOUNT EVEREST of Hebrew prophecy," resembles the Bible in miniature. Its first thirty-nine chapters correspond to the thirty-nine books of the Old Testament and stress the righteousness, holiness, and justice of God. The prophet announces judgment upon immoral and idolatrous people beginning with Judah, then Judah's neighboring nations, and finally the whole world. Surely there is cause to groan under God's chastening hand.

But the last twenty-seven chapters correspond to the twenty-seven books of the New Testament and portray God's glory, compassion, and undeserved favor. Messiah will come as a Savior to bear a cross and as a Sovereign to wear a crown. Therefore, " 'Comfort, yes comfort My people!' says your God" (40:1).

Focus	Prophecies of Condemnation					Historical Parenthesis	Prophecies of Comfort		
	1:1				35:10	36:1　　　39:8	40:1		66:24
Divisions	Prophecies Against Judah	Prophecies Against the Nation	Prophecies of the Day of the Lord	Prophecies of Judgment and Blessing		Hezekiah's Salvation, Sickness and Sin	Israel's Deliverance	Israel's Deliverer	Israel's Glorious Future
	1:1　12:6	13:1　23:18	24:1　27:13	28:1　35:10		36:1　　　39:8	40:1　48:22	49:1　57:21	58:1　66:24
Topics	Prophetic					Historic	Messianic		
	Judgment					Transition	Hope		
Place	Israel & Judah								
Time	740–680 B.C.								

Introduction and Title

Isaiah is like a miniature Bible. The first thirty-nine chapters (like the thirty-nine books of the Old Testament) are filled with judgment upon immoral and idolatrous men. Judah has sinned; the surrounding nations have sinned; the whole earth has sinned. Judgment must come, for God cannot allow such blatant sin to go unpunished forever. But the final twenty-seven chapters (like the twenty-seven books of the New Testament) declare a message of hope. The Messiah is coming as a Savior and a Sovereign to bear a cross and to wear a crown.

Isaiah's prophetic ministry, spanning the reigns of four kings of Judah, covers at least forty years.

Yesha'yahu and its shortened form *yeshaiah* mean "Yahweh is Salvation." This name is an excellent summary of the contents of the book. The Greek form in the Septuagint is *Hesaias,* and the Latin form is *Esaias* or *Isaias.*

Author

Isaiah, the "Saint Paul of the Old Testament," was evidently from a distinguished Jewish family. His education is evident in his impressive vocabulary and style. His work is comprehensive in scope and beautifully communicated. Isaiah maintained close contact with the royal court, but his exhortations against alliances with foreign powers were not always well received. This great poet and prophet was uncompromising, sincere, and compassionate. His wife was a prophetess and he fathered at least two sons (7:3; 8:3). He spent most of his time in Jerusalem, and talmudic tradition says his persecutors sawed him in two during the reign of Manasseh (cf. Heb. 11:37).

The unity of this book has been challenged by critics who hold that a "Deutero-Isaiah" wrote chapters 40—66 after the Babylonian captivity. They argue that chapters 1—39 have an Assyrian background, while chapters 40—66 are set against a Babylonian background. But Babylon is mentioned more than twice as often in chapters 1—39 as in chapters 40—66. The only shift is one of perspective from present time to future time. Critics also argue that there are radical differences in the language, style, and theology of the two sections. Actually, the resemblances between chapters 1—39 and chapters 40—66 are greater than the differences. These include similarities in thoughts, images, rhetorical ornaments, characteristic expressions, and local coloring. It is true that the first section is more terse and rational, while the second section is more flowing and emotional, but much of this is caused by the different subject matter, condemnation versus consolation. Critics often forget that content, time, and circumstances typically affect any author's style. In addition, there is no theological contradiction between the emphasis on the Messiah as King in chapters 1—39 and as Suffering Servant in chapters 40—66. While the thrust is different, the Messiah is seen in both sections as Servant and King. Another critical argument is that Isaiah could not have predicted the Babylonian captivity and the return under Cyrus (mentioned by name in 44—45) 150 years in advance. This view is based on the mere assumption that divine prophecy is impossible, rejecting the predictive claims of the book (42:9). The theory cannot explain the amazing messianic prophecies of Isaiah that were literally fulfilled in the life of Christ (see "Christ in Isaiah").

The unity of Isaiah is supported by the Book of Ecclesiasticus, the Septuagint, and the Talmud. The New Testament also claims that Isaiah wrote both sections. John 12:37–41 quotes from Isaiah 6:9–10; 53:1 and attributes it all to Isaiah. In Romans 9:27; 10:16–21, Paul quotes from Isaiah (10; 53; 65) and gives the credit to Isaiah. The same is true of Matthew 3:3; 12:17–21; Luke 3:4–6; and Acts 8:28.

If 40—66 was written by another prophet after the events took place, it is a misleading and deceptive work. Furthermore, it would lead to the strange conclusion that one of Israel's greatest prophets would be the only writing prophet of the Old Testament to go unnamed.

Date and Setting

Isaiah's long ministry ranged from about 740 to 680 B.C. (1:1). He began his ministry near the end of Uzziah's reign (790–739 B.C.) and continued through the reigns of Jotham (739–731 B.C.), Ahaz (731–715 B.C.), and Hezekiah (715–686 B.C.). Assyria was growing in power under Tiglath-pileser who turned toward the west after his conquests in the east. He plucked up the small nations that dotted the Mediterranean coast including Israel and much of Judah. Isaiah lived during this time of military threat to Judah, and warned its kings against trusting in alliances with other countries rather than the power of Yahweh. As a contemporary of Hosea and Micah, he prophesied during the last years of the northern kingdom but ministered to the southern kingdom of Judah who was following the sins of her sister Israel. After Israel's demise in 722 B.C., he warned Judah of judgment not by Assyria but by Babylonia, even though Babylonia had not yet risen to power.

Isaiah ministered from the time of Tiglath-pileser (745–727 B.C.) to the time of Sennacherib (705–681 B.C.) of Assyria. He outdated Hezekiah by a few years because chapter 37, verse 38, records the death of Sennacherib in 681 B.C. Hezekiah was succeeded by his wicked son Manasseh who overthrew the worship of Yahweh and no doubt opposed the work of Isaiah.

Theme and Purpose

The basic theme of this book is found in Isaiah's name: *salvation* is of the Lord. The word "salvation" appears twenty-six times in Isaiah but only seven times in all the other prophets combined. Chapters 1—39 portray man's great need for salvation, and chapters 40—66 reveal God's great provision of salvation. Salvation is of God, not man, and He is seen as the supreme Ruler, the sovereign Lord of history, and the only Savior. Isaiah solemnly warned Judah of approaching judgment because of moral depravity, political corruption, social injustice, and especially spiritual idolatry. Because the nation would not turn away from its sinful practice, Isaiah announced the ultimate overthrow of Judah. Nevertheless, God would remain faithful to His covenant by preserving a godly remnant and promising salvation and deliverance through the coming Messiah. The Savior will come out of Judah and accomplish the twin work of redemption and restoration. The Gentiles will come to His light and universal blessing will finally come.

Keys to Isaiah

Key Word: Salvation

Key Verses (9:6–7; 53:6)—"For unto us a Child is born, unto us a Son is given; and the government will be upon His shoulder. And His name will be called Wonderful, Counselor, Mighty God, Everlasting Father, Prince of Peace. Of the increase of *His* government and peace *there will be* no end, upon the throne of David and over his kingdom, to order it and establish it with judgment and justice from that time forward, even forever. The zeal of the LORD of hosts will perform this" (9:6–7).

"All we like sheep have gone astray; we have turned, every one, to his own way; and the LORD has laid on Him the iniquity of us all" (53:6).

Key Chapter (53)—Along with Psalm 22, Isaiah 53 lists the most remarkable and specific prophecies of the atonement of the Messiah. Fulfilling each clear prophecy, the Jewish nation later proved the messiahship of Jesus.

Christ in Isaiah

When he speaks about Christ, Isaiah sounds more like a New Testament writer than an Old Testament prophet. His messianic prophecies are clearer and more explicit than those of any other Old Testament book. They describe many aspects of the person and work of Christ in His first and second advents, and often blend the two together. Here are a few of the christological prophecies with their New Testament fulfillments: 7:14 (Matt. 1:22–23); 9:1–2 (Matt. 4:12–16); 9:6 (Luke 2:11; Eph. 2:14–18); 11:1 (Luke 3:23, 32; Acts 13:22–23); 11:2 (Luke 3:22); 28:16 (1 Pet. 2:4–6); 40:3–5 (Matt. 3:1–3); 42:1–4 (Matt. 12:15–21); 42:6 (Luke 2:29–32); 50:6 (Matt. 26:67; 27:26, 30); 52:14 (Phil. 2:7–11); 53:3 (Luke 23:18; John 1:11; 7:5); 53:4–5 (Rom. 5:6, 8); 53:7 (Matt. 27:12–14; John 1:29; 1 Pet. 1:18–19); 53:9 (Matt. 27:57–60); 53:12 (Mark 15:28); 61:1 (Luke 4:17–19, 21). The Old Testament has over three hundred prophecies about the first advent of Christ, and Isaiah contributes a number of them. The odds that even ten of them could be fulfilled by one person is a statistical marvel. Isaiah's messianic prophecies that await fulfillment in the Lord's second advent include: 4:2; 11:2–6, 10; 32:1–8; 49:7; 52:13, 15; 59:20–21; 60:1–3; 61:2–3.

The central passage (52:13—53:12) of the consolation section (40—66) presents five different aspects of the saving work of Christ: (1) 52:13–15—His wholehearted sacrifice (burnt offering); (2) 53:1–3—His perfect character (meal offering); (3) 53:4–6—He brought atonement that issues in peace with God (peace offering); (4) 53:7–9—He paid for the transgression of the people (sin offering); and (5) 53:10–12—He died for the effects of sin (trespass offering).

Contribution to the Bible

Isaiah is quoted in the New Testament far more than any other prophet. He is mentioned twenty-one times by name, and chapter 53 alone is quoted or alluded to at least eighty-five times in the New Testament. Isaiah is characterized by systematic presentation, brilliant imagery, broad scope, clarity, beauty, and power.

Some of his prophecies have been fulfilled but many await fulfillment. Our Lord, for example, quoted Isaiah (61:1–2) in Luke 4:18–20 but stopped mid-sentence: ". . . to preach the acceptable year of the Lord." The next phrase in Isaiah reads "and the day of vengeance of our God." The first part was indeed fulfilled by Christ, but the second awaits fulfillment when He comes again, not as the Suffering Servant, but as the ruling King.

Survey of Isaiah

Isaiah, the "Shakespeare of the prophets," has often been called the "evangelical prophet" because of his incredibly clear and detailed messianic prophecies. The "gospel according to Isaiah" has three major sections: prophecies of condemnation (1—35); historical parenthesis (36—39); and prophecies of comfort (40—66).

Prophecies of Condemnation (1—35): Isaiah's first message of condemnation is aimed at his own countrymen in Judah (1—12). Chapter 1 is a capsulized message of the entire book. Judah is riddled with moral and spiritual disease; the people are neglecting God as they bow to ritualism and selfishness. But Yahweh graciously invites them to repent and return to Him because this is their only hope of avoiding judgment. Isaiah's call to proclaim God's message is found in chapter 6, and this is followed by the book of Immanuel (7—12). These chapters repeatedly refer to the Messiah (see 7:14; 8:14; 9:2, 6–7; 11:1–2) and anticipate the blessing of His future reign.

The prophet moves from local to regional judgment as he proclaims a series of oracles against the surrounding nations (13—23). The eleven nations are Babylon, Assyria, Philistia, Moab, Damascus (Syria), Ethiopia, Egypt, Babylon (again), Edom, Arabia, Jerusalem (Judah), and Tyre. Isaiah's little apocalypse (24—27) depicts universal tribulation followed by the blessings of the kingdom. Chapters 28—33 pronounce six woes on Israel and Judah for specific sins. Isaiah's prophetic condemnation closes with a general picture of international devastation that will precede universal blessing (34—35).

Historical Parenthesis (36—39): This historical parenthesis looks back to the Assyrian invasion of Judah in 701 B.C. and anticipates the coming Babylonian invasion of Judah. Judah escapes captivity by Assyria (36—37; 2 Kin. 18—19), but they will not escape from the hands of Babylon (38—39; 2 Kin. 20). God answers King Hezekiah's prayers and delivers Judah from Assyrian destruction by Sennacherib. Hezekiah also turns to the Lord in his illness and is granted a fifteen-year extension of his life. But he foolishly shows all his treasures to the Babylonian messengers, and Isaiah tells him that the Babylonians will one day carry his treasure and descendants to their land.

Prophecies of Comfort (40—66): Having pronounced Judah's divine condemnation, Isaiah comforts them with God's promises of hope and restoration. The basis for this hope is the sovereignty and majesty of God (40—48). Of the 216 verses in these nine chapters, 115 speak of God's greatness and power. The Creator is contrasted with idols, the creations of men. His sovereign character is Judah's assurance of future restoration. Babylon will indeed carry them off; but Babylon will finally be judged and destroyed, and God's people will be released from captivity.

Chapters 49—57 concentrate on the coming Messiah who will be their Savior and Suffering Servant. This rejected but exalted One will pay for their iniquities and usher in a kingdom of peace and righteousness throughout the earth. All who acknowledge their sins and trust in Him will be delivered (58—66). In that day Jerusalem will be rebuilt, Israel's borders will be enlarged, and the Messiah will reign in Zion. God's people will confess their sins and His enemies will be judged. Peace, prosperity, and justice will prevail, and God will make all things new.

Outline of Isaiah

Part One: Prophecies of Condemnation (1:1—35:10)

I. **Prophecies against Judah,** 1:1—12:6
   A. The Judgment of Judah, 1:1–31
   B. The Day of the Lord, 2:1—4:6
   C. The Parable of the Vineyard, 5:1–30
   D. The Commission of Isaiah, 6:1–13
   E. The Destruction of Israel by Assyria, 7:1—10:4
      1. Sign of Immanuel, 7:1–25
      2. Sign of Maher-Shalal-Hash-Baz, 8:1–22
      3. Prophecy of the Messiah's Birth, 9:1–7
      4. Judgment on Ephraim, 9:8—10:4
   F. The Destruction of Assyria by God, 10:5—12:6
      1. Destruction of Assyria, 10:5–19
      2. Remnant of Israel, 10:20–34
      3. Restoration of the Messiah's Kingdom, 11:1–16
      4. Thanksgiving in the Messiah's Kingdom, 12:1–6

II. **The Prophecies against Other Nations,** 13:1—23:18
   A. Prophecies against Babylon, 13:1—14:23
   B. Prophecies against Assyria, 14:24–27
   C. Prophecies against Philistia, 14:28–32
   D. Prophecies against Moab, 15:1—16:14
   E. Prophecies against Damascus and Samaria, 17:1–14
   F. Prophecies against Ethiopia, 18:1–7
   G. Prophecies against Egypt, 19:1—20:6
   H. Prophecies against Babylon, 21:1–10
   I. Prophecies against Dumah (Edom), 21:11–12

   F. The Messiah's Invitation to the World, 55:1—56:8

   G. The Messiah's Rebuke of the Wicked, 56:9—57:21

III. The Prophecies of Israel's Glorious Future, 58:1—66:24

   A. Blessings of True Worship, 58:1–14

   B. Sins of Israel, 59:1–21

   C. Glory of Israel in the Kingdom, 60:1–22

   D. Advents of the Messiah, 61:1–11

   E. Future of Jerusalem, 62:1–12

   F. Vengeance of God, 63:1–6

   G. Prayer of the Remnant, 63:7—64:12

   H. The Lord's Answer to the Remnant, 65:1–16

   I. Glorious Consummation of History, 65:17—66:24

Jeremiah

JEREMIAH IS THE AUTOBIOGRAPHY of one of Judah's greatest prophets during the nation's darkest days. Apostasy, idolatry, perverted worship, moral decay—these were the conditions under which Jeremiah lived and ministered. An avalanche of judgment is coming, and Jeremiah is called to proclaim that message faithfully for forty years. In response to his sermons, the tender prophet of God experiences intense sorrows at the hands of his countrymen: opposition, beatings, isolation, imprisonment. But though rejected and persecuted, Jeremiah lives to see many of his prophecies come true. The Babylonian army arrives; vengeance falls; and God's holiness and justice are vindicated, though it breaks the prophet's heart.

JEREMIAH

Focus	Call of Jeremiah		Prophecies to Judah				Prophecies to the Gentiles		Fall of Jerusalem
	1:1 1:19	2:1				45:5	46:1 51:64		52:1 52:34
Divisions		Prophetic Commission	Condemnation of Judah	Conflicts of Jeremiah	Future Restoration of Jerusalem	Present Fall of Jerusalem		Condemnation of Nine Nations	Historic Conclusion
	1:1 1:19		2:1 25:38	26:1 29:32	30:1 33:26	34:1 45:5	46:1 51:64		52:1 52:34
Topics	Before the Fall					The Fall	After the Fall		
	Call		Ministry						Retrospect
Place	Judah						Surrounding Nations		Babylonia
Time	c. 627–580 B.C.								

Introduction and Title

The Book of Jeremiah is the prophecy of a man divinely called in his youth from the priest-city of Anathoth. A heartbroken prophet with a heart-breaking message, Jeremiah labors for more than forty years proclaiming a message of doom to the stiff-necked people of Judah. Despised and persecuted by his countrymen, Jeremiah bathes his harsh prophecies in tears of compassion. His broken heart causes him to write a broken book, which is difficult to arrange chronologically or topically. But through his sermons and signs he faithfully declares that surrender to God's will is the only way to escape calamity.

Yirmeyahu or *Yirmeyah* literally means "Yahweh Throws," perhaps in the sense of laying a foundation. It may effectively mean "Yahweh establishes, appoints, or sends." The Greek form of the Hebrew name in the Septuagint is *Hieremias,* and the Latin form is *Jeremias.*

Author

Jeremiah was the son of Hilkiah the priest and lived just over two miles north of Jerusalem in Anathoth. As an object lesson to Judah he was not allowed to marry (16:2). Because of his radical message of God's judgment through the coming Babylonian invasion, he led a life of conflict. He was threatened in his hometown of Anathoth, tried for his life by the priests and prophets of Jerusalem, put in stocks, forced to flee from king Jehoiakim, publicly humiliated by the false prophet Hananiah, and thrown into a cistern.

The book clearly states that Jeremiah is its author (1:1). Jeremiah dictated all his prophecies to his secretary Baruch from the beginning of his ministry until the fourth year of Jehoiakim. After this scroll was destroyed by the king, Jeremiah dictated a more complete edition to Baruch (see 36—38), and later sections were also composed. Only chapter 52 was evidently not written by Jeremiah. This supplement is almost identical to Second Kings 24:18—25:30, and it may have been added by Baruch.

Daniel alludes to Jeremiah's prophecy of the seventy-year captivity (see 25:11–14; 29:10; Dan. 9:2), and Jeremiah's authorship is also confirmed by Ecclesiasticus, Josephus, and the Talmud. The New Testament makes explicit and implicit references to Jeremiah's prophecy: Matthew 2:17–18 (31:15); Matthew 21:13; Mark 11:17; Luke 19:4 (7:11); Romans 11:27 (31:33); and Hebrews 8:8–13 (31:31–34).

Date and Setting

Jeremiah was a contemporary of Zephaniah, Habakkuk, Daniel, and Ezekiel. His ministry stretched from 627 to about 580 B.C. Josiah, Judah's last good king (640–609 B.C.) instituted spiritual reforms when the Book of the Law was discovered in 622 B.C. Jeremiah was on good terms with Josiah and lamented when he was killed in 609 B.C. by Pharaoh Necho of Egypt. By this time, Babylon had already overthrown Nineveh, the capital city of Assyria (612 B.C.). Jehoahaz replaced Josiah as king of Judah, but reigned only three months before he was deposed and taken to Egypt by Necho. Jehoiakim (609–597 B.C.) was Judah's next king, but he reigned as an Egyptian vassal until 605 B.C., when Egypt was defeated by Babylon at Carchemish. Nebuchadnezzar took Palestine and deported key people like Daniel to Babylon. Judah's King Jehoiakim was now a Babylonian vassal, but he rejected Jeremiah's warnings in 601 B.C. and rebelled against Babylon. Jehoiachin became Judah's next king in 597 B.C., but was replaced by Zedekiah three months later when Nebuchadnezzar captured Jerusalem and deported Jehoiachin to Babylon. Zedekiah was the last king of Judah; his attempted alliance with Egypt led to Nebuchadnezzar's occupation and overthrow of Jerusalem in 586 B.C.

Thus, there were three stages in Jeremiah's ministry: (1) From 627 to 605 B.C. he prophesied while Judah was threatened by Assyria and Egypt. (2) From 605 to 586 B.C. he proclaimed God's judgment while Judah was threatened and besieged by Babylon. (3) From 586 to about 580 B.C. he ministered in Jerusalem and Egypt after Judah's downfall.

Theme and Purpose

In Jeremiah, God is seen as patient and holy—He has delayed judgment and appealed to His people to repent before it is too late. As the object lesson at the potter's house demonstrated, a ruined vessel could be repaired while still wet (18:1–4), but once dried, a marred vessel was fit only for the garbage heap (19:10–11). God's warning was clear: Judah's time for repentance would soon pass. Because they defied God's words and refused to repent, the Babylonian captivity was inevitable. Jeremiah listed the moral and spiritual causes for their coming catastrophe, but he also proclaimed God's gracious promise of hope and restoration. There will always be a remnant, and God will establish a new covenant.

Keys to Jeremiah

Key Word: Judah's Last Hour

Key Verses (7:23–24; 8:11–12)—"But this is what I commanded them, saying, 'Obey My voice, and I will be your God, and you shall be My people. And walk in all the ways that I have commanded you, that it may be well with you.' Yet they did not obey or incline their ear, but walked in the counsels *and* in the imagination of their evil heart, and went backward and not forward" (7:23–24).

" 'For they have healed the hurt of the daughter of My people slightly, saying, "Peace, peace!" when *there is* no peace. Were they ashamed when they had committed abomination? No! They were not at all ashamed, nor did they know how to blush. Therefore they shall fall among those who fall; in the time of their punishment they shall be cast down,' says the LORD" (8:11–12).

Key Chapter (31)—Amid all the judgment and condemnation of Jeremiah are the wonderful promises of Jeremiah 31. Even though Judah has broken the covenants of her great King, God will make a new covenant when He will "put My law in their minds, and write it on their hearts; and I will be their God, and they shall be My people" (31:33). The Messiah instituted that new covenant with His death and resurrection (cf. Matt. 26:26–29).

Christ in Jeremiah

The Messiah is clearly seen in chapter 23, verses 1–8, as the coming Shepherd and the righteous Branch who "shall reign and prosper, and execute judgment and righteousness in the earth. In His days Judah will be saved, and Israel will dwell safely; Now this *is* His name by which He will be called: THE LORD OUR RIGHTEOUSNESS" (23:5–6). He will bring in the new covenant (31:31–34), which will fulfill God's covenants with Abraham (Gen. 12:1–3; 17:1–8), Moses and the people (Deut. 28–30), and David (2 Sam. 7:1–17).

The curse on Jehoiachin (Jeconiah, Coniah) meant that no physical descendant would succeed him to the throne (22:28–30). Matthew 1:1–17 traces the genealogy of Christ through Solomon and Jeconiah to His legal (but not His physical) father Joseph. But no son of Joseph could sit upon the throne of David, for he would be under the curse of Jehoiachin. Luke 3:23–38 traces Christ's lineage backward from Mary (His physical parent) through David's other son Nathan (Luke 3:31), thereby avoiding the curse. The Righteous Branch will indeed reign on the throne of David.

Contribution to the Bible

While Isaiah is generally chronological, Jeremiah is not. Following the order of Judah's last kings, this is a possible arrangement of his oracles: Josiah (1—6); Jehoahaz (22:10–12); Jehoiakim (7—20; 25—26; 35—36; 45—46:12; 47—49); Jehoiachin (22—23); Zedekiah (21; 24; 27—34; 37—39); Gedaliah (Nebuchadnezzar's puppet governor of Judah, 40—44).

Jeremiah presents Yahweh as the sovereign Creator and Lord of all people and nations. His love is holy and His compassion is righteous. As the only true God, He hates idolatry and the immorality it produces. Loss of reverence for Yahweh leads to moral degradation and dissolution. During the course of Jeremiah's life, these are the changes that took place:

Beginning	End
Reformation	Retrogression
Assyria in power	Babylon in power
Jews in the land	Jews deported to Babylon
Jeremiah in Jerusalem	Jeremiah in Egypt
Jeremiah addressing the masses	Jeremiah addressing a remnant
Davidic throne occupied	Davidic throne empty

Survey of Jeremiah

Jeremiah is a record of the ministry of one of Judah's greatest prophets during its darkest days. He is called as a prophet during the reign of Josiah, the last of Judah's good kings. But even Josiah's well-intentioned reforms cannot stem the tide of apostasy. The downhill slide of the nation continues virtually unabated through a succession of four godless kings during Jeremiah's ministry. The people wallow in apostasy and idolatry and grow even more treacherous than Israel was before its captivity (3:11). They pervert the worship of the true God and give themselves over to spiritual and moral decay. Because they refuse to repent or even listen to God's prophet, the divine cure requires radical surgery. Jeremiah proclaims an approaching avalanche of judgment. Babylon will be God's instrument of judgment, and this book refers to that nation 164 times, more than the rest of the Bible together.

Jeremiah faithfully proclaims the divine condemnation of rebellious Judah for forty years and is rewarded with opposition, beatings, isolations, and imprisonment. His sympathy and sensitivity cause him to grieve over the rebelliousness and imminent doom of his nation. He often desires to resign from his prophetic office because of the harshness of his message and his reception, but he perseveres to Judah's bitter end. He is the weeping prophet (9:1; 13:17)—lonely, rejected, and persecuted.

Although Jeremiah is not easy to arrange chronologically or thematically, its basic message is clear: surrender to God's will is the only way to escape calamity. Judgment cannot be halted, but promises of restoration are sprinkled through the book. Its divisions are: the call of Jeremiah (1), the prophecies to Judah (2—45), the prophecies to the Gentiles (46—51), the fall of Jerusalem (52).

The Call of Jeremiah (1):—Jeremiah is called and sanctified before birth to be God's prophet. This introductory chapter surveys the identification, inauguration, and instructions of the prophet.

The Prophecies to Judah (2—45):—Jeremiah's message is communicated through a variety of parables, sermons, and object lessons. The prophet's life becomes a daily illustration to Judah, and most of the book's object lessons are found in this section (13:1–14; 14:1–9; 16:1–9; 18:1–8; 19:1–13; 24:1–10; 27:1–11; 32:6–15; 43:8–13). In a series of twelve graphic messages, Jeremiah lists the causes of Judah's coming judgment. The gentile nations are more faithful to their false gods than Judah is to God. They become a false vine by following idols and are without excuse. The people are condemned for their empty profession, disobedience to God's covenant, and spiritual harlotry. God has bound Judah to Himself; but like a rotten waistband, they have become corrupt and useless. Jeremiah offers a confession for the people, but their sin is too great; the prophet can only lament for them. As a sign of imminent judgment he is forbidden to marry and participate in the feasts. Because the nation does not trust God or keep the Sabbath, the land will receive a sabbath rest when they are in captivity. Jerusalem will be invaded and the rulers and people will be deported to Babylon. Restoration will only come under the new Shepherd, the Messiah, the nation's future King. Jeremiah announces the duration of the Captivity as seventy years, in contrast to the messages of the false prophets who insist it will not happen.

Because of his message (2:25), Jeremiah suffers misery and opposition (26—45). He is rejected by the prophets and priests who call for his death, but he is spared by the elders and officials. In his sign of the yoke he proclaims the unpopular message that Judah must submit to divine discipline. But he assures the nation of restoration and hope under a new covenant (30—33). A remnant will be delivered and there will be a coming time of blessing. Jeremiah's personal experiences and sufferings are the focal point of 34—45 as opposition against the prophet mounts. Since he is no longer allowed in the temple, he sends his assistant Baruch to read his prophetic warnings. His scroll is burned by Jehoiakim, and Jeremiah is imprisoned. After the destruction of the city, Jeremiah is taken to Egypt by fleeing Jews, but he prophesies that Nebuchadnezzar will invade Egypt as well.

The Prophecies to the Gentiles (46—51): These chapters are a series of prophetic oracles against nine nations: Egypt, Philistia, Moab, Ammon, Edom, Damascus (Syria), Arabia, Elam, and Babylon. Only Egypt, Moab, Ammon, and Elam are given a promise of restoration.

The Fall of Jerusalem (52): Jeremiah's forty-year declaration of doom was finally vindicated in an event so significant that it is recorded in detail four times in the Scriptures (see 2 Kin. 25; 2 Chr. 36; Jer. 39; 52). In this historical supplement, Jerusalem is captured, destroyed, and plundered. The leaders are killed and the captives taken to Babylon.

Outline of Jeremiah

Part One: The Call of Jeremiah (1:1–19)

I. Jeremiah's Call, 1:1–10

II. Jeremiah's Signs, 1:11–16

III. Jeremiah's Assurance, 1:17–19

Part Two: The Prophecies to Judah (2:1—45:5)

I. The Condemnation of Judah, 2:1—25:38
  A. Jeremiah's First Sermon: Judah Sinned Willfully, 2:1—3:5
  B. Jeremiah's Second Sermon: Judah to Be Judged, 3:6—6:30
    1. Judah Ignores Israel's Example, 3:6–10
    2. Judah Is Called from Backsliding, 3:11—4:4
    3. Judah's Destruction from the North, 4:5–31
    4. Judah's Sins, 5:1–31
    5. Jerusalem to Be Destroyed, 6:1–30

C. Jeremiah's Third Sermon: Judah's Hypocrisy in Worship, 7:1—10:25
   1. Judah's Sin of External Religion, 7:1—8:3
   2. Judah's Judgment Imminent, 8:4–17
   3. Jeremiah's Lament for Judah, 8:18—9:8
   4. Judah's Judgment Is Described, 9:9–26
   5. Judah's Futile Idolatry, 10:1–18
   6. Jeremiah's Prayer for Correction, 10:19–25
D. Jeremiah's Fourth Sermon: Judah's Breach of the Covenant, 11:1—12:17
   1. Judah's Curse because of the Broken Covenant, 11:1–17
   2. Anathoth's Conspiracy against Jeremiah, 11:18–23
   3. Jeremiah's Complaint to God, 12:1–4
   4. God's Reply to Jeremiah, 12:5–17
E. Jeremiah's Fifth Sermon: Judah's Revived Relationship, 13:1–27
   1. Sign of the Marred Sash, 13:1–11
   2. Sign of the Wine Bottles, 13:12–27
F. Jeremiah's Sixth Sermon, 14:1—15:21
   1. Judah's Drought Is Described, 14:1–6
   2. Jeremiah's First Intercession, 14:7–12
   3. Jeremiah's Second Intercession, 14:13–18
   4. Jeremiah's Third Intercession, 14:19—15:9
   5. God Encourages Jeremiah, 15:10–21
G. Jeremiah's Seventh Sermon: Jeremiah's Unmarried State, 16:1—17:27
   1. Jeremiah Is Not to Marry, 16:1–9
   2. Judah's Idolatry, 16:10–13
   3. God's Promise of Judah's Restoration, 16:14–21
   4. Judah's Sins Are Listed, 17:1–18
   5. Jeremiah's Call for Sabbath Observance, 17:19–27
H. Jeremiah's Eighth Sermon: Sign of the Potter's House, 18:1—20:18
   1. Sign of the Potter, 18:1–23
   2. Sign of the Broken Flask, 19:1–15
   3. Jeremiah Is Persecuted by Pashhur, 20:1–6
   4. Jeremiah Complains to God, 20:7–18
I. Jeremiah's Ninth Sermon: Against Judah's Kings, 21:1—23:8
   1. Message against Zedekiah, 21:1—22:9
   2. Message against Shallum, 22:10–12
   3. Message against Jehoiakim, 22:13–23
   4. Message against Coniah (Jehoiachin), 22:24–30
   5. Message of the Righteous King, 23:1–8
J. Jeremiah's Tenth Sermon: Against Judah's False Prophets, 23:9–40
K. Jeremiah's Eleventh Sermon: The Two Baskets of Figs, 24:1–10
L. Jeremiah's Twelfth Sermon: The Seventy-year Captivity, 25:1–38

II. **The Conflicts of Jeremiah,** 26:1–29:32
A. Conflict with the Nation, 26:1–24
B. Conflict with the False Prophets, 27:1–22
C. Conflict with Hananiah, 28:1–17
D. Conflict with Shemaiah, 29:1–32

      1. First Letter to the Exiles, 29:1–23

      2. Letter from Shemaiah, 29:24–29

      3. Second Letter to the Exiles, 29:30–32

III. The Future Restoration of Jerusalem, 30:1—33:26

    A. Restoration to the Land, 30:1–24

    B. Restoration of the Nation, 31:1–40

      1. Israel Is Restored, 31:1–21

      2. Judah Is Restored, 31:22–40

    C. Rebuilding of Jerusalem, 32:1–44

    D. Reconfirming the Covenant, 33:1–26

IV. The Present Fall of Jerusalem, 34:1—45:5

    A. Messages before the Fall, 34:1—36:32

      1. Message to Zedekiah, 34:1–7

      2. Message to the People, 34:8–22

      3. Message to the Rechabites, 35:1–19

      4. Message of the Scroll, 36:1–32

    B. Events before the Fall, 37:1—38:28

      1. First Interview with Zedekiah, 37:1–10

      2. Jeremiah Is Imprisoned in a Dungeon, 37:11–16

      3. Second Interview of Zedekiah, 37:17–21

      4. Jeremiah Is Imprisoned in a Cistern, 38:1–13

      5. Third Interview of Zedekiah, 38:14–28

    C. Events during the Fall, 39:1–18

      1. Jerusalem Falls, 39:1–10

      2. Jeremiah Is Released, 39:11–14

      3. Ebed-Melech Is Rewarded, 39:15–18

    D. Messages after the Fall, 40:1—44:30

      1. Ministry to Remnant in Judah, 40:1—42:22

      2. Ministry to Remnant in Egypt, 43:1—44:30

    E. Message to Baruch, 45:1–5

Part Three: The Prophecies to the Gentiles (46:1—51:64)

  I. Prophecies against Egypt, 46:1–28

  II. Prophecies against Philistia, 47:1–7

  III. Prophecies against Moab, 48:1–47

  IV. Prophecies against Ammon, 49:1–6

  V. Prophecies against Edom, 49:7–22

  VI. Prophecies against Damascus, 49:23–27

  VII. Prophecies against Kedar and Hazor, 49:28–33

  VIII. Prophecies against Elam, 49:34–39

Lamentations

LAMENTATIONS, PERHAPS THE SADDEST BOOK of the Old Testament, is penned by the mourning prophet Jeremiah after the fall of Jerusalem. In five "dirges of death," Jeremiah expresses the horror and helplessness of seeing the Jews' proudest city reduced to rubble. Defeat, slaughter, and ruination—the horrors so long promised and so frequently ignored—now fall from the hands of the brutal Babylonians. And yet, even as the prophet's heart breaks, he pauses to proclaim a ringing testimony of deep faith in the goodness and mercy of God. Though the present is bleak with judgment, the future sparkles with the promise of renewal and restoration—a promise as certain as the dawn. Indeed, "Great is Your faithfulness" (3:23).

	Focus	Destruction of Jerusalem	Anger of Jehovah	Prayer for Mercy	Siege of Jerusalem	Prayer for Restoration
LAMENTATIONS		1:1 — 1:22	2:1 — 2:22	3:1 — 3:66	4:1 — 4:22	5:1 — 5:22
	Divisions	Mourning City	Broken People	Suffering Prophet	Ruined Kingdom	Penitent Nation
		1:1 — 1:22	2:1 — 2:22	3:1 — 3:66	4:1 — 4:22	5:1 — 5:22
	Topics	The Grief	The Cause	The Hope	The Repentance	The Prayer
	Place	Jerusalem				
	Time	c. 586 B.C.				

Introduction and Title

Lamentations describes the funeral of a city. It is a tearstained portrait of the once proud Jerusalem, now reduced to rubble by the invading Babylonian hordes. In a five-poem dirge, Jeremiah exposes his emotions. A death has occurred; Jerusalem lies barren.

Jeremiah writes his lament in acrostic or alphabetical fashion. Beginning each chapter with the first letter A (aleph) he progresses verse by verse through the Hebrew alphabet, literally weeping from A to Z. And then, in the midst of this terrible holocaust, Jeremiah triumphantly cries out, "*Great is* Your faithfulness" (3:23). In the face of death and destruction, with life seemingly coming apart at the seams, Jeremiah turns tragedy into a triumph of faith. God has never failed him in the past. God has promised to remain faithful in the future. In the light of the God he knows and loves, Jeremiah finds hope and comfort.

The Hebrew title of this book comes from the first word of chapters 1—2, and 4: *Ekah,* "Ah, how!" Another Hebrew word *Ginoth* ("Elegies" or "Lamentations") has also been used as the title because it better represents the contents of the book. The Greek title *Threnoi* means "Dirges" or "Laments," and the Latin title *Threni* ("Tears" or "Lamentations") was derived from this word. The subtitle in Jerome's Vulgate reads: "*Id est lamentationes Jeremiae prophetae,*" and this became the basis for the English title "The Lamentations of Jeremiah."

Author

The author of Lamentations is unnamed in the book, but internal and external evidence is consistently in favor of Jeremiah.

External Evidence: The universal consensus of early Jewish and Christian tradition attributes this book to Jeremiah. The superscription to Lamentations in the Septuagint says: "And it came to pass, after Israel had been carried away captive, and Jerusalem had become desolate, that Jeremiah sat weeping, and lamented with this lamentation over Jerusalem, saying . . ." This is also the position of the Talmud, the Aramaic Targum of Jonathan, and early Christian writers, such as Origen and Jerome. In addition, Second Chronicles 35:25 says that "Jeremiah also lamented for Josiah." This was an earlier occasion, but Jeremiah was obviously familiar with the lament form.

Internal Evidence: The scenes in this graphic book were clearly portrayed by an eyewitness of Jerusalem's siege and fall soon after the destruction took place (cf. 1:13–15; 2:6, 9; 4:1–12). Jeremiah witnessed the fall of Jerusalem and remained behind after the captives were deported (see Jer. 39). Although some critics claim that the style of Lamentations is different from the Book of Jeremiah, the similarities are in fact striking and numerous, especially in the poetic sections of Jeremiah. Compare these passages from Lamentations and Jeremiah: 1:2 (Jer. 30:14); 1:15 (Jer. 8:21); 1:16; 2:11 (Jer. 9:1, 18); 2:22 (Jer. 6:25); 4:21 (Jer. 49:12). The same compassion, sympathy, and grief over Judah's downfall are evident in both books.

Date and Setting

The historical background of Lamentations can be found in the Book of Jeremiah ("Date and Setting"). The book was written soon after Jerusalem's destruction (Jer. 39; 52) at the beginning of the Exile. Nebuchadnezzar laid siege to Jerusalem from January 588 B.C. to July 586 B.C. It fell on July 19, and the city and temple were burned on August 15. Jeremiah probably wrote these five elegies before he was taken captive to Egypt by his disobedient countrymen not long after the destruction (Jer. 43:1–7).

Theme and Purpose

There are three themes that run through the five laments of Jeremiah. The most prominent is the theme of mourning over Jerusalem's holocaust. The Holy City has been laid waste and desolate—God's promised judgment for sin has come. In his sorrow, Jeremiah speaks for himself, for the captives, and sometimes for the personified city. The second theme is a confession of sin and acknowledgment of God's righteous and holy judgment upon Judah. The third theme is least prominent but very important: it is a note of hope in God's future restoration of His people. Yahweh has poured out His wrath, but in His mercy He will be faithful to His covenant promises. "*Through* the LORD's mercies we are not consumed, because His compassions fail not. *They are* new every morning; great *is* Your faithfulness" (3:22–23).

Keys to Lamentations

Key Word: Lamentations

Key Verses (2:5–6; 3:22–23)—"The Lord was like an enemy. He has swallowed up Israel, He has swallowed up all her palaces; He has destroyed her strongholds, and has increased mourning and lamentation in the daughter of Judah. He has done violence to His tabernacle, *as if it were* a garden; He has destroyed His place of assembly; the LORD has caused the appointed feasts and Sabbaths to be forgotten in Zion. In His burning indignation He has spurned the king and the priest" (2:5–6).

"*Through* the LORD's mercies we are not consumed, because His compassions fail not. *They are* new every morning; great *is* Your faithfulness" (3:22–23).

Key Chapter (3)—In the midst of five chapters of ruin, destruction, and utter hopelessness, Jeremiah rises and grasps with strong faith the promises and character of God.

Chapter 3, verses 22–25, express a magnificent faith in the mercy of God—especially when placed against the dark backdrop of chapters 1, 2, 4, and 5.

Christ in Lamentations

The weeping prophet Jeremiah is a type of Christ, the Prophet who wept over the same city six centuries later. "O Jerusalem, Jerusalem, the one who kills the prophets and stones those who are sent to her! How often I wanted to gather your children together, as a hen gathers her chicks under *her* wings, but you were not willing! See! Your house is left to you desolate" (Matt. 23:37–38). Like Christ, Jeremiah identified himself personally with the plight of Jerusalem and with human suffering caused by sin.

Lamentations also includes elements that typify Christ's life and ministry as the Man of Sorrows who was acquainted with grief. He was afflicted (1:12; 3:19), despised, and derided by His enemies (2:15–16; 3:14, 30).

Contribution to the Bible

In the Hebrew text, the first four chapters of Lamentations are alphabetic acrostics. The first word in each of the twenty-two verses of chapters 1—2, and 4 begins with the twenty-two successive letters of the Hebrew alphabet. Chapter 3 has sixty-six verses because three verses are allotted to each Hebrew letter. Chapter 5 has twenty-two verses but it is not an acrostic poem. In addition, chapters 1—2 have three lines per verse, chapter 4 has two lines per verse, and chapters 3 and 5 have only one line per verse. This elaborate structure stands in balanced contrast to the passionate and dramatic outpouring of grief in these five lament poems. The acrostic form may have been used to express the full range (from A to Z) of their sufferings, and it may also have been an aid to memory and liturgical use. Jeremiah also chose to use "limping meter" in his poetic lines because this melancholy rhythm was used in funeral dirges. This technique adds to the plaintive mood of lamentation. The Jews publicly read this vivid and tragic book each year to commemorate Jerusalem's destruction in 586 B.C. and again in A.D. 70. In the Hebrew Bible it was placed in the *Megilloth* (the "five rolls") along with the Song of Solomon, Ruth, Esther, and Ecclesiastes. But it follows Jeremiah in the Septuagint as it does in English versions.

While the Book of Jeremiah primarily anticipates the fall of Jerusalem, Lamentations reflects back upon it:

Book of Jeremiah	DEFEAT AND	Book of Lamentations
(Warning) $\rightarrow$	DESOLATION	$\leftarrow$ (Mourning)
Looking Ahead	OF JERUSALEM	Looking Back

Jeremiah's Two Glimpses of Jerusalem's Fall

Survey of Lamentations

For forty years Jeremiah suffers rejection and abuse for his warnings of coming judgment. When Nebuchadnezzar finally comes and destroys Jerusalem in 586 B.C., a lesser man might say, "I told you so!" But Jeremiah compassionately identifies with the tragic overthrow of Jerusalem and composes five beautiful and emotional lament poems as a funeral for the once proud city. These dirges reflect the tender heart of the man who was divinely commissioned to communicate a harsh message to a sinful and stiff-necked people. The city, the temple, the palace, and the walls have been reduced to rubble and its inhabitants have been deported to distant Babylon. Jeremiah's five mournful poems can be entitled: The Destruction of Jerusalem (1);

The Anger of Jehovah (2); The Prayer for Mercy (3); The Siege of Jerusalem (4); and The Prayer for Restoration (5).

The Destruction of Jerusalem (1): This poem consists of a lamentation by Jeremiah (1:1–11) and a lamentation by the personified Jerusalem (1:12–22). The city has been left desolate because of its grievous sins, and her enemies "mocked at her downfall" (1:7). Jerusalem pleads with God to regard her misery and repay her adversaries.

The Anger of Jehovah (2): In his second elegy, Jeremiah moves from Jerusalem's desolation to a description of her destruction. Babylon has destroyed the city, but only as the Lord's instrument of judgment. Jeremiah presents an eyewitness account of the thoroughness and severity of Jerusalem's devastation. Through the Babylonians, God has terminated all religious observances, removed the priests, prophets, and kings, and razed the temple and palaces. Jeremiah grieves over the suffering the people brought on themselves through rebellion against God, and Jerusalem's supplications complete the lament.

The Prayer for Mercy (3): In the first eighteen verses, Jeremiah enters into the miseries and despair of his people and makes them his own. However, we observe an abrupt turn in verses 19–39 as the prophet reflects on the faithfulness and loyal love of the compassionate God of Israel. These truths enable him to find comfort and hope in spite of his dismal circumstances. Jeremiah expresses his deep sorrow and petitions God for deliverance and for God to avenge Jerusalem's misery.

The Siege of Jerusalem (4): The prophet rehearses the siege of Jerusalem and remembers the suffering and starvation of rich and poor. He also reviews the causes of the siege, especially the sins of the prophets and priests, and their foolish trust in human aid. This poem closes with a warning to Edom of future punishment and a glimmer of hope for Jerusalem.

The Prayer for Restoration (5): Jeremiah's last elegy is a melancholy description of his people's lamentable state. Their punishment is complete, and Jeremiah prayerfully desires the restoration of his nation.

Outline of Lamentations

I. **The Destruction of Jerusalem,** 1:1–22
  A. The Lament of the Prophet Jeremiah, 1:1–11
    1. The Desolation of Jerusalem, 1:1–7
    2. The Cause of Jerusalem's Desolation, 1:8–11
  B. The Lament of the City Jerusalem, 1:12–22
    1. The Contrition of Jerusalem, 1:12–19
    2. The Confession of Jerusalem, 1:20–22

II. **The Anger of God,** 2:1–22
  A. The Anger of God, 2:1–9
  B. The Agony of Jerusalem, 2:10–17
  C. The Appeal of Jerusalem, 2:18–22

Ezekiel

EZEKIEL PROPHESIES AMONG THE JEWISH EXILES in Babylon during the last days of Judah's decline and downfall. His ministry is in some ways similar to that of his older contemporary, Jeremiah. But while Jeremiah delivers a chilling message of destruction in Jerusalem, Ezekiel brings a warming message of reconstruction in Babylon. Jeremiah is a man of tears; Ezekiel is a man of visions. And those visions stretch from horror to hope; from condemnation upon Judah's faithless leaders and godless foes, to consolation regarding Judah's future. Through it all, mankind would see the glory of Israel's sovereign God, and "'they shall know that I am the LORD'" (6:10).

EZEKIEL						
Focus	**Commission of Ezekiel** 1:1 — 3:27		**Judgment on Judah** 4:1 — 24:27	**Judgment on Gentiles** 25:1 — 32:32	**Restoration of Israel** 33:1 — 48:35	
Divisions	Ezekiel Sees the Glory	Ezekiel Commissioned to the Word	Signs, Messages, Visions and Parables of Judgment	Judgment on Surrounding Nations	Return of Israel to the Lord	Restoration of Israel in the Kingdom
	1:1 — 1:28	2:1 — 3:27	4:1 — 24:27	25:1 — 32:32	33:1 — 39:29	40:1 — 48:35
Topics	Before the Siege (592–587 B.C.)			During the Siege (586 B.C.)	After the Siege (585–570 B.C.)	
	Judah's Fall			Judah's Foes	Judah's Future	
Place	Babylon					
Time	c. 592–570 B.C.					

Introduction and Title

Ezekiel, a priest and a prophet, ministers during the darkest days of Judah's history: the seventy-year period of Babylonian captivity. Carried to Babylon before the final assault on Jerusalem, Ezekiel uses prophecies, parables, signs, and symbols to dramatize God's message to His exiled people. Though they are like dry bones in the sun, God will reassemble them and breathe life into the nation once again. Present judgment will be followed by future glory so that "you shall know that I *am* the LORD."

The Hebrew name *yehezke'l* means "God strengthens" or "strengthened by God." Ezekiel is indeed strengthened by God for the prophetic ministry to which he is called (3:8–9). The name occurs twice in this book and nowhere else in the Old Testament. The Greek form in the Septuagint is *Iezekiel* and the Latin form in the Vulgate is *Ezechiel*.

Author

Ezekiel the son of Buzi (1:3) had a wife who died as a sign to Judah when Nebuchadnezzar began his final siege on Jerusalem (24:16–24). Like Jeremiah, he was a priest who was called to be a prophet of the Lord. His prophetic ministry shows a priestly emphasis in his concern with the temple, priesthood, sacrifices, and *shekinah* (the glory of God). Ezekiel was privileged to receive a number of visions of the power and plan of God, and he was careful and artistic in his written presentation.

Some objections have been raised, but there is no good reason to overthrow the strong evidence in favor of Ezekiel's authorship. The first person singular is used throughout the book, indicating that it is the work of a single personality. This person is identified as Ezekiel (1:3; 24:24), and internal evidence supports the unity and integrity of Ezekiel's prophetic record. The style, language, and thematic development are consistent through the book; and several distinctive phrases are repeated throughout, such as, "They shall know that I am the LORD," "Son of man," "the word of the LORD came to me," and the "glory of the LORD."

Date and Setting

Nebuchadnezzar destroyed Jerusalem in three stages. First, in 605 B.C., he overcame Jehoiakim and carried off key hostages including Daniel and his friends. Second, in 597 B.C., the rebellion of Jehoiakim and Jehoiachin brought further punishment; and Nebuchadnezzar made Jerusalem submit a second time. He carried off ten thousand hostages including Jehoiachin and Ezekiel. Third, in 586 B.C., Nebuchadnezzar destroyed the city after a long siege and disrupted all of Judah. If "thirtieth year" in chapter 1, verse 1, refers to Ezekiel's age, he was twenty-five years old when he was taken to Babylon and thirty years old when he received his prophetic commission (1:2–3). This means he was about seventeen when Daniel was deported in 605 B.C., so that Ezekiel and Daniel were about the same age. Both men were about twenty years younger than Jeremiah who was ministering in Jerusalem. According to this chronology, Ezekiel was born in 622 B.C. deported to Babylon in 597 B.C., prophesied from 592 B.C. to at least 570 B.C., and died about 560 B.C. Thus, he overlapped the end of Jeremiah's ministry and the beginning of Daniel's ministry. By the time Ezekiel arrived in Babylon, Daniel was already well-known; and he is mentioned three times in Ezekiel's prophecy (14:14, 20; 28:3). Ezekiel's Babylonian home was at Tel Abib, the principal colony of Jewish exiles along the river Chebar, Nebuchadnezzar's "Grand Canal" (1:1; 3:15, 23).

From 592 to 586 B.C., Ezekiel found it necessary to convince the disbelieving Jewish exiles that there was no hope of immediate deliverance. But it was not until they heard that Jerusalem was destroyed that their false hopes of returning were abandoned.

Ezekiel no doubt wrote this book shortly after the incidents recorded in it occurred. His active ministry lasted for at least twenty-two years (1:2; 29:17), and his book was probably completed by 565 B.C.

Theme and Purpose

Like most of the other prophets, Ezekiel's two-fold theme was condemnation (1—32) and consolation (33—48). His ministry to the early Jewish exiles in Babylon was similar to Jeremiah's ministry in Jerusalem. He surveyed the sins which were bringing God's judgment upon the people of Judah and exposed the foolishness of their false hopes of an early return to their homeland. God's judgment on Jerusalem and its temple would surely strike and the Babylonian exile would not be brief. When the city fell, Ezekiel comforted the people by assuring them of God's covenant promise of future blessing and complete restoration. Ezekiel's section on divine consolation is more detailed and extensive than that of his contemporary Jeremiah.

Ezekiel places a strong emphasis on the sovereignty, glory, and faithfulness of God. He concentrates on the temple with its perversion, destruction, and restoration. Another temple-related theme is Ezekiel's fascinating portrayal of God's heavenly glory (1:28; 3:12,23), God's departing glory (9:3; 10:4, 18–19; 11:22–23), and God's earthly glory (43:1–5; 44:4). The sovereign purpose of God through judgment and blessing alike is that His people come to know that He is the Lord.

Keys to Ezekiel

Key Word: Restoration of Israel

Key Verses (36:24–26; 36:33–35)—"For I will take you from among the nations, gather you out of all countries, and bring you into your own land. Then I will sprinkle clean water on you, and you shall be clean; I will cleanse you from all your filthiness and from all your idols. I will give you a new heart and put a new spirit within you; I will take the heart of stone out of your flesh and give you a heart of flesh" (36:24–26).

"Thus says the Lord GOD: On the day that I cleanse you from all your iniquities, I will also enable *you* to dwell in the cities, and the ruins shall be rebuilt. The desolate land shall be tilled instead of lying desolate in the sight of all who pass by. So they will say, 'This land that was desolate has become like the garden of Eden; and the wasted, desolate, and ruined cities *are now* fortified *and* inhabited'" (36:33–35).

Key Chapter (37)—Central to the hope of the restoration of Israel is the vision of the valley of the dry bones. Ezekiel 37 outlines with clear steps Israel's future.

Christ in Ezekiel

Chapter 17, verses 22–24, depicts the Messiah as a tender twig that becomes a stately cedar on a lofty mountain, as He is similarly called the Branch in Isaiah (11:1), Jeremiah (23:5; 33:15), and Zechariah (3:8; 6:12). The Messiah is the King who has the right to rule (21:26–27), and He is the true Shepherd who will deliver and feed His flock (34:11–31).

Contribution to the Bible

Ezekiel is a book of methodical style, careful dating, and diligent organization. But this exacting framework houses an unsurpassed depth of mystery and richness of vibrant imagery, symbolism, parables, allegories, and apocalyptic visions. God told him "I have made you a sign to the house of Israel" (12:6). Nine signs are found in chapters 4—24 and a tenth is in chapter 37 (4:1–3, 4–8, 9–17; 5:1–17; 12:1–7, 17–20; 21:1–17, 18–23; 22:17–31; 24:15–27; 37:15–17). Ezekiel records six visions (1:4–28; 2:9—3:13; 3:22–23; 8–11; 37:1–10; 40–48) and six parables (15:1–8; 16; 17:1–21, 22–24; 23; 24:1–14). Apocalyptic passages are scattered throughout the book (6:1–14; 7:5–12; 20:33–44; 28:25–26; 34:25–31; 36:8–15,33–36; 38–39; 47:1–12). Some of his images and visions are difficult to interpret, and this is especially true of chapters 40—48. Students of the Bible are divided over a spiritual and literal interpretation of these chapters. Those who hold the spiritual view argue that the sacrifical system has been fulfilled and abolished in Christ, that there is no temple in the New Jerusalem (Rev. 21:22), and that these descriptions are being spiritually fulfilled in the church. Those who hold the literal view argue that the detailed measurements and lengthy descriptions would be meaningless unless understood literally, that the sacrifices are memorial in nature, that this will be in effect only in the millennial kingdom before the New Jerusalem of Revelation 21 appears, and that Israel's covenant promises are not fulfilled in the church.

Survey of Ezekiel

Ezekiel prophesies among the Jewish exiles in Babylon during the last days of Judah's decline and downfall. His message of judgment is similar to that of his older contemporary Jeremiah who has remained in Jerusalem. Judah will be judged because of her unfaithfulness, but God promises her future restoration and blessing. Like Isaiah and Jeremiah, Ezekiel proclaims a message of horror and hope, of condemnation and consolation. But Ezekiel places special emphasis on the glory of Israel's sovereign God who says, "They shall know that I *am* the LORD." The book breaks in four sections: (1) The commission of Ezekiel (1—3); (2) the judgment on Judah (4—24); (3) the judgment on the Gentiles (25—32); and (4) the restoration of Israel (33—48).

The Commission of Ezekiel (1—3): God gives Ezekiel an overwhelming vision of His divine glory and commissions him to be His prophet (cf. the experiences of Moses in Ex. 3:1–10, Isaiah in 6:1–10, Daniel in 10:5–14, and John in Rev. 1:12–19). Ezekiel is given instruction, enablement, and responsibility.

The Judgment on Judah (4—24): Ezekiel directs his prophecies against the nation God chose for Himself. The prophet's signs and sermons (4—7) point to the certainty of Judah's judgment. In chapters 8—11, Judah's past sins and coming doom are seen in a series of visions of the abominations in the temple, the slaying of the wicked, and the departing glory of God. The priests and princes are condemned as the Glory leaves the temple, moves to the Mount of Olives, and disappears in the east. Chapters 12—24 speak of the causes and extent of Judah's coming judgment through dramatic signs, powerful sermons, and parables. Judah's prophets are counterfeits and her elders are idolatrous. They have become a fruitless vine and an adulterous wife. Babylon will swoop down like an eagle and pluck them up, and they will not be aided by Egypt. The people are responsible for their own sins, and they are not being unjustly judged for the sins of their ancestors. Judah has been unfaithful, but God promises that her judgment ultimately will be followed by restoration.

The Judgment on the Gentiles (25—32): Judah's nearest neighbors may gloat over her destruction, but they will be next in line. They too will suffer the fate of siege and destruction by Babylon. Ezekiel shows the full circle of judgment on the nations that surround Judah by following them in a clockwise circuit: Ammon, Moab, Edom, Philistia, Tyre, and Sidon (25—28). He spends a disproportionate amount of time on Tyre, and many scholars believe that the "king of Tyre" (28:11–19) may be Satan, the real power behind the nation. Chapters 29—32 contain a series of oracles against Egypt. Unlike the nations in chapters 25—28 that were destroyed by Nebuchadnezzar, Egypt will continue to exist, but as "the lowliest of the kingdoms." Since that time it has never recovered its former glory or influence.

The Restoration of Israel (33—48): The prophecies in these chapters were given after the overthrow of Jerusalem. Now that the promised judgment has come, Ezekiel's message no longer centers on coming judgment but on the positive theme of comfort and consolation. Just as surely as judgment has come, blessing will also come; God's people will be regathered and restored. The mouth of Ezekiel, God's watchman, is opened when he is told that Jerusalem has been taken. Judah has had false shepherds (rulers), but the true Shepherd will lead them in the future. The vision of the valley of dry bones pictures the reanimation of the nation by the Spirit of God. Israel and Judah will be purified and reunited. There will be an invasion by the northern armies of God, but Israel will be saved because the Lord will destroy the invading forces.

In 572 B.C., fourteen years after the destruction of Jerusalem, Ezekiel returns in a vision to the fallen city and is given detailed specifications of the reconstruction of the temple, the city, and the land (40—48). After an intricate description of the new outer court, inner court, and temple (40—42), Ezekiel views the return of the glory of the Lord to the temple from the east. Regulations concerning worship in the coming temple (43—46) are followed by revelations concerning the new land and city (47—48).

Outline of Ezekiel

Part One: The Commission of Ezekiel (1:1—3:27)

I. Ezekiel Sees the Glory of God, 1:1–28
  A. Time of the Vision, 1:1–3
  B. The Four Living Creatures, 1:4–14
  C. The Four Wheels, 1:15–21
  D. The Firmament, 1:22–25
  E. The Appearance of a Man, 1:26–28

II. Ezekiel Is Commissioned to the Word of God, 2:1—3:27
  A. Ezekiel Is Sent to Israel, 2:1—3:3
  B. Ezekiel Is Instructed about His Ministry, 3:4–27

Part Two: Judgment on Judah (4:1—24:27)

I. Four Signs of Coming Judgment, 4:1—5:17
  A. Sign of the Clay Tablet, 4:1–3
  B. Sign of Ezekiel's Lying on His Side, 4:4–8
  C. Sign of the Defiled Bread, 4:9–17
  D. Sign of the Razor and Hair, 5:1–4
  E. Explanation of the Signs, 5:5–17

II. Two Messages of Coming Judgment, 6:1—7:27
  A. Destruction because of Idolatry, 6:1–14
    1. Destruction of High Places, 6:1–7
    2. Salvation of the Remnant, 6:8–10
    3. Desolation of the Land, 6:11–14
  B. Description of the Babylonian Conquest, 7:1–27

III. Four-part Vision of Coming Judgment, 8:1—11:25
  A. Vision of the Glory of God, 8:1–4
  B. Vision of the Abominations in the Temple, 8:5–18
    1. Image of Jealousy, 8:5–6
    2. Paintings on the Wall, 8:7–12
    3. Weeping for Tammuz, 8:13–14
    4. Sun Worship, 8:15–18
  C. Vision of the Slaying in Jerusalem, 9:1–11
    1. Call to the Six Men, 9:1–3
    2. Command to Slay the Wicked, 9:4–7
    3. Weeping of Ezekiel, 9:8–11
  D. Departure of the Glory of God to the Threshold, 10:1–8
  E. Vision of the Wheels and Cherubim, 10:9–22
  F. Vision of the Twenty-five Wicked Rulers, 11:1–12
  G. Promise of the Restoration of the Remnant, 11:13–21
  H. Departure of the Glory of God from the Mount of Olives, 11:22–25

IV. Signs, Parables, and Messages of Judgment, 12:1—24:27
  A. Sign of Belongings for Removing, 12:1–16

B. Sign of Trembling, 12:17–28
C. Message against the False Prophets, 13:1–23
   1. Judgment upon False Prophets, 13:1–16
   2. Judgment upon False Prophetesses, 13:17–23
D. Message against the Elders, 14:1–23
   1. Idolatry of the Elders, 14:1–11
   2. Jerusalem to Be Destroyed, 14:12–23
E. Parable of the Vine, 15:1–8
F. Parable of Israel's Marriage, 16:1–63
   1. God Has Mercy on Israel, 16:1–14
   2. Israel Rejects God, 16:15–34
   3. God Punishes Israel, 16:35–59
   4. God Remembers His Covenant, 16:60–63
G. Parable of the Two Eagles, 17:1–24
H. Message of Personal Judgment for Personal Sin, 18:1–32
I. Lament for the Princes of Israel, 19:1–9
J. Parable of the Withered Vine, 19:10–14
K. Message of Judgment on Jerusalem, 20:1—24:27
   1. Review of God's Past Dealings with Israel, 20:1–32
      a. In Egypt, 20:1–9
      b. In the Wilderness, 20:10–26
      c. In Canaan, 20:27–28
      d. In Ezekiel's Time, 20:29–32
   2. Message of God's Future Restoration of Israel, 20:33–44
   3. Signs of Judgment on Jerusalem, 20:45—21:32
      a. Sign of the Forest Fire, 20:45–49
      b. Sign of the Drawn Sword, 21:1–17
      c. Sign of the Double Stroke of the Sword, 21:18–32
   4. Message of Judgment on Jerusalem, 22:1–31
   5. Parables of Judgment on Jerusalem, 23:1—24:14
      a. Parable of Two Sisters, 23:1–49
      b. Parable of the Boiling Pot, 24:1–14
   6. Sign through the Death of Ezekiel's Wife, 24:15–27

Part Three: Judgment on Gentiles (25:1—32:32)

I. Judgment on Ammon, 25:1–7

II. Judgment on Moab, 25:8–11

III. Judgment on Edom, 25:12–14

IV. Judgment on Philistia, 25:15–17

V. Judgment on Tyre, 26:1—28:19
  A. Destruction of Tyre, 26:1–21
  B. Lament over Tyre, 27:1–36
  C. Fall of the Prince of Tyre, 28:1–19

VI. Judgment on Sidon, 28:20–26

VII. Judgment on Egypt, 29:1—32:32
  A. Egypt to Be Desolate, 29:1–16
  B. Egypt to Be Taken by Babylon, 29:17–21
  C. Egypt to Be Destroyed, 30:1–26
  D. Egypt Is Cut Down like Assyria, 31:1–18
  E. Egypt Is Lamented, 32:1–16
  F. Egypt in Sheol, 32:17–32

Part Four: Restoration of Israel (33:1—48:35)

I. The Return of Israel to the Land, 33:1—39:29
  A. The Appointment of Ezekiel as Watchman, 33:1–33
  B. The Message to the Shepherds, 34:1–31
    1. The False Shepherds, 34:1–10
    2. The True Shepherd, 34:11–31
  C. The Judgment of Edom, 35:1–15
  D. The Prophecies concerning Israel, 36:1—37:28
    1. Judgment on the Nations, 36:1–7
    2. Israel Returns to the Lord, 36:8–38
    3. Israel Is Reborn, 37:1–28
      a. Vision of Dry Bones, 37:1–14
      b. Sign of the Two Sticks, 37:15–28
  E. Prophecies concerning Gog and Magog, 38:1—39:29
    1. Attack by Gog, 38:1–16
    2. Judgment of God, 38:17—39:29

II. The Restoration of Israel in the Kingdom, 40:1—48:35
  A. The New Temple, 40:1—43:27
    1. Vision of the Man with the Measuring Rod, 40:1–4
    2. The Outer Court, 40:5–27
    3. The Inner Court, 40:28–47
    4. The Temple Vestibule, 40:48–49
    5. The Temple Itself, 41:1–26
    6. The Chamber in the Outer Court, 42:1–14
    7. The Place of Separation, 42:15–20
    8. The Return of the Glory of God to the Temple, 43:1–12
    9. The Altar of Burnt Offerings, 43:13–27
  B. The New Worship, 44:1—46:24
    1. Duties of Temple Priests, 44:1–31
    2. Land of the Temple Priests, 45:1–8
    3. Offerings of the Temple Priests, 45:9—46:24
  C. The New Land, 47:1—48:35
    1. River from the Temple, 47:1–12
    2. Boundaries of the Land, 47:13–23
    3. Divisions of the Land, 48:1–29
    4. Gates of the City, 48:30–34
    5. Name of the City, 48:35

Daniel

DANIEL, SOMETIMES REFERRED TO as the "Apocalypse of the Old Testament," presents a majestic sweep of prophetic history. The Babylonians, Persians, Greeks, and Romans will come and go, but God will establish His people forever. Nowhere is this theme more apparent than in the life of Daniel, a young God-fearing Jew transplanted from his homeland and raised in Babylonia. His adventures—and those of his friends—in the palace, the fiery furnace, and the lion's den show that even during the Exile God has not forgotten His chosen nation. And through Daniel, God provides dreams—and interpretations of dreams—designed to convince Jew and Gentile alike that wisdom and power belong to Him alone!

Focus	History of Daniel	Prophetic Plan for the Gentiles				Prophetic Plan of Israel		
	1:1　　　1:21	2:1　　　　　　　　7:28				8:1　　　　　　12:13		
Divisions	Personal Life of Daniel	Visions of Nebuchadnezzar	Vision of Belshazzar	Decree of Darius	Four Beasts	Vision of Ram & He-Goat	Vision of Seventy Weeks	Vision of Israel's Future
	1:1　　　1:21	2:1　　4:37	5:1　5:31	6:1　6:28	7:1　7:28	8:1　　8:27	9:1　　9:27	10:1　12:13
Topics	Daniel's Background	Daniel Interprets Others' Dreams				Angel Interprets Daniel's Dreams		
	Hebrew	Aramaic				Hebrew		
Place	Babylonia/Persia							
Time	c. 605–536 B.C.							

Introduction and Title

Daniel's life and ministry bridge the entire seventy-year period of Babylonian captivity. Deported to Babylon at the age of sixteen, and handpicked for government service, Daniel becomes God's prophetic mouthpiece to the gentile and Jewish world declaring God's present and eternal purpose. Nine of the twelve chapters in his book revolve around dreams, including God-given visions involving trees, animals, beasts, and images. In both his personal adventures and prophetic visions, Daniel shows God's guidance, intervention, and power in the affairs of men.

The name *Daniye'l* or *Dané'el* means "God Is My Judge," and the book is of course named after the author and principal character. The Greek form *Daniel* in the Septuagint is the basis for the Latin and English titles.

Author

Daniel and his three friends were evidently born into noble Judean families and were "young men in whom *there was* no blemish, but good-looking and gifted in all wisdom, possessing knowledge and quick to understand" (1:4). He was given three years of training in the best of Babylon's schools (1:5). As part of the reidentification process, he was given a new name that honored one of the Babylonian deities: *Belteshazzar* meant "Bel Protect His Life" (see 1:7; 4:8; Jer. 51:44). Daniel's wisdom and divinely given interpretive abilities brought him into a position of prominence, especially in the courts of Nebuchadnezzar and Darius. He is one of the few well-known Bible characters about whom nothing negative is ever written. His life was characterized by faith, prayer, courage, consistency, and lack of compromise. This "greatly beloved" man (9:23; 10:11, 19) was mentioned three times by his sixth-century B.C. contemporary Ezekiel as an example of righteousness.

Daniel claimed to write this book (12:4), and he used the autobiographical first person from chapter 7, verse 2, onward. The Jewish Talmud agrees with this testimony, and Christ attributed a quote from chapter 9, verse 27, to "Daniel the prophet" (Matt. 24:15).

Date and Setting

Babylon rebelled against the Assyrian Empire in 626 B.C. and overthrew the Assyrian capital of Nineveh in 612 B.C. Babylon became the master of the Middle East when it defeated the Egyptian armies in 605 B.C. Daniel was among those taken captive to Babylon that year when Nebuchadnezzar subdued Jerusalem. He ministered for the full duration of the Babylonian captivity as a prophet and a government official and continued on after Babylon was overcome by the Medes and Persians in 539 B.C. His prophetic ministry was directed to the gentile courts of Babylon (Nebuchadnezzar and Belshazzar) and Persia (Darius and Cyrus), as well as to his Jewish countrymen. Zerubbabel led a return of the Jews to Jerusalem in the first year of Cyrus, and Daniel lived and ministered at least until the third year of Cyrus (536 B.C. 10:1). Daniel's book was no doubt written by Cyrus' ninth year (c. 530 B.C.). As he predicted, the Persian Empire continued until Alexander the

Great (11:2–3) who stretched the Greek Empire as far east as India. The Romans later displaced the Greeks as rulers of the Middle East.

For various reasons, many critics have argued that Daniel is a fraudulent book that was written in the time of the Maccabees in the second century B.C., not the sixth century B.C. as it claims. But their arguments are not compelling:

1. *The prophetic argument* holds that Daniel could not have made such accurate predictions; it must be a "prophecy after the events." Chapter 11 alone contains over one hundred specific prophecies of historical events that literally came true. The author, the critics say, must have lived at the time of Antiochus Epiphanes (175—163 B.C.) and probably wrote this to strengthen the faith of the Jews. But this argument was developed out of a theological bias that assumes true prophecy cannot take place. It also implies that the work was intentionally deceptive.

2. *The linguistic argument* claims that the book uses a late Aramaic in chapters 2—7 and that the Persian and Greek words also point to a late date. But recent discoveries show that Daniel's Aramaic is actually a form of the early Imperial Aramaic. Daniel's use of some Persian words is no argument for a late date since he continued living in the Persian period under Cyrus. The only Greek words are names of musical instruments in chapter 3, and this comes as no surprise since there were Greek mercenaries in the Assyrian and Babylonian armies. Far more Greek words would be expected if the book were written in the second century B.C.

3. *The historical argument* asserts that Daniel's historical blunders argue for a late date. But recent evidence has demonstrated the historical accuracy of Daniel. Inscriptions found at Haran show that Belshazzar reigned in Babylon while his father Nabonidus was fighting the invading Persians. And Darius the Mede (5:31; 6:1) has been identified as Gubaru, a governor appointed by Cyrus.

Theme and Purpose

Daniel was written to encourage the exiled Jews by revealing God's sovereign program for Israel during and after the period of gentile domination. The Times of the Gentiles began with the Babylonian captivity, and Israel would suffer under gentile powers for many years. But this period is not permanent, and a time will come when God will establish the messianic kingdom which will last forever. Daniel repeatedly emphasizes the sovereignty and power of God over human affairs. "The Most High rules in the kingdom of men, and gives it to whomever He chooses" (4:25b). The God who directs the forces of history has not deserted His people. They must continue to trust in Him, because His promises of preservation and ultimate restoration are as sure as the coming of the Messiah.

Keys to Daniel

Key Word: God's Plan for Israel

Key Verses (2:20–22; 2:44)—"Daniel answered and said: 'Blessed be the name of God forever and ever, for wisdom and might are His. And He changes the times and the seasons; He removes kings and raises up kings; He gives wisdom to the wise and knowledge to those who have understanding. He reveals deep and secret things; he knows what *is* in the darkness, and light dwells with Him'" (2:20–22).

"And in the days of these kings the God of heaven will set up a kingdom which shall never be destroyed; and the kingdom shall not be left to other people; it shall break in pieces and consume all these kingdoms, and it shall stand forever." (2:44).

Key Chapter (9)—Daniel's prophecy of the Seventy Weeks (9:24–27) provides the chronological frame for messianic prediction from the time of Daniel to the establishment of the kingdom on earth. It is clear that the first sixty-nine weeks were fulfilled at Christ's first coming. Some scholars affirm that the last week has not yet been fulfilled because Christ relates its main events to His second coming (Matt. 24:6, 15). Others perceive these words of Christ as applying to the Roman desecration of the temple in A.D. 70.

Christ in Daniel

Christ is the Great Stone who will crush the kingdoms of this world (2:34–35, 44), the Son of Man who is given dominion by the Ancient of Days (7:13–14), and the coming Messiah who will be cut off (9:25–26). It is likely that Daniel's vision (10:5–9) was an appearance of Christ (cf. Rev. 1:12–16).

The vision of the sixty-nine weeks (9:25–26) pinpoints the coming of the Messiah. The decree (9:25) took place on March 4, 444 B.C. (Neh. 2:1–8). The sixty-nine weeks of seven years equals 483 years, or 173,880 days (using 360-day prophetic years). This leads to March 29, A.D. 33, the date of the Triumphal Entry. This is checked by noting that 444 B.C. to A.D. 33 is 476 years, and 476 times 365.24219 days per year equals 173,855 days. Adding twenty-five for the difference between March 4 and March 29 gives 173,880 days.

Contribution to the Bible

While Ezekiel emphasizes the nation's religious restoration, Daniel concentrates on its political restoration. Daniel was clearly a prophet, but he did not occupy the prophetic office by making public proclamations to the people as God's representative like Jeremiah and Ezekiel. Therefore, this book was placed in the Writings, the third division of the Hebrew bible, rather than the Prophets. Because it is apocalyptic literature, Daniel has many similarities to Revelation, particularly in its imagery and symbolism. Some believe that it was fulfilled before or during the first century A.D., but others believe that portions await fulfillment. The second view argues that since the events of the sixty-nine weeks were literally fulfilled in the four kingdoms, the events of the Seventieth Week will be literally fulfilled in the future.

Survey of Daniel

Daniel, the "Apocalypse of the Old Testament," presents a surprisingly detailed and comprehensive sweep of prophetic history. After an introductory chapter in

Hebrew, Daniel switches to Aramaic in chapters 2—7 to describe the future course of the gentile world powers. Then in chapters 8—12, Daniel reverts back to his native language to survey the future of the Jewish nation under gentile dominion. The theme of God's sovereign control in the affairs of world history clearly emerges and provides comfort to the future church, as well as to the Jews whose nation was destroyed by the Babylonians. The Babylonians, Persians, Greeks, and Romans will come and go, but God will establish His kingdom through His redeemed people forever. Daniel's three divisions are: (1) The personal history of Daniel (1); (2) the prophetic plan for the Gentiles (2—7); and (3) the prophetic plan for Israel (8—12).

The Personal History of Daniel (1): This chapter introduces the book by giving the background and preparation of the prophet. Daniel is deported along with other promising youths and placed in an intensive training program in Nebuchadnezzar's court. Their names and diets are changed so that they will lose their Jewish identification, but Daniel's resolve to remain faithful to the Lord is rewarded. He and his friends are granted wisdom and knowledge.

The Prophetic Plan for the Gentiles (2—7): Only Daniel can relate and interpret Nebuchadnezzar's disturbing dream of the great statue (2). God empowers Daniel to foretell the way in which He will sovereignly raise and depose four gentile empires. The Messiah's kingdom will end the "Times of the Gentiles." Because of his position revealed in the dream, Nebuchadnezzar erects a golden image and demands that all bow to it (3). The persecution and preservation of Daniel's friends in the fiery furnace again illustrates the power of God. After Nebuchadnezzar refuses to respond to the warning of his vision of the tree (4), he is humbled until he acknowledges the supremacy of God and the foolishness of his pride. The feast of Belshazzar marks the end of the Babylonian kingdom (5). Belshazzar is judged because of his arrogant defiance of God. In the reign of Darius, a plot against Daniel backfires when he is divinely delivered in the den of lions (6). Daniel's courageous faith is rewarded, and Darius learns a lesson about the might of the God of Israel. The vision of the four beasts (7) supplements the four-part statue vision of chapter 2 in its portrayal of the Babylonian, Persian, Greek, and Roman empires. But once again, "the saints of the Most High shall receive the kingdom, and possess the kingdom forever" (7:18).

The Prophetic Plan for Israel (8—12): The focus in chapter 8 narrows to a vision of the ram and goat that shows Israel under the Medo-Persian and Grecian empires. Alexander the Great is the big horn (8:21) and Antiochus Epiphanes is the little horn (8:23). After Daniel's prayer of confession for his people, he is privileged to receive the revelation of the Seventy Weeks, including the Messiah's atoning death (9). This gives the chronology of God's perfect plan for the redemption and deliverance of His people. Following is a great vision that gives amazing details of Israel's future history (10—11). Chapter 11 chronicles the coming kings of Persia and Greece, the wars between the Ptolemies of Egypt and the Seleucids of Syria, and the persecution led by Antiochus. God's people will be saved out of tribulation resurrected (12).

Outline of Daniel

Part One: The Personal History of Daniel (1:1–21)

I. The Deportation of Daniel to Babylon, 1:1–7

II. The Faithfulness of Daniel in Babylon, 1:8–16

III. The Reputation of Daniel in Babylon, 1:17–21

Part Two: The Prophetic Plan for the Gentiles (2:1—7:28)

I. Nebuchadnezzar's Dream of the Great Image, 2:1–49
   A. Nebuchadnezzar Conceals His Dream, 2:1–13
   B. God Reveals the Dream, 2:14–23
   C. Daniel Interprets the Dream, 2:24–45
   D. Nebuchadnezzar Promotes Daniel, 2:46–49

II. Nebuchadnezzar's Image of Gold, 3:1–30
   A. Nebuchadnezzar's Image Is Erected, 3:1–7
   B. Daniel's Friends Refuse to Worship, 3:8–12
   C. Daniel's Friends Trust God, 3:13–18
   D. Daniel's Friends Are Protected in the Furnace, 3:19–25
   E. Daniel's Friends Are Promoted, 3:26–30

III. Nebuchadnezzar's Vision of a Great Lee, 4:1–37
   A. Nebuchadnezzar's Proclamation, 4:1–3
   B. Nebuchadnezzar's Vision, 4:4–18
   C. Daniel's Interpretation of the Vision, 4:19–27
   D. Nebuchadnezzar's Humiliation, 4:28–33
   E. Nebuchadnezzar's Restoration, 4:34–37

IV. Belshazzar and the Handwriting on the Wall, 5:1–31
   A. Belshazzar Defiles the Temple Vessels, 5:1–4
   B. Belshazzar Sees the Handwriting, 5:5–9
   C. Daniel Interprets the Handwriting, 5:10–29
   D. Belshazzar Is Killed, 5:30–31

V. Darius' Foolish Decree, 6:1–28
   A. Daniel Is Promoted, 6:1–3
   B. Darius Signs the Foolish Decree, 6:4–9
   C. Daniel Prays Faithfully, 6:10–15
   D. Daniel Is Saved in the Lions' Den, 6:16–24
   E. Darius' Wise Decree, 6:25–28

VI. Daniel's Vision of the Four Beasts, 7:1–28
  A. The Revelation of the Vision, 7:1–14
     1. Four Beasts, 7:1–8
     2. "Ancient of Days," 7:9–14
  B. The Interpretation of the Vision, 7:15–28
     1. Interpretation of the Four Beasts, 7:15–23
     2. Interpretation of the Fourth Beast, 7:24–28

Part Three: The Prophetic Plan for Israel (8:1—12:13)

I. Daniel's Vision of the Ram and Male Goat, 8:1–27
  A. The Revelation of the Vision, 8:1–12
     1. The Ram, 8:1–4
     2. The Male Goat, 8:5–8
     3. The Little Horn, 8:9–12
  B. The Length of the Vision, 8:13–14
  C. The Interpretation of the Vision, 8:15–27
     1. Interpretation of the Vision, 8:15–19
     2. Interpretation of the Ram, 8:20
     3. Interpretation of the Male Goat, 8:21–22
     4. Interpretation of the Little Horn, 8:23–26
     5. Response of Daniel, 8:27

II. Daniel's Vision of the Seventy Weeks, 9:1–27
  A. The Understanding of Daniel, 9:1–2
  B. The Intercession of Daniel, 9:3–19
  C. The Intervention of Gabriel, 9:20–23
  D. The Revelation of the Seventy Weeks, 9:24–27

III. Daniel's Vision of Israel's Future, 10:1—12:13
  A. The Preparation of Daniel, 10:1–21
     1. Time of the Vision, 10:1–4
     2. Vision of the Heavenly Messenger, 10:5–9
     3. Touch of the Heavenly Messenger, 10:10–17
     4. Strengthening by the Heavenly Messenger, 10:18–21
  B. The Revelation of the Sixty-Nine Weeks, 11:1–35
     1. The Rule of Persia, 11:1–2
     2. The Rule of Greece, 11:3–35
  C. The Revelation of the Seventieth Week, 11:36—12:3
     1. Prophecy of the Willful King, 11:36–45
     2. Prophecy of the Great Time of Trouble, 12:1
     3. Prophecy of the Resurrections, 12:2–3
  D. The Conclusion of the Visions of Daniel, 12:4–13
     1. Sealing of the Book, 12:4
     2. Questions Regarding the Great Time of Trouble, 12:5–13

Prophets of Israel and Judah

Name	Date	Audience	World Power	Biblical Context	Old Testament References to the Prophet	Theme
Isaiah	c. 740–680	Pre-Exile: Judah	Assyria	2 Kin. 15:1—20:21; 2 Chr. 26:16—32:33	2 Kin. 19—20 (passim); 2 Chr. 26:22; 32:20,32; Isa. (passim)	Salvation is of the Lord
Jeremiah	c. 627–580	Pre-Exile: Judah	Assyria & Babylonia	2 Kin. 22:3—25:30; 2 Chr. 34:1—26:21	2 2 Chr. 35:25; 36:12, 21ff.; Ezra 1:1; Dan. 9:2; Jer. (passim)	Warning of the Coming Judgment
Ezekiel	c. 493–571	Exile: Exiles in Babylonia	Babylonia	2 Kin. 24:8—25:30; 2 Chr. 36:9–21	Ezek. 1:3, 24:24	Glory of the Lord
Daniel	c. 605–535	Exile: Exiles in Babylonia	Babylonia & Medo-Persia	2 Kin. 23:34—25:30; 2 Chr. 36:4–23	Ezek. 14:14, 20; 28:3; Dan. (passim)	Sovereignty of God over men and nations
Hosea	c. 755–715	Pre-Exile: Israel	Assyria	2 Kin. 14:23—18:12	Hos. 1:1–2	Loyal Love of God
Joel	c. 835	Pre-Exile: Judah	Assyria	2 Kin. 12:1–21; 2 Chr. 24:1–27	Joel 1:1	Day of the Lord
Amos	c. 760–753	Pre-Exile: Israel	Assyria	2 Kin 14:23—15:7	Amos 1:1; 7:8–14; 8:2	Judgment on Israel
Obadiah	c. 848–841	Pre-Exile: Edom	Assyria	2 Kin. 8:16–24; 2 Chr. 21:1–20	Obad. 1	Doom on Edom
Jonah	c. 782–753	Pre-exile: Assyria	Assyria	2 Kin. 13:10–25; 14:23–29	2 Kin. 14:25; Jon. (passim)	Salvation to the Gentiles
Micah	c. 735–700	Pre-Exile: Judah	Assyria	2 Kin. 15:32—19:37; 2 Chr. 27:1—32:23	Mic. 1:1; Jer. 26:18	Injustice of Judah and Justice of God
Nahum	c. 664–654	Pre-Exile: Assyria	Assyria	2 Kin. 21:1–18; 2 Chr. 33:1–20	Nah. 1:1	The Destruction of Nineveh
Habakkuk	c. 609–605	Pre-Exile: Judah	Babylonia	2 Kin. 23:31—24:7; 2 Chr. 36:1–8	Hab. 1:1; 3:1	The Just Shall Live by Faith

Prophets of Israel and Judah—*Continued*

Name	Date	Audience	World Power	Biblical Context	Old Testament References to the Prophet	Theme
Zephaniah	c. 632–628	Pre-Exile: Judah	Assyria	2 Kin. 22:1–2 2 Chr. 34:1–7	Zeph. 1:1	Judgment and Blessing in the Day of the Lord
Haggai	c. 520	Post-Exile: Jews who returned to Jesuralem from Babylonia	Medo-Persia	Ezra 5:1—6:15	Ezra 5:1; 6:14 Hag. (passim)	Rebuilding the Temple
Zechariah	c. 520–480	Post-Exile: Jews who returned to Jerusalem from Babylonia	Medo-Persia	Ezra 5:1—6:15	Ezra 5:1; 6:14 Neh. 12:16 Zech. 1:1,7; 7:1,8	Future Blessing for Israel
Malachi	c. 432–424	Post-Exile: Jews who returned to Jerusalem from Babylonia	Medo-Persia	Neh. 13:1–31	Mal. 1:1	Appeal to Backsliders

Introduction to the
Minor Prophets

WHILE THE SEVENTEEN PROPHETIC BOOKS of the Old Testament are the "dark continent of Scripture," people are even more unfamiliar with the twelve minor prophets as a whole than they are with the five major prophets. These twelve books became known as the Minor Prophets late in the 4th century A.D. not because they were considered less important or less inspired, but because they are generally shorter than the five Major Prophets, especially books like Isaiah and Jeremiah. Their messages are more succinct than those of the Major Prophets, but they are just as powerful.

Before the time of Christ these twelve books were joined together to make one scroll known collectively as "The Twelve." Their combined length (sixty-seven chapters) is about equal to that of Isaiah. The only chronological significance of the order of the Minor Prophets in the English Bible is that the first six were written before the last six:

Canonical Order	Chronological Order	Approximate Dates
1. Hosea	1. Obadiah	840
2. Joel	2. Joel	835
3. Amos	3. Jonah	760
4. Obadiah	4. Amos	755
5. Jonah	5. Hosea	740
6. Micah	6. Micah	730
7. Nahum	7. Nahum	660
8. Habakkuk	8. Zephaniah	625
9. Zephaniah	9. Habakkuk	607
10. Haggai	10. Haggai	520
11. Zechariah	11. Zechariah	515
12. Malachi	12. Malachi	430

The Minor Prophets from Obadiah to Malachi cover a four-hundred-year span of history moving through the Assyrian, Babylonian, and Persian Empires. Three were prophets to the northern kingdom (Jonah, Amos, Hosea), six were prophets to the southern kingdom (Obadiah, Joel, Micah, Nahum, Zephaniah, Habakkuk), and three were postexilic prophets (Haggai, Zechariah, Malachi). Although all the minor prophets are named, very little is known about most of them. Their backgrounds and personalities are quite diverse, but the four basic prophetic themes are found in all of them (see "Introduction to the Major Prophets").

Hosea

The unhappy story of Hosea and his faithless wife Gomer illustrates the loyal love of God and the spiritual adultery of Israel. Hosea exposes the sins of Israel and contrasts them to God's holiness. The nation must be judged for its sins but it will be restored in the future because of the love and faithfulness of God.

Joel

This book looks back to a recent locust plague that decimated the land of Judah to illustrate the far more terrifying day of the Lord. The land will be invaded by a fearsome army that will make the locusts seem mild in comparison. Nevertheless, God appeals to the people to repent in order to divert the coming disaster. Because the people will not change, judgment will come, but it will be followed by great blessing.

Amos

The northern kingdom was in its heyday when Amos warned the people of their coming doom. In eight pronouncements of judgment, Amos spirals around the surrounding countries before landing on Israel. He then delivers three sermons to list the sins of the house of Israel and call for repentance. The people reject Amos' warnings and their coming judgment is portrayed in a series of five visions. But Amos closes his book with a brief word of future hope.

Obadiah

This obscure prophet of the southern kingdom directs his brief oracle to the nation of Edom that bordered Judah on the southeast. Edom (descended from Esau) refused to act as his brother's keeper toward Judah (descended from Jacob). Because they gloated when

Jerusalem was invaded, their judgment would be nothing less than total destruction.

Jonah

With a prophetic message of only one line, Jonah is the most biographical of all the prophets. The repentant response of the people of Nineveh to Jonah's terse oracle causes the God of mercy to spare the city. But the central teaching of the book is the lesson on compassion God has to teach His reluctant prophet. Jonah learns to look beyond his nation and trust the Creator of all people.

Micah

The prophecy of Micah begins with a word of divine retribution against Israel and Judah because of the radical corruption on every level of society: rulers, prophets, priests, judges, businessmen, and landlords. But God's covenant promises will be fulfilled in the future kingdom of Messiah. Judgment will ultimately be followed by forgiveness and restoration, and the book ends on a strong note of promise.

Nahum

About 125 years after Nineveh repented under the preaching of Jonah, Micah predicted the imminent destruction of the same city. The people in the Assyrian capital have reverted to idolatry and brutality, and Assyria has overthrown the northern kingdom of Israel. Because of God's holiness and power, Nineveh will surely be destroyed in spite of its apparent invincibility.

Habakkuk

Very close to the end of the kingdom of Judah, Habakkuk asks God why He is not dealing with the wickedness of his nation. When God tells him He is about to use the Babylonians as His rod of judgment, Habakkuk asks a second question: How can He judge Judah with a nation that is even more wicked? After the Lord's second response, the prophet magnifies the name of God for His power and purposes.

Zephaniah

In no uncertain terms, Zephaniah develops the theme of the coming day of the Lord as a day of awesome judgment followed by great blessing. Zephaniah begins with the coming judgment of Judah and broadens his scope to include the Gentiles as well. Because Judah refuses to seek the Lord, it stands condemned. But a remnant will exult when God restores the fortunes of His people.

Haggai

After the Babylonian exile, the Jews began to rebuild the temple but allowed the work to stop while they rebuilt their own houses instead. Because of their failure to put God first, they were not enjoying His blessing in the land. Haggai urges the people to finish the temple because of God's promise that it would be filled with glory. After chastening the people for their contamination, Haggai closes with a promise of future blessing.

Zechariah

A contemporary of Haggai, Zechariah also exhorts the Jews to complete the construction of the temple. Zechariah's method of motivating them is one of encouragement—the temple is central to Israel's spiritual heritage, and it is related to the coming of Messiah. Zechariah's series of visions, messages, and burdens offer some of the clearest messianic prophecies in Scripture. God reveals that His program for his people is far from completed.

Malachi

By the time of the last Old Testament prophet, the spiritual and moral climate of the people has grown cold. Their worship is meaningless and indifferent, and as they grow more distant from God, they become characterized by religious and social compromise. A terrible day of judgment is coming when "all the arrogant and every evildoer will be chaff" to be burned, "But for you who fear My name the sun of righteousness will rise with healing in its wings."

Hosea

HOSEA IS CALLED BY GOD to prophesy during Israel's last hours, just as Jeremiah would be called years later to prophesy to the crumbling kingdom of Judah. Hosea's personal tragedy becomes an intense illustration of Israel's national tragedy. It is a story of one-sided love and faithfulness—between a prophet and his faithless wife (Hosea and Gomer) and Jehovah and His faithless people. Just as Gomer is married to Hosea, Israel is betrothed to God. In both cases the bride plays the harlot and runs after other lovers. But unconditional love keeps seeking even when it is spurned. In Hosea's case, that means buying back his wife from the slave market; for Israel it means purifying punishment followed by restoration to the Land of Promise.

Focus	Adulterous Wife and Faithful Husband			Adulterous Israel and Faithful Lord			
	1:1 — 3:5			4:1 — 14:9			
Divisions	Prophetic Marriage	Application of Gomer to Israel	Restoration of Gomer	Spiritual Adultery of Israel	Refusal of Israel to Repent	Judgment of Israel by God	Restoration of Israel to God
	1:1 — 2:1	2:2 — 2:23	3:1 — 3:5	4:1 — 6:3	6:4 — 8:14	9:1 — 10:15	11:1 — 14:9
Topics	Marriage of Hosea			Message of Hosea			
	Personal			National			
Place	Northern Kingdom of Israel						
Time	c. 755–710 B.C.						

Introduction and Title

Hosea, whose name means "salvation," ministers to the northern kingdom of Israel (also called Ephraim, after its largest tribe). Outwardly, the nation is enjoying a time of prosperity and growth; but inwardly, moral corruption and spiritual adultery permeate the people. Hosea, instructed by God to marry a woman named Gomer, finds his domestic life to be an accurate and tragic dramatization of the unfaithfulness of God's people. During his half century of prophetic ministry, Hosea repeatedly echoes his threefold message: God abhors the sins of His people; judgment is certain; but God's loyal love stands firm.

The names Hosea, Joshua, and Jesus are all derived from the same Hebrew root word. The word *hoshea* means "salvation," but "Joshua" and "Jesus" include an additional idea: "Yahweh Is Salvation" (see "Introduction and Title" in Joshua). As God's messenger, Hosea offers the possibility of salvation if only the nation will turn from idolatry back to God.

Israel's last king, Hoshea, has the same name as the prophet even though the English Bible spells them differently. Hosea in the Greek and Latin is *Osee*.

Author

Few critics refute the claim in chapter 1, verse 1, that Hosea was the author of this book. His place of birth is not given, but his familiarity and obvious concern with the northern kingdom indicate that he lived in Israel, not Judah. This is also seen when he called the king of Samaria "our king" (7:5). Hosea was the son of Beeri (1:1), husband of Gomer (1:3), and father of two sons and a daughter (1:4, 6, 9). Nothing more is known of him since he is not mentioned elsewhere in the Bible.

Hosea had a real compassion for his people, and his personal suffering because of Gomer gave him some understanding of God's grief over their sin. Thus, his words of coming judgment were passionately delivered but tempered with a heart of tenderness. He upbraided his people for their lying, murder, insincerity, ingratitude, idolatry, and covetousness with cutting metaphors and images; but his messages were punctuated with consolation and future hope.

Date and Setting

Hosea addressed the northern kingdom of Israel (5:1), often called Ephraim after the largest tribe (5:3, 5, 11, 13). According to chapter 1, verse 1, he ministered during the reigns of Uzziah (767–739 B.C.), Jotham (739–731 B.C.), Ahaz (731–715 B.C.), and Hezekiah (715–686 B.C.), kings of Judah. When Hosea began his ministry, Jeroboam II (782–753 B.C.) was still reigning in Israel. This makes Hosea a younger contemporary of Amos, another prophet to the northern kingdom. Hosea was also a contemporary of Isaiah and Micah who ministered to the southern kingdom. Hosea's long career continued after the time of Jeroboam II and spanned the reigns of the last six kings of Israel from Zechariah (753–752 B.C.) to Hoshea (732–722 B.C.). Hosea evidently compiled this book in the early years of Hezekiah, and his ministry stretched from about 755 B.C. to about 710 B.C. The Book of Hosea represents approximately forty years of prophetic ministry.

When Hosea began his ministry, Israel was enjoying a temporary period of political and economic prosperity under Jeroboam II. However, the nation began to crumble after Tiglath-pileser III (745–727 B.C.) strengthened Assyria. The reigns of Israel's last six kings were relatively brief since four were murdered and a fifth was carried captive to Assyria. Confusion and decline characterized the last years of the northern kingdom, and her people refused to heed Hosea's warning of imminent judgment. The people were in a spiritual stupor, riddled with sin and idolatry.

Theme and Purpose

The themes of chapters 1—3 echo throughout the rest of the book. The adultery of Gomer (1) illustrates the sin of Israel (4—7); the degradation of Gomer (2) represents the judgment of Israel (8—10); and Hosea's redemption of Gomer (3) pictures the restoration of Israel (11—14). More than any other Old Testament prophet, Hosea's personal experiences illustrated his prophetic message. In his relationship to Gomer, Hosea portrayed God's faithfulness, justice, love, and forgiveness toward His people. The theme of God's holiness is developed in contrast to Israel's corruption and apostasy. Hosea utters about 150 statements concerning the sins of Israel, and more than half deal specifically with idolatry. The theme of God's justice is contrasted with Israel's lack of justice. There was never a good king in Israel, and judgment is long overdue. The theme of God's love is seen in contrast to Israel's hardness and empty ritual. God's loyal love is unconditional and ceaseless; in spite of Israel's manifold sins, God tries every means to bring His people back to Himself. He pleads with the people to return to Him, but they will not. "O Israel, return to the Lord your God, for you have stumbled because of your iniquity" (14:1).

Keys to Hosea

Key Word: God's Loyal Love for Israel

Key Verses (4:1; 11:7–9)—"Hear the word of the Lord, you children of Israel, for the Lord *brings* a charge against the inhabitants of the land: there is no truth or mercy or knowledge of God in the land" (4:1).

"My people are bent on backsliding from Me. Though they call to the Most High, none at all exalt *Him.* How can I give you up, Ephraim? *How* can I hand you over, Israel? How can I make you like Admah? *How* can I set you like Zeboiim? My heart churns within Me; my sympathy is stirred. I will not execute the fierceness of My anger; I will not again destroy Ephraim. For I *am* God, and not man, the Holy One in your midst; and I will not come with terror" (11:7–9).

Key Chapter (4)—The nation of Israel has left the knowledge of the truth and followed the idolatrous ways of their pagan neighbors. Central to the book is verse 6—"My people are destroyed for lack of knowledge. Because you have rejected knowledge, I also will reject you from being priest for Me; because you have forgotten the law of your God, I also will forget your children."

Christ in Hosea

Matthew 2:15 applies chapter 11, verse 1, to Christ in Egypt: "When Israel *was* a child, I loved him, and out of Egypt I called My son." Matthew quotes the second half of this verse to show that the Exodus of Israel from Egypt as a new nation was a prophetic type of Israel's Messiah who was also called out of Egypt in His childhood. Both Israel and Christ left Palestine to take refuge in Egypt.

Christ's identification with our plight and His loving work of redemption can be seen in Hosea's redemption of Gomer from the slavemarket.

Contribution to the Bible

Hosea is the first of the twelve minor prophets, perhaps because of its size. The New Testament quotes or alludes to its vivid statements several times: 1:10 (Rom. 9:25–27; 2 Cor. 6:18); 2:23 (Rom. 9:25–26; 1 Pet. 2:10); 6:6 (Matt. 9:13; 12:7); 10:8 (Luke 23:30; Rev. 6:16); 11:1 (Matt. 2:14–15); 13:14 (1 Cor. 15:55); and 14:2 (Heb. 13:15).

There are different views concerning Hosea's marriage to Gomer. Some see it as a fictional allegory of God and Israel, but there is little basis for this position. Chapters 1—3 are presented as a straightforward narrative, and there are no indications that it is fictitious. Although Hosea was told to take a "wife of harlotry" (1:2), this does not necessarily mean that Gomer was a harlot before her marriage to Hosea. This passage may be looking ahead to what she would become.

Survey of Hosea

Hosea is called by God to prophesy during Israel's last hours just as Jeremiah will prophesy years later to the crumbling kingdom of Judah. As one commentator has noted, "What we see in the prophecy of Hosea are the last few swirls as the kingdom of Israel goes down the drain." This book represents God's last gracious effort to plug the drain. Hosea's personal tragedy is an intense illustration of Israel's national tragedy. It is a story of one-sided love and faithfulness that represents the relationship between Israel and God. Just as Gomer is married to Hosea, Israel is betrothed to God. Both relationships gradually disintegrate—Gomer runs after other men, and Israel runs after other gods. Israel's spiritual adultery is illustrated in Gomer's physical adultery. The development of the book can be traced in two parts: the adulterous wife and faithful husband (1—3) and the adulterous Israel and faithful Lord (4—14).

The Adulterous Wife and Faithful Husband (1—3): Hosea marries a woman named Gomer who bears him three children appropriately named by God as signs to Israel. Jezreel, Lo-Ruhamah, and Lo-Ammi mean "God Scatters," "Not Pitied," and "Not My People." Similarly, God will judge and scatter Israel because of her sin.

Gomer seeks other lovers and deserts Hosea. In spite of the depth to which her sin carries her, Hosea redeems her from the slave market and restores her.

The Adulterous Israel and Faithful Lord (4—14): Because of his own painful experience, Hosea can feel some of the sorrow of God over the sinfulness of His people. His loyal love for Gomer is a reflection of God's concern for Israel. However, Israel has fallen into the dregs of sin and is hardened against God's gracious last appeal to return. The people have flagrantly violated all of God's commandments, and they are indicted by the holy God for their crimes. Even now God wants to heal and redeem them (7:1, 13), but in their arrogance and idolatry they rebel.

Chapters 9—10 give the verdict of the case God has just presented. Israel's disobedience will lead to her dispersion. "For they [sow] the wind" (4—7), "and they . . . reap the whirlwind" (8—10). Israel spurns repentance, and the judgment of God can no longer be delayed.

God is holy (4—7) and just (8—10), but He is also loving and gracious (11—14). God must discipline, but because of His endless love, He will ultimately save and restore His wayward people. "How can I give you up, Ephraim? . . . I will heal their backsliding, I will love them freely, for My anger has turned away from him" (11:8; 14:4).

Outline of Hosea

I. **The Adulterous Wife and Faithful Husband,** 1:1—3:5
    A. The Introduction to the Book of Hosea, 1:1
    B. The Prophetic Marriage of Hosea to Gomer, 1:2—2:1
        1. Hosea's Marriage to Gomer, 1:2
        2. The Children of Hosea and Gomer, 1:3–9
        3. The Application of Future Restoration, 1:10—2:1
    C. The Application of the Adultery of Gomer, 2:2–23
        1. Israel's Sin of Spiritual Adultery, 2:2–5
        2. Judgment of God, 2:6–13
        3. Restoration of Israel, 2:14–23
    D. The Restoration of Gomer to Hosea, 3:1–5

II. **The Adulterous Israel and Faithful Lord,** 4:1—14:9
    A. The Spiritual Adultery of Israel, 4:1—6:3
        1. The Sins of Israel, 4:1–19
            a. Rejection of the Knowledge of God, 4:1–11
            b. Idolatry of Israel, 4:12–19
        2. Judgment on Israel, 5:1–14
        3. Eventual Restoration of Israel, 5:15—6:3
    B. The Refusal of Israel to Repent of Her Adultery, 6:4—8:14
        1. Willful Transgression of the Covenant, 6:4–11
        2. Willful Refusal to Return to the Lord, 7:1–16
        3. Willful Idolatry, 8:1–14
    C. The Judgment of Israel by God, 9:1—10:15
        1. Judgment of Dispersion, 9:1–9
        2. Judgment of Barrenness, 9:10–17
        3. Judgment of Destruction, 10:1–15

D. The Restoration of Israel to the Lord, 11:1—14:9
1. God's Love for Israel, 11:1–12
2. Israel's Continuing Sin, 12:1—13:16
3. God's Promise to Restore Israel, 14:1–9

Joel

JOEL USES A RECENT CALAMITY in the nation of Judah to teach his hearers a prophetic lesson. A locust plague had invaded the land, destroying every green thing in its path. Grapevines were stripped clean; grain fields lay bare; fruit trees stood leafless and unproductive. The devastation was so complete that even grain offerings to God were impossible. Joel uses the locust invasion as the starting point of his sermon. As bad as the locust plague was, it would pale by comparison with what God was about to bring upon His people. An army from the north would come to attack the nation, leaving behind devastation even more complete than that of the locusts. The only hope for Joel's hearers: heartfelt repentance before that terrible day arrives.

Focus	Day of the Lord in Retrospect		Day of the Lord in Prospect	
	1:1 1:20		2:1 3:21	
Divisions	Past Day of the Locust	Past Day of the Drought	Imminent Day of the Lord	Ultimate Day of the Lord
	1:1 1:12	1:13 1:20	2:1 2:27	2:28 3:21
Topics	Historical Invasion		Prophetic Invasion	
	Past Judgment on Judah		Future Judgment and Restoration of Judah	
Place	Southern Kingdom of Judah			
Time	c. 835 Years			

JOEL

Introduction and Title

Disaster strikes the southern kingdom of Judah without warning. An ominous black cloud descends upon the land—the dreaded locusts. In a matter of hours, every living green thing has been stripped bare. Joel, God's spokesman during the reign of Joash (835–796 B.C.), seizes this occasion to proclaim God's message. Although the locust plague has been a terrible judgment for sin, God's future judgments during the day of the Lord will make that plague pale by comparison. In that day, God will destroy His enemies, but bring unparalleled blessing to those who faithfully obey Him.

The Hebrew name *Yo'el* means "Yahweh Is God." This name is appropriate to the theme of the book, which emphasizes God's sovereign work in history. The courses of nature and nations are in His hand. The Greek equivalent is *Ioel,* and the Latin is *Joel.*

Author

Although there are several other Joels in the Bible, the prophet Joel is known only from this book. In the introductory verse, Joel identifies himself as the son of Pethuel (1:1) meaning "persuaded of God." His frequent references to Zion and the house of the Lord (1:9, 13–14; 2:15–17, 23, 32; 3:1, 5–6, 16–17, 20–21) suggest that he probably lived not far from Jerusalem. Because of his statements about the priesthood (1:13–14; 2:17), some think Joel was a priest as well as a prophet. In any case, Joel was a clear, concise, and uncompromising preacher of repentance.

Date and Setting

Since this book includes no explicit time references, it cannot be dated with certainty. Some commentators assign a late date (usually postexilic) to Joel for these reasons: (1) It does not mention the northern kingdom and indicates it was written after the 722 B.C. demise of Israel. (2) The references to priests but not kings fit the postexilic period. (3) Joel does not refer to Assyria, Syria, or Babylon, perhaps because these countries have already been overthrown. (4) If chapter 3, verse 2, refers to the Babylonian captivity, this also supports the postexilic date. (5) The mention of the Greeks (3:6) argues for a late date.

Commentators who believe Joel was written in the ninth century B.C. answer the above arguments in this way: (1) Joel's failure to mention the northern kingdom is an argument from silence. His prophecy was directed to Judah, not Israel. (2) Other early prophets omit references to a king (Obadiah, Jonah, Nahum, and Habakkuk). This also fits the political situation during 841–835 B.C. when Athaliah usurped the throne upon the death of her husband Ahaziah. Joash, the legitimate heir to the throne, was a minor and protected by the high priest Jehoida. When Athaliah was removed from power in 835, Joash came to the throne but ruled under the regency of Jehoiada. Thus, the prominence of the priests and lack of reference to a king in Joel fit this historical context. (3) It is true that Joel does not refer to Assyria or Babylonia, but the countries Joel mentions are more crucial. They include Phoenicia,

Philistia, Egypt, and Edom— countries prominent in the ninth century but not later. Assyria and Babylonia are not mentioned because they had not yet reached a position of power. Also, if Joel were postexilic, a reference to Persia would be expected. (4) Chapter 3, verse 2, does not refer to the Babylonian captivity but to an event that has not yet occurred. (5) Greeks are mentioned in Assyrian records from the eighth century B.C. It is just an assumption to state that the Hebrews had no knowledge of the Greeks at an early time.

Evidence also points to a sharing of material between Joel and Amos (cf. Joel 3:16 and Amos 1:2; Joel 3:18 and Amos 9:13). The context of the books suggests that Amos, an eighth-century prophet, borrowed from Joel. Also, Joel's style is more like that of Hosea and Amos than of the postexilic writers. The evidence seems to favor a date of about 835 B.C. for Joel. Since Joel does not mention idolatry, it may have been written after the purge of Baal worship and most other forms of idolatry in the early reign of Joash under Jehoiada the priest. As an early prophet of Judah, Joel would have been a contemporary of Elisha in Israel.

Theme and Purpose

The key theme of Joel is the day of the Lord in retrospect and prospect. The terrible locust plague that recently occurred in Judah was used by Joel to illustrate the coming Day of Judgment when God directly intervenes in human history to vindicate His righteousness. This will be a time of unparalleled retribution upon Israel (2:1–11) and the nation (3:1–17), but it will culminate in great blessing and salvation for all who trust in the Lord (2:18–32; 3:18–21). "And it shall come to pass *that* whoever calls on the name of the LORD shall be saved" (2:32a).

Joel was written as a warning to the people of Judah of their need to humbly turn to the Lord with repentant hearts (2:12–17) so that God could bless rather than buffet them. If they continue to spurn God's gracious call for repentance, judgment will be inevitable. Joel stresses the sovereign power of Yahweh over nature and nations, and shares how God uses nature to get the attention of men.

Keys to Joel

Key Word: The Day of the Lord

Key Verses (2:11, 28–9)—"The LORD gives voice before His army, for His camp is very great; for strong *is the One* who executes His word. For the day of the LORD *is* great and very terrible; who can endure it?" (2:11).

"And it shall come to pass afterward that I will pour out My Spirit on all flesh; your sons and your daughters shall prophesy, your old men shall dream dreams, your young men shall see visions; And also *My* men-servants and on *My* maidservants I will pour out My spirit in those days" (2:28–29).

Key Chapter (2)—The prophet calls for Judah's repentance and promises God's repentance (2:13–14) from His planned judgment upon Judah if they do indeed turn to Him. Though the offer is clearly given, Judah continues to rebel against the Lord, and judgment is to follow. In that judgment, however, is God's promise of His later outpouring, fulfilled initially on the Day of Pentecost (Acts 2:16ff.) and ultimately when Christ returns for the culmination of the day of the Lord.

Christ in Joel

Christ promised to send the Holy Spirit after His ascension to the Father (see John 16:7–15; Acts 1:8). When this was fulfilled on the Day of Pentecost, Peter said, "This is that which was spoken by the prophet Joel" (see Joel 2:28–32; Acts 2:16–21). Joel also portrays Christ as the One who will judge the nations in the Valley of Jehoshaphat ("God judges," 3:2, 12).

Contribution to the Bible

Joel is characterized by graphic style and vivid descriptions. He makes striking use of a historical event as an illustrative foundation for the overall message of the book. Although Obadiah was the first prophet to mention the day of the Lord (Obad. 15), Joel was the first to develop this important biblical theme. Other references to the day of the Lord include: Isaiah 2:12, 17–20; 3:7–18; 4:1–2; 13:6–9; Jeremiah 46:10; Ezekiel 13:5; 30:3; Amos 5:18; Zephaniah 1:7, 14; Malachi 4:5; First Corinthians 5:5; First Thessalonians 5:2. It is clear from Second Thessalonians 2:2 and Second Peter 3:10 that the day of the Lord is a future event from the New Testament perspective. Peter quoted Joel (2:28–32) in his sermon on the Day of Pentecost in Acts 2:16–21, but stopped in the middle of verse 32. In His Olivet Discourse (Matt. 24:29), Jesus associated the events mentioned in Joel 2:10, 31; 3:15 with the signs of His second coming. The apostle Paul applied chapter 2, verse 32, to the salvation available to Jews and Gentiles who trust in Christ (Rom. 10:12–13).

Survey of Joel

The brief Book of Joel develops the crucial theme of the coming day of the Lord (1:15; 2:1–2, 11, 31; 3:14, 18). It is a time of awesome judgment upon people and nations that have rebelled against God. But it is also a time of future blessing upon those who have trusted in Him. The theme of disaster runs throughout the book (locust plagues, famine, raging fires, invading armies, celestial phenomena), but promises of hope are interspersed with the pronouncements of coming judgment. The basic outline of Joel is: the day of the Lord in retrospect (1:1–20) and the day of the Lord in prospect (2:1—3:21).

The Day of the Lord in Retrospect (1:1–20): Joel begins with an account of a recent locust plague that has devastated the land. The black cloud of insects has stripped the grapevines and fruit trees and ruined the grain harvest. The economy has been brought to a further standstill by a drought and the people are in a desperate situation.

The Day of the Lord in Prospect (2:1—3:21): Joel makes effective use of this natural catastrophe as an illustration of a far greater judgment to come. Compared to the terrible day of the Lord, the destruction by the locusts will seem insignificant. The land will be invaded by a swarming army; like locusts they will be speedy and voracious. The desolation caused by this army will be dreadful: "For the day of the LORD is great and very terrible; who can endure it?" (2:11).

Even so, it is not too late for the people to avert disaster. The prophetic warning is designed to bring them to the point of repentance (2:12–17). " 'Now, therefore,' says the LORD, 'Turn to me with all your heart, with fasting, with weeping, and with mourning' " (2:12). But God's gracious offer falls on deaf ears.

Ultimately, the swarming, creeping, stripping, and gnawing locusts (1:4; 2:25) will come again in a fiercer form. But God promises that judgment will be followed by great blessing in a material (2:18–27) and spiritual (2:28–32) sense.

These rich promises are followed by a solemn description of the judgment of all nations in the valley of decision (3:14) in the end times. The nations will give an account of themselves to the God of Israel who will judge those who have rebelled against Him. God alone controls the course of history. "So shall you know that I *am* the LORD your God, dwelling in Zion My holy mountain" (3:17). Joel ends with the kingdom blessings upon the remnant of faithful Judah: "But Judah shall abide forever, and Jerusalem from generation to generation" (3:20).

Outline of Joel

I. The Day of the Lord in Retrospect, 1:1–20
   - A. The Past Day of the Locust, 1:1–12
   - B. The Past Day of the Drought, 1:13–20

II. The Day of the Lord in Prospect, 2:1—3:21
   - A. The Imminent Day of the Lord, 2:1–27
     1. Prophecy of the Imminent Invasion of Judah, 2:1–11
     2. Conditional Promise of the Salvation of Judah, 2:12–27
   - B. The Ultimate Day of the Lord, 2:28—3:21
     1. Last Events Before the Terrible Day of the Lord, 2:28–32
     2. Events of the Terrible Day of the Lord, 3:1–21
       a. Judgment on the Gentiles, 3:1–16
       b. Restoration of Judah, 3:17–21

Amos

AMOS PROPHESIED DURING A PERIOD of national optimism in Israel. Business was booming and boundaries were bulging. But below the surface, greed and injustice were festering. Hyprocritical religious motions had replaced true worship, creating a false sense of security and a growing callousness to God's disciplining hand. Famine, drought, plagues, death, destruction—nothing could force the people to their knees.

Amos, the country-farmer-turned-prophet, lashes out at sin unflinchingly, trying to visualize the nearness of God's judgment and mobilize the nation to repentance. The nation, like a basket of rotting fruit, stands ripe for judgment because of its hypocrisy and spiritual indifference.

Focus	Eight Prophecies 1:1 — 2:16	Three Sermons 3:1 — 6:14	Five Visions 7:1 — 9:10	Five Promises 9:11 — 9:15
Divisions	Judgment of Israel and Surrounding Nations 1:1 — 2:16	Sin of Israel: Present, Past, and Future 3:1 — 6:14	Pictures of the Judgment of Israel 7:1 — 9:10	Restoration of Israel 9:11 — 9:15
Topics	Pronouncements of Judgment	Provocations for Judgment	Future of Judgment	Promises after Judgment
	Judgment			Hope
Place	Surrounding Nations	Northern Kingdom of Israel		
Time	c. 760–753 Years			

Introduction and Title

Amos prophesies during a period of national optimism in Israel. Business is booming and boundaries are bulging. But below the surface, greed and injustice are festering. Hypocritical religious motions have replaced true worship, creating a false sense of security and a growing callousness to God's disciplining hand. Famine, drought, plagues, death, destruction—nothing can force the people to their knees.

Amos, the farmer-turned-prophet, lashes out at sin unflinchingly, trying to visualize the nearness of God's judgment and mobilize the nation to repentance. The nation, like a basket of rotting fruit, stands ripe for judgment because of its hypocrisy and spiritual indifference.

The name *Amos* is derived from the Hebrew root *Amos,* "to lift a burden, to carry." Thus, his name means "Burden" or "Burden-Bearer." Amos lives up to the meaning of his name by bearing up under his divinely given burden of declaring judgment to rebellious Israel. The Greek and Latin titles are both transliterated in English as *Amos.*

Author

The only Old Testament appearance of the name *Amos* is in this book. (He should not be confused with Amoz, the father of Isaiah.) Concerning his background, Amos said, "I *was* no prophet, nor *was I a* son of a prophet, but I *was* a herdsman and a tender of sycamore fruit" (7:14). But he was gripped by God and divinely commissioned to bring his prophetic burden to Israel (3:8; 7:15). He came from the rural area of Tekoa in Judah, twelve miles south of Jerusalm, where he tended a special breed of small sheep that produced wool of the best quality. As a grower of sycamore figs, he had to puncture the fruit before it ripened to allow the insects inside to escape. Amos lived a disciplined life, and his knowledge of the wilderness often surfaces in his messages (cf. 3:4–5, 12; 5:8, 19; 9:9). Amos was from the country, but he was well-educated in the Scriptures. His keen sense of morality and justice is obvious, and his objective appraisal of Israel's spiritual condition was not well received, especially since he was from Judah. He delivered his message in Beth-el because it was the residence of the king of Israel and a center of idolatry. His frontal attack on the greed, injustice, and self-righteousness of the people of the northern kingdom made his words unpopular.

Date and Setting

Amos prophesied "in the days of Uzziah king of Judah, and in the days of Jeroboam the son of Joash, king of Israel, two years before the earthquake" (1:1). Uzziah reigned from 767 to 739 B.C. and Jeroboam II reigned from 782 to 753 B.C., leaving an overlap from 767 to 753 B.C. Over two hundred years later, Zechariah referred to this earthquake in Uzziah's reign (Zech. 14:5). Amos anticipates the 722 B.C. Assyrian captivity of Israel (7:11) and indicates that at the time of writing, Jeroboam II was not yet dead. Thus, Amos prophesied in Beth-el about 755 B.C. Astronomical calculations indicate that a solar eclipse took place in Israel on June 15, 763 B.C. This event was probably fresh in the minds of Amos' hearers (8:9).

Amos ministered after the time of Obadiah, Joel, and Jonah and just before Hosea, Micah, and Isaiah. At this time Uzziah reigned over a prosperous and militarily successful Judah. He fortified Jerusalem and subdued the Philistines, the Ammonites, and the Edomites. In the north, Israel was ruled by the capable king Jeroboam II. Economic and military circumstances were almost ideal, but prosperity only increased the materialism, immorality, and injustice of the people (2:6–8; 3:10; 4:1; 5:10–12; 8:4–6). During these years, Assyria, Babylonia, Syria, and Egypt were relatively weak. Thus, the people of Israel found it hard to imagine the coming disaster predicted by Amos. However, it was only three decades until the downfall of Israel.

Theme and Purpose

The basic theme of Amos is the coming judgment of Israel because of the holiness of Yahweh and the sinfulness of His covenant people. Amos unflinchingly and relentlessly visualizes the causes and course of Israel's quickly approaching doom. God is gracious and patient, but His justice and righteousness will not allow sin to go unpunished indefinitely. The sins of Israel are heaped as high as heaven: empty ritualism, oppression of the poor, idolatry, deceit, self-righteousness, arrogance, greed, materialism, callousness. The people have repeatedly broken every aspect of their covenant relationship with God. Nevertheless, God's mercy and love are evident in His offer of deliverance if the people will only turn back to Him. God graciously sent Amos as a reformer to warn the people of Israel of their fate if they refused to repent. But they rejected his plea, and the course of judgment could not be altered.

Keys to Amos

Key Word: Judgment of Israel

Key Verses (3:1–2; 8:11–12)—"Hear this word that the Lord has spoken against you, O children of Israel, against the whole family which I brought up from the land of Egypt, saying: You only have I known of all the families of the earth; therefore I will punish you for all your iniquities" (3:1–2).

"'Behold, the days are coming,' says the Lord God, 'that I will send a famine on the land, not a famine of bread, nor a thirst for water, but of hearing the words of the LORD. They shall wander from sea to sea, and from north to east; they shall run to and fro, seeking the word of the LORD, but shall not find it'" (8:11–12).

Key Chapter (9)—Set in the midst of the harsh judgments of Amos are some of the greatest prophecies of restoration of Israel anywhere in Scripture. Within the scope of just five verses the future of Israel becomes clear, as the Abrahamic, Davidic, and Palestinian covenants are focused on their climactic fulfillment in the return of the Messiah.

Christ in Amos

The clearest anticipation of Christ in Amos is found at the end of the book. He has all authority to judge (1:1—9:10), but He will also restore His people (9:11–15).

Contribution to the Bible

The proportion of judgment compared to hope and blessing is higher in Amos than in the other prophets. Only the last five verses offer a word of consolation and promise. Amos stands as one of the Bible's most direct and incisive prophets. Consider, for example, his description of the greedy women of Samaria: "Hear this word, you cows of Bashan, who *are* on the mountain of Samaria" (4:1). Amos was the first of the two writing prophets to the northern kingdom (3:1, 12; 7:10, 14–15). Unlike Hosea, he was a resident of Judah, not Israel. Here are some *generalized* comparisons between their two books.

Hosea	Amos
1. Preaches against idolatry	1. Preaches against injustice
2. Commands the people to know God	2. Commands the people to seek God
3. Rebukes religious inequities	3. Rebukes social inequities
4. Aims at their worship of God	4. Aims at their walk with God
5. Stresses their need for the knowledge of God	5. Stresses their need for justice
6. "I don't delight in your sacrifices"	6. "I hate your offerings"
7. Majors on image worship	7. Little on image worship
8. Describes Israel as a privileged people	8. Describes Israel as a privileged people
9. Much about the loyal love of God	9. Little about the loyal love of God
10. Called for repentance	10. Aroused the conscience
11. Addresses Israel as family	11. Addresses israel as a state
12. Deals with his homeland	12. Deals with foreigners
13. A national message	13. A universal message
14. Refers much to the past	14. Refers little to the past
15. Grace of God	15. Righteousness of God
16. Lovingkindness	16. Wrath
17. Complex character	17. Simple character
18. A poet	18. A philosopher
19. A mystic	19. A moralist
20. Sympathetic	20. Stern

Amos displays a detailed understanding of the Pentateuch. Compare these examples: 2:7 (Deut. 23:17–18); 2:8 (Exod. 22:26); 2:12 (Num. 6:1–21); 4:4 (Deut.

14:28; 26:12); 4:5 (Lev. 2:11; 7:13). Amos is quoted in Matthew, Acts, and Romans: 4:11 (Rom. 9:29); 5:25–27 (Acts 7:42–43); 8:9 (Matt. 24:29); 9:11–12 (Acts 15:16–18).

Survey of Amos

Amos' message of the coming doom of the northern kingdom of Israel seems preposterous to the people. External circumstances have never looked better in the north: it is a time of booming business, bulging boundaries, and soaring optimism. However, the internal conditions have never looked worse: injustice, greed, hypocrisy, oppression, and arrogance. Unsurprisingly, Amos' earnest and forceful message against Israel's sins and abuses is poorly received. The "prophet of Israel's Indian summer" presents a painfully clear message: "Prepare to meet your God, O Israel!" (4:12). The four divisions of Amos are: (1) The eight prophecies (1:1—2:16); (2) the three sermons (3:1—6:14); (3) the five visions (7:1—9:10); and (4) the five promises (9:11–15).

The Eight Prophecies (1:1—2:16): Amos is called by God to the unenviable task of leaving his homeland in Judah to preach a harsh message of judgment to Israel. Each of his eight oracles in chapters 1—2 begins with the statement "For three transgressions of . . . and for four." The fourth transgression is equivalent to the last straw; the iniquity of each of the eight countries is full. Amos begins with the nations that surround Israel as his catalog of catastrophes gradually spirals in on Israel herself. Seven times God declares, "I will send a fire" (1:4, 7, 10, 12, 14; 2:2, 5), a symbol of judgment.

The Three Sermons (3:1—6:14): In these chapters, Amos delivers three sermons, each beginning with the phrase "Hear this word" (3:1; 4:1; 5:1). The first sermon (3) is a general pronouncement of judgment because of Israel's iniquities. The second sermon (4) exposes the crimes of the people and describes the ways God has chastened them in order to draw them back to Himself. Five times He says, "Yet you have not returned to Me" (4:6, 8–11). The third sermon (5—6) lists the sins of the house of Israel and calls the people to repent. But they hate integrity, justice, and compassion, and their refusal to turn to Yahweh will lead to their exile. Although they arrogantly wallow in luxury, their time of prosperity will suddenly come to an end.

The Five Visions (7:1—9:10): Amos' three sermons are followed by five visions of coming judgment upon the northern kingdom. The first two judgments of locusts and fire do not come to pass because of Amos' intercession. The third vision of the plumbline is followed by the only narrative section in the book (7:10–17). Amaziah the priest of Beth-el wants Amos to go back to Judah. The fourth vision pictures Israel as a basket of rotten fruit, overripe for judgment. The fifth vision is a relentless portrayal of Israel's unavoidable judgment.

The Three Promises (9:11–15): Amos has hammered upon the theme of divine retribution with oracles, sermons, and visions. Nevertheless, he ends his book on a note of consolation, not condemnation. God promises to reinstate the Davidic line, to renew the land, and to restore the people.

Outline of Amos

I. **Introduction to Amos,** 1:1–2

II. **The Eight Judgments,** 1:3—2:16
   A. Judgment on Damascus, 1:3–5
   B. Judgment on Gaza, 1:6–8
   C. Judgment on Tyre, 1:9–10
   D. Judgment on Edom, 1:11–12
   E. Judgment on Ammon, 1:13–15
   F. Judgment on Moab, 2:1–3
   G. Judgment on Judah, 2:4–5
   H. Judgment on Israel, 2:6–16

III. **The Three Sermons of Judgment,** 3:1—6:14
   A. The First Sermon: Israel's Present, 3:1–15
      1. Israel's Judgment Is Deserved, 3:1–10
      2. Israel's Judgment Is Described, 3:11–15
   B. The Second Sermon: Israel's Past, 4:1–13
      1. Israel's Judgment Is Deserved, 4:1–5
      2. Israel's Judgment Is Demonstrated, 4:6–11
      3. Israel's Judgment Is Described, 4:12–13
   C. The Third Sermon: Israel's Future, 5:1—6:14
      1. Israel's Judgment Is Deserved, 5:1–15
      2. Israel's Judgment Is Described, 5:16—6:14
         a. The First Woe of Judgment, 5:16–27
         b. The Second Woe of Judgment, 6:1–14

IV. **The Five Visions of Judgment,** 7:1—9:10
   A. Vision of the Locusts, 7:1–3
   B. Vision of the Fire, 7:4–6
   C. Vision of the Plumb Line, 7:7–9
   D. Opposition of Amaziah (Historical Parenthesis), 7:10–17
   E. Vision of the Summer Fruit, 8:1–14
   F. Vision of the Stricken Doorposts, 9:1–10

V. **The Three Promises of the Restoration of Israel,** 9:11–15

Obadiah

FIGHTING AND FEUDING BETWEEN TWIN BROTHERS (Esau and Jacob, Gen. 27) leads to national enmity between their respective peoples (Edomites and Israelites). In an hour of need when Israel's enemies were knocking at the gates of Jerusalem, the Edomites came to the aid of the enemy. For their unwillingness to serve as their brothers' keeper; the Edomites would one day become extinct. Obadiah, an obscure prophet of unknown background, describes how Edom would be "cut off forever" (v. 10), God 's people would be vindicated, and God would be recognized as Judge over all the earth.

OBADIAH

Focus	Judgment of Edom			Restoration of Israel
	1 18			19 21
Divisions	Predictions of Judgment	Reasons for Judgment	Possession of Edom by Israel	Possession of Edom by Israel
	1 9	10 14	15 18	19 21
Topics	Defeat of Israel			Victory of Israel
	Judgment			Hope
Place	Edom and Israel			
Time	c. 840 B.C.			

Introduction and Title

A struggle that began in the womb between twin brothers, Esau and Jacob, eventuates in a struggle between their respective descendants, the Edomites and the Israelites. For the Edomites' stubborn refusal to aid Israel, first during the time of wilderness wandering (Num. 20:14–21) and later during a time of invasion, they are roundly condemned by Obadiah. This little-known prophet describes their crimes, tries their case, and pronounces their judgment: total destruction.

The Hebrew name *Obadyah* means "Worshiper of Yahweh" or "Servant of Yahweh." The Greek title in the Septuagint is *Obdiou,* and the Latin title in the Vulgate is *Abdias.*

Author

Obadiah was an obscure prophet who probably lived in the southern kingdom of Judah. Nothing is known of his hometown or family, but it is not likely that he came out of the kingly or priestly line, because his father is not mentioned (1:1). There are thirteen Obadiahs in the Old Testament, and some scholars have attempted to identify the author of this book with one of the other twelve. Four of the better prospects are: (1) The officer in Ahab's palace who hid God's prophets in a cave (1 Kin. 18:3); (2) one of the officials sent out by Jehoshaphat to teach the law in the cities of Judah (2 Chr. 17:7); (3) one of the overseers who took part in repairing the temple under Josiah (2 Chr. 34:12); or (4) a priest in the time of Nehemiah (Neh. 10:5).

Date and Setting

Obadiah mentions no kings, so verses 10–14 provide the only historical reference point to aid in determining the book's time and setting. However, scholars disagree about which invasion of Jerusalem Obadiah had in mind. There are four possibilities: (1) In 926 B.C., Shishak of Egypt plundered the temple and palace of Jerusalem in the reign of Rehoboam (1 Kin. 14:25–26). At this time, Edom was still subject to Judah. This does not fit verses 10–14, which indicate that Edom was independent of Judah. (2) During the reign of Jehoram (848–841 B.C.), the Philistines and Arabians invaded Judah and looted the palace (see 2 Chr. 21:16–17). Edom revolted during the reign of Jehoram and became a bitter antagonist (see 2 Kin. 8:20–22; 2 Chr. 21:8–20). This fits the description of Obadiah. (3) In 790 B.C., King Jehoash of Israel invaded Judah (see 2 Kin. 14; 2 Chr. 25). However, Obadiah in verse 11 calls the invaders "strangers." This would be an inappropriate term for describing the army of the northern kingdom. (4) In 586 B.C., Nebuchadnezzar of Babylon defeated and destroyed Jerusalem (2 Kin. 24—25).

The two best candidates are (2) and (4). Verses 10–14 seem to fit (2) better than (4) because they do not indicate the total destruction of the city, which took place when Nebuchadnezzar burned the palace and temple and razed the walls. And Nebuchadnezzar certainly would not have "cast lots for Jerusalem" (11) with anyone. Also, all of the other prophets who speak of the destruction of 586 B.C.

identify Nebuchadnezzar and the Babylonians as the agents; but Obadiah leaves the enemy unidentified. For these and other reasons, it appears likely that the plundering of Jerusalem written of in Obadiah was by the Philistines between 848 and 841 B.C. This would make the prophet a contemporary of Elisha, and Obadiah would be the earliest of the writing prophets, predating Joel by a few years.

The history of Edom began with Esau who was given the name Edom ("Red") because of the red stew for which he traded his birthright. Esau moved to the mountainous area of Seir and absorbed the Horites, the original inhabitants. Edom refused to allow Israel to pass through their land on the way to Canaan. The Edomites opposed Saul and were subdued under David and Solomon. They fought against Jehoshaphat and successfully rebelled against Jehoram. They were again conquered by Judah under Amaziah, but they regained their freedom during the reign of Ahaz. Edom was later controlled by Assyria and Babylon; and in the fifth century B.C. the Edomites were forced by the Nabataeans to leave their territory. They moved to the area of southern Palestine and became known as Idumaeans. Herod the Great, an Idumaean, became king of Judea under Rome in 37 B.C. In a sense, the enmity between Esau and Jacob was continued in Herod's attempt to murder Jesus. The Idumaeans participated in the rebellion of Jerusalem against Rome and were defeated along with the Jews by Titus in A.D. 70. Ironically, the Edomites applauded the destruction of Jerusalem in 586 B.C. (see Ps. 137:7) but died trying to defend it in A.D. 70. After that time they were never heard of again. As Obadiah predicted they would be "cut off forever" (10); "and no survivors shall *remain* of the house of Esau" (18).

Theme and Purpose

The major theme of Obadiah is a declaration of Edoms coming doom because of its arrogance and cruelty to Judah: "I will make you small among the nations" (2); "the pride of your heart has deceived you" (3); "how you will be cut off!" (5); "How Esau shall be searched out!" (6); "your mighty men O Teman, shall be dismayed" (9); "shame shall cover you" (10); "you shall be cut off forever" (10); "as you have done, it shall be done to you" (15). Even the last few verses which primarily deal with Israel, speak of Edom's downfall (17–21). The secondary theme of Obadiah is the future restoration of Israel and faithfulness of Yahweh to His covenant promises. God's justice will ultimately prevail.

Keys to Obadiah

Key Word: Judgment of Edom
Key Verses (10, 21)—"For your violence against your brother Jacob, shame shall cover you, and you shall be cut off forever" (10).

"Then saviors shall come to Mount Zion to judge the mountains of Esau, and the kingdom shall be the LORD's" (21).

Christ in Obadiah

Christ is seen in Obadiah as the Judge of the nations (15–16), the Savior of Israel (17—20), and the Possessor of the kingdom (21).

Contribution to the Bible

Obadiah is the most difficult prophetical book to date, but the best candidates are c. 840 B.C. and c. 586 B.C. If the former, Obadiah is the earliest of the writing prophets. His book is extremely short but complete with the two basic prophetic themes of condemnation (1–16) and consolation (17–21). Obadiah concentrates on the judgment of Edom, but other prophets are not silent about Edom's doom: see Isaiah 21; 34; Jeremiah 9; 25; 27; 49; Ezekiel 25; 35–36; Joel 3; Amos 1; Malachi 1. Evidence indicates that the prophets Joel, Amos, and Jeremiah made use of Obadiah: 1 (Jer. 49:14); 2 (Jer. 49:15); 3–4 (Jer. 49:16); 5 (Jer. 49:9); 6 (Jer. 49:10); 8 (Jer. 49:7) 9 (Jer. 49:22); 10 (Joel 3:19); 11 (Joel 3:3); 15 (Joel 1:15); 16 (Jer. 49:12); 17 (Joel 3:17); 18 (Amos 1:12); 19 (Amos 9:12). Obadiah offers one of the clearest biblical examples of pride going before a fall (1 Cor. 10:12).

Survey of Obadiah

The struggle between Esau and Jacob continued in the form of an ongoing struggle between their descendants in the nations of Edom and Israel. Edom (Esau) refused to act as a brother to Judah (Jacob), and maintained a fierce enmity with the offspring of Jacob for over a thousand years. This national rivalry became especially heinous when the Edomites reveled over the defeat and looting of Jerusalem by a foreign power. Instead of being his brother's keeper, Edom participated in the crime.

Obadiah is the shortest book in the Old Testament (twenty-one verses), but it carries one of the strongest messages of judgment in the Old Testament. For Edom there are no pleas to return, no words of consolation or hope. Edom's fate is sealed, and there are no conditions for possible deliverance. God will bring total destruction upon Edom, and there will be no remnant. Obadiah is Edom's day in court, complete with Edom's arraignment, indictment, and sentence. This "prophet of poetic justice" describes how the Judge of the earth will overthrow the pride of Edom and restore the house of Jacob. The two sections of Obadiah are: the judgment of Edom (1–18) and the restoration of Israel (19–21).

The Judgment of Edom (1–18): The first section of Obadiah makes it clear that the coming overthrow of Edom is a certainty, not a condition. Edom is arrogant (3) because of its secure position in Mount Seir, a mountainous region south of the Dead Sea. Its capital city of Sela (Petra) is protected by a narrow canyon that prevents invasion by an army. But God says this will make no difference. Even a thief does not take everything, but when God destroys Edom it will be totally ransacked. Nothing will avert God's complete judgment. Verses 10–14 describe Edom's major crime of gloating over the invasion of Jerusalem. Edom rejoiced when foreigners plundered Jerusalem, and became as one of them. On the day when she should have been allies with Judah, she instead became an aggressor against Judah. Edom will eventually be judged during the coming day of the Lord when Israel "shall be a fire, . . . but the house of Esau *shall be* stubble" (18).

The Restoration of Israel (19–21): The closing verses give hope to God's people that they will possess not only their own land, but also that of Edom and Philistia.

Outline of Obadiah

I. **The Predictions of Judgment on Edom,** 1–9

II. **The Reasons for the Judgment on Edom,** 10–14

III. **The Results of the Judgment on Edom,** 15–18

IV. **The Possession of Edom by Israel,** 19–21

Jonah

NINEVEH WAS NORTHEAST; Tarshish was west. When God called Jonah to preach repentance to the wicked Ninevites, the prophet knew that God's mercy might follow. He turned down the assignment and headed for Tarshish instead. But once God had dampened his spirits (by tossing him out of the boat and into the water) and demonstrated His protection (by moving him out of the water and into the fish), Jonah realized God was serious about His command! Nineveh must hear the word of the Lord, and so Jonah goes. But though the preaching is a success, the preacher comes away angry and discouraged, and must learn firsthand of God's compassion upon sinful men.

Focus	First Commission of Jonah				Second Commission of Jonah			
	1:1 — 2:10				3:1 — 4:11			
Divisions	Disobedience to the First Call	Judgment on Jonah Exacted	Prayer of Jonah in the Fish	Deliverance of Jonah from the Fish	Obedience to the Second Call	Judgment on Nineveh Averted	Prayer of Jonah	Rebuke of Jonah
	1:1 1:3	1:4 1:17	2:1 2:9	2:10	3:1 3:4	3:5 3:10	4:1 4:3	4:4 4:11
Topics	God's Mercy Upon Jonah				God's Mercy Upon Nineveh			
	"I won't go"		"I will go"		"I'm here"		"I shouldn't have come"	
Place	The Great Sea				The Great City			
Time	c. 760 B.C.							

255

Introduction and Title

Nineveh is northeast; Tarshish is west. When God calls Jonah to preach repentance to the wicked Ninevites, the prophet knows that God's mercy may follow. He turns down the assignment and heads for Tarshish instead. But once God has dampened his spirits (by tossing him out of the boat and into the water) and has demonstrated His protection (by moving him out of the water and into the fish), Jonah realizes God is serious about His command. Nineveh must hear the word of the Lord; therefore Jonah goes. Although the preaching is a success, the preacher comes away angry and discouraged, and must learn firsthand of God's compassion for sinful men.

Yonah is the Hebrew word for "dove." The Septuagint Hellenized this word into *Ionas,* and the Latin Vulgate used the title *Jonas.*

Author

The first verse introduces Jonah as "the son of Amittai." Nothing more would be known about him were it not for another reference to him in Second Kings 14:25 as a prophet in the reign of Jeroboam II of Israel. Under Jeroboam, the borders of Israel were expanded "according to the word of the LORD God of Israel, which He had spoken through His servant Jonah the son of Amittai, the prophet who *was* from Gath Hepher." Gath Hepher was three miles north of Nazareth in lower Galilee, making Jonah a prophet of the northern kingdom. The Pharisees were wrong when they said, "Search and look, for no prophet has arisen out of Galilee" (John 7:52), because Jonah was a Galilean. One Jewish tradition says that Jonah was the son of the widow of Zarephath whom Elijah raised from the dead (see 1 Kin. 17:8–24).

Some critics claim that Jonah was written during the fifth to third centuries B.C. as a historical fiction to oppose the "narrow nationalism" of Ezra and Nehemiah by introducing universalistic ideas. They say an anonymous writer created this work to counteract the Jewish practice of excluding the Samaritans from worship and divorcing foreign wives. To support this view, it is noted that the book is written in the third person with no claim that Jonah authored it. The use of Aramaic words and the statement that "Nineveh was an exceedingly great city" (3:3) indicate a late date after Nineveh's fall in 612 B.C.

Conservative scholars challenge this claim with these arguments: (1) The idea of God's inclusion of the Gentiles in His program is found elsewhere in the Scripture (cf. Gen. 9:27; 12:3; Lev. 19:33–34; 1 Sam. 2:10; Is. 2:2; Joel 2:28–32). (2) Aramaic words occur in early as well as late Old Testament books. Aramaic is found in Near Eastern texts as early as 1500 B.C. (3) The fact that the book does not explicitly say that it was written by Jonah is an argument from silence. (4) Use of the third-person style was common among biblical writers. (5) The text (3:3) literally means "had become." At the time of the story, Nineveh had already become a very large city. (6) Jonah was a historical prophet (see 2 Kin. 14:25), and there are no hints that the book is fictional or allegorical. (7) Christ supported the historical accuracy of the book (see Matt. 12:39–41).

Date and Setting

Jonah was a contemporary of Jeroboam II of Israel (782–753 B.C.) who ministered after the time of Elisha and just before the time of Amos and Hosea. Israel under Jeroboam II was enjoying a period of resurgence and prosperity (see "Date and Setting" in Amos). Conditions looked promising after many bleak years, and nationalistic fervor was probably high. During these years, Assyria was in a period of mild decline. Weak rulers had ascended the throne, but Assyria remained a threat. By the time of Jonah, Assyrian cruelty had become legendary. Graphic accounts of their cruel treatment of captives have been found in ancient Assyrian records, especially from the ninth and seventh centuries B.C. The repentance of Nineveh probably occurred in the reign of Ashurdan III (773–755 B.C.). Two plagues (765 and 759 B.C.) and a solar eclipse (763 B.C.) may have prepared the people for Jonah's message of judgment.

Theme and Purpose

Jonah reveals the power of God in nature (1—2; 4) and the mercy of God in human affairs (3—4). The prophet learned that "salvation is of the Lord" (2:9), and God's gracious offer extends to all who repent and turn to Him. Jewish nationalism blinded God's covenant people to an understanding of His concern for the Gentiles. Jonah wanted God to show no mercy to the Ninevites, but he later learned how selfish and unmerciful his position was.

Keys to Jonah

Key Word: Revival in Nineveh

Key Verses (2:8–9; 4:2)—"Those who regard worthless idols forsake their own Mercy. But I will sacrifice to You with the voice of thanksgiving; I will pay what I have vowed. Salvation *is* of the LORD" (2:8–9).

"So he prayed to the LORD, and said, 'Ah, LORD, was not this what I said when I was still in my country? Therefore I fled previously to Tarshish; for I know that You *are* a gracious and merciful God, slow to anger and abundant in lovingkindness, One who relents from doing harm'" (4:2).

Key Chapter (3)—The third chapter of Jonah records perhaps the greatest revival of all time as the entire city of Nineveh "[believes] God, and [proclaims] a fast," and cries out to God.

Christ in Jonah

Jonah is the only prophet whom Jesus likened to Himself. "But he answered and said to them, 'An evil and adulterous generation seeks after a sign, and no sign will be given to it except the sign of the prophet Jonah. For as Jonah was three days and three nights in the belly of the great fish, so will the Son of Man be three days and three nights in the heart of the earth. The men of Nineveh will rise in the judgment with this generation and condemn it, because they repented at the preaching of

Jonah; and indeed a greater than Jonah *is* here'" (see Matt. 12:39–41). Jonah's experience is a type of the death, burial, and resurrection of Christ. (The Hebrew idiom, "three days and three nights," only requires a portion of the first and third days.)

Contribution to the Bible

Unlike the other prophetical books, Jonah places more emphasis on the messenger than the message. In the Hebrew, the prophetic message consists of only five words (3:4). The forty-eight verses of this biographical book provide a clear character development and a powerful portrait of human emotions. Jonah was the only prophet sent directly to the Gentiles and the only prophet who tried to conceal his message. Jonah learned a number of principles: (1) It is impossible to succeed in running away from God. (2) There is no limit to what God can use to get one's attention. (3) Failure does not disqualify a person from God's service. (4) Disobedience to God creates turmoil in the life of a believer. (5) Patriotism should never stand between a believer and the plan of God.

More than any other Old Testament book, Jonah reveals the universal concern of Yahweh for all men. It is interesting that Nineveh responded better to the preaching of Jonah than Israel and Judah ever responded to any of their prophets.

Jonah has often been challenged because of its miraculous elements, especially the great fish. But this is a preconceived view that does not allow the God of creation to directly use His creation for special purposes. In addition, there are published accounts of men who have survived being swallowed by whales—certain whales have the capacity to engorge a man in one swallow. But the Hebrew word does not specify what kind of "fish" was involved in Jonah's case.

Survey of Jonah

Jonah is an unusual book because of its message and messenger. Unlike other Old Testament books, it revolves exclusively around a gentile nation. God is concerned for the Gentiles as well as for His covenant people Israel. But God's messenger is a reluctant prophet who does not want to proclaim his message for fear that the Assyrians will respond and be spared by the compassionate God of Israel. Of all the people and things mentioned in the book—the storm, the lots, the sailors, the fish, the Ninevites, the plant, the worm, and the east wind—only the prophet himself fails to obey God. All these were used to teach Jonah a lesson in compassion and obedience. The four chapters divide into two parts: (1) the first commission of Jonah (1—2); and (2) the second commission of Jonah (3—4).

The First Commission of Jonah (1—2): This chapter records the commission of Jonah (1:1–2), the disobedience of Jonah (1:3), and the judgment on Jonah (1:4–17). Jonah does not want to see God spare the notoriously cruel Assyrians. To preach a message of repentance to them would be like helping Israel's enemy. In his patriotic zeal, Jonah put his country before his God and refused to represent Him in Nineveh.

Instead of going five hundred miles northeast to Nineveh, Jonah attempts to go two thousand miles west to Tarshish (Spain). But the Lord uses a creative series of counter-measures to accomplish His desired result. Jonah's efforts to thwart God's plan are futile.

God prepares a "great fish" to preserve Jonah and deliver him on dry land. The fish and its divinely appointed rendezvous with the sinking prophet became a powerful reminder to Jonah of the sovereignty of God in every circumstance. While inside the fish (2), Jonah utters a declarative praise psalm which alludes to several psalms that were racing through his mind (see Ps. 3:8; 31:22; 42:7; 69:1). In his unique "prayer closet," Jonah offers thanksgiving for his deliverance from drowning. When he acknowledges that "salvation *is* of the LORD" (2:9), he is finally willing to obey and be used by God. After he is cast up on the shore, Jonah has a long time to reflect on his experiences during his eastward trek of five hundred miles to Nineveh.

The Second Commission of Jonah (3—4): Jonah obeys his second commission to go to Nineveh (3:1–4) when he becomes "a sign to the Ninevites" (see Luke 11:30). The prophet is a walking object lesson from God, his skin no doubt bleached from his stay in the fish. As he proceeds through the city, his one-sentence sermon brings incredible results: it is the most responsive evangelistic effort in history. Jonah's words of coming judgment are followed by a proclamation by the king of the city to fast and repent. Because of His great mercy, God "relented from the disaster that He had said He would bring upon them" (3:10).

In the final chapter, God's love and grace are contrasted with Jonah's anger and lack of compassion. He is unhappy with the good results of his message because he knows God will now spare Nineveh. God uses a plant, a worm, and a wind to teach Jonah a lesson in compassion. Jonah's emotions shift from fierce anger (4:1), to despondency (4:3), then to great joy (4:6), and finally to despair (4:8). In a humorous but meaningful account, Jonah is forced to see that he has more concern for a plant than for hundreds of thousands of people (if 120,000 children are in mind in chapter 4, verse 11, the population of the area may have been 600,000). Jonah's lack of a divine perspective makes his repentance a greater problem than the repentance of Nineveh.

Outline of Jonah

I. The First Commission of Jonah, 1:1—2:10
   A. The Disobedience to the First Call, 1:1–3
   B. The Judgment on Jonah Is Exacted, 1:4–17
      1. The Great Storm, 1:4–16
      2. The Great Salvation of Jonah by the Fish, 1:17
   C. The Prayer of Jonah, 2:1–9
   D. The Deliverance of Jonah, 2:10

II. The Second Commission of Jonah, 3:1—4:11

    A. The Obedience to the Second Call, 3:1–4

    B. The Judgment of Nineveh Averted, 3:5–10

        1. The Great Fast, 3:5–9

        2. The Great Salvation of Nineveh by God, 3:10

    C. The Prayer of Jonah, 4:1–3

    D. The Rebuke of Jonah by God, 4:4–11

Micah

MICAH PROPHESIED DURING A PERIOD of intense social injustice in Judah. False prophets preached for riches, not for righteousness. Princes thrived on cruelty, violence, and corruption. Priests ministered more for greed than for God. Landlords stole from the poor and evicted widows. Judges lusted after bribes. Businessmen used deceitful scales and weights. Sin had infiltrated every segment of society. A word from God was mandatory.

Micah enumerates the sins of the nation, sins which will ultimately lead to destruction and captivity. But in the midst of blackness there is hope. A Divine Deliverer will appear and righteousness will prevail. Though justice is now trampled underfoot, it will one day triumph.

Focus	Prediction of Judgment		Prediction of Restoration			Plea for Repentance		
	1:1 — 3:12		4:1 — 5:15			6:1 — 7:20		
Divisions	Judgment on People	Judgment on Leadership	Promise of Coming Kingdom	Promise of Coming Captivities	Promise of Coming King	First Plea of God	Second Plea of God	Promise of Final Salvation
	1:1 — 2:13	3:1 — 3:12	4:1 — 4:5	4:6 — 5:1	5:2 — 5:15	6:1 — 6:9	6:10 — 7:6	7:7 — 7:20
Topics	Punishment		Promise			Pardon		
	Retribution		Restoration			Repentance		
Place	Judah and Israel							
Time	c. 735–710 B.C.							

Introduction and Title

Micah, called from his rustic home to be a prophet, leaves his familiar surroundings to deliver a stern message of judgment to the princes and people of Jerusalem. Burdened by the abusive treatment of the poor by the rich and influential, the prophet turns his verbal rebukes upon any who would use their social or political power for personal gain. One-third of Micah's book exposes the sins of his countrymen; another third pictures the punishment God is about to send; and the final third holds out the hope of restoration once that discipline has ended. Through it all, God's righteous demands upon His people are clear: "to do justly, to love mercy, and to walk humbly with your God" (6:8).

The name *Michayahu* ("Who Is Like God?") is shortened to *Michaia*. In chapter 7, verse 18, Micah hints at his own name with the phrase "Who *is* a God like You?" The Greek and Latin titles of this book are *Michaias* and *Micha*.

Author

Micah's home town of Moresheth Gath (1:14) was located about twenty-five miles southwest of Jerusalem on the border of Judah and Philistia, near Gath. Like Amos, Micah was from the country. His family and occupation are unknown, but Moresheth was in a productive agricultural belt. Micah was not as aware of the political situation as Isaiah or Daniel, but he showed a profound concern for the sufferings of the people. His clear sense of prophetic calling is seen in chapter 3, verse 8: "But truly I am full of power by the Spirit of the LORD, and of justice and might, to declare to Jacob his transgression and to Israel his sin."

Date and Setting

The first verse indicates that Micah prophesied in the days of Jotham (739–731 B.C.), Ahaz (731–715 B.C.), and Hezekiah (715–686 B.C.), kings of Judah. Although Micah deals primarily with Judah, he also addresses the northern kingdom of Israel and predicts the fall of Samaria (1:6). Much of his ministry, therefore, took place before the Assyrian captivity of Israel in 722 B.C. His strong denunciations of idolatry and immorality also suggest that his ministry largely preceded the sweeping religious reforms of Hezekiah. Thus, Micah's prophecies ranged from about 735 to 710 B.C. He was a contemporary of Hosea in the northern kingdom, and of Isaiah in the court of Jerusalem.

After the prosperous reign of Uzziah in Judah (767–739 B.C.), his son Jotham came to power and followed the same policies (739–731 B.C.). He was a good king, although he failed to remove the idolatrous high places. Under the wicked King Ahaz (731–715 B.C.), Judah was threatened by the forces of Assyria and Syria. Hezekiah (715–686 B.C.) opposed the Assyrians and successfully withstood an Assyrian siege with the help of God. He was an unusually good king who guided the people of Judah back to a proper course in their walk with God.

During the ministry of Micah, the kingdom of Israel continued to crumble inwardly and outwardly until its collapse in 722 B.C. The Assyrian Empire under Tiglath-pileser III (745–727 B.C.), Shalmeneser V (727–722 B.C.), Sargon II (722–705 B.C.), and Sennacherib (705–681 B.C.) reached the zenith of its power and became a constant threat to Judah. Babylon was still under Assyrian domination, and Micah's prediction of future Babylonian captivity for Judah (4:10) must have seemed farfetched.

Theme and Purpose

Micah exposes the injustice of Judah and the righteousness and justice of Yahweh. About one-third of the book indicts Israel and Judah for specific sins, including oppression, bribery among judges, prophets, and priests, exploitation of the powerless, coveteousness, cheating, violence, and pride. Another third of Micah predicts the judgment that will come as a result of those sins. The remaining third of the book is a message of hope and consolation. God's justice will triumph and the divine Deliverer will come. True peace and justice will prevail only when Messiah reigns. The "goodness and severity of God" (see Rom. 11:22) are illustrated in Micah's presentation of divine judgment and pardon. This book emphasizes the integral relationship between true spirituality and social ethics. Chapter 6, verse 8, summarizes what God wanted to see in His people: justice and equity tempered with mercy and compassion as the result of a humble and obedient relationship with Him.

Keys to Micah

Key Word: Judgment and Restoration of Judah

Key Verses (6:8; 7:18)—"He has shown you, O man, what *is* good; and what does the LORD require of you but to do justly, to love mercy, and to walk humbly with your God?" (6:8).

"Who *is* a God like You, pardoning iniquity and passing over the transgression of the remnant of His heritage? He does not retain His anger forever, because He delights *in* mercy" (7:18).

Key Chapters (6—7)—The closing section of Micah describes a courtroom scene. God has a controversy against His people, and He calls the mountains and hills together to form the jury as He sets forth His case. The people have replaced heartfelt worship with empty ritual, thinking that this is all God demands. They have divorced God's standards of justice from their daily dealings in order to cover their unscrupulous practices. They have failed to realize what the Lord requires of man. There can only be one verdict: guilty.

Nevertheless, the book closes on a note of hope. The same God who executes judgment also delights to extend mercy. "Who *is* a God like You, pardoning iniquity and passing over the transgression of the remnant of His heritage? He does not retain His anger forever, because He delights *in* mercy" (7:18). No wonder the prophet exclaims, "Therefore I will look to the LORD; I will wait for the God of my salvation; my God will hear me" (7:7).

Christ in Micah

Chapter 5, verse 2, is one of the clearest and most important of all Old Testament prophecies: "But you, Bethlehem Ephrathah, *though* you are little among the thousands of Judah, *yet* out of you shall come forth to Me the One to be ruler in Israel, whose goings forth *have been* from of old, from everlasting." This prophecy about the birthplace and eternity of the Messiah was made seven hundred years before His birth. The chief priests and scribes paraphrased this verse in Matthew (2:5–6) when questioned about the birthplace of the Messiah. Micah offers some of the best Old Testament descriptions of the righteous reign of Christ over the whole world (2:12–13; 4:1–8; 5:4–5).

Contribution to the Bible

In some ways, Micah is an Isaiah in miniature. Both prophets addressed the same people and problems: compare 1:2 (Isa. 1:2); 1:9–16 (Isa. 10:28–32); 2:8–9 (Isa. 10:2), 2:12 (Isa. 10:10–23); 2:13 (Isa. 52:12); 3:5–7 (Isa. 29:9–12); 4:1 (Isa. 2:2); 5:2 (Isa. 7:14); 5:4 (Isa. 40:11); 6:6–8 (Isa. 58:6–7); 7:7 (Isa. 8:17); 7:12 (Isa. 11:11). But Micah focused on moral and social problems while Isaiah placed greater stress on world affairs and political concerns.

A quote from Micah 3:12 a century later in Jeremiah 26:18 concerning the coming destruction of Jerusalem was instrumental in delivering Jeremiah from death. Micah was also quoted in the New Testament: 5:2 (Matt. 2:5–6; John 7:42); 7:6 (Matt. 10:34–36; Mark 13:12; Luke 12:53). Compared with other prophets, Micah's proportion of foretelling relative to forthtelling is high. He has much to say about the future of Israel and the advent and reign of Messiah.

Survey of Micah

Micah is the prophet of the downtrodden and exploited people of Judean society. He prophesies during a time of great social injustice and boldly opposes those who imposed their power upon the poor and weak for selfish ends. Corrupt rulers, false prophets, and ungodly priests all become targets for Micah's prophetic barbs. Micah exposes judges who are bought by bribes, and merchants who use deceptive weights. The pollution of sin has permeated every level of society in Judah and Israel. The whole earth is called to witness God's indictment against His people (1:2; 6:1–2), and the guilty verdict leads to a sentence of destruction and captivity. However, while the three major sections begin with condemnation (1:2—2:11; 4:6—5:1; 6:1—7:6), this condemnation is followed by a clear note of consolation (2:12–13; 5:2–15; 7:7–20). After sin is punished and justice is established, "He will again have compassion on us, and will subdue our iniquities. You will cast all our sins into the depths of the sea" (7:19). The three sections of Micah are: The prediction of judgment (1—3); the prediction of restoration (4—5); and the plea for repentance (6—7).

The Prediction of Judgment (1—3): Micah begins by launching into a general declaration of the condemnation of Israel (Samaria) and Judah (Jerusalem). Both kingdoms will be overthrown because of their rampant treachery. Micah uses a series of wordplays on the names of several cities of Judah in his lamentation over Judah's coming destruction (1:10–16). This is followed by some of the specific causes for judgment: premeditated schemes, covetousness, and cruelty. Nevertheless, God will regather a remnant of His people (2:12–13). The prophet then systematically condemns the princes (3:1–4) and the prophets (3:5–8) and concludes with a warning of coming judgment (3:9–12).

The Prediction of Restoration (4—5): Micah then moves into a two-chapter message of hope, which describes the reinstitution of the kingdom (4:1–5) and the intervening captivity of the kingdom (4:6—5:1), concluding with the coming Ruler of the Kingdom (5:2–15). The prophetic focus gradually narrows from the nations to the remnant to the King.

The Plea for Repentance (6—7): In His two controversies with His people, God calls them into court and presents an unanswerable case against them. The people have spurned God's grace, choosing instead to revel in wickedness. Micah concludes with a sublime series of promises that the Lord will pardon their iniquity and renew their nation in accordance with His covenant.

Outline of Micah

I. The Prediction of Judgment, 1:1—3:12
   A. Introduction to the Book of Micah, 1:1
   B. The Judgment on the People, 1:2—2:13
      1. Judgment on Samaria, 1:2–8
      2. Judgment on Judah, 1:9–16
      3. Cause of the Judgment, 2:1–11
      4. Promise of Future Restoration, 2:12–13
   C. The Judgment on the Leadership, 3:1–12
      1. Judgment on Princes, 3:1–4
      2. Judgment on Prophets, 3:5–8
      3. Promise of Future Judgment, 3:9–12

II. The Prediction of Restoration, 4:1—5:15
   A. The Promise of the Coming Kingdom, 4:1–5
   B. The Promise of the Coming Captivities, 4:6—5:1
   C. The Promise of the Coming King, 5:2–15
      1. Birth of the Messiah, 5:2
      2. Rejection of the Messiah, 5:3
      3. Work of the Messiah, 5:4–15

III. The Plea for Repentance, 6:1—7:20
   A. The First Plea of God, 6:1–9
      1. God Pleads, 6:1–5
      2. Micah Replies, 6:6–9
   B. The Second Plea of God, 6:10—7:6
      1. God Pleads, 6:10–16
      2. Micah Replies, 7:1–6
   C. The Promise of Final Salvation, 7:7–20

Nahum

NINEVEH WAS A CITY BUILT to last. Surrounded by high walls, fortified with two hundred towers, encircled by a deep moat, it was truly an invincible and impregnable fortress—or so the Ninevites thought! But according to the prophet Nahum, the proud city and its inhabitants would be powerless to stand before God's coming wrath. In the 150 years since Jonah's remarkable revival, the people of Nineveh had returned to their defiant, immoral ways. Nahum's preaching is not a call to repentance (like Jonah's), but a decree of death for an evil people who have "worn out" the patience of God.

		Destruction of Nineveh Decreed		Destruction of Nineveh Described		Destruction of Nineveh Deserved	
Focus		1:1 ... 1:15		2:1 ... 2:13		3:1 ... 3:19	
Divisions		General Principles of Divine Judgment	Destruction of Nineveh and Deliverance of Judah	Call to Battle	Description of the Destruction of Nineveh	Reasons for the Destruction of Nineveh	Destruction of Nineveh Is Inevitable
		1:1 — 1:8	1:9 — 1:15	2:1 — 2:2	2:3 — 2:13	3:1 — 3:7	3:12 — 3:19
Topics		Verdict of Vengeance		Vision of Vengeance		Vindication of Vengeance	
		What God Will Do		How God Will Do It		Why God Will Do It	
Place		In Judah against Nineveh, Capital of Assyria					
Time		c. 660 B.C.					

NAHUM

266

Introduction and Title

"For everyone to whom much is given, from him much will be required" (Luke 12:48). Nineveh had been given the privilege of knowing the one true God. Under Jonah's preaching this great gentile city had repented, and God had graciously stayed His judgment. However, a hundred years later, Nahum proclaims the downfall of this same city. The Assyrians have forgotten their revival and have returned to their habits of violence, idolatry, and arrogance. As a result, Babylon will so destroy the city that no trace of it will remain—a prophecy fulfilled in painful detail.

The Hebrew word *nahum* ("comfort, consolation") is a shortened form of Nehemiah ("Comfort of Yahweh"). The destruction of the capital city of Assyria is a message of comfort and consolation to Judah and all who live in fear of the cruelty of the Assyrians. The title of this book in the Greek and Latin Bibles is *Naoum* and *Nahum*.

Author

The only mention of Nahum in the Old Testament is found in chapter 1, verse 1, where he is called an Elkoshite. At least four locations have been proposed for Elkosh: (1) A sixteenth-century tradition identifies Elkosh with Al-Qush in Iraq, north of the site of Nineveh on the Tigris River. (2) Jerome believed that Elkesi, a city near Ramah in Galilee, was Elkosh because of the similarity of the consonants. (3) Capernaum means "City of Nahum" (*Kephar-Nahum*), and many believe that the name Elkosh was changed to Capernaum in Nahum's honor. (4) Most conservative scholars believe that Elkosh was a city of southern Judah (later called Elcesei) between Jerusalem and Gaza. This would make Nahum a prophet of the southern kingdom and may explain his interest in the triumph of Judah (1:15; 2:2).

Date and Setting

The fall of Nineveh to the Babylonians in 612 B.C. is seen by Nahum as a future event. Critics who deny predictive prophecy naturally date Nahum after 612 B.C., but this is not based upon exegetical or historical considerations. Nahum (3:8–10) refers to the fall of Thebes as a recent event, so this book must be dated after 664 B.C., the year when this took place. Thus, Nahum can safely be placed between 663 and 612 B.C. Thebes was restored a decade after its defeat, and Nahum's failure to mention this restoration has led several scholars to the conclusion that Nahum was written before 654 B.C. The fact that Nahum mentions no king in the introduction to his book (1:1) may point to the reign of the wicked King Manasseh (686–642 B.C.).

The conversion of the Ninevites in response to Jonah's message of judgment took place about 760 B.C. The revival was evidently short-lived, because the Assyrians soon returned to their ruthless practices. In 722 B.C., Sargon II of Assyria destroyed Samaria, the capital of the northern kingdom of Israel, and scattered the ten tribes. Led by Sennacherib, the Assyrians also came close to capturing Jerusalem in the reign of King Hezekiah in 701 B.C. By the time of Nahum (c. 660 B.C.), Assyria reached the peak of its prosperity and power under Ashurbanipal (669–633 B.C.).

This king extended Assyria's influence farther than had any of his predecessors. Nineveh became the mightiest city on earth with walls 100 feet high and wide enough to accommodate three chariots riding abreast. Dotted around the walls were huge towers that stretched an additional 100 feet above the top of the walls. In addition, the walls were surrounded by a moat 150 feet wide and 60 feet deep. Nineveh appeared impregnable and could withstand a twenty-year siege. Thus, Nahum's prophecy of Nineveh's overthrow seemed unlikely indeed.

Assyrian power faded under Ashurbanipal's sons, Ashuretililani (633–629 B.C.) and Sinsharishkun (629–612 B.C.). Nahum predicted that Nineveh would end "with an overflowing flood" (1:8), and this is precisely what occurred. The Tigris River overflowed its banks and the flood destroyed part of Nineveh's wall. The Babylonians invaded through this breach in the wall, plundered the city, and set it on fire. Nahum also predicted that Nineveh would "be hidden" (3:11). After its destruction in 612 B.C. the site was not discovered until A.D. 1842.

Theme and Purpose

Beginning with chapter 1, verse 9, the single thrust of Nahum's prophecy is the retribution of God against the wickedness of Nineveh. Nineveh's judgment is irreversibly decreed by the righteous God who will no longer delay His wrath. Assyria's arrogance and cruelty to other nations will come to a sudden end—her power will be useless against the mighty hand of Yahweh.

Chapter 1, verses 2–8, portray the patience, power, holiness, and justice of the living God. He is slow to wrath, but He settles in full. This book concerns the downfall of Assyria but it was written for the benefit of the surviving kingdom of Judah (Israel had already been swallowed up by Assyria). The people in Judah who trusted in the Lord would be comforted to hear of God's judgment upon the proud and brutal Assyrians (1:15; 2:2).

Keys to Nahum

Key Word: Judgment Nineveh

Key Verses (1:7–8; 3:5–7)—"The LORD *is* good, a stronghold in the day of trouble; and He knows those who trust in Him. But with an overflowing flood He will make an utter end of its place, and darkness will pursue His enemies" (1:7–8).

" 'Behold, I am against you,' says the LORD of hosts; 'I will lift your skirts over your face, I will show the nations your nakedness, and the kingdoms your shame. I will cast abominable filth upon you, make you vile, and make you a spectacle. It shall come to pass that all who look upon you will flee from you, and say, "Nineveh is laid waste! Who will bemoan her?" Where shall I seek comforters for you?' " (3:5–7).

Key Chapter (1)—The first chapter of Nahum records the principles of divine judgment resulting in the decree of the destruction of Nineveh and the deliverance and celebration of Judah. Nahum's prophecy proclaims God's retribution upon Nineveh because of its wickedness. God will delay no longer, and Assyria will be destroyed for its cruelty toward the nations and its arrogance toward God. While God is slow to wrath, His judgment is sure. The people in Judah who read this prophecy and saw the storm clouds brewing had to have been comforted with these words of judgment (1:15; 2:2).

Christ in Nahum

While there are no direct messianic prophecies in Nahum, the divine attributes (1:2–8) are consistent with Christ's work as the judge of the nations in His second advent.

Contribution to the Bible

Nahum is one of the three prophets who primarily focused on the judgment of Judah's enemies. The other two are Obadiah (Edom) and Habakkuk (Babylonia). In spite of Judah's wickedness in the time of Nahum, this book does not contain one word of condemnation against Judah and it has no call to repentance or reformation. That was the calling of Nahum's younger contemporaries, Zephaniah, Jeremiah, and Habakkuk.

In this book, Jonah's hoped for judgment upon Nineveh is dramatically described with brilliant imagery.

Jonah	Nahum
The Mercy of God	The Judgment of God
c. 760 B.C.	c. 660 B.C.
Repentance of Nineveh	Rebellion of Nineveh
Emphasis on the Prophet	Emphasis on the Prophecy
Disobedient Prophet	Obedient Prophet
Obedient Nation	Disobedient Nation
Deliverance from Water	Destruction by Water
The Great Fish	Great Fulfillment

Nahum's very specific prophetic details include: Nineveh destroyed by a flood (1:8; 2:6) and by fire (1:10; 2:13; 3:13,15); the profaning of Nineveh's temples and images (1:14); the city never to be rebuilt (1:14; 2:11,13); the leaders will flee (2:9; 3:17); the easy capture of the fortresses around the city (3:12); the destruction of the gates (3:13); and the lengthy siege and frantic efforts to strengthen its defenses (3:14). All these events have been authenticated in archaeological finds and historical accounts.

There are only forty-seven verses in this book, but it contains nearly fifty references to nature (see 1:3, 10; 2:11; 3:15). Nahum is not quoted in the New Testament.

Survey of Nahum

When God finally convinces His prophet Jonah to preach to the people of Nineveh, the whole city responds with repentance and Nineveh escapes destruction. The people humble themselves before the one true God, but their humility soon changes to arrogance as Assyria reaches its zenith as the most powerful empire in the world. About a century after the preaching of Jonah, God calls Nahum to proclaim the coming destruction of Nineveh. This time there will be no escape, because their measure of wickedness is full. Unlike Jonah, Nahum does not go to the city but declares his oracle from afar. There is is no hope of repentance. Nineveh's destruction is decreed (1), described (2), and deserved (3).

The Destruction of Nineveh Is Decreed (1): Nahum begins with a very clear description of the character of Yahweh. Because of His righteousness, He is a God of vengeance (1:2). God is also characterized by patience (1:3) and power (1:3–6). He is gracious to all who respond to Him, but those who rebel against Him will be overthrown (1:7–8). God is holy, and Nineveh stands condemned because of its sins (1:9–14). Nothing can stand in the way of its judgment, and this is a message of comfort to the people of Judah (1:15). The threat of Assyrian invasion will soon be over.

The Destruction of Nineveh Is Described (2): Assyria will be conquered, but Judah will be restored (2:1–2). Nahum's description of the siege of Nineveh (2:3–7) and the sack of Nineveh (2:8–13) is one of the most vivid portraits of battle in Scripture. The storming warriors and chariots can almost be seen as they enter the city through a breach in the wall. As the Ninevites flee in terror, the invading army plunders the treasures of the city. Nineveh is burned and cut off forever.

The Destruction of Nineveh Is Deserved (3): Nahum closes his brief book of judgment with God's reasons for Nineveh's coming overthrow. The city is characterized by cruelty and corruption (3:1–7). Just as Assyria crushed the Egyptian capital city of Thebes (No Amon), Assyria's capital city will also be destroyed (3:8–10). Nineveh is fortified so well that defeat seems impossible, but God proclaims that its destruction is inevitable (3:11–19). None of its resources can deter divine judgment.

Outline of Nahum

I. **The Destruction of Nineveh Is Decreed,** 1:1–15
  A. The General Principles of Divine Judgment, 1:1–8
    1. God's Vengeance in Judgment, 1:1–2
    2. God's Power in Judgment, 1:3–8
  B. The Destruction of Nineveh and Deliverance of Judah, 1:9–15

II. **The Destruction of Nineveh Is Described,** 2:1–13
  A. The Call to Battle, 2:1–2
  B. The Destruction of Nineveh, 2:3–13

Habakkuk

HABAKKUK LOOKS AT HIS NATIVE JUDAH, observes the violence and injustice on every hand, and cries out to God with some perplexing questions: Why are the wicked prospering in the midst of God's people? Why are the righteous beaten down? And why is God seemingly inactive and indifferent in a day of wickedness? God's reply is even more shocking than the conditions in Judah. God assures His prophet He is doing something. The Chaldeans—a people even more corrupt than God's chosen nation—are about to descend as God's rod of chastening. When Habakkuk reacts with shock and dismay, God patiently instructs His messengers until at last the prophet is able to respond with a psalm of praise: "I will rejoice in the LORD, I will joy in the God of my salvation" (3:18).

HABAKKUK	Focus	Problems of Habakkuk				Praise of Habakkuk
		1:1 2:20				3:1 3:19
	Divisions	First Problem of Habakkuk	First Reply of God	Second Problem of Habakkuk	Second Reply of God	Prayer of Praise of Habakkuk
		1:1 1:4	1:5 1:11	1:12 2:1	2:2 2:20	3:1 3:19
	Topics	Faith Troubled				Faith Triumphant
		What God Is Doing				Who God Is
	Place	The Nation of Judah				
	Time	c. 607 B.C.				

Introduction and Title

Habakkuk ministers during the "death throes" of the nation of Judah. Though repeatedly called to repentance, the nation stubbornly refuses to change her sinful ways. Habakkuk, knowing the hardheartedness of his countrymen, asks God how long this intolerable condition can continue. God replies that the Babylonians will be His chastening rod upon the nation—an announcement that sends the prophet to his knees. He acknowledges that the just in any generation shall live by faith (2:4) not by sight. Habakkuk concludes by praising God's wisdom even though he doesn't fully understand God's ways.

Habaqquq is an unusual Hebrew name derived from the verb *habaq,* "embrace." Thus his name probably means "One Who Embraces" or "Clings." At the end of his book this name becomes appropriate because Habakkuk chooses to cling firmly to God regardless of what happens to his nation (3:16–19). The Greek title in the Septuagint is *Ambakouk,* and the Latin title in Jerome's Vulgate is *Habacuc.*

Author

In the introduction to the book (1:1) and the closing psalm (3:1), the author identifies himself as Habakkuk the prophet. This special designation seems to indicate that Habakkuk was a professional prophet. The closing statement at the end of the psalm ("To the Chief Musician. With my stringed instruments.") suggests that Habakkuk may have been a priest connected with the temple worship in Jerusalem. He mentions nothing of his genealogy or location, but speculative attempts have been made to identify him with certain unnamed Old Testament characters. In the apocryphal book of Bel and the Dragon, Daniel is rescued a second time by the prophet Habakkuk.

Date and Setting

The only explicit time reference in Habakkuk is to the Babylonian invasion as an imminent event (1:6; 2:1; 3:16). Some scholars suggest Habakkuk was written during the reign of Manasseh (686–642 B.C.) or Amon (642–640 B.C.) because of the list of Judah's sins in 1:2–4. However, the descriptions of the Chaldeans indicate that Babylon had become a world power; and this was not true in the time of Manasseh when Babylon was under the thumb of Assyria. It is also unlikely that this prophecy took place in the time of King Josiah (640–609 B.C.), because the moral and spiritual reforms of Josiah do not fit the situation (1:2–4). The most likely date for the book is in the early part of Jehoiakim's reign (609–597 B.C.). Jehoiakim was a godless king who led the nation down the path of destruction (cf. 2 Kin. 23:34—24:5; Jer. 22:17).

The Babylonians began to rise in power during the reign of Nabopolassar (626–605 B.C.), and in 612 B.C. they destroyed the Assyrian capital of Nineveh. By the time of Jehoiakim, Babylon was the uncontested world power. Nabopolassar's successor, Nebuchadnezzar, came to power in 605 B.C. and carried out successful military expeditions in the west, advancing into Palestine and Egypt. Nebuchadnezzar's first invasion of Judah occurred in his first year, when he deported ten thousand of

Jerusalem's leaders to Babylon. The nobles who oppressed and extorted from the poor were the first to be carried away. Since Habakkuk prophesied prior to the Babylonian invasion, the probable date for this book is c. 607 B.C.

Theme and Purpose

The circumstances of life sometimes appear to contradict God's revelation concerning His power and purposes. Habakkuk struggled in his faith when he saw men flagrantly violate God's law and distort justice on every level without fear of divine intervention. He wanted to know why God was allowing growing iniquity to go unpunished. When God revealed His intention to use Babylonia as His rod of judgment, Habakkuk was even more troubled, because that nation was more corrupt than Judah. God's answer (2:2–20) satisfied Habakkuk that he could trust Him even in the worst of circumstances because of His matchless wisdom, goodness, and power. God's plan is perfect, and nothing is big enough to stand in the way of its ultimate fulfillment. In spite of appearances to the contrary, God is still on the throne as the Lord of history and the Ruler of the nations. Yahweh may be slow to wrath, but all iniquity will eventually be punished. He is the worthiest object of faith, and the righteous man will trust in Him at all times.

Keys to Habakkuk

Key Word: Faith

Key Verses (2:4; 3:17–19)—"Behold the proud, his soul is not upright in him; but the just shall live by his faith" (2:4).

"Though the fig tree may not blossom, nor fruit be on the vines; though the labor of the olive may fail, and the fields yield no food; though the flock be cut off from the fold, and there be no herd in the stalls—yet I will rejoice in the LORD, I will joy in the God of my salvation. The LORD God is my strength; He will make my feet like deer's feet, and He will make me walk on my high hills. To the Chief Musician. With my stringed instruments" (3:17–19).

Key Chapter (3)—The book of Habakkuk builds to a triumphant climax reached in the last three verses (3:17–19). The beginning of the book and the ending stand in stark contrast: mystery to certainty, questioning to affirming, and complaint to confidence. Chapter 3 is one of the most majestic of all Scripture and records the glory of God in past history and in future history (prophecy).

Christ in Habakkuk

The word "salvation" appears three times (3:13, 18) and is the root word front which the name "Jesus" is derived (cf. Matt. 1:21). When He comes again, "the earth will be filled with the knowledge of the glory of the LORD, as the waters cover the sea" (2:14).

Contribution to the Bible

Habakkuk was a daring thinker who openly expressed his doubt to God. He was a man of integrity who was concerned with the character and program of

Yahweh. Habakkuk's unusually extended dialogue with God (about two-thirds of the book) was initiated by the prophet. Normally, the prophetic process was begun by God. After receiving the divine oracle, Habakkuk transmitted it to the people of Judah.

Both Jonah and Habakkuk faced severe tests of their faith. But they approached their problems differently:

Jonah	Habakkuk
God called on Jonah	Habakkuk called on God
Jonah ran *from* God	Habakkuk ran *to* God
Prayer and trouble (ch. 2)	Prayer after trouble (ch. 3)
Ends in foolishness	Ends in faith
Salvation of God to the Gentiles	Sovereignty of God over the Gentiles
In the fish	On the watchtower (2:4)

Habakkuk moves from burden to blessing, from wondering to worship, from restlessness to rest, from a problem to God's person, and from a complaint to consolation. The best known passage is "the just shall live by his faith" (2:4). This concept was central to the argument of Habakkuk and influential in the thought of three New Testament books (see Rom. 1:17; Gal. 3:11; Heb. 10:38). It also powerfully affected the lives of Luther and Wesley.

The concluding psalm of praise, in chapter 3, is one of the greatest psalms in the Old Testament. This magnificent declaration of faith in the character and ways of God has much in common with Psalms 18 and 68.

Survey of Habakkuk

Habakkuk is a freethinking prophet who is not afraid to wrestle with issues that test his faith. He openly and honestly directs his problems to God and waits to see how He will respond to his probing questions. After two rounds of dialogue with the Lord, Habakkuk's increased understanding of the person, power, and plan of God cause him to conclude with a psalm of unqualified praise. The more he knows about the Planner, the more he can trust His plans. No matter what God brings to pass, "the just shall live by his faith" (2:4). The two divisions of this book are: The problems of Habakkuk (1—2); and the praise of Habakkuk (3).

The Problems of Habakkuk (1—2): Habakkuk's first dialogue with God takes place in chapter 1, verses 1–11. The prophet asks God how long He will allow the wickedness of Judah to go unpunished (1:1–4). The people of Judah sin with impunity, and justice is perverted. God's startling answer is given (1:5–11): He is raising up the fierce Babylonians as His rod of judgment upon sinful Judah. The Chaldeans will come against Judah swiftly, violently, and completely. The coming storm from the east will be God's answer to Judah's crimes.

This answer leads to Habakkuk's second dialogue with God (1:12—2:20). The prophet is more perplexed than ever and asks how the righteous God can punish Judah with a nation that is even more wicked (1:12—2:1). Will the God whose eyes are too pure to approve evil reward the Babylonians for their cruelty and idolatry? Habakkuk stands upon a watchtower to wait for God's reply. The Lord answers with a series of five woes of—greed and aggression (2:5–8), exploitation and extortion (2:9–11), violence (2:12–14), immorality (2:15–17), and idolatry (2:18–20). God is aware of the sins of the Babylonians, and they will not escape His terrible judgment. But Judah is guilty of the same offenses and stands under the same condemnation. Jehovah concludes His answer with a statement of His sovereign majesty: "But the LORD is in His holy temple. Let all the earth keep silence before Him" (2:20).

The Praise of Habakkuk (3): Habakkuk begins by questioning God, but he concludes his book with a psalm of praise for the person (3:1–3), power (3:4–12), and plan (3:13–19) of God. He now acknowledges God's wisdom in the coming invasion of Judah, and though it terrifies him, he will trust the Lord. God's creative and redemptive work in the past gives the prophet confidence in the divine purposes, and hope at a time when he would otherwise despair. "Yet I will rejoice in the LORD, I will joy in the God of my salvation" (3:18).

Outline of Habakkuk

I. **The Problems of Habakkuk,** 1:1—2:20
   A. The First Problem of Habakkuk, 1:1–4
   B. God's First Reply, 1:5–11
   C. The Second Problem of Habakkuk, 1:12—2:1
   D. God's Second Reply, 2:2–20

II. **The Praise of Habakkuk,** 3:1–19
   A. Habakkuk Prays for God's Mercy, 3:1–2
   B. Habakkuk Remembers God's Mercy, 3:3–15
      1. The Glory of the Person of God, 3:3–4
      2. The Power of the Saving Acts of God, 3:5–15
   C. Habakkuk Trusts in God's Salvation, 3:16–19

Zephaniah

DURING JUDAH'S HECTIC POLITICAL and religious history, reform would come from time to time. Zephaniah's forceful prophecy may have been a factor in the reform which occurred during Josiah's reign—a "revival" which produced outward change but could not remove the inward heart of corruption which characterized the leadership of the nation. Zephaniah hammers home his message repeatedly that the day of the Lord, Judgment Day, is coming when the malignancy of sin will be dealt with. Israel and her gentile neighbors will soon experience the crushing hand of God's wrath. But after the chastening process is complete, blessing will come in the person of Messiah, who will be the cause for praise and singing.

ZEPHANIAH

Focus	Judgment in the Day of the Lord					Salvation in the Day of the Lord	
	1:1				3:8	3:9	3:20
Divisions	Judgment on the Whole Earth	Judgment on the Nation of Judah	Judgment on the Nations Surrounding Judah	Judgment on the City of Jerusalem	Judgment on the Whole Earth	Promise of Conversion	Promise of Restoration
	1:1 — 1:3	1:4 — 2:3	2:4 — 2:15	3:1 — 3:7	3:8	3:9 — 3:13	3:14 — 3:20
Topics	Day of Wrath					Day of Joy	
	Judgment on Judah					Restoration for Judah	
Place	Judah and the Nations						
Time	c. 630 B.C.						

277

Introduction and Title

During Judah's hectic political and religious history, reform comes from time to time. Zephaniah's forceful prophecy may be a factor in the reform that occurs during Josiah's reign—a "revival" that produces outward change, but does not fully remove the inward heart of corruption which characterizes the nation. Zephaniah hammers home his message repeatedly that the day of the Lord, Judgment Day, is coming when the malignancy of sin will be dealt with. Israel and her gentile neighbors will soon experience the crushing hand of God's wrath. But after the chastening process is complete, blessing will come in the person of Messiah, who will be the cause for praise and singing.

Tsephan-yah means "Yahweh Hides" or "Yahweh Has Hidden." Zephaniah was evidently born during the latter part of the reign of King Manasseh. His name may mean that he was "hidden" from Manasseh's atrocities. The Greek and Latin title is *Sophonias*.

Author

The first verse is very unusual in that Zephaniah traces his lineage back four generations to Hezekiah. This is probably Hezekiah the king of Judah, since this would best explain the genealogy. If Zephaniah was the great-great-grandson of the godly king Hezekiah, he was the only prophet of royal descent. This may have given the prophet freer access to the court of King Josiah in whose reign he ministered. Because Zephaniah used the phrase "this place" (1:4) to refer to Jerusalem and was quite familiar with its features (cf. 1:9–10; 3:1–7), he was probably an inhabitant of Judah's royal city.

Date and Setting

Zephaniah solves the dating problem by fixing his prophecy "in the days of Josiah son of Amos, king of Judah" (1:1). Josiah reigned from 640 to 609 B.C. and chapter 2, verse 13, indicates that the destruction of Nineveh (612 B.C.) was still a future event. Thus, Zephaniah's prophecy can be dated between 640 and 612 B.C.

However, the sins catalogued (1:3–13; 3:1–7) indicate a date prior to Josiah's reforms when the sins from the reign of Manasseh and Amon still predominated. It is therefore likely that Zephaniah's ministry played a significant role in preparing Judah for the revivals that took place in the reign of the nation's last righteous king. Josiah became king of Judah at the age of eight, and by the age of sixteen his heart had already begun to turn toward God. His first reform took place in the twelfth year of his reign (628 B.C.; 2 Chr. 34:3–7) when he tore down all the altars of Baal, destroyed the foreign incense altars, burned the bones of the false prophets on their altars, and broke the Asherim (carved images) and molten images in pieces. Six years later (622 B.C.), Josiah's second reform was kindled when Hilkiah the priest found the Book of the Law in the temple (see 2 Chr. 34:8—35:19). Thus, Zephaniah's prophecy can be dated more precisely as occurring between 630 and 625 B.C.

The evil reigns or Manasseh and Amon (a total of fifty-seven years) had such a profound effect upon Judah that it never recovered. Josiah's reforms were too little and too late, and the people reverted to their crass idolatry and teaching soon after Josiah was gone. As a contemporary of Jeremiah and Habakkuk, Zephaniah was one of the eleventh-hour prophets to Judah.

Theme and Purpose

The bulk of Zephaniah (1:1—3:8) describes the coming Day of Judgment upon Judah and the nations. Yahweh is holy and must vindicate His righteousness by calling all the nations of the world into account before Him. The sovereign God will judge not only His own people but also the whole world—no one escapes from His authority and dominion. The day of the Lord will have universal impact. That day came for Judah and all the nations (2:4–15), but there is a future aspect when all the earth will be judged. Chapter 3, verses 9–20, speak of another side of the day of the Lord: it will be a day of blessing after the judgment is complete. A righteous remnant will survive and all who call upon Him, Jew or Gentile, will be blessed. God will regather and restore His people, and there will be worldwide rejoicing.

Zephaniah was also written as a warning to Judah and a call to repentance (2:1–3). God wanted to spare the people but they ultimately rejected Him. His judgment would be great, but in His covenant loyalty God promised His people a future day of hope and joy. Wrath and mercy, severity and kindness cannot be separated in the character of God.

Keys to Zephaniah

Key Word: Judgment and Restoration in the Day of the Lord

Key Verses (1:14–15; 2:3)—"The great day of the LORD *is* near; *it is* near and hastens quickly. The noise of the day of the LORD is bitter; there the mighty men shall cry out. That day *is* a day of wrath, a day of trouble and distress, a day of devastation and desolation, a day of darkness and gloominess, a day of clouds and thick darkness" (1:14–15).

"Seek the LORD, all you meek of the earth, who have upheld His justice. Seek righteousness, seek humility. It may be that you will be hidden in the day of the LORD's anger" (2:3).

Key Chapter (3)—The last chapter of Zephaniah records the two distinct parts of the day of the Lord: judgment and restoration. Following the conversion of the nation, Israel finally is fully restored. Under the righteous rule of God, Israel fully inherits the blessings contained in the biblical covenants.

Christ in Zephaniah

Jesus alluded to Zephaniah on two occasions (cf. Zeph. 1:3; Matt. 13:41 and cf. Zeph. 1:15; Matt. 24:29). Both of these passages about the day of the Lord are associated with Christ's second advent. Although the Messiah is not specifically mentioned in Zephaniah, it is clear that He is the One who will fulfill the great promises (3:9–20). He will gather His people and reign in victory: "The LORD has taken away your judgments, He has cast out your enemy. The King of Israel, the LORD, is in your midst; you shall see disaster no more" (3:15).

Contribution to the Bible

Both Joel and Zephaniah deal almost exclusively with the concept of the coming day of the Lord. Using different expressions, Zephaniah refers to it twenty-three times in only three chapters. This book expands this important theme and includes these elements: the day of the Lord will fall upon all creation (1:2–3), it is imminent (1:14), it is a day of terror and judgment upon sin (1:15, 17), it will involve the nations of the world (2:4–15; 3:8), a remnant will return on that day (3:9–13), and it will bring great blessing (3:14–20).

Zephaniah, Habakkuk, and Lamentations chronologically follow each other and deal with the fall of Jerusalem:

Zephaniah	Habakkuk	Lamentations
Decades before the fall of Jerusalem (c. 630)	Just before the fall of Jerusalem (c. 607)	Just after the fall of Jerusalem (586)
God will judge	God, when will you judge?	God has judged
Preview of trouble	Promise of trouble	Presence of trouble
Declaration	Dialogue	Dirge
Day of the Lord	Dominion of the Lord	Destruction of the Lord
God is in your midst (see 3:15, 17)	God is your strength (see 3:19)	God is your portion (see 3:35)

Survey of Zephaniah

On the whole, Zephaniah is a fierce and grim book of warning about the coming day of the Lord. Desolation, darkness, and ruin will strike Judah and the nations because of the wrath of God upon sin. Zephaniah looks beyond judgment, however, to a time of joy when God will cleanse the nations and restore the fortunes of His people Israel. The book begins with God's declaration, "I will utterly consume all *things* from the face of land" (1:2); but it ends with this promise, "At that time I will bring you back" and "return your captives before your eyes" (3:20). Zephaniah moves three times from the general to the specific: (1) From universal judgment (1:1–3) to judgment upon Judah (1:4—2:3); (2) from judgment upon surrounding nations (2:4–15) to judgment upon Jerusalem (3:1–7); and (3) from judgment and cleansing of all nations (3:8–10) to restoration of Israel (3:11–20). The two broad divisions of the book are: the judgment in the day of the Lord (1:1—3:8) and the salvation in the day of the Lord (3:9–20).

The Judgment in the Day of the Lord (1:1—3:8): The prophetic oracle begins with an awesome statement of God's coming judgment upon the entire earth because of the sins of men (1:2–3). Zephaniah then concentrates on the judgment of Judah (1:4–18), listing some of the offenses that will cause it to come. Judah is polluted with idolatrous priests who promote the worship of Baal and nature, and her officials and princes are completely corrupt. Therefore, the day of the Lord is imminent; and it will be characterized by terror, desolation, and distress. However, by His grace, Yahweh appeals to His people to repent and humble themselves to avert the coming disaster before it is too late (2:1–3).

Zephaniah pronounces God's coming judgment upon the nations that surround Judah (2:4–15). He looks in all four directions: Philistia (west), Moab and Ammon (east), Ethiopia (south), and Assyria (north). Then he focuses on Jerusalem, the center of God's dealings (3:1–7). Jerusalem is characterized by spiritual rebellion and moral treachery. "She has not obeyed *His* voice, she has not received correction; she has not trusted in the LORD; she has not drawn near to her God" (3:2).

The Salvation in the Day of the Lord (3:9–20): After a broad statement of the judgment of all nations (3:8), Zephaniah changes the tone of the remainder of his book to blessing; for this, too, is an aspect of the day of the Lord. The nations will be cleansed and will call on the name of the Lord (3:9–10). The remnant of Israel will be regathered, redeemed, and restored (3:11–20). They will rejoice in their Redeemer, and He will be in their midst. Zephaniah opens with idolatry, wrath, and judgment, but closes with true worship, rejoicing, and blessing.

Outline of Zephaniah

Haggai

WITH THE BABYLONIAN EXILE now history and a newly returned group of Jews back in the land, the work of rebuilding the temple can begin. But sixteen years after the process is begun, the people have yet to finish the project, for their personal affairs have interfered with God's business. Haggai preaches a fiery series of sermonettes designed to stir up the nation to finish the temple. He calls the builders to renewed courage in the Lord, renewed holiness in life, and renewed faith in God who controls the future.

Focus	Completion of the Latter Temple	Glory of the Latter Temple	Present Blessing of Obedience	Future Blessing through Promise
	1:1 1:15	2:1 2:9	2:10 2:19	2:20 2:23
Divisions	"Consider your ways! . . . My house that is in ruins"	"The glory of this latter temple shall be greater"	"From this day forward I will bless you"	"I will shake heaven and earth"
	1:1 1:15	2:1 2:9	2:10 2:19	2:20 2:23
Topics	Temple of God		Blessing of God	
	First Rebuke (Present)	First Encouragement (Future)	Second Rebuke (Present)	Second Encouragement (Future)
Place	Jerusalem			
Time	September 1, 520 B.C.	October 21, 520 B.C.	December 24, 520 B.C.	December 24, 520 B.C.

Introduction and Title

With the Babylonian exile in the past, and a newly returned group of Jews back in the land, the work of rebuilding the temple can begin. However, sixteen years after the process is begun, the people have yet to finish the project, for their personal affairs have interfered with God's business. Haggai preaches a fiery series of sermonettes designed to stir up the nation to finish the temple. He calls the builders to renewed courage in the Lord, renewed holiness of life, and renewed faith in God who controls the future.

The etymology and meaning of *haggay* is uncertain, but it is probably derived from the Hebrew word *hag*, "festival." It may also be an abbreviated form of *haggiah*, "festival of Yahweh." Thus, Haggai's name means "Festal" or "Festive," possibly because he was born on the day of a major feast, such as Tabernacles (Haggai's second message takes place during that feast, 2:1). The title in the Septuagint is *Aggaios*, and in the Vulgate it is *Aggaeus*.

Author

Haggai's name is mentioned nine times (1:1, 3, 12–13; 2:1, 10, 13–14, 20); the authorship and date of the book are virtually uncontested. The unity of theme, style, and dating is obvious. Haggai is known only from this book and from two references to him in Ezra 5:1 and 6:14. There he is seen working alongside the younger prophet Zechariah in the ministry of encouraging the rebuilding of the temple. Haggai returned from Babylon with the remnant under Zerubbabel and evidently lived in Jerusalem. Some think chapter 2, verse 3, may mean that he was born in Judah before the 586 B.C. Captivity and was one of the small company who could remember the former temple before its destruction. This would mean Haggai was about seventy-five when he prophesied in 520 B.C. It is equally likely, however, that he was born in Babylon during the Captivity.

Date and Setting

In 538 B.C. Cyrus of Persia issued a decree allowing the Jews to return to their land and rebuild their temple. The first return was led by Zerubbabel, and in 536 B.C. work on the temple began. Ezra 4—6 gives the background to the Book of Haggai and describes how the Samaritans hindered the building of the temple and wrote a letter to the Persian king. This opposition only added to the growing discouragement of the Jewish remnant. Their initial optimism upon returning to their homeland was dampened by the desolation of the land, crop failure, hard work, hostility, and other hardships. They gave up the relative comfort of Babylonian culture to pioneer in a land that seemed unproductive and full of enemies. Finding it easier to stop building than to fight their neighbors, the work on the temple ceased in 534 B.C. The pessimism of the people led to spiritual lethargy, and they became preoccupied with their own building projects. They used political opposition and a theory that the temple was not to be rebuilt until some later time (perhaps after Jerusalem was rebuilt) as excuses for neglecting the house of the Lord.

It was in this context that God called His prophets Haggai and Zechariah to the same task of urging the people to complete the temple. Both books are precisely dated: Haggai 1:1, September 1, 520 B.C.; Haggai 1:15, September 24, 520 B.C.; Haggai 2:1, October 21, 520 B.C.; Zechariah 1:1, November, 520 B.C.; Haggai 2:10, 20, December 24, 520 B.C.; Zechariah 1:7, February 24, 519 B.C.; Zechariah 7:1, December 4, 518 B.C. Zechariah's prophecy commenced between Haggai's second and third messages. Thus, after fourteen years of neglect, work on the temple was resumed in 520 B.C. and was completed in 516 B.C. (Ezra 6:15). The Talmud indicates that the ark of the covenant, the *shekinah* glory, and the Urim and Thummim were not in the rebuilt temple.

Darius I (521–486 B.C.) was king of Persia during the ministries of Haggai and Zechariah. He was a strong ruler who consolidated his kingdom by defeating a number of revolting nations.

Theme and Purpose

Haggai's basic theme is clear: the remnant must reorder its priorities and complete the temple before they can expect the blessing of God upon their efforts. Because of spiritual indifference they failed to respond to God's attempts to get their attention. In their despondency, they did not realize that their hardships were divinely given symptoms of their spiritual disease. Haggai brought them to an understanding that circumstances become difficult when people place their own selfish interests before God's. When they put God first and seek to do His will, He will bring His people joy and prosperity.

Keys to Haggai

Key Word: Reconstruction of the Temple

Key Verses (1:7–8; 2:7–9)—"Thus says the LORD of hosts: 'Consider your ways! Go up to the mountains and bring wood and build the temple, that I may take pleasure in it and be glorified,' says the LORD" (1:7–8).

" ' "And I will shake all nations, and they shall come to the Desire of All Nations, and I will fill this temple with glory," says the LORD of hosts. "The silver *is* Mine, and the gold *is* Mine," says the LORD of hosts. "The glory of this latter temple shall be greater than the former," says the LORD of hosts. "And in this place I will give peace," says the LORD of hosts' " (2:7–9).

Key Chapter (2)—Verses 6–9 record some of the most startling prophecies in Scripture concerning the coming of the Messiah: " 'For thus says the LORD of hosts: "Once more (it *is* a little while) I will shake heaven and earth, the sea and dry land; and I will shake all nations, and they shall come to the Desire of All Nations, and I will fill this temple with glory," says the LORD of hosts. "The silver *is* Mine, and the gold *is* Mine," says the LORD of hosts. "The glory of this latter temple shall be greater than the former," says the LORD of hosts. "And in this place I will give peace," says the LORD of hosts.' "

Christ in Haggai

The promise of chapter 2, verse 9, points ahead to the crucial role the second temple is to have in God's redemptive plan. Herod the Great later spent a fortune on the project of enlarging and enriching this temple, and it was filled with the glory of God incarnate every time Christ came to Jerusalem.

The Messiah is also portrayed in the person of Zerubbabel: " 'I will take you, Zerubbabel . . . and I will make you as a signet *ring;* for I have chosen you' " (2:23). Zerubbabel becomes the center of the messianic line and is like a signet ring, sealing both branches together.

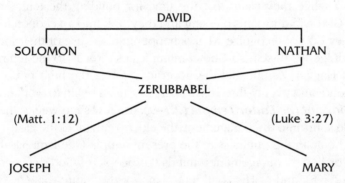

Contribution to the Bible

Haggai was one of the few prophets whose message brought quick and tangible results. Only twenty-three days after his first oracle, the people began to work on the temple for the first time in fourteen years. Founding the second temple marked a major turning point in God's dealing with His covenant people: "But from this day forward I will bless *you*" (2:19). This was because of the centrality of the sanctuary to the whole religious life in the Mosaic Law. It was not only the focus of the whole system of offerings and sacrifices, priests, and worship; it was also the symbol of Israel's spiritual identity and a visible reminder of the person, power, and presence of God. Now that the Davidic throne was gone, it was especially important that the temple be built to bind the remnant together as the continuing covenant people of God.

Haggai lacks the vivid imagery and poetry of other prophets like Isaiah and Nahum, but his concise and austere messages were successful. His words ring with divine authority ("thus says the LORD" and similar expressions appear twenty-six times in Haggai's thirty-eight verses).

Survey of Haggai

Haggai is second only to Obadiah in brevity among Old Testament books, but this strong and frank series of four terse sermons accomplishes its intended effect.

The work on the temple has ceased, and the people have become more concerned with the beautification of their own houses than with the building of the central sanctuary of God. Because of their misplaced priorities, their labor is no longer blessed by God. Only when the people put the Lord first by completing the task He has set before them will His hand of blessing once again be upon them. Haggai acts as God's man in God's hour, and his four messages are: the completion of the latter temple (1:1–15), the glory of the latter temple (2:1–9), the present blessings of obedience (2:10–19), and the future blessings of promise (2:20–23).

The Completion of the Latter Temple (1:1–15): When the remnant returns from Babylon under Zerubbabel, they begin to rebuild the temple of the Lord. However, the work soon stops and the people find excuses to ignore it as the years pass. They have no problem in building rich dwellings for themselves ("paneled houses," 1:4) while they claim that the time for building the temple has not yet come (1:2). God withdraws his blessing and they sink into an economic depression. However, they do not recognize what is happening because of their indifference to God and indulgence of self; so God communicates directly to the remnant through His prophet Haggai. Zerubbabel the governor, Joshua the high priest, and all the people respond; and twenty-three days later they again begin to work on the temple.

The Glory of the Latter Temple (2:1–9): In a few short weeks, the enthusiasm of the people sours into discouragement; the elders remember the glory of Solomon's temple and bemoan the puniness of the present temple (see Ezra 3:8–13). Haggai's prophetic word of encouragement reminds the people of God's covenant promises in the past (2:4–5), and of His confident plans for the future (2:6–9): "The glory of this latter temple shall be greater than the former" (2:9).

The Present Blessings of Obedience (2:10–19): Haggai's message to the priests illustrates the concept of contamination (2:11–13) and applies it to the nation (2:14–19). The Lord requires holiness and obedience, and the contamination of sin blocks the blessing of God. Because the people have obeyed God in building the temple, they will be blessed from that day forward.

The Future Blessings of Promise (2:20–23): On the same day that Haggai addresses the priests, he gives a second message to Zerubbabel. God will move in judgment, and in His power He will overthrow the nations of the earth (2:21–22). At that time, Zerubbabel, a symbol of the Messiah to come, will be honored.

Outline of Haggai

I. **The Completion of the Latter Temple,** 1:1–15
   A. The Temple Is Not Complete, 1:1–6
   B. The Temple Must Be Completed, 1:7–15

II. **The Glory of the Latter Temple,** 2:1–9
   A. The Latter Temple Is Not as Glorious as the First, 2:1–3
   B. The Latter Temple Will Be More Glorious than the First, 2:4–9

III. The Present Blessings of Obedience, 2:10–19
   A. The Disobedience of the Remnant, 2:10–14
   B. The Solution: The Obedience of the Remnant, 2:15–19

IV. The Future Blessings through Promise, 2:20–23
   A. The Future Destruction of the Nations, 2:20–22
   B. The Future Recognition of Zerubbabel, 2:23

Zechariah

FOR A DOZEN YEARS or more, the task of rebuilding the temple has stood half completed. Zechariah is commissioned by God to encourage the people in the unfinished responsibility. Rather than exhorting them to action with strong words of rebuke, Zechariah seeks to encourage them to action by reminding them of the future importance of the temple. The temple must be built, for one day Messiah's glory will inhabit it. But future blessing is contingent upon present obedience. The people are not merely building a structure; they are building the future. With that as their motivation, they can enter into the building project with wholehearted zeal, for their Messiah is coming!

	Focus	**Eight Visions**			**Four Messages**		**Two Burdens**	
ZECHARIAH		1:1 ——— 6:15			7:1 ——— 8:23		9:1 ——— 14:21	
	Divisions	Call to Repentance	Eight Visions	Crowning of Joshua	Question of the Fasts		First Burden: Rejection of the Messiah	Second Burden: Reign of the Messiah
		1:1 1:6	1:7 6:8	6:9 6:15	7:1 8:23		9:1 11:17	12:1 14:21
	Topics	Pictures			Problems		Predictions	
		Israel's Fortune			Israel's Fasting		Israel's Future	
	Place	Jerusalem						
	Time	While Building the Temple 520–518 B.C.					After Building the Temple c. 480–470 B.C.	

Introduction and Title

For a dozen years or more, the task of rebuilding the temple has stood half completed. Zechariah is commissioned by God to encourage the people in their unfinished responsibility. Rather than exhorting them to action with strong words of rebuke, Zechariah seeks to encourage them to action by reminding them of the future importance of the temple. The temple must be built, for one day the Messiah's glory will inhabit it. But future blessing is contingent upon present obedience. The people are not merely building a building; they are building the future. With that as their motivation, they can enter into the building project with wholehearted zeal, for their Messiah is coming.

Zekar-yah means "God Remembers" or "God Has Remembered." This theme dominates the whole book: Israel will be blessed because Yahweh remembers the covenant He made with the fathers. The Greek and Latin version of his name is *Zacharias*.

Author

Zechariah ("God Remembers") was a popular name shared by no fewer than twenty-nine Old Testament characters. It may have been given out of gratitude for God's gift of a baby boy. Like his predecessors, Jeremiah and Ezekiel, Zechariah was of priestly lineage as the son of Berechiah and grandson of Iddo (see 1:1, 7; Ezra 5:1; 6:14; Neh. 12:4, 16). He was born in Babylonia and was brought by his grandfather to Palestine when the Jewish exiles returned under Zerubbabel and Joshua the high priest. If he was the "young man" of chapter 2, verse 4, he was called to prophesy at an early age in 520 B.C. According to Jewish tradition, Zechariah was a member of the Great Synagogue that collected and preserved the canon of revealed Scripture. Matthew 23:35 indicates he was "murdered between the temple and the altar" in the same way that an earlier Zechariah was martyred (see 2 Chr. 24:20–21). The universal testimony of Jewish and Christian tradition affirms Zechariah as the author of the entire book.

Date and Setting

Zechariah was a younger contemporary of Haggai the prophet, Zerubbabel the governor, and Joshua the high priest. The historical setting for chapters 1—8 (520–518 B.C.) is identical to that of Haggai (see "Date and Setting" in Haggai). Work was resumed on the temple in 520 B.C. and the project was completed in 516 B.C. Chapters 9—14 are undated, but stylistic differences and references to Greece indicate a date of between 480 and 470 B.C. This would mean that Darius I (521–486 B.C.) had passed from the scene and had been succeeded by Xerxes (486–464 B.C.), the king who deposed Queen Vashti and made Esther queen of Persia.

Theme and Purpose

The first eight chapters frequently allude to the temple and encouraged the people to complete their great work on the new sanctuary. As they built the temple, they were building their future, because that very structure will be used by the coming Messiah when He comes to bring salvation. Zechariah eloquently attests to Yahweh's covenant faithfulness toward Israel through the work of the Messiah, especially in chapters 9—14. This book outlines God's program for His people during the Times of the Gentiles until Messiah comes to deliver them and reign upon the earth. This hope of glory was a source of reassurance to the Jewish remnant at a time when circumstances were trying. Zechariah was also written to promote spiritual revival so that the people would call upon the Lord with humble hearts and commit their ways to Him.

Keys to Zechariah

Key Word: Preparation for the Messiah

Key Verses (8:3; 9:9)—"Thus says the LORD: 'I will return to Zion, and dwell in the midst of Jerusalem. Jerusalem shall be called the City of Truth, the Mountain of the LORD of hosts, the Holy Mountain'" (8:3).

"Rejoice greatly, O daughter of Zion! Shout, O daughter of Jerusalem! Behold, your King is coming to you; He *is* just and having salvation, lowly and riding on a donkey, a colt, the foal of a donkey" (9:9).

Key Chapter (14)—Zechariah builds to a tremendous climax in chapter 14 where he discloses the last siege of Jerusalem, the initial victory of the enemies of Israel, the cleaving of the Mount of Olives, the Lord's defense of Jerusalem with His visible appearance on Olivet, judgment on the confederated nations, the topographical changes in the land of Israel, the Feast of Tabernacles in the Millennium, and the ultimate holiness of Jerusalem and her people.

Christ in Zechariah

Very clear messianic passages abound in this book. Christ is portrayed in His two advents as both Servant and King, Man and God. The following are a few of Zechariah's explicit anticipations of Christ: The angel of the Lord (3:1–2); the righteous Branch (3:8; 6:12–13), the stone with seven eyes (3:9); the King-Priest (6:13); the humble King (9:9–10); the cornerstone, tent peg, and bow of battle (10:4); the good Shepherd who is rejected and sold for thirty shekels of silver, the price of a slave (11:4–13); the pierced One (12:10); the cleansing fountain (13:1); the smitten Shepherd who is abandoned (13:7); and the coming Judge and righteous King (14).

Contribution to the Bible

Zechariah is the "major Minor Prophet"—the longest of the Minor Prophets and second only to Isaiah among the prophets in messianic passages. There is considerable variety in this book with its visions, messages, and apocalyptic oracles. As a counterpart to Daniel, Zechariah emphasizes the history of Israel during gentile domination, while Daniel also develops God's prophetic plan for the Gentiles.

Haggai and Zechariah ministered together in motivating the remnant to build the second temple, but their approaches were different. Here are some *general* contrasts:

Haggai	Zechariah
Exhortation	Encouragement
More concrete	More abstract
Concise	Expanded
Present concern	Future concern
Take part!	Take heart!
Older activist	Younger visionary

Survey of Zechariah

Zechariah uses a series of eight visions, four messages, and two burdens to portray God's future plans for His covenant people. The first eight chapters were written to encourage the remnant while they were rebuilding the temple; the last six chapters were written after the completion of the temple to anticipate Israel's coming Messiah. Zechariah moves from gentile domination to messianic rule, from persecution to peace, and from uncleanness to holiness. The book divides into the eight visions (1—6), the four messages (7—8), and the two burdens (9—14).

The Eight Visions (1—6): The book opens with an introductory appeal to the people to repent and return to God, unlike their fathers who rejected the warnings of the prophets (1:1–6). A few months later, Zechariah has a series of eight night visions, evidently in one troubled night (February 15, 519 B.C.; 1:7). The angel who speaks with him interprets the visions, but some of the symbols are not explained. The visions mix the work of the Messiah in both Advents, and like the other prophets, Zechariah sees only the peaks of God's program without the intervening valleys. The first five are visions of comfort, and the last three are visions of judgment: (1) The horsemen among the myrtle trees—God will rebuild Zion and His people (1:7–17). (2) The four horns and craftsmen—Israel's oppressors will be judged (1:18–21). (3) The man with a measuring line—God will protect and glorify Jerusalem (2:1–13). (4) The cleansing of Joshua the high priest—Israel will be cleansed and restored by the coming Branch (3:1–10). (5) The golden lampstand—God's spirit is empowering Zerubbabel and Joshua (4:1–14). (6) The flying scroll—individual sin will be judged (5:1–4). (7) The woman in the basket—national sin will be removed (5:5–11). (8) The four chariots—God's judgment will descend on the nations (6:1–8). The crowning of Joshua (6:9–15) anticipates the coming of the Branch who will be King and Priest (the composite crown).

The Four Messages (7—8): In response to a question about the continuation of the fasts (7:1–3), God gives Zechariah a series of four messages: (1) A rebuke of empty ritualism (7:4–7); (2) a reminder of past disobedience (7:8–14); (3) the restoration and consolation of Israel (8:1–17); and (4) the recovery of joy in the kingdom (8:18–23).

The Two Burdens (9—14): The first burden (9—11) concerns the First Advent and rejection of Israel's coming King. Alexander the Great will conquer Israel's neighbors, but will spare Jerusalem (9:1–8) which will be preserved for her King (the Messiah; 9:9–10). Israel will succeed against Greece (the Maccabean revolt; 9:11–17), and although they will later be scattered, the Messiah will bless them and bring them back (10:1—11:3). Israel will reject her Shepherd-King and be led astray by false shepherds (11:4–17). The second burden (12—14) concerns the second advent of Christ and the acceptance of Israel's King. The nations will attack Jerusalem, but the Messiah will come and deliver His people (12). They will be cleansed of impurity and falsehood (13), and the Messiah will come in power to judge the nations and reign in Jerusalem over the whole earth (14).

Outline of Zechariah

I. **The Call to Repentance,** 1:1–6

II. **The Eight Visions of Zechariah,** 1:7–6:8
    A. The Horses among the Myrtle Trees, 1:7–17
    B. The Four Horns and Four Craftsmen, 1:18–21
    C. The Man with the Measuring Line, 2:1–13
    D. The Cleansing of Joshua, the High Priest, 3:1–10
    E. The Golden Lampstand and Olive Trees, 4:1–14
    F. The Flying Scroll, 5:1–4
    G. The Woman in the Basket, 5:5–11
    H. The Four Chariots, 6:1–8

III. **The Crowning of Joshua,** 6:9–15

IV. **The Question of Fasting,** 7:1–3

V. **The Four Messages of Zechariah,** 7:4—8:23
    A. Rebuke of Hypocrisy, 7:4–7
    B. Repent of Disobedience, 7:8–14
    C. Restoration of Israel, 8:1–17
    D. Rejoice in Israel's Future, 8:18–23

VI. **The Two Burdens of Zechariah,** 9:1—14:21
    A. The First Burden: The Rejection of the Messiah, 9:1—11:17
        1. Judgment on Surrounding Nations, 9:1–8
        2. Coming of the Messiah, 9:9—10:12
            a. First Coming of the Messiah, 9:9
            b. Second Coming of the Messiah, 9:10—10:12
        3. Rejection of the Messiah, 11:1–17

B. The Second Burden: The Reign of the Messiah, 12:1—14:21
  1. Deliverance of Israel, 12:1—13:9
     a. Physical Salvation of Judah, 12:1–9
     b. Spiritual Salvation of Judah, 12:10—13:9
  2. Reign of the Messiah, 14:1–21
     a. Final Siege of Jerusalem, 14:1–2
     b. Second Coming of the Messiah, 14:3–8
     c. Kingdom of the Messiah, 14:9–21

Malachi

MALACHI MARKS THE CLOSE of Old Testament prophecy, and the beginning of four hundred years of silence between the Old and New Testaments. Having learned little from their captivity, the people soon lapse into many of the same sins that resulted in their exile in the first place: covetousness, idolatry, mixed marriages with pagan people, abuse of the poor, calloused hearts. In a question-and-answer format, Malachi highlights Judah's hardheartedness and pronounces God's curse upon all who practice such things. It will remain for John the Baptist—the promised forerunner who would come in the power and spirit of Elijah—to bring a hope-filled message, "Behold! The Lamb of God" (John 1:29).

MALACHI							
Focus	Privilege of the Nation 1:1 — 1:5	**Pollution of the Nation** 1:6 — 3:15			**Promise to the Nation** 3:16 — 4:6		
Divisions	Love of God for the Nation 1:1 — 1:5	Sin of the Priests 1:6 — 2:9	Sin of the People 2:10 — 3:15		Book of Remembrance 3:16 — 3:18	Coming of Christ 4:1 — 4:3	Coming of Elijah 4:4 — 4:6
Topics	Past	Present			Future		
	Care of God	Complaint of God			Coming of God		
Place	Jerusalem						
Time	c. 432–425 B.C.						

Introduction and Title

Malachi, a prophet in the days of Nehemiah, directs his message of judgment to a people plagued with corrupt priests, wicked practices, and a false sense of security in their privileged relationship with God. Using the question-and-answer method, Malachi probes deeply into their problems of hypocrisy, infidelity, mixed marriages, divorce, false worship, and arrogance. So sinful has the nation become that God's words to the people no longer have any impact. For four hundred years after Malachi's ringing condemnations, God remains silent. Only with the coming of John the Baptist (3:1) does God again communicate to His people through a prophet's voice.

The meaning of the name *Mal'aki* ("My Messenger") is probably a shortened form of *Mal'akya,* "Messenger of Yahweh," and it is appropriate to the book which speaks of the coming of the "messenger of the covenant" ("messenger" is mentioned three times; see 2:7; 3:1). The Septuagint used the title *Malachias* even though it also translated it "by the hand of his messenger." The Latin title is *Maleachi.*

Author

The only Old Testament mention of Malachi is in chapter 1, verse 1. The authorship, date, and unity of Malachi have never been seriously challenged. The unity of the book can be seen in the dialectic style that binds it together. Nothing is known of Malachi (not even his father's name), but a Jewish tradition says that he was a member of the Great Synagogue (see "Author" in Zechariah).

Date and Setting

Although an exact date cannot be established for Malachi, internal evidence can be used to deduce an approximate date. The Persian term for governor, *pechah* (1:8; cf. Neh. 5:14; Hag. 1:1, 14; 2:21) indicates that this book was written during the Persian domination of Israel (539–333 B.C.). Sacrifices were being offered in the temple (1:7–10; 3:8), which was rebuilt in 516 B.C. Evidently many years had passed since the offerings were instituted, because the priests had grown tired of them and corruptions had crept into the system. In addition, Malachi's oracle was inspired by the same problems that Nehemiah faced: corrupt priests (1:6—2:9; Neh. 13:1–9); neglect of tithes and offerings (3:7–12; Neh. 13:10–13); and intermarriage with pagan wives (2:10–16; Neh. 13:23–28). Nehemiah came to Jerusalem in 444 B.C. to rebuild the city walls, thirteen years after Ezra's return and reforms (457 B.C.). Nehemiah returned to Persia in 432 B.C., but came back to Palestine about 425 B.C., and dealt with the sins described in Malachi. It is therefore likely that Malachi proclaimed his message while Nehemiah was absent between 432 B.C. and 425 B.C., almost a century after Haggai and Zechariah began to prophesy (520 B.C.).

Theme and Purpose

The divine dialogue in Malachi's prophecy was designed as an appeal that would break through the barrier of Israel's disbelief, disappointment, and discouragement.

The promised time of prosperity had not yet come, and the prevailing attitude that it was not worth serving Yahweh became evident in their moral and religious corruption. But God revealed His continuing love in spite of Israel's lethargy. His appeal in this oracle was that the people and priests would stop to realize that their lack of blessing was not caused by His lack of concern, but by their own compromise and disobedience to the covenant law. When they repent and return to God with sincere hearts, the obstacles to the flow of divine blessing will be removed. Malachi also reminds the people that a day of reckoning will surely come when God will judge the righteous and the wicked.

Keys to Malachi

Key Word: Appeal to Backsliders

Key Verses (2:17—3:1; 4:5–6)—"You have wearied the LORD with your words; Yet you say, 'In what way have we wearied *Him?*' In that you say, 'Everyone who does evil *is* good in the sight of the LORD, and He delights in them' or, 'Where *is* the God of justice?' 'Behold, I send My messenger, and he will prepare the way before Me. And the Lord, whom you seek, will suddenly come to His temple, even the Messenger of the covenant, in whom you delight. Behold, He is coming,' says the LORD of hosts" (2:17—3:1).

"Behold, I will send you Elijah the prophet before the coming of the great and dreadful day of the LORD. And he shall turn the hearts of the fathers to the children, and the hearts of the children to their fathers, lest I come and strike the earth with a curse" (4:5–6).

Key Chapter (3)—The last book of the Old Testament concludes with a dramatic prophecy of the coming of the Lord and John the Baptist: "I will send my messenger, and he will prepare the way before Me" (3:1). Israel flocked to the Jordan four hundred years later when "The voice of one crying in the wilderness: Prepare the way of the LORD" (Matt. 3:3) appeared, breaking the long silence of prophetic revelation. Malachi 3—4 records the coming of the Messiah and His forerunner.

Christ in Malachi

The Book of Malachi is the prelude to four hundred years of prophetic silence, broken finally by the words of the next prophet, John the Baptist: "Behold! The Lamb of God who takes away the sin of the world!" (John 1:29). Malachi predicts the coming of the messenger who will clear the way before the Lord (3:1; cf. Is. 40:3). John the Baptist later fulfills this prophecy, but the next few verses (3:2–5) jump ahead to Christ in His second advent. This is also true of the prophecy of the appearance of "Elijah the prophet" (4:5). John the Baptist was this Elijah (see Matt. 3:3; 11:10–14; 17:9–13; Mark 1:2–3; 9:10–13; Luke 1:17; 3:4; John 1:23), but Elijah will also appear before the Second Coming of Christ.

Contribution to the Bible

Malachi's structure is built upon a recurring pattern of accusation ("You are robbing Me!"), interrogation ("How have we robbed Thee?"), and refutation ("In tithes and offerings"). Over and over, the false conclusions and rationalizations of the people ("but you say" and similar expressions appear more than a dozen times) are overcome by irrefutable and convicting arguments. Of the fifty-five verses in Malachi, forty-seven are spoken by God, the highest proportion of all the prophets. Malachi is also the only prophet who ends his book with judgment. While Joel and Zephaniah present the theme of the day of the Lord with greater intensity than Malachi (3:2,17; 4:1,3,5), they end on a theme of hope and blessing. But Malachi is a fitting conclusion to the Old Testament because it underscores the sinful human condition and anticipates God's solution in the work of the coming Messiah.

Survey of Malachi

The great prophecies of Haggai and Zechariah are not yet fulfilled, and the people of Israel become disillusioned and doubtful. They begin to question God's providence as their faith imperceptibly degenerates into cynicism. Internally, they wonder whether it is worth serving God after all; and externally, these attitudes surface in mechanical observances, empty ritual, cheating on tithes and offerings, and crass indifference to God's moral and ceremonial law. Their priests are corrupt and their practices wicked, but they are so spiritually insensitive that they wonder why they are not being blessed by God.

Using a probing series of questions and answers, God seeks to pierce their hearts of stone. In each case the divine accusations are denied: How has God loved us? (1:2–5); How have we (priests) despised God's name? (1:6—2:9); How have we (people) profaned the covenant? (2:10–16); How have we wearied God? (2:17—3:6); How have we robbed God? (3:7–12); and How have we spoken against God? (3:13–15). In effect, the people sneer, "Oh, come on now: it's not that bad!" However, their rebellion is quiet, not open. As their perception of God grows dim, the resulting materialism and externalism become a settled characteristic that later grips the religious parties of the Pharisees and Sadducees. In spite of all this, God still loves His people and once again extends His grace to any who will humbly turn to Him. Malachi explores: the privilege of the nation (1:1–5); the pollution of the nation (1:6—3:15); and the promise to the nation (3:16—4:16).

The Privilege of the Nation (1:1–5): The Israelites blind themselves to God's love for them. Wallowing in the problems of the present, they are forgetful of God's works for them in the past. God gives them a reminder of His special love by contrasting the fates of Esau (Edom) and Jacob (Israel).

The Pollution of the Nation (1:6—3:15): The priests have lost all respect for God's name and in their greed offer only diseased and imperfect animals on the altar. They have more respect for the Persian governor than they do for the living God. Moreover, God is withholding His blessings from them because of their disobedience to God's covenant and their insincere teaching.

The people are indicted for their treachery in divorcing the wives of their youth in order to marry foreign women (2:10–16). In response to their questioning the justice of God, they receive a promise of the Messiah's coming but also a warning of the judgment that He will bring (2:17—3:6). The people have robbed God of the tithes and offerings due Him, but God is ready to bless them with abundance if they will put Him first (3:7–12). The final problem is the arrogant challenge to the character of God (3:13–15), and this challenge is answered in the remainder of the book.

The Promise to the Nation (3:16—4:6): The Lord assures His people that a time is coming when the wicked will be judged and those who fear Him will be blessed. The day of the Lord will reveal that it is not "vain to serve God" (3:14).

Malachi ends on the bitter word "curse." Although the people are finally cured of idolatry, there is little spiritual progress in Israel's history. Sin abounds, and the need for the coming Messiah is greater than ever.

Outline of Malachi

   I. **The Privilege of the Nation,** 1:1–5

   II. **The Pollution of the Nation,** 1:6—3:15
   - A. The Sin of the Priests of Israel, 1:6—2:9
     1. The Priests Despise the Name of the Lord, 1:6–14
     2. The Lord Curses the Priest, 2:1–9
   - B. The Sin of the People of Israel, 2:10—3:15
     1. The People Commit Idolatry, 2:10–13
     2. The People Divorce, 2:14–16
     3. The Lord Will Judge at His Coming, 2:17—3:5
     4. The People Rob God, 3:6–12
     5. The People Doubt the Character of God, 3:13–15

   III. **The Promises to the Nation,** 3:16—4:6
   - A. The Rewards of the Book of Remembrance, 3:16–18
   - B. The Rewards of the Coming of Christ, 4:1–3
   - C. The Prophecy of the Coming of Elijah, 4:4–6

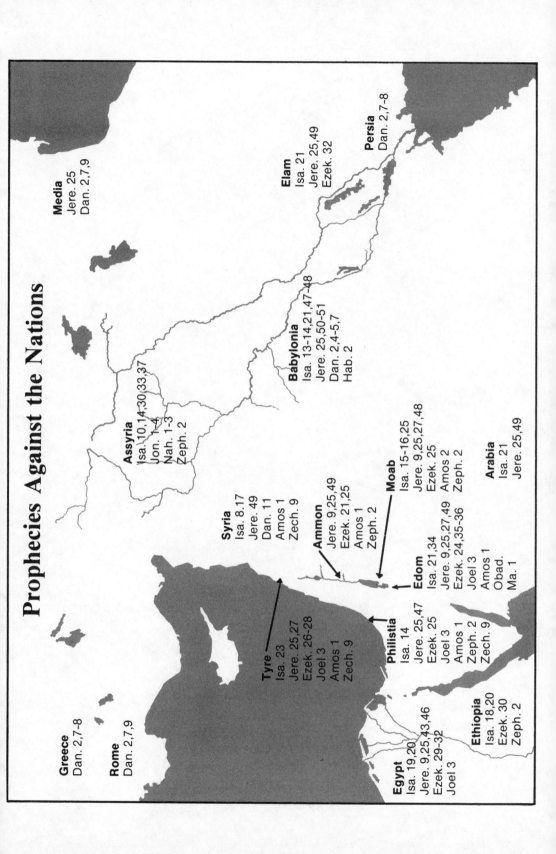

Prophecies Against the Nations

Media
Jere. 25
Dan. 2,7,9

Greece
Dan. 2,7-8

Rome
Dan. 2,7,9

Persia
Dan. 2,7-8

Elam
Isa. 21
Jere. 25,49
Ezek. 32

Babylonia
Isa. 13-14,21,47-48
Jere. 25,50-51
Dan. 2,4-5,7
Hab. 2

Assyria
Isa. 10,14,30,33,37
Jon. 1-4
Nah. 1-3
Zeph. 2

Syria
Isa. 8.17
Jere. 49
Dan. 11
Amos 1
Zech. 9

Ammon
Jere. 9,25,49
Ezek. 21,25
Amos 1
Zeph. 2

Moab
Isa. 15-16,25
Jere. 9,25,27,48
Ezek. 25
Amos 2
Zeph. 2

Arabia
Isa. 21
Jere. 25,49

Tyre
Isa. 23
Jere. 25,27
Ezek. 26-28
Joel 3
Amos 1
Zech. 9

Edom
Isa. 21,34
Jere. 9,25,27,49
Ezek. 24,35-36
Joel 3
Amos 1
Obad.
Ma. 1

Philistia
Isa. 14
Jere. 25,47
Ezek. 25
Joel 3
Amos 1
Zeph. 2
Zech. 9

Ethiopia
Isa. 18,20
Ezek. 30
Zeph. 2

Egypt
Isa. 19,20
Jere. 9,25,43,46
Ezek. 29-32
Joel 3

Introduction to the
New Testament

THE HISTORIANS, POETS, AND PROPHETS who wrote the thirty-nine books of the Old Testament were men who passionately anticipated the fulfillment of Yahweh's redemptive program and the coming of His Anointed One. Their inspired predictions were gloriously realized in the coming of Jesus the Messiah. Thus, the New Testament completes the cosmic story begun in the Old Testament of God's plan to bring salvation upon the earth.

He Kaine Diatheke (Latin, *Novum Testamentum*) literally means "The New Covenant." The Greek work *diatheke* speaks of a last will and testament that came into effect upon the death of the testator. The New Covenant was ratified with the blood of Christ, and a person enters into that covenant relationship when he comes to God on *His* terms. This redemptive covenant is a unifying theme that binds the books of the New Testament together (see Luke 22:20; 1 Cor. 11:25; Heb. 8:7–13; 9:15–17).

Like the Old Testament, the New Testament is not one book but an anthology of books that ranged in length from a single sheet of papyrus to a full scroll. The twenty-seven books of the New Testament reflect a wide diversity of themes, personalities, literary forms and achievement, backgrounds, and purposes, so that each book has a unique contribution to make. The New Testament, less than one-third the length of the Old Testament, was written from about A.D. 45–95 in *Koine* ("common") Greek, the international language of the people. The language was not only widely used, but it was clear, precise, and flexible. The New Testament books were separately circulated and gradually collected together. Their inspiration and apostolic authority guaranteed them a place in the canon of Scripture as they were set apart from other writings in the early church. As these books were copied and distributed throughout the Roman Empire, they were eventually placed in a standard order (more logical than chronological).

Of the nine New Testament authors, only Luke was a full Gentile. Paul wrote thirteen books, John wrote five, Luke and Peter wrote two, and Matthew, Mark, James, Jude, and the author of Hebrews each wrote one. Sometimes these books are arranged into three periods: (1) The lifetime of Christ, 4 B.C. to A.D. 33 (Matthew, Mark, Luke, John); (2) the expansion of the church in Acts, A.D. 33–62 (Acts, Romans, First and Second Corinthians, Galatians, Ephesians, Philippians, Colossians, First and Second Thessalonians, Philemon, James); and (3) the post-Acts consolidation of the church, A.D. 62–95 (First and Second Timothy, Titus, Hebrews, First and Second Peter, First, Second, and Third John, Jude, Revelation). A more common classification is the threefold division into the Historical books, the Pauline Epistles, and the Non-Pauline Epistles and the Revelation. This can be modified into the following chart:

The Structure of the New Testament			
Pauline Epistles: Individuals			
First Timothy	Second Timothy	Titus	Philemon
Second Thessalonians			Hebrews
First Thessalonians			James
Colossians			First Peter
Philippians			Second Peter
Ephesians			First John
Galatians			Second John
Second Corinthians			Third John
First Corinthians			Jude
Romans			Revelation
Acts			
Matthew	Mark	Luke	John
Historical Books			

Left vertical label: Pauline Epistles: Churches
Right vertical label: Non-Pauline Epistles and Revelation

Historical Books

These five books depict key events in the life of Christ, the foundation of the church, and the early spread of Christianity. The Old Testament anticipated the person and works of the Lord Jesus in manifold ways, and the hope of the prophets was incarnated in the form of the God-man, the Word who became flesh (John 1:1,14). After His Resurrection, He empowered His apostles to spread the glad tidings of salvation beginning in Jerusalem and reaching to Rome and beyond.

Pauline Epistles

The Epistles as a whole develop the seed doctrines in the Gospels and show how they can transform the lives of believers. Paul wrote nine letters to churches and four to individuals as he sought to instruct, correct, and encourage believers throughout the Roman Empire. Paul wanted Christians to base their practice upon the reality of their position in Christ.

Non-Pauline Epistles and Revelation

Peter, John, James, and the author of Hebrews dealt frankly and firmly with a multitude of problems that were creeping into the churches. They pointed to the person and power of the resurrected Christ as the believer's source of life and godliness. Revelation is a fitting conclusion to the New Testament as it looks ahead to the hope of Christ's return, the vindication of God's righteousness, and the culmination of His eternal plan in the new heavens and new earth.

Introduction to the
Historical Books

THE FOUR GOSPELS COMPRISE about 46 percent of the New Testament, and when the Book of Acts is added, the figure goes up to 60 percent. The early church placed the Gospels at the beginning of the New Testament canon, not because they were the first books to be written, but because they are the foundation upon which Acts and the Epistles are built. The Gospels are at once rooted in and the fulfillment of the Old Testament, and they provide the historical and theological backdrop for the rest of the New Testament.

The Greek word *euaggelion* refers to the "glad tidings" or "good news" about Jesus Christ that was orally proclaimed. It later came to be applied to the written accounts as well. The English word "gospel" is a derivative of the Anglo-Saxon *godspell* which can mean "God story" or "good story." Although later gospels were written, the early church regarded only the four Gospels as we know them to be authoritative and divinely inspired. They were distinguished from one another by the Greek preposition *kata* ("according to") followed by the name of the writer. The present order of the four Gospels goes back at least to the late second century, and it was thought to be the order in which they were written. Although there are some who have theorized that the Gospels were originally written in Aramaic, there is no real evidence for this position. The inhabitants of Palestine were primarily bilingual (Aramaic and Greek), and many were trilingual (Hebrew or Latin). But Greek was the common language of the whole empire, and thus the most suitable vehicle for the gospel accounts.

The literary form of the Gospels had no counterpart in Hellenistic literature. Although they are full of biographical material, they are really thematic portraits that almost entirely overlook the thirty-plus years of preparation for Christ's relatively brief public ministry. Even this portion of His life is presented in a highly skewed fashion with the emphasis on His last week. In all, only about fifty days of Jesus' ministry are touched upon in the combined Gospels.

The four complementary accounts provide a composite picture of the person and work of the Savior, working together to give depth and clarity to our understanding of the most unique figure in human history. In them He is seen as divine and human, the sovereign Servant, the God-man. Each gospel has a distinctive dimension to add, so that the total is greater than the sum of the parts.

Topics	Matthew	Mark	Luke	John
Probable Date	A.D. 58–58	A.D. 55–65	A.D. 60–68	A.D. 80–90
Place of Writing	Syrian Antioch or Palestine	Rome	Rome/ Greece	Ephesus
Original Audience	Jewish Mind (Religious)	Roman Mind (Pragmatic)	Greek Mind (Idealistic)	Universal
Theme	Messiah-King	Servant-Redeemer	Perfect Man	Son of God
Traditional Picture of Christ (cf. Ezek. 1:10; Rev. 4:6–8)	The Lion (strength, authority)	The Bull (service, power)	The Man (wisdom, character)	The Eagle (deity, person)

The Gospels were written to awaken and strengthen faith in Christ and to answer objections and misconceptions about Him. They were also designed to guide believers into a fuller understanding of His person and power. As Christianity spread beyond Palestine, the oral testimony of the apostles was no longer adequate. Their message was multiplied and preserved through the medium of the written word.

Matthew, Mark, and Luke are known as the *synoptic Gospels*. The Greek word synoptikos means "seeing together," and it is an appropriate description of these gospels because of their common viewpoint and similar characteristics, especially in contrast to John, the *supplemental gospel*.

Topics	Synoptics (Matthew, Mark, Luke)	John
Portrait of Christ	God-*man*	*God*-man
Perspective	Historical	Theological
Unique Material	Less unique (Matthew, 42%; Mark, 7%; Luke 59%)	More unique (92%)
Chronology	Only one Passover mentioned	Three or four Passovers mentioned
Geography	Concentrate on Galilean ministry	Concentrates on Judean ministry
Discourse Material	More Public	More Private
Teaching Method	Parables	Allegories
Teaching Emphasis	More on ethical, practical teachings	More on the person of Christ
Relationship to Other Gospels	Complementary	Supplementary

The agreements and differences among the synoptics have led to the "synoptic problem" of determining their literary relationship. The agreements include selection of materials, broad chronological outline, and literary structure. The differences include unique material, differences in some parallel accounts, and different historical contexts for some episodes. There are many proposed solutions to this problem, but most are variations on three basic suggestions: (1) oral tradition, (2) interdependence, and (3) documentary sources. The two-document theory proposes that Mark and an unknown source document named Q were the basis for Matthew and Luke. Multiple-documents theories propose additional hypothetical source documents. The most satisfactory approach involves four elements: (1) direct knowledge, (2) oral tradition, (3) use of documents, and (4) the superintending ministry of the Holy Spirit (cf. John 14:26).

Christ indeed came in "the fullness of the time" (Gal. 4:4). Politically, the Roman Empire provided universal peace, improved travel (Roman roads), and a common language (Greek) that would facilitate the spread of the gospel. Economically, conditions of high taxation, poverty, and unrest put most people in a state of need. Spiritually, Judaism had lost its vitality and the Roman gods were dead or dying. It was in this context that Christianty flourished in its crucial beginning years.

Matthew

The first Gospel presents Jesus as the Christ, Israel's messianic King. Jesus' genealogy, fulfillment of Old Testament prophecy, authority, and power are emphasized as His messianic credentials. In spite of His unique words and works, gradually mounting opposition culminates in His Crucifixion. But the King left an empty tomb and will come again.

Mark

The second Gospel presents Jesus as the Servant who came to "give His life a ransom for many." In the beginning of His ministry He was a servant to the multitudes, but as His departure grew near, Jesus concentrated on teaching and ministering to His disciples. A full 37 percent of this gospel is devoted to the events of His last and most important week.

Luke

The third Gospel presents Jesus as the perfect Son of Man whose mission was "to seek and to save that which was lost." This lucid historical portrait of Christ traces His advent, activities, admonitions, affliction, and authentication to demonstrate His perfect character and redemptive work.

John

The fourth Gospel presents Jesus as the eternal Son of God who offered eternal life to all who would believe in Him. John uses a carefully chosen series of seven signs to demonstrate that Jesus is the Christ. Five chapters of this gospel record Jesus' parting discourse to His disciples only a few hours before His death. After His victorious Resurrection, Christ further instructed His men in a number of appearances.

Acts

There are four gospel accounts, but only one canonical Book of Acts. Thus, this book provides the only historical portrait of the period from the Ascension to the travels and trials of Paul. Acts chronicles some of the key events in the spread of the gospel from Judea to Samaria, Syria, and the rest of the Roman Empire.

Matthew

THE OLD TESTAMENT PROPHETS predicted and longed for the coming of the Anointed One who would enter history to bring redemption and deliverance. The first verse of Matthew announces that long-awaited event: "The book of the genealogy of Jesus Christ, the Son of David, the Son of Abraham." Matthew provides the essential bridge between the Old and New Testaments. Through a carefully selected series of Old Testament quotations, Matthew documents Jesus Christ's claim to be Messiah. Jesus possesses the credentials of Messiah, ministers in the predicted pattern of Messiah, preaches messages only Messiah could preach, and finally dies the death only Messiah could die.

MATTHEW

Focus	Offer of the King				Rejection of the King			
	1:1			11:1	11:2			28:20
Divisions	Presentation of the King	Proclamation of the King	Power of the King	Progressive Rejection of the King	Preparation of the King's Disciples	Presentation and Rejection of the King	Proof of the King	
	1:1 4:11	4:12 7:29	8:1 11:1	11:2 16:12	16:13 20:28	20:29 27:66	28:1 28:20	
Topics	Teaching the Throngs				Teaching the Twelve			
	Topical			Chronological				
Place	Bethlehem & Nazareth	Galilee			Judea			
Time	c. 4 B.C.–A.D. 33							

Introduction and Title

Matthew is the gospel written by a Jew to Jews about a Jew. Matthew is the writer, his countrymen are the readers, and Jesus Christ is the subject. Matthew's design is to present Jesus as the King of the Jews, the long-awaited Messiah. Through a carefully selected series of Old Testament quotations, Matthew documents Jesus Christ's claim to be Messiah. His genealogy, baptism, messages, and miracles all point to the same inescapable conclusion: Christ is King. Even in His death, seeming defeat is turned to victory by the Resurrection, and the message again echoes forth: the King of the Jews lives.

At an early date this gospel was given the title *Kata Matthaion,* "According to Matthew." As this title suggests, other gospel accounts were known at that time (the word *gospel* was added later). Matthew ("Gift of the Lord") was also surnamed Levi (Mark 2:14; Luke 5:27).

Author

The early church uniformly attributed this gospel to Matthew, and no tradition to the contrary ever emerged. This book was known early and accepted quickly. In his Ecclesiastical History (A.D. 323), Eusebius quoted a statement by Papias (c. A.D. 140) that Matthew wrote *logia* ("sayings") in Aramaic. No Aramaic gospel of Matthew has been found, and it is evident that Matthew is not a Greek translation of an Aramaic original. Some believe that Matthew wrote an abbreviated version of Jesus' sayings in Aramaic before writing his gospel in Greek for a larger circle of readers.

Matthew, the son of Alphaeus (Mark 2:14), occupied the unpopular post of tax collector in Capernaum for the Roman government. As a publican he was no doubt disliked by his Jewish countrymen. When Jesus called him to discipleship (see 9:9–13; Mark 2:14; Luke 5:27–28), his quick response probably meant that he had already been stirred by Jesus' public preaching. He gave a large reception for Jesus in his house so that his associates could meet Jesus. He was chosen as one of the twelve apostles, and the last appearance of his name in the Bible is in Acts 1:13. Matthew's life from that point is veiled in tradition.

Modern scholars often deny the apostolic origin of this gospel because it does not have as many lifelike touches as the other gospels and because an apostle like Matthew would not have depended so heavily on a non-apostolic writer like Mark. While there are problems, the first argument is more a matter of stylistic approach, and the second argument overlooks the apostolic origin of Mark's gospel (Peter) and Matthew's critical use of Mark (if he used it at all). The arguments against Matthean authorship are much weaker than the external and internal evidence for the traditional view. The early church uniformly attributed this gospel to Matthew, and no contrary tradition ever developed. This book was known early and quickly accepted.

Date and Setting

Like all the Gospels, Matthew is not easy to date: suggestions have ranged from A.D. 40 to 140. The two expressions "to this day" (27:8), and "until this day" (28:15) indicate that a substantial period of time has passed since the events described in the book, but they also point to a date prior to the destruction of Jerusalem in A.D.

70. The Olivet Discourse (24—25) also anticipates this event. The strong Jewish flavor of this gospel is another argument for a date prior to A.D. 70. If Matthew depended on Mark's gospel as a source, the date of Mark would determine the earliest date for Matthew. The likely time frame for this book is A.D. 58–68. It may have been written in Palestine or Syrian Antioch.

Theme and Purpose

Although Matthew has no purpose statement, it was clearly written to proclaim the words and works of Jesus Christ so that the reader could make an intelligent decision about Him. The opening genealogy reaches back into the Old Testament, and the many references to Christ's fulfillment of specific prophecies show that Israel's long-awaited Messiah had come. By quoting repeatedly from the Old Testament, Matthew validates Christ's claims that He is, in fact, the prophesied Messiah (the Anointed One) of Israel. Everything about this King is unique: His miraculous birth and obscure yet carefully prophesied birthplace, His flight into Egypt, His announcement by John, His battle with Satan in the wilderness, all support the only possible conclusion—Jesus is the culmination of promises delivered by the prophets over a period of a thousand years. Thus God's redemptive plan is alive and well, even after four hundred years of prophetic silence. Matthew was no doubt used by Jewish believers as an evangelistic tool to reach other Jews.

It is evident that Matthew also had an instructional purpose in writing his gospel. It systematically presents the claims, credentials, authority, ethical teachings, and theological teachings of the Lord Jesus. As such, it has been used as a teaching manual since the early years of the church.

Keys to Matthew

Key Word: Jesus the King

Key Verses (16:16–19; 28:18–20)—"And Simon Peter answered and said, 'You are the Christ, the Son of the living God.' Jesus answered and said to him, 'Blessed are you, Simon Bar-Jonah, for flesh and blood has not revealed *this* to you, but My Father who is in heaven. And I also say to you that you are Peter, and on this rock I will build My church, and the gates of Hades shall not prevail against it. And I will give you the keys of the kingdom of heaven, and whatever you bind on earth will be bound in heaven, and whatever you loose on earth will be loosed in heaven'" (16:16–19).

"Then Jesus came and spoke to them, saying, 'All authority has been given to Me in heaven and on earth. Go therefore and make disciples of all the nations, baptizing them in the name of the Father and of the Son and of the Holy Spirit, teaching them to observe all things that I have commanded you; and lo, I am with you always, *even* to the end of the age.' Amen" (28:18–20).

Key Chapter (12)—The turning point of Matthew comes in the twelfth chapter when the Pharisees, acting as the leadership of the nation of Israel, formally reject Jesus Christ as the Messiah, saying that His power comes not from God but from Satan. Christ's ministry changes immediately with His new teaching of parables, increased attention given to His disciples, and His repeated statement that His death is now near.

Christ in Matthew

Matthew presents Jesus as Israel's promised messianic King (1:23; 2:2, 6; 3:17; 4:15–17; 21:5, 9; 22:44–45; 26:64; 27:11, 27–37). The phrase "the king of heaven" appears thirty-two times in Matthew but nowhere else in the New Testament. To show that Jesus fulfills the qualifications for the Messiah, Matthew uses more Old Testament quotations and allusions than any other book (almost 130). Often used in this gospel is the revealing phrase "that what was spoken through the prophet might be fulfilled," which appears nine times in Matthew and not once in the other gospels. Jesus is the climax of the prophets (12:39–40; 13:13–15, 35; 17:5–13), "the Son of man" (24:30ff.), the "Servant" of the Lord (12:17–21), and the "Son of David" (the Davidic references occurs nine times in Matthew, but only six times in all of the other gospels).

Contribution to the Bible

The most striking feature of the first Gospel is its Jewish emphasis. Matthew traces the genealogy of Jesus back to Abraham and frequently calls Him the son of David. He strongly stresses the fulfillment of messianic prophecies in the life of Christ. Also prominent are Jewish customs and traditions (without explanations), the place of the Mosaic Law in Jesus' teaching, the "lost sheep of the house of Israel," and the scribes and Pharisees. Matthew develops the theme of the kingdom because the Jewish reader would wonder why Jesus did not establish the promised kingdom if He was indeed Messiah.

The Good News of this book reaches beyond the Jews to the rest of the world as well. Gentile women are found in Christ's genealogy; Gentiles worshiped Him after His birth, "the field is the world" (13:38); and the Great Commission is to "make disciples of all the nations" (28:19; see also 8:11–12; 21:33–43).

Fully 60 percent of Matthew's 1,071 verses contain the spoken word of Jesus. Matthew paints a broad picture of Christ's life without going into the fine details that are often seen in the other gospels. The highly organized content of this gospel (discourses, miracles, parables, questions) is thematically arranged to stress the combined thrust of the Savior's words and work. Matthew builds his themes in such a way that they all join together in the climax of the book.

Survey of Matthew

The Old Testament prophets predicted and longed for the coming of the Anointed One who would enter history to bring redemption and deliverance. The first verse of Matthew succinctly announces the fulfillment of Israel's hope in the coming of Christ: "The book of the genealogy of Jesus Christ, the Son of David, the Son of Abraham." Matthew was placed first in the canon of New Testament books by the early church because it is a natural bridge between the Testaments. This gospel describes the person and work of Israel's messianic King. An important part of Matthew's structure is revealed in the phrase "when Jesus had ended" (7:28; 13:53; 19:1; 26:1; cf. 11:1), which is used to conclude the five key discourses of the book: The Sermon on the Mount (5:3—7:27), Instruction of the Disciples (10:5–42), Parables of the Kingdom (13:3–52), Terms of Discipleship (18:3–35), and the Olivet

Discourse (24:4—25:46). Matthew can be outlined as follows: The presentation of the King (1:1—4:11); the proclamation of the King (4:12—7:29); the power of the King (8:1—11:1); the progressive rejection of the King (11:2—16:12); the preparation of the King's disciples (16:13—20:28); the presentation and rejection of the King (20:29—27:66); and the proof of the King (28:1-20).

The Presentation of the King (1:1—4:11): The promise to Abraham was that "in you all the families of the earth shall be blessed" (Gen. 12:3). Jesus Christ, the Savior of the world, is "the Son of Abraham" (1:1). However, He is also "the Son of David"; and as David's direct descendant, He is qualified to be Israel's King. The magi know that the "King of the Jews" (2:2) has been born and come to worship Him. John the Baptist, the messianic forerunner who breaks the four hundred years of prophetic silence, also bears witness of Him (cf. Mal. 3:1). The sinlessness of the King is proved when He overcomes the satanic temptations to disobey the will of the Father.

The Proclamation of the King (4:12—7:29): In this section, Matthew uses a topical rather than a chronological arrangement of his material in order to develop a crucial pattern in Christ's ministry. The words of the Lord are found in the Sermon on the Mount (5—7). This discourse requires less than fifteen minutes to read, but its brevity has not diminished its profound influence on the world. The Sermon on the Mount presents new laws and standards for God's people.

The Power of the King (8:1—11:1): The works of the Lord are presented in a series of ten miracles (8—9) that reveal His authority over every realm (disease, demons, death, and nature). Thus, the words of the Lord are supported by His works; His claims are verified by His credentials.

The Progressive Rejection of the King (11:2—16:12): Here we note a series of reactions to Christ's words and works. Because of increasing opposition, Jesus begins to spend proportionately more time with His disciples as He prepares them for His coming death and departure.

The Preparation of the King's Disciples (16:13—20:28): In a series of discourses, Jesus communicates the significance of accepting or rejecting His offer of righteousness. His teaching (16:13—21:11) is primarily directed to those who accept Him.

The Presentation and Rejection of the King (20:29—27:66): The majority of Christ's words in this section are aimed at those who reject their King. The Lord predicts the terrible that will fall on Jerusalem, resulting in the dispersion of the Jewish people. Looking beyond these events (fulfilled in A.D. 70), He also describes His Second Coming as the Judge and Lord of the earth.

The Proof of the King (28): Authenticating His words and works are the empty tomb, Resurrection, and appearance, all proving that Jesus Christ is indeed the prophesied Messiah, the very Son of God.

Christ's final ministry in Judea (beginning in 19:1) reaches a climax at the Cross as the King willingly gives up His life to redeem sinful persons. Jesus endures awesome human hatred in this great demonstration of divine love (cf. Rom. 5:7–8). His perfect sacrifice is acceptable, and this gospel concludes with His glorious Resurrection.

Outline of Matthew

Part One: The Presentation of the King (1:1—4:11)

I. The Advent of the King, 1:1—2:23
- A. Genealogy of Christ, 1:1–17
- B. Birth of Christ, 1:18–25
- C. Visit of the Wise Men, 2:1–12
- D. Flight into Egypt, 2:13–15
- E. Herod Kills the Children, 2:16–18
- F. Jesus Returns to Nazareth, 2:19–23

II. The Announcer of the King, 3:1–12
- A. The Person of John the Baptist, 3:1–6
- B. The Preaching of John the Baptist, 3:7–12

III. The Approval of the King, 3:13—4:11
- A. Baptism of Jesus, 3:13–17
- B. Temptation of Jesus, 4:1–11
  - 1. First Temptation, 4:1–4
  - 2. Second Temptation, 4:5–7
  - 3. Third Temptation, 4:8–11

Part Two: The Proclamation of the King (4:12—7:29)

I. The Background for the Sermon, 4:12–25
- A. Jesus Begins His Ministry, 4:12–17
- B. Jesus Calls His First Disciples, 4:18–22
- C. Jesus Ministers in Galilee, 4:23–25

II. The Sermon on the Mount, 5:1—7:29
- A. The Subjects of the Kingdom, 5:1–16
  - 1. The Beatitudes, 5:1–12
  - 2. The Similitudes, 5:13–16
- B. The Relationship of Jesus to the Law, 5:17—7:6
  - 1. Jesus Fulfills the Law, 5:17–19
  - 2. Jesus Rejects Pharisaic Interpretation, 5:20–48
    - a. Murder, 5:20–26
    - b. Adultery, 5:27–30
    - c. Divorce, 5:31–32
    - d. Oaths, 5:33–37
    - e. Retaliation, 5:38–42
    - f. Love, 5:43–48
  - 3. Jesus Rejects Pharisaic Practices, 6:1—7:6
    - a. Charitable Deeds, 6:1–4
    - b. Prayer, 6:5–15
    - c. Fasting, 6:16–18
    - d. Wealth, 6:19–34
    - e. Judging, 7:1–6

C. Jesus Instructs on Entering the Kingdom, 7:7–27
   1. "Ask, and It Will Be Given," 7:7–11
   2. Golden Rule, 7:12
   3. Two Ways of Life, 7:13–14
   4. False and True Teaching, 7:15–20
   5. True Way into the Kingdom, 7:21–23
   6. Parable of the Two Builders, 7:24–27
D. Response to the Sermon, 7:28–29

Part Three: The Power of the King (8:1—11:1)

I. The Demonstration of the King's Power, 8:1—9:34
A. Miracles of Healing, 8:1–17
   1. The Leper Is Cleansed, 8:1–4
   2. The Centurion's Servant Is Healed, 8:5–13
   3. Peter's Mother-in-Law Is Healed, 8:14–17
B. Demands of Discipleship, 8:18–22
C. Miracles of Power, 8:23—9:8
   1. The Sea Is Stilled, 8:23–27
   2. Demons Are Cast into Swine, 8:28–34
   3. The Paralytic Is Forgiven, 9:1–8
D. Distinctions of Disciples, 9:9–17
   1. Matthew Is Called, 9:9
   2. The Disciples Eat with Sinners, 9:10–13
   3. The Disciples Do Not Fast, 9:14–17
E. Miracles of Restoration, 9:18–34
   1. Life Is Restored, 9:18–26
   2. Sight Is Restored, 9:27–31
   3. Speech Is Restored, 9:32–34

II. The Delegation of the King's Power, 9:35—11:1
A. The Need for Delegation of Power, 9:35–38
B. The Twelve Apostles Are Sent, 10:1–4
C. The Twelve Apostles Are Instructed, 10:5—11:1

Part Four: The Progressive Rejection of the King (11:2—16:12)

I. The Commencement of Rejection, 11:2–30
A. Rejection of John the Baptist, 11:2–15
B. Rejection by Jesus' Generation, 11:16–19
C. Rejection of Chorazin, Bethsaida, and Capernaum, 11:20–24
D. Invitation to Come unto Jesus, 11:25–30

II. The Rejection of Christ by the Pharisees, 12:1–50
A. Controversy over Sabbath-Labor, 12:1–8
B. Controversy over Sabbath-Healing, 12:9–13
C. Pharisees Plan to Destroy Christ, 12:14–21
D. Pharisees Blaspheme the Holy Spirit, 12:22–30
E. Pharisees Commit the Unpardonable Sin, 12:31–37

F. Pharisees Demand a Sign, 12:38–45
G. Jesus and the True Brethren, 12:46–50

III. The Consequences of the Rejection, 13:1–53
A. Parables Spoken to the Multitude, 13:1–35
    1. Parable of the Soils, 13:1–23
    2. Parable of the Wheat and Tares, 13:24–30
    3. Parable of the Mustard Seed, 13:31–32
    4. Parable of the Leaven, 13:33–35
B. Parables Spoken to the Disciples, 13:36–53
    1. Parable of the Tares Explained, 13:36–43
    2. Parable of the Hidden Treasure, 13:44
    3. Parable of the Pearl of Great Price, 13:45–46
    4. Parable of the Dragnet, 13:47–50
    5. Parable of the Householder, 13:51–53

IV. The Continuing Rejection of the King, 13:54—16:12
A. Rejection at Nazareth, 13:54–58
B. Rejection by Herod, 14:1–36
    1. Reaction of Herod, 14:1–12
        a. Present Response to Jesus, 14:1–2
        b. Recount of the Murder of John the Baptist, 14:3–12
    2. Withdrawal of Jesus, 14:13–36
        a. Desert: Feeds Five Thousand, 14:13–21
        b. Sea: Walks on Water, 14:22–33
        c. Gennesaret: Heals Many, 14:34–36
C. Rejection by Scribes and Pharisees, 15:1–39
    1. Debate over Tradition, 15:1–20
    2. Withdrawal of Jesus, 15:21–39
        a. Tyre and Sidon: Heals the Gentile Woman, 15:21–28
        b. Mountains: Heals Many, 15:29–31
        c. Decapolis: Feeds Four Thousand Gentiles, 15:32–39
D. Rejection by Pharisees and Sadducees, 16:1–12
    1. Debate over a Sign from Heaven, 16:1–4
    2. Withdrawal of Jesus, 16:5–12

Part Five: The Preparation of the King's Disciples (16:13—20:28)

I. The Revelation in View of Rejection, 16:13—17:13
A. Revelation of the Person of the King, 16:13—17
B. Revelation of the Program of the King, 16:18—17:13
    1. Revelation of the Church, 16:18–20
    2. Revelation of Jesus' Death, 16:21–23
    3. Revelation of Jesus' Reward, 16:24–26
    4. The Prophecy of the Second Coming, 16:27–28
    5. The Transfiguration 17:1–13

II. The Instruction in View of Rejection, 17:14—20:28
A. Instruction about Faith, 17:14–21

    1. Parable of the Fig Tree, 24:32–35
    2. Illustration of the Days of Noah, 24:36–44
    3. Illustration of the Two Servants, 24:45–51
  E. Jesus Predicts Judgment at His Coming, 25:1–46
    1. Parable of the Ten Virgins, 25:1–13
    2. Parable of the Talents, 25:14–30
    3. Judgment of the Gentiles, 25:31–46

VI. The Passion of the King, 26:1—27:66
  A. The Religious Leaders Plot to Kill Jesus, 26:1–5
  B. Mary Anoints Jesus for Burial, 26:6–13
  C. Judas Agrees to Betray Jesus, 26:14–16
  D. The Disciples Celebrate the Passover, 26:17–35
    1. The Passover Is Prepared, 26:17–19
    2. The Passover Is Celebrated, 26:20–25
    3. The Lord's Supper Is Instituted, 26:26–29
    4. Peter's Denial Is Predicted, 26:30–35
  E. Jesus Is Arrested in Gethsemane, 26:36–56
    1. Jesus' Three Prayers, 26:36–46
    2. Jesus' Betrayal and Arrest, 26:47–56
  F. Jesus Is Tried, 26:57—27:25
    1. The Trial before Caiaphas, 26:57–75
      a. Two False Witnesses, 26:57–68
      b. Three Denials of Peter, 26:69–75
    2. The Trial before Pilate, 27:1–25
      a. Jesus Is Delivered to Pilate, 27:1–2
      b. Judas Repents, 27:3–10
      c. Jesus Is Examined, 27:11–14
      d. Barabbas Is Freed, 27:15–25
  G. Jesus Is Crucified, 27:26–56
    1. Jesus Is Scourged, 27:26–28
    2. Jesus Is Led to Golgotha, 27:29–33
    3. Jesus Is Crucified, 27:34–44
    4. Jesus Dies, 27:45–50
    5. Signs Accompanying Jesus' Death, 27:51–56
  H. Jesus Is Buried, 27:57–66

Part Seven: The Proof of the King (28:1–20)

I. The Empty Tomb, 28:1–8

II. The Appearance of Jesus to the Women, 28:9–10

III. The Bribery of the Soldiers, 28:11–15

IV. The Appearance of Jesus to the Disciples, 28:16–17

V. The Great Commission, 28:18–20

Mark

MARK, THE SHORTEST AND SIMPLEST of the four Gospels, gives a crisp and fast-moving account of the life of Christ. With few comments, Mark lets the narrative speak for itself as it tells the story of the Servant who is constantly on the move preaching, healing, teaching, and finally dying for sinful men. A ministry that begins with the masses soon narrows to the twelve disciples, and finally culminates on the Cross. There the Servant who "'did not come to be served,'" makes the supreme sacrifice of servanthood by giving "'His life a ransom for many'" (10:45). And that pattern of selfless service becomes the model for those who follow in the Servant's steps.

MARK

Focus	To Serve			To Sacrifice	
	1:1 ... 10:52			11:1 ... 16:20	
Divisions	Presentation of the Servant	Opposition to the Servant	Instruction by the Servant	Rejection of the Servant	Ressurection of the Servant
	1:1 — 2:12	2:13 — 8:26	8:27 — 10:52	11:1 — 15:47	16:1 — 16:20
Topics	Sayings and Signs			Suffering	
Place	Galilee and Perea			Judea and Jerusalem	
Time	c. 3 Years		c. 6 Months	8 Days	
	c. A.D. 29–33				

Introduction and Title

The message of Mark's gospel is captured in a single verse: "For even the Son of Man did not come to be served, but to serve, and to give His life a ransom for many" (10:45). Chapter by chapter, the book unfolds the dual focus of Christ's life: service and sacrifice.

Mark portrays Jesus as a Servant on the move, instantly responsive to the will of the Father. By preaching, teaching, and healing, He ministers to the needs of others even to the point of death. After the Resurrection, He commissions His followers to continue His work in His power—servants following in the steps of the perfect Servant.

The ancient title for this gospel was *Kata Markon,* "According to Mark." The author is best known by his Latin name *Marcus,* but in Jewish circles he was called by his Hebrew name *John.* Acts 12:12, 25; 15:37 refer to him as "John, whose surname was Mark."

Author

According to Acts 12:12, Mark's mother Mary had a large house that was used as a meeting place for believers in Jerusalem. Peter apparently went to this house often because the servant girl recognized his voice at the gate (Acts 12:13–16). Barnabas was Mark's cousin (Col. 4:10), but Peter may have been the person who led him to Christ (Peter called him "Mark my son," 1 Pet. 5:13). It was this close association with Peter that lent apostolic authority to Mark's gospel, since Peter was evidently Mark's primary source of information. It has been suggested that Mark was referring to himself in his account of "a certain young man" in Gethsemane (14:51–52). Since all the disciples had abandoned Jesus (14:50), this little incident may have been a firsthand account.

Barnabas and Saul took Mark along with them when they returned from Jerusalem to Antioch (Acts 12:25) and again when they left on the first missionary journey (Acts 13:5). However, Mark left early and returned to Jerusalem (Acts 13:13). When Barnabas wanted to bring Mark on the second missionary journey, Paul's refusal led to a disagreement. The result was that Barnabas took Mark to Cyprus and Paul took Silas through Syria and Cilicia (Acts 15:36–41). Nevertheless, Paul wrote that Mark was with him during his first Roman imprisonment (see Col. 4:10; Philem. 24) about twelve years later, so there must have been a reconciliation. In fact, at the end of his life Paul sent for Mark, saying, "he is useful to me for ministry" (2 Tim. 4:11).

The early church uniformly attested that Mark wrote this gospel. Papias, Irenaeus, Clement of Alexandria, and Origen are among the church fathers who affirmed Marcan authorship.

Date and Setting

Many scholars believe that Mark was the first of the four Gospels, but there is uncertainty over its date. Because of the prophecy about the destruction of the temple (13:2), it should be dated before A.D. 70, but early traditions disagree as to whether it was written before or after the martyrdom of Peter (c. A.D. 64). The probable range for this book is A.D. 55–65.

Mark was evidently directed to a Roman readership and early tradition indicates that it originated in Rome. This may be why Mark omitted a number of items that would not have been meaningful to Gentiles, such as the genealogy of Christ, fulfilled prophecy, references to the Law, and certain Jewish customs that are found in other gospels. Mark interpreted Aramaic words (3:17; 5:41; 7:34; 15:22) and used a number of Latin terms in place of their Greek equivalents (4:21; 6:27; 12:14, 42; 15:15–16, 39).

Theme and Purpose

Even in the first verse it is obvious that this gospel centers on the person and mission of the Son of God. Mark's theme is captured well in chapter 10, verse 45, because Jesus is portrayed in this book as a Servant and as the Redeemer of men (cf. Phil. 2:5–11). Like the other gospels, Mark is not a biography but a topical narrative. Mark juxtaposes Christ's teachings and works to show how they authenticate each other. Miracles are predominant in this book (there are eighteen), and they are used to demonstrate not only the power of Christ but also His compassion. Mark shows his Gentile readers how the Son of God was rejected by His own people, achieving ultimate victory through apparent defeat. There was no doubt an evangelistic purpose behind this gospel as Mark directed his words to a Gentile audience that knew little about Old Testament theology. This book may also have been used to instruct and encourage Roman believers.

Keys to Mark

Key Word: Jesus the Servant

Key Verses (10:43–45; 8:34–37)—"Yet it shall not be so among you; but whoever desires to become great among you shall be your servant. And whoever of you desires to be first shall be slave of all. For even the Son of Man did not come to be served, but to serve, and to give His life a ransom for many" (10:43–45).

"And when He had called the people to *Him,* with His disciples also, He said, to them 'Whoever desires to come after Me, let him deny himself, and take up his cross, and follow Me. For whoever desires to save his life will lose it, but whoever loses his life for My sake and the gospel's will save it. For what will it profit a man if he gains the whole world, and loses his own soul? Or what will a man give in exchange for his soul?'" (8:34–37).

Key Chapter (8)—As in the Book of Matthew, Mark's gospel contains a pivotal chapter showing the change of emphasis in Jesus' ministry. In Matthew it is chapter 12; in Mark it is chapter 8. The pivotal event lies in Peter's confession, "You are the Christ." That faith-inspired response triggers a new phase in both the content and the course of Jesus' ministry. Until this point He has sought to validate His claims as Messiah. But now He begins to fortify His men for His forthcoming suffering and death at the hands of the religious leaders. Jesus' steps begin to take Him daily closer to Jerusalem— the place where the Perfect Servant will demonstrate the full extent of His servanthood.

Christ in Mark

The Lord is presented as an active, compassionate, and obedient Servant who constantly ministers to the physical and spiritual needs of others. Because this is the story of a Servant, Mark omits Jesus' ancestry and birth and moves right into His busy public ministry. The distinctive word of this book is *euthus,* translated "immediately" or "straightway," and it appears more often in this compact gospel (forty-two times) than in the rest of the New Testament. Christ is constantly moving toward a goal that is hidden to almost all. Mark clearly shows the power and authority of this unique Servant, identifying Him as no less than the Son of God (1:1, 11; 3:11; 5:7; 9:7; 13:32; 14:61; 15:39).

Contribution to the Bible

Mark uses a simple and unvarnished style that is brisk and clear. The narrative moves vigorously and efficiently, very, appropriate for a gospel that depicts the divine Servant at work. The quick pace and brevity of this book (it has only two extended discourses: 4:1–34; 13:3–37) reflect Mark's emphasis on action more than words, making it suitable to the, practical orientation of the Roman mind. Only eighteen out of Christ's seventy parables are found in Mark—and some of these are only one sentence in length—but he lists over half of Christ's thirty-five miracles, the highest proportion in the Gospels. Mark's language is characterized by broken sentence structure, colloquialisms, and extra expressions that may reproduce Peter's style of speaking. He uses the historic present tense 151 times to depict action in progress. The vivid descriptions in this book are often more detailed than the parallel accounts in Matthew and Luke. Mark records a wide range of emotional reactions: "they were all amazed" (1:27), "they feared exceedingly" (4:41), "they laughed Him to scorn" (5:40), "they were offended at Him" (6:3), "they were astonished beyond measure" (7:37). Jesus' own reactions of compassion, anger, grief, sorrow, warmth, distress, sympathy, and indignation are also very evident.

Survey of Mark

Mark, the shortest and simplest of the four Gospels, gives a crisp and fast-moving look at the life of Christ. With few comments, Mark lets the narrative speak for itself as it tells the story of the Servant who constantly ministers to others through preaching, healing, teaching, and, ultimately, His own death. Mark traces the steady building of hostility and opposition to Jesus as He resolutely moves toward the fulfillment of His earthly mission. Almost 40 percent of this gospel is devoted to a detailed account of the last eight days of Jesus' life, climaxing in His Resurrection. The Lord is vividly portrayed in this book in two parts: to serve (1—10); to sacrifice (11—16).

To Serve (1—10): Mark passes over the birth and early years of Jesus' life and begins with the events that immediately precede the inauguration of His public ministry—His baptism by John and His temptation by Satan (1:1–13). The first four chapters emphasize the words of the Servant while chapters 5—7 accent His works. However, in both sections there is a frequent alternation between Christ's messages and miracles in order to reveal His person and power. Though He has come to serve others, Jesus' authority prevails over many realms.

Although Jesus has already been teaching and testing His disciples (see ch. 4), His ministry with them becomes more intense from this point on as He begins to prepare them for His departure. The religious leaders are growing more antagonistic, and Christ's "hour" is only about six months away. Chapter 8, verse 31, is the pivotal point in the gospel as the Son of Man speaks clearly to His disciples about His coming death and Resurrection. The disciples struggle with this difficult revelation, but Jesus' steps head inexorably to Jerusalem.

To Sacrifice (11—16): Mark allots a disproportionate space to the last weeks of the Servant's redemptive ministry. During the last seven days in Jerusalem, hostility from the chief priests, scribes, elders, Pharisees, Herodians, and Sadducees reaches crisis proportions as Jesus publicly refutes their arguments in the temple. After His Last Supper with the disciples, Jesus offers no resistance to His arrest, abuse, and agonizing Crucifixion. His willingness to bear countless human sins is the epitome of servanthood.

Outline of Mark

    C. Parable of the Growing Seed, 4:26–29

    D. Parable of the Mustard Seed, 4:30–34

III. The Miracles of the Servant, 4:35—5:43

    A. The Sea Is Stilled, 4:35–41

    B. Demons Are Cast into Swine, 5:1–20

    C. Jairus Pleads for His Daughter, 5:21–24

    D. A Woman with Issue Is Healed, 5:25–34

    E. Jairus' Daughter Is Healed, 5:35–43

IV. The Growing Opposition to the Servant, 6:1—8:26

    A. Jesus Is Rejected at Nazareth, 6:1–6

    B. Twelve Are Sent to Serve, 6:7–13

    C. John the Baptist Is Murdered, 6:14–29

    D. Twelve Return, 6:30–31

    E. Five Thousand Are Fed, 6:32–44

    F. Jesus Walks on Water, 6:45–52

    G. Jesus Heals at Gennesaret, 6:53–56

    H. Pharisees and Defilement, 7:1–23

    I. Withdrawal to the Gentiles, 7:24—8:9

        1. Syro-Phoenician Woman Is Healed, 7:24–30

        2. Deaf and Dumb Man Is Healed, 7:31–37

        3. Four Thousand Are Fed, 8:1–9

    J. Pharisees Seek a Sign, 8:10–13

    K. Disciples Do Not Understand, 8:14–21

    L. A Blind Man Is Healed, 8:22–26

Part Three: The Instruction by the Servant (8:27—10:52)

I. Peter's Confession of Christ, 8:27–33

II. Cost of Discipleship, 8:34–38

III. The Transfiguration, 9:1–13

IV. Demon-possessed Son Is Delivered, 9:14–29

V. Jesus Foretells His Death, 9:30–32

VI. Jesus Teaches to Prepare the Disciples, 9:33—10:45

    A. Attitude of Servanthood, 9:33–41

    B. Warning about Hell, 9:42–50

    C. Marriage and Divorce, 10:1–12

    D. Children and the Kingdom, 10:13–16

    E. Wealth, 10:17–31

        1. Rich Young Ruler, 10:17–22

        2. Difficulty of Riches, 10:23–27

        3. Eternal Reward, 10:28–31

    F. Coming Crucifixion, 10:32–34

    G. "Whoever Desires to Become Great", 10:35–45

VII. Blind Bartimaeus Is Healed, 10:46–52

Part Four: The Rejection of the Servant (11:1—15:47)

I. The Formal Presentation of the Servant, 11:1–19
    A. The Triumphal Entry, 11:1–11
    B. A Fig Tree Is Cursed, 11:12–14
    C. The Temple Is Cleansed, 11:15–19

II. The Instruction on Prayer, 11:20–26
    A. Power of Faith, 11:20–24
    B. Necessity of Forgiveness, 11:25–26

III. The Opposition by the Leaders, 11:27—12:44
    A. Question of Authority, 11:27–33
    B. Parable of the Vineyard Owner, 12:1–12
    C. Question of Taxes, 12:13–17
    D. Question of the Resurrection, 12:18–27
    E. Question of the Greatest Commandment, 12:28–34
    F. Jesus Questions the Leaders, 12:35–37
    G. Jesus Condemns the Leaders, 12:38–44

IV. The Instruction on the Future, 13:1–37
    A. Questions from the Disciples, 13:1–4
    B. The Tribulation, 13:5–23
    C. The Second Coming, 13:24–27
    D. Parable of the Fig Tree, 13:28–31
    E. Exhortation to Watch, 13:32–37

V. The Passion of the Servant, 14:1—15:47
    A. Leaders Plot to Kill Jesus, 14:1–2
    B. Mary Anoints Jesus, 14:3–9
    C. Judas Plans to Betray Jesus, 14:10–11
    D. The Passover Is Prepared, 14:12–16
    E. The Passover Is Celebrated, 14:17–21
    F. The Lord's Supper Is Instituted, 14:22–25
    G. Jesus Predicts Peter's Denial, 14:26–31
    H. Jesus Prays in Gethsemane, 14:32–42
    I. Judas Betrays Jesus, 14:43–52
    J. Jesus Is Tried, 14:53—15:14
        1. The Sanhedrin Tries Jesus, 14:53–65
        2. Peter Denies Jesus, 14:66–72
        3. Pilate Tries Jesus, 15:1–14
    K. Jesus Is Beaten, 15:15–23
    L. Jesus Is Crucified, 15:24–41
    M. Jesus Is Buried, 15:42–47

Part Five: The Resurrection of the Servant (16:1–20)

I. The Resurrection of Jesus, 16:1–8

II. The Appearances of Jesus, 16:9–18

III. The Ascension of Jesus, 16:19–20

Luke

LUKE, A GENTILE PHYSICIAN, builds his gospel narrative around a historical, chronological presentation of Jesus' life. Luke's is the longest and most comprehensive of the four Gospels, presenting Jesus Christ as the Perfect Man who came to seek and save sinful men. Growing belief and growing opposition develop side by side. Those who believe His claims are challenged to count the cost of discipleship; those who oppose Him will not be satisfied until the Son of Man hangs lifeless on a cross. But the Resurrection insures that His ministry of seeking and saving the lost will continue in the person of His disciples once they have been equipped with His power.

LUKE

Focus	Introduction of Son of Man	Ministry of Son of Man	Rejection of Son of Man	Crucifixion and Resurrection of Son of Man
	1:1 — 4:13	4:14 — 9:50	9:51 — 19:27	19:28 — 24:53
Divisions	Advent	Activities	Antagonism and Admonition	Application and Authentication
	1:1 — 4:13	4:14 — 9:50	9:51 — 19:27	19:28 — 24:53
Topics	Seeking the Lost			Saving the Lost
	Miracles Prominent		Teaching Prominent	
Place	Israel	Galilee	Israel	Jerusalem
Time	c. 4 B.C.–A.D. 33			

Introduction and Title

Luke, a physician, writes with the compassion and warmth of a family doctor as he carefully documents the perfect humanity of the Son of Man, Jesus Christ. Luke emphasizes Jesus' ancestry, birth, and early life before moving carefully and chronologically through His earthly ministry. Growing belief and growing opposition develop side by side. Those who believe are challenged to count the cost of discipleship. Those who oppose will not be satisfied until the Son of Man hangs lifeless on a cross. But the Resurrection insures that His purpose will be fulfilled: "to seek and to save that which was lost" (19:10).

Kata Loukon, "According to Luke," is the ancient title that was added to this gospel at a very early date. The Greek name *Luke* appears only three times in the New Testament (see Col. 4:14; 2 Tim. 4:11; Philem. 24).

Author

It is evident from the prologues to Luke and Acts (see 1:1–4; Acts 1:1–5) that both books were addressed to Theophilus as a two-volume work (Luke is called "the former treatise"). Acts begins with a summary of Luke and continues the story from where the Gospel of Luke concludes. The style and language of both books are quite similar. The "we" portions of Acts (see Acts 16:1–17; 20:5—21:18; 27:1—28:16) reveal that the author was a close associate and traveling companion of Paul. Because all but two of Paul's associates are named in the third person, the list can be narrowed to Titus and Luke. Titus has never been seriously regarded as a possible author of Acts, and Luke best fits the requirements. He was with Paul during his first Roman imprisonment, and Paul referred to him as "Luke, the beloved physician" (see Col. 4:14; cf. Philem. 24). During his second Roman inprisonment, Paul wrote "Only Luke is with me" (2 Tim. 4:11), an evidence of Luke's loyalty to the apostle in the face of profound danger.

Luke may have been a Hellenistic Jew, but it is more likely that he was a Gentile (this would make him the only Gentile contributor to the New Testament). In Colossians 4:10–14, Paul lists three fellow workers who are "of the circumcision" (Col. 4:10–11) and then includes Luke's name with two Gentiles (Col. 4:12–14). Luke's obvious skill with the Greek language and his phrase "their own language" in Acts 1:19 also imply that he was not Jewish. It has been suggested that Luke may have been a Greek physician to a Roman family who at some point was set free and given Roman citizenship. Another guess is that he was the "brother" referred to in Second Corinthians 8:18–19. Ancient traditions (including the Muratorian Fragment, Irenaeus, Tertullian, Clement of Alexandria, Origen, Eusebius, and Jerome) strongly support Luke as the author of Luke and Acts. Tradition also says that Luke was from Syrian Antioch, remained unmarried, and died at the age of eighty-four.

Date and Setting

Luke was not an eyewitness of the events in his gospel, but he relied on the testimony of eyewitnesses and written sources (1:1–4). He carefully investigated and arranged his material and presented it to Theophilus ("Friend of God"). The title "most excellent," or "most noble" (see Acts 23:26; 24:3; 26:25), indicates that Theophilus was a man of high social standing. He probably assumed responsibility for publishing Luke and Acts so that they would be available to Gentile readers. Luke translates Aramaic terms with Greek words and explains Jewish customs and geography to make his gospel more intelligible to his original Greek readership. During Paul's two-year Caesarean imprisonment, Luke may have traveled in Palestine to gather information from eyewitnesses of Jesus' ministry. The date of this gospel depends on that of Acts since this was the first volume (see "Date and Setting" in Acts). If Luke was written during Paul's first imprisonment in Rome it would be dated in the early 60s. However, it may have been given final form in Greece. In all probability, its publication preceded the destruction of Jerusalem (A.D. 70).

Theme and Purpose

Luke clearly states his purpose in the prologue of his gospel: ". . . to write to you an orderly account . . . that you may know the certainty of those things in which you were instructed" (1:3–4). Luke wanted to create an accurate, chronological, and comprehensive account of the unique life of Jesus the Christ to strengthen the faith of Gentile believers and stimulate saving faith among nonbelievers. Luke may also have had a secondary purpose of showing that Christianity was not a politically subversive sect. He records Pilate's acknowledgment of Christ's innocence three times (23:4,14,22). The theme of this gospel is the perfect Son of Man who came "to seek and to save that which was lost" (19:10).

Keys to Luke

Key Word: Jesus the Son of Man

Key Verses (1:3–4; 19:10)—"It seemed good to me also, having had perfect understanding of all things from the very first, to write to you an orderly account, most excellent Theophilus, that you may know the certainty of those things in which you were instructed" (1:3–4).

" 'For the Son of Man has come to seek and to save that which was lost' " (19:10).

Key Chapter (15)—Captured in the three parables of the Lost Sheep, Lost Coin, and Lost Son is the crux of this gospel: that God through Christ has come to seek and to save that which was lost.

Christ in Luke

The humanity and compassion of Jesus are repeatedly stressed in Luke's gospel. Luke gives the most complete account of Christ's ancestry, birth, and development. He is the ideal Son of Man who identified with the sorrow and plight of sinful men in order to carry our sorrows and offer us the priceless gift of salvation. Jesus alone fulfills the Greek ideal of human perfection.

Contribution to the Bible

Luke, the longest book in the New Testament is the most comprehensive and precise of the Gospels. The combined books of Luke and Acts constitute 28 percent of the New Testament, making Luke the most prolific of its contributors (2,138 verses; Paul wrote 2,033). Not only was this gospel carefully recorded and documented, but it was also written in the most refined Greek in the New Testament—only the Epistle to the Hebrews is comparable. Luke's large vocabulary and great breadth of expressions and constructions give his work a literary richness and beauty that make his gospel the favorite of many. Luke alone contains the four beautiful hymns commonly known as the *Magnificat* of Mary (1:46–55), the *Benedictus* of Zacharias (1:67–79), the *Gloria in Excelsis* of the heavenly host (2:14), and the *Nunc Dimittis* of Simeon (2:28–32).

Luke's strong interest in people is evident from his portraits of Zacharias, the Good Samaritan, the Prodigal Son, the repentant tax gatherer, Zaccheus, and the two disciples on the Emmaus road. He also gives a special place to women (e.g., Elizabeth, Mary, Anna, Martha, Mary of Bethany) and children (e.g., the childhoods of John and Jesus). Other themes that are developed in Luke include prayer, the work of the Holy Spirit, poverty and wealth, medical topics, praise and thanksgiving, and domestic life. Luke's gospel shows the universality of the Christian message, describing the Son of Man as the Savior for all men: Jews, Samaritans, Gentiles; poor and rich; respectable and despised; publicans and religious leaders.

Survey of Luke

Luke builds the gospel narrative on the platform of historical reliability. His emphasis on chronological and historical accuracy makes this the most comprehensive of the four Gospels. This is also the longest and most literary gospel, and it presents Jesus Christ as the Perfect Man who came to seek and to save sinful men. This book can be divided into four sections: (1) The introduction of the Son of Man (1:1—4:13); (2) the ministry of the Son of Man (4:14—9:50); (3) the rejection of the Son of Man (9:51—19:27); and (4) the Crucifixion and Resurrection of the Son of Man (19:28—24:53).

The Introduction of the Son of Man (1:1—4:13): Luke places a strong emphasis on the ancestry, birth, and early years of the Perfect Man and of His forerunner John the Baptist. Their infancy stories are intertwined as Luke records their birth announcements, advents, and temple presentations. Jesus prepares over thirty years (summarized in one verse, 2:52) for a public ministry of only three years. The ancestry of the Son of Man is traced back to the first man Adam, and His ministry commences after His Baptism and temptation.

The Ministry of the Son of Man (4:14—9:50): The authority of the Son of Man over every realm is demonstrated in this section (4:14—6:49). His authority over demons, disease, nature, the effects of sin, tradition, and all people is presented as a prelude to His diverse ministry of preaching, healing, and discipling (7:1—9:50).

The Rejection of the Son of Man (9:51—19:27): The dual response of growing belief and growing rejection has already been introduced in the gospel (cf. 4:14; 6:11), but from this time forward the intensity of opposition to the ministry of the Son of Man increases. When the religious leaders accuse Him of being demonized,

Jesus pronounces a series of divine woes upon them (11). Knowing that He is on His last journey to Jerusalem, Jesus instructs His disciples on a number of practical matters including prayer, covetousness, faithfulness, repentance, humility, discipleship, evangelism, money, forgiveness, service, thankfulness, the Second Advent, and salvation (12:1—19:27).

The Crucifixion and Resurrection of the Son of Man (19:28—24:53): After His triumphal entry into Jerusalem, Jesus encounters the opposition of the priests, Sadducees, and scribes and predicts the overthrow of Jerusalem (19:28—21:38). The Son of Man instructs His disciples for the last time before His betrayal in Gethsemane. The three religious and three civil trials culminate in His Crucifixion. The glory and foundation of the Christian message is the historical Resurrection of Jesus Christ. The Lord conquers the grave as He has promised, and appears on a number of occasions to His disciples before His Ascension to the Father.

Outline of Luke

Part One: The Introduction of the Son of Man (1:1—4:13)

I. **The Purpose and Method of Luke's Gospel,** 1:1–4

II. **The Events Preceding Christ's Birth,** 1:5–56
   A. John the Baptist's Birth Is Foretold, 1:5–25
      1. Zacharias Ministers in the Temple, 1:5–10
      2. An Angel Announces the Birth of John the Baptist, 1:11–17
      3. Zacharias Is Unable to Speak, 1:18–25
   B. Jesus the Christ's Birth Is Foretold, 1:26–56
      1. Gabriel Announces Christ's Birth, 1:26–33
      2. Mary Miraculously Conceives, 1:34–38
      3. Mary Visits Elizabeth, 1:39–56

III. **The Events Accompanying Christ's Birth,** 1:57—2:38
   A. The Birth of John the Baptist, 1:57–80
      1. Elizabeth Gives Birth to John, 1:57–66
      2. Zacharias Prophesies of John's Ministry, 1:67–80
   B. The Birth of Jesus the Christ, 2:1–38
      1. Christ Is Born, 2:1–7
      2. The Angels Announce Jesus to the Shepherds, 2:8–14
      3. The Shepherds Visit Jesus, 2:15–20
      4. Christ Is Presented at the Temple, 2:21–38
         a. Christ Is Circumcised, 2:21–24
         b. Simeon's Prophecy, 2:25–35
         c. Anna's Testimony, 2:36–38

IV. **The Events During Christ's Childhood,** 2:39–52
   A. Jesus Returns to Nazareth, 2:39–40
   B. Jesus Celebrates the Passover, 2:41–50
   C. Jesus Grows in Wisdom, 2:51–52

V. The Events Preceding Christ's Presentation, 3:1—4:13

A. The Ministry of John the Baptist, 3:1–20
B. The Baptism of Christ, 3:21–22
C. The Genealogy of Christ through Mary, 3:23–38
D. The Temptation of Christ, 4:1–13

Part Two: The Ministry of the Son of Man (4:14—9:50)

I. The Presentation of Christ, 4:14–30

A. Acceptance throughout Galilee, 4:14–15
B. Rejection at Nazareth, 4:16–30

II. The Demonstration of Christ's Powers, 4:31—5:28

A. Demons Are Cast Out, 4:31–37
B. Peter's Mother-in-Law Is Healed, 4:38–39
C. Jesus Ministers throughout Galilee, 4:40–44
D. The First Disciples Are Called, 5:1–11
E. A Leper Is Cleansed, 5:12–15
F. A Paralytic Is Healed, 5:16–26
G. Matthew Is Called, 5:27–28

III. The Explanation of Christ's Program, 5:29—6:49

A. Jesus Teaches the Pharisees, 5:29—6:11
  1. Jesus Eats with Sinners, 5:29–32
  2. Jesus Teaches about Fasting, 5:33–35
  3. Parable of the Cloth and Wineskins, 5:36–39
  4. Jesus Works on the Sabbath, 6:1–5
  5. Jesus Heals on the Sabbath, 6:6–11
B. Jesus Teaches the Disciples, 6:12–49
  1. Selection of the Twelve Apostles, 6:12–19
  2. The Beatitudes, 6:20–26
  3. Rules of Kingdom Life, 6:27–38
  4. Parable of the Blind Leading the Blind, 6:39–45
  5. Parable of the Two Foundations, 6:46–49

IV. The Expansion of Christ's Program, 7:1—9:50

A. A Centurion's Servant Is Healed, 7:1–10
B. A Widow's Son Is Raised, 7:11–16
C. Christ Comments on John the Baptist, 7:17–35
  1. John's Questions Are Answered, 7:17–23
  2. Jesus Praises John, 7:24–30
  3. Jesus Criticizes His Generation, 7:31–35
D. Christ Dines at a Pharisee's Home, 7:36–50
  1. A Woman Anoints Jesus' Feet, 7:36–39
  2. The Parable of the Two Debtors, 7:40–50
E. Certain Women Minister to Christ, 8:1–3
F. Parable of the Sower and Soils, 8:4–15
G. Parable of the Lamp, 8:16–18
H. Christ's True Brethren, 8:19–21

I. The Storm Is Stilled, 8:22–25
J. Demons Are Cast into Swine, 8:26–40
K. A Woman with Issue Is Healed, 8:41–48
L. Jairus' Daughter Is Raised, 8:49–56
M. Twelve Are Sent to Preach, 9:1–11
N. Five Thousand Are Fed, 9:12–17
O. Peter's Confession of Faith, 9:18–22
P. True Cost of Discipleship, 9:23–26
Q. The Transfiguration, 9:27–36
R. Demoniac Son Is Healed, 9:37–42
S. Christ Prophesies His Coming Death, 9:43–45
T. True Greatness, 9:46–50

Part Three: The Rejection of the Son of Man (9:51—19:27)

I. **The Increasing Opposition to Christ,** 9:51—11:54
  A. Samaria Rejects Christ, 9:51–56
  B. True Cost of Discipleship, 9:57–62
  C. Seventy Disciples Are Sent Out, 10:1–24
    1. Mission of the Seventy, 10:1–16
    2. Return of the Seventy, 10:17–24
  D. Lawyer Tests Christ, 10:25–37
    1. How to Inherit Eternal Life, 10:25–28
    2. Parable of the Good Samaritan, 10:29–37
  E. Mary and Martha Are Contrasted, 10:38–42
  F. Christ Teaches on Prayer, 11:1–13
    1. The Lord's Prayer, 11:1–4
    2. Parable of the Persistent Friend, 11:5–10
    3. Parable of the Good Father, 11:11–13
  G. Christ Is Rejected by the Religious Leaders, 11:14–36
    1. Christ Heals the Demoniac, 11:14
    2. Christ's Power Not from Satan, 11:15–28
    3. Christ's Only Sign Is Jonah, 11:29–32
    4. Parable of the Lighted Lamp, 11:33–36
  H. Religious Leaders Are Rejected by Christ, 11:37–54
    1. "Woes" on the Pharisees, 11:37–44
    2. "Woes" on the Lawyers, 11:45–54

II. **The Instruction in View of Christ's Rejection,** 12:1—19:27
  A. Christ Warns about Hypocrisy, 12:1–12
  B. Christ Warns about Covetousness, 12:13–34
    1. Parable of the Rich Fool, 12:13–21
    2. Seek the Kingdom of God, 12:22–34
  C. Christ Warns about the Second Coming, 12:35–48
    1. Parable of the Expectant Steward, 12:35–40
    2. Parable of the Faithful Steward, 12:41–48
  D. Christ Warns of the Costs of Discipleship, 12:49–53
  E. Christ Warns of Not Discerning the Times, 12:54–59

F. Christ Teaches on Repentance, 13:1–9
G. Christ Heals the Crippled Woman, 13:10–17
   1. A Woman Glorifies Christ, 13:10–13
   2. The Rulers Criticize Christ, 13:14–17
H. Christ Teaches on the Kingdom of Heaven, 13:18–30
   1. Parable of the Mustard Seed, 13:18–19
   2. Parable of the Leaven, 13:20–21
   3. The Way into the Kingdom, 13:22–30
I. Christ Mourns over Jerusalem, 13:31–35
J. Christ Teaches the Pharisees, 14:1–24
   1. Instruction on the Sabbath, 14:1–6
   2. Parable of the Ambitious Guest, 14:7–14
   3. Parable of the Great Supper, 14:15–24
K. Christ Teaches on Discipleship, 14:25–35
   1. Cost of Discipleship, 14:25–27
   2. Parable of the Tower, 14:28–30
   3. Parable of the King Contemplating War, 14:31–33
   4. Parable of the Savorless Salt, 14:34–35
L. Christ Teaches on Repentance, 15:1–32
   1. Parable of the Lost Sheep, 15:1–7
   2. Parable of the Lost Coin, 15:8–10
   3. Parable of the Lost Son, 15:11–32
M. Christ Teaches on Stewardship, 16:1–31
   1. Parable of the Unjust Servant, 16:1–13
   2. Christ Warns the Pharisees, 16:14–17
   3. Christ Teaches on Divorce, 16:18
   4. Parable of the Rich Man and Lazarus, 16:19–31
N. Christ Teaches on Offenses, 17:1–10
O. Christ Cleanses Ten Lepers, 17:11–19
P. Christ Teaches on the Second Coming, 17:20–37
Q. Christ Teaches on Prayer, 18:1–14
   1. Parable of the Woman and the Judge, 18:1–8
   2. Parable of the Pharisee and the Tax Collector, 18:9–14
R. Christ Blesses the Children, 18:15–17
S. Christ Teaches on Sacrifice, 18:18–30
   1. Rich Young Ruler, 18:18–27
   2. Christ Will Reward Sacrifice, 18:28–30
T. Christ Foretells His Death and Resurrection, 18:31–34
U. Christ Heals Bartimaeus, 18:35–43
V. Christ Abides with Zacchaeus, 19:1–10
W. Christ Gives the Parable of the Ten Minas, 19:11–27

Part Four: The Crucifixion and Resurrection of the Son of Man (19:28—24:53)

I. **The Last Week of Christ,** 19:28—23:56
A. Sunday: The Triumphal Entry, 19:28–44
B. Monday: Cleansing the Temple, 19:45–48

C. Tuesday: Public Ministry, 20:1—22:6
1. Religious Leaders Question Christ's Authority, 20:1–8
2. Parable of the Vineyard Owner, 20:9–18
3. Herodians Question Tribute Money, 20:19–26
4. Sadducees Question Resurrection, 20:27–38
5. Christ Questions the Scribes, 20:39–47
6. Christ Teaches on the Widow's Mites, 21:1–4
7. Olivet Discourse, 21:5—22:6
   a. The Disciples' Two Questions—"What?" and "When?", 21:5–7
   b. Signs of Christ's Coming, 21:8–19
   c. Destruction of Jerusalem, 21:20–24
   d. The Second Coming, 21:25–28
   e. Parable of the Fig Tree, 21:29–33
   f. Warning to Watch for His Coming, 21:34–38
   g. Judas Agrees to Betray Christ, 22:1–6
D. Thursday: Passover and Arrest, 22:7–53
1. The Upper Room Is Prepared, 22:7–13
2. The Passover Is Celebrated, 22:14–18
3. The Lord's Supper Is Instituted, 22:19–20
4. Christ Predicts His Betrayer, 22:21–23
5. The Disciples Argue over Who Is the Greatest, 22:24–30
6. Christ Predicts Peter's Denial, 22:31–34
7. Christ Predicts Coming Conflict, 22:35–38
8. Christ Prays in Gethsemane, 22:39–46
9. Judas Betrays Christ, 22:47–53
E. Friday: Trials and Crucifixion, 22:54—23:55
1. Peter Denies Christ, 22:54–62
2. Christ Is Beaten, 22:63–65
3. The Sanhedrin Tries Christ, 22:66–71
4. Pilate Tries Christ, 23:1–7
5. Herod Tries Christ, 23:8–12
6. Pilate Tries Christ Again, 23:13–25
7. Christ Is Crucified, 23:26–49
8. Christ Is Buried, 23:50–55
F. Saturday: In the Grave, 23:56

II. The Authentication of Christ, 24:1–53
A. The Resurrection, 24:1–12
B. Christ Appears on the Road to Emmaus, 24:13–32
C. Christ Appears to the Eleven, 24:33–53
1. The Proof of His Resurrection, 24:33–43
2. The Great Commission, 24:44–48
3. The Ascension, 24:49–53

John

THE GOSPEL OF JOHN is a gospel apart. Matthew, Mark, and Luke are called the "synoptic gospels" because, despite their individual emphases, they describe many of the same events in the life of Jesus of Nazareth. John draws mainly upon events and discourses not found in the other gospels to prove to his readers that Jesus is God in the flesh, the eternal Word come to earth, born to die as God's sacrifice for human sin. Seven miraculous signs prove that "Jesus is the Christ, the Son of God, and that believing you may have life in His name" (20:31).

Focus	Incarnation of the Son of God	Presentation of the Son of God	Opposition to the Son of God	Preparation of the Son's Disciples	Crucifixion and Resurrection of the Son of God
	1:1　　　1:18	1:19　　　4:54	5:1　　　12:50	13:1　　　17:26	18:1　　　21:25
Divisions	Introduction to Christ	Revelation of Christ	Rejection of Christ	Revelation from Christ	Rejection of Christ
	1:1　　　1:18	1:19　　　4:54	5:1　　　12:50	13:1　　　17:26	18:1　　　21:25
Topics	Seven Miracles			Upper Room Discourse	Supreme Miracle
	"That You May Believe"			"That You May Have Life"	
Place	Israel				
Time	A Few Years			A Few Hours	A Few Weeks

Introduction and Title

Just as a coin has two sides, both valid, so Jesus Christ has two natures, both valid. Luke presents Christ in His humanity as the Son of Man; John portrays Him in His deity as the Son of God. John's purpose is crystal clear: to set forth Christ in His deity in order to spark believing faith in his readers. John's gospel is topical, not primarily chronological, and it revolves around seven miracles and seven "I am" statements of Christ.

Following an extended eyewitness description of the Upper Room meal and Discourse, John records events leading up to the Resurrection, the final climactic proof that Jesus is who He claims to be—the Son of God.

The title of the fourth Gospel follows the same format as the titles of the synoptic Gospels: *Kata Ioannen,* "According to John." As with the others, the word "Gospel" was later added. *Ioannes* is derived from the Hebrew name *Johanan,* "Yahweh Has Been Gracious."

Author

Jesus nicknamed John and his brother, James, "Sons of Thunder" (Mark 3:17). Their father was Zebedee, and their mother, Salome, served Jesus in Galilee and was present at His Crucifixion (see Mark 15:40–41). John was evidently among the Galileans who followed John the Baptist until they were called to follow Jesus at the outset of His public ministry (1:19–51). These Galileans were later called to become fulltime disciples of the Lord (Luke 5:1–11), and John was among the twelve men who were selected to be apostles (Luke 6:12–16). After Christ's Ascension, John became one of the "pillars" of the church in Jerusalem along with James and Peter (Gal. 2:9). He is mentioned three times by name in Acts (3:1; 4:13; 8:14), each time in association with Peter. Tradition says that John later went to Ephesus (perhaps just before the destruction of Jerusalem). He was eventually exiled by the Romans for a time to the island of Patmos (Rev. 1:9).

Date and Setting

In spite of the strong internal and external testimony supporting Johannine authorship of this gospel, theological assumptions have motivated a number of critics to deny this claim. Until recently it was popular to propose a second-century date for this book. The discovery of the John Rylands Papyrus 52 containing portions of chapter 18, verses 31–33, 37–38, has overthrown this conjecture. This fragment has been dated at about A.D. 135, and a considerable period of time must have been required for John's gospel to be copied and circulated before it reached Egypt, where this papyrus was found.

On the other hand, John was written after the last of the synoptic Gospels (c. A.D. 66–68). His familiarity with the topography of Jerusalem (e.g., 5:2; 19:13) does not necessarily require a date before A.D. 70. Since John's three epistles and Revelation were written after his gospel, the probable range for this work is A.D. 60–

90. By this time, John would have been one of the last surviving eyewitnesses of the Lord. According to tradition, John wrote this gospel in Ephesus.

The author of this gospel is identified only as the disciple "whom Jesus loved" (13:23; 20:2; 21:7, 20; cf. 19:26). His knowledge of Palestinian geography and Jewish customs makes it clear that he was a Palestinian Jew, and his meticulous attention to numbers (2:6; 6:13, 19; 21:8, 11) and names (1:45; 3:1; 11:1; 18:10) indicates that he was an eyewitness. This fits his own claim to be a witness of the events he described (1:14; 19:35; 21:24–25). The disciple "whom Jesus loved" was part of the inner circle of disciples and was closely associated with Peter. The synoptic Gospels name this inner circle as Peter, James, and John. Since Peter is separate from the beloved disciple, only James and John are left. James was martyred too early to be the author (Acts 12:1–2), so the apostle John was the author of this gospel. This conclusion from internal evidence is consistent with the external testimony of the early church. Irenaeus (c. A.D. 185) was a disciple of Polycarp who was in turn a disciple of the apostle John. In his *Against Heresies,* Irenaeus bore witness to Johannine authorship of this gospel and noted that John lived until the time of the emperor Trajan (A.D. 98–117). Clement of Alexandria, Theophilus of Antioch, Origen, and others also ascribe this book to John.

Theme and Purpose

The fourth Gospel has the clearest purpose statement in the Bible: "But these are written that you may believe that Jesus is the Christ, the Son of God, and that believing you may have life in His name" (20:31). John selected the signs he used with the apologetic purpose of creating intellectual ("that you may believe") and spiritual ("that believing you may have life") conviction about the Son of God. The key verb in John is "believe," and requires both knowledge (8:32; 10:38) and volition (1:12; 3:19; 7:17).

The predominant theme of this gospel is the dual response of faith and unbelief in the person of Jesus Christ. Those who place their faith in the Son of God have eternal life, but those who reject Him are under the condemnation of God (3:36; 5:24–29; 10:27–29)—this is the basic issue. Chapter 1, verses 11–12, summarize the reactions of reception and rejection that are traced through the rest of the book. His rejection by His own people can be seen over and over in chapters 2—19 (". . . those who were His own did not receive Him"), but John also lists a number of men and women who believed in Him ("But as many as received Him . . .").

Some of the key words in this thematic presentation of portions of Jesus' life are truth, light, darkness, word, knowledge, belief, abide, love, world, witness, and judgment. This gospel is not only evangelistic, but it is also designed to build believers in their faith and understanding of spiritual principles. John was no doubt familiar with the synoptic Gospels and created this fourth Gospel as a spiritual supplement to the others. While the other gospels focus on the Galilean ministry, John practically avoids it and concentrates on the Judean ministry.

Keys to John

Key Word: Jesus the Son of God

Key Verses (1:11–13; 20:30–31)—"He came to His own, and His own did not receive Him. But as many as received Him, to them He gave the right to become children of God, *even* to those who believe in His name: who were born, not of blood, nor of the will of the flesh, nor of the will of man, but of God" (1:11–13).

"And truly Jesus did many other signs in the presence of His disciples, which are not written in this book; but these are written that you may believe that Jesus is the Christ, the Son of God, and that believing you may have life in His name" (20:30–31).

Key Chapter (3)—John 3:16 is without doubt the most quoted and preached verse in all of Scripture. Captured in it is the gospel in its clearest and simplest form: that salvation is a gift of God and is obtainable only through belief. The conversation with Nicodemus and the testimony of John the Baptist provide the setting that clearly points out that being "born again" is the only way to find the "kingdom of God."

Christ in John

This book presents the most powerful case in all the Bible for the deity of the incarnate Son of God. "A Man called Jesus" (9:11) is also "Christ, the Son of the living God" (6:69). The deity of Christ can be seen in His seven "I am" statements: "I am the bread of life" (6:35, 48); "I am the light of the world" (8:12; 9:5); "I am the door" (10:7, 9); "I am the good shepherd" (10:11, 14); "I am the resurrection, and the life" (11:25); "I am the way, the truth, and the life" (14:6); "I am the true vine" (15:1–5). The seven signs (1—12) and the five witnesses (5:30–40) also point to His divine character. On certain occasions, Jesus equates Himself with the Old Testament "I AM," or Yahweh (see 4:25–26; 8:24, 28, 58; 13:19; 18:5–6, 8). Some of the most crucial affirmations of His deity are found here (1:1; 8:58; 10:30; 14:9; 20:28).

The Word was God (1:1), but the Word also became flesh (1:14). The humanity of Jesus can be seen in His weariness (4:6), thirst (4:7), dependence (5:19), grief (11:35), troubled soul (12:27), and His anguish and death (19).

Contribution to the Bible

John is the most selective, topical, and theological of the Gospels. Its simple style and vocabulary somehow capture the most profound theological concepts, making the book itself reminiscent of the teaching techniques of Jesus. John uses simple linguistic constructions and avoids the complex sentence structure characteristic of the Pauline epistles. He is particularly adept at parallelism (e.g., light versus darkness), which is an important feature in Hebrew poetry. Unlike the Synoptics, John contains no parables; he uses allegories instead (e.g., the Good Shepherd in 10:1–18, and the True Vine in 15:1–6).

Although John is more fragmentary and selective in his use of material (21:25), the structure of his narratives and discourses is tighter and more coherent than that of the other gospels. The discourses in John are logical units that develop unified themes, and the frequent sprinkling of questions and objections help to develop these themes. These discourses are inter-woven with the narrative sections and John uses them to explain the spiritual significance of the "signs." In this way the narratives of this gospel become symbolic. Of the eight miracles in chapters 1—12 and 21, only the feeding of the multitudes and the walking on the water are found in the Synoptics.

One of the unique features of John's gospel is the highly theological prologue. It gives a matchless portrayal of the incarnation of the truth, life, and glory of the eternal God. John shows the relevance of the Living Word to all men (3:16; 10:16; 12:32).

Survey of John

This most unusual gospel, with its distinct content and style, serves as a supplement to the three Synoptics. It is easily the simplest and yet the most profound of the Gospels, and for many people it is the greatest and most powerful. John writes his gospel for the specific purpose of bringing people to spiritual life through belief in the person and work of Jesus Christ. The five basic sections of this gospel are: (1) The incarnation of the Son of God (1:1–18); (2) the presentation of the Son of God (1:19—4:54); (3) the opposition to the Son of God (5:1—12:50); (4) the preparation of the disciples by the Son of God (13:1—17:26); and (5) the Crucifixion and Resurrection of the Son of God (18:1—21:25).

The Incarnation of the Son of God (1:1–18): This prologue introduces the rest of the book and gives the background for the historical narrative that follows. It dates the nature of Jesus, introduces His forerunner, clarifies His mission, and notes the rejection and acceptance He will find during His ministry.

The Presentation of the Son of God (1:19—4:54): In this section Christ is under careful consideration and scrutiny by Israel. He is introduced by John the Baptist who directs his own disciples to Christ. Shortly the author begins listing the seven signs, which continue through the next section. John carefully selects seven miracles out of the many that Christ accomplished (cf. John 21:25) in order to build a concise case for His deity. They are called signs because they symbolize the life-changing results of belief in Jesus—(1) water to wine: the ritual of law is replaced by the reality of grace (2:1–11); (2) healing the nobleman's son: the gospel brings spiritual restoration (4:46–54); (3) healing the paralytic: weakness is replaced by strength (5:1–16); (4) feeding the multitude: Christ satisfies spiritual hunger (6:1–13); (5) walking on water: the Lord transforms fear to faith (6:16–21); (6) sight to the man born blind: Jesus overcomes darkness and brings in light (9:1–7); (7) raising of Lazarus: the gospel brings people from death to life (11:1–44). These signs combine to show that Jesus is indeed the Son of God.

The Opposition to the Son of God (5:1—12:50): John's unusual pattern in these chapters is to record the reactions of belief and disbelief after the performance of one miracle before moving to the next. In a series of growing confrontations, John portrays the intense opposition that will culminate in the Lord's final rejection on the Cross. Even though many people received Him, the inevitable Crucifixion is foreshadowed in several places (2:4, 21–22; 7:6, 39; 11:51–52; 12:16).

The Preparation of the Disciples by the Son of God (13:1—17:26): John surveys the incarnation and public ministry of Jesus in twelve chapters, but radically changes the pace in the next five chapters to give a detailed account of a few crucial hours. In this clear and vivid recollection of Jesus' last discourse to His intimate disciples, John captures the Lord's words of comfort and assurance to a group of fearful and confused followers. Jesus knows that in less than twenty-four hours He will be on the Cross. Therefore, His last words speak of all the resources that will be at the disciples' disposal after His departure: They will be indwelled and empowered by the triune Godhead. The Upper Room Discourse contains the message of the Epistles in capsule form as it reveals God's pattern for Christian living. In it, the key themes of servanthood, the Holy Spirit, and abiding in Christ are developed.

The Crucifuxion and Resurrection of the Son of God (18:1—21:25): After recording Christ's high priestly prayer on behalf of His disciples and all who believe in Him "through their word" (17:20), John immediately launches into a dramatic description of Christ's arrest and trials before Annas, Caiaphas, and Pilate. In His Crucifixion, Jesus willingly fulfills John the Baptist's prophetic words: "Behold! The Lamb of God who takes away the sin of the world!" (1:29). John closes his profound gospel with a particularly detailed account of the post-Resurrection appearances of the Lord. The Resurrection is the ultimate sign that points to Jesus as the Son of God.

Outline of John

Part One: The Incarnation of the Son of God (1:1–18)

I. The Deity of Christ, 1:1–2

II. The Preincarnate Work of Christ, 1:3–5

III. The Forerunner of Christ, 1:6–8

IV. The Rejection of Christ, 1:9–11

V. The Acceptance of Christ, 1:12–13

VI. The Incarnation of Christ, 1:14–18

Part Two: The Presentation of the Son of God (1:19—4:54)

I. The Presentation of Christ by John the Baptist, 1:19–34
    A. John's Witness to the Priests and Levites, 1:19–28
    B. John's Witness at Christ's Baptism, 1:29–34

II. The Presentation of Christ to John's Disciples, 1:35–51
    A. Andrew and Peter Follow Christ, 1:35–42
    B. Philip and Nathanael Follow Christ, 1:43–51

III. The Presentation of Christ in Galilee, 2:1–12
    A. First Sign: Christ Changes Water to Wine, 2:1–10
    B. The Disciples Believe, 2:11–12

IV. The Presentation of Christ in Judea, 2:13—3:36
    A. Christ Cleanses the Temple, 2:13–25
    B. Christ Witnesses to Nicodemus, 3:1–21
    C. John the Baptist Witnesses Concerning Christ, 3:22–36

V. The Presentation of Christ in Samaria, 4:1–42
    A. Christ Witnesses to the Woman at the Well, 4:1–26
    B. Christ Witnesses to the Disciples, 4:27–38
    C. Christ Witnesses to the Samaritans, 4:39–42

VI. The Presentation of Christ in Galilee, 4:43–54
    A. Christ Is Received by the Galileans, 4:43–45
    B. Second Sign: Christ Heals the Nobleman's Son, 4:46–54

Part Three: The Opposition to the Son of God (5:1—12:50)

I. The Opposition at the Feast in Jerusalem, 5:1–47
    A. Third Sign: Christ Heals the Impotent Man, 5:1–9
    B. Jews Reject Christ, 5:10–47
        1. Christ Breaks the Sabbath, 5:10–16
        2. Christ Claims Equality with God, 5:17–30
            a. Equality with God in Nature, 5:17–18
            b. Equality with God in Power, 5:19–21
            c. Equality with God in Authority, 5:22–30
        3. Christ Lists Other Witnesses to His Person, 5:31–47
            a. Witness of John the Baptist, 5:31–35
            b. Witness of the Works of Christ, 5:36
            c. Witness of the Father, 5:37–38
            d. Witness of the Scriptures, 5:39–47

II. The Opposition during Passover Time in Galilee, 6:1–71
    A. Fourth Sign: Christ Feeds 5,000, 6:1–14
    B. Fifth Sign: Christ Walks on the Water, 6:15–21
    C. Christ Announces: "I Am the Bread of Life," 6:22–71
        1. To the Crowds, 6:22–40
        2. To the Jews, 6:41–59
        3. To the Disciples, 6:60–71
            a. Rejection by Many Followers, 6:60–66
            b. Confession by Peter, 6:67–71

III. The Opposition at the Feast of Tabernacles in Jerusalem, 7:1—10:21
    A. Before the Feast of Tabernacles, 7:1–13
        1. Christ's Brothers Do Not Believe, 7:1–9
        2. Christ Secretly Goes to the Feast, 7:10–13

B. In the Middle of the Feast of Tabernacles, 7:14–36
1. Christ's Authority from the Father, 7:14–24
2. Christ's Origin from the Father, 7:25–31
3. Christ's Departure to the Father, 7:32–36
C. In the Last Day of the Feast of Tabernacles, 7:37–53
1. Christ Reveals the "Living Water," 7:37–39
2. Israel Is Divided over Christ, 7:40–44
3. The Sanhedrin Is Confused over Christ, 7:45–53
D. After the Feast of Tabernacles, 8:1—10:21
1. A Woman Is Caught in Adultery, 8:1–11
2. Christ Announces: "I Am the Light of the World," 8:12–59
3. Sixth Sign: Christ Heals the Blind Man, 9:1–41
4. Christ Announces: "I Am the Good Shepherd," 10:1–21

IV. **The Opposition at the Feast of Dedication in Jerusalem,** 10:22–42

V. **The Opposition at Bethany,** 11:1—12:11
A. Seventh Sign: Christ Raises Lazarus, 11:1–44
B. The Pharisees Plan to Kill Christ, 11:45–57
C. Mary Anoints Christ, 12:1–11

VI. **The Opposition at Jerusalem,** 12:12–50
A. The Triumphal Entry, 12:12–22
B. The Messiah Teaches, 12:23–50

Part Four: The Preparation of the Disciples by the Son of God (13:1—17:26)

I. **The Preparation in the Upper Room,** 13:1—14:31
A. Christ Washes the Disciples Feet, 15:1—16:33
B. Christ Announces Judas, the Betrayer, 13:21–30
C. Christ Gives the Upper Room Discourse, 13:31—14:31
1. Christ Announces His Departure, 13:31–35
2. Christ Foretells Peter's Denial, 13:36–38
3. Christ Comforts His Disciples, 14:1–4
4. Christ Answers Thomas, 14:5–7
5. Christ Answers Philip, 14:8–21
6. Christ Answers Judas, 14:22–31

II. **The Preparation on the Way to the Garden,** 15:1—17:26
A. Christ Instructs the Disciples, 15:1—16:33
1. The Relationship of Believers to Christ, 15:1–11
2. The Relationship of Believers to Each Other, 15:12–17
3. The Relationship of Believers to the World, 15:18–25
4. The Promise of the Holy Spirit, 15:26—16:15
5. The Predictions of Christ's Death and Resurrection, 16:16–33

B. Christ Intercedes with the Father, 17:1–26
   1. Christ Prays for Himself, 17:1–5
   2. Christ Prays for His Disciples, 17:6–19
   3. Christ Prays for All Believers, 17:20–26

Part Five: The Crucifixion and Resurrection of the Son of God (18:1—21:25)

I. The Rejection of Christ, 18:1—19:16
  A. The Arrest of Christ, 18:1–11
  B. The Trials of Christ, 18:12—19:16
    1. First Jewish Trial before Annas, 18:12–23
    2. Second Jewish Trial before Caiaphas, 18:24–27
    3. First Roman Trial before Pilate, 18:28–38
    4. Second Roman Trial before Pilate, 18:39—19:16

II. The Crucifixion of Christ, 19:17–37
  A. Christ's Crucifixion, 19:17–18
  B. Pilate's Inscription, 19:19–22
  C. Soldiers Cast Lots, 19:23–24
  D. Mary's Committal, 19:25–27
  E. Christ's Death, 19:28–37

III. The Burial of Christ, 19:38–42

IV. The Resurrection of Christ, 20:1–10

V. The Appearances of Christ, 20:11—21:25
  A. Christ Appears to Mary Magdalene, 20:11–18
  B. Christ Appears to the Disciples (Thomas Absent), 20:19–25
  C. Christ Appears to the Disciples (Thomas Present), 20:26–29
  D. The Purpose of John's Gospel, 20:30–31
  E. Christ Appears to the Seven Disciples, 21:1–14
  F. Christ Speaks to Peter, 21:15–23
  G. The Conclusion of John's Gospel, 21:24–25

Geography of the Gospels

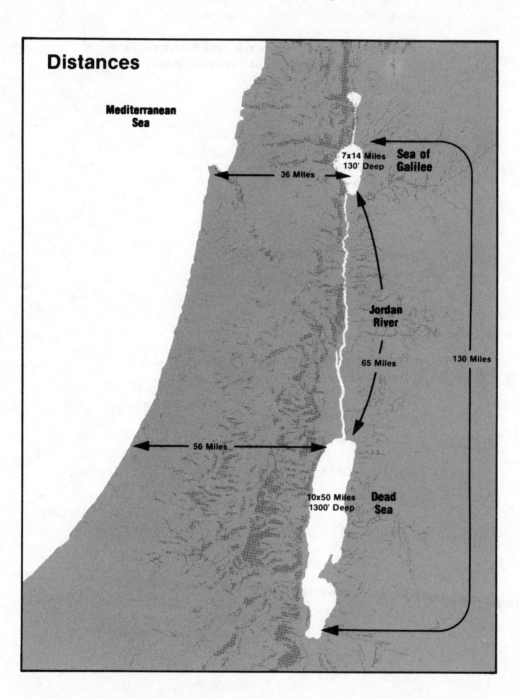

Distances

Mediterranean
Sea

Sea of
Galilee

7x14 Miles
130' Deep

36 Miles

Jordan
River

65 Miles

130 Miles

56 Miles

10x50 Miles
1300' Deep

Dead
Sea

Every Geographical Location in the Gospels

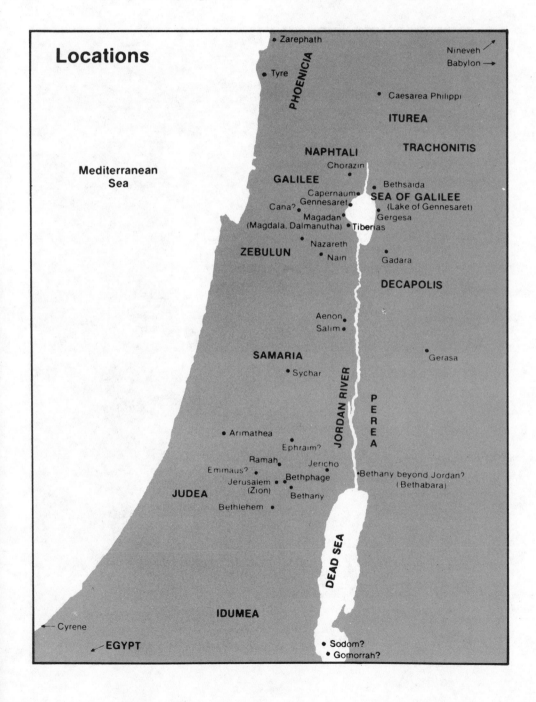

Locations

Mediterranean Sea

Zarephath

PHOENICIA

Tyre

Nineveh

Babylon →

Caesarea Philippi

ITUREA

TRACHONITIS

NAPHTALI

Chorazin

GALILEE

Bethsaida

Capernaum

Gennesaret

SEA OF GALILEE

(Lake of Gennesaret)

Cana?

Magadan

Gergesa

(Magdala, Dalmanutha)

Tiberias

Nazareth

ZEBULUN

Nain

Gadara

DECAPOLIS

Aenon

Salim

Gerasa

SAMARIA

Sychar

JORDAN RIVER

P E R E A

Arimathea

Ephraim?

Ramah

Jericho

Emmaus?

Bethphage

Jerusalem

Bethany beyond Jordan?

(Zion)

(Bethabara)

Bethany

JUDEA

Bethlehem

DEAD SEA

IDUMEA

Cyrene

EGYPT

Sodom?

Gomorrah?

Geography of the Gospels: Travel Routes/Economy

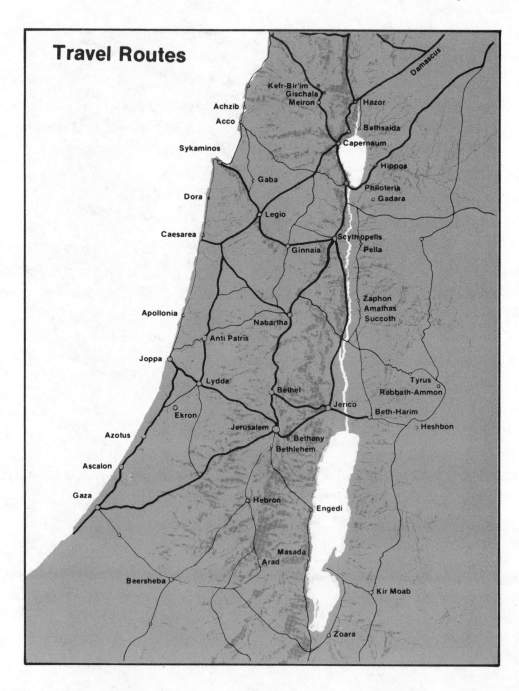

Travel Routes

Kefr-Bir'im
Gischala
Meiron
Achzib
Acco
Hazor
Bethsaida
Capernaum
Sykaminos
Hippos
Gaba
Philoteria
Gadara
Dora
Legio
Caesarea
Scythopelis
Ginnaia
Pella
Zaphon
Amathas
Succoth
Apollonia
Nabartha
Anti Patris
Joppa
Tyrus
Lydda
Rabbath-Ammon
Bethel
Ekron
Jerico
Beth-Harim
Heshbon
Azotus
Jerusalem
Bethany
Bethlehem
Ascalon
Gaza
Hebron
Engedi
Masada
Arad
Beersheba
Kir Moab
Zoara

Damascus

Chronology of the Life of Christ

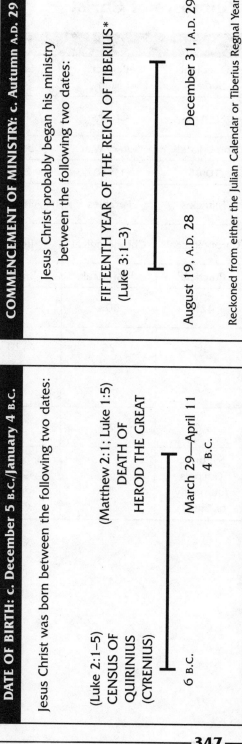

DATE OF BIRTH: c. December 5 B.C./January 4 B.C.

Jesus Christ was born between the following two dates:

(Luke 2:1–5)
CENSUS OF
QUIRINIUS
(CYRENIUS)

(Matthew 2:1; Luke 1:5)
DEATH OF
HEROD THE GREAT

6 B.C.

March 29—April 11
4 B.C.

COMMENCEMENT OF MINISTRY: c. Autumn A.D. 29

Jesus Christ probably began his ministry between the following two dates:

FIFTEENTH YEAR OF THE REIGN OF TIBERIUS*
(Luke 3:1–3)

August 19, A.D. 28

December 31, A.D. 29

Reckoned from either the Julian Calendar or Tiberius Regnal Year

DURATION OF MINISTRY: Autumn A.D. 29—April 14, A.D. 33 (THREE AND ONE-HALF YEARS)

Commencement
of Christ's
Ministry

Autumn
A.D. 29

Passover #1
April 7,
A.D. 30

John 2:13,23

Passover #2

Unstated
Mark 2:23–28
Luke 6:1–5
Matthew 12:1–8

Passover #3
April 25,
A.D. 32

John 6:4

Passover #4
April 14,
A.D. 33

John 11:55—12:1

*Basic Dating: Harold W. Hoehner, ''Chronological Aspects of the Life of Christ,'' Bibliotheca Sacra, vol. 130, 131.

Four Gospel Glimpses of Christ

	Matthew	Mark	Luke	John
Christ Portrayed as	Prophesied King	Obedient Servant	Perfect Man	Son of God
Original Audience	Jews	Romans	Greeks	All Men
Key Word	"fulfilled"	"immediately"	"Son of Man"	"believe"
Key Verse	21:5	10:45	19:10	20:31
Outstanding Feature	Sermons	Miracles	Parables	Allegories
Arrangement of Material	Tropical	Chronological	Chronological	Tropical
Tone	Prophetic	Practical	Historical	Spiritual
Percent Spoken by Christ	60%	42%	50%	50%
Quotations from Old Testament	53	36	25	20
Allusions to Old Testament	76	27	42	105
Unique Material	42%	59%	7%	92%
Broad Division		Synoptic Gospels (humanity of Christ)		Supplemental Gospel (deity of Christ)

Major Themes in the Life of Christ

1. WHO IS HE?

OFFICE	PROPHESIED	FULFILLED	ROLE
Prophet	Deuteronomy 18:15–18	John 6:14	Standard Bearer
Priest	Psalm 110:4	Hebrews 5:5–10	Sacrifice
King	Isaiah 9:6–7	John 12:13	Sovereign

2. WHAT DID HE SAY?

MESSAGE	THEME
Sermon on the Mount (Matt. 5—7)	Requirements of Righteousness
Upper Room Discourse (John 13—17)	Resources of Righteousness
Olivet Discourse (Matt. 24—25)	Results of Rejecting Righteousness

3. WHAT DID HE DO?

MESSAGE VALIDATED	MIRACLE	SCRIPTURE
"I am the resurrection and the life"	Raising Lazarus	John 11
"I am the bread of life"	Feeding Five Thousand	John 6
"Man, your sins are forgiven you."	Healing Paralytic	Luke 5
"Authority" of Jesus	Various Miracles	Matthew 5—9

4. HOW DID THE PEOPLE RESPOND?

	ACCEPTANCE	REJECTION
L E A D E R S	Few Believed	Because: 1. Claims to deity (John 5:18) 2. Company He kept (Mark 2:16) 3. Challenge to their traditions (Mark 7:1–13)
M U L T I T U D E S	Many Believed	Because: 1. Lack of conformity to their expectations (John 6:14–15) 2. refusal to accept moral demands (John 3:19–21) 3. Mob psychology (Mark 15:11–13)

349

Acts

LUKE BEGINS THE BOOK OF ACTS where he left off in his gospel. Acts records the initial fulfillment of the Great Commission of Matthew 28:19–20 as it traces the beginning and growth of the New Testament church. Christ's last words before His Ascension were so perfectly realized in the Book of Acts that they effectively and concisely outline its contents: " 'You shall be witnesses to Me in Jerusalem [chs. 1—7], and in all Judea and Samaria [chs. 8—12], and to the end of the earth [chs. 13—28]' " (1:8). Thus, Acts traces the rapid expansion of the gospel, beginning in Jerusalem and spreading throughout the Roman Empire.

ACTS						
Focus	**Witness in Jerusalem**		**Witness in Judea & Samaria**	**Witness to the Ends of the Earth**		
	1:1	8:4	8:5 12:25	13:1		28:31
Divisions	Power of the Church	Progress of the Church	Expansion of the Church	Paul's Three Journeys		Paul's Three Trials
	1:1 2:47	3:1 8:4	8:5 12:25	13:1 21:16	21:17	28:31
Topics	Jews		Samaritans	Gentiles		
	Peter		Philip	Paul		
Place	Jerusalem		Judea & Samaria	Uttermost Part		
Time	2 Years (A.D. 33–35)		13 Years (A.D. 35–48)	14 Years (A.D. 48–62)		

Introduction and Title

Jesus' last recorded words have come to be known as the Great Commission: ". . . You shall be witnesses to Me in Jerusalem, and in all Judea and Samaria, and to the end of the earth" (1:8). The Book of Acts, written by Luke, is the story of the men and women who took that commission seriously and began to spread the news of a risen Savior to the most remote corners of the known world.

Each section of the book (1—7; 8—12; 13—28) focuses on a particular audience, a key personality, and a significant phase in the expansion of the gospel message.

As the second volume in a two-part work by Luke, this book probably had no separate title. But all available Greek manuscripts designate it by the title *Praxeis*, "Acts," or by an expanded title like "The Acts of the Apostles." *Praxeis* was commonly used in Greek literature to summarize the accomplishments of outstanding men. While the apostles are mentioned collectively at several points, this book really records the acts of Peter (1—12) and of Paul (13—28).

Author

Chapter 1, verse 1, refers Theophilus to "The former account," that is, the Gospel of Luke. (See "Author" in Luke for the internal and external support for Lucan authorship of Luke.) Luke's source for the "we" sections in this book (16:10–17; 20:5—21:18; 27:1—28:16) was his own memory if not some kind of diary. For the remainder of this book, Luke no doubt followed the same careful investigative procedures that he used in writing his gospel (Luke 1:1–4). As a close traveling companion of Paul, Luke had access to the principal eyewitness for chapters 13—28. It is also likely that he had opportunities to interview such key witnesses in Jerusalem as Peter and John for the information in chapters 1—12. Acts indicates that Luke may have used written documents as well (see 15:23–29; 23:26–30).

Date and Setting

Suggested dates for the writing of Acts range from A.D. 62 to the middle of the second century. Twentieth-century archaeological discoveries have strikingly confirmed the trustworthiness and precision of Luke as a historian and show that his work should be dated in the first century. Luke's perplexingly abrupt ending with Paul awaiting trial in Rome has led many to believe that Acts was completed prior to Paul's trial (A.D. 62). If it was written after this crucial event, why didn't Luke mention the outcome? Luke may have had a reason, but the simplest explanation of his silence is that Paul had not yet stood before Caesar. Acts gives no hint of the persecution under Nero (A.D. 64), Paul's death (A.D. 68), or the destruction of Jerusalem (A.D. 70).

Theme and Purpose

While there are four accounts of the life of Jesus, this is the only book that carries on the story from the Ascension to the period of the New Testament epistles.

Thus, Acts is the historical link between the Gospels and the Epistles. Because of Luke's strong emphasis on the ministry of the Holy Spirit, this book should really be regarded as the Acts of the Spirit of Christ working in and through the apostles. As a missionary himself, Luke's interest in the progressive spread of the gospel is obviously reflected in this apostolic history. Luke was personally involved in the process of this story, so it was not written from a detached point of view. But this does not detract from the authority and coherence of this primary historical document.

From a theological standpoint, Acts was written to trace the development of the body of Christ over the one-generation transition from a primarily Jewish to a predominantly Gentile membership. This apologetic work presents Christianity as distinct from Judaism but also as its fulfillment.

Keys to Acts

Key Word: Growth of the Church
Key Verses (1:8; 2:42–47)—"But you shall receive power when the Holy Spirit has come upon you; and you shall be witnesses to Me in Jerusalem, and in all Judea and Samaria, and to the end of the earth" (1:8).

"And they continued steadfastly in the apostles' doctrine and fellowship, in the breaking of bread, and in prayers. Then fear came upon every soul, and many wonders and signs were done through the apostles. Now all who believed were together, and had all things in common, and sold their possessions and goods, and divided them among all, as anyone had need. So continuing daily with one accord in the temple, and breaking bread from house to house, they ate their food with gladness and simplicity of heart, praising God and having favor with all the people. And the Lord added to the church daily those who were being saved" (2:42–47).

Key Chapter (2)—Chapter 2 records the earth-changing events of the Day of Pentecost when the Holy Spirit comes, fulfilling Christ's promise to wait until the Holy Spirit arrives to empower and direct the witness. The Spirit transforms a small group of fearful men into a thriving, worldwide church that is ever moving forward and fulfilling the Great Commission.

Christ in Acts

The resurrected Savior is the central theme of the sermons and defenses in Acts. The Old Testament Scriptures, the historical resurrection, the apostolic testimony, and the convicting power of the Holy Spirit all bear witness that Jesus is both Lord and Christ (see Peter's sermons in 2:22–36; 10:34–43). "To Him all the prophets witness that, through His name, whoever believes in Him will receive remission of sins" (10:43). "Nor is there salvation in any other, for there is no other name under heaven given among men by which we must be saved" (4:12).

Contribution to the Bible

Acts is highly selective in its content, and it does not attempt to be a comprehensive survey of the first thirty years of the Christian church. Nevertheless, it is invaluable as the background history for most of the Epistles. Without it the Epistles would be quite difficult to understand, and the history of the early church would be a vague patchwork. There are certain problems in harmonizing the events in Acts with the information about Paul in his epistles, but these events generally fit well together.

When Luke and Acts are joined together, they offer a monumental account of the foundation and initial development of Christianity. Their style and literary quality are unsurpassed in the New Testament. Luke uses over seven hundred words not found in the other twenty-five New Testament books—he must have been steeped in the Septuagint, because nine-tenths of these words were used in it.

Luke includes about eighty geographical references and mentions over one hundred people by name in Acts. His precision in citing locations (e.g., provinces, cities, specific sites) and titles (e.g., consul, tetrarch, proconsul, Asiarch) was once challenged by critics but is now verified by archaeological evidence. Another prominent feature of this book is the amount of space given to speeches and sermons; no less than twenty-four messages are found in its twenty-eight chapters.

Survey of Acts

Luke begins the Book of Acts where he left off in his gospel. Acts records the initial fulfillment of the Great Commission of Matthew 28:19–20 as it traces the beginning and growth of the New Testament church (This growth pattern can be seen in 1:15; 2:41, 47; 4:4; 5:14; 6:7; 9:31; 12:24; 13:49; 16:5; 19:20). Christ's last words before His Ascension are so perfectly realized in the Book of Acts that they effectively outline its contents: "But you shall receive power when the Holy Spirit has come upon you; and you shall be witnesses to Me in Jerusalem, and in all Judea and Samaria, and to the end of the earth" (1:8). Acts traces important events in the early history of Christianity from the Ascension of Christ to the outpouring of the Holy Spirit to the rapid progress of the gospel, beginning in Jerusalem and spreading throughout the Roman Empire.

Acts is a pivotal book of transitions: from the Gospels to the Epistles (history), from Judaism to Christianity (religion), from law to grace (divine dealing), from Jews alone to Jews and Gentiles (people of God), and from kingdom to church (program of God). The profound changes that took place on the Cross required about a generation to be effected in time (Acts covers c. thirty years). Acts is a history of extraordinary events. The three movements in Acts follow its key verse (1:8): (1) Witness in Jerusalem (1:1—8:4); (2) witness in Judea and Samaria (8:5—12:25); and (3) witness to the uttermost part of the world (13—28).

Witness in Jerusalem (1:1—8:4): After appearing to His disciples for "forty days" (1:3), the Lord tells them to wait in Jerusalem for the fulfillment of His promise concerning the Holy Spirit. Ten days after His Ascension, this promise is significantly fulfilled as the disciples are suddenly empowered and filled with the Holy Spirit. This takes place on the Feast of Weeks (Pentecost), fifty days after Firstfruits (the Resurrection). Because every Jewish male is required to appear at the sanctuary for this feast (see Ex. 23:14–17; Deut. 16:16), Jerusalem swells with Jews and proselytes from throughout the Roman Empire. The disciples are transformed and filled with courage to proclaim the brand new message of the resurrected Savior. Peter's powerful sermon, like all the sermons in Acts, is built upon the Resurrection; and three thousand people respond with saving faith. After dramatically healing a man who was lame from birth, Peter delivers a second crucial message to the people of Israel resulting in thousands of additional responses. The religious leaders arrest the apostles, and this gives Peter an opportunity to preach a special sermon to them.

The enthusiasm and joy of the infant church are marred by internal and external problems. Ananias and Sapphira receive the ultimate form of discipline because of their treachery, and the apostles are imprisoned and persecuted because of their witness. Seven men, including Stephen and Philip, are selected to assist the apostles. Stephen is brought before the Sanhedrin; and in his defense there, he surveys the Scriptures to prove that the Man they condemned and killed was the Messiah Himself. The members of the Sanhedrin react to Stephen's words by dragging him out of the city and making him the first Christian martyr.

Witness in Judea and Samaria (8:5—12:25): Philip goes to the province of Samaria and successfully proclaims the new message to a people who are hated by the Jews. Peter and John confirm his work and exercise their apostolic authority by imparting the Holy Spirit to these new members of the body of Christ. God sovereignly transforms Saul the persecutor into Paul the Apostle to the Gentiles, but He uses Peter to introduce the gospel to the Gentiles. In a special vision Peter realizes that Christ has broken down the barrier between Jews and Gentiles. After Cornelius and other Gentiles come to Christ through his preaching, Peter convinces the Jewish believers in Jerusalem that "the Gentiles had also received the word of God" (11:1). Even while experiencing more and more persecution, the church continues to increase, spreading throughout the Roman Empire.

Witness to the Uttermost Part of the World (13—28): Beginning with chapter 13, Luke switches the focus of Acts from Peter to Paul. Antioch in Syria gradually replaces Jerusalem as the headquarters of the church, and all three of Paul's missionary journeys originate from that city. The first journey (A.D. 48–49) concentrates on the Galatian cities of Pisidian Antioch, Iconium, Lystra, and Derbe. After this journey, a council is held among the apostles and elders of the church in Jerusalem to determine that the Gentile converts need not submit to the Law of Moses. The second missionary journey (A.D. 50–52) brings Paul once again to the Galatian churches, and then for the first time on to Macedonia and Greece. Paul spends much of his time in the cities of Philippi, Thessalonica, and Corinth, and later returns to Jerusalem and Antioch. In his third missionary journey (A.D. 53–57), Paul spends almost three years in the Asian city of Ephesus before visiting Macedonia and Greece for the second time. Although he is warned not to go to Jerusalem, Paul cannot be dissuaded.

It is not long before Paul is falsely accused of bringing Gentiles into the temple.

Only the Roman commander's intervention prevents his being killed by the mob. Paul's defense before the people and before the Sanhedrin evokes violent reactions. When the commander learns of a conspiracy to assassinate Paul, he sends his prisoner to Felix, the governor in Caesarea. During his two-year imprisonment there (A.D. 57–59), Paul defends the Christian faith before Felix, Festus, and Agrippa. His appeal to Caesar requires a long voyage to Rome, where he is placed under house arrest until his trial.

Outline of Acts

Part One: The Witness in Jerusalem (1:1—8:4)

I. **The Power of the Church,** 1:1—2:47
    A. Prologue to Acts, 1:1–2
    B. Appearances of the Resurrected Christ, 1:3–8
    C. Ascension of Christ, 1:9–11
    D. Anticipation of the Spirit, 1:12–14
    E. Appointment of Matthias, 1:15–26
    F. Filling with the Holy Spirit, 2:1–4
    G. Speaking with Other Tongues, 2:5–13
    H. Peter Explains Pentecost, 2:14–41
    I. Practices of the Early Church, 2:42–47

II. **The Progress of the Church,** 3:1—8:4
    A. Peter Heals the Lame Man, 3:1–11
    B. Peter's Second Sermon, 3:12–26
    C. Peter and John Are Put into Custody, 4:1–4
    D. Peter Preaches to the Sanhedrin, 4:5–12
    E. Sanhedrin Commands Peter Not to Preach, 4:13–22
    F. Apostles' Prayer for Boldness, 4:23–31
    G. Early Church Voluntarily Shares, 4:32–37
    H. Ananias and Sapphira Lie, 5:1–11
    I. Apostles' Mighty Miracles, 5:12–16
    J. Apostles' Persecution, 5:17–42
        1. Apostles Are Miraculously Freed from Prison, 5:17–28
        2. Apostles Preach to the Council, 5:29–32
        3. Gamaliel's Advice, 5:33–39
        4. Apostles Are Beaten, 5:40–42
    K. Deacons Are Appointed, 6:1–8
    L. Stephen Is Martyred, 6:9—7:60
        1. Stephen Is Brought before the Council, 6:9–15
        2. Stephen Preaches to the Council, 7:1–60
    M. Saul Persecutes the Church, 8:1–4

Part Two: The Witness in Judea and Samaria (8:5—12:25)

I. The Witness of Philip, 8:5–40
  A. Philip Witnesses to the Samaritans, 8:5–25
  B. Philip Witnesses to the Ethiopian Treasurer, 8:26–40

II. The Conversion of Saul, 9:1–31
  A. Saul Is Converted and Blinded, 9:1–9
  B. Saul Is Filled with the Spirit, 9:10–19
  C. Saul Preaches at Damascus, 9:20–22
  D. Saul Witnesses in Jerusalem, 9:23–31

III. The Witness of Peter, 9:32—11:18
  A. Peter Heals Aeneas at Lydda, 9:32–35
  B. Peter Raises Dorcas at Joppa, 9:36–43
  C. Peter Witnesses to Cornelius at Caesarea, 10:1—11:18
    1. Cornelius Sends for Peter, 10:1–8
    2. Peter Sees the Great Sheet, 10:9–22
    3. Peter Preaches to the Gentiles, 10:23–43
    4. Gentiles Are Converted and Speak in Tongues, 10:44–48
    5. Peter Defends His Ministry to the Gentiles, 11:1–18

IV. The Witness of the Early Church, 11:19—12:25
  A. The Witness of the Antioch Church, 11:19–30
  B. The Persecution by Herod, 12:1–25
    1. Herod Kills James, 12:1–2
    2. Peter Is Miraculously Released from Prison, 12:3–19
    3. Herod Blasphemes and Dies, 12:20–25

Part Three: The Witness to the End of the Earth (13:1—28:31)

I. The First Missionary Journey, 13:1—14:28
  A. Barnabas and Saul Are Sent from Antioch, 13:1–3
  B. Ministry at Cyprus, 13:4–13
    1. Preaching in the Synagogues, 13:4–5
    2. Controversy with Bar-Jesus, 13:6–13
  C. Ministry at Antioch, 13:14–50
    1. Paul Preaches on First Sabbath, 13:14–43
    2. Paul Preaches on Second Sabbath, 13:44–50
  D. Ministry at Iconium, 13:51—14:5
  E. Ministry at Lystra, 14:6–20
    1. A Lame Man Is Healed, 14:6–10
    2. Paul and Barnabas Are Deified, 14:11–18
    3. Paul Is Stoned, 14:19–20
  F. Ministry on the Return Trip, 14:21–25
  G. Report on the First Missionary Journey, 14:26–28

II. The Jerusalem Council, 15:1–35

    A. Debate over Gentiles Keeping the Law, 15:1–5

    B. Peter Preaches Salvation through Grace, 15:6–11

    C. Paul and Barnabas Testify, 15:12

    D. James Proves Gentiles Are Free from the Law, 15:13–21

    E. The Council Sends an Official Letter, 15:22–29

    F. Report to Antioch, 15:30–35

III. The Second Missionary Journey, 15:36—18:22

    A. Contention over John Mark, 15:36–41

    B. Derbe and Lystra: Timothy Is Circumcised, 16:1–5

    C. Troas: Macedonian Call, 16:6–10

    D. Philippi: Extensive Ministry, 16:11–40

        1. Lydia Is Converted, 16:11–15

        2. Spirit of Divination Is Cast Out, 16:16–24

        3. Philippian Jailer Is Converted, 16:25–34

        4. Paul Is Released from Prison, 16:35–40

    E. Thessalonica: "Turn the World Upside Down," 17:1–9

    F. Berea: Many Receive the Word, 17:10–15

    G. Athens: Paul's Sermon on Mars' Hill, 17:16–34

    H. Corinth: One-and-a-half Years of Ministry, 18:1–17

        1. Paul Works with Aquila and Priscilla, 18:1–3

        2. Jews Reject Paul, 18:4–6

        3. Crispus, the Gentile, Is Converted, 18:7–11

        4. Gallio Will Not Try Paul, 18:12–17

    I. Return Trip to Antioch, 18:18–22

IV. The Third Missionary Journey, 18:23—21:16

    A. Galatia and Phrygia: Strengthening the Disciples, 18:23

    B. Ephesus: Three Years of Ministry, 18:24—19:41

        1. Apollos Teaches Effectively, 18:24–28

        2. Disciples of John Receive the Holy Spirit, 19:1–7

        3. Paul Teaches in Tyrannus' School, 19:8–10

        4. Miracles Are Performed at Ephesus, 19:11–20

        5. Timothy and Erastus Are Sent to Macedonia, 19:21–22

        6. Demetrius Causes Uproar at Ephesus, 19:23–41

    C. Macedonia: Three Months of Ministry, 20:1–5

    D. Troas: Eutychus Falls from Loft, 20:6–12

    E. Miletus: Paul Bids Farewell to Ephesian Elders, 20:13–38

    F. Tyre: Paul Is Warned about Jerusalem, 21:1–6

    G. Caesarea: Agabus' Prediction, 21:7–16

V. The Trip to Rome, 21:17—28:31

    A. Paul Witnesses in Jerusalem, 21:17—23:33

        1. Paul Conforms to Jewish Customs, 21:17–26

        2. Paul's Arrest, 21:27–39

        3. Paul's Defense before the Crowd, 21:40—22:23

        4. Paul's Defense before the Centurion, 22:24–29

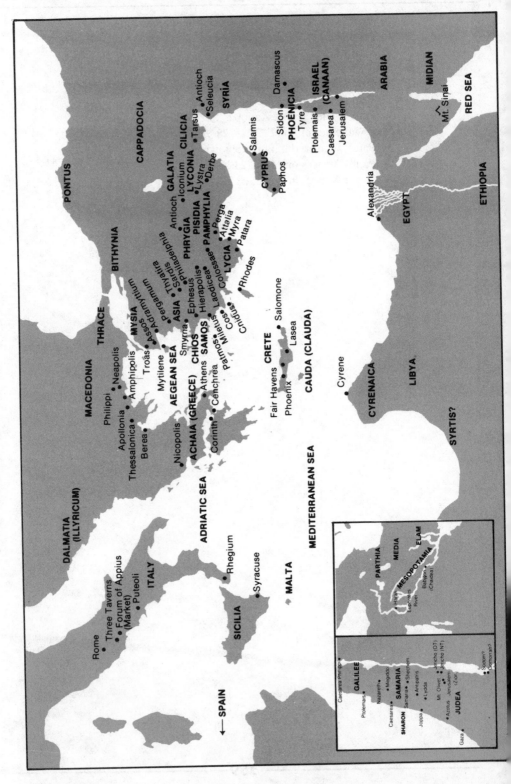

Every Geographical Location in Acts/Epistles

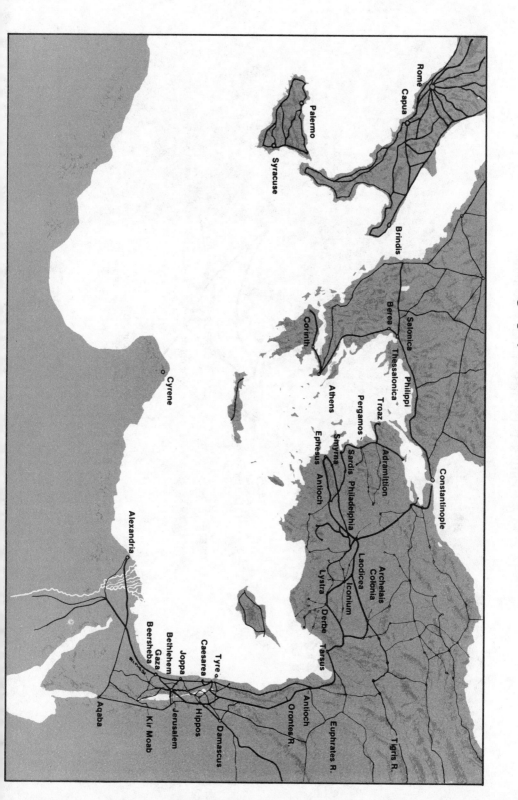

Geography of the Book of Acts: Travel Routes

Paul's First Missionary Journey

Acts 13:2–14:28 April 48–September 49

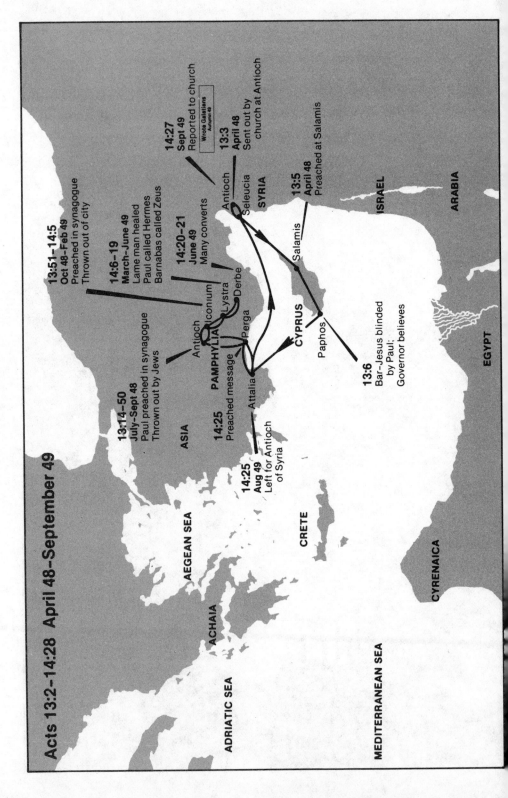

13:14–50
July–Sept 48
Paul preached in synagogue
Thrown out by Jews

13:51–14:5
Oct 48–Feb 49
Preached in synagogue
Thrown out of city

14:6–19
March–June 49
Lame man healed
Paul called Hermes
Barnabas called Zeus

14:20–21
June 49
Many converts

14:27
Sept 49
Reported to church

Wrote Galatians
Autumn 49

13:3
April 48
Sent out by
church at Antioch

13:5
April 48
Preached at Salamis

14:25
Preached message

14:25
Aug 49
Left for Antioch
of Syria

13:6
Bar-Jesus blinded
by Paul;
Governor believes

Antioch
Seleucia
SYRIA
Salamis
CYPRUS
Paphos
ISRAEL
ARABIA
EGYPT
Antioch
Iconium
Lystra
Derbe
Perga
PAMPHYLIA
Attalia
ASIA
AEGEAN SEA
CRETE
ACHAIA
ADRIATIC SEA
MEDITERRANEAN SEA
CYRENAICA

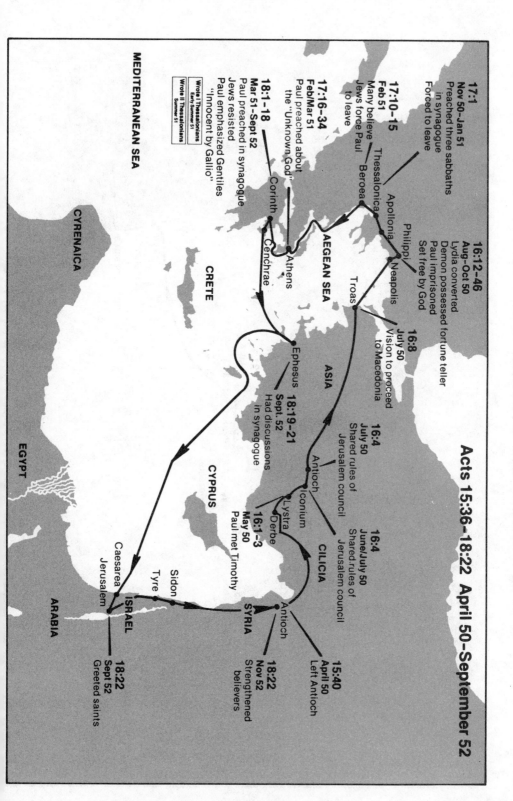

Paul's Second Missionary Journey

Acts 15:36–18:22 April 50–September 52

MEDITERRANEAN SEA

CYRENAICA

EGYPT

CRETE

CYPRUS

AEGEAN SEA

ASIA

CILICIA

SYRIA

ISRAEL

ARABIA

17:1
Nov 50–Jan 51
Preached three sabbaths
in synagogue
Forced to leave

17:10–15
Feb 51
Many believe
Jews force Paul
to leave

17:16–34
Feb/Mar 51
Paul preached about
the "Unknown God"

18:1–18
Mar 51–Sept 52
Paul preached in synagogue
Jews resisted
Paul emphasized Gentiles
"Innocent by Gallio"

Wrote I Thessalonians
Early Summer 51

Wrote II Thessalonians
Summer 51

16:12–46
Aug–Oct 50
Lydia converted
Demon possessed fortune teller
Paul imprisoned
Set free by God

16:8
July 50
Vision to proceed
to Macedonia

18:19–21
Sept. 52
Had discussions
in synagogue

16:4
July 50
Shared rules of
Jerusalem council

16:4
June/July 50
Shared rules of
Jerusalem council

16:1–3
May 50
Paul met Timothy

15:40
April 50
Left Antioch

18:22
Nov 52
Strengthened
believers

18:22
Sept 52
Greeted saints

Thessalonica
Beroea
Apollonia
Philippi
Neapolis
Troas
Corinth
Cenchrae
Athens
Ephesus
Antioch
Iconium
Lystra
Derbe
Caesarea
Jerusalem
Tyre
Sidon
Antioch

Paul's Third Missionary Journey

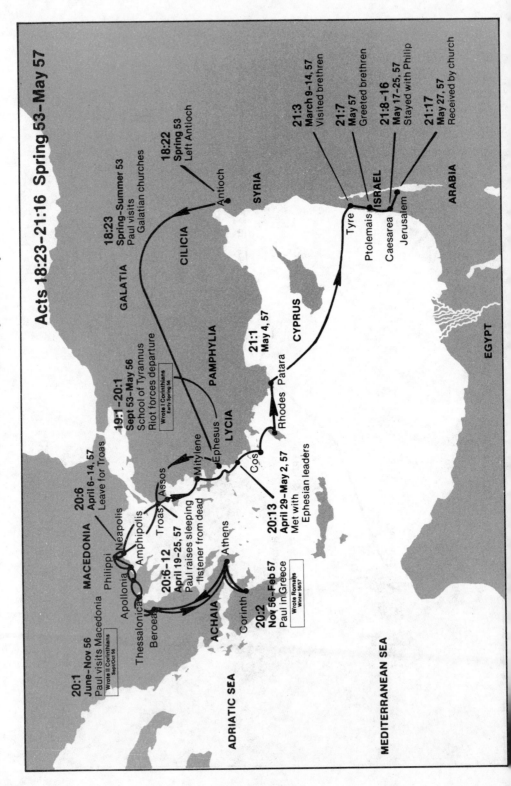

Acts 18:23–21:16 Spring 53–May 57

18:22 Spring 53 Left Antioch

18:23 Spring-Summer 53 Paul visits Galatian churches

19:1–20:1 Sept 53–May 56 School of Tyrannus Riot forces departure

Wrote I Corinthians Early Spring 56

20:1 June–Nov 56 Paul visits Macedonia

Wrote II Corinthians Sept/Oct 56

20:6 April 6–14, 57 Leave for Troas

20:6–12 April 19–25, 57 Paul raises sleeping listener from dead

20:2 Nov 56–Feb 57 Paul in Greece

Wrote Romans Winter 56/57

20:13 April 29–May 2, 57 Met with Ephesian leaders

21:1 May 4, 57

21:3 March 9–14, 57 Visited brethren

21:7 May 57 Greeted brethren

21:8–16 May 17–25, 57 Stayed with Philip

21:17 May 27, 57 Received by church

GALATIA

CILICIA

PAMPHYLIA

LYCIA

SYRIA

CYPRUS

ISRAEL

ARABIA

EGYPT

MACEDONIA

ACHAIA

ADRIATIC SEA

MEDITERRANEAN SEA

Antioch

Tyre

Ptolemais

Caesarea

Jerusalem

Patara

Rhodes

Cos

Ephesus

Mitylene

Assos

Troas

Neapolis

Philippi

Apollonia

Amphipolis

Thessalonica

Beroea

Athens

Corinth

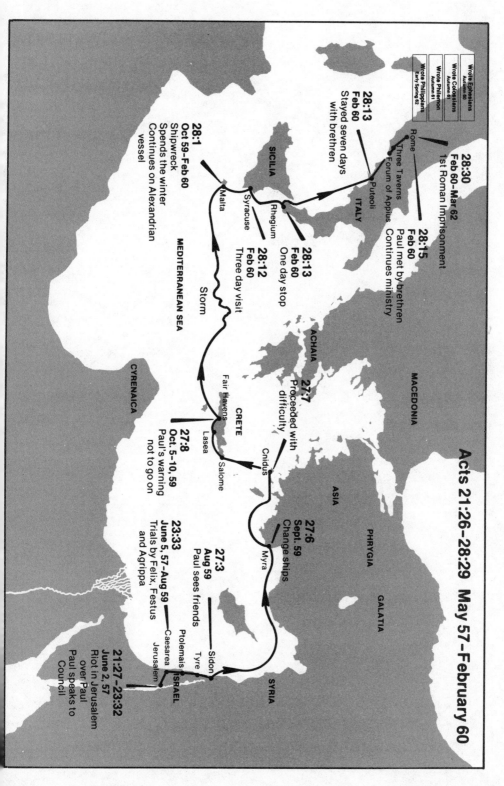

Paul's Trials and Imprisonments

Acts 21:26–28:29 May 57–February 60

28:30
Feb 60–Mar 62
1st Roman Imprisonment

28:13
Feb 60
Stayed seven days
with brethren

28:1
Oct 59–Feb 60
Shipwreck
Spends the winter
Continues on Alexandrian
vessel

28:15
Feb 60
Paul met by brethren
Continues ministry

28:13
Feb 60
One day stop

28:12
Feb 60
Three day visit

Storm

MEDITERRANEAN SEA

27:7
Proceeded with
difficulty

27:8
Oct. 5–10, 59
Paul's warning
not to go on

27:6
Sept. 59
Change ships

27:3
Aug 59
Paul sees friends

23:33
June 5, 57–Aug 59
Trials by Felix, Festus
and Agrippa

21:27–23:32
June 2, 57
Riot in Jerusalem
over Paul
Paul speaks to
Council

Rome
Three Taverns
Forum of Appius
Puteoli
SICILIA
ITALY
Malta
Syracuse
Rhegium
ACHAIA
MACEDONIA
Fair Havens
Lasea
CRETE
Salome
Cnidus
CYRENAICA
ASIA
PHRYGIA
GALATIA
Myra
Sidon
Tyre
Ptolemais
Caesarea
Jerusalem
ISRAEL
SYRIA

Wrote Ephesians
Autumn 60

Wrote Colossians
Autumn 60

Wrote Philemon
Autumn 61

Wrote Philippians
Early Spring 62

Introduction to the
Pauline Epistles

THE PAULINE EPISTLES ARE of inestimable value because Paul, under the inspiration of the Holy Spirit, was able to address specific problems and issues of his time with perspectives that are universal and timeless. In these thirteen epistles, even the most mundane matters stimulated lofty thoughts in the mind of the apostle which he was able to express with astounding versatility. Paul constantly adapted his style to the changing situations he encountered; he could be logical, personal, rhetorical, lyrical, formal, practical, or emotional. These pithy epistles condense an enormous number of ideas into a small space, so that every reading can yield new insights.

The use of the epistle as a medium of divine revelation was unheard of until the time of Paul and his contemporaries. This very personal form of communication was appropriate to the new message that believers have been made adopted children in the household of God by His grace. The epistles of Paul and others are intimately related to the needs and contingencies of real life, and they issue out of the affliction, joy, sorrow, and compassion of these godly writers. The Epistles have an abundance of doctrine, but it is designed for practical application, not theoretical speculation.

Because of their form and personal character, Paul's writings are properly called "letters." They generally follow the standard form of letters in Paul's day: the sender's name and office, the name of the recipient, a greeting or wish for prosperity, the main body of the letter, a farewell with closing greetings and good wishes, and the signature. This shell was filled with the richness of revelation, and a transformation took place that makes it appropriate to call these writings "epistles" as well as letters. Their literary quality and length distinguished them from ordinary letters. Even Philemon (335 words) is considerably longer than the usual letters of Paul's day which easily fit on one sheet of papyrus. Paul's epistles required a number of these sheets to be joined and rolled into scrolls.

Paul followed the usual procedure of using a scribe or *amanuensis* for the final form of his letters, but he wrote the concluding lines and signature with his own hand to guarantee authenticity (see Rom. 16:22; 1 Cor. 16:21; Gal. 6:11; Col. 4:18; 2 Thess. 3:17; Philemon was evidently an exception; Philem. 19). It is clear from letters like Romans and Ephesians that Paul had carefully thought out the details of his argument in advance, but the process of dictation allowed a freedom and freshness of speech. Since the limited imperial postal service was only for official business, Paul relied on helpers to carry his letters, but they also conveyed supplementary messages (see Eph. 6:21–22; Phil. 2:25–28; Col. 4:7–8).

The New Testament contains nine Pauline letters to churches and four to individuals. It is evident, however, that Paul wrote letters that are now lost (see 1 Cor. 5:9; 2 Cor. 10:9–10; Col. 4:16; 2 Thess. 3:17). Paul's thirteen canonical epistles are arranged so that the first nine (to churches) and the last four (to individuals) are in order of decreasing length. The probable chronological order is: Galatians, First Thessalonians, Second Thessalonians, First Corinthians, Second Corinthians, Romans, Colossians, Philemon, Ephesians, Philippians, First Timothy, Titus, and Second Timothy.

Saul was born a Roman citizen in Tarsus of Cilicia, a center of learning. He may have received a Greek education (cf. Acts 17:28; Titus 1:12) before his family moved to Jerusalem. He learned the trade of tent-making (Acts 18:3), but as a full-blooded Jew of the tribe of Benjamin he received the privilege of being educated under Rabbi Gamaliel (Acts 22:3). His keen mind and religious zeal advanced him in Judaism beyond his contemporaries (Gal. 1:14), and as a young Pharisee, Saul was present at the stoning of Stephen (see Acts 7:58; 8:1). He energetically persecuted Christians in Judea and decided to carry his campaign northeast to Damascus when his encounter with the resurrected Christ completely changed his life. He spent three years in Arabia and Damascus (Gal. 1:17–18) before being introduced by Barnabas to the apostles in Jerusalem. After fifteen days, a plot against him forced his departure (see Acts 9:26–30; Gal. 1:18–21), and he spent about ten years in Cilicia and Syria (primarily Tarsus and Antioch).

Barnabas and Paul brought a contribution from Antioch to Jerusalem for the famine relief of the brethren in Judea (Acts 11:25–30). After their return to Antioch, Barnabas, Paul, and Mark embarked on the first missionary journey (Acts 13—14). Mark left early, but Barnabas and Paul ministered in Cyprus, Pamphylia, and Galatia. After the journey, they went to Jerusalem to settle the issue of the Gentiles and the Mosaic Law (Acts 15), and then returned to Antioch. Paul took Silas on his second missionary Journey (Acts 15:36—18:22) which concentrated on Macedonia and Greece. Paul's third missionary journey, again originating in Antioch, focused on Asia with Ephesus as his headquarters (Acts 18:23—21:16). Paul went to Jerusalem for the last time with a collection for the poor but he was soon accused of violating the temple and a riot broke out. The Romans brought him to Caesarea where the governor Felix kept him imprisoned for two years (Acts 24:27). Paul defended himself before Felix, his replacement Festus, and Agrippa before his arduous journey to Rome (Acts 24—28:16). There he was imprisoned for two years, and although the Book of Acts stops at this point, evidence from Paul's letters to Timothy and Titus and from the early church fathers indicates that he was released from prison. He apparently had an opportunity to visit Spain, Crete, Asia, Macedonia, and Greece before his second Roman imprisonment and execution under Nero in A.D. 67–68.

Paul's Christian life was characterized by unflagging dedication to the cause of Christ in the face of suffering. He had a clear sense of divine calling, a strong love for his converts, an unshakable conviction and authority, and a constant spirit of dependence upon Christ in all that he did.

Romans

This most systematic of all the Epistles traces the story of the gospel from condemnation to justification to sanctification to glorification. It explains God's program for Jews and Gentiles and concludes with practical exhortations for the outworking of righteousness among believers.

First Corinthians

This epistle of correction and reproof firmly handles the problems of factions, immorality, lawsuits, and abuse of the Lord's Supper that were destroying the testimony of the Corinthians. Paul also responds to questions raised by the Corinthians on marriage, meat offered to idols, public worship, and the Resurrection.

Second Corinthians

Paul wrote this very personal letter to defend his apostolic character, call, and credentials in view of a recent rebellion against him that was led by certain false apostles. Paul was comforted by the repentance of the majority but concerned about the unrepentant minority.

Galatians

This polemic epistle refutes the error of legalism that had suddenly ensnared the churches of Galatia. Paul uses a biographical, theological, and moral argument to demonstrate the superiority of grace over law and magnify the life of liberty over legalism and license.

Ephesians

The first three chapters of Ephesians are one of the most sublime and profound texts in the Bible, because they extol the believer's position in Christ. The remaining three chapters exhort believers to maintain a spiritual walk that is based upon their spiritual wealth.

Philippians

In this joyous letter of affection and gratitude for the Philippians, Paul speaks of the latest developments in his imprisonment and urges his readers to a lifestyle of unity, humility, and godliness. He also warns them about the error of legalism.

Colossians

This may be the most Christocentric epistle in the New Testament, because in it Paul demonstrates the preeminence of Christ in creation, redemption, and the relationships of life. The Christian is complete in Christ and has no need of other systems of speculation or religious observances.

First Thessalonians

The first three chapters give a summary of Paul's ministry with the Thessalonians. He commends them for their faith and reminds them of his motives and concerns on their behalf. Chapters 4—5 exhort them to purity of life and teach them about the coming of the Lord.

Second Thessalonians

The Thessalonians were arriving at incorrect conclusions about the day of the Lord and they were becoming anxious about their persecution. Paul explains what must precede this awesome event and exhorts them to remain diligent.

First Timothy

This letter is Paul's leadership manual for his entrusted servant who was put in charge of the work in Ephesus. In it, Paul counsels Timothy on the problems of false teachers, public prayer, the role of women, the requirements for elders and deacons, and miscellaneous duties.

Second Timothy

Paul's last letter is a combat manual which is designed to build up and encourage Timothy to boldness and steadfastness in view of the hardships of the spiritual warfare. Paul knew his earthly course was over, and in his last recorded testimony he urges Timothy on.

Titus

Titus was left by Paul in Crete to oversee the work there and appoint elders. This conduct manual lists the requirements for elders and instructs Titus in his duties relative to the various groups in the churches.

Philemon

Onesimus, Philemon's runaway slave, had become a believer under Paul's ministry and now he was being sent back to his master with this letter. In it, Paul appeals to Philemon to forgive Onesimus and to regard him no longer as a slave but as a brother in Christ.

Romans

ROMANS, PAUL'S MAGNUM OPUS, is placed first among his thirteen epistles in the New Testament. While the four Gospels present the words and works of Jesus Christ, Romans explores the significance of His sacrificial death. Using a question-and-answer format, Paul records the most systematic presentation of doctrine in the Bible. But Romans is more than a book of theology; it is also a book of practical exhortations. The good news of Jesus Christ is more than facts to be believed; it is also a life to be lived—a life of righteousness befitting the person "justified freely by His [God's] grace through the redemption that is in Christ Jesus" (3:24).

ROMANS

Focus	Revelation of the Righteousness of God			Vindication of the Righteousness of God			Application of the Righteousness of God	
	1:1 8:39			9:1 11:36			12:1 16:27	
Divisions	Condemnation: Need for God's Righteousness	Justification: Inspiration of God's Righteousness	Sanctification: Demonstration of God's Righteousness	Israel's Past: Election	Israel's Present: Rejection	Israel's Future: Restoration	Christian Duties	Christian Liberties
	1:1 3:20	3:21 5:21	6:1 8:39	9:1 9:29	9:30 10:21	11:1 11:36	12:1 13:14	14:1 16:27
Topics	Sin	Salvation	Sanctification	Sovereignty			Service	
	Doctrinal						Behavioral	
Place	Probably Written in Corinth							
Time	C. A.D. 57							

373

Introduction and Title

Romans, Paul's greatest work, is placed first among his thirteen epistles in the New Testament. While the four Gospels present the words and works of Jesus Christ, Romans explores the significance of His sacrificial death. Using a question-and-answer format, Paul records the most systematic presentation of doctrine in the Bible. Romans is more than a book of theology; it is also a book of practical exhortation. The good news of Jesus Christ is more than facts to be believed; it is also a life to be lived—a life of righteousness befitting the person "justified freely by His [God's] grace through the redemption that is in Christ Jesus" (3:24).

Although some manuscripts omit "in Rome" in chapter 1, verses 7, 15, the title *Pros Romaious*, "To the Romans," has been associated with the epistle almost from the beginning.

Author

All critical schools agree on the Pauline authorship (1:1) of this foundational book. The vocabulary, style, logic, and theological development are consistent with Paul's other epistles. Paul dictated this letter to a secretary named Tertius (16:22), who was allowed to add his own greeting.

The problem arises not with the authorship but with the disunity of the epistle. Some Latin (but no Greek) manuscripts omit a portion (15:1—16:24). The closing doxology (16:25–27) is placed at the end of chapter 14 in some manuscripts. These variations have led some scholars to conclude that the last two chapters were not originally part of the epistle, or that Paul issued it in two editions. However, most scholars believe that chapter 15 fits in logically with the rest of the epistle. There is more debate over chapter 16, because Paul greets by name twenty-six people in a church he has never visited. Some scholars contend that it was a separate letter, perhaps written to Ephesus, that was appended to this epistle. Such a letter would be surprising, to say the least (nothing but greetings), especially in the ancient world. It is simpler to understand the list of greetings as Paul's effort as a stranger to the Roman church to list his mutual friends. Paul met these people in the cities of his missionary journeys. Significantly, the only other Pauline Epistle that lists individual greetings was addressed to the believers at Colossae, another church Paul had never visited. It may be that this portion was omitted from some copies of Romans because it did not seem relevant.

Date and Setting

Paul did not found the church at Rome, and the tradition that Peter was its founder is contrary to the evidence. It is possible that it began when some of the Jews and proselytes to Judaism who became followers of Christ on the Day of Pentecost (cf. Acts 2:10) returned to Rome, but it is more likely that Christians from churches established by Paul in Asia, Macedonia, and Greece settled in Rome and led others to Christ. According to this epistle, Gentiles were predominant in the church at Rome (1:13; 11:13; 11:28–31; 15:15–16), but there were also Jewish believers (2:17—3:8; 3:21—4:1; 7:1–14; 14:1—15:12).

Rome was founded in 753 B.C., and by the time of Paul it was the greatest city in the world with over one million inhabitants (one inscription says over four million). It was full of magnificent buildings, but the majority of people were slaves: opulence and squalor coexisted in the Imperial City. The church in Rome was well known (1:8), and it had been established for several years by the time of this letter (14:14; 15:23). The believers there were probably numerous, and evidently they met in several places (16:1–16). The historian Tacitus referred to the Christians who were persecuted under Nero in A.D. 64 as "an immense multitude." The gospel filled the gap left by the practically defunct polytheism of Roman religion.

Paul wrote Romans in A.D. 57, near the end of his third missionary journey (Acts 18:23—21:14; cf. Rom. 15:19). It was evidently written during his three-month stay in Greece (Acts 20:3–6), more specifically, in Corinth. Paul was staying with Gaius of Corinth (16:23; cf. 1 Cor. 1:14), and he also mentioned "Erastus, the treasurer of the city" (16:23). A first-century inscription in Corinth mentions him: "Erastus, the commissioner of public works, laid this pavement at his own expense." Paul's collection from the churches of Macedonia and Achaia for the needy Christians in Jerusalem was complete (15:26), and he was ready to deliver it (15:25). Instead of sailing directly to Jerusalem, Paul avoided a plot by the Jews by first going north to Philippi. He evidently gave this letter to Phoebe from the church at Cenchrea, near Corinth, and she carried it to Rome (16:1–2).

Theme and Purpose

The theme of Romans is found in chapter 1, verses 16–17: God offers the gift of His righteousness to everyone who comes to Christ by faith. Paul wrote Romans to reveal God's sovereign plan of salvation (1—8), to show how Jews and Gentiles fit into that plan (9—11), and to exhort them to live righteous and harmonious lives (12—16). In his sweeping presentation of God's plan of salvation, Paul moves from condemnation to glorification, and from positional truth to practical truth. Key words like *righteousness, faith, law, all,* and *sin* each appear at least sixty times in this epistle.

Paul did not write Romans to address specific problems in the church but to prepare the brethren for his long-awaited visit to that strategic church (15:22–24). He had laid the foundation for the gospel in the eastern provinces through his three missionary journeys, and now he desires to begin a significant work in the western provinces. Rome, the most influential city in the Empire, would be the logical base of operations for Paul's future missionary endeavors, just as Antioch was during his first three journeys. Paul had tried to visit Rome a number of times in the past, but each time he had been hindered (1:13; 15:22). By writing this letter, Paul hoped to build up the believers there in their knowledge and faith and to encourage this mixed church of Jews and Gentiles to work together as one body. Paul also asked them for their prayer support because of the dangerous opposition that awaited him in Jerusalem.

Keys to Romans

Key Word: The Righteous

Key Verses (1:16–17; 3:21–25)—"For I am not ashamed of the gospel of Christ, for it is the power of God to salvation for everyone who believes, for the Jew first and also for the Greek. For in it the righteousness of God is revealed from faith to faith; as it is written *'The just shall live by faith'*" (1:16–17).

"But now the righteousness of God apart from the law is revealed, being witnessed by the Law and the Prophets, even the righteousness of God *which is* through faith in Jesus Christ to all and on all who believe. For there is no difference; for all have sinned and fall short of the glory of God, being justified freely by His grace through the redemption that is in Christ Jesus, whom God set forth *to be* a propitiation by His blood, through faith, to demonstrate His righteousness, because in His forbearance God had passed over the sins that were previously committed" (3:21–25).

Key Chapters (6—8)—Foundational to all teaching on the spiritual life is the central passage of chapters 6—8. The answers to the questions of how to be delivered from sin, how to live a balanced life under grace, and how to live the victorious Christian life through the power of the Holy Spirit are all contained here. Many consider this to be the principal passage on conforming to the image of Jesus Christ.

Christ in Romans

Paul presents Jesus Christ as the Second Adam whose righteousness and substitutionary death have provided justification for all who place their faith in Him. He offers His righteousness as a gracious gift to sinful men, having borne God's condemnation and wrath for their sinfulness. His death and Resurrection are the basis for the believer's redemption, justification, reconciliation, salvation, and glorification.

Contribution to the Bible

Romans was not the first of Paul's epistles, but it was appropriately placed at the beginning of the Pauline corpus not only because it was Paul's longest work, but because it provides the doctrinal foundation upon which the other epistles are built. It is the most systematic and detailed exposition of theological truth in the Scriptures. Romans concentrates on the doctrines of hamartiology (sin) and soteriology (salvation): just as all men (Jews and Gentiles) are sinners, so God has graciously extended His offer of salvation to all who will place their faith in Christ.

Romans is the most formal of Paul's writings—it is more of a treatise than a letter. Paul was a stranger to most of the Roman believers (hence the long introduction), and he did not seek to refute any specific errors in their church. This is primarily a preventative, not a corrective epistle, and Paul made skillful use of a debate format to refute the kinds of objections he had encountered during two decades of reflecting upon and defending the gospel. The result is one of the most forceful, logical, and eloquent works ever penned. It is safe to say Romans has influenced the subsequent history of the church more than any other epistle.

Survey of Romans

The poet Samuel Taylor Coleridge regarded Romans as "the most profound book in existence," and the commentator Godet called it "the cathedral of the Christian faith." Because of its majestic declaration of the divine plan of salvation, Martin Luther wrote: "This epistle is the chief part of the New Testament and the very purest gospel. . . . It can never be read or pondered too much, and the more it is dealt with the more precious it becomes, and the better it tastes." The four Gospels present the words and works of the Lord Jesus, but Romans, "the Gospel According to Paul," delves more into the significance of His life. The theology of Romans is balanced by practical exhortation, because Paul sees the believer's position as the basis for his practice. The theme of righteousness that runs through the book is reflected in the following outline: The revelation of the righteousness of God (1—8); the vindication of the righteousness of God (9—11); and the application of the righteousness of God (12—16).

The Revelation of the Righteousness of God (1—8): The prologue (1:1–17) consists of a salutation (1:1–7), a statement of Paul's desire to minister in Rome (1:8–15), and the theme of the book (1:16–17). This two-verse theme is the basic text of Romans because it combines the three crucial concepts of salvation, righteousness, and faith. *Salvation:* a believer is saved *from* the penalty of sin (past), the power of sin (present), and the presence of sin (future); and he is saved *to* a new position, a new life, and an entrance into God's heavenly presence. *Righteousness:* this speaks of perfect conformity to an unchanging standard; the sinner who trusts in Christ receives the righteousness of Christ in his position before God. *Faith:* as the instrumentality for salvation and a gracious gift of God, faith includes an acknowledgement of need and a trust in Christ alone for salvation.

In 1:18—3:20, Paul builds a solid case for the condemnation of all people under the holy God. Paul's perceptive diagnosis of the human condition shows that Gentiles and Jews seek to justify themselves by using relative standards, not realizing that God's required standard is nothing short of perfection. Paul knows that the bad news (condemnation) must be understood before the good news (justification) can be appreciated. The Gentiles are without excuse because they have suppressed the knowledge of God they received from nature and their conscience (1:18–32; their seven-step regression is traced in 1:21–31). The Jews are also under the condemnation of God, and Paul overcomes every objection they could raise to this conclusion (2:1—3:8). God judges according to truth (2:2–5), works (2:6–10), and impartially (2:11–16), and both the moral and religious Jews fail to meet His standard. Paul concludes his discussion of the reasons for the guilt of the Jews by reminding them they do not obey the Law (2:17–29) nor believe the Oracles of God (3:1–8). The divine verdict (3:9–20) is universal: "all have sinned and fall short of the glory of God" (3:23).

The section on justification (3:21—5:21) centers on and develops the theme of God's provision for man's need. The first verses are the core of the book (3:21–31), revealing that in Christ, God is both Judge and Savior. Three crucial words are found in these verses: (1) *Justification:* this judicial term means that the believer in Christ is declared righteous by the holy God. The Lord is not unjust when He justifies sinners because He bases this pronouncement upon the death of Christ on their behalf. (2) *Redemption:* through His death, Christ has paid the ransom price of sin by purchasing believers out of slavery to sin and setting them free from the penalty of sin. (3) *Propitiation:* the blood of Christ has satisfied the demands of the righteous God who cannot overlook sin. God in Christ does not give the believer his due, because His holy wrath has been appeased by the sacrifice of His sinless Son. Justification is by grace (the source of salvation; 3:21–24), by blood (the basis of salvation; 3:25–26), and by faith (the condition of salvation; 3:27–31).

Chapter 4 illustrates the principle of justification by faith apart from works in the life of Abraham. Justification issues in reconciliation between God and man (5:1–11). *Reconciliation* speaks of the change in a person's state of alienation from and hostility toward God because of the substitutionary work of Jesus Christ on his behalf. It is brought about by the love of God which is causeless (5:6), measureless (5:7–8), and ceaseless (5:9–11). In 5:12–21 Paul contrasts the two Adams and the opposite results of their two acts. The disobedience of the first Adam made him the head of all who are under sin, but the obedience of the Second Adam (Christ) made Him the head of the race of redeemed humanity. The sin of the first Adam was *imputed* to us (placed on our account), leading to alienation. But the righteousness of the Second Adam is imputed to all who trust in Him, leading to reconciliation.

Chapter 6 describes the believer's relationship to sin: in his position he is dead to the principle of sin (6:1–14) and the practice of sin (6:15–23). The reality of identification with Christ is the basis for the sanctified Christian life. The believer must *know* his position in Christ, *reckon* it as true, and present himself to God as dead to sin but alive to God in Christ Jesus. Paul views devotion as a response to spiritual truth, not as a condition of it. After describing the Christian's emancipation from the Law (7), Paul looks at the work of the Holy Spirit who indwells and empowers every believer (8:1–17). The next major topic after condemnation, justification, and sanctification is glorification (8:18–39). All Christians can anticipate a time when they will be perfectly conformed to Jesus Christ not only in their position (present) but also in their practice (the future resurrection).

The Vindication of the Righteousness of God (9—11): It appears that God has rejected His people, Israel, but it is really Israel who has rejected her Messiah. Paul deals with the problem of Israel in the plan of God in three ways: (1) God is the sovereign Lord who is responsible to no one for His work of election and rejection (9). He elected Israel in the past, but because of her disbelief, the nation has been set aside in the *present.* (2) Although God is sovereign, humans are responsible for the consequences of their decisions (10), and this is true of their decision to accept or reject Jesus. (3) Israelites, the "natural branches" (11:21) of God's olive tree, have been cut off and Gentiles have been added (11). But God's rejection of Israel is only *partial* (there is a spiritual "remnant" that has trusted in Christ) and *temporary* (they will be grafted back; 11:23–27). Paul appropriately quotes frequently from the Old Testament in this section, and he emphasizes that God will be faithful to His covenant promises and restore Israel.

The Application of the Righteousness of God (12—16): Paul recognizes that behavior must be built upon belief, and this is why the practical exhortations of this epistle appear after his teaching on the believer's position in Christ. The salvation described in the first eleven chapters should transform a Christian's life in relation to God (12:1–2), society (12:3–21), higher powers (13:1–7), and one's neighbors (13:8–14). In chapters 14—15 the apostle discusses the whole concept of Christian liberty, noting its principles (14) and its practice (15:1–13). A changed life is not a condition for salvation, but it should be the natural outcome of saving faith. The epistle closes with Paul's statement of his plans (15:14–33), a long series of personal greetings (16:1–16), and an admonition followed by a doxology (16:17–27).

Outline of Romans

Part One: The Revelation of the Righteousness of God (1:1—8:39)

   I. Introduction, 1:1–17

   II. Condemnation: The Need for God's Righteousness, 1:18—3:20
- A. Guilt of the Gentile, 1:18–32
  1. Reason for Gentile Guilt, 1:18–23
  2. Results of Gentile Guilt, 1:24–32
- B. Guilt of the Jew, 2:1—3:8
  1. Jews Are Judged According to Truth, 2:1–5
  2. Jews Are Judged by Their Works, 2:6–10
  3. Jews Are Judged with Impartiality, 2:11–16
  4. Jews Do Not Obey the Law, 2:17–29
  5. Jews Do Not Believe the Oracles, 3:1–8
- C. Conclusion: All Are Guilty before God, 3:9–20

   III. Justification: The Imputation of God's Righteousness, 3:21—5:21
- A. Description of Righteousness, 3:21–31
- B. Illustration of Righteousness, 4:1–25
  1. Abraham's Righteousness Apart from Works, 4:1–8
  2. Abraham's Righteousness Apart from Circumcision, 4:9–12
  3. Abraham's Righteousness Apart from the Law, 4:13–15
  4. Abraham's Righteousness Was by Faith, 4:16–25
- C. Benefits of Righteousness, 5:1–11
  1. Peace with God, 5:1–2
  2. Joy in Tribulation, 5:3–8
  3. Salvation from God's Wrath, 5:9–11
- D. Contrast of Righteousness and Condemnation, 5:12–21

IV. Sanctification: The Demonstration of God's Righteousness, 6:1—8:39
  A. Sanctification and Sin, 6:1–23
    1. Believer's Death to Sin in Principle, 6:1–14
    2. Believer's Death to Sin in Practice, 6:15–23
  B. Sanctification and the Law, 7:1–25
    1. Dead to the Law but Alive to God, 7:1–6
    2. Law Cannot Deliver from Sin, 7:7–25
  C. Sanctification and the Spirit, 8:1–39
    1. The Spirit Delivers from the Power of the Flesh, 8:1–11
    2. The Spirit Gives Sonship, 8:12–17
    3. The Spirit Assures of Future Glory, 8:18–30
    4. The Spirit Assures of Final Victory, 8:31–39

Part Two: The Vindication of the Righteousness of God (9:1—11:36)

I. Israel's Past: The Election of God, 9:1–29
  A. Paul's Sorrow, 9:1–5
  B. God's Sovereignty, 9:6–29

II. Israel's Present: The Rejection of God, 9:30—10:21
  A. Israel Seeks Righteousness by Works, 9:30–33
  B. Israel Rejects Christ, 10:1–15
  C. Israel Rejects the Prophets, 10:16–21

III. Israel's Future: The Restoration by God, 11:1–36
  A. Israel's Rejection Is Not Total, 11:1–10
  B. Israel's Rejection Is Not Final, 11:11–32
    1. Purpose of Israel's Rejection, 11:11–24
    2. Promise of Israel's Restoration, 11:25–32
  C. Israel's Restoration: The Occasion for Glorifying God, 11:33–36

Part Three: The Application of the Righteousness of God (12:1—16:27)

I. Righteousness of God Demonstrated in Christian Duties, 12:1—13:14
  A. Responsibilities Toward God, 12:1–2
  B. Responsibilities Toward Society, 12:3–21
  C. Responsibilities Toward Higher Powers, 13:1–7
  D. Responsibilities Toward Neighbors, 13:8–14

II. Righteousness of God Demonstrated in Christian Liberties, 14:1—15:13
  A. Principles of Christian Liberty, 14:1–23
  B. Practices of Christian Liberty, 15:1–13

III. Conclusion, 15:14—16:27
  A. Paul's Purposes for Writing, 15:14–21
  B. Paul's Plans for Traveling, 15:22–33
  C. Paul's Praise and Greetings, 16:1–27

First Corinthians

FIRST-CENTURY CORINTH WAS the leading commercial center of southern Greece. The city was infamous for its immorality and paganism. But in spite of great obstacles, Paul was able to plant a Christian church there on his second missionary journey (Acts 18:1–17). Though gifted and growing, the church was plagued with problems: moral and ethical, doctrinal and practical, corporate and private. Paul writes the letter of First Corinthians to deal with some of these disorders, and to answer questions which the Christians in Corinth had raised on crucial issues.

FIRST CORINTHIANS	Focus	Answer to Chloe's Report of Divisions		Answer to Report of Fornication			Answer to Letter of Questions				
		1:1 4:21		5:1 6:20			7:1 16:24				
	Divisions	Report of Divisions	Reason for Divisions	Incest	Litigation between Believers	Sexual Immorality	Counsel Concerning Marriage	Counsel Concerning Things Offered to Idols	Counsel Concerning Public Worship	Counsel Concerning Resurrection	Counsel Concerning Collection for Jerusalem
		1:1 1:17	1:18 4:21	5:1 5:13	6:1 6:11	6:12 6:20	7:1 7:40	8:1 11:1	11:2 14:40	15:1 15:50	16:1 16:24
	Topics	Divisions in the Church		Disorder in the Church			Difficulties in the Church				
		Concern		Condemnation			Counsel				
	Place	Written in Ephesus									
	Time	c. A.D. 56									

Introduction and Title

Corinth, the most important city in Greece during Paul's day, was a bustling hub of worldwide commerce, degraded culture, and idolatrous religion. There Paul founded a church (Acts 18:1–17), and two of his letters are addressed "To the church of God which is at Corinth."

First Corinthians reveals the problems, pressures, and struggles of a church called out of a pagan society. Paul addresses a variety of problems in the life-style of the Corinthian church: factions, lawsuits, immorality, questionable practices, abuse of the Lord's Supper and spiritual gifts. In addition to words of discipline, Paul shares words of counsel in answer to questions raised by the Corinthian believers.

The oldest recorded title of this epistle is *Pros Korinthious A,* in effect, the "First to the Corinthians." The *A* was no doubt a later addition to distinguish this book from Second Corinthians.

Author

Pauline authorship of First Corinthians is almost universally accepted. Instances of this widely held belief can be found as early as A.D. 95, when Clement of Rome wrote to the Corinthian church and cited this epistle in regard to their continuing problem of factions among themselves.

Date and Setting

Corinth was a key city in ancient Greece until it was destroyed by the Romans in 146 B.C. Julius Caesar rebuilt it as a Roman colony in 46 B.C. and it grew and prospered, becoming the capital of the province of Achaia. Its official language was Latin, but the common language remained Greek. In Paul's day Corinth was the metropolis of the Peloponnesus since it was strategically located on a narrow isthmus between the Aegean Sea and the Adriatic Sea that connects the Peloponnesus with northern Greece. Because of its two seaports it became a commercial center, and many small ships were rolled or dragged across the Corinthian isthmus to avoid the dangerous 200-mile voyage around southern Greece. Nero and others attempted to build a canal at the narrowest point, but this was not achieved until 1893. The city was filled with shrines and temples, but the most prominent was the Temple of Aphrodite on top of an 1,800-foot promontory called the Acrocorinthus. Worshipers of the "goddess of love" made free use of the 1,000 Hieroduli (consecrated prostitutes). This cosmopolitan center thrived on commerce, entertainment, vice, and corruption; pleasure-seekers came there to spend money on a holiday from morality. Corinth became so notorious for its evils that the term *Korinthiazomai* ("to act like a Corinthian") became a synonym for debauchery and prostitution.

In Paul's day the population of Corinth was approximately 700,000, about two-thirds of whom were slaves. The diverse population produced no philosophers, but Greek philosophy influenced any speculative thought that was there. In spite of these obstacles to the gospel, Paul was able to establish a church in Corinth on his second missionary journey (3:6, 10; 4:15; Acts 18:1–7). Persecution in Macedonia drove him south to Athens, and from there he proceeded to Corinth. He made tents with Aquila and Priscilla and reasoned with the Jews in the synagogue. Silas and Timothy joined him (they evidently brought a gift from Philippi; see 2 Cor. 11:8–9; Phil. 4:15), and Paul began to devote all his time to spreading the gospel. Paul wrote First and Second Thessalonians, moved his ministry from the synagogue to the house of Titius Justus because of opposition, and converted Crispus, the leader of the synagogue. Paul taught the Word of God in Corinth for eighteen months in A.D. 51–52. After Paul's departure, Apollos came from Ephesus to minister in the Corinthian church (3:6; Acts 18:24–28).

When Paul was teaching and preaching in Ephesus during his third missionary journey, he was disturbed by reports from the household of Chloe concerning quarrels in the church at Corinth (1:11). The church sent a delegation of three men (16:17), who apparently brought a letter that requested Paul's judgment on certain issues (7:1). Paul wrote this epistle as his response to the problems and questions of the Corinthians (he had already written a previous letter; 5:9). It may be that the men who came from Corinth took this letter back with them. Paul was planning to leave Ephesus (16:5–8), indicating that First Corinthians was written in A.D. 56.

Themes and Purpose

The basic theme of this epistle is the application of Christian principles on an individual and social level. The Cross of Christ is a message that is designed to transform the lives of believers and make them different, as people and as a corporate body, from the surrounding world. But the Corinthians were destroying their Christian testimony because of immorality and disunity. Paul wrote this letter as his corrective response to the news of problems and disorders among the Corinthians. It was designed to refute improper attitudes and conduct and to promote a spirit of unity among the brethren in their relationships and worship. Paul's concern as their spiritual father (4:14–15) was tempered with love, and he wanted to avoid visiting them "with a rod" (4:21).

Keys to First Corinthians

Key Word: Correction

Key Verses (6:19–20; 10:12–13)—"Or do you not know that your body is the temple of the Holy Spirit *who is* in you, whom you have from God, and you are not your own? For you were bought at a price; therefore glorify God in your body and in your spirit, which are God's" (6:19–20).

"Therefore let him who thinks he stands take heed lest he fall. No temptation has overtaken you except such as is common to man; but God *is* faithful, who will not allow you to be tempted beyond what you are able, but with the temptation will also make the way of escape, that you may be able to bear *it*" (10:12–13).

Key Chapter (13)—Read at weddings and often the text for sermons, First Corinthians, chapter 13, has won the hearts of people across the world as the best definition of "love" ever penned. Standing in stark contrast to the idea that love is an emotion or that one can fall into or fall out of love, this chapter clearly reveals that true love is primarily action. This is why when "God so loved the world that He gave . . ." (John 3:16).

Christ in First Corinthians

This book proclaims the relevance of Christ Jesus to every area of the believer's life. He "became for us wisdom from God—and righteousness and sanctification and redemption—" (1:30), and these are the themes Paul addresses in this epistle.

Contribution to the Bible

This epistle is extremely practical in its thrust, and it focuses on basic social, moral, and spiritual issues. Unlike Romans, First Corinthians is not rhetorically elegant; it is plain, earnest, and unvarnished. The unusual simplicity and directness of this letter is appropriate to the practical content. The sentences are uncomplicated, and Paul forcefully amplifies his thoughts with abundant literary devices (narrative, sarcasm, appeal, etc.). Although it is informal, First Corinthians makes several important contributions to New Testament doctrine. This is particularly true of the doctrines of the church as an organism, the role of spiritual gifts, and the Resurrection.

No other epistle gives a better look at the problems and conditions in an apostolic church. Even though planted and nurtured by Paul himself, the church at Corinth bristled with social, ethical, spiritual, and doctrinal problems. This was a difficult letter for Paul to write, but his profound wisdom and insight dominate its pages and reveal the apostle's patient love and self-control.

The wide variety of subjects discussed in this long epistle (only Romans is longer) is easy to follow because of its logical and orderly development.

Survey of First Corinthians

Through the missionary efforts of Paul and others, the church has been established in Corinth, but Paul finds it very difficult to keep Corinth out of the church. The pagan life-style of Corinth exerts a profound influence upon the Christians in that corrupt city—problems of every kind plague them. In this disciplinary letter, Paul is forced to exercise his apostolic authority as he deals firmly with problems of divisiveness, immorality, lawsuits, selfishness, abuses of the Lord's Supper and spiritual gifts, and denials of the Resurrection. This epistle is quite orderly in its approach as it sequentially addresses a group of problems that have come to Paul's attention. Paul also gives a series of perspectives on various questions and issues raised by the Corinthians in a letter. He uses the introductory phrase "Now concerning" or "Now . . . " to delineate those topics (7:1, 25; 8:1; 11:2; 12:1; 16:1). The three divisions of First Corinthians are: (1) Answer to Chloe's report of divisions (1—4); (2) answer to report of fornication (5—6); and (3) answer to letter of questions (7—16).

Answer to Chloe's Report of Divisions (1—4): Personality cults centering around Paul, Apollos, and Peter have led to divisions and false pride among the Corinthians (1). It is not their wisdom or cleverness that has brought them to Christ, because divine wisdom is contrary to human wisdom. The truth of the gospel is spiritually apprehended (2). Factions that exist among the saints at Corinth are indications of their spiritual immaturity (3). They should pride themselves in Christ, not in human leaders who are merely His servants (4).

Answer To Report of Fornication (5—6): The next problem Paul addresses is that of incest between a member of the church and his stepmother (5). The Corinthians have exercised no church discipline in this matter, and Paul orders them to remove the offender from their fellowship until he repents. Another source of poor testimony is the legal action of believer against believer in civil courts (6:1–8). They must learn to arbitrate their differences within the Christian community. Paul concludes this section with a warning against immorality in general (6:9–20).

Answer To Letter of Questions (7—16): In these chapters the apostle Paul gives authoritative answers to thorny questions raised by the Corinthians. His first counsel concerns the issues of marriage, celibacy, divorce, and remarriage (7). The next three chapters are related to the problem of meat offered to idols (8:1—11:1). Paul illustrates from his own life the twin principles of Christian liberty and the law of love, and he concludes that believers must sometimes limit their liberty for the sake of weaker brothers (cf. Rom. 14). The apostle then turns to matters concerning public worship, including improper observance of the Lord's Supper and the selfish use of spiritual gifts (11:2—14:40). Gifts are to be exercised in love for the edification of the whole body. The Corinthians also have problems with the Resurrection, which Paul seeks to correct (15). His historical and theological defense of the Resurrection includes teaching on the nature of the resurrection body. The Corinthians probably have been struggling over this issue because the idea of a resurrected body is disdainful in Greek thought. The epistle closes with Paul's instruction for the collection he will make for the saints in Jerusalem (16:1–4), followed by miscellaneous exhortations and greetings (16:5–24).

Outline of First Corinthians

Part One: In Answer to Chloe's Report of Divisions (1:1—4:21)

I. **Introduction,** 1:1–9
   A. Greetings of Grace, 1:1–3
   B. Prayer of Thanksgiving, 1:4–9

II. **Report of Divisions,** 1:10–17

III. **Reasons for Divisions,** 1:18—4:21
   A. Misunderstanding of the Gospel Message, 1:18—3:4
      1. The Gospel Is Not Earthly Wisdom, 1:18—2:5
      2. The Gospel Is Heavenly Wisdom, 2:6—3:4
   B. Misunderstanding of the Gospel Messenger, 3:5—4:5
      1. Ministers Are Fellow Workers with God, 3:5–17
      2. Ministers Are Accountable to God, 3:18—4:5
   C. Misunderstanding of Paul's Ministry, 4:6–21

Part Two: In Answer to Reports of Fornication (5:1—6:20)

I. On Incest, 5:1–13
  A. Deliver the Fornicators for Discipline, 5:1–8
  B. Separate Yourselves from Immoral Believers, 5:9–13

II. Concerning Litigation between Believers, 6:1–11

III. Warning against Sexual Immorality, 6:12–20

Part Three: In Answer to the Letter of Questions (7:1—16:24)

I. Counsel Concerning Marriage, 7:1–40
  A. Principles for Married Life, 7:1–9
  B. Principles for the Married Believer, 7:10–16
  C. Principle of Abiding in God's Call, 7:17–24
  D. Principles for the Unmarried, 7:25–38
  E. Principles for Remarriage, 7:39–40

II. Counsel Concerning Things Offered to Idols, 8:1—11:1
  A. Principles of Liberty and the Weaker Brother, 8:1–13
  B. Illustration of Paul and His Liberty, 9:1–27
    1. Paul Lists His Rights as a Minister, 9:1–14
    2. Paul Limits His Rights for Ministry, 9:15–27
  C. Warning against Forfeiting Liberty, 10:1–13
  D. Exhortation to Use Liberty to Glorify God, 10:14—11:1

III. Counsel Concerning Public Worship, 11:2—14:40
  A. Principles of Public Prayer, 11:2–16
  B. Rebuke of Disorders at the Lord's Supper, 11:17–34
  C. Principles of Exercising Spiritual Gifts, 12:1—14:40
    1. Test of the Spirit's Control, 12:1–3
    2. Diversity of the Gifts, 12:4–11
    3. Importance of All Gifts, 12:12–31
    4. Exercise Gifts with Love, 13:1–13
    5. Superiority of Prophecy, 14:1–6
    6. Gift of Tongues, 14:7–25
    7. Exercising Gifts in Public Worship, 14:26–40

IV. Counsel Concerning the Resurrection, 15:1–58
  A. Fact of Christ's Resurrection, 15:1–11
  B. Importance of Christ's Resurrection, 15:12–19
  C. Order of the Resurrections, 15:20–28
  D. Moral Implications of Christ's Resurrection, 15:29–34
  E. Bodies of the Resurrected Dead, 15:35–50
  F. Bodies of the Translated Living, 15:51–58

V. Counsel Concerning the Collection for Jerusalem, 16:1–4

VI. Conclusion, 16:5–24

Second Corinthians

SINCE PAUL'S FIRST LETTER, the Corinthian church had been swayed by false teachers who stirred the people against Paul. They claimed he was fickle, proud, unimpressive in appearance and speech, dishonest, and unqualified as an apostle of Jesus Christ. Paul sent Titus to Corinth to deal with these difficulties, and upon his return, rejoiced to hear of the Corinthians' change of heart. Paul wrote this letter to express his thanksgiving for the repentant majority, and to appeal to the rebellious minority to accept his authority.

Focus	Explanation of Paul's Ministry			Collection for the Saints		Vindication of Paul's Apostleship		
	1:1 · · · 7:16			8:1 · · · 9:15		10:1 · · · 13:14		
Divisions	Paul's Explanation of His Change of Plans	Paul's Philosophy of Ministry	Paul's Exhortations to the Corinthians	Example of the Macedonians	Exhortation to the Corinthians	Paul Answers His Accusers	Paul Defends His Apostleship	Paul Announces His Upcoming Visit
	1:1 2:13	2:14 6:10	6:11 7:16	8:1 8:6	8:7 9:15	10:1 10:18	11:1 12:13	12:14 13:14
Topics	Character of Paul			Collection for Saints		Credentials of Paul		
	Ephesus to Macedonia: Change of Itinerary			Macedonia: Preparation for Visit to Corinth		To Corinth: Imminence of Paul's Visit		
Place	Written in Macedonia							
Time	C. A.D. 56							

Introduction and Title

Since Paul's first letter, the Corinthian church had been swayed by false teachers who stirred the people against Paul. They claimed he was fickle, proud, unimpressive in appearance and speech, dishonest, and unqualified as an apostle of Jesus Christ. Paul sent Titus to Corinth to deal with these difficulties, and upon his return, rejoiced to hear of the Corinthians' change of heart. Paul wrote this letter to express his thanksgiving for the repentant majority and to appeal to the rebellious minority to accept his authority. Throughout the book he defends his conduct, character, and calling as an apostle of Jesus Christ.

To distinguish this epistle from First Corinthians, it was given the title *Pros Korinthious B*, the "Second to the Corinthians." The A and B were probably later additions to *Pros Korinthious*.

Author

External and internal evidence amply support the Pauline authorship of this letter. As with Romans, the problem of Second Corinthians is with its lack of unity, not with its authorship. Many critics theorize that chapters 10—13 were not a part of this letter in its original form because their tone contrasts with that of chapters 1—9. It is held that the sudden change from a spirit of joy and comfort to a spirit of concern and self-defense points to a "seam" between two different letters. Many hypotheses have been advanced to explain the problem, but the most popular is that chapters 10—13 belong to a lost letter referred to in chapter 2, verse 4. Several problems arise with these attempts to dissect Second Corinthians. Chapters 10—13 do not fit Paul's description of the "lost" letter of chapter 2 because they are firm but not sorrowful and because they do not refer to the offender about whom that letter was written (2:5–11). Also, this earlier material would have been appended at the beginning of Second Corinthians, not at the end. There is simply no external (manuscripts, church fathers, tradition) or internal basis for challenging the unity of this epistle. The difference in tone between chapters 1—9 and chapters 10—13 is easily explained by the change of focus from the repentant majority to the rebellious minority.

Date and Setting

Part of the background of Second Corinthians can be found in "Date and Setting" in First Corinthians. Paul was in Ephesus when he wrote First Corinthians and expected Timothy to visit Corinth and return to him (1 Cor. 16:10–11). Timothy apparently brought Paul a report of the opposition that had developed against him in Corinth, and Paul made a brief and painful visit to the Corinthians (this visit is not mentioned in Acts, but it can be inferred from 2 Cor. 2:1; 12:14; 13:1–2). Upon returning to Ephesus, Paul regretfully wrote his sorrowful letter to urge the church to discipline the leader of the opposition (2:1–11; 7:8). Titus carried this letter. Paul, anxious to learn the results, went to Troas and then to Macedonia to meet Titus on his return trip (2:12–13; 7:5–16). Paul was greatly relieved by Titus' report that the majority of the Corinthians had repented of their rebelliousness against Paul's apostolic authority. However, a minority opposition still persisted, evidently led by a group of Judaizers (10—13). There in Macedonia Paul wrote Second Corinthians and sent it with Titus and another brother (8:16–24). This took place late in A.D. 56, and the Macedonian city from which it was written may have been Philippi. Paul then made his third trip to Corinth (12:14; 13:1–2; Acts 20:1–3) where he wrote his letter to the Romans.

There is an alternate view that the anguished letter (2:4 and 7:8) is in fact First Corinthians and not a lost letter. This would require that the offender (2:5–11; 7:12) be identified with the offender of First Corinthians 5.

Theme and Purpose

The major theme of Second Corinthians is Paul's defense of his apostolic credentials and authority. This is especially evident in the portion directed to the still rebellious minority (10—13), but the theme of vindication is also clear in chapters 1—9. Certain "false apostles" mounted an effective campaign against Paul in the church at Corinth, and Paul had to take a number of steps to overcome the opposition. This epistle expresses the apostle's joy over the triumph of the true gospel in Corinth (1—7), and it acknowledges the "godly sorrow" and repentance of the bulk of the believers there. It also urges the Corinthians to fulfill their promise of making a liberal contribution for the poor among the Christians in Judea (8—9). This collection would not only assist the poor, but it would also demonstrate the concern of Gentile Christians in Macedonia and Achaia for Jewish Christians in Judea, thus displaying the unity of Jews and Gentiles in the body of Christ.

The opposition addressed in 10—13 apparently consisted of Jews (Palestinean or Hellenistic; 11:22) who claimed to be apostles (11:5,13; 12:11) but who preached a false gospel (11:4) and were enslaving in their leadership (11:20). Chapters 10—13 were written to expose these "deceitful workers" and defend Paul's God-given authority and ministry as an apostle of Jesus Christ.

Keys to Second Corinthians

Key Word: Paul's Defense of His Authority

Key Verses (4:5–6; 5:17–19)—"For we do not preach ourselves, but Christ Jesus the Lord, and ourselves your servants for Jesus' sake. For it is the God who commanded light to shine out of darkness who has shone in our hearts to *give* the light of the knowledge of the glory of God in the face of Jesus Christ" (4:5–6).

"Therefore, if anyone is in Christ, *he is* a new creation; old things have passed away; behold, all things have become new. Now all things *are* of God, who has reconciled us to Himself through Jesus Christ, and has given us the ministry of reconciliation, that is, that God was in Christ reconciling the world to Himself, not imputing their trespasses to them, and has committed to us the word of reconciliation" (5:17–19).

Key Chapters (8—9)—Chapters 8—9 are really one unit and comprise the most complete revelation of God's plan for giving found anywhere in the Scriptures. Contained therein are the principles for giving (8:1–6), the purposes for giving (8:7–15), the policies to be followed in giving (8:16—9:5), and the promises to be realized in giving (9:6–15).

Christ in Second Corinthians

Christ is presented as the believer's comfort (1:5), triumph (2:14), Lord (4:5), light (4:6), judge (5:10), reconciliation (5:19), substitute (5:21), gift (9:15), owner (10:7), and power (12:9).

Contribution to the Bible

This epistle is full of autobiographical material and many regard it as the most personal book in the New Testament. The mind of Paul is prominent in Romans, but Second Corinthians reveals the apostle's heart. His character, motives, priorities, desires, and emotions are exposed more clearly in this epistle than in any other. The personal anecdotes offer a glimpse into aspects of Paul's personal life that would otherwise be unknown. These include persecution and hardships not recorded in Acts (11:23–27), extra details of his escape from Damascus (11:32–33), his vision and revelation of Paradise (12:1–7), and his thorn in the flesh (12:7–10).

The language of this epistle is characterized by unusual constructions, broken sentences, mixed metaphors, and sudden shifts in feeling and tone. Paul's emotional stress can also be seen in the many digressions; Second Corinthians is perhaps the most unsystematic of all his writings. Nevertheless, this book makes important doctrinal contributions to the Bible. In it, Paul contrasts the old and the new covenants (3), explains the supernatural warfare over the reception of the gospel (4:1–7), gives a proper perspective on suffering for Christ (4:8–18), contributes new insights on the resurrection and judgment of Christians (5:1–13), describes the ministry of reconciliation and the double imputation of Christ (5:14–21), affirms the importance of separation from the ways of the world (6:14—7:1), offers the most thorough biblical perspective on Christian giving (8—9), and exposes the strategies of Satan (2:10–11; 4:4; 11:3, 13–15; 12:7).

Survey of Second Corinthians

Second Corinthians describes the anatomy of an apostle. The Corinthian church has been swayed by false teachers who have stirred the people against Paul, especially in response to First Corinthians, Paul's disciplinary letter. Throughout this letter (Second Corinthians) Paul defends his apostolic conduct, character, and call. The three major sections are: (1) Paul's explanation of his ministry (1—7); (2) Paul's collection for the saints (8—9); and (3) Paul's vindication of his apostleship (10—13).

Paul's Explanation of His Ministry (1—7): After his salutation and thanksgiving for God's comfort in his afflictions and perils (1:1–11), Paul explains why he has delayed his planned visit to Corinth. It is not a matter of vacillation: the apostle wants them to have enough time to repent (1:12—2:4). Paul graciously asks them to restore the repentant offender to fellowship (2:5–13). At this point, Paul embarks on an extended defense of his ministry in terms of his message, circumstances, motives, and conduct (2:14—6:10). He then admonishes the believers to separate themselves from defilement (6:11—7:1), and expresses his comfort at Titus' news of their change of heart (7:2–16).

Paul's Collection for the Saints (8—9): This is the longest discussion of the principles and practice of giving in the New Testament. The example of the Macedonians' liberal giving for the needy brethren in Jerusalem (8:1–6) is followed by an appeal to the Corinthians to keep their promise by doing the same (8:7—9:15). In this connection, Paul commends the messengers he has sent to Corinth to make arrangements for the large gift they have promised. Their generosity will be more than amply rewarded by God.

Paul's Vindication of His Apostleship (10—13): Paul concludes this epistle with a defense of his apostolic authority and credentials that is directed to the still rebellious minority in the Corinthian Church. His meekness in their presence in no way diminishes his authority as an apostle (10). To demonstrate his apostolic credentials, Paul is forced to boast about his knowledge, integrity, accomplishments, sufferings, visions, and miracles (11:1—12:13). He reveals his plans to visit them for the third time and urges them to repent so that he will not have to use severity when he comes (12:14—13:10). The letter ends with an exhortation, greetings, and a benediction (13:11–14).

Outline of Second Corinthians

Part One: Paul's Explanation of His Ministry (1:1—7:16)

I. **Introduction,** 1:1–11
  - A. Paul's Thanksgiving to God, 1:1–7
  - B. Paul's Trouble in Asia, 1:8–11

II. **Paul's Explanation of His Change of Plans,** 1:12—2:13
  - A. Paul's Original Plan, 1:12–22
  - B. Paul's Change of Plans, 1:23—2:4
  - C. Paul's Appeal to Forgive, 2:5–13

III. **Paul's Philosophy of Ministry,** 2:14—6:10
  - A. Christ Causes Us to Triumph, 2:14–17
  - B. Changed Lives Prove Ministry, 3:1–5
  - C. New Covenant Is the Basis of Ministry, 3:6–18
  - D. Christ Is the Theme of Ministry, 4:1–7
  - E. Trials Abound in the Ministry, 4:8–15
  - F. Motivation in the Ministry, 4:16—5:21
    1. Motivation of External Perspective, 4:16–18
    2. Motivation of the Future Presence of Christ, 5:1–8
    3. Motivation of Future Reward, 5:9–10

    4. Motivation of the Love of Christ, 5:11–16
    5. Motivation of the Message of Reconciliation, 5:17–21
  G. Giving No Offense in the Ministry, 6:1–10

IV. Paul's Exhortations to the Corinthians, 6:11—7:16
  A. Paul's Appeal for Reconciliation, 6:11–13
  B. Paul's Appeal for Separation from Unbelievers, 6:14—7:1
  C. Paul's Meeting with Titus, 7:2–7
  D. Corinthians' Response to Paul's Letter, 7:8–16

Part Two: Paul's Collection for the Saints (8:1—9:15)

I. Example of the Macedonians, 8:1–6

II. Exhortation to the Corinthians, 8:7—9:15
  A. Example of Christ, 8:7–9
  B. Purpose of Giving, 8:10–15
  C. Explanation of the Delegation, 8:16—9:5
    1. Policies in Giving, 8:16–24
    2. Readiness in Giving, 9:1–5
  D. Exhortation to Giving, 9:6–15
    1. Principles in Giving, 9:6–7
    2. Promises Giving, 9:8–15

Part Three: Paul's Vindication of His Apostleship (10:1—13:14)

I. Paul Answers His Accusers, 10:1–18
  A. The Charge of Cowardice Is Answered, 10:1–2
  B. The Charge of Walking in the Flesh Is Answered, 10:3–9
  C. The Charge of Personal Weakness Is Answered, 10:10–18

II. Paul Defends His Apostleship, 11:1—12:13
  A. Paul's Declaration of His Apostleship, 11:1–15
  B. Paul's Sufferings Support His Apostleship, 11:16–33
  C. Paul's Revelations Support His Apostleship, 12:1–10
    1. Vision of Paradise, 12:1–6
    2. Thorn in the Flesh, 12:7–10
  D. Paul's Signs Support His Apostleship, 12:11–13

III. Paul Announces His Upcoming Visit, 12:14—13:10
  A. Paul's Concern Not to Be a Financial Burden, 12:14–18
  B. Paul's Concern Not to Find Them Carnal, 12:19–21
  C. Paul's Warning To Examine Yourselves, 13:1–10

IV. Conclusion, 13:11–14

Galatians

THE EPISTLE TO THE GALATIANS has been called "the charter of Christian liberty." It is Paul's manifesto of justification by faith and the liberty it produces. Paul directs this great charter of Christian freedom to a people who are willing to give up the priceless liberty they possess in Christ. Certain Jewish legalists are influencing the believers in Galatia to trade their freedom in Christ for bondage to the Law. Paul writes to refute their false gospel of works, and to demonstrate the superiority of justification by faith.

GALATIANS	Focus	Gospel of Grace Defended		Gospel of Grace Explained			Gospel of Grace Applied		
		1:1 2:21		3:1 4:31			5:1 6:18		
	Divisions	Paul's Apostleship	Paul's Authority	Justification by Faith Not Works	Justification by Faith Not the Law	Law and Grace Cannot Co-exist	Position and Practice of Liberty	Power for Liberty	Performance in Liberty: Fruits of the Spirit
		1:1 1:24	2:1 2:21	3:1 3:9	3:10 4:20	4:21 4:31	5:1 5:15	5:16 5:26	6:1 6:18
	Topics	Biographical Explanation		Doctrinal Exposition			Practical Exhortation		
		Authentication of Liberty		Argumentation for Liberty			Application of Liberty		
	Place	South Galatian Theory: Syrian Antioch North Galatian Theory: Ephesus or Macedonia							
	Time	South Galatian Theory: A.D. 49 North Galatian Theory: A.D. 53–56							

Introduction and Title

The Galatians, having launched their Christian experience by faith, seem content to leave their voyage of faith and chart a new course based on works—a course Paul finds disturbing. His letter to the Galatians is a vigorous attack against the gospel of works, and a defense of the gospel of faith.

Paul begins by setting forth his credentials as an apostle with a message from God: blessing comes from God on the basis of *faith*, not *law*. The law declares men guilty and imprisons them; faith sets men free to enjoy liberty in Christ. But liberty is not license. Freedom in Christ means freedom to produce the fruits of righteousness through a Spirit-led lifestyle.

The book is called *Pros Galatas*, "To the Galatians," and it is the only letter of Paul that is specifically addressed to a number of churches ("To the churches of Galatia" in 1:2). The name *Galatians* was given to this Celtic people because they originally lived in Gaul before their migration to Asia Minor.

Author

The Pauline authorship and the unity of this epistle are virtually unchallenged. The first verse clearly identifies the author as "Paul, an apostle." Also in chapter 5, verse 2, we read, "Indeed I, Paul, say to you." In fact, Paul actually wrote Galatians (6:11) instead of dictating it to a secretary, as was his usual practice.

Date and Setting

The term *Galatia* was used in an ethnographic sense (that is cultural and geographic origin) and in a political sense. The original ethnographic sense refers to the central part of Asia Minor where these Celtic tribes eventually settled after their conflicts with the Romans and Macedonians. Later, in 189 B.C. Galatia came under Roman domination, and in 25 B.C. Augustus declared it a Roman province. The political or provincial Galatia included territory to the south that was not originally considered part of Galatia (e.g., the cities of Pisidian Antioch, Iconium, Lystra, and Derbe). There are two theories regarding the date and setting of Galatians.

The *North Galatian Theory* holds that Paul was speaking of Galatia in its earlier, more restricted sense. According to this theory, the churches of Galatia were north of the cities Paul visited on his first missionary journey. Paul visited the ethnographic Galatia (the smaller region to the North) for the first time on his second missionary journey, probably while he was on his way to Troas (Acts 16:6). On his third missionary journey, Paul revisited the Galatian churches he had established (Acts 18:23) and wrote this epistle either in Ephesus (A.D. 53–56) or in Macedonia (A.D. 56). This theory is supported by the church fathers, but this may be due to the exclusive use of the ethnographic sense of Galatia by the second century. Advocates of this view also point to Luke's apparent use of Galatia in the northern sense (Acts 16:6; 18:23). Similarities between Galatians and Romans (written in A.D. 57) also help to support this late-date theory for Galatians. But it is hurt by the fact that Acts does not say

Paul evangelized in North Galatia. In fact, he would have had to have taken a radical detour to the northeast on his second missionary journey to do so, whereas no such detour would have been necessary if he went to South Galatia.

According to the *South Galatian Theory,* Paul was referring to Galatia in its wider political sense as a province of Rome. This means that the churches he had in mind in this epistle were in the cities he evangelized during his first missionary journey with Barnabas (Acts 13:13—14:23). This was just prior to the Jerusalem Council (Acts 15), so the Jerusalem visit in Galatians 2:1–10 must have been the Acts 11:27–30 famine-relief visit. Galatians was probably written in Syrian Antioch in A.D. 49 just before Paul went to the Council in Jerusalem. This theory is supported in several ways: (1) Paul consistently referred to geography in the political sense in his epistles. (2) If Galatians was written after the Jerusalem Council as the North Galatian theory holds, it is probable that Paul would have referred to that authoritative decree to bolster his argument in this epistle, yet it is not mentioned. (3) It is unlikely that Peter would have acted as he did (Gal. 2:11–21) after the Jerusalem Council. (4) This theory fits against the background in Acts 13—14, but the North Galatian theory has no corresponding background. (5) The South Galatian cities that Paul visited were more strategic from an evangelistic point of view than those in the North because of their location, population, and commerce. (6) Barnabas (mentioned three times in 2) would have been more familiar to the South Galatian churches than to the North Galatian churches because he was not with Paul on his second missionary journey, when the churches in North Galatia were supposedly established.

Paul wrote this epistle in response to a report that the Galatian churches were suddenly taken over by the false teaching of certain Judaizers who professed Jesus yet sought to place Gentile converts under the requirements of the Mosaic Law (1:7; 4:17, 21; 5:2–12; 6:12–13).

Theme and Purpose

Justification by faith apart from works of the Law is the theme of this urgent and corrective book. The three major sections reveal three purposes for which Galatians was written: Chapters 1—2 were written to defend Paul's apostolic authority, because this establishes his gospel message. Chapters 3—4 were written to give a theological defense of the principle of justification by faith to refute the false teaching of justification by law. Paul used the Law itself to build his case. Chapters 5—6 were written to show that liberty from the Law does not mean lawlessness, as Paul's opponents evidently claimed. This epistle shows that the believer is no longer under the Law but is saved by faith alone. It has been said that Judaism was the cradle of Christianity, but also that it was very nearly its grave as well. God raised up Paul as the Moses of the Christian church to deliver them from this bondage. Galatians is the Christian's Declaration of Independence. The power of the Holy Spirit enables the Christian to enjoy freedom within the law of love.

Keys to Galatians

Key Word: Freedom from the Law

Key Verses (2:20–21; 5:1)—"I have been crucified with Christ; it is no longer I who live, but Christ lives in me; and the *life* which I now live in the flesh I live by faith in the Son of God, who loved me and gave Himself for me. I do not set aside the grace of God; for if righteousness *comes* through the law, then Christ died in vain" (2:20–21).

"Stand fast therefore in the liberty by which Christ has made us free, and do not be entangled again with a yoke of bondage" (5:1).

Key Chapter (5)—The impact of the truth concerning freedom is staggering: freedom must not be used "as an opportunity for the flesh" but "through love serve one another" (5:13). This chapter records the power, "Walk in the Spirit" (5:16) and the results, "The fruit of the Spirit" (5:22), of that freedom.

Christ in Galatians

Christ has freed the believer from bondage to the Law (legalism) and to sin (license) and has placed him in a position of liberty. The transforming Cross provides for the believer's deliverance from the curse of sin, law, and self (1:4; 2:20; 3:13; 4:5; 5:24; 6:14).

Contribution to the Bible

Although Galatians and Romans have several themes in common, the polemic tone of Galatians stands in contrast to the irenic tone of Romans. Galatians is written in the sharp language of conflict, its severe words reflecting the urgency of the crisis that had so quickly come upon the believers in that region. Avoiding even his customary thanksgiving, Paul immediately launches into his rebuke. The logical development of Galatians is uninterrupted by digressions as Paul carefully develops his crucial theme. But there is a wide variety of feelings and approaches in this epistle. The severity is broken by tender appeals, and Paul uses personal experience, Old Testament exegesis, logic, warning, rebuke, and even an allegory to develop his argument. This epistle has had a profound impact upon the history of the church.

Survey of Galatians

The Epistle to the Galatians has been called "the Magna Carta of Christian liberty." It is Paul's manifesto of justification by faith, and the resulting liberty. Paul directs this great charter of Christian freedom to a people who are willing to give up the priceless liberty they possess in Christ. The oppressive theology of certain Jewish legalizers has been causing the believers in Galatia to trade their freedom in Christ for bondage to the Law. Paul writes this forceful epistle to do away with the false gospel of works and demonstrate the superiority of justification by faith. This carefully written polemic approaches the problem from three directions: the gospel of grace defended (1—2); the gospel of grace explained (3—4); and the gospel of grace applied (5—6).

The Gospel of Grace Defended (1—2): Paul affirms his divinely given apostleship and presents the gospel (1:1–5) because it has been distorted by false teachers among the Galatians (1:6–10). Paul launches into his biographical argument for the true gospel of justification by faith In showing that he received his message not from men but directly from God (1:11–24). When he submits his teaching of Christian liberty to the apostles in Jerusalem, they all acknowledge the validity and authority of his message (2:1–10). Paul also must correct Peter on the matter of freedom from the Law (2:11–21).

The Gospel of Grace Explained (3—4): In this section Paul uses eight lines of reasoning to develop his theological defense of justification by faith: (1) The Galatians began by faith, and their growth in Christ must continue to be by faith (3:1–5). (2) Abraham was justified by faith, and the same principle applies today (3:6–9). (3) Christ has redeemed all who trust in Him from the curse of the Law (3:10–14). (4) The promise made to Abraham was not nullified by the Law (3:15–18). (5) The Law was given to drive men to faith, not to save them (3:19–22). (6) Believers in Christ are adopted sons of God and are no longer bound by the Law (3:23—4:7). (7) The Galatians must recognize their inconsistency and regain their original freedom in Christ (4:8–20). (8) Abraham's two sons allegorically reveal the superiority of the Abrahamic promise to the Mosaic Law (4:21–31).

The Gospel of Grace Applied (5—6): The Judaizers seek to place the Galatians under bondage to their perverted gospel of justification by law, but Paul warns them that the law and grace are two contrary principles (5:1–12). So far, Paul has been contrasting the liberty of faith with the legalism of law, but at this point he warns the Galatians of the opposite extreme of license or *antinomianism* (5:13—6:10). The Christian is not only set free from bondage of law, but he is also free of the bondage of sin because of the power of the indwelling Spirit. Liberty is not an excuse to indulge in the deeds of the flesh; rather, it provides the privilege of bearing the fruit of the Spirit by walking in dependence upon Him. This letter closes with a contrast between the Judaizers—who are motivated by pride and a desire to avoid persecution—and Paul, who has suffered for the true gospel, but boasts only in Christ (6:11–18).

Outline of Galatians

I. The Gospel of Grace Defended, 1:1—2:21
   A. Introduction, 1:1–9
      1. Salutation: The Ground of Grace, 1:1–5
      2. Situation: The Departure from Grace, 1:6–9
   B. Gospel of Grace Is Given by Divine Revelation, 1:10–24
   C. Gospel of Grace Is Approved by Jerusalem Leadership, 2:1–10
   D. Gospel of Grace Is Vindicated by Rebuking Peter, 2:11–21

II. **The Gospel of Grace Explained,** 3:1—4:31
   A. Holy Spirit Is Given by Faith, Not by Works, 3:1–5
   B. Abraham Was Justified by Faith, Not by Works, 3:6–9
   C. Justification Is by Faith, Not by the Law, 3:10—4:11
      1. Christ Redeems Us from the Curse of the Law, 3:10–14
      2. Abrahamic Covenant Is Not Voided by the Law, 3:15–18
      3. Law Given to Drive Us to Faith, 3:19–22
      4. Believers Are Free from the Law, 3:23—4:11
   D. Galatians Receive Blessings by Faith, Not by the Law, 4:12–20
   E. Law and Grace Cannot Co-exist, 4:21–31

III. **The Gospel of Grace Applied,** 5:1—6:18
   A. Position of Liberty: Stand Fast, 5:1–12
   B. Practice of Liberty: Love One Another, 5:13–15
   C. Power for Liberty: Walk in the Spirit, 5:16–26
      1. Conflict between the Spirit and the Flesh, 5:16–18
      2. Works of the Flesh, 5:19–21
      3. Fruit of the Spirit, 5:22–26
   D. Performance in Liberty: Do Good to All Men, 6:1–10
      1. Bear One Another's Burdens, 6:1–5
      2. Do Not Be Weary while Doing Good, 6:6–10
   E. Conclusion, 6:11–18
      1. Motives of the Circumcised, 6:11–13
      2. Motives of the Apostle Paul, 6:14–18

Ephesians

EPHESIANS IS ADDRESSED to a group of believers who are indescribably rich in Jesus Christ, but living a beggarly existence because they are ignorant of their wealth. And because they have not appropriated their wealth, they are walking like they are spiritual paupers! Paul begins by describing in chapter 1—3 the contents of the Christian's heavenly "bank account": adoption, acceptance, redemption, forgiveness, wisdom, inheritance, the seal of the Holy Spirit, life, grace, citizenship—in short, every spiritual blessing! Drawing upon that huge spiritual endowment, the Christian has all the resources he needs to live a life "to the praise of the glory of His grace" (1:6). Chapters 4—6 resemble an orthopedic clinic, where the Christian learns a spiritual walk rooted in his spiritual wealth.

<table>
<tr><td rowspan="13" style="writing-mode:vertical">EPHESIANS</td></tr>
<tr><td>Focus</td><td colspan="4">Position
of the Christian</td><td colspan="4">Practice
of the Christian</td></tr>
<tr><td></td><td colspan="4">1:1   3:21</td><td colspan="4">4:1   6:24</td></tr>
<tr><td>Divisions</td><td>Praise for Redemption</td><td>Prayer for Revelation</td><td>Position of the Christian</td><td>Prayer for Realization</td><td>Unity in the Church</td><td>Holiness in Life</td><td>Responsibilities at Home and Work</td><td>Conduct in the Conflict</td></tr>
<tr><td></td><td>1:1   1:14</td><td>1:15   1:23</td><td>1:24   3:13</td><td>3:14   3:21</td><td>4:1   4:16</td><td>4:17   5:21</td><td>5:22   6:9</td><td>6:10   6:24</td></tr>
<tr><td rowspan="2">Topics</td><td colspan="4">Belief</td><td colspan="4">Behavior</td></tr>
<tr><td colspan="4">Privileges of the Christian</td><td colspan="4">Responsibilities of the Christian</td></tr>
<tr><td>Place</td><td colspan="8">Rome</td></tr>
<tr><td>Time</td><td colspan="8">A.D. 60–61</td></tr>
</table>

Introduction and Title

Ephesians is addressed to a group of believers who are rich beyond measure in Jesus Christ, yet living as beggars, and only because they are ignorant of their wealth. Since they have yet to accept their wealth, they relegate themselves to living as spiritual paupers. Paul begins by describing in chapters 1—3 the contents of the Christian's heavenly "bank account": adoption, acceptance, redemption, forgiveness, wisdom, inheritance, the seal of the Holy Spirit, life, grace, citizenship—in short, every spiritual blessing. Drawing upon that huge spiritual endowment, the Christian has all the resources needed for living "to the praise of the glory of His grace" (1:6). Chapters 4—6 resemble an orthopedic clinic, where the Christian learns a spiritual walk rooted in his spiritual wealth. "For we are His workmanship, created in Christ Jesus (1—3) for good works, . . . that we should walk in them" (2:10).

The traditional title of this epistle is *Pros Ephesious,* "To the Ephesians." Many ancient manuscripts, however, omit *en Epheso,* "in Ephesus," in chapter 1, verse 1. This has led a number of scholars to challenge the traditional view that this message was directed specifically to the Ephesians. The encyclical theory proposes that it was a circular letter sent by Paul to the churches of Asia. It is argued that Ephesians is really a Christian treatise designed for general use: it involves no controversy and deals with no specific problems in any particular church. This is also supported by the formal tone (no terms of endearment) and distant phraseology ("after I heard of your faith," 1:15; if they "have heard" of his message, 3:2). These things seem inconsistent with the relationship Paul must have had with the Ephesians after a ministry of almost three years among them. On the other hand, the absence of personal greetings is not a support for the encyclical theory because Paul would have done this to avoid favoritism. The only letters that greet specific people are Romans and Colossians, and they were addressed to churches Paul had not visited. Some scholars accept an ancient tradition that Ephesians is Paul's letter to the Laodiceans (Col. 4:16), but there is no way to be sure. If Ephesians began as a circular letter, it eventually became associated with Ephesus, the foremost of the Asian churches. Another plausible option is that this epistle was directly addressed to the Ephesians, but written in such a way as to make it helpful for all the churches in Asia.

Author

All internal (1:1) and external evidence strongly supports the Pauline authorship of Ephesians. In recent years, however, critics have turned to internal grounds to challenge this unanimous ancient tradition. It has been argued that the vocabulary and style are different from other Pauline Epistles, but this overlooks Paul's flexibility under different circumstances (cf. Rom. and 2 Cor.). The theology of Ephesians in some ways reflects a later development, but this must be attributed to Paul's own growth and meditation on the church as the body of Christ. Since the epistle clearly names the author in the opening verse, it is not necessary to theorize that Ephesians was written by one of Paul's pupils or admirers, such as Timothy, Luke, Tychicus, or Onesimus.

Date and Setting

At the end of his second missionary journey, Paul visited Ephesus where he left Priscilla and Aquila (Acts 18:18–21). This strategic city was the commercial center of Asia Minor, but heavy silting required a special canal to be maintained so that ships could reach the harbor. Ephesus was a religious center as well, famous especially for its magnificent temple of Diana (Roman name) or Artemis (Greek name), a structure considered to be one of the seven wonders of the ancient world (cf. Acts 19:35). The practice of magic and the local economy were clearly related to this temple. Paul remained in Ephesus for nearly three years on his third missionary journey (Acts 19; 20:30); the Word of God was spread throughout the province of Asia. Paul's effective ministry began to seriously hurt the traffic in magic and images, leading to an uproar in the huge Ephesian theater. Paul then left for Macedonia, but afterward he met with the Ephesian elders while on his way to Jerusalem (Acts 20:17–38).

Paul wrote the "Prison Epistles" (Ephesians, Philippians, Colossians, and Philemon) during his first Roman imprisonment in A.D. 60–62. These epistles all refer to his imprisonment (Eph. 3:1; 4:1; 6:20; Phil. 1:7, 13–14; Col. 4:3, 10, 18; Philem. 9–10, 13, 23), and fit well against the background in Acts 28:16–31. This is especially true of Paul's references to the "palace guard" (governor's official residential guard, Phil. 1:13) and "Caesar's household" (Phil. 4:22). Some commentators believe that the imprisonment in one or more of these epistles refers to Paul's Caesarean imprisonment or to a hypothetical Ephesian imprisonment, but the weight of evidence favors the traditional view that they were written in Rome. Ephesians, Colossians, and Philemon were evidently written about the same time (cf. Eph. 6:21–22; Col. 4:7–9) in A.D. 60–61. Philippians was written in A.D. 62, not long before Paul's release.

Theme and Purpose

The theme of Ephesians is the believer's responsibility to walk in accordance with his heavenly calling in Christ Jesus (4:1). Ephesians was not written to correct specific errors in a local church, but to prevent problems in the church as a whole by encouraging the body of Christ to mature in Him. It was also written to make believers more aware of their position in Christ because this is the basis for their practice on every level of life.

Keys to Ephesians

Key Word: Building the Body of Christ

Key Verses (2:8–10; 4:1–3)—"For by grace you have been saved through faith, and that not of yourselves; *it is* the gift of God, not of works, lest anyone should boast. For we are His workmanship, created in Christ Jesus for good works, which God prepared beforehand that we should walk in them" (2:8–10).

"I, therefore, the prisoner of the Lord, beseech you to have a walk worthy of the calling with which you were called, with all lowliness and gentleness, with longsuffering, bearing with one another in love, endeavoring to keep the unity of the Spirit in the bond of peace" (4:1–3).

Key Chapter (6)—Even though the Christian is blessed "with every spiritual blessing in the heavenly *places* in Christ" (1:3), spiritual warfare is still the daily experience of the Christian while in the world. Chapter 6 is the clearest advice for how to "be strong in the Lord and in the power of His might" (6:10).

Christ in Ephesians

Paul's important phrase "in Christ" (or its equivalent) appears about thirty-five times, more than in any other New Testament book. The believer is in Christ (1:1), in the heavenly places in Christ (1:3), chosen in Him (1:4), adopted through Christ (1:5), in the Beloved (1:6), redeemed in Him (1:7), given an inheritance in Him (1:11), given hope in Him (1:12), sealed in Him (1:13), made alive together with Christ (2:5), raised and seated with Him (2:6), created in Christ (2:10), brought near by His blood (2:13), growing in Christ (2:21), a partaker of the promise in Christ (3:6), and given access through faith in Him (3:12).

Contribution to the Bible

Unlike Galatians, which is a very personal and controversial letter, Ephesians is formal and impersonal in its style and noncontroversial in its subject matter. Paul communicates only two facts about himself in this epistle: his imprisonment and his reason for sending Tychicus. And unlike the rest of his epistles, the benediction is in the third person (6:23–24) Ephesians abounds with sublime thought and rich vocabulary, especially in chapters 1—3, where theology and worship are intertwined. Many regard it as the most profound book in the New Testament.

Survey of Ephesians

Paul wrote this epistle to make Christians more aware of their position in Christ and to motivate them to draw upon their spiritual source in daily living: "walk worthy of the calling with which you were called" (4:1; see 2:10). The first half of Ephesians lists the believer's heavenly possessions: adoption, redemption, inheritance, power, life, grace, citizenship, and the love of Christ. There are no imperatives in chapters 1—3, which focus only on divine gifts. But chapters 4—6 include thirty-five directives in the last half of Ephesians that speak of the believer's responsibility to conduct himself according to his individual calling. So Ephesians begins in heaven, but concludes in the home and in all other relationships of daily life. The two divisions are: the position of the Christian (1:1—3:21) and the practice of the Christian (4:1—6:20).

The Position of the Christian (1:1—3:21): After a two-verse prologue, in one long Greek sentence Paul extols the triune God for the riches of redemption (1:3–14). This hymn to God's grace praises the Father for choosing us (1:3–6), the Son for redeeming us (1:7–12), and the Spirit for sealing us (1:13–14). The saving work of each divine Person is "to the praise of the glory of His grace" (see 1:6, 12, 14). Before continuing, Paul offers the first of two very significant prayers (1:15–23; cf. 3:14–21). Here he asks that the readers receive spiritual illumination so that they may come to perceive what is in fact true. Next, Paul describes the power of God's grace by contrasting their former condition with their present spiritual life in Christ, a salvation attained not by human works but by divine grace (2:1–10). This redemption includes Jews, yet also extends to those Gentiles who previously were "strangers from the covenants of promise" (2:12). In Christ, the two for the first time have become members of one body (2:11–22). The truth that Gentiles would become "fellow heirs, of the same body" (3:6) was formerly a mystery that has now been revealed (3:1–13). Paul's second prayer (3:14–21) expresses his desire that the readers be strengthened with the power of the Spirit and fully apprehend the love of Christ.

The Practice of the Christian (4:1—6:24): The pivotal verse of Ephesians (4:1) draws a sharp line between the doctrinal and the practical divisions of this book. There is a cause and effect relationship between chapters 1—3 and 4—6 because the spiritual walk of a Christian must be rooted in his spiritual wealth. As Paul emphasized in Romans, behavior does not determine blessing; instead, blessing should determine behavior.

Because of the unity of all believers in the body of Christ, growth and maturity come from "the effective working by which every part does its share" (4:16). This involves the exercise of spiritual gifts in love. Paul exhorts the readers to "put off, concerning your former conduct, the old man" (4:22) "and put on the new man" (4:24) that will be manifested by a walk of integrity in the midst of all people. They are also to maintain a walk of holiness as children of light (5:1–21). Every relationship (wives, husbands, children, parents, slaves, masters) must be transformed by their new life in Christ (5:22—6:9). Paul's colorful description of the spiritual warfare and the armor of God (6:10–20) is followed by a word about Tychicus and then a benediction (6:21–24).

Outline of Ephesians

Part One: The Position of the Christian (1:1—3:21)

I. Praise for Redemption, 1:1–14
    A. Salutation from Paul, 1:1–2
    B. Chosen by the Father, 1:3–6
    C. Redeemed by the Son, 1:7–12
    D. Sealed by the Spirit, 1:13–14

II. Prayer for Revelation, 1:15–23

III. Position of the Christian, 2:1—3:13
    A. The Christian's Position Individually, 2:1–10
      1. Old Condition: Dead to God, 2:1–3
      2. New Condition: Alive to God, 2:4–10

B. The Christian's Position Corporately, 2:11—3:13
   1. Reconciliation of Jews and Gentiles, 2:11–22
   2. Revelation of the Mystery of the Church, 3:1–13

IV. **Prayer for Realization,** 3:14–21

Part Two: The Practice of the Christian (4:1—6:24)

I. **Unity in the Church,** 4:1–6
   A. Exhortation to Unity, 4:1–3
   B. Explanation of Unity, 4:4–6
   C. Means for Unity: The Gifts, 4:7–11
   D. Purpose of the Gifts, 4:12–16

II. **Holiness in Life,** 4:17—5:21
   A. Put Off the Old Man, 4:17–22
   B. Put On the New Man, 4:23–29
   C. Grieve Not the Holy Spirit, 4:30–32
   D. Walk as Children of Light, 5:1–17
   E. Be Filled with the Spirit, 5:18–21

III. **Responsibilities in the Home and at Work,** 5:22—6:9
   A. Wives: Submit to Your Husbands, 5:22–24
   B. Husbands: Love Your Wives, 5:25–33
   C. Children: Obey Your Parents, 6:1–4
   D. Service on the Job, 6:5–9

IV. **Conduct in the Conflict,** 6:10–24
   A. Put On the Armor of God, 6:10–17
   B. Play for Boldness, 6:18–20
   C. Conclusion, 6:21–24

Philippians

PHILIPPIANS IS THE EPISTLE OF JOY and encouragement in the midst of adverse circumstances. In it, Paul freely expresses his fond affection for the Philippians in view of their consistent testimony and support, and lovingly urges them to center their actions and thoughts on the person, pursuit, and power of Jesus Christ. Paul also seeks to correct a problem with disunity and rivalry, urging his readers to imitate Christ in His humility and servanthood. In this way the work of the gospel will go forward as believers seek to stand fast, be of the same mind, rejoice always, and pray about everything.

Focus	Account of Circumstances		Appeal to Have the Mind of Christ		Appeal to Have the Knowledge of Christ		Appeal to Have the Peace of Christ	
	1:1	1:30	2:1	2:30	3:1	3:21	4:1	4:23
Divisions	Partakers of Christ		People of Christ		Pursuit of Christ		Power of Christ	
	1:1	1:30	2:1	2:30	3:1	3:21	4:1	4:23
Topics	Suffering		Submission		Salvation		Sanctification	
	Experience		Examples		Exhortation			
Place	Rome							
Time	c. A.D. 62							

Introduction and Title

Paul writes a thank-you note to the believers at Philippi for their help in his hour of need, and he uses the occasion to send along some instruction on Christian unity. His central thought is simple: Only in Christ are real unity and joy possible. With Christ as your model of humility and service, you can enjoy a oneness of purpose, attitude, goal, and labor—a truth which Paul illustrates from his own life, and one the Philippians desperately need to hear. Within their own ranks, fellow workers in the Philippian church are at odds, hindering the work in proclaiming new life in Christ. Because of this, Paul exhorts the church to "stand fast. . . . be of the same mind. . . . rejoice in the Lord always. . . . but in everything by prayer and supplication, with thanksgiving, let your requests be made known. . . . and the peace of God, which surpasses all understanding, will guard your hearts and minds through Christ Jesus" (4:1, 2, 4, 6, 7).

This epistle is called *Pros Philippesious,* "To the Philippians." The church at Philippi was the first church Paul founded in Macedonia.

Author

The external and internal evidence for the Pauline authorship of Philippians is very strong, and there is scarcely any doubt that anyone but Paul wrote it.

Date and Setting

In 356 B.C., King Philip of Macedonia (the father of Alexander the Great) took this town and expanded it, renaming it Philippi. The Romans captured it in 168 B.C. and in 42 B.C., the defeat of the forces of Brutus and Cassius by those of Anthony and Octavian (later Augustus) took place outside the city. Octavian turned Philippi into a Roman colony (cf. Acts 16:12) and a military outpost. The citizens of this colony were regarded as citizens of Rome and given a number of special privileges. Because Philippi was a military city and not a commercial center, there were not enough Jews for a synagogue when Paul came (Acts 16:13).

Paul's "Macedonian Call" in Troas during his second missionary journey led to his ministry in Philippi with the conversion of Lydia and others. Paul and Silas were beaten and imprisoned, but this resulted in the conversion of the Philippian jailer. The magistrates were placed in a dangerous position by beating Roman citizens without a trial (Acts 16:37–40), and that embarrassment may have prevented future reprisals against the new Christians in Philippi. Paul visited the Philippians again on his third missionary journey (Acts 20:1, 6). When they heard of his Roman imprisonment, the Philippian church sent Epaphroditus with financial help (4:18); they had helped Paul in this way on at least two other occasions (4:16). Epaphroditus almost died of an illness, yet remained with Paul long enough for the Philippians to receive word of his malady. Upon his recovery, Paul sent this letter back with him to Philippi. (2:25–30).

Silas, Timothy, Luke, and Paul first came to Philippi in A.D. 51, eleven years before Paul wrote this letter. Certain references (1:13; 4:22) suggest that it was written from Rome, although some commentators argue for Caesarea or Ephesus. Paul's life was at stake, and he was evidently awaiting the verdict of the Imperial Court (2:20–26).

Theme and Purpose

This letter was written to convey Paul's love and gratitude for the believers at Philippi and to exhort them to a lifestyle of unity, holiness, and joy. Paul evidently enjoyed a very warm relationship with the Philippian church, perhaps his favorite. They were more sensitive and responsive to his financial needs than any other church (see 4:15–18; 2 Cor. 8:11) and appeared to have no major problems in their midst. Philippians was not written because of any crisis, but to express Paul's affection for them, his gratitude for their gift, his encouragement concerning their Christian growth, his admonitions against false teaching, and his thoughts about his circumstances. Paul gave the Philippians the latest news of his imprisonment and growing ministry in the propagation of the gospel (1:12–20), and prepared them for the coming of Timothy and possibly himself (2:19–24). He warned them of the twin dangers of legalism and antinomianism (3), but this was more of a preventative than a corrective measure. On the other hand, Paul recognized a growing problem of disunity in the Philippian church and sought to correct it before it became severe.

Keys to Philippians

Key Word: To Live Is Christ

Key Verses (1:21; 4:12)—"For to me, to live *is* Christ, and to die *is* gain" (1:21).

"I know how to be abased, and I know how to abound. Everywhere and in all things I have learned both to be full and to be hungry, both to abound and to suffer need" (4:12).

Key Chapter (2)—The grandeur of the truth of the New Testament seldom exceeds the revelation of the humility of Jesus Christ when He left heaven to become a servant of man. Christ is clearly the Christian's example, and Paul encourages, "Let this mind be in you which was also in Christ Jesus" (2:5).

Christ in Philippians

The great *kenosis* passage is one of several portraits of Christ in this epistle. In chapter 1, Paul sees Christ as his life ("For to me, to live *is* Christ," 1:21). In chapter 2, Christ is the model of true humility ("Let this mind be in you which was also in Christ Jesus," 2:5). Chapter 3 presents Him as the One "who will transform our lowly body that it may be conformed to His glorious body" (3:21). In chapter 4, He is the source of Paul's power over circumstances ("I can do all things through Christ who strengthens me," 4:13).

Contribution to the Bible

This warm and informal letter verbalizes Paul's love for a group of people to an unparalleled degree. The spontaneous words of affection to the "beloved" Philippians are not diluted by the problems of doctrine, discipline, or disorder that persistently marred Paul's relationship with some churches. Because of its informality, Philippians rapidly shifts from topic to topic without regard to a strict outline, just as one would expect from a personal letter. It also reveals Paul's true motivation and devotion to the cause of the gospel (see especially chapter 3). One of the predominant words in this epistle is *joy* or *rejoice,* appearing sixteen times in its four chapters. By the power of God, Paul was enabled to live above his difficult circumstances with joy, and he sought the same for his Philippian readers. Other significant words are *attitude* or *think* (used ten times) and *gospel* (used nine times). Although there is a small amount of doctrinal teaching, Philippians is centered around the person and power of Christ, and perhaps the most crucial christological passage in the Pauline Epistles is chapter 2, verses 5–11. It was written to illustrate practical humility as a means of unity among believers, but it is in fact one of the most sublime texts in Scripture. Condensed in these seven verses are profound insights concerning the preexistence, incarnation, humiliation, and exaltation of Jesus Christ.

Survey of Philippians

Philippians is the epistle of joy and encouragement in the midst of adverse circumstances. Paul freely expresses his fond affection for the Philippians, appreciates their consistent testimony and support, and lovingly urges them to center their actions and thoughts on the pursuit of the person and power of Christ. Paul also seeks to correct the problems of disunity and rivalry (2:2–4) and to prevent the problems of legalism and antinomianism (3:1–19). Philippians focuses on: Paul's account of his present circumstances (1); Paul's appeal to have the mind of Christ (2); Paul's appeal to have the knowledge of Christ (3); and Paul's appeal to have the peace of Christ (4).

Paul's Account of His Present Circumstances (1): Paul's usual salutation (1:1–2) is followed by his thanksgiving, warm regard, and prayer on behalf of the Philippians (1:3–11). For years, they have participated in the apostle's ministry, and he prays for their continued growth in the real knowledge of Christ. Paul shares the circumstances of his imprisonment and rejoices in the spread of the gospel in spite of and because of his situation (1:12–26). As he considers the outcome of his approaching trial, he expresses his willingness to "depart and be with Christ" (1:23) or to continue in ministry. Paul encourages the Philippians to remain steadfast in the face of opposition and coming persecution (1:27–30).

Paul's Appeal To Have the Mind of Christ (2): Paul exhorts the Philippians to have a spirit of unity and mutual concern by embracing the attitude of humility (2:1–4), the greatest example of which is the Incarnation and Crucifixion of Christ (2:5–11). The *kenosis,* or "emptying" of Christ, does not mean that He divested Himself of His deity, but that He withheld His preincarnate glory and voluntarily restricted His use of certain attributes (e.g., omnipresence and omniscience). Paul asks the Philippians to apply this attitude to their lives (2:12–18), and he gives two more examples of sacrifice, the ministries of Timothy and Epaphroditus (2:19–30).

Paul's Appeal To Have the Knowledge of Christ (3): It appears that Paul is about to close his letter ("Finally, my brethren," 3:1) when he launches into a warning about the continuing problem of legalism (3:1–9). Paul refutes this teaching with revealing autobiographical details about his previous attainments in Judaism. Compared to the goal of knowing Christ, those pursuits are as nothing. True righteousness is received through faith, not by mechanical obedience to any law. Paul scornfully refers to the Judaizers as "dogs" (*their* term for Gentiles) and "evil workers" (that is, the attempt to achieve salvation by works). Paul could be refuting the opposite extreme of antinomianism (3:17–21). Some, however, believe this may still refer to the legalists. Paul yearns for the promised attainment of the resurrected body.

Paul's Appeal To Have the Peace of Christ (4): In a series of exhortations, Paul urges the Philippians to have peace with the brethren by living a lifestyle of unity, prayerful dependence, and holiness (4:13). In chapter 4, verses 4–9, Paul describes the secrets of having the peace of God as well as peace with God. He then rejoices over their gift, but explains that the power of Christ enables him to live above his circumstances (4:10–20). This joyous letter from prison closes with greetings and a benediction (4:21–23).

Outline of Philippians

I. **Paul's Account of His Present Circumstance,** 1:1–30
   A. Paul's Prayer of Thanksgiving, 1:1–11
   B. Paul's Afflictions Promote the Gospel, 1:12–18
   C. Paul's Afflictions Exalt the Lord, 1:19–26
   D. Paul's Exhortation to the Afflicted, 1:27–30

II. **Paul's Appeal to Have the Mind of Christ,** 2:1–30
   A. Paul's Exhortation to Humility, 2:1–4
   B. Christ's Example of Humility, 2:5–16
   C. Paul's Example of Humility, 2:17–18
   D. Timothy's Example of Humility, 2:19–24
   E. Epaphroditus' Example of Humility, 2:25–30

III. **Paul's Appeal to Have the Knowledge of Christ,** 3:1–21
   A. Warning against Confidence in the Flesh, 3:1–9
   B. Exhortation to Know Christ, 3:10–16
   C. Warning against Living for the Flesh, 3:17–21

IV. **Paul's Appeal to Have the Peace of Christ,** 4:1–23
   A. Peace with the Brethren, 4:1–3
   B. Peace with the Lord, 4:4–9
   C. Peace in All Circumstances, 4:10–19
   D. Conclusion, 4:20–23

Colossians

COLOSSIANS IS ONE OF THE MOST Christ-centered books of the Bible. In it, Paul stresses the supremacy of the person of Christ and the completeness of the salvation He provides in order to combat a growing heresy in the church at Colossae. Christ, the Lord of creation and Head of the body which is His church, is completely sufficient for every spiritual and practical need of the believer. The believer's union with Christ in His death, Resurrection, and exaltation is the foundation upon which his earthly life must be built. Relationship inside and outside the home can demonstrate daily the transformation that faith in Jesus Christ in the walk of the believer.

COLOSSIANS							
Focus	**Supremacy of Christ**			**Submission to Christ**			
	1:1		2:23	3:1			4:18
Divisions	Introduction	Preeminence of Christ	Freedom in Christ	Position of the Believer	Practice of the Believer		Conclusion
	1:1　　1:14	1:15　　2:3	2:4　　2:23	3:1　　3:4	3:5　　4:6		4:7　　4:18
Topics	Doctrinal			Practical			
	What Christ Did for Us			What Christ Does Through Us			
Place	Rome						
Time	A.D. 60–61						

Introduction and Title

If Ephesians can be labeled the epistle portraying the "Church of Christ," then Colossians must surely be the "Christ of the Church." Ephesians focuses on the Body, Colossians on the Head. Like Ephesians, the little Book of Colossians divides neatly in half with the first portion doctrinal (1—2) and the second practical (3—4). Paul's purpose is to show that Christ is preeminent—first and foremost in everything—and the Christian's life should reflect that priority. Because believers are rooted in Him, alive with Him, hidden in Him, and complete in Him, it is utterly inconsistent for them to live life without Him. Clothed in His love, with His peace ruling in their hearts, they are equipped to make Christ first in every area of life.

This epistle became known as *Pros Kolossaeis,* "To the Colossians," because of chapter 1, verse 2. Paul also wanted it to be read in the neighboring church at Laodicea (4:16).

Author

The external testimony to the Pauline authorship of Colossians is ancient and consistent, and the internal evidence also is very good. It not only claims to be written by Paul (1:1, 23; 4:18), but the personal details and close parallels with Ephesians and Philemon make the case even stronger. Nevertheless, the authenticity of this letter has been challenged on the internal grounds of vocabulary and thought. In its four chapters, Colossians uses fifty-five Greek words that do not appear in Paul's other epistles. However, Paul commanded a wide vocabulary; and the circumstances and subject of this epistle, especially the references to the Colossian heresy, account for these additional words. The high christology of Colossians has been compared to John's later concept that Christ is the Logos (cf. 1:15–23; John 1:1–18), with the conclusion that these concepts were too late for Paul's time. However, there is no reason to assume that Paul was unaware of Christ's work as Creator, especially in view of Philippians 2:5–11. It is also wrong to assume that the heresy refuted in chapter 2 refers to the fully developed form of Gnosticism that did not appear until the second century. The parallels only indicate that Paul was dealing with an early form of Gnosticism.

Date and Setting

Colossae was a minor city about one hundred miles east of Ephesus in the region of the seven Asian churches of Revelation 1—3. Located in the fertile Lycus Valley by a mountain pass on the road from Ephesus to the East, Colossae once was a populous center of commerce, famous for its glossy black wool. By the time of Paul, it had been eclipsed by its neighboring cities, Laodicea and Hierapolis (cf. 4:13), and was on the decline. Apart from this letter, Colossae exerted almost no influence on early church history. It is evident that Paul had never visited the church at Colossae, which was founded by Epaphras (1:4–8; 2:1). On his third missionary journey, Paul devoted almost three years to an Asian ministry centered in Ephesus (cf. Acts 19:10; 20:31); and Epaphras probably came to Christ during this time. He carried the gospel to the cities in the Lycus Valley and years later came to visit Paul in his imprisonment (4:12–13; Philem. 23).

Colossians, Philemon, and Ephesians were evidently written about the same time and under the same circumstances, judging by the overlapping themes and personal names (cf. Col. 4:9–17; Philem. 2, 10, 23–24). Although Caesarea and Ephesus have been suggested as the location of authorship, the bulk of the evidence indicates that Paul wrote all four Prison Epistles during his first Roman imprisonment (see "Date and Setting" in Ephesians and in Philippians). If so, Paul wrote it in A.D. 60 or 61 and sent it with Tychicus and the converted slave Onesimus to Colossae (4:7–9; see Eph. 6:21; Philem. 10–12).

Epaphras' visit and report about the conditions in Colossae prompted this letter. Although the Colossians had not yet succumbed (2:1–5), an encroaching heresy was threatening the predominantly Gentile (1:21, 27; 2:13) Colossian church. The nature of this heresy can only be deduced from Paul's incidental references to it in his refutation (2:8–23). It was apparently a religious system that combined elements from Greek speculation (2:4, 8–10), Jewish legalism (2:11–17), and Oriental mysticism (2:18–23). It involved a low view of the body (2:20–23) and probably nature as a whole. Circumcision, dietary regulations, and ritual observances were included in this system, which utilized asceticism, worship of angels as intermediaries, and mystical experiences as an approach to the spiritual realm. Any attempt to fit Christ into such a system would undermine His person and redemptive work.

Theme and Purpose

The resounding theme in Colossians is the preeminence and sufficiency of Christ in all things. The believer is complete in Him alone and lacks nothing because "in Him dwells all the fullness of the Godhead bodily" (2:9); He has "all the treasures of wisdom and knowledge" (2:3). There is no need for speculation, mystical visions, or ritualistic regulations as though faith in Christ were insufficient. Paul's predominant purpose, then, was to refute a threatening heresy that was devaluating Christ by a positive presentation of His true attributes and accomplishments. A proper view of Christ is the antidote for heresy. Paul also wrote this epistle to encourage the Colossians to "continue in the faith, grounded and steadfast" (1:23) so that they will grow and bear fruit in the knowledge of Christ (1:10). A firm adherence to the true gospel will give them stability and resistance to opposing influences. Another purpose in the mind of the apostle is reflected in 3:1—4:6. Paul wanted the Colossians to understand the implications of the preeminence of Christ not only for doctrine, but also for practice. The supremacy of Christ is one side of the coin—submission to Christ is the other. The believer's position in Him (3:1–4) provides the basis and power for a transformed life in every area.

Keys to Colossians

Key Word: Preeminence of Christ
Key Verses (2:9–10; 3:1–2)—"For in Him dwells all the fullness of the Godhead bodily; and you are complete in Him, who is the head of all principality and power" (2:9–10).

"If then you were raised with Christ, seek those things which are above, where Christ is, sitting at the right hand of God. Set your mind on things above, not on things on the earth" (3:1–2).

Key Chapter (3)—Chapter 3 links the three themes of Colossians together showing their cause and effect relationships. Because the believer is risen with Christ (3:1–4), he is to put off the old man and put on the new (3:5–17), which will result in holiness in all relationships (3:18–25).

Christ in Colossians

This singularly christological book is centered on the cosmic Christ—"the head of all principality and power" (2:10), the Lord of creation (1:16–17), and the Author of reconciliation (1:20–22; 2:13–15). He is the basis for the believer's hope (1:5, 23, 27), the source of the believer's power for a new life (1:11, 29), the believer's Redeemer and Reconciler (1:14, 20–22; 2:11–15), the embodiment of full deity (1:15, 19; 2:9), the Creator and Sustainer of all things (1:16–17), the Head of the church (1:18), the resurrected God-Man (1:18; 3:1), and the all-sufficient Savior (1:28; 2:3, 10; 3:1–4).

Contribution to the Bible

Colossians is characterized by its high christology: as the exalted Creator and Redeemer, He is central to all belief and behavior. Paul uses rich language and even redefines the terms used by the heretical movement by filling them with orthodox meaning (e.g., *pleroma*, "fulness," and *gnosis*, "knowledge"). Even though the style is not as piercing or rigorous as that in Galatians or Romans, the intense concepts betray an underlying controversy. There are no Old Testament references in this epistle.

The twin epistles Ephesians and Colossians can be compared and contrasted in several ways:

Ephesians	Colossians
Written in prison, carried by Tychicus	Written in prison, carried by Tychicus
Stresses wisdom, knowledge, fullness, mystery	Stresses wisdom, knowledge, fullness, mystery
Similar passages: (1) 1:7; (2) 1:10; (3) 1:15–17; (4) 1:18; (5) 1:19–20; (6) 1:21–23	Similar passages: (1) 1:4; (2) 1:20; (3) 1:3–4; (4) 1:27; (5) 2:12; (6) 1:16–19
Emphasizes the church as the body of Christ	Emphasizes Christ as the Head of the body
General, universal	Specific, local
First half—position; second half—practice	First half—position; second half—practice
Irenic, calm	Polemic, concern
Reflective, quiet	Spiritual conflict

Survey of Colossians

Colossians is perhaps the most Christ-centered book in the Bible. In it Paul stresses the preeminence of the person of Christ and the completeness of the salvation He provides, in order to combat a growing heresy that is threatening the church at Colossae. This heresy seeks to devaluate Christ by elevating speculation, ritualism, mysticism, and asceticism. But Christ, the Lord of creation and Head of the body, is completely sufficient for every spiritual and practical need of the believer. The last half of this epistle explores the application of these principles to daily life, because doctrinal truth (1—2) must bear fruit in practical conduct (3—4). The two major topics are: supremacy of Christ (1—2) and submission to Christ (3—4).

Supremacy of Christ (1—2): Paul's greeting (1:1–2) is followed by an unusually extended thanksgiving (1:3–8) and prayer (1:9–14) on behalf of the believers at Colossae. Paul expresses his concern that the Colossians come to a deeper understanding of the person and power of Christ. Even here Paul begins to develop his major theme of the preeminence of Christ, but the most potent statement of this theme is in chapter 1, verses 15–23. He is supreme both in creation (1:15–18) and in redemption (1:19–23), and this majestic passage builds a positive case for Christ as the most effective refutation of the heresy that will be exposed in chapter 2. Paul describes his own ministry of proclaiming the mystery of "Christ in you, the hope of glory" (1:27) to the Gentiles and assures his readers that although he has not personally met them, he strongly desires that they become deeply rooted in Christ alone, who is preeminent in the Church (1:24—2:3). This is especially important in view of false teachers who would defraud them through enticing rationalisms (2:4–7), vain philosophy (2:8–10), legalistic rituals (2:11–17), improper mysticism (2:18–19), and useless asceticism (2:20–23). In each case, Paul contrasts the error with the corresponding truth about Christ.

Submission to Christ (3—4): The believer's union with Christ in His death, Resurrection, and exaltation is the foundation upon which his earthly life must be built (3:1–4). Because of his death with Christ, the Christian must regard himself as dead to the old sins and put them aside (3:5–11); because of his resurrection with Christ, the believer must regard himself as alive to Him in righteousness and put on the new qualities that are prompted by Christian love (3:12–17). Turning from the inward life (3:1–17) to the outward life (3:18—4:6), Paul outlines the transformation that faith in Christ should make in relationships inside and outside the home. This epistle concludes with a statement concerning its bearers (Tychicus and Onesimus), greetings and instructions, and a farewell note (4:7–18).

Outline of Colossians

Part One: The Supremacy of Christ in the Church (1:1—2:23)

    I. Introduction, 1:1–14

        A. Paul's Greeting to the Colossians, 1:1–2

        B. Paul's Thanksgiving for the Colossians, 1:3–8

        C. Paul's Prayer for the Colossians, 1:9–14

II. The Preeminence of Christ, 1:15—2:3
    A. Christ Is Preeminent in Creation, 1:15–18
    B. Christ Is Preeminent in Redemption, 1:19–23
    C. Christ Is Preeminent in the Church, 1:24—2:3

III. The Freedom in Christ, 2:4–23
    A. Freedom from Enticing Words, 2:4–7
    B. Freedom from Vain Philosophy, 2:8–10
    C. Freedom from the Judgment of Men, 2:11–17
    D. Freedom from Improper Worship, 2:18–19
    E. Freedom from the Doctrine of Men, 2:20–23

Part Two: The Submission to Christ in the Church (3:1—4:18)

I. The Position of the Believer, 3:1–4

II. The Practice of the Believer, 3:5—4:6
    A. Put Off the Old Man, 3:5–11
    B. Put On the New Man, 3:12–17
    C. Personal Commands for Holiness, 3:18—4:6
        1. Holiness in Family Life, 3:18–21
        2. Holiness in Work Life, 3:22—4:1
        3. Holiness in Public Life, 4:2–6

III. Conclusion, 4:7–18
    A. Commendation of Tychicus, 4:7–9
    B. Greetings from Paul's Friends, 4:10–14
    C. Instruction Regarding This Letter, 4:15–18

First Thessalonians

THE CHURCH AT THESSALONICA was in many ways a model church. Paul had many things to commend the believers for: their exemplary faith, diligent service, patient steadfastness, and overflowing joy. But in the midst of his commendation, Paul voices a word of caution. Abounding in the work of the Lord is only one step removed from abandoning the work of the Lord through complacency. Thus, Paul exhorts the Thessalonians to excel in their faith, to increase in their love for one another, and to give thanks always for all things. In short, Paul encourages them to "stay on target" as they labor for the Lord.

Focus	Reflections on the Thessalonians			Instructions to the Thessalonians			
	1:1 3:13			4:1 5:28			
Divisions	Paul's Commendation of Their Growth	Paul's Founding of the Church	Timothy's Strengthening of the Church	Direction for the Thessalonians' Growth	Revelation Concerning the Dead in Christ	Description of the Day of the Lord	Instructions for Holy Living
	1:1 1:10	2:1 2:16	2:17 3:13	4:1 4:12	4:13 4:18	5:1 5:11	5:1 25:28
Topics	Personal Experience			Practical Exhortation			
	Looking Back			Looking Forward Through Us			
Place	Written in Corinth						
Time	C. A.D. 51						

FIRST THESSALONIANS

Introduction and Title

Paul has many pleasant memories of the days he spent with the infant Thessalonian church. Their faith, hope, love, and perseverance in the face of persecution are exemplary. Paul's labors as a spiritual parent to the fledgling church have been richly rewarded, and his affection is visible in every line of his letter.

Paul encourages them to excel in their new-found faith, to increase in their love for one another, and to rejoice, pray, and give thanks always. He closes his letter with instruction regarding the return of the Lord, whose Advent signifies hope and comfort for believers both living and dead.

Because this is the first of Paul's two canonical letters to the church at Thessalonica, it received the title *Pros Thessalonikeis A,* the "First to the Thessalonians."

Author

First Thessalonians went unchallenged as a Pauline Epistle until the nineteenth century, when radical critics claimed that its dearth of doctrinal content made its authenticity suspect. But this is a weak objection on two counts: (1) The proportion of doctrinal teaching in Paul's epistles varies widely; and (2) 4:13—5:11 is a foundational passage for New Testament eschatology (future events). Paul had quickly grounded the Thessalonians in Christian doctrine, and the only problematic issue when this epistle was written concerned the matter of Christ's return. The external and internal evidence points clearly to Paul.

Date and Setting

In Paul's time, Thessalonica was the prominent seaport and the capital of the Roman province of Macedonia. This prosperous city was located on the Via Egnatia, the main road from Rome to the East, within sight of Mount Olympus, legendary home of the Greek pantheon. Cassander expanded and strengthened this site around 315 B.C. and renamed it after his wife, the half-sister of Alexander the Great. The Romans conquered Macedonia in 168 B.C. and organized it into a single province twenty-two years later with Thessalonica as the capital city. It became a "free city" under Augustus with its own authority to appoint a governing board of magistrates who were called "politarchs." Its strategic location assured it of commercial success, and it boasted a population of perhaps 200,000 in the first century. It survives under the shortened name Salonika.

Thessalonica had a sizable Jewish population, and the ethical monotheism of Judaism attracted many Gentiles who had become disenchanted with Greek paganism. These God-fearers quickly responded to Paul's reasoning in the synagogue when he ministered there on his second missionary journey (Acts 17:1). The Jews became jealous of Paul's success and organized a mob to oppose the Christian missionaries. Not finding Paul and Silas, they dragged Jason, Paul and Silas' host, before the politarchs, and accused him of harboring traitors of Rome. The politarchs extracted a pledge guaranteeing the departure of Paul and Silas, who left that night for Berea. After a time, the Thessalonian Jews raised an uproar in Berea so that Paul departed for Athens, leaving orders for Silas and Timothy to join him there (Acts 17:11–16). Because of Luke's account in Acts some scholars have reasoned that Paul was in Thessalonica for less than a month ("three Sabbaths," 17:2), but other evidence suggests a longer stay: (1) Paul received two separate offerings from Philippi, one hundred miles away, while he was in Thessalonica (Phil. 4:15–16). (2) Most of the Thessalonian converts were Gentiles who came out of idolatry (1:9; 2:14–16). This would imply an extensive ministry directed to the Gentiles after Paul's initial work with the Jews and Gentile God-fearers. (3) Paul worked "night and day" (see 2:9; 2 Thess. 3:7–9) during his time there. He may have begun to work immediately, but Paul supported himself by tentmaking, which took many hours away from his ministry, requiring a longer stay to accomplish the extensive ministry of evangelism and teaching that took place in that city. After Silas and Timothy met Paul in Athens (3:1–2), he sent Timothy to Thessalonica (Silas also went back to Macedonia, probably Philippi), and his assistants later rejoined him in Corinth (Acts 18:5; cf. 1 Thess. 1:1 where Silas is called Silvanus). There he wrote this epistle in A.D. 51 as his response to Timothy's good report.

Theme and Purpose

The basic theme of this epistle is the salvation and sanctification of the Thessalonians. The contents reveal five basic purposes for which First Thessalonians was written: (1) Paul wanted to express his thanksgiving for their faith and love now that he heard of their steadfastness in the face of persecution. (2) Paul defended himself against slanderous attacks that evidently originated from the Jewish opposition. He reminds the Thessalonians of his conduct and motives while among them, in refutation of those who claimed that he was a religious charlatan and mercenary. (3) The Thessalonians needed encouragement and exhortation to resist the temptations of moral impurity and slothful behavior. (4) Paul sought to dispel their ignorance about the relationship of the dead in Christ to His *parousia*. He comforted them with the revelation that Christians who are alive when Christ comes to meet them will have no advantage over those who have already died, since both groups will "meet the Lord in the air." (5) Paul instructed the Thessalonians concerning their spiritual leaders, conduct, and worship (5:12–22).

Keys to First Thessalonians

Key Word: Sanctification

Key Verses (3:12–13; 4:16–18)—"And may the Lord make you increase and abound in love to one another and to all, just as we *do* to you, so that He may establish your hearts blameless in holiness before our God and Father at the coming of our Lord Jesus Christ with all His saints" (3:12–13).

"For the Lord Himself will descend from heaven with a shout, with the voice of an archangel, and with the trumpet of God. And the dead in Christ will rise first. Then we who are alive *and* remain shall be caught up together with them in the clouds to meet the Lord in the air. And thus we shall always be with the Lord. Therefore comfort one another with these words" (4:16–18).

Key Chapter (4)—Chapter 4 includes the central passage of the epistle on the coming of the Lord when the dead in Christ shall rise first, and those who remain are caught up together with them in the clouds.

Christ in First Thessalonians

Christ is seen as the believer's hope of salvation both now and at His Coming. When He returns, He will deliver (1:10; 5:4–11), reward (2:19), perfect (3:13), resurrect (4:13–18), and sanctify (5:23) all who trust Him.

Contribution to the Bible

This book contains one of the most helpful and illuminating biblical passages on the return of the Redeemer (4:13—5:11). In fact, all five chapters refer to this great event: 1:10; 2:19; 3:13; 4:13–18; 5:1–11, 23. First Thessalonians alludes to several other doctrines, but Paul did not feel a need to develop them. He evidently taught them well during his short stay, and wanted to make this more of a personal than a doctrinal letter. Like Second Corinthians, it reveals Paul's tenderness, affection, and great concern for the spiritual welfare of his converts. The purity of his motives, compassion, and dedication—in short, his innermost feelings—are manifest in these pages.

Survey of First Thessalonians

After Paul's forced separation from the Thessalonians, he grows increasingly concerned about the progress of their faith. His great relief upon hearing Timothy's positive report prompts him to write this warm epistle of commendation, exhortation, and consolation. They are commended for remaining steadfast under afflictions, exhorted to excel still more in their Christian walk, and consoled concerning their loved ones who have died in Christ. The theme of the coming of the Lord recurs throughout this epistle, and chapter 4, verse 13—chapter 5, verse 11, is one of the fullest New Testament developments of this crucial truth. The two major sections of First Thessalonians are: (1) Paul's personal reflections of the Thessalonians (1—3) and (2) Paul's instructions for the Thessalonians (4—5).

Paul's Personal Reflections of the Thessalonians (1—3): Paul's typical salutation in the first verse combines the customary Greek ("grace") and Hebrew ("peace") greetings of his day and enriches them with Christian content. The opening chapter is a declaration of thanksgiving for the Thessalonians' metamorphosis from heathenism to Christian hope. Faith, love, and hope (1:3) properly characterize the new lives of these believers. Paul reviews his brief ministry in Thessalonica and defends his conduct and motives, apparently to answer enemies who are trying to impugn his character and message (2:1–16). His devotion to the Thessalonian believers is evident from his affection (like a mother, 2:7) and admonition (like a father, 2:11). Prevented from returning to Thessalonica, Paul becomes troubled because of uncertainty over their spiritual condition. He sends Timothy to minister to them and is greatly relieved when Timothy reports the stability of their faith and love (2:17—3:10). Paul therefore closes this historical section with a prayer that their faith may continue to deepen (3:11–13).

Paul's Instructions for the Thessalonians (4—5): The apostle deftly moves into a series of exhortations and instructions by encouraging the Thessalonians to continue progressing. He reminds them of his previous teaching on sexual and social matters (4:1–12), since these Gentile believers lack the moral upbringing in the Mosaic Law provided in the Jewish community. Now rooted in the Word of God (2:13), the readers must resist the constant pressures of a pagan society.

Paul has taught them about the return of Christ, and they have become distressed over the deaths of some among them. Paul comforts them with the assurance that all who die in Christ will be resurrected at His *parousia* ("presence, coming, advent," see 4:13–18). The apostle continues his discourse on eschatology by describing the coming day of the Lord (5:1–11). In anticipation of this day, believers are to "watch and be sober" as "children of light" who are destined for salvation, not wrath. Paul requests the readers to deal with integrity toward one another and to continue growing spiritually (5:12–22). The epistle closes with a wish for their sanctification, three requests, and a benediction (5:23–28).

Outline of First Thessalonians

I. Paul's Personal Reflections on the Thessalonians, 1:1—3:13
  A. Paul's Commendation for Their Growth, 1:1–10
  B. Paul's Founding of the Church, 2:1–16
  C. Timothy's Strengthening of the Church, 2:17—3:13
    1. Satan Hinders Paul, 2:17–20
    2. Paul Sends Timothy, 3:1–5
    3. Timothy's Encouraging Report, 3:6–10
    4. Paul's Desire to Visit Them, 3:11–13

II. Paul's Instructions to the Thessalonians, 4:1—5:28
  A. Directions for Growth, 4:1–12
  B. Revelation Concerning the Dead in Christ, 4:13–18
  C. Description of the Day of the Lord, 5:1–11
  D. Instruction for Holy Living, 5:12–22
  E. Conclusion, 5:23–28

Second Thessalonians

SINCE PAUL'S FIRST LETTER to the Thessalonians, problems had arisen in the church. False teachers had upset the saints by claiming that the "day of Christ" had already occurred. Such news prompted Paul to prescribe strong medicine to cure the problem: "of anyone will not work, neither shall he eat" (3:10) Paul reminds the Thessalonians that those undergoing persecution can take heart, knowing that God's righteous judgment will settle all accounts equitably. Paul exhorts his readers to be steadfast and diligent, buying up the opportunities, rather than merely biding their time.

SECOND THESSALONIANS

Focus	Encouragement in Persecution			Explanation of the Day of the Lord		Exhortation to the Church		
	1:1 — 1:12			2:1 — 2:17		3:1 — 3:18		
Divisions	Thanksgiving for Their Growth	Encouragement in Their Persecution	Prayer for God's Blessing	Events Preceding the Day of the Lord	Comfort of the Believer on the Day of the Lord	Wait Patiently for Christ	Withdraw from the Disorderly	Conclusion
	1:1 — 1:4	1:5 — 1:10	1:11 — 1:12	2:1 — 2:12	2:13 — 2:17	3:1 — 3:5	3:6 — 3:15	3:16 — 3:18
Topics	Discouraged Believers			Disturbed Believers		Disobedient Believers		
	Thanksgiving for Their Life			Instruction of Their Doctrine		Correction of Their Behavior		
Place	Written in Corinth							
Time	C. A.D. 51							

Introduction and Title

Since Paul's first letter, the seeds of false doctrine have been sown among the Thessalonians, causing them to waver in their faith. Paul removes these destructive seeds and again plants the seeds of truth. He begins by commending the believers on their faithfulness in the midst of persecution and encouraging them that present suffering will be repaid with future glory. Therefore, in the midst of persecution, expectation can be high.

Paul then deals with the central matter of his letter: a misunderstanding spawned by false teachers regarding the coming day of the Lord. Despite reports to the contrary, that day has not yet come, and Paul recounts the events that must first take place. Laboring for the gospel, rather than lazy resignation, is the proper response.

As the second letter in Paul's Thessalonian correspondence, this was entitled *Pros Thessalonikeis B,* the "Second to the Thessalonians."

Author

The external attestation to the authenticity of Second Thessalonians as a Pauline epistle is even stronger than that for First Thessalonians. Internally, the vocabulary, style, and doctrinal content support the claims that it was written by Paul (1:1; 3:17).

Date and Setting

See "Date and Setting" in First Thessalonians for the background to the Thessalonian correspondence. This letter was probably written a few months after First Thessalonians, while Paul was still in Corinth with Silas and Timothy (1:1; cf. Acts 18:5). The bearer of the first epistle may have brought Paul an update on the new developments, prompting him to write this letter. They were still undergoing persecution, and the false teaching about the day of the Lord led some of them to overreact by giving up their jobs. The problem of idleness recorded in First Thessalonians, chapter 4, verses 11–12, had become more serious (3:6–15). By this time, Paul was beginning to see the opposition he would face in his ministry in Corinth (3:2; see Acts 18:5–10).

Theme and Purpose

The theme of this epistle is Paul's comfort and correction of the Thessalonians in view of their problems of religious persecution, doctrinal misunderstanding, and practical abuse. Paul's three major purposes correspond to the three chapters: (1) The apostle wanted to applaud their continuing growth in faith and love and encourage them to endure their persecution in the knowledge that God will vindicate His name and glorify all who have trusted in Christ. (2) The second chapter was written to correct the fallacious teaching that the day of the Lord was already upon them. This teaching, coupled with the afflictions they were suffering, was causing great disturbances among the Thessalonian believers who were wondering when their "gathering together to Him" (2:1; cf. 1 Thess. 4:13–18) would take place. Paul made it clear that the day of the Lord had not overtaken them (cf. 1 Thess. 5:4). (3) The doctrinal error of chapter 2 was causing a practical error that Paul sought to overcome in chapter 3. Some of the believers abandoned their work and began to live off others, apparently assuming that the end was at hand. Paul commanded them to follow his example by supporting themselves and instructed the rest of the church to discipline them if they failed to do so.

Keys to Second Thessalonians

Key Word: Expectation of the Day of the Lord

Key Verses (2:2–3; 3:4–5)—"Not to be soon shaken in mind or troubled, either by spirit or by word or by letter, as if from us, as though the day of Christ had come. Let no one deceive you by any means; for *that Day will not come* unless the falling away comes first, and the man of sin is revealed, the son of perdition" (2:2–3).

"Now may the Lord direct your hearts into the love of God and into the patience of Christ. But we command you, brethren, in the name of our Lord Jesus Christ, that you withdraw from every brother who walks disorderly and not according to the tradition which he received from us" (3:5–6).

Key Chapter (2)—This chapter corrects a serious error that had crept into the Thessalonian church. This error taught that the day of the Lord had already come; as a result, the believers had become confused and had begun to question when they would go to be with Him (2:1). Paul clearly teaches that the day of the Lord has not yet come and that certain events, which they will be able to identify, must take place before Christ returns.

Christ in Second Thessalonians

The return of Christ is mentioned more times (318) in the New Testament than any other doctrine, and this is certainly the major concept in chapters 1–2 of this epistle. The return of the Lord Jesus is a reassuring and joyful hope for believers, but His revelation from heaven holds awesome and terrifying implications for those who have not trusted in Him (1:6–10; 2:8–12).

Contribution to the Bible

This is the shortest of Paul's nine letters to churches, but it provides crucial information concerning the end times and clarifies issues that would otherwise be very obscure. Even so, there has been a wide difference of opinion regarding the nature of the man of lawlessness and the restrainer. The two Thessalonian epistles, along with the Olivet Discourse (Matt. 24—25) and the Book of Revelation, form the three major prophetic texts of the New Testament. Their early date places them among the first New Testament books to be written and reveals that apostolic doctrine had already become a settled body of truth. Paul refers to his teaching among the Thessalonians as "the traditions" which they had received (2:15; 3:6). These two epistles refer to almost every central doctrine of the Christian faith even though they are not doctrinal treatises like Romans or Ephesians.

In spite of its brevity, Paul offers four prayers on behalf of the readers of this letter (1:11–12; 2:16–17; 3:5; 3:16). It closes with a greeting in his own handwriting as a mark of authentication against the possibility of fraud (3:17; cf. 2:2).

Survey of Second Thessalonians

This epistle is the theological sequel to First Thessalonians, which developed the theme of the coming day of the Lord (1 Thess. 5:1–11). However, not long after the Thessalonians receive that letter, they fall prey to false teaching or outright deception, thinking the day of the Lord has already begun. Paul writes this brief letter to correct the error and also to encourage those believers whose faith is being tested by the difficulties presented by persecution. He also reproves those who have decided to cease working because they believe the coming of Christ is near. Second Thessalonians deals with Paul's encouragement in persecution (1); Paul's explanation of the day of the Lord (2); and Paul's exhortation to the church (3).

Paul's Encouragement in Persecution (1): After his two-verse salutation, Paul gives thanks to the growing faith and love of the Thessalonians and assures them of their ultimate deliverance from those who are persecuting them (1:3–10). They are encouraged to patiently endure their afflictions, knowing that the Lord Jesus will judge their persecutors when He is "revealed from heaven with His mighty angels, in flaming fire" (1:7–8). Before Paul moves to the next topic, he concludes this section with a prayer for the spiritual welfare of his readers (1:11–12).

Paul's Explanation of the Day of the Lord (2): Because of the severity of their afflictions, the Thessalonians have become susceptible to false teaching (and possibly a fraudulent letter in the name of Paul), claiming that they are already in the day of the Lord (2:1–2). This was particularly disturbing because Paul's previous letter had given them the comforting hope that they were not destined for the wrath of that day (1 Thess. 5:9). Paul therefore assures them that the day of the Lord is yet in the future and will not arrive unannounced. Specifically, a great spiritual rebellion must take place, climaxed by the revealing of the satanically empowered man of lawlessness (2:3–4, 8–9). A comparison of this passage with Daniel 9:27; 12:11; Matthew 24:15; First John 2:18; Revelation 11:7; 13:1–10 shows that the man of lawlessness is the Antichrist who will be fully manifested when the restrainer is removed (2:6–9). The Thessalonians knew the identity of this restrainer, but we cannot be sure of what Paul had in mind. The prominent views of the identity of the restrainer are the Holy Spirit, the church, or civil government. In any case, the conflict of lawlessness and of Christ will continue until the climax of Christ's victorious appearance. Paul then concludes with a word of encouragement and a benedictory prayer of comfort before moving to his next topic (2:13–17).

Paul's Exhortation to the Church (3:1–18): Paul requests the Thessalonian church to pray on his behalf and to wait patiently for the Lord (3:1–5). Having thus commended, corrected, and comforted his readers, the tactful apostle closes his letter with a sharp word of command to those who have been using the truth of Christ's return as an excuse for disorderly conduct (3:6–15; cf. 1 Thess. 4:11–12). The doctrine of the Lord's return requires a balance between waiting and working. It is a perspective that should encourage holiness, not idleness. This final section, like the first two, closes on a benedictory note (3:16–18).

Outline of Second Thessalonians

I. **Paul's Encouragement in Persecution,** 1:1–12
   A. Thanksgiving for Their Growth, 1:1–4
   B. Encouragement in Their Persecution, 1:5–10
   C. Prayer for God's Blessing, 1:11–12

II. **Paul's Explanation of the Day of the Lord,** 2:1–17
   A. The Events Preceding the Day of the Lord, 2:1–12
      1. First a Falling Away, 2:1–3
      2. The Man of Sin Is Revealed, 2:4–5
      3. The Restrainer Is Taken Out of the Way, 2:6–7
      4. The Second Coming of Christ, 2:8–12
   B. The Comfort of the Believer on the Day of the Lord, 2:13–17

III. **Paul's Exhortation to the Church,** 3:1–18
   A. Wait Patiently for Christ, 3:1–5
   B. Withdraw from the Disorderly, 3:6–15
   C. Conclusion, 3:16–18

First Timothy

PAUL, THE AGED AND EXPERIENCED APOSTLE, writes to young pastor Timothy who is facing a heavy burden of responsibility in the church at Ephesus. The task is challenging: false doctrine must be erased, public worship safeguarded, and mature leadership developed. In addition to the conduct of the church, Paul talks pointedly about the conduct of the minister. Timothy must be on his guard lest his youthfulness become a liability, rather than an asset to the gospel. He must be careful to avoid false teachers and greedy motives, pursuing instead righteousness, godliness, faith, love, perseverance, and gentleness as befitting a man of God.

	Doctrine	Public Worship	False Teachers	Church Discipline	Pastoral Motives
Focus	1:1 1:20	2:1 3:16	4:1 4:16	5:1 5:25	6:1 6:21
Divisions	Problem of False Doctrine	Public Worship and Leadership	Preserve True Doctrine	Prescriptions for Widows and Elders	Pastoral Motivations
	1:1 1:20	2:1 3:16	4:1 4:16	5:1 5:25	6:1 6:21
Topics	Warning	Worship	Wisdom	Widows	Wealth
	Dangers of False Doctrine	Directions for Worship	Defense against False Teachers	Duties toward Others	Dealings with Riches
Place	Written in Macedonia					
Time	c. A.D. 62–63					

FIRST TIMOTHY

Introduction and Title

Paul, the aged and experienced apostle, writes to the young pastor Timothy who is facing a heavy burden of responsibility in the church at Ephesus. The task is challenging: false doctrine must be erased, public worship safeguarded, and mature leadership developed. In addition to the conduct of the church, Paul talks pointedly about the conduct of the minister. Timothy must be on his guard lest his youthfulness become a liability, rather than an asset, to the gospel. He must be careful to avoid false teachers and greedy motives, pursuing instead righteousness, godliness, faith, love, perseverance, and the gentleness that befits a man of God.

The Greek title for this letter is *Pros Timotheon A,* the "First to Timothy." Timothy means "honoring God" or "honored by God," and probably was given to him by his mother Eunice.

Author

Since the early nineteenth century, the Pastoral Epistles have been attacked more than any other Pauline Epistles on the issue of authenticity. The similarity of these epistles requires that they be treated as a unit in terms of authorship because they stand or fall together.

The external evidence solidly supports the conservative position that Paul wrote the letters to Timothy and Titus. Postapostolic church fathers, such as Polycarp and Clement of Rome, allude to them as Paul's writing. In addition, these epistles are identified as Pauline by Irenaeus, Tertullian, Clement of Alexandria, and the Muratorian Canon. Only Romans and First Corinthians have better attestation among the Pauline Epistles.

Suggestions of an author other than Paul are supported wholly on the basis of internal evidence. Even though these letters claim to be written by Paul (1:1; 2 Tim. 1:1; Titus 1:1), critics assert that they are "pious forgeries" that appeared in the second century. There are several problems with this: (1) Pseudonymous writing was unacceptable to Paul (see 2 Thess. 2:2; 3:17) and to the early church, which was very sensitive to the problem of forgeries. (2) The adjective "pious" should deceive no one: a forgery was as deliberately deceptive then as it is now. (3) The many personal facts and names that appear in the Pastoral Epistles would have been avoided by a forger who would have taken refuge in vagueness. Nor would a forger have used expressions like those in chapter 1, verses 13 and 15, if he had been an admirer of Paul. The doctrinal teaching and autobiographical details (cf. 1:12–17; 2:7; 2 Tim. 1:8–12; 4:9–22; Titus 1:5; 3:12–13) fit very well with "Paul, the aged" (Philem. 9). (4) What purpose or advantage would these epistles serve as forgeries written years later? There are too many personal elements, and the doctrinal refutations do not refer to second-century Gnosticsm. (5) The style and content of the postapostolic writings or apocryphal books differ greatly with these three letters.

Date and Setting

Pauline authorship of the Pastoral Epistles requires Paul's release from his Roman imprisonment (Acts 28), the continuation of his missionary endeavors, and his imprisonment for a second time in Rome. Unfortunately, the order of events can only be reconstructed from hints, because there is no concurrent history paralleling Acts to chronicle the last years of the apostle. The following reconstruction, therefore, is only tentative:

As he anticipated (Phil. 1:19, 25–26; 2:24), Paul was released from his first Roman imprisonment. It is possible that his Jewish accusers decided not to appear at his trial before Caesar. In fulfillment of his promise to the Philippians (Phil. 2:19–23), he sends Timothy to Philippi to relate the good news. Paul himself went to Ephesus (in spite of his earlier expectations in Acts 20:38) and to other Asian churches like Colossae (see Philem. 22). When Timothy rejoined him in Ephesus, Paul instructed his assistant to "remain in Ephesus" (1:3) while he journeyed to Macedonia. When he saw that he might be delayed in Macedonia, Paul wrote First Timothy, perhaps from Philippi (3:14–15). After he saw Timothy in Ephesus, the apostle journeyed on to the island of Crete where, after a period of ministry, he left Titus to continue the work (Titus 1:5). In Corinth, Paul decided to write a letter to Titus because Zenas and Apollos were making a journey that would take them by way of Crete (Titus 3:13). He instructed Titus to join him in Nicopolis after the arrival of his replacement in Crete, Artemas or Tychicus (Titus 3:12).

If he went to Spain as he had planned (Rom. 15:24, 28), Paul probably departed with Titus for that western province after his winter in Nicopolis. Early church tradition holds that Paul did go to Spain. Before the end of the first century, Clement of Rome said that Paul "reached the limits of the West" (1 Clement 5:7). Since he was writing from Rome, he evidently had Spain in mind. Paul may have been in Spain from A.D. 64 to 66. He returned to Greece and Asia, to Corinth, Miletus, and Troas (2 Tim. 4:13, 20), and may have been arrested in Troas where he left his valuable books and parchments (2 Tim. 4:13, 15).

Now that Christianity had become an illegal religion in the Empire (the burning of Rome took place in A.D. 64), Paul's enemies were able to successfully accuse him. He was imprisoned in A.D. 67 and wrote Second Timothy from his Roman cell after his first defense before the Imperial Court (2 Tim. 1:8–17; 2:9; 4:16–17). He was delivered from condemnation, but he held no hope of release and expected to be executed (2 Tim. 4:6–8, 18). He urged Timothy to come before that happened (2 Tim. 4:9, 21); and, according to tradition, the apostle was beheaded west of Rome on the Ostian Way.

Paul wrote First Timothy from Macedonia in A.D. 62 or 63 while Timothy was serving as his representative in Ephesus and perhaps in other churches in the province of Asia. Timothy was to appoint elders, combat false doctrine, and supervise church life as an apostolic representative.

Theme and Purpose

The theme of this epistle is Timothy's organization and oversight of the Asian churches as a faithful minister of God. Paul wrote this letter as a leadership manual so that Timothy would have effective guidance in his responsibilities during Paul's absence in Macedonia (3:14–15). Paul wanted to encourage and exhort his younger assistant to become an example to others, exercise his spiritual gifts, and "Fight the good fight of faith" (6:12; cf. 1:18; 4:12–16; 6:20). Timothy's personal and public life must be beyond reproach, and he must know how to deal with matters of false teaching, organization, discipline, proclamation of the Scriptures, poverty and wealth, and the role of various groups. Negatively, he was to refute error (1:7–11; 6:3–5); positively, he was to teach the truth (4:13–16; 6:2, 17–18).

Keys to First Timothy

Key Word: Leadership Manual

Key Verses (3:15–16; 6:11–12)—"But if I am delayed, I *write* so that you may know how you ought to conduct yourself in the house of God, which is the church of the living God, the pillar and ground of the truth. And without controversy great is the mystery of godliness: God was manifested in the flesh, justified in the Spirit, seen by angels, preached among the Gentiles, believed on in the world, received up in glory" (3:15–16).

"But you, O man of God, flee these things and pursue righteousness, godliness, faith, love, patience, gentleness. Fight the good fight of faith, lay hold on eternal life, to which you were also called and have confessed the good confession in the presence of many witnesses" (6:11–12).

Key Chapter (3)—Listed in chapter 3 are the qualifications for the leaders of God's church, the elders and deacons. Notably absent are qualities of worldly success or position. Instead, Paul enumerates character qualities demonstrating that true leadership emanates from our walk with God rather than from achievements or vocational success.

Christ in First Timothy

Christ is the "one Mediator between God and men" (2:5). "God was manifested in the flesh, justified in the Spirit, seen by angels, preached among the Gentiles, believed on in the world, received up in glory" (3:16). He is the source of spiritual strength, faith, and love (1:12, 14). He "came into the world to save sinners" (1:15) and "gave Himself a ransom for all" (2:6) as "the Savior of all men, especially of those who believe" (4:10).

Contribution to the Bible

This is a personal letter, but it is rich in principles that are relevant to every Christian worker and Christian church. Because it was written to Timothy, this epistle assumes rather than develops doctrine. Its primary concern is with the practical outworking of Christian truth on an individual and corporate level. First Timothy, along with Titus, provides the most explicit directions for church leadership and organization in the Bible.

The phrase, "It is a trustworthy statement" (see 1 Tim. 1:15; 3:1; 4:9; 2 Tim.

2:11; Titus 3:8) is peculiar to the Pastoral Epistles. Paul used it in his later years to refer to Christian sayings and confessions.

Survey of First Timothy

Paul's last three recorded letters, written near the end of his full and fruitful life, were addressed to his authorized representatives Timothy and Titus. These were the only letters Paul wrote exclusively to individuals (Philemon was addressed primarily to its namesake, but also to others), and they were designed to exhort and encourage Timothy and Titus in their ministry of solidifying the churches in Ephesus and Crete. In the eighteenth century, these epistles came to be known as the Pastoral Epistles even though they do not use any terms, such as "shepherd, pastor, flock, or sheep." Still, this title is appropriate for First Timothy and Titus, since they focus on the oversight of church life. It is less appropriate in the case of Second Timothy, which is a more personal than church-oriented letter. The Pastoral Epistles abound with principles for leadership and righteous living.

In his first letter to Timothy, Paul seeks to guide his younger and less experienced assistant in his weighty responsibility as the overseer of the work at Ephesus and other Asian cities. He writes, in effect, a challenge to Timothy to fulfill the task before him: combating false teaching with sound doctrine, developing qualified leadership, teaching God's Word, and encouraging Christian conduct. Because of the personal and conversational character of this letter, it is loosely structured around five clear charges that end each section (1:18–20; 3:14–16; 4:11–16; 5:21–25; 6:20–21): Paul's charges concerning doctrine (1); Paul's charge concerning public worship (2—3); Paul's charge concerning false teachers (4); Paul's charge concerning church discipline (5); and Paul's charge concerning pastoral motives (6).

Paul's Charge Concerning Doctrine (1): After his greetings (1:1–2), Paul warns Timothy about the growing problem of false doctrines, particularly as they relate to the misuse of the Mosaic Law (1:3–11). The aging apostle then recounts his radical conversion to Christ and subsequent calling to the ministry (1:12–17). Timothy, too, has received a divine calling, and Paul charges him to fulfill it without wavering in doctrine or conduct (1:18–20).

Paul's Charge Concerning Public Worship (2—3): Turning his attention to the church at large, Paul addresses the issues of church worship and leadership. Efficacious public prayer should be a part of worship, and Paul associates this with the role of men in the church (2:1–8). He then turns to the role of women (2:9–15), wherein he emphasizes the importance of the inner quality of godliness. In chapter 3, verses 1–7, Paul lists several qualifications for overseers or bishops. The word for "overseer" (*episkopos*) is used synonymously with the word for "elder" (*presbuteros*) in the New Testament, because both originally referred to the same office (see Acts 20:17, 28; Titus 1:5, 7). The qualifications for the office of deacon (*diakonos,* "servant") are listed in 3:8–13.

Paul's Charge Concerning False Teachers (4): Timothy obviously had difficulties with some of the older men (5:1) who had left the faith. Paul carefully advises on the issues of marriage, food, and exercise. The closing charge exhorts Timothy not to neglect the spiritual gift given to him.

Paul's Charge Concerning Church Discipline (5): One of the most difficult pastoral duties for the young minister is to lead in the exercise of church discipline. Commencing with the general advice of treating all members of the church as family (5:1–2), Paul concentrates on the two special areas of widows and elders, focusing on Timothy's responsibility and providing practical instruction.

Paul's Charge Concerning Pastoral Duties (6): In addition, the insidious doctrine was being taught that godliness will eventually result in material blessing. Paul, in no uncertain terms, states "from such withdraw yourself" (6:5). The book closes with an extended charge (6:11–21), which is supplemented by an additional charge that Timothy is to give to the wealthy of this age (6:17–19).

Outline of First Timothy

Second Timothy

SECOND TIMOTHY IS PAUL'S LAST WILL and testament to his spiritual son Timothy. Writing from a Roman prison cell, Paul imparts his final words of wisdom and encouragement to Timothy who is ministering in the midst of opposition and hardship in Ephesus. Paul stresses the importance of godly living, preaching the Word both in and out of season, and preparing for the coming apostasy within the church. Underlying all that Paul says is the importance of God's Word—the only foundation strong enough to withstand persecution from without and problems from within!

SECOND TIMOTHY	Focus	Persevere in Present Testings			Endure in Future Testings		
		1:1 2:26			3:1 4:22		
	Divisions	Thanksgiving for Timothy's Faith	Reminder of Timothy's Responsibility	Characteristics of a Faithful Minister	Approaching Day of Apostasy	Charge to Preach the Word	Approaching Death of Paul
		1:1 1:5	1:6 1:18	2:1 2:26	3:1 3:17	4:1 4:5	4:6 4:22
	Topics	Power of the Gospel		Perseverance of the Gospel Message	Protector of the Gospel	Proclamation of the Gospel	
		Reminder		Requirements	Resistance	Requests	
	Place	Roman Prison					
	Time	c. A.D. 67					

Introduction and Title

Prison is the last place from which to expect a letter of encouragement, but that is where Paul's second letter to Timothy originates. He begins by assuring Timothy of his continuing love and prayers, and reminds him of his spiritual heritage and responsibilities. Only the one who perseveres, whether as a soldier, athlete, farmer, or minister of Jesus Christ, will reap the reward. Paul warns Timothy that his teaching will come under attack as men desert the truth for ear "itching" words (4:3). But Timothy has Paul's example to guide him and God's Word to fortify him as he faces growing opposition and glowing opportunities in the last days.

Paul's last epistle received the title *Pros Timotheon B,* the "Second to Timothy." When Paul's epistles were collected together the B was probably added to distinguish this letter from the first letter he wrote to Timothy.

Author

Since the Pastoral Epistles have to be treated as a unit on the matter of authorship, see "Author" in First Timothy for comments on the origin of Second Timothy.

Timothy's name is found more often in the salutations of the Pauline Epistles than any other (see 2 Cor.; Phil.; Col.; 1 and 2 Thess.; 1 and 2 Tim.; Philem.). His father was a Greek (Acts 16:1), but his Jewish mother Eunice and grandmother Lois raised him in the knowledge of the Hebrew Scriptures (1:5; 3:15). Timothy evidently became a convert of Paul (see 1 Cor. 4:17; 1 Tim. 1:2; 2 Tim. 1:2) when the apostle was in Lystra on his first missionary journey (Acts 14:8–20). When he visited Lystra on his second missionary journey, Paul decided to take Timothy along with him and circumcised him because of the Jews (Acts 16:1–3). Timothy was ordained to the ministry (1 Tim. 4:14; 2 Tim. 1:6) and served as a devoted companion and assistant to Paul in Troas, Berea, Thessalonica, and Corinth (Acts 16—18; 1 Thess. 3:1–2). During the third missionary journey, Timothy labored with Paul and ministered for him as his representative in Ephesus, Macedonia, and Corinth. He was with Paul during his first Roman imprisonment and evidently went to Philippi (Phil. 2:19–23) after Paul's release. Paul left him in Ephesus to supervise the work there (1 Tim. 1:3) and years later summoned him to Rome (4:9, 21). According to Hebrews 13:23, Timothy was imprisoned and released, but the passage does not say where. Timothy was sickly (1 Tim. 5:23), timid (1:7), and youthful (1 Tim. 4:12), but he was a gifted teacher who was trustworthy and diligent.

Date and Setting

For a tentative reconstruction of the events following Paul's first Roman imprisonment, see "Date and Setting" in First Timothy. The cruel and unbalanced Nero, emperor of Rome from A.D. 54 to 68, was responsible for the beginning of the Roman persecution of Christians. Half of Rome was destroyed in July, A.D. 64 by a fire, and mounting suspicion that Nero was responsible for the conflagration caused him to use the unpopular Christians as his scapegoat. Christianity thus became a *religio illicita,* and persecution of those who professed Christ became severe. By the time of Paul's return from Spain to Asia in A.D. 66, his enemies were able to use the official Roman position against Christianity to their advantage. Fearing for their own lives, the Asian believers failed to support Paul after his arrest (1:15) and no one supported him at his first defense before the Imperial Court (4:16). Abandoned by almost everyone (4:10–11), the apostle found himself in circumstances very different from those of his first Roman imprisonment (Acts 28:16–31). At that time he was merely under house arrest, people could freely visit him, and he had the hope of release. Now he was in a cold Roman cell (4:13), regarded "as an evildoer" (2:9), and without hope of acquittal in spite of the success of his initial defense (4:6–8, 17–18). Under these conditions, Paul wrote this epistle in the fall of A.D. 67, hoping that Timothy would be able to visit him before the approaching winter (4:21). Timothy evidently was in Ephesus at the time of this letter (see 1:18, 4:19), and on his way to Rome he would go through Troas (4:13) and Macedonia. Priscilla and Aquila (4:19) probably returned from Rome (Rom. 16:3) to Ephesus after the burning of Rome and the beginning of the persecution. Tychicus may have been the bearer of this letter (4:12).

Theme and Purpose

In this letter, Paul commissions Timothy to faithfully carry on the work that the condemned apostle must now relinquish. This combat manual exhorts Timothy to put the spiritual equipment of the Word of God to constant use to overcome growing obstacles to the spread of the gospel. Timothy was in great need of encouragement because of the hardships that he was facing, and Paul used this letter to instruct him on how to handle persecution from without and dissension and deception from within. As a spiritual father, Paul urged his son Timothy to overcome his natural timidity and boldly proclaim the gospel even if it meant that he would suffer for doing so. Paul also wrote this letter to summon Timothy and Mark to visit him in Rome as soon as possible and to bring his papyrus and parchment scrolls along with his cloak. In case they did not reach him in time, this letter would serve as Paul's closing testimony to the believer's victory in Christ in the face of death.

Keys to Second Timothy

Key Word: Endurance in Ministry

Key Verses (2:3–4; 3:14–17)—"You therefore must endure hardship as a good soldier of Jesus Christ. No one engaged in warfare entangles himself with the affairs of *this* life, that he may please him who enlisted him as a soldier" (2:3–4).

"But *as for you,* continue in the things which you have learned and have been assured of, knowing from whom you have learned *them,* and that from childhood you have known the Holy Scriptures, which are able to make you wise for salvation through faith which is in Christ Jesus. All Scripture is given by inspiration of God, and is profitable for doctrine, for reproof, for correction, for instruction in righteousness, that the man of God may be complete, thoroughly equipped for every good work" (3:14–17).

Key Chapter (2)—The second chapter of Second Timothy ought to be required daily reading for every pastor and full-time Christian worker. Paul lists the keys to an enduring successful ministry: A reproducing ministry (1—2); an enduring ministry (3—13); a studying ministry (14—18); and a holy ministry (19—26).

Christ in Second Timothy

Christ Jesus appeared on earth, "abolished death and brought life and immortality to light through the gospel" (1:10). He rose from the dead (2:8) and provides salvation and "eternal glory" (2:10); for if believers "died with *Him*" they will "also live with *Him*" (2:11). All who love His appearing will receive the "crown of righteousness" (4:8) and "reign with *Him*" (2:12).

Contribution to the Bible

Second Timothy is, in effect, Paul's last will and testament, and in it Paul reviews the past, analyzes the present, and anticipates his future deliverance to God's heavenly kingdom. This book has provided comfort, encouragement, and motivation to distressed Christian workers over the centuries. It emphasizes the centrality of the Scriptures and contains the clearest biblical statement of their inspiration (3:16–17; see also 4:2).

This little epistle is full of personal references to Paul, Timothy, and over twenty other people, a number of whom are mentioned nowhere else in Scripture. It also contains two important prophecies about coming conditions of apostasy, empty profession, and spiritual deception (3:1–9; 4:3–4)

Survey of Second Timothy

Paul knows as he writes this final epistle that his days on earth are quickly drawing to a close. About to relinquish his heavy burdens, the godly apostle seeks to challenge and strengthen his somewhat timid but faithful associate, Timothy, in his difficult ministry in Ephesus. In spite of Paul's bleak circumstances, this is a letter of encouragement that urges Timothy on to steadfastness in the fulfillment of his divinely appointed task. Paul calls Timothy a "good soldier of Jesus Christ" (2:3), and it is clear from the sharp imperatives that this letter is really a combat manual for use in the spiritual warfare: "stir up" (1:6); "Do not be ashamed" (cf. 1:8, 12–13); "share with me in the sufferings" (1:8); "Hold fast . . . sound words" (1:13); "That good thing . . . keep" (1:14); "be strong" (2:1); "endure hardship" (2:3); "Be diligent to present yourself approved" (2:15); "Flee . . . pursue" (2:22); "avoid" (2:23); "You . . . must beware" (4:15). Central to everything in Second Timothy is the sure foundation of the Word of God. Paul focuses on the need to persevere in present testing (1—2), and to endure in future testing (3—4).

Persevere in Present Testing (1—2): After his salutation to his "beloved son" (1:1–2), Paul expresses his thanksgiving for Timothy's "genuine faith" (1:3–5). He then encourages Timothy to stand firm in the power of the gospel and to overcome any fear in the face of opposition. At personal risk, Onesiphorus boldly sought out Paul in Rome, but most of the Asian Christians failed to stand behind Paul at the time of his arrest. Timothy must remain faithful and not fear possible persecution. Paul then exhorts his spiritual son to reproduce in the lives of others what he has received in Christ (four generations are mentioned in 2:2). He is responsible to work hard and discipline himself like a teacher, a soldier, a farmer, a workman, a vessel, and a servant, following the example of Paul's perseverance (2:1–13). In his dealings with others, Timothy must not become entangled in false speculation, foolish quarrels, or youthful lusts, which would hamper his effectiveness. As he pursues "righteousness, faith, love, peace" (2:22), he must know how to graciously overcome error.

Endure in Future Testing (3—4): Paul anticipates a time of growing apostasy and wickedness when men and women will be increasingly susceptible to empty religiosity and false teaching (3:1–9). Arrogance and godlessness will breed further deception and persecution, but Timothy must not waiver in using the Scripture to combat doctrinal error and moral evil (3:10–17). The Scriptures are inspired ("God-breathed") and with them Timothy is equipped to carry out the ministry to which he was called. Paul's final exhortation to Timothy (4:1–5) is a classic summary of the task of the man of God to proclaim the gospel in spite of opposing circumstances. This very personal letter closes with an update of Paul's situation in Rome along with certain requests (4:6–22). Paul longs to see Timothy before the end, and he also needs certain articles, especially "the parchments" (probably portions of the Old Testament Scriptures).

Outline of Second Timothy

I. **Persevere in Present Testings,** 1:1—2:26
- A. Thanksgiving for Timothy's Faith, 1:1–5
- B. Reminder of Timothy's Responsibility, 1:6–18
- C. Characteristics of a Faithful Minister, 2:1–26
  1. Discipling Teacher, 2:1–2
  2. Single-minded Soldier, 2:3–5
  3. Enduring Farmer, 2:6–13
  4. Diligent Workman, 2:14–19
  5. Sanctified Vessel, 2:20–23
  6. Gentle Servant, 2:24–26

II. **Endure in Future Testings,** 3:1—4:22
- A. Approaching Day of Apostasy, 3:1–17
  1. Coming of Apostasy, 3:1–9
  2. Confronting Apostasy, 3:10–17
- B. Charge to Preach the Word, 4:1–5
- C. Approaching Death of Paul, 4:6–22
  1. Paul's Hope in Death, 4:6–8
  2. Paul's Situation in Prison, 4:9–18
  3. Paul's Closing Greetings, 4:19–22

Titus

Titus, a young minister, is left on the island of Crete by Paul to begin the challenging task of organizing new converts into local churches. In this letter, Paul shares with Titus some practical wisdom regarding church organization and administration. Leaders must be chosen on the basis of proven character and conduct; false teachers must be quickly detected and removed; church members of all ages must be encouraged to live lives worthy of the gospel they claim to believe. Young and old, leader and laity, must demonstrate the reality of their faith by being "careful to maintain good works" (3:8).

TITUS	Focus	Appoint Elders		Set Things in Order	
		1:1 — 1:16		2:1 — 3:15	
	Divisions	Ordain Qualified Elders	Rebuke False Teachers	Speak Sound Doctrine	Maintain Good Works
		1:1 — 1:9	1:10 — 1:16	2:1 — 2:15	3:1 — 3:15
	Topics	Protection of Sound Doctrine		Practice of Sound Doctrine	
		Organization	Offenders	Operation	Obedience
	Place	Probably Written in Corinth			
	Time	c. A.D. 63			

Introduction and Title

Titus, a young pastor, faces the unenviable assignment of setting in order the church at Crete. Paul writes advising him to appoint elders, men of proven spiritual character in their homes and businesses, to oversee the work of the church. But elders are not the only individuals in the church who are required to excel spiritually. Men and women, young and old, each have their vital functions to fulfill in the church if they are to be living examples of the doctrine they profess. Throughout his letter to Titus, Paul stresses the necessary, practical working out of salvation in the daily lives of both the elders and the congregation. Good works are desirable and profitable for all believers.

This third Pastoral Epistle is simply titled *Pros Titon,* "To Titus." Ironically, this was also the name of the Roman general who destroyed Jerusalem in A.D. 70 and succeeded his father Vespasian as emperor.

Author

Since the Pastoral Epistles have to be treated as a unit on the matter of authorship, see "Author" in First Timothy for the authorship of Titus.

Titus is not mentioned in Acts, but the thirteen references to him in the Pauline Epistles make it clear that he was one of Paul's closest and most trusted companions. This convert of Paul ("*my* true son in *our* common faith," 1:4) was probably from Syrian Antioch, if he was one of the disciples of Acts 11:26. Paul brought this uncircumcised Greek believer to Jerusalem (Gal. 2:3) where he became a test case on the matter of Gentiles and liberty from the Law. Years later when Paul set out from Antioch on his third missionary journey (Acts 18:22), Titus must have accompanied him because he was sent by the apostle to Corinth on three occasions during that time (see 2 Cor. 2:12–13; 7:5–7, 13–15; 8:6, 16–24). He is not mentioned again until Paul leaves him in Crete to carry on the work (1:5). He was with Paul during his second Roman imprisonment but left to go to Dalmatia (2 Tim. 4:10), possibly on an evangelistic mission. Paul spoke of this reliable and gifted associate as his "brother" (2 Cor. 2:13), his "partner and fellow worker" (2 Cor. 8:23), and his "son" (1:4). He lauded Titus' character and conduct in Second Corinthians 7:13–15; 8:16–17.

Date and Setting

For a tentative reconstruction of the events following Paul's first Roman imprisonment, see "Date and Setting" in First Timothy.

The Mediterranean island of Crete is 156 miles long and up to 30 miles wide, and its first-century inhabitants were notorious for untruthfulness and immorality (1:12–13). "To act the Cretan" became an idiom meaning "to play the liar." A number of Jews from Crete were present in Jerusalem at the time of Peter's sermon on the Day of Pentecost (Acts 2:11), and some of them may have believed in Christ and introduced the gospel to their countrymen. Certainly Paul would not have had opportunity to do evangelistic work during his brief sojourn in Crete while he was en route to Rome (Acts 27:7–13). The apostle spread the gospel in the cities of Crete after his release from Roman imprisonment and left Titus there to finish organizing the churches (1:5). Because of the problem of immorality among the Cretans, it was important for Titus to stress the need for righteousness in Christian living. False teachers, especially "those of the circumcision" (1:10), were also misleading and divisive. Paul wrote this letter c. A.D. 63, perhaps from Corinth, taking advantage of the journey of Zenas and Apollos (3:13), whose destination would take them by way of Crete. Paul was planning to spend the winter in Nicopolis (western Greece), and he urged Titus in this letter to join him there upon his replacement by Artemas or Tychicus (3:12). Paul may have been planning to leave Nicopolis for Spain in the spring, and he wanted his useful companion Titus to accompany him.

Theme and Purpose

This brief letter focuses on Titus' role and responsibility in the organization and supervision of the churches in Crete. It was written to strengthen and exhort Titus to firmly exercise his authority as an apostolic representative in a situation where churches needed to be put in order, false teachers and dissenters needed to be refuted, and immoral behavior needed to be replaced by good deeds. Paul used this letter to remind Titus of some of the details related to his task, including the qualifications for elders and the behavior expected of various groups in the churches. Paul included three doctrinal sections in this letter to stress that proper belief (orthodoxy) gives the basis for proper behavior (orthopraxy). Because of the opposition Titus would face (1:11,13; 2:15; 3:9–11), this letter was also written to provide official apostolic warrant for Titus' authority. Paul also used this letter to give Titus certain personal instructions (3:12–13).

Keys to Titus

Key Word: Conduct Manual

Key Verses (1:5; 3:8)—"For this reason I left you in Crete, that you should set in order the things that are lacking, and appoint elders in every city as I commanded you—" (1:5).

"This is a faithful saying, and these things I want you to affirm constantly, that those who have believed in God should be careful to maintain good works. These things are good and profitable to men" (3:8).

Key Chapter (2)—Summarized in Titus 2 are the key commands to be obeyed which insure godly relationships within the church. Paul includes all categories of people, instructing them to show "all good fidelity, that they may adorn the doctrine of God our Savior in all things" (2:10).

Christ in Titus

The deity and redemptive work of Christ are beautifully stated: "Looking for the blessed hope and glorious appearing of our great God and Savior Jesus Christ, who gave Himself for us, that He might redeem us from every lawless deed and purify for Himself *His* own special people, zealous for good works" (2:13–14).

Contribution to the Bible

Titus and First Timothy are similar in date, circumstances, and purposes. Both give instructions on qualifications for leadership, how to deal with false teaching, and the need for sound doctrine and behavior. Both contain encouragement and exhortation to Paul's representatives, but Titus is briefer, more official, and less personal than First Timothy. The situation at Ephesus required a stronger emphasis on sound doctrine, while that at Crete required more concentration on conduct. Even so, Titus offers three excellent summaries of Christian theology (1:1–4; 2:11–14; 3:4–7), and the last two are among the most sublime New Testament portraits of the grace of God.

Survey of Titus

Titus, like First Timothy, was written by Paul after his release from Roman imprisonment and was also written to an associate who was given the task of organizing and supervising a large work as an apostolic representative. Paul left Titus on the island of Crete to "set in order the things that are lacking, and appoint elders in every city" (1:5). Not long after Paul's departure from Crete, he wrote this letter to encourage and assist Titus in his task. It stresses sound doctrine and warns against those who distort the truth, but it also is a conduct manual that emphasizes good deeds and the proper conduct of various groups within the churches. This epistle falls into two major sections: the appointment of elders (1); setting things in order (2—3).

Appoint Elders (1): The salutation to Titus is actually a compact doctrinal statement, which lifts up "His word" as the source of the truth that reveals the way to eternal life (1:1–4). Paul reminds Titus of his responsibility to organize the churches of Crete by appointing elders (also called overseers; see 1:7) and rehearses the qualifications these spiritual leaders must meet (1:5–9). This is especially important in view of the disturbances that are being caused by false teachers who are upsetting a number of the believers with their Judaic myths and commandments (1:10–16). The natural tendency toward moral laxity among the Cretans coupled with that kind of deception is a dangerous force that must be overcome by godly leadership and sound doctrine.

Set Things in Order (2—3): Titus is given the charge to "speak the things which are proper for sound doctrine" (2:1), and Paul delineates Titus' role with regard to various groups in the church, including older men, older women, young women, young men, and servants (2:2–10). The knowledge of Christ must effect a transformation in each of these groups so that their testimony will "adorn the doctrine of God" (2:10). The second doctrinal statement of Titus (2:11–14) gives the basis for the appeals Paul has just made for righteous living. God in His grace redeems believers from being slaves of sin, assuring them the "blessed hope" of the coming of Christ that will eventually be realized. Paul urges Titus to authoritatively proclaim these truths (2:15).

In chapter 3, Paul moves from conduct in groups (2:1–10) to conduct in general (3:1–11). The behavior of believers as citizens must be different from the behavior of unbelievers because of their regeneration and renewal by the Holy Spirit. The third doctrinal statement in this book (3:4–7) emphasizes the kindness, love, and mercy of God who saves us "not by works of righteousness which we have done" (3:5). Nevertheless, the need for good deeds as a result of salvation is stressed six times in the three chapters of Titus (1:16; 2:7, 14; 3:1, 8, 14). Paul exhorts Titus to deal firmly with dissenters who would cause factions and controversies (3:9–11) and closes the letter with three instructions, a greeting, and a benediction (3:12–15).

Outline of Titus

I. Appoint Elders, 1:1–16
    A. Introduction, 1:1–4
    B. Ordain Qualified Elders, 1:5–9
    C. Rebuke False Teachers, 1:10–16

II. Set Things in Order, 2:1—3:15
    A. Speak Sound Doctrine, 2:1–15
    B. Maintain Good Works, 3:1–11
    C. Conclusion, 3:12–15

Philemon

PAUL'S "POSTCARD" TO PHILEMON is the shortest and perhaps the most intimate of all his letters. It is a masterpiece of diplomacy and tact in dealing with a festering social sore in the Roman Empire: human slavery. Onesimus, a slave of Philemon, had stolen from his master and run away to Rome. There he came in contact with Paul (who was under house arrest, Acts 28:16–30) and with the claims of Jesus Christ. After his conversion, Onesimus faced yet another confrontation, this time with his estranged master Philemon. Paul sends him back with this letter in hand, urging Philemon to extend forgiveness. Onesimus had left him as his bond servant. Now he was returning as his brother in the Lord. Therefore, Paul exhorts, "Receive him as you would me" (v. 17).

	Focus	Prayer of Thanksgiving		Petition for Onesimus		Promise to Philemon	
		1	7	8	16	17	25
PHILEMON	**Divisions**	Commendation of Philemon's Love		Intercession for Onesimus		Confidence in Philemon's Obedience	
		1	7	8	16	17	25
	Topics	Praise of Philemon		Plea of Paul		Pledge of Paul	
		Character of Philemon		Conversion of Onesimus		Confidence of Paul	
	Place	Rome					
	Time	C. A.D. 60–61					

Introduction and Title

Does Christian brotherly love really work, even in situations of extraordinary tension and difficulty? Will it work, for example, between a prominent slave owner and one of his runaway slaves? Paul has no doubt! He writes a "postcard" to Philemon, his beloved brother and fellow worker, on behalf of Onesimus—a deserter, thief, and formerly worthless slave, but now Philemon's brother in Christ. With much tact and tenderness, Paul asks Philemon to receive Onesimus back with the same gentleness with which he would receive Paul himself. Any debt Onesimus owes, Paul promises to make good. Knowing Philemon, Paul is confident that brotherly love and forgiveness will carry the day.

Since this letter is addressed to Philemon in verse 1, it becomes known as *Pros Philemona,* "To Philemon." Like First and Second Timothy and Titus, it is addressed to an individual, but unlike the Pastoral Epistles, Philemon is also addressed to a family and a church (v. 2).

Author

The authenticity of Philemon was not called into question until the fourth century, when certain theologians concluded that its lack of doctrinal content made it unworthy of the apostle Paul. But men like Jerome and Chrysostom soon vindicated this epistle, and it was not challenged again until the nineteenth century. Some radical critics who denied the authenticity of Colossians also turned against the Pauline authorship of Philemon because of the close connection between the two epistles (e.g., the same people are associated with Paul in both letters: cf. Col. 4:9–10, 12, 14; Philem. 10, 23–24). The general consensus of scholarship, however, recognized Philemon as Paul's work. There could have been no doctrinal motive for its forgery, and it is supported externally by consistent tradition and internally by no less than three references to Paul (vv. 1, 9, 19).

Date and Setting

Reconstructing the background of this letter, it appears that a slave named Onesimus had robbed or in some other way wronged his master Philemon and had escaped. He had made his way from Colossae to Rome where he had found relative safety among the masses in the Imperial City. Somehow Onesimus had come into contact with Paul: it is possible that he had even sought out the apostle for help (Onesimus no doubt had heard Philemon speak of Paul). Paul had led him to Christ (v. 10), and although Onesimus had become a real asset to Paul, both knew that as a Christian, Onesimus had a responsibility to return to Philemon. That day came when Paul wrote his epistle to the Colossians. Tychicus was the bearer of that letter. Paul decided to send Onesimus along with Tychicus to Colossae (see Col. 4:7–9; Philem. 12), knowing that it would be safer, in view of slave-catchers, to send Onesimus with a companion.

Philemon is one of the four Prison Epistles (see Ephesians, Philippians, and especially "Date and Setting" in Colossians for background). It was written in A.D. 60

or 61 and dispatched at the same time as Colossians during Paul's first Roman imprisonment (vv. 1, 9–10, 13, 23). Philemon 22 reflects Paul's confident hope of release: "prepare a guest room for me, for I trust that through your prayers I shall be granted to you."

Philemon was a resident of Colossae (Philem. 1–2) and a convert of Paul (v. 19), perhaps through an encounter with Paul in Ephesus during Paul's third missionary journey. Philemon's house was large enough to serve as the meeting place for the church there (v. 2). He was benevolent to other believers (vv. 5–7), and his son Archippus evidently held a position of leadership in the church (see Col. 4:17; Philem. 2). Philemon may have had other slaves in addition to Onesimus, and he was not alone as a slave owner among the Colossian believers (Col. 4:1). Thus this letter and his response would provide guidelines for other master-slave relationships.

According to Roman law, runaway slaves such as Onesimus could be severely punished or condemned to a violent death. It is doubtful that Onesimus would have returned to Philemon even with this letter if he had not become a believer in Christ.

Theme and Purpose

Philemon develops the transition from bondage to brotherhood that is brought about by Christian love and forgiveness. Just as Philemon was shown mercy through the grace of Christ, so he must graciously forgive his repentant runaway who has returned as a brother in Christ. Paul wrote this letter as his personal appeal that Philemon receive Onesimus even as he would receive Paul. This letter was also addressed to other Christians in Philemon's circle, because Paul wanted it to have an impact on the Colossian church as a whole.

Keys to Philemon

Key Word: Forgiveness
Key Verses (16–17)—"No longer as a slave but more than a slave, as a beloved brother, especially to me but how much more to you, both in the flesh and in the Lord. If then you count me as a partner, receive him as *you would* me" (vv. 16–17).

Christ in Philemon

The forgiveness that the believer finds in Christ is beautifully portrayed by analogy in Philemon. Onesimus, guilty of a great offense (vv. 11, 18), is motivated by Paul's love to intercede on his behalf (vv. 10–17). Paul lays aside his rights (v. 8) and becomes Onesimus' substitute by assuming his debt (vv. 18–19). By Philemon's gracious act, Onesimus is restored and placed in a new relationship (vv. 15–16). In this analogy, we are as Onesimus. Paul's advocacy before Philemon is parallel to Christ's work of mediation before the Father. Onesimus was condemned by law but saved by grace.

Contribution to the Bible

In this very personal and persuasive letter, Paul skillfully handled a delicate matter with supreme tactfulness and genuine warmth. As in his other epistles, he was able to apply the highest principles to the most mundane affairs. Christian love and courtesy dominate Philemon, and though it is not written with elegance and formality, its content is marked by loftiness and dignity. Unlike his other epistles, Paul wrote Philemon entirely in his own hand (v. 19), apparently to emphasize the urgency and personal nature of the request. Paul does not minimize Onesimus' offense, but acting as his advocate and intercessor, he puts himself in Onesimus' place.

Philemon was not written to impart doctrine but to apply it in such a way that the life-changing effects of Christianity would have an impact on social conditions. The power of the gospel overcomes sociological barriers ("neither slave nor free," Gal. 3:28; cf. Col. 3:11), and Paul is a vivid illustration of this truth: this once self-righteous Pharisee now refers to a gentile slave as "my son Onesimus, whom I have begotten" (v. 10). Philemon is not a direct attack on the institution of slavery, but its Christian principles would ultimately lead to the renunciation of slavery.

Survey of Philemon

This briefest of Paul's epistles (only 334 words in the Greek text) is a model of courtesy, discretion, and loving concern for the forgiveness of one who would otherwise face the sentence of death. This tactful and highly personal letter can be divided into three components: prayer of thanksgiving for Philemon (vv. 1–7); petition of Paul for Onesimus (vv. 8–16); promise of Paul to Philemon (vv. 17–25).

Prayer of Thanksgiving for Philemon (vv. 1–7): Writing this letter as a "prisoner of Christ Jesus" Paul addresses it personally to Philemon (a Christian leader in Colossae), to Apphia and Archippus (evidently Philemon's wife and son), as well as to the church that meets in Philemon's house. The main body of this compact letter begins with a prayer of thanksgiving for Philemon's faith and love.

Petition of Paul for Onesimus (vv. 8–16): Basing his appeal on Philemon's character, Paul refuses to command Philemon to pardon and receive Onesimus. Instead, Paul seeks to persuade his friend of his Christian responsibility to forgive even as he was forgiven by Christ. Paul urges Philemon not to punish Onesimus but to receive him "no longer as a slave" but as "a beloved brother" (v. 16).

Promise of Paul to Philemon (vv. 17–25): Paul places Onesimus' debt on his account, but then reminds Philemon of the greater spiritual debt which Philemon himself owes as a convert to Christ (vv. 17–19).

Paul closes this effective epistle with a hopeful request (v. 22), greetings from his companions (vv. 23–24), and a benediction (v. 25). The fact that it was preserved indicates Philemon's favorable response to Paul's pleas.

Outline of Philemon

I. The Prayer of Thanksgiving for Philemon, 1–7

II. The Petition of Paul for Onesimus, 8–16

III. The Promise of Paul to Philemon, 17–25

Talk Thru the Pauline Epistles

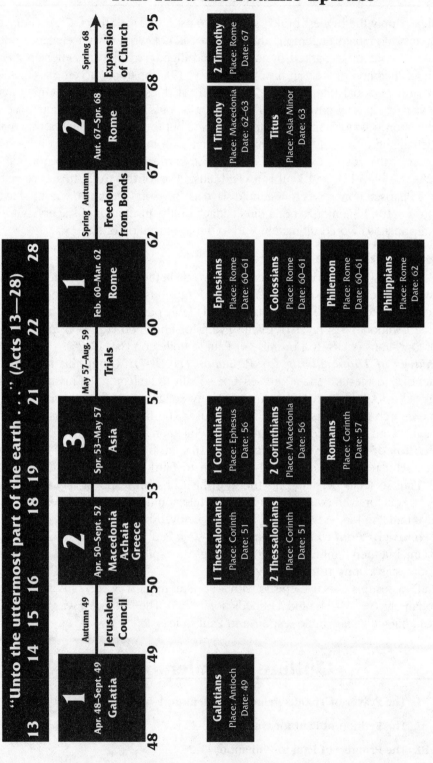

Summary of the Pauline Epistles

Book	No. of Chapters	Author	Key Words	Place Written	Date Written	Recipients
Romans	16	Paul	Paid in Full	Corinth	57	Beloved of God in Rome
1 Corinthians	16	Paul	Spanking the Saints	Ephesus	56	Church of God at Corinth, those sanctified in Christ Jesus
2 Corinthians	13	Paul	Anatomy of an Apostle	Macedonia	56	Church of God at Corinth and all Saints throughout Achaia
Galatians	6	Paul	Unshackled	Antioch	49	Churches of Galatia
Ephesians	6	Paul	Body-building	Rome	60–61	Saints in Ephesus
Phillipians	4	Paul	How to Be Happy Though Humble	Rome	62	Saints in Christ Jesus in Philippi
Colossians	4	Paul	Commander-in-Chief	Rome	60–61	Saints and faithful brothers in Christ at Colosse
1 Thessalonians	5	Paul	Stay on Target	Corinth	51	Church of the Thessalonians
2 Thessalonians	3	Paul	Working Waiters	Corinth	51	Church of the Thessalonians
1 Timothy	6	Paul	Leadership Manual	Macedonia	62–63	Timothy, my true child in the faith
2 Timothy	4	Paul	Combat Manual	Rome	67	Timothy, my beloved son
Titus	3	Paul	Conduct Manual	Corinth	63	Titus, my true child in a common faith
Philemon	1	Paul	Bondage to Brotherhood	Rome	60–61	Philemon, our beloved brother

Introduction to
The Non-Pauline Epistles and Revelation

THE NON-PAULINE EPISTLES

These eight epistles exert an influence out of proportion to their length (less than 10 percent of the New Testament). They supplement the thirteen Pauline Epistles by offering different perspectives on the richness of Christian truth. Each of the five authors—James, Peter, John, Jude, and the author of Hebrews—has a distinctive contribution to make from his own point of view. Like the four complementary approaches to the life of Christ in the Gospels, these writers provide a sweeping portrait of the Christian life in which the total is greater than the sum of the parts. Great as Paul's epistles are, the New Testament revelation after Acts would be severely limited by one apostolic perspective if the writings of these five men were not included.

With the exception of James, these letters were written near the end of Paul's life or after his time. As Paul anticipated in Acts 20:29–30; First Timothy 4:1–3; and Second Timothy 4:3–4, the problem of heretical teachings would reach alarming proportions in the church. It is significant that most of the non-Pauline Epistles deal rather firmly with these dangerous doctrines. The churches of this time were threatened not only by external opposition and persecution, but also by internal attacks from false prophets.

The term "general epistle" appears in the King James Version titles of James, First and Second Peter, First John, and Jude, but it was not used in the oldest manuscripts. These epistles were not addressed to specific churches or individuals, and they came to be known as the general or "catholic" (universal) Epistles. The epistles of Second and Third John are also included in this group even though they are addressed to specific people. Because of this problem, and because Hebrews is not regarded as a general epistle, it would be safer to designate Hebrews, James, First and Second Peter, First, Second, and Third John, and Jude as the non-Pauline Epistles (assuming that Paul did not write

Hebrews; see Hebrews, "Author"). The Pauline Epistles are titled by their addressees, but the non-Pauline Epistles (except Hebrews) are titled by their authors.

These epistles were usually placed before the Pauline Epistles in Greek manuscripts, but early catalogs of the canonical New Testament books generally listed them in the order used today. This seems preferable because of their date, length, and content. It also reflects the delay most of them endured in being admitted into the canon of authoritative books. All but the first epistles of Peter and John were disputed for a period of time for various reasons before being officially recognized as canonical. This illustrates the great care taken by the early church in critically distinguishing between authoritative and later apocryphal books.

Hebrews

This beautifully styled epistle was written to demonstrate the superiority of Christ over all that preceded Him. The readers were evidently in danger of slipping back into Judaism because of growing opposition to them as Christians. They needed to mature and become stable in their faith. The author presents the superiority of Christ's person, priesthood, and power.

James

James wrote this incisive and practical catalog of the characteristics of true faith to exhort his Hebrew-Christian readers to examine the reality of their own faith. If it does not produce a qualitative change in character or control (1—3), its genuineness must be questioned. James also rebukes those who succumb to the pursuit of worldly pleasure and wealth rather than God, and encourages a patient endurance in light of the coming of the Lord.

First Peter

The recipients of this letter were being maligned for their faith in Christ and needed Peter's words of comfort and counsel. He begins by giving them a fresh perspective on the riches of their salvation and their need for holy lives. He then encourages them to develop an attitude of submission in view of their suffering. Undeserved suffering for the name of Christ must be met by an attitude of humble dependence on God.

Second Peter

Unlike First Peter, which dealt with external opposition, Second Peter copes with the problem of internal opposition, in the dangerous form of false teachers who would entice believers into their errors of belief and conduct. Peter counters this peril with an appeal for growth in the true knowledge of Christ as the best way to overcome the seduction of heresy.

First John

John's first epistle explores the dimensions of fellowship between redeemed people and God. He is a God of light, and believers must walk in integrity before Him; He is a God of love, and believers must manifest love for one another; and He is a God of life, and believers can be assured of eternal life in Christ.

Second John

This note was written to commend the readers for remaining steadfast in apostolic truth and to remind them to walk in love in obedience to the Lord's commandment. John also urged them not to show hospitality to any teachers whose doctrine about Christ is unsound.

Third John

John had received a report from the traveling teachers he commissioned, telling of Gaius' warm hospitality on their behalf. The apostle personally thanks Gaius for his walk in the truth and support of these missionaries, in contrast to Diotrephes, who rejected them and told others to do the same.

Jude

In spite of its brevity, this is the most intense exposé of false teachers in the New Testament. Jude reveals their conduct and character and makes liberal use of the Old Testament to predict their judgment. On the positive side, Jude encourages his readers to build themselves up in the truth and contend earnestly for the faith.

Revelation

This most controversial book is the culmination, not only of the New Testament but of the Bible as a whole, since it completes the story begun in Genesis. As the only New Testament book that concentrates on prophecy, the Apocalypse has been approached from a number of interpretive directions.

After a dramatic description of his overwhelming vision of the glorious Christ, John records seven messages to seven Asian churches (1—3). Chapters 4—19 portray unparalleled judgment upon rebellious mankind, the scenes shifting back and forth from heaven to earth. Jesus Christ is not only the Lamb that was slain, but also the Lion who has received all authority to stand in judgment of men and angels. After describing the Second Advent and the judgments that follow, John records his vision of the new heaven and new earth and surveys the marvels of the New Jerusalem (20—22).

Hebrews

MANY JEWISH BELIEVERS, HAVING STEPPED OUT of Judaism into Christianity, wanted to reverse their course in order to escape persecution by their countrymen. The writer of Hebrews exhorts them to "press on" to maturity in Christ. His appeal is based on the superiority of Christ over the Judaic system. Christ is better than the angels, for they worship Him. He is better than Moses, for Moses was created by Him. He is better than the Aaronic priesthood, for His sacrifice was once for all time. He is better than the Law, for He mediates a better covenant. In short, there is more to be gained by suffering for Christ than by reverting to Judaism. Pressing on to maturity produces tested faith, self-discipline, and a visible love seen in good works.

HEBREWS

Focus	Superiority of Christ's Person			Superiority of Christ's Work			Superiority of the Christian's Walk		
	1:1 4:13			4:14 10:18			10:19 13:25		
Divisions	Christ over the Prophets	Christ over the Angels	Christ over Moses	Christ's Priesthood	Christ's Covenant	Christ's Sanctuary and Sacrifice	Full Assurance of Faith	Endurance of Faith	Exhortation of Love
	1:1 1:3	1:4 2:18	3:1 4:13	4:14 7:28	8:1 8:13	9:1 10:18	10:19 11:40	12:1 12:29	13:1 13:25
Topics	Majesty of Christ			Ministry of Christ			Ministers for Christ		
	Doctrine						Discipline		
Place	Place of Writing Unknown								
Time	C. A.D. 64–68								

Introduction and Title

Many Jewish believers, having stepped out of Judaism into Christianity, want to reverse their course in order to escape persecution by their countrymen. The writer of Hebrews exhorts them to "go on to perfection" (6:1). His appeal is based on the superiority of Christ over the Judaic system. Christ is better than the angels, for they worship Him. He is better than Moses, for He created him. He is better than the Aaronic priesthood, for His sacrifice was once for all time. He is better than the Law, for He mediates a better covenant. In short, there is more to be gained in Christ than to be lost in Judaism. Pressing on in Christ produces tested faith, self-discipline, and a visible love seen in good works.

Although the King James Version uses the title "The Epistle of Paul the Apostle to the Hebrews," there is no early manuscript evidence to support it. The oldest and most reliable title is simply *Pros Ebraious,* "To Hebrews."

Author

Like the ancestry of Melchizedek, the origin of Hebrews is unknown. Uncertainty plagues not only its authorship, but also where it was written, its date, and its readership. The question of authorship delayed its recognition in the West as part of the New Testament canon in spite of early support by Clement of Rome. Not until the fourth century was it generally accepted as authoritative in the Western church, when the testimonies of Jerome and Augustine settled the issue. In the Eastern church, there was no problem of canonical acceptance because it was regarded as one of the "fourteen" epistles of Paul. The issue of its canonicity was again raised during the Reformation, but the spiritual depth and quality of Hebrews bore witness to its inspiration, despite its anonymity.

Chapter 13, verses 18–24, tell us that this book was not anonymous to the original readers; they evidently knew the author. For some reason, however, early church tradition is divided over the identity of the author. Part of the church attributed it to Paul; others preferred Barnabas, Luke, or Clement; and some chose anonymity. Thus, external evidence will not help determine the author.

Internal evidence must be the final court of appeal, but here too, the results are ambiguous. Some aspects of the language, style, and theology of Hebrews are very similar to Paul's epistles, and the author also refers to Timothy (13:23). However, significant differences have led the majority of biblical scholars to reject Pauline authorship of this book: (1) The Greek style of Hebrews is far more polished and refined than that found in any of Paul's recognized epistles. (2) In view of Paul's consistent claims to be an apostle and an eyewitness of Christ, it is very doubtful that he would have used the phraseology found in chapter 2, verse 3: "which at the first began to be spoken by the Lord, and was confirmed to us by those who heard *Him.*" (3) The lack of Paul's customary salutation, which includes his name, goes against the firm pattern found in all his other epistles. (4) While Paul used both the Hebrew text and the Septuagint to quote from the Old Testament, the writer of

Hebrews apparently did not know Hebrew and quoted exclusively from the Septuagint. (5) Paul's common use of compound titles to refer to the Son of God is not followed in Hebrews, which usually refers to Him as Christ, Jesus, and Lord. (6) Hebrews concentrates on Christ's present priestly ministry, but Paul's writings have very little to say about the present work of Christ. Thus, Hebrews appears not to have been written by Paul although the writer shows a Pauline influence. The authority of Hebrews in no way depends upon Pauline authorship, especially since it does not claim to have been written by Paul.

Tertullian referred to Barnabas as the author of Hebrews, but it is unlikely that this resident of Jerusalem (Acts 4:36–37) would include himself as one of those who relied on others for eyewitness testimony about Jesus (2:3). Other suggestions include Luke, Clement of Rome, Apollos, Silvanus (Silas), Philip, and even Priscilla. Some of these are possibilities, but we must agree with the third-century theologian Origen who wrote: "Who it was that really wrote the Epistle, God only knows."

Date and Setting

Because of the exclusive use of the Septuagint (Greek translation of the Hebrew Old Testament) and the elegant Greek style found in Hebrews, some recent scholars have argued that this book was written to a Gentile readership. However, the bulk of the evidence favors the traditional view that the original recipients of this letter were Jewish Christians. In addition to the ancient title "To Hebrews," there is also the frequent use of the Old Testament as an unquestioned authority, the assumed knowledge of the sacrificial ritual, and the many contrasts between Christianity and Judaism, which are designed to prevent the readers from lapsing into Judaism.

Many places have been suggested for the locality of the readers, but this letter's destination cannot be determined with any certainty. In the past, Jerusalem was most frequently suggested, but this view is hindered by four problems: (1) It is unlikely that a book addressed to Palestineans would quote exclusively from the Septuagint rather than the Hebrew Old Testament. (2) Palestinean believers were poor (Rom. 15:26), but these readers were able to financially assist other Christians (6:10). (3) Residents of Jerusalem would not be characterized by the description in chapter 2, verse 3, because some would have been eyewitnesses of the ministry of Christ. (4) "You have not yet resisted to bloodshed" (12:4) does not fit the situation in Jerusalem. The majority view today is that the recipients of Hebrews probably lived in Rome. The statement "Those from Italy greet you" seems to suggest that Italians away from Italy are sending their greetings home (13:24).

The recipients of this letter were believers (3:1) who had come to faith through the testimony of eyewitnesses of Christ (2:3). They were not novices (5:12), and they had successfully endured hardships because of their stand for the gospel (10:32–34). Unfortunately, they had become "dull of hearing" (5:11) and were in danger of drifting away (2:1; 3:12). This made them particularly susceptible to the renewed persecutions that were coming upon them (12:4–12), and the author found it necessary to check the downward spiral with "the word of exhortation" (13:22). While there is disagreement over the specific danger involved, the classic position that the readers were on the verge of lapsing into Judaism to avoid persecution directed at Christians seems to be supported by the whole tenor of the book. Hebrews' repeated emphasis on the superiority of Christianity over Judaism would have been pointless if the readers were about to return to Gnosticism or heathenism.

The place of writing is unknown, but a reasonable estimate of the date can be made. Hebrews was quoted in A.D. 95 by Clement of Rome, but its failure to mention the ending of the Old Testament sacrificial system with the destruction of Jerusalem in A.D. 70 indicates that it was written prior to that date. Timothy was still alive (13:23), persecution was mounting, and the old Jewish system was about to be removed (12:26–27). All this suggests a date between A.D. 64 and 68.

Theme and Purpose

The basic theme of Hebrews is found in the use of the word "better" (1:4; 6:9; 7:7,19,22; 8:6; 9:23; 10:34; 11:16,35,40; 12:24). The words "perfect" and "heavenly" are also prominent in describing the superiority of Christ in His person and work. He offers a better revelation, position, priesthood, covenant, sacrifice, and power. The writer develops this theme to prevent the readers from giving up the substance for the shadow by abandoning Christianity and retreating into the old Judaic system. This epistle was also written to exhort them to become mature in Christ and put away their spiritual dullness and degeneration. Thus, it places heavy stress on doctrine, concentrating on christology and soteriology (salvation).

Keys to Hebrews

Key Word: Superiority of Christ

Key Verses (4:14–16; 12:1–2)—"Seeing then that we have a great High Priest who has passed through the heavens, Jesus the Son of God, let us fold fast our confession. For we do not have a High Priest who cannot sympathize with our weaknesses, but was in all *points* tempted as *we are,* yet without sin. Let us therefore come boldly to the throne of grace, that we may obtain mercy and find grace to help in time of need" (4:14–16).

"Therefore we also, since we are surrounded by so great a cloud of witnesses, let us lay aside every weight, and the sin which so easily ensnares *us,* and let us run with endurance the race that is set before us, looking unto Jesus, the author and finisher of *our* faith, who for the joy that was set before Him endured the Cross, despising the shame, and has sat down at the right hand of the throne of God" (12:1–2).

Key Chapter (11)—The Hall of Fame of the Scriptures is located in chapter 11 and records those who willingly took God at His word even when there was nothing to cling to but His promise. Inherent to all those listed is the recognition that "without faith *it is* impossible to please *Him,* for he who comes to God must believe that He is, and *that* He is a rewarder of those who diligently seek Him" (Heb. 11:6).

Christ in Hebrews

Christ is our eternal High Priest according to the order of Melchizedek. He identified with man in His Incarnation and offered no less a sacrifice than Himself on our behalf.

Sacrifices Under the Law (10:1–4)	Sacrifice of Christ (10:5–18)
Reminders of sin	Remover of sin
Repeated constantly	Once for all time
Anticipation	Fulfillment
Shadows	Substance
Blood of animals	Blood of Christ
Involuntary	Voluntary

Hebrews presents Christ as the divine-human Prophet, Priest, and King. His deity (1:1–3, 8) and humanity (2:9, 14, 17–18) are asserted with equal force, and over twenty titles are used to describe His attributes and accomplishments (e.g., heir of all things, Apostle and High Priest, mediator, author and perfecter of faith). He is superior to all who went before and offers the supreme sacrifice, priesthood, and covenant.

Contribution to the Bible

Among the New Testament epistles Hebrews is unique in form. It has no introductory salutation like other letters, and there is no evidence that such a salutation was ever removed at some early point. Hebrews instead launches immediately into its theme, and it reads more like a sermonic essay than a letter. The author regarded it as a "word of exhortation" (13:22), and it may have been a modified sermon or series of sermons. Only 13:18–25 sounds like a real epistle. Hebrews is characterized by a very precise and scholarly style, elegantly written and carefully constructed. Its literary quality and vigorous rhetoric are unexcelled in the New Testament. This book abounds with quotations and allusions to the Old Testament which are authoritatively used to demonstrate the superiority and finality of the person and priesthood of Christ. Hebrews makes important doctrinal contributions to the New Testament, especially in its revelation of the present priestly ministry of Christ on behalf of the believer. It develops the doctrine of the atoning work of Christ in relation to the New Covenant. It also explores the typological significance of the offerings and feasts in Leviticus; Hebrews is a divine commentary on the prophetic meaning of the ceremonial law. Throughout this epistle, the application of doctrine to practice is stressed in its negative warnings and positive exhortations (see "let us . . ." in 4:1,11,14,16; 6:1; 10:22–24; 12:1 two times, 28; 13:13,15).

Survey of Hebrews

Hebrews stands alone among the New Testament epistles in its style and approach, and it is the only New Testament book whose authorship remains a real mystery. This profound work builds a case for the superiority of Christ through a cumulative argument in which Christ is presented as "better" in every respect. In His person He is better than the angels, Moses, and Joshua; and in His performance He provides a better priesthood, covenant, sanctuary, and sacrifice. Evidently, the readers are in danger of reverting to Judaism because of the suffering they are beginning to experience for their faith in Christ. However, by doing so, they would be retreating from the substance back into the shadow. In addition to his positive presentation of the supremacy of Christ, the writer intersperses five solemn warnings about the peril of turning away from Christ (2:1–4; 3:7—4:13; 5:11—6:20; 10:19–39; 12:25–29). These parenthetical warnings include cautions against neglect (2:1–4) and refusal (12:25–29). After using the Old Testament to demonstrate the superiority of Christ's person (1:1—4:13) and the superiority of Christ's work (4:14—10:18), the writer applies these truths in a practical way to show the superiority of the Christian's walk of faith (10:19—13:25).

The Superiority of Christ's Person (1:1—4:13): Instead of the usual salutation, this epistle immediately launches into its theme—the supremacy of Christ even over the Old Testament prophets (1:1–3). Christianity is built upon the highest form of divine disclosure: the personal revelation of God through His incarnate Son. Christ is therefore greater than the prophets, and He is also greater than the angels, the mediators of the Mosaic Law (1:4—2:18; see also 2:2; Acts 7:53). This is seen in His name, His position, His worship by the angels, and His Incarnation. The Son of God partook of flesh and blood and was "made like *His* brethren" in all things (2:17) in order to bring "many sons to glory" (2:10). Christ is also superior to Moses (3:1–6), for Moses was a servant in the house of God, but Christ is the Son over God's household. Because of these truths, the readers are exhorted to avoid the divine judgment that is visited upon unbelief (3:7—4:13). Their disbelief had prevented the generation of the Exodus from becoming the generation of the conquest, and the rest that Christ offers is so much greater than what was provided by Joshua. The readers are therefore urged to enter the eternal rest that is possessed by faith in Christ.

The Superiority of Christ's Work (4:14—10:18): The high priesthood of Christ is superior to the Aaronic priesthood (4:14—7:28). Because of His Incarnation, Christ can "sympathize with our weaknesses," having been "in all *points* tempted as *we are, yet* without sin" (4:15). Christ was not a Levite, but He qualified for a higher priesthood according to the order of Melchizedek. The superiority of Melchizedek to Levi is seen in the fact that Levi, in effect, paid tithes through Abraham to Melchizedek (7:9–10). Abraham was blessed by Melchizedek, and "the lesser is blessed by the better" (7:7). The parenthetical warning in 5:11—6:20 exhorts the readers to "go on to perfection," (6:1), by moving beyond the basics of salvation and repentance.

By divine oath (7:21), Christ has become a permanent and perfect High Priest and "the Mediator of a better covenant" (8:6). The New Covenant has made the old covenant obsolete (8:6–13). Our Great High Priest similarly ministers in "the greater and more perfect tabernacle not made with hands, that is, not of this creation" (9:11). And unlike the former priests, He offers Himself as a sinless and voluntary sacrifice once and for all (9:1—10:18).

The Superiority of the Christian's Walk of Faith (10:19—13:25): The author applies what he has been saying about the superiority of Christ by warning his readers of the danger of discarding their faith in Christ (10:19–39). The faith that the readers must maintain is defined in chapter 11, verses 1–3, and illustrated in chapter 11, verses 4–40. The triumphs and accomplishments of faith in the lives of Old Testament believers should encourage the recipients of "something better" (11:40) in Christ to look "unto Jesus, the author and finisher of *our* faith" (12:2). Just as Jesus endured great hostility, those who believe in Him will sometimes have to endure divine discipline for the sake of holiness (12:1–29). The readers are warned not to turn away from Christ during such times, but to place their hope in Him. The character of their lives must be shaped by their dedication to Christ (13:1–19), and this will be manifested in their love of each other through their hospitality, concern, purity, contentment, and obedience. The author concludes this epistle with one of the finest benedictions in Scripture (13:20–21) and some personal words (13:22–25).

Outline of Hebrews

Part One: The Superiority of Christ's Person (1:1—4:13)

I. The Superiority of Christ over the Prophets, 1:1–3

II. The Superiority of Christ over the Angels, 1:4—2:18
   A. Christ Is Superior because of His Deity, 1:4–14
   B. First Warning: Danger of Neglect, 2:1–4
   C. Christ Is Superior because of His Humanity, 2:5–18

III. The Superiority of Christ over Moses, 3:1—4:13
   A. Christ Is Superior to Moses in His Work, 3:1–4
   B. Christ Is Superior to Moses in His Person, 3:5–6
   C. Second Warning: Danger of Unbelief, 3:7—4:13
      1. Danger of Hardening the Heart, 3:7–19
      2. Challenge to Enter His Rest, 4:1–13

Part Two: The Superiority of Christ's Work (4:14—10:18)

I. The Superiority of Christ's Priesthood, 4:14—7:28
  A. Christ Is Superior in His Position, 4:14–16
  B. Christ Is Superior in His Qualifications, 5:1–10
    1. Aaronic Priesthood, 5:1–4
    2. Melchizedekian Priesthood, 5:5–10
  C. Third Warning: Danger of Not Maturing, 5:11—6:20
    1. Dullness of Hearing, 5:11–14
    2. Need for Maturity, 6:1–8
    3. Exhortation to Maturity, 6:9–20
  D. Christ Is Superior in His Priestly Order, 7:1–28
    1. Description of Melchizedek, 7:1–3
    2. Superiority of Melchizedek, 7:4–10
    3. Imperfection of Aaronic Priesthood, 7:11–28

II. The Superiority of Christ's Covenant, 8:1–13
  A. A Better Covenant, 8:1–6
  B. A New Covenant, 8:7–13

III. The Superiority of Christ's Sanctuary and Sacrifice, 9:1—10:18
  A. Old Covenant's Sanctuary and Sacrifice, 9:1–10
    1. Old Covenant's Sanctuary, 9:1–5
    2. Old Covenant's Sacrifice, 9:6–10
  B. New Covenant's Sanctuary and Sacrifice, 9:11—10:18
    1. New Covenant's Sanctuary, 9:11
    2. New Covenant's Sacrifice, 9:12—10:18

Part Three: The Superiority of the Christian's Walk of Faith (10:19—13:25)

I. Exhortation to Full Assurance of Faith, 10:19—11:40
  A. Hold Fast the Confession of Faith, 10:19–25
  B. Fourth Warning: Danger of Drawing Back, 10:26–39
  C. Definition of Faith, 11:1–3
  D. Examples of Faith, 11:4–40
    1. Abel, 11:4
    2. Enoch, 11:5–6
    3. Noah, 11:7
    4. Abraham and Sarah, 11:8–19
    5. Isaac, 11:20
    6. Jacob, 11:21
    7. Joseph, 11:22
    8. Moses' Parents, 11:23
    9. Moses, 11:24–29
    10. Joshua and Rahab, 11:30–31
    11. Many Other Heroes of Faith, 11:32–40

II. Endurance of Faith, 12:1–29

    A. Example of Christ's Endurance, 12:1–4

    B. Exhortation to Endure God's Chastening, 12:5–24

    C. Fifth Warning: Danger of Refusing God, 12:25–29

III. Exhortation to Love, 13:1–17

    A. Love in the Social Realm, 13:1–6

    B. Love in the Religious Realm, 13:7–17

IV. Conclusion, 13:18–25

James

FAITH WITHOUT WORKS CANNOT be called faith. It is dead, and a dead faith is worse than no faith at all. Faith must work; it must produce; it must be visible. Verbal faith is not enough; mental faith is insufficient. Faith must move into action. Throughout his epistle to Jewish believers, James integrates true faith and everyday practical experience by stressing that true faith "works." It endures trials; it obeys God's Word; it produces doers; it harbors no prejudice; it controls the tongue; it acts wisely; it provides the power to resist the devil; it waits patiently for the coming of the Lord.

JAMES							
Focus	**Test of Faith**		**Characteristics of Faith**		**Triumph of Faith**		
	1:1 — 1:18		1:19 — 5:6		5:7 — 5:20		
Divisions	Purpose of Tests	Source of Temptation	The Outward Demonstration of the Inner Faith		Endures Awaiting Christ's Return	Prays for the Afflicted	Confronts the Erring Brother
	1:1 — 1:12	1:13 — 1:18	1:19 — 5:6		5:7 — 5:12	5:13 — 5:18	5:19 — 5:20
Topics	Development of Faith		Works of Faith		Power of Faith		
	Response of Faith		Reality of Faith		Reassurance of Faith		
Place	Probably Jerusalem						
Time	A.D. 46–49						

Introduction and Title

Faith without works cannot be called faith. Faith without works is dead, and a dead faith is worse than no faith at all. Faith must work; it must produce; it must be visible. Verbal faith is not enough; mental faith is insufficient. Faith must be there, but it must be more. It must inspire action. Throughout his epistle to Jewish believers, James integrates true faith and everyday practical experience by stressing that true faith must manifest itself in works of faith.

Faith endures trials. Trials come and go, but a strong faith will face them head-on and develop endurance. Faith understands temptations. It will not allow us to consent to our lust and slide into sin. Faith obeys the Word. It will not merely hear and not do. Faith produces doers. Faith harbors no prejudice. For James, faith and favoritism cannot coexist. Faith displays itself in works. Faith is more than mere words; it is more than knowledge; it is demonstrated by obedience; and it overtly responds to the promises of God. Faith controls the tongue. This small but immensely powerful part of the body must be held in check. Faith can do it. Faith acts wisely. It gives us the ability to choose wisdom that is heavenly and to shun wisdom that is earthly. Faith produces separation from the world and submission to God. It provides us with the ability to resist the devil and humbly to draw near to God. Finally, faith waits patiently for the coming of the Lord. Through trouble and trial it stifles complaining.

The name *Jakobos* (James in 1:1) is the basis for the early title *Jakobou Epistole,* "Epistle of James." *Jakobos* is the Greek form of the Hebrew name Jacob, a Jewish name common in the first century.

Author

Four men are named James in the New Testament: (1) James, the father of Judas (not Iscariot), is mentioned twice (see Luke 6:16; Acts 1:13) as the father of one of the twelve disciples, but is otherwise completely unknown. (2) James, the son of Alphaeus (see Matt. 10:3; Mark 3:18; Luke 6:15; Acts 1:13), elsewhere called James the Less (Mark 15:40), was one of the twelve disciples. Apart from being listed with the other disciples, this James is completley obscure, and it is doubtful that he is the authoritative figure behind the epistle. Some attempts have been made to identify this James with the Lord's brother (Gal. 1:19), but this view is difficult to reconcile with the gospel accounts. (3) James, the son of Zebedee and brother of John (see Matt. 4:21; 10:2; 17:1; Mark 3:17; 10:35; 13:3; Luke 9:54; Acts 1:13), was one of Jesus' intimate disciples, but his martyrdom by A.D. 44 (Acts 12:2) makes it very unlikely that he wrote this epistle. (4) James, the Lord's brother (see Matt. 13:55; Mark 6:3; Gal. 1:19), was one of the "pillars" in the church in Jerusalem (see Acts 12:17; 15:13–21; 21:18; Gal. 2:9, 12). Tradition points to this prominent figure as the author of the epistle, and this best fits the evidence of Scripture. There are several clear parallels between the language of the letter drafted under his leadership in Acts 15:23–29 and the epistle of James (e.g., the unusual word *chairein,* "greeting," is found only in Acts 15:23; 23:26; and James 1:1). The Jewish character of this epistle with its stress upon the Law, along with the evident influence by the Sermon on the Mount (e.g., 4:11–12; 5:12), complement what we know about James "the Just" from Scripture and early tradition.

It has been argued that the Greek of this epistle is too sophisticated for a Galilean such as James, but this assumes that he never had the opportunity or aptitude to develop proficiency in Koine ("common") Greek. As a prominent church leader, it would have been to his advantage to become fluent in the universal language of the Roman Empire.

For various reasons, some assert that James was a stepbrother of Jesus by a previous marriage of Joseph, or that the "brothers" of Jesus mentioned in Matthew 13:55 and Mark 6:3 were really His cousins. However, the most natural understanding of the gospel accounts is that James was the half brother of Jesus, being the offspring of Joseph and Mary after the birth of Jesus (Matt. 1:24–25). He apparently did not accept the claims of Jesus until the Lord appeared to him after His Resurrection (1 Cor. 15:7). He and his brothers were among the believers who awaited the coming of the Holy Spirit on the day of Pentecost (Acts 1:14). It was not long before he became an acknowledged leader of the Jerusalem church (see Acts 12:17; Gal. 2:9, 12), and he was a central figure in the Jerusalem Council in Acts 15. Even after Paul's third missionary journey, James continued to observe the Mosaic Law as a testimony to other Jews (Acts 21:18–25). Early tradition stresses his Jewish piety and his role in bringing others to an understanding of Jesus as the Messiah. He suffered a violent martyr's death not long before the fall of Jerusalem.

The brevity and limited doctrinal emphasis of James kept it from wide circulation; and by the time it became known in the church as a whole, there was uncertainty about the identity of the James (1:1). Growing recognition that it was written by the Lord's brother led to its acceptance as a canonical book.

Date and Setting

James is addressed "To the twelve tribes which are scattered abroad" (1:1), and it is apparent from verses like 1:19 and 2:1, 7 that this greeting refers to Hebrew Christians outside of Palestine. Their place of meeting is called a "synagogue" in the Greek text (2:2), and the whole epistle reflects Jewish thought and expressions (e.g., 2:19, 21; 4:11–12; 5:4, 12). There are no references to slavery or idolatry, and this also fits an originally Jewish readership.

These Jewish believers were beset with problems that were testing their faith, and James was concerned that they were succumbing to impatience, bitterness, materialism, disunity, and spiritual apathy. As a resident of Jerusalem and a leader of the church, James no doubt had frequent contact with Jewish Christians from a number of Roman provinces. He therefore felt a responsibility to exhort and encourage them in their struggles of faith.

According to Josephus, James was martyred in A.D. 62 (Hegesippus, quoted in Eusebius, fixed the date of James's death at A.D. 66). Those who accept him as the author of this epistle have proposed a date of writing ranging from A.D. 45 to the end of his life. However, several factors indicate that this letter may have been the earliest writing of the New Testament (c. A.D. 46–49): (1) There is no mention of Gentile Christians or their relationship to Jewish Christians as would be expected in a later epistle. (2) Apart from references to the Person of Christ, there is practically no distinctive theology in James, suggesting an early date when Christianity was viewed in terms of Messianic Judaism. (3) The allusions to the teachings of Christ have such little verbal agreement with the synoptic Gospels that they probably preceded them. (4) James uses the word "synagogue" (assembly, 2:2) in addition to "church" and indicates a very simple organization of elders and masters, that is, teachers (3:1; 5:14), which was patterned after the early synagogue. (5) James does not mention the issues involved in the Acts 15 Council in Jerusalem (A.D. 49).

Theme and Purpose

Throughout his epistle, James develops the theme of the characteristics of true faith. He effectively uses these characteristics as a series of tests to help his reader evaluate the reality of their relationship to Christ. The purpose of this work is not doctrinal or apologetic but practical, as James seeks to challenge these believers to examine the quality of their daily lives in terms of attitudes and actions. A genuine faith will produce real changes in a person's conduct and character, and the absence of change is a symptom of a dead faith.

Keys to James

Key Word: Faith That Works

Key Verses (1:19–22; 2:14–17)—"Therefore, my beloved brethren, let every man be swift to hear, slow to speak, slow to wrath; for the wrath of man does not produce the righteousness of God. Therefore lay aside all filthiness and overflow of wickedness, and receive with meekness the implanted Word, which is able to save your souls. But be doers of the Word, and not hearers only, deceiving yourselves" (1:19–22).

"What *does it* profit, my brethren, if someone says he has faith but does not have works? Can faith save him? If a brother or sister is naked and destitute of daily food, and one of you says to them, 'Depart in peace, be warmed and filled,' but you do not give them the things which are needed for the body, what *does it* profit? Thus also faith by itself, if it does not have works, is dead." (2:14–17).

Key Chapter (1)—One of the most difficult areas of the Christian life is that of testings and temptation. James reveals our correct response to both: to testings, count them all joy; to temptations, realize that God is not their source.

Christ in James

James refers to the "Lord Jesus Christ" (1:1; 2:1), and he anticipates "the coming of the Lord" (5:7–8). Compared to other New Testament writers. James says little about Christ, and yet his speech is virtually saturated with allusions to the teaching of Christ. The Sermon on the Mount is especially prominent in James' thinking (there are c. fifteen indirect references; e.g., James 1:2 and Matt. 5:10–12; James 1:4 and Matt. 5:48; James 2:13 and Matt. 6:14–15; James 4:11 and Matt. 7:1–2; James 5:2 and Matt. 6:19). This epistle portrays Christ in the context of early messianic Judaism.

Contribution to the Bible

Martin Luther took a dim view of James and called it "a right strawy epistle" compared to other New Testament books that bear clearer testimony to the work of Christ and the way of salvation. But James and Paul are supplementary, not contradictory, and this epistle assumes a knowledge of these doctrines on the part of the readers. Because of its very practical nature, James has little formal theology, but it is not devoid of doctrinal statements (1:12–13, 17–18; 2:1, 10–13, 19; 3:9; 4:5; 5:7–9).

James writes with a very concise, authoritative, and unvarnished style. Combining the pithy maxims of Wisdom Literature with the impassioned rhetoric of Amos, James' pointed barbs are borne out of an uncompromising ethical stance. His Greek is of a good quality and he communicates his thoughts effectively by means of vivid imagery (especially from nature), illustrations, and figures of speech. Unlike Paul, James says nothing about his personal circumstances. This is a formal and sometimes severe epistle, authoritatively written and full of imperatives (54 in only 108 verses). Nevertheless, its liberal use of "[my] brethren" (eleven times) and "my beloved brethren" (three times) tempers the harshness with warmth and concern.

James was probably written before or during Paul's first missionary journey at a time when the church was almost exclusively made up of Jewish believers. This explains its strong Jewish perspective with its abundant references to the Law and Old Testament imagery (James alludes to twenty-two Old Testament books).

As the most practical book in the New Testament, James is as relevant today as it was in the first century. Its exhortations concerning trials and temptations, response to the Word, preferential treatment because of social status, control of the tongue, and the lure of worldliness are strongly needed in the contemporary church.

Chapter 3, verses 15–17, describes human and divine wisdom in terms strikingly similar to those found in the Book of Proverbs. Human wisdom *is earthly* (Prov. 14:2), *natural* (Prov. 7:18), *demonic* (Prov. 27:20), *jealous* (Prov. 6:34), *selfish* (Prov. 28:25), *disorderly* (Prov. 11:29), and *evil* (Prov. 8:13). By contrast, divine wisdom *is pure* (Prov. 15:26), *peaceable* (Prov. 3:1–2), *gentle* (Prov. 11:2), *reasonable* (Prov. 14:15), *full of mercy and good fruits* (Prov. 11:17; 3:18), *unwavering* (Prov. 21:6), and *without hypocrisy* (Prov. 28:13).

Survey of James

James is an intensely practical manual on the outworking of true faith in everyday life. It explores Christian conduct from several perspectives and shifts abruptly from topic to topic. Faith perseveres under trials, resists temptations, responds to the Word, overcomes prejudice, produces good works, controls the tongue, manifests wisdom, submits to God rather than worldly pleasure, depends on God rather than wealth, and waits patiently for the return of the Lord. Biblical faith moves from assent to actions, from words to works.

James is the "Proverbs of the New Testament" because it is written in the terse moralistic style of Wisdom Literature. It is evident that James was profoundly influenced by the Old Testament (especially by its Wisdom Literature) and by the Sermon on the Mount. But James' impassioned preaching against inequity and social injustice also earns him the title of the "Amos of the New Testament." Because of the many subjects in this epistle, it is difficult to outline; suggestions have ranged from no connection between the various topics to a unified scheme. The outline used here is: the test of faith (1:1–18); the characteristics of faith (1:19—5:6); and the triumph of faith (5:7–20).

The Test of Faith (1:1–18): The first part of this epistle develops the qualities of genuine faith in regard to trials and temptations. After a one-verse salutation to geographically dispersed Hebrew Christians (1:1), James quickly introduces his first subject, outward tests of faith (1:2–12). These trials are designed to produce mature endurance and a sense of dependence upon God, to whom the believer turns for wisdom and enablement. Inward temptations (1:13–18) do not come from the One who bestows "Every good gift" (1:17). These solicitations to evil must be checked at an early stage or they may result in disastrous consequences.

The Characteristics of Faith (1:19—5:6): A righteous response to testing requires that one be "swift to hear, slow to speak, slow to wrath" (1:19), and this broadly summarizes the remainder of the epistle. Quickness of hearing involves an obedient response to God's Word (1:19–27). True hearing means more than mere listening; the Word must be received and applied. After stating this principle (1:21–22), James develops it with an illustration (1:23–25) and an application (1:26–27). A genuine faith should produce a change in attitude from partiality to the rich to a love for the poor as well as the rich (2:1–13). True faith should also result in actions (2:14–26). In Romans 4, Paul used the example of Abraham to show that justification is by faith, not by works. But James says that Abraham was justified by works (2:21). In spite of the apparent contradiction, Romans 4 and James 2 are really two sides of the same coin. In context, Paul is writing about justification before God while James writes of the evidence of justification before men. A faith that produces no change is not saving faith.

Moving from works to words, James shows how a living faith controls the tongue ("slow to speak," 1:19). The tongue is small, but it has the power to accomplish great good or equally great evil. Only the power of God applied by an active faith can tame the tongue (3:1–12). Boasting comes from an untamed tongue, but James contrasts seven characteristics of human wisdom with seven qualities of divine wisdom (3:13–18).

The strong pulls of worldliness (4:1–12) and wealth (4:13—5:6) create conflicts that are harmful to the growth of faith. The world system is at enmity with God, and the pursuit of its pleasures produces covetousness, envy, fighting, and arrogance (4:1–6). The believer's only alternative is submission to God out of a humble and repentant spirit. This will produce a transformed attitude toward others as well (4:7–12). This spirit of submission and humility should be applied to any attempts to accrue wealth (4:13–17), especially because wealth can lead to pride, injustice, and selfishness (5:1–6).

The Triumph of Faith (5:7–20): James encourages his readers to patiently endure the sufferings of the present life in view of the future prospect of the coming of the Lord (5:7–12). They may be oppressed by the rich or by other circumstances, but as the example of Job teaches, believers can be sure that God has a gracious purpose in His dealings with them. James concludes his epistle with some practical words on prayer and restoration (5:13–20). The prayers of righteous men (e.g., elders in local churches) are efficacious for the healing and restoration of believers. When sin is not dealt with, it can contribute to illness and even death.

Outline of James

I. The Test of Faith, 1:1–18
   A. The Purpose of Tests, 1:1–12
   B. The Source of Temptations, 1:13–18

II. The Characteristics of Faith, 1:19—5:6
   A. Faith Obeys the Word, 1:19–27
   B. Faith Removes Discriminations, 2:1–13
   C. Faith Proves Itself by Works, 2:14–26
   D. Faith Controls the Tongue, 3:1–12
   E. Faith Produces Wisdom, 3:13–18
   F. Faith Produces Humility, 4:1–12
   G. Faith Produces Dependence on God, 4:13—5:6

III. The Triumph of Faith, 5:7–20
   A. Faith Endures awaiting Christ's Return, 5:7–12
   B. Faith Prays for the Afflicted, 5:13–18
   C. Faith Confronts the Erring Brother, 5:19–20

First Peter

PERSECUTION CAN EITHER CAUSE YOU to grow or grumble in the Christian life. It all depends on your response! In writing to Jewish believers struggling in the midst of persecution, Peter reminds them of their "roots." They have been born again to a living hope, and therefore both their character and conduct can be above reproach as they imitate the Holy One who called them. The fruit of that proven character will be actions rooted in submission: law-abiding citizens, obedient employees, submissive wives, loving husbands.

FIRST PETER

Focus	Salvation of the Believer		Submission of the Believer				Suffering of the Believer			
	1:1 2:12		2:13 3:12				3:13 5:14			
Divisions	Salvation of the Believer	Sanctification of the Believer	Submission to the Government	Submission in Business	Submission in Marriage	Submission in All of Life	Conduct in Suffering	Christ's Example of Suffering	Commands in Suffering	Minister in Suffering
	1:1 1:12	1:13 2:12	2:13 2:17	2:18 2:25	3:1 3:8	3:9 3:12	3:13 3:17	3:18 4:6	4:7 4:19	5:1 5:14
Topics	Belief of Christians		Behavior of Christians				Buffeting of Christians			
	Holiness		Harmony				Humility			
Place	Either Rome or Babylon									
Time	c. A.D. 63–64									

Introduction and Title

Persecution can cause either growth or bitterness in the Christian life. Response determines the result. In writing to Jewish believers struggling in the midst of persecution, Peter encourages them to conduct themselves courageously for the person and program of Christ. Both their character and conduct must be above reproach. Having been born again to a living hope, they are to imitate the Holy One who has called them. The fruit of that character will be conduct rooted in submission: citizens to government, servants to masters, wives to husbands, husbands to wives, and Christians to one another. Only after submission is fully understood does Peter deal with the difficult area of suffering. The Christians are not to think it "strange concerning the fiery trial which is to try you, as though some strange thing happened to you" (4:12), but are to rejoice as partakers of the suffering of Christ. That response to life is truly the climax of one's submission to the good hand of God.

This epistle begins with the phrase *Petros apostolos Iesou Christou,* "Peter, an apostle of Jesus Christ." This is the basis of the early title *Petrou A,* the "First of Peter."

Author

The early church universally acknowledged the authenticity and authority of First Peter. The internal evidence supports this consistent external testimony in several ways. The apostle Peter's name is given (1:1) and there are definite similarities between certain phrases in this letter and Peter's sermons as recorded in the Book of Acts (cf. 1 Pet. 1:20 and Acts 2:23; 1 Pet. 4:5 and Acts 10:42). Twice in Acts, Peter used the Greek word *xylon,* "wood, tree," to speak of the cross, and this distinctive use is also found in First Peter (see Acts 5:30; 10:39; 1 Pet. 2:24). The epistle contains a number of allusions to events in the life of Christ that held special significance for Peter (e.g., 2:23; 3:18; 4:1; 5:1; cf. 5:5; John 13:4).

Nevertheless, critics since the nineteenth century have challenged the authenticity of First Peter on several grounds. Some claim that chapter 1, verses 1–2, (see also 4:12—5:14) were later additions that turned an anonymous address or a baptismal sermon into a Petrine Epistle. Others argue that the sufferings experienced by readers of this letter must refer to the persecution of Christians that took place after the time of Peter in the reigns of the emperors Domitian (A.D. 81–96) and Trajan (A.D. 98–117). There is no basis for the first argument, and the second argument falsely assumes that Christians were not being reviled for their faith during the life of Peter. Another challenge asserts that the quality of the Greek of this epistle is too high for a Galilean like Peter. But Galileans were bilingual (Aramaic and Greek), and writers such as Matthew and James were skillful in their use of Greek. It is also likely that Peter used Silvanus as his scribe (5:12; Paul calls him Silvanus in 2 Cor. 1:19; 1 Thess. 1:1; 2 Thess. 1:1; Luke calls him Silas in Acts 15:40—18:5), and Silvanus may have smoothed out Peter's speech in the process.

Date and Setting

This letter is addressed "to the strangers scattered," or more literally, "pilgrims of the Dispersion" (1:1). This, coupled with the injunction to keep their behavior "honorable among the Gentiles" (2:12), gives the initial appearance that the bulk of the readers are Hebrew Christians. A closer look, however, forms the opposite view that most of these believers were Gentiles. They were called "out of darkness" (2:9), and they "once *were* not a people but *are* now the people of God" (2:10). Their former "aimless conduct *received* by tradition from [their] fathers" was characterized by ignorance and futility (1:18; cf. Eph. 4:17). Because they no longer engage in debauchery and idolatry, they are maligned by their countrymen (4:3–4). These descriptions do not fit a predominantly Hebrew Christian readership. Though Peter was an apostle "to the circumcised" (Gal. 2:9), he also ministered to Gentiles (Acts 10:34–48; Gal. 2:12), and a letter like this would not be beyond the scope of his ministry.

This epistle was addressed to Christians throughout Asia Minor, indicating the spread of the gospel in regions not evangelized when Acts was written (Pontus, Cappadocia, Bithynia; 1:1). It is possible that Peter visited and ministered in some of these areas, but there is no evidence. He wrote this letter in response to the news of growing opposition to the believers in Asia Minor (1:6; 3:13–17; 4:12–19; 5:9–10). Hostility and suspicion were mounting against Christians in the empire, and they were being reviled and abused for their life-styles and subversive talk about another Kingdom. Christianity had not yet received the official Roman ban, but the stage was being set for the persecution and martyrdom of the near future.

Peter's life was dramatically changed after the Resurrection, and he occupied a central role in the early church and in the spread of the gospel to the Samaritans and Gentiles (Acts 2—10). After the Jerusalem Council in Acts 15, little is recorded of Peter's activities. He evidently traveled extensively with his wife (1 Cor. 9:5) and ministered in various Roman provinces. According to tradition, Peter was crucified upside down in Rome prior to Nero's death in A.D. 68.

This epistle was written from Babylon (5:13), but scholars are divided as to whether this refers literally to Babylon in Mesopotamia or symbolically to Rome. There is no tradition that Peter went to Babylon, and in his day it had few inhabitants. On the other hand, tradition consistently indicates that Peter spent the last years of his life in Rome. As a center of idolatry, the term "Babylon" was an appropriate figurative designation for Rome (cf. the later use of Babylon in Rev. 17—18). Peter used other figurative expressions in this epistle, and it is not surprising that he would do the same with Rome. His mention of Mark (5:13) also fits this view because Mark was in Rome during Paul's first imprisonment (Col. 4:10). This epistle was probably written shortly before the outbreak of persecution under Nero in A.D. 64.

Theme and Purpose

The basic theme of First Peter is the proper response to Christian suffering. Knowing that his readers would be facing more persecution than ever before, Peter wrote this letter to give them a divine perspective on these trials so that they would be able to endure them without wavering in their faith. They should not be surprised at their ordeal because the One they follow also suffered and died (2:21; 3:18; 4:1,12–14). Rather, they should count it a privilege to share the sufferings of Christ. Peter therefore exhorts them to be sure that their hardships are not being caused by their own wrongdoings, but for their Christian testimony. They are not the only believers who are suffering (5:9), and they must recognize that God brings these things in the lives of His children not as a punishment but as a stimulus to growth in Christlikeness. Peter wanted to overcome an attitude of bitterness and anxiety and replace it with dependence on and confidence in God.

Another theme is stated in chapter 5, verse 12: "I have written to you briefly, exhorting and testifying that this is the true grace of God." In this epistle, Peter frequently speaks of the believer's position in Christ and future hope, and he does so to remind his readers that they are merely sojourners on this planet—their true destiny is eternal glory at the revelation of Jesus Christ. The grace of God in their *salvation* (1:1—2:10) should give them an attitude of *submission* (2:11—3:12) in the context of *suffering* for the name of Christ (3:13—5:14).

Keys to First Peter

Key Word: Suffering for Christ

Key Verses (1:10–12; 4:12–13)—"Of this salvation the prophets have inquired and searched diligently, who prophesied of the grace *that would come* to you, searching what, or what manner of time, the Spirit of Christ who was in them was indicating when He testified beforehand the sufferings of Christ and the glories that would follow. To them it was revealed that, not to themselves, but to us they were ministering the things which now have been reported to you through those who have preached the gospel to you by the Holy Spirit sent from heaven—things which angels desire to look into" (1:10–12).

"Beloved, do not think it strange concerning the fiery trial which is to try you, as though some strange thing happened to you; but rejoice to the extent that you partake of Christ's sufferings, that when His glory is revealed, you may also be glad with exceeding joy" (4:12–13).

Key Chapter (4)—Central in the New Testament revelation concerning how to handle persecution and suffering caused by one's Christian testimony is chapter 4. Not only is Christ's suffering to be our model (4:1–2), but also we are to rejoice in that we can share in His suffering (4:12–14).

Christ in First Peter

This epistle presents Christ as the believer's example and hope in times of suffering in a spiritually hostile world. He is the basis for the Christian's "living hope" and "inheritance" (1:3–4), and the love relationship available with Him by faith is a source of inexpressible joy (1:8). His suffering and death provide redemption for all who trust in Him: "who Himself bore our sins in His own body on the tree, that we, having died to sins, might live for righteousness—by Whose stripes you were healed"

(2:24; cf. 1:18–19; 3:18). Christ is the Chief Shepherd and Guardian of believers (2:25; 5:4), and when He appears, those who know Him will be glorified.

Contribution to the Bible

There are evidences of Pauline influence in the style and content of First Peter. Peter knew Paul and his epistles, but the similarities do not imply that Peter was dependent on Paul, since both men shared common apostolic doctrine. Peter wrote this letter with real warmth and sympathy for the plight of his readers, but this does not diminish its forcefulness. The chain of thirty-four imperatives from 1:13 to 5:9 is highly authoritative, yet borne out of a heart of compassion. In some ways, First Peter is the Job of the New Testament because of its theme of undeserved suffering and steadfast submission to the sovereignty of God. This epistle, like Peter's sermon in Acts 2, reveals a thorough acquaintance with the Old Testament and an effective use of its contents. It is also characterized by a number of allusions to Peter's personal experiences with Christ and to the future prospect of all believers in Christ. Some passages make a significant contribution to the theology of the New Testament (1:2–12, 18–20; 2:21–25; 3:18–22; 4:12–19).

Survey of First Peter

Peter addresses this epistle to "pilgrims" in a world that is growing increasingly hostile to Christians. These believers are beginning to suffer because of their stand for Christ, and Peter uses this letter to give them counsel and comfort by stressing the reality of their living hope in the Lord. By standing firm in the grace of God (5:12) they will be able to endure their "fiery trial" (4:12), knowing that there is a divine purpose behind their pain. This letter logically proceeds through the themes of the salvation of the believer (1:1—2:12); the submission of the believer (2:13—3:12); and the suffering of the believer (3:13—5:14).

The Salvation of the Believer (1:1—2:12): Addressing his letter to believers in several Roman Provinces, Peter briefly describes the saving work of the triune Godhead in his salutation (1:1–2). He then extols God for the riches of this salvation by looking in three temporal directions (1:3–12). First, Peter anticipates the future realization of the Christian's manifold inheritance (1:3–5). Second, he looks at the present joy that this living hope produces in spite of various trials (1:6–9). Third, he reflects upon the prophets of the past who predicted the gospel of God's grace in Christ (1:10–12).

The proper response to this salvation is the pursuit of sanctification or holiness (1:13—2:12). This involves a purifying departure from conformity with the world to godliness in behavior and love. With this in mind, Peter exhorts his readers to "desire the pure milk of the Word, that [they] may grow" (2:2) by applying "the Word of God which lives and abides forever" (1:23) and acting as a holy priesthood of believers.

The Submission of the Believer (2:13—3:12): Peter turns to the believer's relationships in the world and appeals for an attitude of submission as the Christlike way to harmony and true freedom. Submission for the Lord's sake to those in governmental (2:13–17) and social (2:18–20) authority will foster a good testimony to outsiders.

Before moving on to submission in marital relationships (3:1–7), Peter again picks up the theme of Christian suffering (mentioned in 1:6–7; 2:12, 18–20) and uses Christ as the supreme model: He suffered sinlessly, silently, and as a substitute for the salvation of others (2:21–25; cf. Is. 52:13—53:12). Peter summarizes his appeal for Christlike submission and humility (3:8–11).

The Suffering of the Believer (3:13—5:14): Anticipating that growing opposition to Christianity will require a number of his readers to defend their faith and conduct, Peter encourages them to be ready to do so in an intelligent and gracious way (3:13–16). Three times he tells them that if they must suffer, it should be for righteousness' sake and not as a result of sinful behavior (3:17; see 2:20; 4:15–16). The end of this chapter (3:18–22) is an extremely difficult passage to interpret, and several options have been offered. Verses 19–20 may mean that Christ, during the period between His death and Resurrection, addressed demonic spirits or the spirits of those who were alive before the Flood. Another interpretation is that Christ preached through Noah to his pre-Flood contemporaries. Verse 21 teaches that the inner attitude of repentance and identification with the work of Christ saves a person, and this attitude is reflected in water baptism.

As believers in Christ, the readers are no longer to pursue the lusts of the flesh as they did formerly, but rather the will of God (4:1–6). In view of the hardships that they may suffer, Peter exhorts them to be strong in their mutual love and to exercise their spiritual gifts in the power of God so that they will be built up (4:7–11). They should not be surprised when they are slandered and reviled for their faith because the sovereign God has a purpose in all things, and the time of judgment will come when His name and all who trust in Him will be vindicated (4:12–19). They must therefore "commit their souls *to Him* in doing good" (4:19).

In a special word to the elders of the churches in these Roman provinces, Peter urges them to be diligent but gentle shepherds over the flocks that have been divinely placed under their care (5:1–4). The readers as a whole are told to clothe themselves with humility toward one another and toward God who will exalt them at the proper time (5:5–7). They are to resist the adversary in the sure knowledge that their calling to God's eternal glory in Christ will be realized (5:8–11). Peter ends his epistle by stating his theme ("the true grace of God") and conveying greetings and a benediction (5:12–14).

Outline of First Peter

Part One: The Salvation of the Believer (1:1—2:12)

I. Salutation, 1:1–2

II. Salvation of the Believer, 1:3–12
    A. Hope for the Future, 1:3–4
    B. Trials for the Present, 1:5–9
    C. Anticipation in the Past, 1:10–12

III. Sanctification of the Believer, 1:13—2:12
   A. "Be Holy," 1:13–21
   B. "Love One Another," 1:22–25
   C. "Desire the Pure Milk of the Word," 2:1–3
   D. "Offer Up Spiritual Sacrifices," 2:4–10
   E. "Abstain from Fleshly Lusts," 2:11–12

Part Two: The Submission of the Believer (2:13—3:12)

I. Submission to the Government, 2:13–17

II. Submission in Business, 2:18–25

III. Submission in Marriage, 3:1–8

IV. Submission in All of Life, 3:9–12

Part Three: The Suffering of the Believer (3:13—5:14)

I. Conduct in Suffering, 3:13–17

II. Christ's Example of Suffering, 3:18—4:6

III. Commands in Suffering, 4:7–19

IV. Minister in Suffering, 5:1–9
   A. Elders, Shepherd the Flock, 5:1–4
   B. Saints, Humble Yourselves, 5:5–9

V. Benediction, 5:10–14

Second Peter

WHILE PETER'S AUDIENCE IS THE SAME in his second letter (3:1), his theme and purpose are different. Persecution from unbelievers can be hard for Christians to bear (First Peter); but defection within the community of believers can be even more devastating (Second Peter). To counteract the effects of this "poison in the pews," Peter reminds his readers of the timeless truths of the faith, and exhorts them to continue growing toward Christian maturity. Those who scoff at the thought of future judgment will find, like Sodom and Gomorrah, that ignoring God's Word will ultimately lead to destruction every time! The warning for believers is clear: "Do not forget. . . . be diligent. . . . beware!" (3:8, 14, 17).

SECOND PETER

Focus	Cultivation of Christian Character			Condemnation of False Teachers			Confidence of Christ's Return		
	1:1 ————— 1:21			2:1 ————— 2:22			3:1 ————— 3:18		
Divisions	Salutation	Growth in Christ	Grounds of Belief	Danger of False Teachers	Destruction of False Teachers	Description of False Teachers	Mockery in the Last Days	Manifestation of the Day of the Lord	Maturity in View of the Day of the Lord
	1:1 — 1:2	1:3 — 1:14	1:15 — 1:21	2:1 — 2:3	2:4 — 2:9	2:10 — 2:22	3:1 — 3:7	3:8 — 3:10	3:11 — 3:18
Topics	True Prophecy			False Prophets			Prophecy of the Day of the Lord		
	Holiness			Heresy			Hope		
Place	Probably Rome								
Time	c. A.D. 64–66								

Introduction and Title

First Peter deals with problems from the outside; Second Peter deals with problems from the inside. Peter writes to warn the believers about the false teachers who are peddling damaging doctrine. He begins by urging them to keep close watch on their personal lives. The Christian life demands diligence in pursuing moral excellence, knowledge, self-control, perseverance, godliness, brotherly kindness, and selfless love. By contrast, the false teachers are sensual, arrogant, greedy, and covetous. They scoff at the thought of future judgment and live their lives as if the present would be the pattern for the future. Peter reminds them that although God may be long-suffering in sending judgment, ultimately it will come. In view of that fact, believers should live lives of godliness, blamelessness, and steadfastness.

The statement of authorship (1:1) is very clear: "Simon Peter, a servant and apostle of Jesus Christ." To distinguish this epistle from the first by Peter it was given the Greek title *Petrou B,* "Second of Peter."

Author

No other book in the New Testament poses as many problems of authenticity as does Second Peter. Unlike First Peter, this letter has very weak external testimony, and its genuineness is hurt by internal difficulties as well. Because of these obstacles, many scholars reject the Petrine authorship of this epistle, but this does not mean that there is no case for the opposite position.

External Evidence: The external testimony for the Petrine authorship of Second Peter is weaker than that for any other New Testament book, but by the fourth century it became generally recognized as an authentic work of the apostle Peter. There are no undisputed second-century quotations from Second Peter, but in the third century it is quoted in the writings of several church fathers, notably Origen and Clement of Alexandria. Third-century writers were generally aware of Second Peter and respected its contents, but it was still cataloged as a disputed book. The fourth century saw the official acknowledgment of the authority of Second Peter in spite of some lingering doubts. For several reasons Second Peter was not quickly accepted as a canonical book: (1) Slow circulation kept it from being widely known. (2) Its brevity and contents greatly limited the number of quotations from it in the writings of early church leaders. (3) The delay in recognition meant that Second Peter had to compete with several later works which falsely claimed to be Petrine (e.g., the Apocalypse of Peter). (4) Stylistic differences between First and Second Peter also raised doubts.

Internal Evidence: On the positive side, Second Peter bears abundant testimony to its apostolic origin. It claims to be by "Simon Peter" (1:1), and chapter 3, verse 1, says "Beloved, I now write to you this second epistle." The writer refers to the Lord's prediction about the apostle's death (1:14; cf. John 21:18–19) and says he was an eyewitness of the Transfiguration (1:16–18). As an apostle (1:1), he places himself on an equal level with Paul (3:15). There are also distinctive words that are found in Second Peter's sermons in Acts, as well as unusual words and phrases shared by First and Second Peter.

On the negative side, a number of troublesome areas challenge the traditional position: (1) There are differences between the style and vocabulary of First and Second Peter. The Greek of Second Peter is rough and awkward compared to that of First Peter, and there are also differences in informality and in the use of the Old Testament. But these differences are often exaggerated, and they can be explained by Peter's use of Silvanus as his secretary for First Peter and his own hand for Second Peter. (2) It is argued that Second Peter used a passage from Jude to describe false teachers, and that Jude was written after Peter's death. However, this is a debated issue, and it is possible that Jude quoted from Peter or that both used a common source (see "Author" in Jude). (3) The reference to a collection of Paul's letters (3:15–16) implies a late date for this epistle. But it is not necessary to conclude that all of Paul's letters were in mind here. Peter's contact with Paul and his associates no doubt made him familiar with several Pauline Epistles. (4) Some scholars claim that the false teaching mentioned in Second Peter was a form of Gnosticism that emerged after Peter's day, but there is insufficient evidence to support this stand.

The alternative to Petrine authorship is a later forgery done in the name of Peter. Even the claim that Second Peter was written by a disciple of Peter cannot overcome the problem of misrepresentation. In addition, Second Peter is clearly superior to any pseudonymous writings. In spite of the external and internal problems, the traditional position of Petrine authorship overcomes more difficulties than any other option.

Date and Setting

Most scholars regard chapter 3, verse 1, ("Beloved, I now write to you this second epistle") as a reference to First Peter. If this is so, Peter had the same readers of Asia Minor in mind (see "Date and Setting" in First Peter), although the more general salutation (1:1) would also allow for a wider audience. Peter wrote this epistle in response to the spread of heretical teachings which were all the more insidious because they emerged from within the churches. These false teachers perverted the doctrine of justification and promoted a rebellious and immoral way of life.

This epistle was written just before the apostle's death (1:14), probably from Rome. His martyrdom took place between A.D. 64 and 66 (if Peter were alive in 67 when Paul wrote Second Timothy during his second Roman imprisonment, it is likely that Paul would have mentioned him).

Theme and Purpose

The basic theme that runs through Second Peter is the contrast between the knowledge and practice of truth versus falsehood. This epistle was written to expose the dangerous and seductive work of false teachers and to warn believers to be on their guard so that they will not be "led away with the error of the wicked" (3:17).

It was also written to exhort the readers to "grow in the grace and knowledge of our Lord and Savior Jesus Christ" (3:18), because this growth into Christian maturity is the best defense against spiritual counterfeits. Another purpose of this letter was to provide a "reminder" (1:12–13; 3:1–2) to the readers of the foundational elements in the Christian life from which they must not waver. This includes the certainty of the Lord's return in power and judgment.

Keys to Second Peter

Key Word: Against False Teachers

Key Verses (1:20–21; 3:9–11)—"Knowing this first, that no prophecy of Scripture is of any private interpretation, for prophecy never came by the will of man, but holy men of God spoke *as they were* moved by the Holy Spirit" (1:20–21).

"The Lord is not slack concerning *His* promise, as some count slackness, but is long-suffering toward us, not willing that any should perish but that all should come to repentance. But the day of the Lord will come as a thief in the night, in which the heavens will pass away with a great noise, and the elements will melt with fervent heat; both the earth and the works that are in it will be burned up. Therefore, since all these things will be dissolved, what manner *of persons* ought you to be in holy conduct and godliness" (3:9–11).

Key Chapter (1)—The Scripture clearest in defining the relationship between God and man on the issue of inspiration is contained in chapter 1, verses 19–21. Three distinct principles surface: (1) that the interpretation of Scriptures is not limited to a favored elect but is open for all who "rightly dividing the word of truth" (2 Tim. 2:15); (2) that the divinely inspired prophet did not initiate the Scripture himself; and (3) that the Holy Ghost (not the emotion or circumstances of the moment) moved holy men.

Christ in Second Peter

Apart from the first verse of his epistle, Peter employs the title "Lord" every time he names the Savior. The Lord Jesus Christ is the source of full knowledge and power for the attainment of spiritual maturity (1:2–3, 8; 3:18). Peter recalls the glory of His Transfiguration on the holy mountain and anticipates His *parousia*, "Coming," when the whole world, not just three men on a mountain, will behold His glory.

Contribution to the Bible

While First Peter dealt with submission to God as the proper response to suffering from without, Second Peter concentrates on knowledge of the truth as the proper response to error from within. The words "suffering" in First Peter and "knowledge" in Second Peter appear sixteen times in various forms. The "knowledge" of Second Peter involves not only intellectual comprehension but experiential realization as well. It is based on the application of spiritual truth to growth in the life of the believer.

The two epistles of Peter can be contrasted in several ways:

First Peter	Second Peter
External Opposition	Internal Opposition
Hostility	Heresy
Antagonism	Apostasy
Endurance	Steadfastness
Waiting	Warning
Suffering	Error
Submission	Knowledge
Comfort	Caution
Hope in the Lord's Return	Confidence in the Lord's Return
Holiness	Maturity
"Pain with a Purpose"	"Poison in the Pew"

Peter's scenario from the creation of the present heavens and earth to the dissolution of the universe and creation of the new heavens and earth is one of the most astonishing passages in all of Scripture (3:5–13).

Survey of Second Peter

Peter wrote his first epistle to encourage his readers to respond properly to external opposition. His second epistle focuses on internal opposition caused by false teachers whose "destructive heresies" (2:1) can seduce believers into error and immorality. While First Peter speaks of the new birth through the living Word, Second Peter stresses the need for growth in the grace and knowledge of Christ. The best antidote for error is a mature understanding of the truth. Second Peter divides into three parts: cultivation of Christian character (1); condemnation of false teachers (2); and confidence of Christ's return (3).

Cultivation of Christian Character (1): Peter's salutation (1:1–2) is an introduction to the major theme of chapter 1, that is, the true knowledge of Jesus Christ. The readers are reminded of the "great and precious promises" that are theirs because of their calling to faith in Christ (1:3–4). They have been called away from the corruption of the world to conformity with Christ, and Peter urges them to progress by forging a chain of eight Christian virtues from faith to love (1:5–7). If a believer does not transform profession into practice, he becomes spiritually useless, perverting the purpose for which he was called (1:8–11).

This letter was written not long before Peter's death (1:14) to remind believers of the riches of their position in Christ and their responsibility to hold fast to the truth (1:12–21). Peter knew that his departure from this earth was imminent, and he left this letter as a written legacy. As an eyewitness of the life of Christ (he illustrates this with a portrait of the Transfiguration in 1:16–18), Peter affirms the authority and reliability of the prophetic word. The clearest biblical description of the divine-human process of inspiration is found in chapter 1, verse 21: "but holy men of God spoke *as they were* moved by the Holy Spirit."

Condemnation of False Teachers (2): Peter's discussion of true prophecy leads him to an extended denunciation of false prophecy in the churches. These false teachers were especially dangerous because they arose within the church and undermined the confidence of believers (2:1–3). Peter's extended description of the characteristics of these false teachers (2:10–22) exposes the futility and corruption of their strategies. Their teachings and life-styles reek of arrogance and selfishness, but their crafty words are capable of enticing immature believers.

Confidence of Christ's Return (3): Again Peter states that this letter is designed to stir up the minds of his readers "by way of reminder" (3:1; cf. 1:13). This very timely chapter is designed to remind them of the certain truth of the imminent *parousia* (this Greek word, used in 3:4, 12, refers to the Second Coming or the advent of Christ) and to refute those mockers who will deny this doctrine in the last days. These scoffers will claim that God does not powerfully intervene in world affairs, but Peter calls attention to two past and one future divinely induced catastrophic events: the Creation, the Flood, and the dissolution of the present heavens and earth (3:1–7). It may appear that the promise of Christ's return will not be fulfilled, but this is untrue for two reasons: God's perspective on the passing of time is quite unlike that of men, and the apparent delay in the *parousia* is due to His patience in waiting for more individuals to come to a knowledge of Christ (3:8–9). Nevertheless, the day of consummation will come, and all the matter of this universe will evidently be transformed into energy from which God will fashion a new cosmos (3:10–13).

In light of this coming day of the Lord, Peter exhorts his readers to live lives of holiness, steadfastness, and growth (3:14–18). He mentions the letters of "our beloved brother Paul" and significantly places them on a level with the Old Testament Scriptures (3:15–16). After a final warning about the danger of false teachers, the epistle closes with an appeal to growth, and a doxology.

Outline of Second Peter

I. Cultivation of Christian Character, 1:1–21
    A. Salutation, 1:1–2
    B. Growth in Christ, 1:3–14
    C. Grounds of Belief, 1:15–21
        1. Experience of the Transfiguration, 1:15–18
        2. Certainty of the Scriptures, 1:19–21

II. Condemnation of False Teachers, 2:1–22
   A. Danger of False Teachers, 2:1–3
   B. Destruction of False Teachers, 2:4–9
   C. Description of False Teachers, 2:10–22

III. Confidence of Christ's Return, 3:1–18
   A. Mockery in the Last Days, 3:1–7
   B. Manifestation of the Day of the Lord, 3:8–10
   C. Maturity in View of the Day of the Lord, 3:11–18

First John

JOHN, THE "BELOVED" APOSTLE with a pastor's heart, writes to his "little children" (2:1,18,28; 3:7,18; 5:21) and "beloved" ones in the faith (3:2, 21; 4:1, 7,11). His letter has at least five purposes: to promote fellowship (1:3), to produce happiness (1:4), to protect holiness (2:1), to prevent heresy (2:26), and to provide hope (5:13). Fellowship with God is not a vague, nebulous experience. It can be an objective daily reality. John sets forth at least three tests which can act as a "fellowship barometer" for his spiritual children in their daily walk with God:

(1) Have I confessed all known sins to God? (1:9).
(2) Am I walking in obedience to the light of God's Word? (2:4–5).
(3) Am I demonstrating a love for the brethren? (2:9–10).

FIRST JOHN					
Focus	**Basis of Fellowship**		**Behavior of Fellowship**		
	1:1 2:27		2:28 5:21		
Divisions	Conditions for Fellowship	Cautions to Fellowship	Characteristics of Fellowship	Consequences of Fellowship	
	1:1 2:14	2:15 2:27	2:28 5:3	5:4 5:21	
Topics	Meaning of Fellowship		Manifestations of Fellowship		
	Abiding in God's Light		Abiding in God's Love		
Place	Written in Ephesus				
Time	C. A.D. 90				

483

Introduction and Title

God is light; God is love; and God is life. John is enjoying a delightful fellowship with that God of light, love, and life, and he desperately desires that his spiritual children enjoy the same fellowship.

God is light. Therefore, to engage in fellowship with Him we must walk in light and not in darkness. As we walk in the light, we will regularly confess our sins, allowing the blood of Christ to continually cleanse us. Christ will act as our defense attorney before the Father. Proof of our "walk in the light" will be keeping the commandments of God and replacing any hatred we have toward our brother with love. Two major roadblocks to hinder this walk will be falling in love with the world and falling for the alluring lies of false teachers.

God is love. Since we are His children we must walk in love. In fact, John says that if we do not love, we do not know God. Additionally, our love needs to be practical. Love is more than just words; it is actions. Love is giving, not getting. Biblical love is unconditional in its nature. It is an "in spite of" love. Christ's love fulfilled those qualities and when that brand of love characterizes us, we will be free of self-condemnation and experience confidence before God.

God is life. Those who fellowship with Him must possess His quality of life. Spiritual life begins with spiritual birth. Spiritual birth occurs through faith in Jesus Christ. Faith in Jesus Christ infuses us with God's life—eternal life. Therefore, one who walks in fellowship with God will walk in light, love, and life.

Although the apostle John's name is not found in this book, it was given the title *Ioannou A,* "First of John."

Author

The external evidence for the authorship of First John shows that from the beginning it was universally received without dispute as authoritative. It was used by Polycarp (who knew John in his youth) and Papias in the early second century, and later in that century Irenaeus (who knew Polycarp in his youth) specifically attributed it to the apostle John. All the Greek and Latin church fathers accepted this epistle as Johannine.

The internal evidence supports this universal tradition because the "we" (apostles), "you" (readers), and "they" (false teachers) phraseology places the writer in the sphere of the apostolic eyewitness (cf. 1:1–3; 4:14). John's name was well known to the readers, and it was unnecessary for him to mention it. The style and vocabulary of First John are so similar to those of the fourth Gospel that most scholars acknowledge these books to be by the same hand (see "Author" in John). Both share many distinctively Johannine phrases, and the characteristics of limited vocabulary and frequent contrast of opposites are also common to them. Even so, some critics have assailed this conclusion on various grounds, but the theological and stylistic differences are not substantial enough to overcome the abundant similarities.

The traditional view is also rejected by those who hold that the fourth Gospel and these three epistles were written by John the "elder" or "presbyter," who is to be distinguished from John the apostle. But the only basis for this distinction is Eusebius' interpretation in his *Ecclesiastical History* (A.D. 323) of a statement by Papias. Eusebius understood the passage to refer to two distinct Johns, but the wording does not require this; the elder John and the apostle John may be one and the same. Even if they were different, there is no evidence for contradicting the consistent acknowledgment by the early church that this book was written by the apostle John.

Date and Setting

In Acts 8:14, John is associated with "the apostles who were at Jerusalem," and Paul calls him one of the "pillars" of the Jerusalem church in Galatians 2:9. Apart from Revelation 1, the New Testament is silent about his later years, but early Christian tradition uniformly tells us that he left Jerusalem (probably not long before its destruction in A.D. 70) and that he ministered in and around Ephesus. The seven churches in the Roman province of Asia, mentioned in Revelation 2 and 3, were evidently a part of this ministry. Although there is no address in First John, it is likely that the apostle directed this epistle to the Asian churches that were within the realm of his oversight.

The believers in these congregations were well established in Christian truth, and John wrote to them not as novices but as brethren grounded in apostolic doctrine (2:7, 18–27; 3:11). The apostle does not mention his own affairs, but his use of such terms of address as "beloved" and "my little children" gives this letter a personal touch that reveals his close relationship to the original recipients. First John was probably written in Ephesus after the Gospel of John, but the date cannot be fixed with certainty. No persecution is mentioned, suggesting a date prior to A.D. 95 when persecution broke out during the end of Domitian's reign (A.D. 81–96).

Advanced in years, John wrote this fatherly epistle out of loving concern for his "children," whose steadfastness in the truth was being threatened by the lure of worldliness and the guile of false teachers. The Gnostic heresy taught that matter is inherently evil, and a divine being therefore could not take on human flesh. This resulted in the distinction between the man Jesus and the spiritual Christ who came upon Jesus at His Baptism but departed prior to His Crucifixion. Another variation was Docetism (from *dokeo,* "to seem"), the doctrine that Christ only seemed to have a human body. The result in both cases was the same—a flat denial of the Incarnation.

The Gnostics also believed that their understanding of the hidden knowledge (*gnosis*) made them a kind of spiritual elite, who were above the normal distinctions of right and wrong. This led in most cases to deplorable conduct and complete disregard for Christian ethics.

Theme and Purpose

The major theme of First John is fellowship with God. John wanted his readers to have assurance of the indwelling God through their abiding relationship with Him (2:28; 5:13). Belief in Christ should be manifested in the practice of righteousness and love for the brethren which in turn produces joy and confidence before God. John wrote this epistle to encourage this kind of fellowship and to emphasize the importance of holding fast to apostolic doctrine.

First John was also written to refute the destructive teachings of the Gnostics by stressing the reality of the Incarnation and the emptiness of profession without practice. These "antichrists" failed the three tests of righteous living, love for the brethren, and belief that Jesus is the Christ, the incarnate God-man.

Keys to First John

Key Word: Fellowship

Key Verses (1:3–4; 5:11–13)—"That which we have seen and heard we declare to you, that you also may have fellowship with us; and truly our fellowship *is* with the Father and with His Son Jesus Christ. And these things we write to you that your joy may be full" (1:3–4).

"And this is the testimony: that God has given us eternal life, and this life is in His Son. He who has the Son has life; he who does not have the Son of God does not have life. These things I have written to you who believe in the name of the Son of God, that you may know that you have eternal life, and that you may *continue to* believe in the name of the Son of God" (5:11–13).

Key Chapter (1)—The two central passages in the New Testament for continued fellowship with God are John 15 and First John 1. The former relates the positive side of fellowship, that is, abiding in Christ. The latter unfolds the other side, pointing out that when Christians do not abide in Christ, they must seek forgiveness before fellowship can be restored.

Christ in First John

The present ministry of Christ is portrayed in this epistle (1:5—2:22). His blood continually cleanses the believer from all sin, and He is our righteous Advocate before the Father. This epistle places particular stress on the Incarnation of God the Son and the identity of Jesus as the Christ (2:22; 4:2–3), in refutation of Gnostic doctrine. Jesus Christ "came by water and blood" (5:6); He was the same indivisible person from the beginning (His Baptism) to the end (His Crucifixion) of His public ministry.

Contribution to the Bible

The usual characteristics of a letter (salutation, address, greetings, benediction) are absent in First John, and some scholars regard it as a transcribed sermon. But John had a definite audience and historical situation in mind, and he composed this work ("I am writing these things to you," 2:1; cf. 1:4; 2:7–8, 12–14, 21, 26; 5:13) with their specific interests in mind. Thus, we can regard First John as an epistle written in a sermonic mood.

Like the fourth Gospel, John's first epistle is written with disarming simplicity of style and vocabulary. John skillfully uses this simplicity as his vehicle for expressing some of the most profound concepts in all Scripture. Certain ideas like light, love, life, truth, and righteousness are frequently repeated, not monotonously, but as developing motifs that are enriched as the epistle progresses. There is also an abundance of antithetical parallelism: light vs. darkness, truth vs. falsehood, love vs. hatred, love of the world vs. love of the Father, Christ vs. antichrists, children of God vs. children of the devil, righteousness vs. sin, the Spirit of God vs. the spirit of the Antichrist, and life vs. death.

First John is characterized by its authoritative declaration of truth and stern denunciation of error, and yet a spirit of love prevails. The structure of the book is subtle, making it difficult to outline, especially because of the way John intertwines motifs. Surpisingly, there are no quotations from the Old Testament, and only one Old Testament incident is mentioned (Cain, 3:12). Finally, John's gospel and first epistle are complementary works in their contents and purposes (cf. 2:28; 5:13; John 20:30–31).

Survey of First John

John writes his first epistle at a time when apostolic doctrine is being challenged by a proliferation of false teachings. Like Second Peter and Jude, First John has a negative and a positive thrust: it refutes erroneous doctrine and encourages its readership to walk in the knowledge of the truth. John lists the criteria and characteristics of fellowship with God and shows that those who abide in Christ can have confidence and assurance before Him. This simply written but profound work develops the basis of fellowship (1:1—2:27) and the behavior of fellowship (2:28—5:21).

The Basis of Fellowship (1:1—2:27): John's prologue (1:1–4) recalls the beginning of apostolic contact with Christ. It relates his desire to transmit this apostolic witness to his readers so that they may share the same fellowship with Jesus Christ, the personification of life. This proclamation is followed by a description of the conditions of fellowship (1:5—2:14). Fellowship with a God of light is made possible by the blood of Christ, which cleanses the believer and propitiates (satisfies) the Father's righteous demands. Believers must walk in integrity and openness to what the light reveals, with a willingness to confess failures exposed by the light. While no specific instance of sin should be seen as inevitable in a Christian's life, complete sinlessness will not be a reality until we stand before God (3:2).

The readers' sins have been forgiven and they enjoy fellowship with God. As a result, they know "Him *Who is* from the beginning" and are strengthened to overcome the temptations of the evil one (2:12–14). The cautions to fellowship are both practical (the lusts of the corrupt world system which opposes God, 2:15–17) and doctrinal (the teachings of those who differentiate between Jesus and the Christ, 2:18–23). In contrast to these "antichrists," the readers have the knowledge of the truth and an anointing from the Holy One. Therefore, it would be foolish for them to turn away from the teachings of the apostles to the innovations of the antichrists. The antidote to these heretical teachings is abiding in the apostolic truths that they "heard from the beginning," which are authenticated by the anointing they have received (2:24–27).

The Behavior of Fellowship (2:28—5:21): The basic theme of First John is summarized in 2:28—assurance through abiding in Christ. The next verse introduces the motif of regeneration, and argues that regeneration is manifested in the practice of righteousness (2:29—3:10). Because we are children of God through faith in Christ, we have a firm hope of being fully conformed to Him when He appears (3:1–3). Our present likeness to Christ places us in a position of incompatibility with sin, because sin is contrary to the person and work of Christ (3:4–6). The concept (3:6) does not contradict chapter 1, verse 8, because it is saying that the abider, insofar as he abides, does not sin. When the believer sins, he does not reflect the regenerate new man but Satan, the original sinner (3:7–10).

Regeneration is shown in righteousness (2:29—3:10), and righteousness is manifested in love (3:10–23). The apostle uses the example of Cain to illustrate what love is not: hatred is murdering in spirit, and it arises from the worldly sphere of death. John then uses the example of Christ to illustrate what love is: love is practiced in self sacrifice, not mere profession. This practical expression of love results in assurance before God and answered prayers because the believer is walking in obedience to God's commands to believe in Christ and love one another.

John introduces two important motifs (3:24), which are developed in chapter 4, verses 1–16: the indwelling God, and the Spirit as a mark of this indwelling. The Spirit of God confesses the incarnate Christ and confirms apostolic doctrine (4:1–6). The mutual abiding of the believer in God and God in the believer is manifested in love for others, and this love produces a divine and human fellowship that testifies to and reflects the reality of the Incarnation (4:7–16). It also anticipates the perfect fellowship to come and creates a readiness to face the One from whom all love is derived (4:17–19).

John joins the concepts he has presented into a circular chain of six links that begins with love for the brethren (4:20—5:17): (1) Love for believers is the inseparable product of love for God (4:20—5:1). (2) Love for God arises out of obedience to His commandments (5:2–3). (3) Obedience to God is the result of faith in His Son (5:4–5). (4) This faith is in Jesus, who was the Christ not only at His baptism (the water), but also at His death (the blood; 5:6–8). (5) The divine witness to the person of Christ is worthy of complete belief (5:9–13). (6) This belief produces confident access to God in prayer (5:14–17). Since intercessory prayer is a manifestation of love for others, the chain has come full circle.

The epilogue (5:18–21) summarizes the conclusions of the epistle in a series of three certainties: (1) Sin is a threat to fellowship, and it should be regarded as foreign to the believer's position in Christ (cf. Rom. 6). (2) The believer stands with

God against the satanic world system. (3) The Incarnation produces true knowledge and communion with Christ. Since He is "the true God and eternal life," the one who knows Him should avoid the lure of any substitute.

Outline of First John

Part One: The Basis of Fellowship (1:1—2:27)

I. Introduction, 1:1–4

II. The Conditions for Fellowship, 1:5—2:14
    A. Walk in the Light, 1:5–7
    B. Confession of Sin, 1:8—2:2
    C. Obedience to His Commandments, 2:3–6
    D. Love for One Another, 2:7–14

III. The Cautions to Fellowship, 2:15–27
    A. Love of the World, 2:15–17
    B. Spirit of the Antichrist, 2:18–27

Part Two: The Behavior of Fellowship (2:28—5:21)

I. Characteristics of Fellowship, 2:28—5:3
    A. Purity of Life, 2:28—3:3
    B. Practice of Righteousness, 3:4–12
    C. Love in Deed and Truth, 3:13–24
    D. Testing the Spirits, 4:1–6
    E. Love as Christ Loved, 4:7—5:3

II. Consequences of Fellowship, 5:4–21
    A. Victory over the World, 5:4–5
    B. Assurance of Salvation, 5:6–13
    C. Guidance in Prayer, 5:14–17
    D. Freedom from Habitual Sin, 5:18–21

Second John

JOHN'S FIRST EPISTLE WAS WRITTEN to a group of believers in danger of following false teachers. His second letter is addressed to a chosen lady and her children who are undergoing similar temptations. John wastes no words in making his point: "If anyone comes to you and does not bring this doctrine, do not receive him into your house, nor greet him" (v. 10). Though John commends love as a necessary ingredient of the Christian life, it must not sentimentally embrace those who willfully seek to destroy the truth. To do so is to diminish the proper love which Christians must have for one another. John's warning is stern, but he knows a letter is not the best place to elaborate. He promises to deal more fully with the problem when he makes a personal visit.

SECOND JOHN							
Focus	**Abide in God's Commandments** 1		6	**Abide Not with False Teachers** 7			13
Divisions	Salutation 1 3	Walk in Truth 4	Walk in Love 5 6	Doctrine of False Teachers 7 9	Avoid the False Teachers 10 11	Benediction 12 13	
Topics	Walk in Commandments			Watch for Counterfeits			
	Practice the Truth			Protect the Truth			
Place	Written in Ephesus						
Time	C. A.D. 90						

Introduction and Title

"Let him who thinks he stands take heed lest he fall" (1 Cor. 10:12). These words of the apostle Paul could well stand as a subtitle for John's little epistle. The recipients, a chosen lady and her children, were obviously standing. They were walking in truth, remaining faithful to the commandments they had received from the Father. John is deeply pleased to be able to commend them. But he takes nothing for granted. Realizing that standing is just one bad step removed from falling, he does not hesitate to issue a reminder: love one another. The apostle admits that this is not new revelation, but he views it sufficiently important to repeat. Loving one another, he stresses, is equivalent to walking according to God's commandments.

John indicates, however, that this love must be discerning. It is not a naive, unthinking, "open to anything and anyone" kind of love. Biblical love is a matter of choice; it is dangerous and foolish to float through life with undiscerning love. False teachers abound who do not acknowledge Christ as having come in the flesh. The chosen lady is to guard herself against this teaching, since those who believe it have a "God-void" in their lives; they do not belong to Him. John even warns her not to receive into her house anyone who rejects the teaching of Christ, which she had previously learned. It is false charity to open the door to false teaching. We must have fellowship with God. We must have fellowship with Christians. But we must not have fellowship with false teachers.

The "elder" of verse 1 has been traditionally identified with the apostle John, resulting in the Greek title *Ioannou B.* "Second of John."

Author

Because of the similarity of the contents and circumstances of Second and Third John, the authorship of both will be considered here. These letters were not widely circulated at the beginning because of their brevity and their specific address to a small number of people. This limited circulation, combined with the fact that they have few distinctive ideas to add that are not found in First John, meant that they were seldom quoted in the patristic writings of the early church. Their place in the canon of New Testament books was disputed for a time, but it is significant that there was no question in the minds of those church fathers who lived closest to the time of John that these two epistles were written by the apostle. The second-century writers Irenaeus and Clement of Alexandria entertained no other view. Only as the details of their origin were forgotten did doubts arise, but the positive evidence in their favor eventually won for them the official recognition of the whole church.

It is obvious that the recipients of Second and Third John well knew the author's identity, although he did not use his name. Instead, he designated himself in the first verse of both letters as "the elder." This is not an argument against the Johannine authorship of Second and Third John, since the context of these epistles reveals that his authority was far greater than that of an elder in a local church. The apostle Peter also referred to himself as an elder (1 Pet. 5:1), and John uses the distinguishing term "the elder."

The similarity of style, vocabulary, structure, and mood between Second and Third John makes it clear that these letters were written by the same author. In addition, both (especially Second John) bear strong resemblances to First John and to the fourth Gospel. Thus, the external and internal evidence lends clear support to the traditional view that these epistles were written by the apostle John.

Date and Setting

The identification of the original readers of this epistle is difficult because of disagreement regarding the interpretation of "the elect lady and her children" (v. 1). Some scholars believe the address should be taken literally to refer to a specific woman and her children, while others prefer to take it as a figurative description of a local church.

The evidence is insufficient for a decisive conclusion, but in either case, the readers were well known to John and probably lived in the province of Asia, not far from Ephesus. If the figurative view is taken, "the children of your elect sister," (v. 13) refers to the members of a sister church.

In his first epistle, John wrote that a number of false teachers had split away from the church ("They went out from us, but they were not of us," 2:19). Some of these became traveling teachers who depended on the hospitality of individuals while they sought to infiltrate churches with their teachings.

Judging by the content and circumstances of Second John, it was evidently contemporaneous with First John or was written slightly later. It was probably written about A.D. 90. All three of John's epistles may have been written in Ephesus (see "Date and Setting" in First John).

Theme and Purpose

The basic theme of this brief letter is steadfastness in the practice and purity of the apostolic doctrine that the readers "have heard from the beginning" (v. 6). John wrote it as a reminder to continue walking in obedience to God's commandment to love one another (practical exhortation, vv. 4–6). He also wrote it as a warning not to associate with or assist teachers who do not acknowledge the truth about Jesus Christ (doctrinal exhortation, vv. 7–11).

It has been suggested that Second and Third John were written as covering letters for First John to provide a personal word to a church (Second John) and to Gaius (Third John) that would supplement the longer epistle. However, there is no way to be sure.

Keys to Second John

Key Word: Avoid False Teachers

Key Verses (9–10)—"Whoever transgresses and does not abide in the doctrine of Christ does not have God. He who abides in the doctrine of Christ has both the Father and the Son. If anyone comes to you and does not bring this doctrine, do not receive him into your house nor greet him" (vv. 9–10).

Christ in Second John

John refutes the same error regarding the person of Christ in this epistle as he did in his first epistle. Again he stresses that those "who do not confess Jesus Christ *as* coming in the flesh" (v. 7) are deceivers who must be avoided. One must abide "in the doctrine of Christ" (v. 9) to have a relationship with God. The doctrine of the person and work of Jesus Christ affects every other area of theology.

Contribution to the Bible

All three of John's epistles develop the theme of fellowship. The first focuses on fellowship with God, the second on fellowship with enemies of the truth, and the third on fellowship with proclaimers of the truth.

This letter is the second shortest book in the Bible (Third John is slightly shorter), and it originally fit on a single sheet of papyrus paper. The first six verses are positive in nature, mentioning "truth" five times and "love" four times. The last half of the letter is a negative warning, and these two words are not mentioned at all. If the literal view of "chosen lady" is taken, Second John is the only biblical book that is addressed to a woman.

Survey of Second John

This brief letter has much in common with First John, including a warning about the danger of false teachers who deny the Incarnation of Jesus Christ. John encourages the readers to continue walking in love but exhorts them to be discerning in their expression of love. Truth without love produces autocratic severity, but love without truth leads to blind sentimentality. Walking in love must not be separated from walking in truth (cf. Eph. 4:15, "speaking the truth in love"), and believers must not show hospitality to false teachers who distort the central teaching of Christianity—the person and work of Jesus Christ. Second John breaks into two parts: abide in God's commandments (vv. 1–6) and abide not with false teachers (vv. 7–13).

Abide In God's Commandments (vv. 1–6): The salutation (vv. 1–3) centers on the concept of abiding in the truth (mentioned four times in these three verses). The recipients are loved for their adherence to the truth by "all those who have known the truth." The apostle commends his readers on their walk in truth in obedience to God's commandment (v. 4), and reminds them that this commandment entails the practice of love for one another (vv. 5–6). The divine command is given in verse 5 and the human response follows in verse 6.

Abide Not with False Teachers (vv. 7–13): Moving from the basic test of Christian behavior (love for the brethren) to the basic test of Christian belief (the person of Christ), John admonishes the readers to beware of deceivers "who do not confess Jesus Christ *as* coming in the flesh" (vv. 7–9). In no uncertain terms, the apostle enjoins the readers to deny even the slightest assistance or encouragement to itinerant teachers who promote an erroneous view of Christ (and hence of salvation; vv. 10–11).

This letter closes with John's explanation of its brevity: he anticipates a future visit during which he will be able to "speak face to face" with his readers (v. 12). The meaning of the greeting in verse 13 relates to the interpretation of verse 1.

Outline of Second John

I. Abide in God's Commandments, 1–6
  A. Salutation, 1–3
  B. Walk in Truth, 4
  C. Walk in Love, 5–6

II. Abide Not with False Teachers, 7–13
  A. Doctrine of the False Teachers, 7–9
  B. Avoid the False Teachers, 10–11
  C. Benediction, 12–13

Third John

IN FIRST JOHN THE APOSTLE DISCUSSES fellowship with God; in Second
John he forbids fellowship with false teachers; and in Third John he
encourages fellowship with Christian brothers. Following his expression of love for Gaius, John voices his joy that Gaius is persistently
walking in the truth and showing hospitality to the messengers of the
gospel. But John cannot commend certain others in the assembly.
Diotrephes, for example, has allowed pride to replace love in his life,
even rejecting the disciplining words of John. Everything that Gaius is,
Diotrephes is not! John uses this negative example as an opportunity
to encourage Gaius. Godly character and loyalty to the truth are never
easy, but they bring God's richest commendation—and John's as well!

THIRD JOHN

Focus	Commendation of Gaius			Condemnation of Diotrephes		
	1　　　　　　　　　　　8			9　　　　　　　　　　　14		
Divisions	Salutation	Godliness of Gaius	Generosity of Gaius	Pride of Diotrephes	Praise for Demetrius	Benediction
	1	2　　　4	5　　　8	9　　　11	12	13　　　14
Topics	Servanthood			Selfishness		
	Duty of Hospitality			Danger of Haughtiness		
Place	Written in Ephesus					
Time	C. A.D. 90					

495

Introduction and Title

In First John the apostle discusses fellowship with God; in Second John he forbids fellowship with false teachers; and in Third John he encourages fellowship with Christian brothers. Following his expression of love for Gaius, John assures him of his prayers for his health and voices his joy over Gaius' persistent walk in truth and for the manner in which he shows hospitality and support for missionaries who have come to his church. The phrase "send them forward on their journey" means to provide help for the missionaries' endeavors. Included in this help can be food, money, arrangements for companions, and means of travel. By supporting these men who are ministering for Christ, Gaius has become a fellow worker of the truth.

But not everyone in the church feels the same way. Diotrephes' heart is 180 degrees removed from Gaius' heart. He is no longer living in love. Pride has taken precedence in his life. He has refused a letter John has written for the church, fearing that his authority might be superseded by that of the apostle. He also has accused John of evil words and refused to accept missionaries. He forbids others to do so and even expels them from the church if they disobey him. John uses this negative example as an opportunity to encourage Gaius to continue his hospitality. Demetrius has a good testimony and may even be one of those turned away by Diotrephes. He is widely known for his good character and his loyalty to the truth. Here he is well commended by John and stands as a positive example for Gaius.

The Greek titles of First, Second, and Third John are *Ioannou, A, B, and G.* The *G* is *gamma,* the third letter of the Greek alphabet; *Ioannou G* means "Third of John."

Author

The authorship of Second and Third John was considered together because the contents and circumstances of both books are similar (see "Author" in Second John). Although the external evidence for Second and Third John is limited (there is even less for Third John than for Second John), what little there is consistently points to the apostle John as author. The internal evidence is stronger, and it, too, supports the apostolic origin of both letters.

Date and Setting

The parallels between Second and Third John suggest that these epistles were written at about the same time (A.D. 90). Early Christian writers are unified in their testimony that the headquarters of John's later ministry was in Ephesus, the principal city of the Roman province of Asia (see "Date and Setting" in First John). John evidently commissioned a number of traveling teachers to spread the gospel and to solidify the Asian churches, and these teachers were supported by believers who received them into their homes.

Third John, probably delivered by Demetrius, was occasioned by the report of some of these emissaries (called "brethren" in this letter), who returned to the apostle and informed him of the hospitality of Gaius and the hostility of Diotrephes. The arrogant Diotrephes seized the reins of an Asian church and vaunted himself as its preeminent authority. He maligned John's authorship and rejected the teachers sent out by John, expelling those in his church who wanted to receive them.

Gaius was a common name in the Roman Empire, and three other men by that name are mentioned in the New Testament: (1) Gaius, one of Paul's traveling companions from Macedonia (Acts 19:29); (2) Gaius of Derbe (Acts 20:4); and (3) Gaius, Paul's host in Corinth, one of the few Corinthians Paul baptized (see Rom. 16:23; 1 Cor. 1:14). The Gaius of Third John evidently lived in Asia, and it is best to distinguish him from these other men.

In verse 9, John alludes to a previous letter that Diotrephes had spurned. This may have been First or Second John, but it is more likely a letter that has been lost or perhaps destroyed by Diotrephes.

Theme and Purposes

The basic theme of this letter is the contrast between the truth and servanthood of Gaius and the error and selfishness of Diotrephes. Moving through Third John, five specific purposes can be discerned from its contents: (1) To commend Gaius for his adherence to the truth and his hospitality to the emissaries sent out by John (1–6a); (2) to encourage Gaius to continue his support of these brethren (6b–8); (3) to rebuke Diotrephes for his pride and misconduct (9–11); (4) to provide a recommendation for Demetrius (12); and (5) to inform Gaius of John's intention to visit and straighten out the difficulties (10a,13–14).

Keys to Third John

Key Word: Fellowship with the Brethren
Key Verse (11)—"Beloved, do not imitate what is evil, but what is good. He who does good is of God, but he who does evil has not seen God" (v. 11).

Christ in Third John

Unlike First and Second John, Third John makes no mention of the name of Jesus Christ. But verse 7 says they "went forth for His name's sake" an indirect reference to our Lord (cf. Acts 5:41, where the identical Greek construction is used to refer to "the name of Jesus" in Acts 5:40). The concept of truth runs throughout this letter, and Christ is the source and incarnation of truth, as is obvious from John's other writings.

Contribution to the Bible

This epistle is characteristically Johannine, emphasizing the themes of love, truth, and joy which are so prominent in John's gospel and other epistles. The length, style, and mood of Second and Third John are quite similar. Both epistles use similar phraseology and structure:

Second John	Third John
"Love" (4 times)	"Love" (2 times) "beloved" (4 times)
"Truth" (5 times)	"Truth" (6 times)
"The elder . . . whom I love in truth" (1)	"The elder . . . whom I love in truth" (1)
Expresses joy over the report of the readers	Expresses joy over the report of the reader
"Walking in truth" (4)	"Walk in (the) truth" (3–4)
Warns against hospitality to enemies of the truth	Encourages hospitality to teachers of the truth
Commendation followed by rebuke	Commendation followed by rebuke
Condemnation of bad doctrine	Condemnation of bad conduct
Short letter due to planned visit (12)	Short letter due to planned visit (13–14)

While Second and Third John do not make any real doctrinal contributions to the Bible that are not found in First John, they give important insights into the life and struggles of the church at the close of the apostolic age. Even the churches that were under the care of the apostle John were constantly threatened by unorthodox doctrine and conduct.

In spite of its brevity, Third John skillfully develops the characters of Gaius and Diotrephes with surprising vividness. This letter gives us a glimpse into the kind of frank and personal correspondence that the apostle John and other early Christian leaders maintained.

Survey of Third John

Third John is the shortest book in the Bible, but it is very personal and vivid. It offers a stark contrast between two men who respond in opposite ways to the itinerant teachers who have been sent out by the apostle. The faithful Gaius responds with generosity and hospitality, but the faithless Diotrephes responds with arrogance and opposition. Thus, John writes this letter to commend Gaius for walking in the truth (vv. 1–8) and to condemn Diotrephes for walking in error (vv. 9–14).

Commendation of Gaius (vv. 1–8): The "elder" writes to one of his beloved "children" whose godly behavior has given the apostles great joy (vv. 1–4). The "brethren," upon returning to John, have informed him of Gaius' faithfulness, love, and generosity in their behalf. The apostle acknowledges these actions and urges Gaius to continue supporting traveling teachers and missionaries who go out "for His [Jesus'] name's sake" (vv. 5–8).

Condemnation of Diotrephes (vv. 9–14): The epistle suddenly shifts to a negative note as John describes a man whose actions are diametrically opposed to those of Gaius (vv. 9–11). Diotrephes boldly rejects John's apostolic authority and refuses to receive the itinerant teachers sent out by the apostle. Diotrephes evidently has been orthodox in his doctrine, but his evil actions indicate a blindness to God in his practice.

By contrast, John gives his full recommendation to Demetrius, another emissary and probably the bearer of this letter to Gaius (v. 12). John expresses his hope of a personal visit in the closing remarks (vv. 13–14), as he does in Second John.

Outline of Third John

I. The Commendation of Gaius, 1–8
   A. Salutation, 1
   B. Godliness of Gaius, 2–4
   C. Generosity of Gaius, 5–8

II. The Condemnation of Diotrephes, 9–14
   A. Pride of Diotrephes, 9–11
   B. Praise for Demetrius, 12
   C. Benediction, 13–14

Jude

JUDE ORIGINALLY INTENDED TO WRITE on the theme of salvation. But because of pressing threats to his readers, he turns his attention instead to those who would seek to destroy the gospel. The dangers of false doctrine and rebellion are not new in the history of God's dealings with men. Disobedient Israel, fallen angels, Sodom and Gomorrah, Cain, Balaam, Torah—each has experienced God's judgment. How then can a believer resist such onslaughts? By "building yourselves up on [in] your most holy faith" (v. 20).

Focus	Purpose of Jude	Description of False Teachers			Defense against False Teachers	Doxology of Jude
	1　　　　4	15 　　　　　　　　　　　16			17 　　　　　23	24 　　25
Divisions	Introduction	Past Judgment	Present Characteristics	Future Judgment	Duty of Believers	Conclusion
	1　　　4	5　　7	8　　13	14　　16	17　　　　23	24　　25
Topics	Reason to Contend				How to Contend	
	Anatomy of Apostasy				Antidote for Apostasy	
Place	Unknown					
Time	C. A.D. 66–80					

JUDE

500

Introduction and Title

Fight! Contend! Do battle! When apostasy arises, when false teachers emerge, when the truth of God is attacked, it is time to fight for the faith. Only believers who are spiritually "in shape" can answer the summons. At the beginning of his letter Jude focuses on the believers' common salvation, but then feels compelled to challenge them to contend for the faith. The danger is real. False teachers have crept into the church, turning God's grace into unbounded license to do as they please. Jude reminds such men of God's past dealings with unbelieving Israel, disobedient angels, and wicked Sodom and Gomorrah. In the face of such danger Christians should not be caught off guard. The challenge is great, but so is the God who is able to keep them from stumbling.

The Greek title *Iouda,* "Of Jude," comes from the name *Ioudas* which appears in verse 1. This name, which can be translated Jude or Judas, was popular in the first century because of Judas Maccabaeus (d. 160 B.C.), a leader of the Jewish resistance against Syria during the Maccabean revolt.

Author

In spite of its limited subject matter and size, Jude was accepted as authentic and quoted by early church fathers. There may be some older allusions, but undisputed references to this epistle appear in the last quarter of the second century. It was included in the Muratorian Canon (c. A.D. 170) and accepted as part of Scripture by early leaders, such as Tertullian and Origen. Nevertheless, doubts arose concerning the place of Jude in the Canon because of its use of the Apocrypha. It was a disputed book in some parts of the church, but it eventually won universal recognition.

The author identifies himself as "a servant of Jesus Christ, and brother of James" (v. 1). This designation, combined with the reference in verse 17 to the apostles, makes it unlikely that this is the apostle Jude, called "Judas *the son* of James" in Luke 6:16 and in Acts 1:13. The Greek construction is better rendered in most modern translations as "Judas the son of James," so that the apostle Jude does not fit the description in Jude 1. This leaves the traditional view that Jude was one of the Lord's brothers, called Judas in Matthew 13:55 and Mark 6:3 (see "Author" in James). His older brother James (note his position on the two lists) was the famous leader of the Jerusalem church (Acts 15:13–21) and author of the epistle that bears his name. Like his brothers, Jude did not believe in Jesus before the Resurrection (John 7:1–9; Acts 1:14). The only other biblical allusion to him is in First Corinthians 9:5 where it is recorded that "the brothers of the Lord" took their wives along on their missionary journeys (the Judas of Acts 15:22, 32 may be another reference to him). Extrabiblical tradition adds nothing to our limited knowledge of Jude.

Date and Setting

Jude's general address does not mark out any particular circle of readers, and there are no geographical restrictions. Nevertheless, he probably had in mind a specific region that was being troubled by false teachers. There is not enough information in the epistle to settle the question of whether his readers were predominately Jewish or Gentile Christians (there is probably a mixture of both). In any case, the progress of the faith in their region was threatened by a number of apostates who rejected Christ in practice and principle. These proud libertines were especially dangerous because of their deceptive flattery (v. 16) and infiltration of Christian meetings (v. 12). They perverted the grace of God (v. 4) and caused divisions in the church (v. 19).

Jude's description of these heretics is reminiscent of that found in Second Peter and leads to the issue of the relationship between the two epistles (see "Author" in Second Peter). The strong similarity between Second Peter 2:1—3:4 and verses 4–18 can hardly be coincidental, but the equally obvious differences rule out the possibility that one is a mere copy of the other. It is also doubtful that both authors independently drew from an unknown third source, so the two remaining options are that Peter used Jude or Jude used Peter. Both views have their advocates, and a number of arguments have been raised in support of either side. But two arguments for the priority of Second Peter are so strong that they tip the scales in favor of this position: (1) A comparison of the two books shows that Second Peter anticipates the future rise of apostate teachers (2 Pet. 2:1–2; 3:3) while Jude records the historical fulfillment of Peter's words (vv. 4, 11–12, 17–18); (2) Jude directly quotes Second Peter 3:3 and acknowledges it as a quote from "the apostles" (cf. 1 Tim. 4:1; 2 Tim. 3:1).

Because of the silence of the New Testament and tradition concerning Jude's later years, we cannot know where this epistle was written. Nor is there any way to be certain of its date. Assuming the priority of Second Peter (A.D. 64–66), the probable range is A.D. 66–80. (Jude's silence concerning the destruction of Jerusalem does not prove that he wrote this letter before A.D. 70.)

Theme and Purpose

This epistle is intensely concerned with the threat of heretical teachers in the church and the believer's proper response to that threat. The contents reveal two major purposes: (1) To condemn the practices of the ungodly libertines who were infesting the churches and corrupting believers; and (2) to counsel the readers to stand firm, grow in their faith, and contend for the truth. Jude says little about the actual doctrines of these "hidden reefs," but they might have held to an antinomian version of Gnosticism (see "Date and Setting" in First John). The readers are encouraged to reach out to those who have been misled by these men.

Keys to Jude

Key Word: Contend for the Faith

Key Verse (3)—"Beloved, while I was very diligent to write to you concerning our common salvation, I found it necessary to write to you exhorting you to contend earnestly for the faith which was once for all delivered to the saints" (v. 3).

Christ in Jude

In contrast to those who stand condemned by their licentiousness and denial of Christ (v. 4), the believer is "preserved in Jesus Christ" (v. 1). Jude tells his readers to "keep yourselves in the love of God, looking for the mercy of our Lord Jesus Christ unto eternal life" (v. 21). But at the same time, the Lord "is able to keep you from stumbling, and to present *you* faultless before the presence of His glory with exceeding joy" (v. 24).

Contribution to the Bible

Like his brother James, Jude used highly descriptive and stinging words to describe those who compromise the truth. Both use considerable nature imagery and a highly succinct style. Both lay strong stress on ethical purity and display loving concern for their readers in spite of the stern approach. Errorists were not to be persecuted but rescued and shown mercy. Though James and Jude were raised in the same household with Jesus, they both humbly refer to themselves as His bond-servants.

One unusual feature of this epistle is its abundant use of triads of thought. Examples can be found in verse 1 (Jude, servant, brother; called, sanctified, preserved), verse 2 (mercy, peace, love), verses 5–7 (people, angels, those who did not believe), verse 11 (Cain, Balaam, Korah), verses 22–23 (some, others, them), and verses 24–25 (before, now, forever). The letter itself naturally breaks into three divisions (1–4, 5–16, 17–25).

Jude makes a surprising number of references to Old Testament characters and events in view of its brevity. But many have been troubled by its evident use of two first-century pseudepigraphal books. Verse 9 apparently alludes to the Assumption of Moses, and verses 14–15 clearly quote from the Book of Enoch (see 1:9). But this does not mean that Jude was thereby affirming the authority of these books; he was merely using them to illustrate a point much like Paul when he cited the Greek poets Aratus (see Acts 17:28), Menander (see 1 Cor. 15:33), and Epimenides (see Titus 1:12).

Survey of Jude

A surprisingly large number of the Pauline and non-Pauline Epistles confront the problem of false teachers, and almost all of them allude to it. But Jude goes beyond all other New Testament epistles in its relentless and passionate denunciation of the apostate teachers who have "crept in unnoticed" (v. 4). With the exception of its salutation (vv. 1–2) and doxology (vv. 24–25), the entire epistle revolves around this alarming problem. Combining the theme of Second Peter with the style of James,

Jude is potent in spite of its brevity. This urgent letter has four major sections: purpose of Jude (vv. 1–4); description of false teachers (vv. 5–16); defense against false teachers (vv. 17–23); and doxology of Jude (vv. 24–25).

Purpose of Jude (vv. 1–4): Jude addresses his letter to believers who are "sanctified, preserved," and "called," and wishes for them the threefold blessing of mercy, peace, and love (vv. 1–2). Grim news about the encroachment of false teachers in the churches has impelled Jude to put aside his commentary on salvation to write this timely word of rebuke and warning (vv. 3–4). In view of apostates who turn "the grace of our God into licentiousness" and deny Christ, it is crucial that believers "contend earnestly for the faith."

Description of False Teachers (vv. 5–16): Jude begins his extended expose of the apostate teachers by illustrating their ultimate doom with three examples of divine judgment from the Pentateuch (vv. 5–7). God impartially judged: (1) Those from among His chosen people who refused to believe (v. 5); (2) fallen angels (v. 6; cf. Gen. 6:1–4; 2 Pet. 2:4); and (3) the immoral Gentiles described in Genesis 18—19 (v. 7).

Like unreasoning animals, these apostates are ruled by the things they revile, and they are destroyed by the things they practice (vv. 8–10). Even the archangel Michael is more careful in his dealings with superhuman powers than are these arrogant men. Jude focuses more on the teachers of the heresy than on the heresy of the teachers, assuming that his readers are familiar with the details. He compares these men to three spiritually rebellious men from Genesis (Cain) and Numbers (Balaam and Korah) who incurred the condemnation of God (v. 11). Verses 12–13 succinctly summarize their character with five highly descriptive metaphors taken from nature: spots in your feasts, clouds without water, uprooted trees, raging waves, and wandering stars. After affirming the judgment of God upon such ungodly men with a quote from the noncanonical book of Enoch (vv. 14–15), Jude catalogs some of their practices (v. 16).

Defense Against False Teachers (vv. 17–23): This letter has been exposing apostate teachers (vv. 8, 10, 12, 14, 16), but now Jude directly addresses his readers ("But you, beloved, remember" v. 17). He reminds them of the apostolic warning that such men would come (vv. 17–19) and encourages them to protect themselves against the onslaught of apostasy (vv. 20–21). The readers must become mature in their own faith so that they will be able to rescue those who are enticed or already ensnared by error (vv. 22–23). Believers are to show mercy, not belligerence, when contending for the faith. They should hate the heresy but have compassion on those who are victimized.

Doxology of Jude (vv. 24–25): Jude closes with one of the greatest doxologies in the Bible. It emphasizes the power of Christ to keep those who trust in Him from being overthrown by error.

Outline of Jude

I. Purpose of Jude, 1–4

II. Description of False Teachers, 5–16
    A. Past Judgment of False Teachers 5–7
    B. Present Characteristics of False Teachers 8–13
    C. Future Judgment of False Teachers 14–16

III. Defense against False Teachers, 17–23

IV. Doxology of Jude, 24–25

Talk Thru the Non-Pauline Epistles

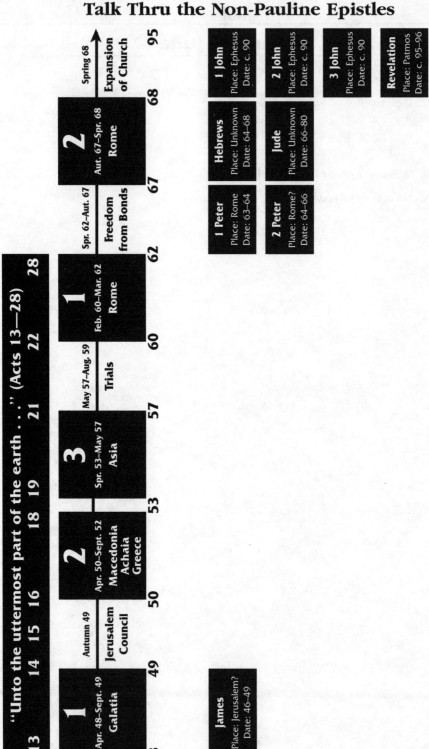

"Unto the uttermost part of the earth . . ." (Acts 13—28)

13 14 15 16 18 19 21 22 28

| 1 Apr. 48–Sept. 49 Galatia | Autumn 49 Jerusalem Council | 2 Apr. 50–Sept. 52 Macedonia Achaia Greece | 3 Spr. 53–May 57 Asia | May 57–Aug. 59 Trials | 1 Feb. 60–Mar. 62 Rome | Spr. 62–Aut. 67 Freedom from Bonds | 2 Aut. 67–Spr. 68 Rome | Spring 68 Expansion of Church |

48 49 50 53 57 60 62 67 68 95

James
Place: Jerusalem?
Date: 46–49

1 Peter
Place: Rome
Date: 63–64

Hebrews
Place: Unknown
Date: 64–68

1 John
Place: Ephesus
Date: c. 90

2 Peter
Place: Rome?
Date: 64–66

Jude
Place: Unknown
Date: 66–80

2 John
Place: Ephesus
Date: c. 90

3 John
Place: Ephesus
Date: c. 90

Revelation
Place: Patmos
Date: c. 95–96

Summary of the Non-Pauline Epistles

Book	No. of Chapters	Author	Key Words	Place Written	Date Written	Recipients
Hebrews	13	Unknown	Milk to Meat	Unknown	64–68	Unstated
James	5	James	Faith Gauge	Jerusalem?	46–49	The twelve tribes dispersed abroad
1 Peter	5	Peter	Pain with a Purpose	Rome?	63–64	Those who reside as aliens
2 Peter	3	Peter	Poison in the Pew	Rome?	64–66	Those who have received a faith the same as ours
1 John	5	John	Fellowship Barometer	Ephesus	c. 90	My little children
2 John	1	John	Bolt the Door	Ephesus	c. 90	The chosen lady and her children
3 John	1	John	Open the Door	Ephesus	c. 90	The beloved Gaius
Jude	1	Jude	Fight for the Faith	Unknown	66–80	Those who are the called, beloved in God the Father, and kept for Jesus Christ
Revelation	22	John	Coming Events	Patmos	95–96	The seven churches in Asia

Revelation

JUST AS GENESIS IS THE BOOK of the beginnings, Revelation is the book of consummation. In it, the divine program of redemption is brought to fruition, and the holy name of God is vindicated before all creation. Although there are numerous prophecies in the Gospels and Epistles, Revelation is the only New Testament book that focuses primarily on prophetic events. Its title means "unveiling" or "disclosure." thus, the book is an unveiling of the character and program of God. Penned by John during his exile on the island of Patmos, Revelation centers around visions and symbols of the resurrected Christ who alone has authority to judge the earth, remake it, and rule it in righteousness.

REVELATION

Focus	"Things Which You Have Seen" 1:1 1:20	"Things Which Are" 2:1 3:22	"Things Which Will Take Place" (1:19) 4:1 22:21				
Divisions	The Lord Jesus Christ 1:1 1:20	The Seven Churches 2:1 3:22	The Judge 4:1 5:14	The Tribulation 6:1 19:6	The Second Coming 19:7 19:21	The Millennium 20:1 20:15	The Eternal State 21:1 22:21
Topics	Vision of Christ		Vision of Consummation				
	Theophany	Talks	Tribulations		Trumpets		Together!
Place	Written on the Island of Patmos						
Time	C. A.D. 95–96						

Introduction and Title

Just as Genesis is the book of beginnings, Revelation is the book of consummation. In it, the divine program of redemption is brought to fruition, and the holy name of God is vindicated before all creation. Although there are numerous prophecies in the Gospels and Epistles, Revelation is the only New Testament book that focuses primarily on prophetic events. Its title means "unveiling" or "disclosure." Thus, the book is an unveiling of the character and program of God. Penned by John during his exile on the island of Patmos, Revelation centers around visions and symbols of the resurrected Christ, who alone has authority to judge the earth, to remake it, and to rule it in righteousness.

The title of this book in the Greek text is *Apokalypsis Ioannou,* "Revelation of John." It is also known as the Apocalypse, a transliteration of the word *apokalypsis,* meaning "unveiling," "disclosure," or "revelation." Thus, the book is an unveiling of that which otherwise could not be known. A better title comes from the first verse: *Apokalypsis Iesou Christoue,* "Revelation of Jesus Christ." This could be taken as a revelation which came from Christ or as a revelation which is about Christ—both are appropriate. Because of the unified contents of this book, it should not be called "Revelations."

Author

The style, symmetry, and plan of Revelation show that it was written by one author, four times named "John" (1:1, 4, 9; 22:8; see "Author" in John). Because of its contents and its address to seven churches, Revelation quickly circulated and became widely known and accepted in the early church. It was frequently mentioned and quoted by second- and third-century Christian writers and was received as part of the canon of New Testament books. From the beginning, Revelation was considered an authentic work of the apostle John, the same John who wrote the gospel and three epistles. This was held to be true by Justin Martyr, the Shepherd of Hermas, Melito, Irenaeus, the Muratorian Canon, Tertullian, Clement of Alexandria, Origen, and others.

This view was seldom questioned until the middle of the third century when Dionysius presented several arguments against the apostolic authorship of Revelation. He observed a clear difference in style and thought between Revelation and the books that he accepted as Johannine, and concluded that the Apocalypse must have been penned by a different John. Indeed, the internal evidence does pose some problems for the traditional view: (1) The Greek grammar of Revelation is not on par with the Fourth Gospel or the Johannine Epistles. (2) There are also differences in vocabulary and expressions used. (3) The theological content of this book differs from John's other writings in emphasis and presentation. (4) John's other writings avoid the use of his name, but it is found four times in this book. While these difficulties exist, two things should be kept in mind: (1) There are a number of remarkable similarities between the Apocalypse and the other books traditionally associated with the apostle John (e.g., the distinctive use of terms, such as "word," "lamb," and "true," and the careful development of conflicting themes, such as light and darkness, love and hatred, good and evil). (2) Many of the differences can be explained by the unusual circumstances surrounding this book. The apocalyptic subject matter demands a different treatment, and John received the contents not by reflection but by a series of startling and ecstatic visions. It is also possible that John used a secretary who smoothed out the Greek style of his other writings, and that his exile on Patmos prevented the use of such a scribe when he wrote Revelation.

Thus, the internal evidence, while problematic, need not overrule the early and strong external testimony to the apostolic origin of this important book. The author was obviously well-known to the recipients in the seven Asian churches, and this fits the unqualified use of the name John and the uniform tradition about his ministry in Asia. Alternate suggestions, such as John the Elder or a prophet named John create more problems than they solve.

Date and Setting

John directed this prophetic word to seven selected churches in the Roman province of Asia (1:3–4). The messages to these churches in chapters 2 and 3 begin with Ephesus, the most prominent, and continue in a clockwise direction until Laodicea is reached. It is likely that this book was initially carried along this circular route. While each of these messages had particular significance for these churches, they were also relevant for the church as a whole ("He who has an ear, let him hear what the Spirit says to the churches," 2:7,29).

John's effective testimony for Christ led the Roman authorities to exile him to the small, desolate island of Patmos in the Aegean Sea (1:9). This island of volcanic rock was one of several places to which the Romans banished criminals and political offenders.

Revelation was written at a time when Roman hostility to Christianity was erupting into overt persecution (1:9; 2:10, 13). Some scholars believe that it should be given an early date during the persecution of Christians under Nero after the A.D. 64 burning of Rome. The Hebrew letters for Nero Caesar (Neron Kesar) add up to 666, the number of the beast (13:18), and there was a legend that Nero would reappear in the East after his apparent death (cf. 13:3, 12, 14). This kind of evidence is weak, and a later date near the end of the reign of the emperor Domitian (A.D. 81–96) is preferable for several reasons: (1) This was the testimony of Irenaeus (disciple of Polycarp who was a disciple of John) and other early Christian writers. (2) John probably did not move from Jerusalem to Ephesus until C. A.D. 67, shortly before the Roman destruction of Jerusalem in A.D. 70. The early dating would not give him enough time to have established an ongoing ministry in Asia by the time he wrote this book. (3) The churches of Asia appear to have been in existence for a number of years, long enough for some to reach a point of complacency and decline (cf. 2:4; 3:1, 15–18). (4) The deeds of Domitian are more relevant than those of Nero to the themes of the Apocalypse. Worship of deceased emperors had been practiced for years, but Domitian was the first emperor to demand worship while he was alive. This led to a greater clash between the state and the church, especially in Asia, where the worship of Caesar was widely practiced. The persecution under Domitian presaged the more severe persecutions to follow.

Thus, it is likely that John wrote this book in A.D. 95 or 96. The date of his release from Patmos is unknown, but he was probably allowed to return to Ephesus after the reign of Domitian. Some passages suggest that the book was completed before John's release (1:11; 22:7, 9–10, 18–19).

Themes and Purpose

The purposes for which Revelation was written depend to some extent on how the book as a whole is interpreted. Because of its complex imagery and symbolism, Revelation is the most difficult biblical book to interpret, and there are four major alternatives: (1) The *symbolic* or *idealist* view maintains that Revelation is not a predictive prophecy but a symbolic portrait of the cosmic conflict of spiritual principles. In this way the book is divorced from the realm of history and placed exclusively in the realm of ideas. (2) The *preterist* view (the Latin word *praeter* means "past") also denies the prophetic aspect of the Apocalypse, limiting it solely to the events of the first century. It is a symbolic description of the Roman persecution of the church, emperor worship, and the divine judgment of Rome. (3) The *historicist* view approaches Revelation as an allegorical panorama of the history of the (Western) church from the first century to the Second Advent. The lack of objective criteria combined with the changing historical climate from one generation to another has led to a wide range of conflicting interpretations within this school. (4) The *futurist* view acknowledges the obvious influence that the first-century conflict between Roman power and the church had upon the themes of this book. But it also accepts the bulk of Revelation (chs. 4—22) as an inspired look into the time immediately preceding the Second Advent (the "Tribulation," usually seen as seven years; 4—18), and extending from the return of Christ to the creation of the new cosmos (19—22). According to this view, the Apocalypse centers around the second advent of Christ who will return in power and glory as the Judge of all who rejected His offer of salvation. Futurists attempt to discern the literal meanings behind the symbolism of Revelation whenever this is permitted by the context or by comparison with other Scripture.

Generally speaking, proponents of the first three views are postmillennial or amillennial, while futurists are premillennial. Postmillennialists believe that the spread of the gospel will lead to a golden age of peace on earth followed by the return of Christ; amillennialists believe that the Christian's present heavenly position in Christ is the true "millennium," not an earthly kingdom; and premillennialists believe that the six appearances of "a thousand years" (20:2–7) are to be taken literally as the duration of the earthly kingdom that Christ will establish between the Second Advent and the creation of the new universe.

Advocates of all four interpretive approaches to Revelation agree that it was written to assure the recipients of the ultimate triumph of Christ over all who rise up against Him and His saints. The readers were facing dark times of persecution, and even worse times would follow. Therefore they needed to be encouraged to persevere by standing firm in Christ in view of God's plan for the righteous and the wicked. This plan is especially clear in the stirring words of the epilogue (22:6–21). The book was also written to challenge complacent Christians to stop compromising with the world. According to futurists, Revelation serves the additional purpose of providing a perspective on end-time events that would have meaning and relevance to the spiritual lives of all succeeding generations of Christians.

Keys to Revelation

Key Word: Revelation of Jesus Christ

Key Verses (1:19; 19:11–15)—" 'Write the things which you have seen, and the things which are, and the things which will take place after this' " (1:19).

"Then I saw heaven opened, and behold, a white horse. And He who sat on him was called Faithful and True, and in righteousness He judges and makes war. His eyes *were* like a flame of fire, and on His head *were* many crowns. He had a name written that no one knew except Himself. He *was* clothed with a robe dipped in blood, and His name is called The Word of God. And the armies in heaven, clothed in fine linen, white and clean, followed Him on white horses. Now out of His mouth goes a sharp sword, that with it He should strike the nations. And He Himself will rule them with a rod of iron. He Himself treads the winepress of the fierceness and wrath of Almighty God" (19:11–15).

Key Chapters (19—22)—When the end of history is fully understood, its impact radically affects the present. In Revelation 19—22 the plans of God for the last days and for all of eternity are recorded in explicit terms. Careful study of and obedience to them will bring the blessings that are promised (1:3). Uppermost in the mind and deep in the heart should be guarded the words of Jesus, "Behold, I am coming quickly!"

Christ in Revelation

Revelation has much to say about all three persons of the Godhead, but it is especially clear in its presentation of the awesome resurrected Christ who has received all authority to judge the earth. He is called Jesus Christ (1:1), the faithful witness, the firstborn from the dead, the ruler over the kings of the earth (1:5), the First and the Last (1:17), He who lives (1:18), the Son of God (2:18), holy and true (3:7), the Amen, the Faithful and True Witness, the Beginning of the creation of God (3:14), the Lion of the tribe of Judah, the Root of David (5:5), a Lamb (5:6), Faithful and True (19:11), The Word of God (19:13), KING OF KINGS, AND LORD OF LORDS (19:16), Alpha and Omega (22:13), the Bright and Morning Star (22:16), and the Lord Jesus (22:21).

This book is indeed "The Revelation of Jesus Christ" (1:1) since it comes from Him and centers on Him. It begins with a vision of His glory, wisdom, and power (1), and portrays His authority over the entire church (2—3). He is the Lamb who was slain and declared worthy to open the book of judgment (5). His righteous wrath is poured out upon the whole earth (6—18), and He returns in power to judge His enemies and to reign as the Lord over all (19—20). He will rule forever over the heavenly city in the presence of all who know Him (21—22).

The Scriptures close with His great promise: "'Behold, I am coming quickly'" (22:7, 12). "'Surely I am coming quickly.' Amen. Even so, come, Lord Jesus" (22:20).

Contribution to the Bible

Revelation is a unique blend of apocalyptic, prophetic, and epistolary literature. The contents of Revelation are apocalyptic, as can be seen by a comparison with Isaiah 24—27, Ezekiel, Daniel, Joel, and Zechariah, as well as intertestamental apocalypses like the Book of Enoch, the Apocalypse of Baruch, and the Apocalypse of Ezra (2 Esdras 3—14). Such literature is characterized by symbolic language, ecstatic visions, catastrophic judgments, and eschatological material. The theme and message of Revelation are prophetic, according to the book's own claim (1:3; 22:7, 10, 18–19). The form of Revelation is epistolary, with its salutation (1:4–6), its seven individual letters (chs. 2—3), and its closing benediction (22:21).

Revelation means an "unveiling" or "disclosure," but many regard its content as veiled or closed because of the heavy symbolism. This leads to the view that the book should not be studied because its undecipherable nature will only lead the student into error. The opposite extreme is the overconfident approach which asserts that every symbolic nuance can be captured. This can lead to unhealthy speculation and "newspaper exegesis." The interpreter should steer a middle course between these extremes by seeking to understand as much as possible while acknowledging that this understanding will be limited. Hundreds of symbolic objects and acts are used in Revelation, but most of these are either explained in the context (e.g., 1:20) or in the rest of the Bible (e.g., the Book of Daniel). John's frequent use of comparative descriptions ("like," "as it were") in his attempt to convey visions that are beyond words should be kept in mind. Numerical symbolism also appears frequently; seven, the number of completion or perfection, appears over 50 times (the numbers 4, 10, and 12 are also significant). Familiarity with the Old Testament is an important prerequisite to an understanding of many things in Revelation. While there are no direct citations, scholars have found between 250 and 550 allusions to the Hebrew Scriptures in the Apocalypse. For example, note the obvious similarities between the 10 plagues of Exodus 7:14—12:36 and the judgments of chapters 8 and 16. Another interpretive ingredient in Revelation is the fact that its visions are not always in chronological sequence—they sometimes dart back and forth.

Revelation is characterized by its dramatic interplay between heaven and earth. God is on His throne (4) as the sovereign Ruler of all creation. The earth is the center of the massive spiritual conflict portrayed in Revelation, and it is viewed from a global perspective. Satan gives the beast authority "over every tribe, tongue, and nation" (13:7), but his power and time are limited (12:12), and he will be permanently judged (20:10). This is a book of divine judgment which culminates at the second advent of Messiah and the later Great White Throne Judgment. God will righteously deal with all evil and vindicate His holy name. It is significant that interspersed between the judgments of this book are songs and declarations of praise for the character and works of God. Revelation abounds with joyful worship for the worthy Lord of creation and redemption (e.g. 4:2—5:14; 7:9–17; 15:2–8; 19:1–7).

This book is more relevant now than ever before, especially in view of modern political, economic, military, technological, and communicative developments. Some of the once mysterious descriptions now have contemporary analogies.

The Apocalypse has been given an appropriate place as the last book in the canon of Scripture because it ties the themes of the Bible together. There is an especially striking contrast between the first and last three charters of the Bible:

Genesis 1—3	Revelation 20—22
"In the beginning God created the heavens and the earth" (1:1)	"I saw a new heaven and a new earth" (21:1)
"The darkness He called Night" (1:5)	"There shall be no night there" (21:25)
"God made two great lights" (sun and moon; 1:16)	"The city had no need of the sun or of the moon" (21:23)
"In the day that you eat of it you shall surely die" (2:17)	"There shall be no more death" (21:4)
Satan appears as deceiver of mankind (3:1)	Satan disappears forever (20:10)
Shown a garden into which defilement entered (3:6–7)	Shown a city into which defilement will never enter (21:27)
Walk of God with man interrupted (3:8–10)	Walk of God with man resumed (21:3)
Initial triumph of the serpent (3:13)	Ultimate triumph of the Lamb (20:10; 22:3)
"I will greatly multiply your sorrow" (3:16)	"There shall be no more death or sorrow, nor crying; and there shall be no more pain" (21:4)
"Cursed is the ground for your sake" (3:17)	"There shall be no more curse" (22:3)
Man's dominion broken in the fall of the first man, Adam (3:19)	Man's dominion restored in the rule of the new man, Christ (22:5)
First paradise closed (3:23)	New paradise opened (21:25)
Access to the tree of life disinherited in Adam (3:24)	Access to the tree of life reinstated in Christ (22:14)
They were driven from God's presence (3:24)	"They shall see His face" (22:4)

In a very real sense, chapters 21—22 are the new Genesis, but this time there will be no fall. In broadest terms, the Bible gives the story of God's work in creation, redemption, and re-creation, and it centers on the incarnation of the God-man:

A   †   Ω

CREATION   REDEMPTION   NEW CREATION

Survey of Revelation

Revelation is written in the form of apocalyptic literature (cf. Daniel and Zechariah) by a prophet (10:11; 22:9) and refers to itself as a prophetic book (1:3; 22:7, 10, 18–19). The three major movements in this profound unveiling are captured in 1:19: "the things which you have seen" (1); "the things which are" (2—3); and "the things which will take place after this" (4—22).

"The Things Which You Have Seen" (1): Revelation contains a prologue (1:1–3) before the usual salutation (1:4–8). The Revelation was received by Christ from the Father and communicated by an angel to John. This is the only biblical book that specifically promises a blessing to those who read it (1:3), but it also promises a curse to those who add to or detract from it (22:18–19). The salutation and closing benediction show that it was originally written as an epistle to seven Asian churches.

A rich theological portrait of the triune God (1:4–8) is followed by an overwhelming theophany (visible manifestation of God) in chapter 1, verses 9–20. The omnipotent and omniscient Christ who will subjugate all things under His authority is the central figure in this book.

"The Things Which Are" (2—3): The messages to the seven churches (2—3) refer back to an aspect of John's vision of Christ and contain a command, a commendation and/or condemnation, a correction, and a challenge. These messages are tailored to the needs of each of the seven churches, and some expositors have also seen in them a relevance that goes beyond the first-century context. Others see them as portraying some of the general movements in the history of the Christian church.

"The Things Which Will Take Place after This" (4—22): John is translated into heaven where he is given a vision of the divine majesty. In it, the Father ("one sat on the throne") and the Son (The Lion/Lamb) are worshiped by the twenty-four elders, the four living creatures, and the angelic host because of who they are and what they have done (creation and redemption; 4—5). Christ is declared worthy to judge the earth as the Redeemer of men, and He is about to open the seven seals of the book of judgment.

Three cycles of seven judgments in chapters 6—16 consist of seven seals, seven trumpets, and seven bowls. There is a prophetic insert between the sixth and seventh seal and trumpet judgments and an extended insert between the trumpet and bowl judgments. Because of the similarity of the seventh judgment in each series, it is possible that the three sets of judgments take place concurrently or with some overlap so that they all terminate with the return of Christ. An alternate approach views them as three consecutive series of judgments, so that the seventh seal is the seven trumpets and the seventh trumpet is the seven bowls.

The seven seals (6:1—8:5) are generated in large part by the sinfulness of man. They include war, the famine and death that are associated with war, and persecution. The prophetic insert between the sixth and seventh seals (7) describes the protective sealing of 144,000 "children of Israel," 12,000 from every tribe. It also looks ahead to the multitudes from every part of the earth who come "out of the great tribulation." The seven trumpets (8:2—11:19) appear to be largely associated with satanic and demonic activity, judging by the symbolism that is used. The catastrophic events in most of the trumpet judgments are called "woes." The prophetic interlude between the sixth and seventh trumpets (10:1—11:14) adds more details about the nature of the Tribulation Period and mentions a fourth set of seven judgments (the "seven thunders"), which would have extended it if they had not been withdrawn. Two unnamed witnesses will minister during the last three-and-a-half years of the Tribulation (forty-two months or 1,260 days). At the end of their ministry they will be overcome by the beast, but their resurrection and ascension will confound their enemies.

Chapters 12—14 contain a number of miscellaneous prophecies that are inserted between the trumpet and bowl judgments to give further background on the Time of Tribulation. The woman of chapter 12 is evidently Israel, her child is Christ, and the dragon is Satan. After he is cast down to earth, Satan will seek to destroy the woman but will not succeed. Chapter 13 gives a graphic description of the Antichrist and his false prophet, both empowered by Satan. The first beast is given political, economic, and religious authority; and because of his power and the lying miracles performed by the second beast, he is worshiped as the ruler of the earth. Chapter 14 contains a series of visions including the 144,000 at the end of the Tribulation, the fate of those who follow the beast, and the outpouring of the wrath of God.

The seven bowl judgments of chapter 16 are prefaced by a heavenly vision of the power, holiness, and glory of God in chapter 15. This final series of judgments appears to take place just prior to the return of Christ, and it stems from the righteous wrath of God.

Chapters 17—18 anticipate the final downfall of the religio-political system of the revived Roman empire. Babylon is symbolically used to refer both to a system and to a city. Commentators disagree, but chapter 17 may focus on the false religious aspect of Babylon while chapter 18 deals with the overthrow of political and commercial Babylon.

Christ Himself is about to return to the earth, and heaven wells up with praise to God. With His triumphant and glorious coming He vindicates His righteousness and all who have been persecuted for His name. The messianic marriage banquet is ready to take place, and the awesome King of Kings appears to overthrow His enemies in one consummating judgment (19). The Antichrist and False Prophet are thrown into the lake of fire, the followers perish, and Satan is bound for a thousand years. During this one thousand-year period Christ reigns over the earth with His resurrected saints, but by the end of this Millennium, many will have been born who refuse to submit their hearts to Christ. Satan will be released for a time and these people will become evident when they are satanically inspired to wage war with the Lord. However, Satan is permanently thrown into the lake of fire, the heavens and earth disappear, and the final Great White Throne judgment of those who have rejected Christ takes place (20).

A new universe is created, this time unspoiled by sin, death, pain, or sorrow. The New Jerusalem (described in 21:9—22:5), is shaped like a gigantic cube, one thousand five hundred miles in length, width, and height (the most holy place in the Old Testament tabernacle and the temple was also a perfect cube). Its multicolored stones will reflect the glory of God, and it will continually be filled with light. But the greatest thing of all is that believers will be in the presence of God "and they shall see his face."

Revelation concludes with an epilogue (22:6–21), which reassures the readers that Christ is coming quickly (22:7, 12, 20) and invites all who wish to "take the water of life freely" (22:17) to come to the Alpha and Omega, the Bright and Morning Star.

Outline of Revelation

Part One: "The Things Which You Have Seen" (1:1–20)

I. Introduction, 1:1–8

II. Revelation of Christ, 1:9–20

Part Two: "The Things Which Are" (2:1—3:22)

I. Message to Ephesus, 2:1–7

II. Message to Smyrna, 2:8–11

III. Message to Pergamos, 2:12–17

IV. Message to Thyatira, 2:18–29

V. Message to Sardis, 3:1–6

VI. Message to Philadelphia, 3:7–13

VII. Message to Laodicea, 3:14–22

Part Three: "The Things Which Will Take Place after This" (4:1—22:21)

I. Person of the Judge, 4:1—5:14
   A. The Throne of God, 4:1–11
   B. The Sealed Book, 5:1–14

II. Prophecies of Tribulation, 6:1—19:6
   A. Seven Seals of Judgment, 6:1—8:5
      1. First Seal, 6:1–2
      2. Second Seal, 6:3–4
      3. Third Seal, 6:5–6

IV. Prophecies of the Millennium, 20:1–15

    A. Satan Is Bound 1000 Years, 20:1–3

    B. Saints Reign 1000 Years, 20:4–6

    C. Satan Is Released and Leads Rebellion, 20:7–9

    D. Satan Is Tormented Forever, 20:10

    E. Great White Throne Judgment, 20:11–15

V. Prophecies of the Eternal State, 21:1—22:5

    A. New Heaven and Earth Are Created, 21:1

    B. New Jerusalem Descends, 21:2–8

    C. New Jerusalem Is Described, 21:9—22:5

VI. Conclusion, 22:6–21

Integration of the New Testament

Historical Books	Matthew **1**	Mark **2**	Luke **3**	John **4**	1	13	16	Acts **5**	18	21	28	Freedom / From Bondage	Second Roman Imprisonment	Expansion of the Church

Historical Books

Matthew 1 | Mark 2 | Luke 3 | John 4 | Acts 5

Pauline Epistles (To Churches)

Galatians | 1 Thessalonians | 2 Thessalonians | 1 Corinthians | 2 Corinthians | Romans | Ephesians | Colossians | Philippians

Pauline Epistles (To Pastors)

Philemon | 1 Timothy | Titus | 2 Timothy

General Epistles

James | 1 Peter | 2 Peter | Hebrews | Jude | 1 John | 2 John | 3 John | Revelation

Authors of the New Testament

Name	Nationality	Home Town	Occupation	Relationships	Chapters Written	Verses Written	Books Written
Matthew	Jew	Capernaum	Tax Collector	Apostle of Jesus Christ	28	1,071	Gospel of Matthew
Mark	Jew/Roman	Jerusalem	Missionary	Disciple of Peter	16	678	Gospel of Mark
Luke	Greek	Antioch	Physician	Disciple of Paul	52	2,158	Gospel of Luke Acts
John	Jew	Bethsaida or Capernaum	Fisherman	Apostle of Jesus Christ	50	1,414	Gospel of John 1 John 2 John 3 John Revelation
Paul	Jew	Tarsus	Tentmaker	Apostle of Jesus Christ	87 (100)*	2,033 (2,336)*	Romans 1 Corinthians 2 Corinthians Galatians Ephesians Philippians Colossians Philemon 1 Thessalonians 2 Thessalonians 1 Timothy 2 Timothy Titus (Hebrews?)
James	Jew	Nazareth	Carpenter?	Brother of Jesus Christ	5	108	James
Peter	Jew	Bethsaida	Fisherman	Apostle of Jesus Christ	8	166	1 Peter 2 Peter
Jude	Jew	Nazareth	Carpenter?	Brother of Jesus Christ	1	25	Jude

*Indicates total if Hebrews is assigned to Paul.

The Links of Scripture

"Even so, come, Lord Jesus"

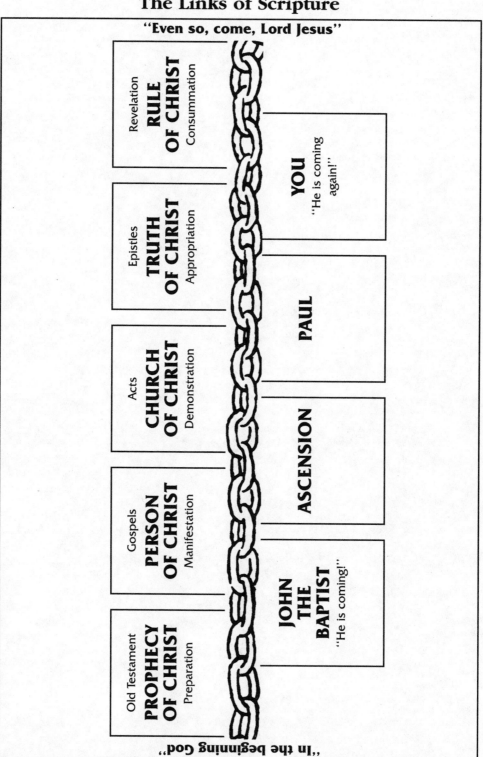

Old Testament	Gospels	Acts	Epistles	Revelation
PROPHECY OF CHRIST	**PERSON OF CHRIST**	**CHURCH OF CHRIST**	**TRUTH OF CHRIST**	**RULE OF CHRIST**
Preparation	Manifestation	Demonstration	Appropriation	Consummation

JOHN THE BAPTIST "He is coming!"   **ASCENSION**   **PAUL**   **YOU** "He is coming again!"

"In the beginning God"

523

VISUAL SURVEY OF THE BIBLE

Introduction
to the Visual Survey
of the Bible

The Visual Survey gives you a complete overview of the Bible. Taking people, events, and themes of the Bible as focus points, this handy study tool unfolds for you the contents of Scripture. Quotations from the Bible are taken from the King James Version.

Take a moment to familiarize yourself with the first chart, which compares the Old and New Testaments. Note particularly the time-line at the bottom of the page. This time-line divides the Old Testament into five periods and the New Testament into two. It is the key to the rest of the charts.

As you look through the following pages, notice that each chart has its own time-line containing both biblical and extrabiblical events. The maps portray the major movement of each period; the boxes present the key topics. The charts also summarize the themes of the Old Testament poetic and prophetic books, and the themes of the New Testament Epistles.

The ten Life Applications are an important part of this Survey. Based on the flow of each period, they crystallize the central spiritual truths of Scripture. Each principle leads into the next, and all of them relate to your own life.

VISUAL SURVEY...

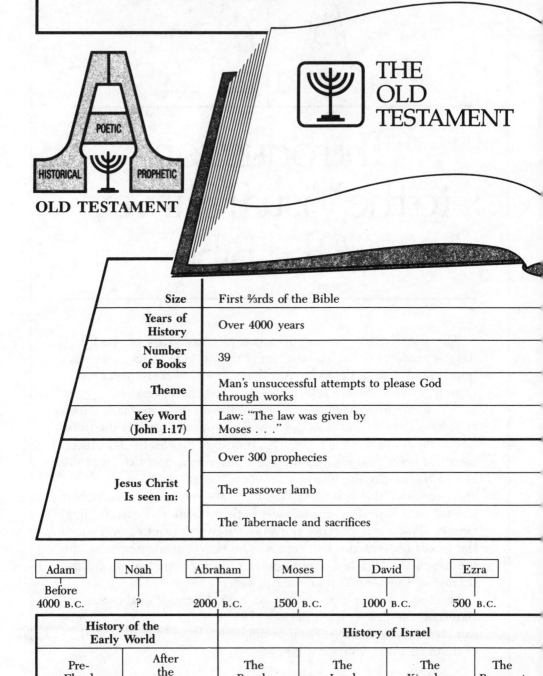

OLD TESTAMENT

THE OLD TESTAMENT

Size	First ⅔rds of the Bible
Years of History	Over 4000 years
Number of Books	39
Theme	Man's unsuccessful attempts to please God through works
Key Word (John 1:17)	Law: "The law was given by Moses . . ."
Jesus Christ Is seen in:	Over 300 prophecies
	The passover lamb
	The Tabernacle and sacrifices

Adam	Noah	Abraham	Moses	David	Ezra
Before 4000 B.C.	?	2000 B.C.	1500 B.C.	1000 B.C.	500 B.C.

History of the Early World		History of Israel			
Pre-Flood	After the Flood	The People	The Land	The Kingdom	The Remnant
11 Chapters (Gen. 1—11)		Over 38 Books (Gen. 12—Mal.)			

...OF THE BIBLE

THE NEW TESTAMENT

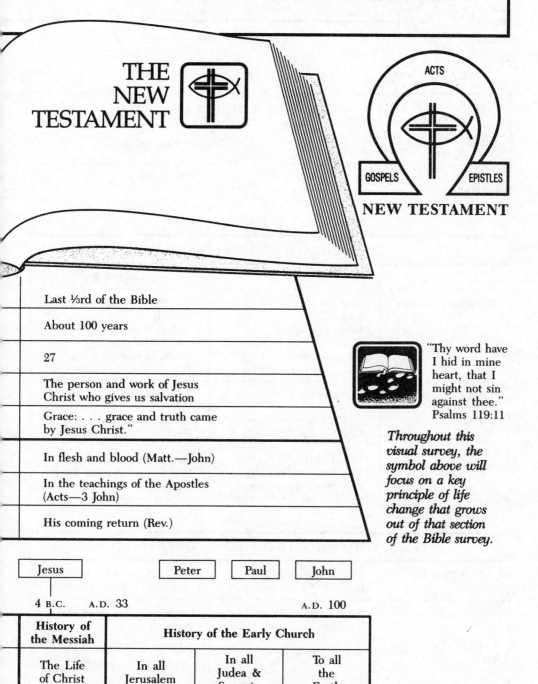

ACTS

GOSPELS   EPISTLES

NEW TESTAMENT

Last ⅓rd of the Bible	
About 100 years	
27	
The person and work of Jesus Christ who gives us salvation	
Grace: . . . grace and truth came by Jesus Christ."	
In flesh and blood (Matt.—John)	
In the teachings of the Apostles (Acts—3 John)	
His coming return (Rev.)	

"Thy word have I hid in mine heart, that I might not sin against thee." Psalms 119:11

Throughout this visual survey, the symbol above will focus on a key principle of life change that grows out of that section of the Bible survey.

Jesus		Peter	Paul	John

4 B.C.   A.D. 33   A.D. 100

History of the Messiah	History of the Early Church		
The Life of Christ	In all Jerusalem	In all Judea & Samaria	To all the Earth
(Matt.—John)	(Acts—Rev.)		

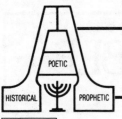

POETIC

HISTORICAL | PROPHETIC

HISTORY OF THE EARLY WORLD

Adam

Before
4000 B.C.

BEFORE THE FLOOD

CREATION (Origin of man)	FALL (Origin of sin)	SPREAD OF SIN
Gen. 1; 2	Gen. 3	Gen. 4—9

THE CREATIVE WORK OF GOD

	Genesis 1	Genesis 2
Creation Accounts	God the creator Elohim God as powerful Creation of the universe Climaxes with man The six days of creation	God the covenant-keeper Yahweh God as personal Creation of man Climaxes with marriage The sixth day of creation
Genesis 1:2	"without form . . ."	". . . and void"
Six Days of Creation	In the first three days, God shaped the Creation Day 1: light Day 2: water, atmosphere Day 3: earth, vegetation	In the second three days, God populated the Creation Day 4: sun, moon, stars Day 5: sea creatures, birds Day 6: animals

TEMPTATION: THE TWO ADAMS CONTRASTED

1 John 2:16	Genesis 3:6 (First Adam)	Luke 4:1–13 (Second Adam—Christ)
"the lust of the flesh"	"the tree was good for food"	"command this stone that it be made bread"
"the lust of the eyes"	"it was pleasant to the eyes"	"the devil . . . shewed unto him all the kingdoms"
"the pride of life"	"a tree to be desired to make one wise"	"cast thyself down from hence"

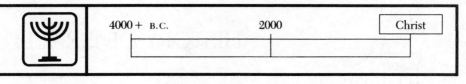

| 4000 + B.C. | 2000 | Christ |

| Noah | | Abraham |

2500 B.C. ?   2000 B.C.

AFTER THE FLOOD	
FLOOD (Judgment of sin)	SPREAD OF NATIONS
Gen. 6—9	Gen. 10—11

AGES OF THE PATRIARCHS
(Before and after the Flood)

The patriarchs who lived before the Flood had an average life span of about 900 years (Gen. 5). The ages of post-Flood patriarchs dropped rapidly and gradually leveled off (Gen. 11). Some suggest that this is due to major environmental changes brought about by the Flood.

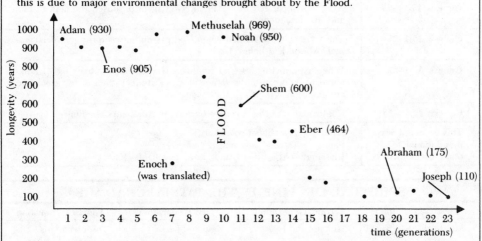

Principle: Righteousness is creative; sin is destructive (Gen. 2:17; Rom. 6:23).

Practice: Genesis 1—11, the prologue not only to Genesis, but to the entire Bible, begins with the ordered and life-giving activity of the holy Creator. The fall of man and the consequent spread of sin stand in stark contrast to the work of God and illustrate the disorder and death that always accompanies rebellion against the purposes of the Lord. God is not mocked; in a moral and spiritual universe, sin must be judged. What must you do, according to Romans 3:21–26, to escape the condemnation of your Creator?

HISTORY OF ISRAEL:

Abraham	Joseph
2000 B.C.	1975 B.C.

THE PEOPLE

THE PATRIARCHS		BONDAGE IN EGYPT	
2135 Birth of Abraham	1991 Beginning of Egyptian Middle Kingdom	Jacob Enters Egypt with His Family	1790 Code of Hammurabi

THE ABRAHAMIC COVENANT

Genesis 12:1–3	God initiated His covenant with Abram when he was living in Ur of the Chaldeans, promising a land, descendants, and blessing.
Genesis 12:4, 5	Abram went with his family to Haran, lived there for a time, and left at the age of 75.
Genesis 13:14–17	After Lot separated from Abram, God again promised the land to him and his descendants.
Genesis 15:1–21	This covenant was ratified when God passed between the sacrificial animals Abram laid before God.
Genesis 17:1–27	When Abram was 99 God renewed His covenant, changing Abram's name to Abraham ("the father of a multitude"). Sign of the covenant: circumcision.
Genesis 22:15–18	Confirmation of the covenant because of Abraham's obedience.
This covenant was foundational to other covenants.	Land: Palestinian covenant (Deut. 30). Seed: Davidic covenant (2 Sam. 7). Blessing: "old" (Ex. 19) and "new" covenants (Jer. 31).

SPIRITUAL DECLINE IN THE PATRIARCHAL AGE

First Generation	Second Generation	Third Generation	Fourth Generation
Abraham	Ishmael and Isaac	Esau and Jacob	Joseph and his eleven brothers

Abraham:
  man of faith
  believed God
	Ishmael:
	  not son of
	  promise
	Isaac:
	  called on God
	  believed God
		Esau:
		  unspiritual
		  little faith
		Jacob:
		  at first compromised, later turned to the Lord
			Joseph:
			  man of God
			  showed faith
			Brothers:
			  treachery, immorality, lack of separation from Canaanites

Abraham:
  built altars to
  God (Gen. 12:7, 8; 13:4, 18; 22:9)
	Isaac:
	  built an altar to
	  God (Gen. 26:25)
		Jacob:
		  built altars to
		  God (Gen. 33:20; 35:1, 3, 7)
			No altars were built to God in the fourth generation

THE PEOPLE		2000	1500	1000	500	Christ
		People	Land	Kingdom	Remnant	

Moses

1500 B.C.

(430 years until Exodus, Ex. 12:40; Gal. 3:17)

c. 1750 Beginning of Hittite Empire	1570 Beginning of Egyptian New Kingdom	1525 Birth of Moses	1445 The Exodus

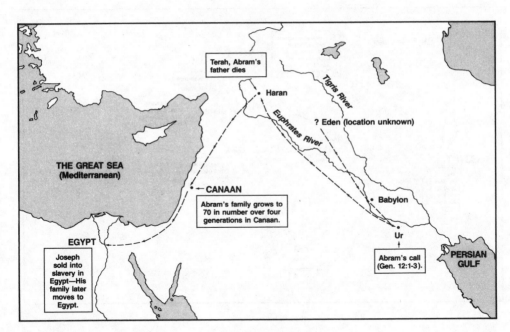

Principle: The destructiveness of sin is overcome by a faith that takes God at His word in spite of appearances and circumstances to the contrary (Gen. 15:6; John 3:16; Heb. 11:8–22).

Practice: Beginning in Genesis 12, God drew forth a man who would be the father of the people from whom and to whom the Messiah would come. Abraham became a friend of God through faith. In spite of appearances to the contrary, he went to a land he had not seen, believed God's promise of a son, and offered up that son at the same area where God's own Son would be crucified. Because he believed God, his faith was accounted to him for righteousness. In the same way, you can enter into a relationship with God by placing your trust in the person and work of His Son. Have you made that decision?

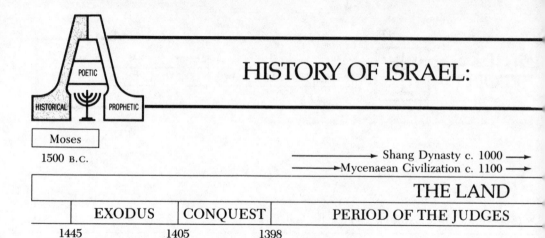

HISTORY OF ISRAEL:

POETIC

HISTORICAL PROPHETIC

Moses

1500 B.C.

Shang Dynasty c. 1000 →
Mycenaean Civilization c. 1100 →

THE LAND

EXODUS	CONQUEST	PERIOD OF THE JUDGES

1445   1405   1398
1450 ———————— 1423   Reign of Amenhotep II of Egypt

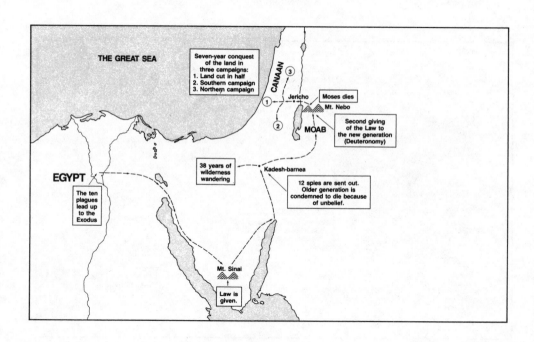

THE GREAT SEA

Seven-year conquest
of the land in
three campaigns:
1. Land cut in half
2. Southern campaign
3. Northern campaign

CANAAN

① Jericho

Moses dies

Mt. Nebo

② MOAB

Second giving
of the Law to
the new generation
(Deuteronomy)

38 years of
wilderness
wandering

Kadesh-barnea

12 spies are sent out.
Older generation is
condemned to die because
of unbelief.

EGYPT

The ten
plagues
lead up
to the
Exodus

Mt. Sinai

Law is
given.

Principle: Revelation demands obedience, and obedience brings blessing (Deut. 6:1–15; Josh. 1:8; John 15:12–17).

Practice: After redeeming His people from bondage, the Lord spoke to them in power and glory at Mt. Sinai. The revelation of the Mosaic law required a response of obedience. Their success as individuals and as a nation would depend on the degree of their conformity to God's moral, civil, and ceremonial law. Likewise, disobedience would lead to disaster (e.g., the wilderness wandering and servitude in the time of the Judges). As believers in Christ, our success is measured by the degree of our conformity to His character. To what extent is Christ the Lord of your life?

	Samuel	David
	1105–1020	1000 B.C.

c. 1100 Greek Dark Ages ———▶

1191
Gideon beats Midianites

1043
Saul anointed King

 THE LAW After their deliverance from Egyptian bondage, the children of Israel needed to learn to walk with their God. The Law was given to instruct the people about the person and the ways of their Redeemer so that they could be set apart to a life of holiness and obedience, not to save anyone but to reveal the people's need to trust in the Lord. As Paul told the Galatians, "Wherefore the law was our schoolmaster to bring us unto Christ, that we might be justified by faith (Gal. 3:24).

The Law combines poetry, salvation history, legislation, and exhortation. The three major divisions of the Law (Deut. 4:44) are the testimonies (moral duties), the statutes (ceremonial duties), and the judgments or ordinances (civil and social duties). The moral portion of the Law is summarized in the Ten Commandments (Ex. 20:1–17; Deut. 5:6–21):

THE TEN COMMANDMENTS (Moral Law)

1–4	Duties to God	"Thou shalt love the Lord thy God" (Matt. 22:37).
5–10	Duties to man	"Thou shalt love thy neighbour" (Matt. 22:39).

THE JUDGES: A CASE STUDY IN DISOBEDIENCE

Each of the seven cycles found in Judges 3:5—16:31 has five steps: sin, servitude, supplication, salvation, and silence. The cycles connect as a descending spiral of sin (2:19), with Israel vacillating between obedience and apostasy.

Cycle	Oppressor	Years of Oppression	Judge/Deliverer	Years of Peace
1. (3:7–11)	Mesopotamians	8	Othniel	40
2. (3:12–30)	Moabites	18	Ehud	80
(3:31)	Philistines		Shamgar	
3. (4:1—5:31)	Canaanites	20	Deborah/Barak	40
4. (6:1—8:32)	Midianites	7	Gideon	40
5. (8:33—10:5)	Abimelech	3	Tola/Jair	45
6. (10:6—12:15)	Ammonites	18	Jephthah/Ibzan/Elon/Abdon	6/7/10/8
7. (13:1—16:31)	Philistines	40	Samson	20

HISTORY OF ISRAEL:

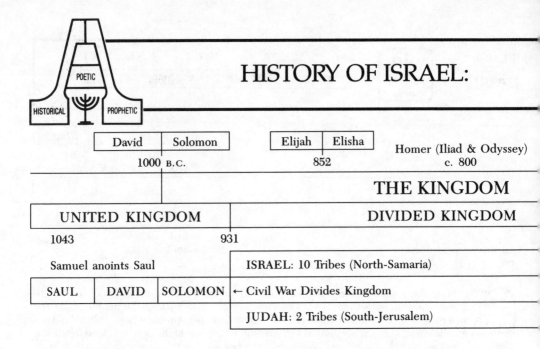

POETIC					
HISTORICAL	PROPHETIC				

David	Solomon		Elijah	Elisha	Homer (Iliad & Odyssey)
1000 B.C.			852		c. 800

THE KINGDOM

UNITED KINGDOM	DIVIDED KINGDOM
1043	931

Samuel anoints Saul

SAUL	DAVID	SOLOMON	← Civil War Divides Kingdom

ISRAEL: 10 Tribes (North-Samaria)

JUDAH: 2 Tribes (South-Jerusalem)

THE LIFE OF DAVID: A Man after God's own heart

1041 B.C.				1011			971 B.C.
DAVID'S 70 YEARS							
David as Subject (30 Years)				David as King (40 Years)			
As a son to his father	As a servant to King Saul			King over the South	King over all 12 tribes		
	His rise over Saul	Rejected by Saul	Refuge with Philistines	Growing	Growing		
	17–18	19–26	27–31	Success			Crisis
Psalms	1 Samuel			2 Samuel			1 Kings
23	17	19:1–10	31	7	11	14–18 24	2:10
David the Shepherd	Kills Goliath		Saul and Jonathan killed at Gilboa	Promise of Christ		Absalom's Rebellion	David Dies
		Protected by Jonathan			Sins with Bathsheba	David's Census	

Principle: Obedience grows out of a heart for God (Deut. 6:5; 1 Sam. 13:14; 1 Chr. 28:9; Acts 13:22).

Practice: Saul and David are a study in contrasts. The key to Saul's failure was his lack of a heart for God; the key to David's greatness was his obvious love for the Lord. David's relationship with God became the standard by which all the kings of Judah would be measured. To know God is to love Him, and to love Him is to desire to obey Him. Read Psalms 23 as a model of a man who was intimate with God. What are the things that may be hindering your growth in the knowledge of God?

THE KINGDOM

2000	1500	1000	500	Christ
People	Land	Kingdom	Remnant	

Rome Founded
753

Births of Buddha, Confucius
563   551

Ezra
450 B.C.

EXILE | RETURN

722   586   538

← Assyria Conquers Israel

Babylon Conquers Judah →

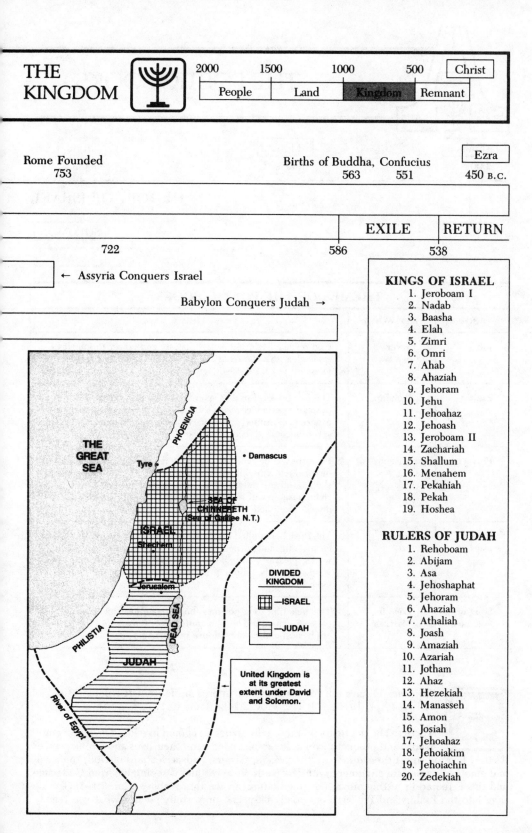

THE
GREAT
SEA

PHOENICIA

Tyre • Damascus

SEA OF
CHINNERETH
(Sea of Galilee N.T.)

ISRAEL

Shechem

Jerusalem

DEAD SEA

PHILISTIA

JUDAH

River of Egypt

**DIVIDED
KINGDOM**

▦ —ISRAEL

▤ —JUDAH

**United Kingdom is
at its greatest
extent under David
and Solomon.**

KINGS OF ISRAEL
1. Jeroboam I
2. Nadab
3. Baasha
4. Elah
5. Zimri
6. Omri
7. Ahab
8. Ahaziah
9. Jehoram
10. Jehu
11. Jehoahaz
12. Jehoash
13. Jeroboam II
14. Zachariah
15. Shallum
16. Menahem
17. Pekahiah
18. Pekah
19. Hoshea

RULERS OF JUDAH
1. Rehoboam
2. Abijam
3. Asa
4. Jehoshaphat
5. Jehoram
6. Ahaziah
7. Athaliah
8. Joash
9. Amaziah
10. Azariah
11. Jotham
12. Ahaz
13. Hezekiah
14. Manasseh
15. Amon
16. Josiah
17. Jehoahaz
18. Jehoiakim
19. Jehoiachin
20. Zedekiah

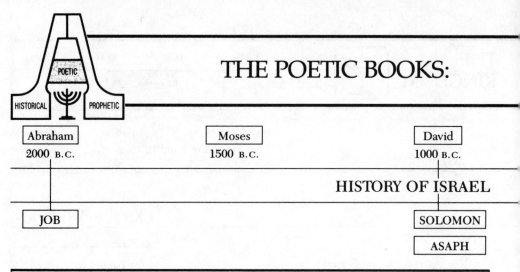

THE POETIC BOOKS:

Abraham	Moses	David
2000 B.C.	1500 B.C.	1000 B.C.

HISTORY OF ISRAEL

JOB

SOLOMON

ASAPH

THEMES OF THE POETIC BOOKS		
BOOK	**KEY WORD**	**THEME**
Job	Sovereignty	God revealed Himself in His majesty and power to Job. It became clear that the real issue was not Job's suffering (caused by Job's sin) but God's sovereignty.
Psalms	Worship	The five books of psalms span the centuries from Moses to the postexilic period, covering the full range of human emotions and experiences. Suited for service as the temple hymnal, they were set to music and focused on worship.
Proverbs	Wisdom	Proverbs was designed to equip the reader in practical wisdom, discernment, discipline, and discretion. The development of skills in all the details of life are stressed, so that beauty and righteousness will replace foolishness and evil through dependence upon God.
Ecclesiastes	Vanity	The Preacher applied his great mind and resources to the quest for meaning and purpose in life. He found that wisdom, wealth, works, pleasure, and power all led to futility and striving after wind. The only source of ultimate meaning and fulfillment is God Himself.
Song of Solomon	Love in Marriage	This beautiful song portrays the intimate love relationship between Solomon and his Shulamite bride. It magnifies the virtues of physical and emotional love in marriage.

Principle: To have a heart for God is to approach life from His perspective (Job 42:1–6; Ps. 1; 19; 63; 73; 119; Prov. 2:1–9; Rom. 12:1–3).

Practice: The poetic books record the struggles of men like Job, David, Solomon, Asaph, and others to gain a divine perspective on their lives and circumstances. As they learned to set their minds on the person, powers, and perfections of God, their wills and emotions came into alignment with His truth. True wisdom is seeing life from God's side, and this is rooted in setting our minds (meditating) on the things above (Col. 3:1–3). Try dipping into the Psalms and Proverbs on a daily basis and prayerfully ponder what you read.

THE HEART OF THE JEWS

Ezra	Christ
500 B.C.	4 B.C.

THE PATH TO TRUE SUCCESS	
Question	**Principle**
1. What is wisdom?	Wisdom is the key to a life of beauty, fulfillment, and purpose (Prov. 3:15–18). Wisdom is the skill in the art of living life with every area under the dominion of God. It is the ability to use the best means at the best time to accomplish the best ends.
2. How do we pursue wisdom?	The treasure of wisdom rests in the hands of God. Since it comes from above (Prov. 2:6; cf. James 3:17), we cannot attain it apart from Him.
3. What are the conditions for attaining wisdom?	True wisdom can only be gained by cultivating the fear of the Lord (Job 28:28; Ps. 86:11; 111:10; Prov. 1:7; 9:10).
4. What is the fear of the Lord?	To fear God is to have an attitude of awe and humility before Him (Prov. 15:33). It is to recognize Him as our Creator and our complete dependence upon Him in every activity of our lives.
5. Why have so few people developed this fear of God?	The temporal value system of this world is based on what is seen, while the eternal value system of Scripture is based on what is unseen (2 Cor. 4:16–18; 5:7). The former exerts a powerful influence upon us, and we struggle with giving up the seen for the unseen.
6. What can enable us to choose the eternal value system?	This choice is based on faith (believing God in spite of appearances and circumstances), and faith is based on trust.
7. How do we grow in faith?	Our ability to trust God is directly proportional to our knowledge of God. The better we know Him, the more we can trust Him.
8. How can we increase in our knowledge of God?	We become intimate with God as we talk with Him in prayer and listen to His voice in Scripture. The better we know God, the more we love Him and want to respond to His desires for our lives. Faith in God is simply trusting Him as a person, and trust is manifested in action.

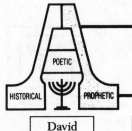

THE PROPHETIC BOOKS:

David		Elijah	Elisha		Zerubbabel	Ezra	Nehemiah
1000 B.C.		852				500	

THE KINGDOM

UNITED KINGDOM	DIVIDED KINGDOM	EXILE	RETURN

UNITED KINGDOM	ISRAEL	← 722	70 Years in Babylon	3 stage return
	← 931			1st Zerubbabel
		586 →		2nd Ezra
	JUDAH			3rd Nehemiah

PROPHETS BEFORE THE EXILE		EXILE PROPHETS	PROPHETS AFTER THE EXILE
To Israel: Amos (760) Hosea (755) **To Nineveh:** Jonah (760) Nahum (660) **To Edom:** Obadiah (840)	**To Judah:** Joel (835) Isaiah (740) Micah (735) Zephaniah (630) Jeremiah (627) Habakkuk (607) Lamentations (586)	**To Jews in Babylon:** Daniel (605) Ezekiel (592)	To the Remnant after returning: Haggai (520) Zechariah (520) Malachi (432)

Principle: God's disciplines are designed to restore a heart for Himself (Jer. 17:5, 7; Joel 2:12, 13; Heb. 12:5–11).

Practice: God had to discipline His people because of their moral and spiritual rebellion and their refusal to heed the warnings of His prophets. Reproof is designed to bring repentance and repentance brings restoration. The same prophets who pronounced the condemnation of God also announced the consolation of God. Similarly, because God loves us, He must sometimes chasten us as His children to train us in the ways of righteousness. How do you respond during these times? Are you teachable or intractable?

THE HOPE OF THE JEWS

Christ
4 B.C.

THE REMNANT

400 YEARS UNTIL CHRIST

THEMES OF THE PROPHETIC BOOKS

The Major Prophets

BOOK	KEY WORD	THEME
Isaiah	Salvation Is of the Lord	Twofold message of condemnation (1–39) and consolation (40–66). God's judgment on the sins of Judah, the surrounding nations, and the world, followed by future salvation and restoration.
Jeremiah	Judah's Last Hour	Declaration of certain judgment of God against Judah. God promises to establish a new covenant with His people.
Lamentations	Lamentations	This beautifully structured series of five lament poems is a funeral dirge for the fallen city of Jerusalem.
Ezekiel	Future Restoration	Ministry to the Jewish captives in Babylon before and after the fall of Jerusalem. The fate of Judah's foes and an apocalyptic vision of Judah's future.
Daniel	God's Program for Israel	Outlines God's plan for the gentile nations (2–7) and portrays Israel during the time of gentile domination (8–12).

The Minor Prophets

BOOK	KEY WORD	THEME
Hosea	God's Love for Israel	The story of Hosea and his faithless wife illustrates the loyal love of God and the spiritual adultery of Israel.
Joel	Day of the Lord	A recent locust plague illustrates the far more terrifying day of the Lord. God appeals to the people to repent in order to avert the coming disaster.
Amos	Judgment of Israel	In eight pronouncements of judgment, Amos spirals around the surrounding countries before landing on Israel. He lists the sins of Israel and calls for repentance.
Obadiah	Judgment of Edom	Condemns the nation of Edom (descended from Esau) for refusing to act as a brother toward Judah (descended from Jacob).
Jonah	Revival in Nineveh	The repentant response of the people of Nineveh to Jonah's one-line prophetic message caused the God of mercy to spare the city.
Micah	Judgment and Restoration of Judah	In spite of divine retribution against the corruption of Israel and Judah, God's covenant with them will be fulfilled in Messiah's future kingdom.
Nahum	Judgment of Nineveh	About 125 years after Nineveh repented under the preaching of Jonah, Micah predicted the destruction of the city because of its idolatry and brutality.
Habakkuk	Live by Faith	Troubled with God's plan to use the Babylonians as His rod of judgment on Judah, Habakkuk praises the Lord after gaining a better perspective on His power and purposes.
Zephaniah	Day of the Lord	The coming day of the Lord is a time of awesome judgment followed by great blessing. Judah stands condemned, but God will restore the fortunes of the remnant.
Haggai	Reconstruction of the Temple	After the Babylonian exile, Haggai urges the Jews to put God first and finish the Temple they had begun so that they can enjoy God's blessing.
Zechariah	Prepare for the Messiah	Like Haggai, Zechariah exhorts the Jews to complete the construction of the Temple. He relates it to the coming of Messiah in a series of visions and messianic prophecies.
Malachi	Appeal to Backsliders	The spiritual climate of the people had grown cold, and Malachi rebukes them for their religious and social compromise. If they return to God with sincere hearts, they will be blessed.

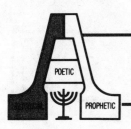

HISTORY OF ISRAEL: THE REMNANT

	Ezra
	450 B.C.

HISTORY OF ISRAEL

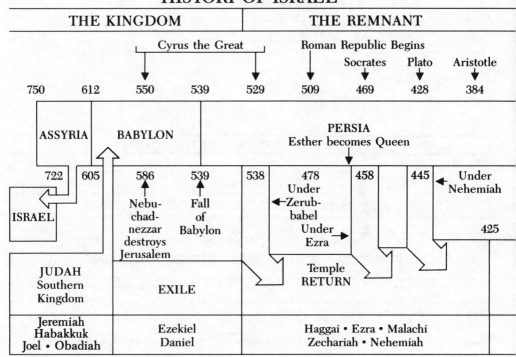

THE KINGDOM					THE REMNANT			
		Cyrus the Great			Roman Republic Begins			
						Socrates	Plato	Aristotle
750	612	550	539	529	509	469	428	384

ASSYRIA		BABYLON			PERSIA — Esther becomes Queen			
722	605	586	539	538	478	458	445	Under Nehemiah
ISRAEL		Nebu-chad-nezzar destroys Jerusalem	Fall of Babylon		Under ←Zerub-babel Under Ezra→			425
JUDAH Southern Kingdom		EXILE			Temple RETURN			
Jeremiah Habakkuk Joel • Obadiah		Ezekiel Daniel			Haggai • Ezra • Malachi Zechariah • Nehemiah			

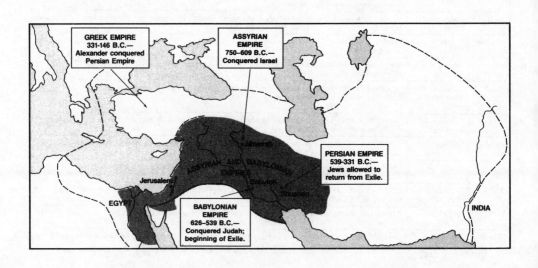

GREEK EMPIRE
331-146 B.C.—
Alexander conquered
Persian Empire

ASSYRIAN
EMPIRE
750–609 B.C.—
Conquered Israel

PERSIAN EMPIRE
539-331 B.C.—
Jews allowed to
return from Exile.

Jerusalem

EGYPT

BABYLONIAN
EMPIRE
626–539 B.C.—
Conquered Judah;
beginning of Exile.

INDIA

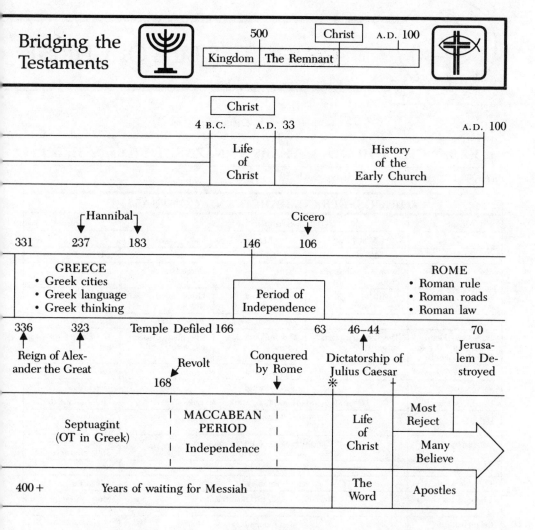

Bridging the Testaments

	500	Christ	A.D. 100
	Kingdom	The Remnant	

	Christ		
	4 B.C.	A.D. 33	A.D. 100
	Life of Christ	History of the Early Church	

	Hannibal		Cicero		
331	237	183	146	106	

GREECE		ROME
• Greek cities • Greek language • Greek thinking	Period of Independence	• Roman rule • Roman roads • Roman law

336	323	Temple Defiled 166		63	46–44	70
Reign of Alexander the Great		Revolt 168	Conquered by Rome	Dictatorship of Julius Caesar		Jerusalem Destroyed

Septuagint (OT in Greek)	MACCABEAN PERIOD Independence		Life of Christ	Most Reject	
				Many Believe	
400 +	Years of waiting for Messiah		The Word	Apostles	

Principle: True restoration results from being molded by the Word within rather than the world without (Ezra 7:10; 9:10–15; Is. 46:3, 4; Acts 7:51–53).

Practice: Even after the chastening of the Exile, most of the returning Jews became enmeshed once again in the affairs of the world and neglected their relationship with God. For some, the problem was external religiosity without internal reality; for others, the problem was being more influenced by culture than Scripture. God has always had to work with a faithful minority who love Him enough to stand against the tide of the world system. Is your quality of life different from that of those who love the world more than the Lord?

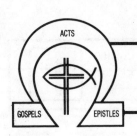

ACTS

GOSPELS   EPISTLES

THE LIFE OF CHRIST

4 B.C.   A.D. 9 (Temple Discussion)

EARLY CHILDHOOD	YEARS AT NAZARETH (Luke 2:51, 52)

Birth   Luke 2:41–50

THE GOSPELS COMPARED AND CONTRASTED				
Topics	The Synoptic Gospels			John
	Matthew	Mark	Luke	
Probable Date	A.D. 58–68	A.D. 55–65	A.D. 60–68	A.D. 80–90
Place of Writing	Syria Antioch or Palestine	Rome	Rome/Greece	Ephesus
Original Audience	Jewish mind (Religious)	Roman mind (Pragmatic)	Greek mind (Idealistic)	Universal
Theme	Messiah-King	Servant-Redeemer	Perfect Man	Son of God
Traditional Picture of Christ (cf. Ezek. 1:10; Rev. 4:6–8)	The Lion (strength, authority)	The Bull (service, power)	The Man (wisdom, character)	The Eagle (deity, person)
Portrait of Christ	God-man			God-man
Perspective	Historical			Theological
Unique Material	Less unique (Matthew, 42%; Mark, 7%; Luke, 59%)			More unique (92%)
Chronology	Only one Passover mentioned			Three or four Passovers mentioned
Geography	Concentrates on Galilean ministry			Concentrates on Judean ministry
Discourse Material	More public			More private
Teaching Method	Parables			Allegories
Teaching Emphasis	More on ethical, practical teachings			More on the person of Christ
Relationship to Other Gospels	Complementary			Supplementary

CHRIST'S PUBLIC MINISTRY

Masses drawn to His miracles and teachings →

Popularity peaks
Leaders attribute His miracles

A.D. 29	30	31
Opening events	Early Judaean ministry	Great Galilean ministry
Year of curious acceptance		Year of growing hostility

Baptized by John Matt. 3	First miracle John 2	Nicodemus learns of new birth John 3	Woman at well John 4	Rejected at Nazareth Luke 4	Apostles selected Mark 3

Sermon on Mount
Matt. 5—7

A.D. 29   A.D. 33

PUBLIC MINISTRY

Principle: Jesus, the living Word, lives His life in and through us as we walk in dependence upon Him (John 1:11, 12; 10:10; 15:4, 5; Gal. 2:20).

Practice: In Christ, God personally revealed Himself in human flesh: to see Him is to see God (John 12:45; 14:9), to know Him is to know God (John 8:19), to receive Him is to receive God (Mark 9:37), to honor Him is to honor God (John 5:23), and to reject Him is to reject God (Luke 10:16). He is the vine, the source of life; we are the branches, the channels of life. It is only as we draw our life from Him that we bear lasting fruit. To what extent are you looking to Jesus as the true source of your security, significance, and fulfillment?

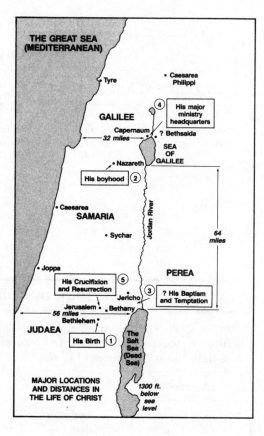

THE GREAT SEA (MEDITERRANEAN)

• Tyre
• Caesarea Philippi

GALILEE

④ His major ministry headquarters

Capernaum — 32 miles —
? Bethsaida

SEA OF GALILEE

• Nazareth

His boyhood ②

• Caesarea

SAMARIA

• Sychar

Jordan River

64 miles

• Joppa

PEREA

His Crucifixion and Resurrection ⑤

Jericho

③ ? His Baptism and Temptation

Jerusalem • — 56 miles — • Bethany

JUDAEA

Bethlehem •

His Birth ①

The Salt Sea (Dead Sea)

MAJOR LOCATIONS AND DISTANCES IN THE LIFE OF CHRIST

1300 ft. below sea level

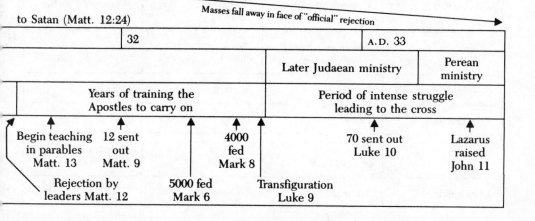

to Satan (Matt. 12:24)

Masses fall away in face of "official" rejection

| 32 | A.D. 33 |

| | Later Judaean ministry | Perean ministry |

| Years of training the Apostles to carry on | Period of intense struggle leading to the cross |

Begin teaching in parables Matt. 13   12 sent out Matt. 9   4000 fed Mark 8   70 sent out Luke 10   Lazarus raised John 11

Rejection by leaders Matt. 12   5000 fed Mark 6   Transfiguration Luke 9

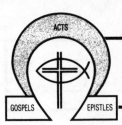

HISTORY OF THE EARLY CHURCH

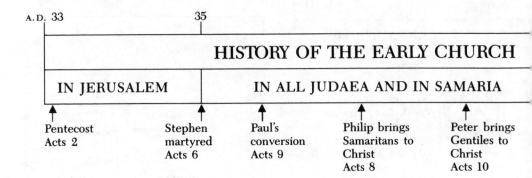

A.D. 33	35			
HISTORY OF THE EARLY CHURCH				
IN JERUSALEM	**IN ALL JUDAEA AND IN SAMARIA**			

Pentecost
Acts 2

Stephen
martyred
Acts 6

Paul's
conversion
Acts 9

Philip brings
Samaritans to
Christ
Acts 8

Peter brings
Gentiles to
Christ
Acts 10

THE BOOK OF ACTS IN OVERVIEW			
"But ye shall receive power, after that the Holy Ghost is come upon you: and ye shall be witnesses unto me both in *Jerusalem*, and in all *Judaea*, and in *Samaria*, and unto the *uttermost part of the earth*" (Acts 1:8).			
Chapters	**Acts 1–7**	**Acts 8–12**	**Acts 13–28**
Spread of the Church	The church in Jerusalem	The church in all Judaea and Samaria	The church to all the earth
The Gospel	Witnessing in the city	Witnessing in the provinces	Witnessing in the world
Theme	Power and progress of the church	Expansion of the church	Paul's three journeys and trials
People Addressed	Jews	Samaritans	Gentiles
Key Person	Peter	Philip	Paul
Time	2 years (A.D. 33–35)	13 years (A.D. 35–48)	14 years (A.D. 48–62)
Development	Triumph	Transition	Travels and trials

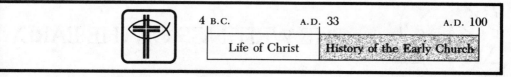

| 48 | 58 (Acts Ends) | 68 | 70 | A.D. 100 |

UNTO THE UTTERMOST PART OF THE EARTH

Missionary Journeys   Paul Imprisoned   Peter Executed   Jerusalem Destroyed   John Dies

Jerusalem Council
Acts 15

Paul Executed

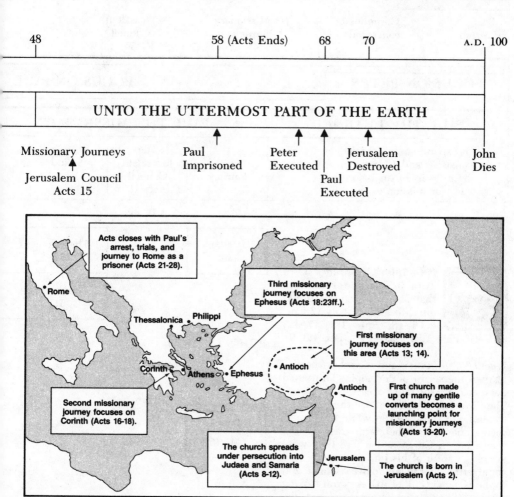

Acts closes with Paul's arrest, trials, and journey to Rome as a prisoner (Acts 21-28).

Rome

Third missionary journey focuses on Ephesus (Acts 18:23ff.).

Thessalonica · Philippi

First missionary journey focuses on this area (Acts 13; 14).

Corinth · Athens · Ephesus · Antioch

Second missionary journey focuses on Corinth (Acts 16-18).

Antioch

First church made up of many gentile converts becomes a launching point for missionary journeys (Acts 13-20).

The church spreads under persecution into Judaea and Samaria (Acts 8-12).

Jerusalem

The church is born in Jerusalem (Acts 2).

Principle: Christ's life is reproduced in others when we take the initiative to witness in the power of the Holy Spirit (Matt. 28:18–20; Acts 1:8; Col. 4:2–6).

Practice: The Book of Acts records the spread of the gospel from the city of Jerusalem to the whole province of Judea and Samaria, and ultimately through the Roman Empire and beyond. These first-century Christians were sold out for the cause of Christ and transformed their world as their lives became living epistles of the Good News. God has called us to a life-style of evangelism in which we build relationships with non-Christians. These friendships in turn become natural bridges for communicating the gospel. Take a close look at Colossians 4:2–6 to learn how to become more effective as an instrument of the Holy Spirit to reproduce the life of Christ in others.

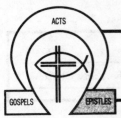

THE WRITINGS OF THE EARLY

Paul converted A.D. 34	Cornelius converted 40	1st Missionary Journey 48	Jerusalem Council 50

FOCUS ON PETER	FOCUS ON PAUL

PAUL THE LEARNER	PAUL THE MISSIONARY		
Paul spends nearly 3 years at Damascus and 10 years in obscurity in Tarsus before he is ready for mission work.	1st Journey	The Jerusalem Council Acts 15	2nd Journey

A.D. 50

Principle: God wants us to grow in our understanding that Christ's life and destiny is our life and destiny (2 Cor. 4:16–18; Eph. 1:3, 17–19; 3:16–19; Phil. 1:21; 3:20, 21; 1 Pet. 1:3–9).

Practice: Paul, Peter, and the other apostles learned the secret of developing an eternal perspective in the midst of earthly problems. They were able to live above their circumstances and rejoice even while being persecuted because of their firm grasp on who they were in Christ and where they were going. In spite of his imprisonment, Paul could write, "For to me, to live is Christ, and to die is gain" (Phil. 1:21). Are you looking more at "the things which are seen" or at "the things which are not seen"? The former are temporary, but the latter are eternal (2 Cor. 4:18).

Galatians (49)		1 Thessalonians (51)
		2 Thessalonians (51)

PAUL'S LETTERS

James (44, 45)

LETTERS BY OTHERS

GOSPELS & ACTS

Matthew (c. 40's)

CHURCH		A.D. 33	49		A.D. 100
			James		John

Paul imprisoned 58	Peter executed 64	Paul executed 68	Jerusalem destroyed 70	John dies A.D. 100

FOCUS ON JOHN

PAUL THE PRISONER

3rd Journey	1st Imprisonment	Freedom	2nd Imprisonment	JOHN'S WRITINGS
1 Corinthians (56)	Ephesians (60)	1 Timothy (62)	2 Timothy (67)	
2 Corinthians (56)	Colossians (61)	Titus (66)		
Romans (56, 57)	Philemon (61)			
	Philippians (62)			
		1 Peter (64)	Hebrews (66–69)	1 John (85–90)
		2 Peter (64)	Jude (75)	2 John (85–90)
				3 John (85–90)
				Revelation (95–96)
	Acts (62)			
	Luke (58–60)	Mark (60)		John (65–70)

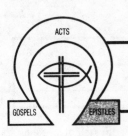

THE THEMES OF THE NEW TESTAMENT LETTERS

PAUL'S LETTERS TO CHURCHES

BOOK	KEY WORD	THEME
Romans	Righteousness of God	Portrays the gospel from condemnation to justification to sanctification to glorification (1–8). Presents God's program for Jews and Gentiles (9–11) and practical exhortations for believers (12–16).
1 Corinthians	Correction of Carnal Living	Corrects problems of factions, immorality, lawsuits, and abuse of the Lord's Supper (1–6). Replies to questions concerning marriage, meat offered to idols, public worship, and the Resurrection (7–16).
2 Corinthians	Paul Defends His Ministry	Defends Paul's apostolic character, call, and credentials. The majority had repented of their rebellion against Paul, but there was still an unrepentant minority.
Galatians	Freedom from the Law	Refutes the error of legalism that had ensnared the churches of Galatia. Demonstrates the superiority of grace over law, and magnifies the life of liberty over legalism and license.
Ephesians	Building the Body of Christ	Extols the believer's position in Christ (1–3), and exhorts the readers to maintain a spiritual walk that is based upon their spiritual wealth (4–6).
Philippians	To Live Is Christ	Paul speaks of the latest developments in his imprisonment and urges his readers to a life-style of unity, humility, and godliness.
Colossians	The Preeminence of Christ	Demonstrates the preeminence of Christ in creation, redemption, and the relationships of life. The Christian is complete in Christ and needs nothing else.
1 Thessalonians	Holiness in Light of Christ's Return	Paul commends the Thessalonians for their faith and reminds them of his motives and concerns on their behalf. He exhorts them to purity of life and teaches them about the coming of the Lord.
2 Thessalonians	Understanding the Day of the Lord	Paul corrects false conclusions about the day of the Lord, explains what must precede this awesome event, and exhorts his readers to remain diligent.

PAUL'S LETTERS TO PEOPLE

BOOK	KEY WORD	THEME
1 Timothy	Leadership Manual for Churches	Paul counsels Timothy on the problems of false teachers, public prayer, the role of women, and the requirements for elders and deacons.
2 Timothy	Endurance in Ministry	A combat manual designed to build up and encourage Timothy to boldness and steadfastness in view of the hardships of the spiritual warfare.
Titus	Conduct Manual for Churches	Lists the requirements for elders and instructs Titus in his duties relative to the various groups in the churches.
Philemon	Forgiveness from Slavery	Paul appeals to Philemon to forgive Onesimus and to regard him no longer as a slave but as a brother in Christ.

LETTERS FROM OTHERS

BOOK	KEY WORD	THEME
Hebrews	Superiority of Christ	Demonstrates the superiority of Christ's person, priesthood, and power over all that preceded Him to encourage the readers to mature and to become stable in their faith.
James	Faith that Works	A practical catalog of the characteristics of true faith written to exhort James' Hebrew-Christian readers to examine the reality of their own faith.
1 Peter	Suffering for Christ	Comfort and counsel to those who were being maligned for their faith in Christ. They are encouraged to develop an attitude of submission in view of their suffering.
2 Peter	Guard Against False Prophets	Copes with internal opposition in the form of false teachers who were enticing believers into their errors of belief and conduct. Appeals for growth in the true knowledge of Christ.
1 John	Fellowship with God	Explores the dimensions of fellowship between redeemed people and God. Believers must walk in His light, manifest His love, and abide in His life.
2 John	Avoid Fellowship with False Teachers	John commends his readers for remaining steadfast in apostolic truth and reminds them to walk in love and avoid false teachers.
3 John	Enjoy Fellowship with the Brethren	John thanks Gaius for his support of traveling teachers of the truth, in contrast to Diotrephes, who rejected them and told others to do the same.
Jude	Contend for the Faith	This expose of false teachers reveals their conduct and character and predicts their judgment. Jude encourages his readers to build themselves up in the truth and contend earnestly for the faith.
Revelation	Revelation of the Coming Christ	The glorified Christ gives seven messages to the church (1–3). Visions of unparalleled judgment upon rebellious mankind are followed by the Second Advent (4–19). The Apocalypse concludes with a description of the new heaven and new earth and the marvels of the new Jerusalem (20–22).